Faulkner's County

The Fred W. Morrison Series in Southern Studies

Faulkner's County

The Historical Roots

of Yoknapatawpha

Don H. Doyle The

University of North

Carolina Chapel

Hill and London

© 2001 The University of North Carolina Press ❦ All rights reserved ❦ Designed by April

Leidig-Higgins ❦ Set in Quadraat by Tseng Information Systems, Inc. ❦ Manufactured

in the United States of America ❦ The paper in this book meets the guidelines for

permanence and durability of the Committee on Production Guidelines for Book Lon-

gevity of the Council on Library Resources. Selections from *Requiem for a Nun* copyright

© 1950, 1951 by William Faulkner. Reprinted by permission of Random House, Inc. ❦

Library of Congress Cataloging-in-Publication Data ❦ Doyle, Don Harrison, 1946– Faulk-

ner's county: the historical roots of Yoknapatawpha / Don H. Doyle. p. cm.—(The Fred W.

Morrison Series in Southern Studies) Includes bibliographical references and index. ❦

ISBN 0-8078-2615-4 (alk. paper) ❦ ISBN 0-8078-4931-6 (pbk.: alk. paper) ❦ 1. Lafayette

County (Miss.)—History. 2. Yoknapatawpha County (Imaginary place). 3. Faulkner, William,

1897–1962—Settings. I. Title. II. Series.

F347.L2 D69 2001 976.2'83—dc21 00-047951

05 04 03 02 01 5 4 3 2 1

For Mike, Kathy,
and the memory
of our mother

contents

illustrations

maps, figures, & table

This book had its origins in a telephone call from Ann Abadie one afternoon long ago, in 1982. She was calling from the Center for the Study of Southern Culture at the University of Mississippi about a project involving the history of Lafayette County, Mississippi, the main source of William Faulkner's fictional Yoknapatawpha. By chance, I had made my first pilgrimage to Faulkner country the previous fall and was reading his short stories and letters. The idea of doing a history of a place so richly complemented by historical fiction struck me as an exciting idea. It stayed in my mind—and in Ann's—for years. It was sometime in 1988 that I called Ann to inquire whatever happened to this plan for a history of Faulkner's county. "It's waiting for you," she told me. Later that summer I drove down to Oxford with my daughters, Carrie and Kelly, met with Ann and Charles Wilson at the Center and talked about what might be done to revive this dream of Ann's. We had lunch at Smitty's, visited Square Books, and drove around Yoknapatawpha/Lafayette County. I was already hooked, but it would be another two years before I could begin research. Once I waded into the history of this place, I realized what a rich trove of material Faulkner had to work with. The more I read of his "apocryphal" and "actual" county (as he once distinguished them), the more I admired his achievement not only as a writer but also as a historian—an interpreter of the past.

This book is a history of a small but characteristic little piece of the American South, a "postage stamp of native soil," Faulkner called it. It stretches back to the early Chickasaws, before the first entry of Europeans into this part of the world in 1540, and up to the modern civil rights movement in 1962, the year of Faulkner's death. The central idea of this book is to use Faulkner's fiction to inform my historical interpretation and, to a lesser extent, use the history to illuminate Faulkner's imaginary world. There are numerous books that have made connections between the factual and fictional, and those are a fascinating but peripheral aspect of what I am trying to achieve here. I was more interested in Faulkner's larger themes and interpretations of the past, especially his part of the South, the new country in Mississippi that was on the edge of the western cotton frontier. Faulkner is wonderfully quotable, and throughout the book, I lay on excerpts from his prose as much as to savor and enjoy his rich language and imagery as to illustrate his capacity to imagine the past. Faulkner provided far more than just literary sauce over the historical meat; I soon found that his imagined history helped me see and understand things in ways I might otherwise never have.

I wrote this book with the idea that readers may or may not bring to it a deep knowledge of Faulkner or southern history and that few would have both in any case. I hope everyone who enjoys Faulkner will want to read this book and that others not familiar with Faulkner will want to dive into his fictional world having learned about his nonfictional world. Those who know their Faulkner will enjoy numerous parallels with the historical world described here, only some of which I have pointed out along the way. My goal, however, was to tell the story of the people who lived in Lafayette County, rather than the fictional characters who occupy Yoknapatawpha County. I tried to capture the voices of the historical actors and let them speak, but the historian's job is also to help tell their story, to work out a plot, decide on which characters and events to put in the foreground, and to make connections they might have been blind to. I have read and profited from dozens of other historians and Faulkner scholars during these past several years, but most readers will not be interested in hearing our academic debates, so I kept them offstage.

There are many people and institutions I owe thanks for supporting my work in connection with this project. Vanderbilt University has offered a wonderful place to work with colleagues and students who have shaped my thinking on this book in countless ways. The College of Arts and Sciences granted me research leaves in 1990–91 and 1994–95; I am grateful to Vanderbilt's College of Arts and Science for allowing me this time for research and writing.

Vanderbilt University Research Council provided grants that helped defray expenses for travel and research. The American Philosophical Society awarded me a Research Grant in 1991, for which I am most grateful. The National Endowment for the Humanities granted me a Summer Fellowship in 1992 and sponsored a Summer Seminar for College Teachers on Southern History and Faulkner in 1993, which I directed. The group of professors, in English and history, who came from Mississippi, the Midwest, Morocco, Ghana, Denmark, and places in between, provided a wonderfully stimulating experience that helped shape my thinking at an early stage in this project.

Vanderbilt's Jean and Alexander Heard Library, particularly Joe Mount, Peter Brush, Jim Toplin, and Marilyn Pilley, the latter two at the Interlibrary Loan department, provided superb support of my research efforts over the years. Not least, the many students in the College Scholars Program who took Honors 184 on Faulkner and Southern History over the past several years were an enormously important stimulus to my thinking on this book. No less helpful were the students in Rome and Genoa, Italy, where I taught as a Fulbright professor, and Leeds, England, where I spent a year directing the Vanderbilt-in-England program. I have always enjoyed integrating my research passions with teaching, in part because I find there is no better way to learn a subject than to teach it. Some students patiently suffered my initial ignorance of the subject, and all of them provided astute comments, questions, and insights. John Barrow aided me one summer as a research assistant, and Bill Fletcher loaned some of his computer expertise in preparing some of the databases for this project.

My deepest thanks goes to Ann Abadie and the Center for the Study of Southern Culture at the University of Mississippi, for reasons I have already explained. In addition to inspiring this book, Ann and her husband, Dale, have been extraordinarily hospitable to me over the years. Bill Ferris and Charles Wilson, successive directors of the Center, have offered constant moral support and practical aid. Charles Eagles, Brenda Eagles, Ted Ownby, and others at Ole Miss have been friendly companions and helpful colleagues during my many visits to Oxford. Special Collections at the John Williams Library, University of Mississippi, was one of the most important sources for research on this book, and Debbie Landi was especially helpful to me during my many visits there. Jennifer Ford helped locate several photographs in their collections.

Thanks also to the staff of the University Museums in Oxford. Michele Desrosiers was very helpful in making photographs from their collections available.

Few people knew Faulkner country better than Evans Harrington, former professor of English at the University of Mississippi. Evans had an uncanny way of relating his tours of the county to Faulkner stories. I brought my Vanderbilt honors seminar down to Oxford one spring and, after one of his long and seemingly disconnected — but always complete — stories, one of my students turned to me to say: "Dr. Doyle, he talks just like Faulkner writes!" I was deeply saddened to learn of Evans Harrington's death just as I was finishing my first draft of this book. He helped me in many ways.

The Center for the Study of Southern Culture sponsors an annual Faulkner and Yoknapatawpha conference; part festival and part scholarly conference, it is an occasion for scholars and fans to meet, to share ideas, and to immerse themselves in the literary and literal world of Faulkner. For a historian crossing disciplinary boundaries, it provided a short course in Faulkner criticism, one I gladly repeated whenever I could. In 1995, Don Kartiganer and the conference board invited me to give a paper on "Faulkner and History," and this offered me a welcome opportunity to share some of my early thoughts about the relation of Yoknapatawpha and Lafayette County. The many friends and acquaintances I have made at the annual Faulkner conference have been immensely helpful, generous, and welcoming.

Early in my research, Ann Abadie introduced me to the Skipwith Historical and Genealogical Society, and I became a dues-paying member. Many of the Skipwith members are rather indifferent to William Faulkner, but they were all enthusiastic and cordial in helping an outsider learn the history of their county. The late Sybil Metts Hill and her husband, W. C. Hill, were a constant source of help and information. I will never forget the day the three of us, with Mark Vinson at the wheel, drove over to the Old Dallas neighborhood to find the grave of Elizabeth Ragland and see the house where she was murdered. Walker Coffey, another Skipwith stalwart, gave up part of an afternoon to share with me his remarkable knowledge of local history. I had no idea at the time how important his work as a historian and autobiographer would be to my work. Annette Waite of the Skipwith Society helped me at every stage in countless ways. One hot afternoon, she, Sybil, and I spent out at an abandoned school for blacks near Taylor's that was filled with discarded county records, dust, and wasps—a day in the archives like no other.

Others in Oxford and Lafayette County were generous with their time and information. Susie Marshall, a wise source of local black history, sat with me on her front porch and told me stories that never made it into the usual narratives of local history. Guy Turnbow gave me access to the diaries and family letters of his ancestor Rebecca Pegues, who figures prominently in this book. Richard Stanley of Austin, Texas, also related to the Pegues family, graciously allowed me access to some of the original diaries, along with photos and letters. The Reverend Leroy Wadlington directed me to several useful sources on African American history. Nathan Hodges Jr. shared with me the secret history of the local civil rights movement. Elmo Howell, a Faulkner scholar and Mississippian, and Mary Metcalfe, the niece of former governor Lee Russell, generously shared their knowledge with me. I am grateful to them and to several others who unlocked the doors of local history.

Another important site for research was the Mississippi Department of Archives and History in Jackson. I spent several weeks there working through the records, each time managing, with help from Anne Webster and her staff, to unearth more material from their rich collections. Patricia Galloway's extensive understanding of Mississippi Indian history immediately accelerated my own primitive knowledge. Jeff Rogers helped track down several illustrations. Mississippi has one of the finest state archives I have had the pleasure to work in, and I am grateful for their helpful and friendly assistance. The Holly Springs Historical Society had some collections that proved relevant to my subject, and I am grateful for the hospitality its staff showed me during two visits.

The National Archives, NARA, was an unusually rich resource for the making of this book. Steve Miller at the Freedmen and Southern Society Project, University of Maryland, generously gave me advice by telephone on the resources of NARA. Susan Aloha and Mike Musik at NARA were very helpful to my work. Joyce Ray was a great help in guiding me through the bureaucracy of NARA, and her husband, Dr. F. G. Gosling, kept me distracted evenings while I stayed with them in Washington.

Many others helped track down sources and lend their expertise. Anastatia Sims identified several sources at the Southern Historical Collection at University of North Carolina, and Louis Kyriakoudes aided me by going through the Barringer Collection there. Stephen Cresswell shared his knowledge of Mississippi politics with me. Gaines Foster kindly sent a valuable letter I never would have found. Chris Everett helped me understand the Chickasaw trade. Dozens of others, some I may never know, helped answer queries I had posted on the Internet discussion groups, which I found to be a remarkably obliging community of scholars.

Several friends and colleagues have read parts of the manuscript at various stages of its production and provided useful comments. My colleague David Carlton has been a sharp reader and helpful adviser at every stage. Mary DeCredico, a former graduate student of mine, brought her remarkable knowledge of the Civil War and southern history to her reading of most of the manuscript in its first draft. Bruce McTavish generously shared sources and insights from his own fine work on northern Mississippi, and he gave an immensely helpful reading of my manuscript. Randy Shifflett's insights and comments at various stages of this project have been valuable and much appreciated. Andrew McMichael, Jane Landers, Chaz Joyner, and Ed Countryman each gave me their reactions to the chapter on slavery, which proved very useful. Christopher Morris gave me very perceptive comments on this chapter and another. I presented the chapter on the slaves to the Southern Social History Group, an informal discussion group of Vanderbilt graduate students and faculty; their many comments were of great help. Ed Harcourt, one of the group, used his keen editorial eye on several chapters and helped proof final copy. Tom McHaney read the introduction and gave me several useful comments. Jeanette Keith, a former student, shared her uncanny knowledge of southern country people while reading chapters on the last two chapters. My former dean and fellow historian Jacque Voegeli cast his sharp eye and extraordinary knowledge of southern history over an early draft of the manuscript. He saved me from many errors, pointed out biases and blind spots, and in many small and large ways made this a better book. I presented early versions of parts of this book at the annual meeting of the Organization of American Historians, where Clarence

Mohr and Wayne Durrill gave me their reactions to my work on the Civil War in Lafayette County. Another paper on Reconstruction was presented at the Southern Historical Association meeting, where Brenda Stevenson and Michael Les Benedict provided useful criticism. There were dozens of others in the academy, Internet discussion groups, local people in Lafayette County, or students at Vanderbilt, or in Italy and England, who helped me along the way.

Finally, thanks to Lew Bateman, David Perry, and Pam Upton for all they did to help this project go from idea to manuscript to book at the University of North Carolina Press.

Fièsole, Italy
May 2000

Map 1. Northern Mississippi

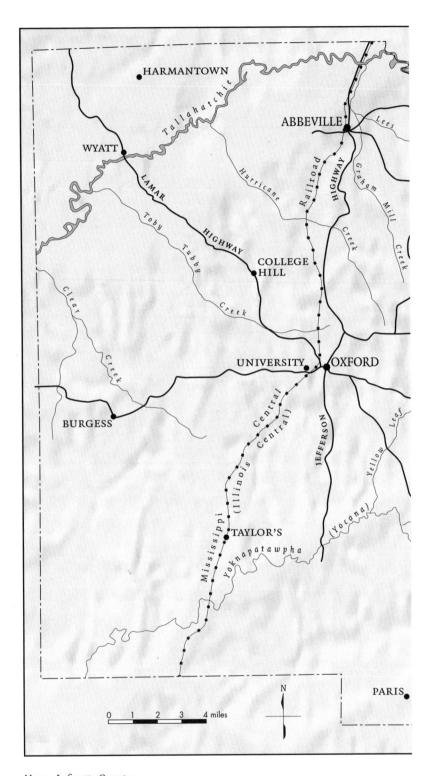

Map 2. Lafayette County

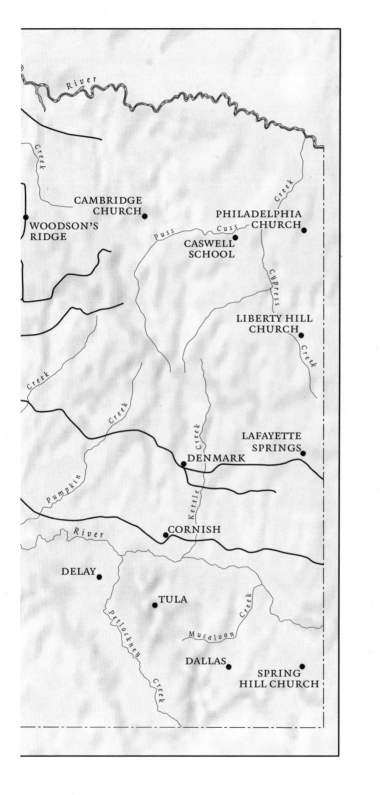

Faulkner's County

We have a few old mouth-to-mouth tales; we exhume from old trunks and boxes and drawers letters without salutation or signature, in which men and women who once lived and breathed are now merely initials or nicknames out of some now incomprehensible affection which sound to us like Sanskrit or Choctaw; we see dimly people, the people in whose living blood and seed we ourselves lay dormant and waiting, in this shadowy attenuation of time possessing now heroic proportions, performing their acts of simple passion and simple violence, impervious to time and inexplicable. —WILLIAM FAULKNER, Absalom, Absalom!*

introduction Listen, Stranger

This book is about the history of a real place, Lafayette County, Mississippi, the main source of William Faulkner's Yoknapatawpha County, and the storied past they shared. It was one of several counties formed in northern Mississippi in the 1830s, after the Chickasaw people were forced to leave for Indian Territory. They called the area Yoknapatawpha, and a river flowing through the county still bears that name in abbreviated form. The human history of this place goes back long before the creation of Lafayette County and before 1540, when the first Europeans, Spanish soldiers with Hernando DeSoto, entered the Chickasaw domain.

Three centuries following that first fateful encounter, the Chickasaws made their exit westward while a swarm of cotton planters, slaves, yeomen, and poor whites came in from the East. Almost overnight the new claimants to the land built a plantation economy based on cotton and slavery with towns, hamlets, roads, bridges, railroads, a courthouse, and government all in service to that economic and social order.

Twenty-five years after its founding, pushed by an ardent corps of fire-eating secessionists, the citizens of Lafayette County joined a revolutionary struggle to become independent from a nation they feared would destroy slavery. During four years of war that followed, Union armies invaded northern Mississippi, plundering the land and encouraging slaves to rise and flee. One day in August 1864 a Union force, including former slaves among its troops, invaded the county and sacked and burned Oxford, the county seat, leaving the courthouse and public square, along with several mansions in town, nothing but blackened ruins. What the Union invaders had not pillaged or destroyed, the Confederate armies foraged for themselves. Roving bands of bushwhackers, white southerners preying on defenseless families in a war-torn society, took much of what remained. Lafayette County was as decimated by war as almost any part of the South. The revolution for independence was defeated and, instead, a revolution that destroyed slavery had succeeded.

Another war ensued, this one over the status of former slaves, who made up nearly half the population. Reconstruction continued the Civil War in new form. It was a political contest and an armed struggle that pitted Democrats against Republicans, whites against freedmen, Ku Klux Klan terrorists against federal marshals. Ten bloody years after the war for southern independence was lost, the war for white supremacy was triumphant in Mississippi. The losers, the former slaves, began their dark journey into violent subjugation and segregation, an ordeal they would endure the better part of a century until the civil rights movement—the Second Reconstruction—brought relief.

Once part of a frontier full of promise, following the Civil War and Reconstruction, Lafayette County, along with much of the rural Deep South, became a backward region burdened by conditions of poverty, poor health, illiteracy, and misery that bore heavily on both races. The domain of abundant forests, wildlife, and fertile fields the Chickasaws had ceded to whites was now a largely ruined landscape of washed-out gullies, silt-laden creeks, and fields exhausted by the repeated planting of cotton. Forests once teeming with deer, bear, and other wild game were depleted, while the voracious advance of itinerant sawmills denuded wide swaths through them. Lafayette County was part of a nation that congratulated itself on a history of triumph, prosperity, opportunity, tolerance, and progress. In this part of America, however, a history of defeat, poverty, racism, and fatalistic despair cast a deep shadow across the land. These conditions would not begin to lift until after the Great Depression, when a combination of forces brought change to the economy, politics, and race relations of the South. It was toward the end of this prolonged era of gloom that William Faulkner, a fourth-generation Mississippian, began writing about his native land and the history that haunted it. He wrote fiction and made up characters and stories, but his subject, his source material, was the very real people and the history that his family had been part of since the time white Americans first settled in northern Mississippi.

Quite apart from Faulkner's unique contribution to the history of this county and region, Lafayette County, Mississippi, stands on its own as a southern community whose history can reveal much about the larger past of which it is part. We can learn from this kind of case study, not because Lafayette County was in any way exceptional or because events took place here of great significance to the nation's history. On the contrary, this county and its people present a rather typical, even ordinary, portrait of the southern past. Founded during the high tide of Old South expansion, it offers a view of southern society as it formed on the coarse western edge of the expanding cotton frontier. Much of our understanding of the Old South rests on images of older, more settled and finished eastern states like Virginia and South Carolina. In Mississippi, we witness the freshest expression of a dynamic southern society as it regenerated itself in the West.

Lafayette County also replicates in some rough fashion the social diversity of the Deep South. Straddling the piney hills and broad, fertile tablelands and river bottomlands near the Tallahatchie and Yoknapatawpha Rivers, the county included a range of wealth and social classes. There were hardscrabble, semisubsistence farmers in the hills who lived in unpainted dog-trot cabins, rich cotton planters and slave owners who lived in grand mansions with ostentatious white columns, and, in between, a wide strata of yeoman farmers who owned few or no slaves. Over 40 percent of the white families owned slaves, half of them owned less than five, but a few had well over one hundred. Slaves made up nearly half the people of the county, and blacks still claimed between 40 and 50 percent of the county's population a century after emancipation. Serving the isolated plantations and small farms of the countryside were several scattered hamlets that dotted the county's landscape, some emerging, others disappearing over time. Clustered around a country store, a cotton gin, or a blacksmith shop, these remote outposts of the marketplace connected, in turn, to Oxford, the economic hub and political center of local society. There, a distinctive town society led by the more prosperous families of planters, merchants, lawyers, government officials, and artisans fostered a genteel middle-class culture.

The University of Mississippi, founded in the 1840s, was the foundation of Oxford's identity as a cultural outpost in Mississippi. Faulkner had the freedom to take the university out of his fictional Jefferson, probably because it seemed atypical of the southern town life he was depicting. Historians do not possess the same license to remove or even ignore such things, but if the university makes Oxford seem exceptional, its impact on the local economy and society was limited before the twentieth century and never so great as to make the entire county significantly different.

The history of Lafayette County, as told in this book, does not always parallel the fictional historical portraits that Faulkner created for Yoknapatawpha County. The earlier history of Lafayette County and the crisis of the Civil War and Reconstruction receive far more attention here than in Faulkner's accounts of Yoknapatawpha. Slaves are present in Faulkner's fiction usually as anonymous background figures, but the slaves and descendants of slaves in Lafayette County are an integral part of this history. African slaves were the main source of labor for the cotton economy. Moreover, slavery and the destiny of former slaves were of central and continuing importance to the way history happened in this part of the world.

The faith underlying a local historical study such as this is that by knowing one small place well we can understand better the larger society of which it is a part. It is a premise not unlike that underlying a biopsy or blood sample examined by a physician. We know there is much to be learned about the larger organism by close inspection of one small part, not because it contains all the features of the larger body but because it includes many of its essential elements. No local sample of one county can ever be truly representative of such a large and diverse region as the American South, especially over more than a century. Whatever anomalies might exist in our Lafayette County sample, it nevertheless contains enough of the essential traits of the larger society to serve as a plausible specimen of the South.

To study a small community is more than just a convenient way of sampling; it is the context within which people experienced what we call social history. All social history, to rephrase Tip O'Neil's famous comment on politics, is local. Important national events, the Chickasaw treaties, the Panic of 1837, Fort Sumter, and Appomattox, always impinged on life as people experienced it in Lafayette County, to be sure. They lived in a nation with laws, wars, and markets that framed their lives in many ways. But to a remarkable degree people well into the twentieth century lived out their lives within a network of local connections. Political parties rested on grassroots organizations and were led by men who were known to local voters. When Lafayette County sent its men to war in 1861, they were told they were fighting for the altars and hearths of their loved ones at home. Those men fought—or deserted—based on their own calculation of personal and family advantage. Politics and economics, along with many other types of history, must take place within a broader, national or international framework, but social history requires us to scale down to the local context within which ordinary people lived.

Whatever one can say for Lafayette County as a representative case study, let me hasten to admit that the real reason I chose it was that William Faulkner chose it before me. Lafayette County was the primary source for what is the most famous imaginary place in American literature: Yoknapatawpha County, Mississippi. The "sole owner and proprietor" of this domain was William Faulkner, but his frequent references to the actual past remind us that the apocryphal Yoknapatawpha was also a product of the actual history. In sixteen novels and dozens of short stories, Faulkner conceived this fictional county, mapped its geographical landmarks, and filled it with characters he created. Yoknapatawpha was a place of the imagination, invented by Faulkner as a vehicle for developing a coherent body of fiction, but the raw materials from which he created this place and its people lay right at his front porch. His main subject was the history of this place, these people, and the larger South of which they were part. There is no single place in America that offers such a rich and extensive body of historical fiction.

Table 1 illustrates in schematic outline the broad historical periods of the sixteen novels in the Yoknapatawpha opus. This listing necessarily oversimplifies what were often complicated relationships between the present time of narration and flashbacks to earlier historical periods. A few of Faulkner's stories float loosely in time without the specific historical detail to allow precise definition of the chronological location, which sometimes must be deduced from knowledge of a character from another story.[1] Faulkner's treatment of the past was more seamless than this table suggests, but it nonetheless illustrates his continued probing of his people's history during a career of writing.

Interest in the relationship between the world Faulkner lived in and the one he created in fiction has generally focused on the anecdotal connections between particular people, places, and incidents in fact and fiction. Following Faulkner's belated rise to fame in the years after World War II, journalists, scholars, and local residents began outlining the parallels and connections between Yoknapatawpha and Lafayette County. Ward Miner's *The World of William Faulkner* (1952) was a pioneering attempt to connect the actual and apocryphal and to place Yoknapatawpha within a broad framework of historical interpretation. Joseph Blotner's meticulous biography of William Faulkner, published in 1974, unearthed a vast and fascinating web of connections between the fictional characters and events of Faulk-

William Faulkner, 1925. (Southern Media Archive, Center for the Study of Southern Culture, University of Mississippi)

ner's Yoknapatawpha and their local counterparts. Many other scholars have added to our understanding of how Faulkner made such extensive use of local characters and stories. Often they have relied on interviews with Lafayette County people and research into historical records to connect the fictional and factual. Among his neighbors, it became a local sport to try to guess the real-life counterparts to Faulkner's characters, "the one literary criticism of the town being 'How in the hell did he remember all that.' "[2] There may be no finer tribute to Faulkner's authenticity.

These links between people or incidents in famous literature and the

Table 1. Faulkner's Yoknapatawpha Novels and History

| | | Approximate Historical Period | | | | |
Novel	Year Published	Pre-1830	Ante-bellum	War/Recon-struction	New South	Since WWI
Sartoris	1929			x		
The Sound and the Fury	1929				x	x
As I Lay Dying	1930					x
Sanctuary	1931					x
Light in August	1932			x		x
Absalom, Absalom!	1936		x	x	x	
The Unvanquished	1938			x	x	
The Hamlet	1940				x	
Go Down, Moses	1941		x		x	x
Intruder in the Dust	1948					x
Knight's Gambit	1949				x	x
Requiem for a Nun	1951	x	x	x	x	x
Big Woods	1955	x			x	x
The Town	1957				x	x
The Mansion	1959				x	x
The Reivers	1962				x	

"real world" hold a certain fascination for readers, in part, because they seem to validate the notion that literature relates to life. I initially approached this project with the historian's instinctive skepticism toward fictional representations of history and with the unspoken expectation that my own empirical research into the historical sources of Yoknapatawpha would cast doubt on Faulkner as an authority on southern history. But the deeper I took my research into the history of this place, the more my respect grew for Faulkner, not as a historian dealing with facts and evidence but as an intuitive interpreter of the past and an astute observer of his contemporary social environment. I disagree with those who assume that because he was indifferent to "facts" that his fiction does not document accurately the social and historical reality of the world he was exploring. Writing history is not just sorting out facts; it is interpreting the past from the evidence left to us. At the same time, I came to appreciate more than ever the limitations of empirical historical research alone in understanding the past. Faulkner, I have often told my friends in literature, is much too important to leave solely to literary scholars. What I learned from Faulkner is that history, the interpretation of the past, is too important to leave exclusively to historians.

Many historians before me have seen in Faulkner a credible authority on the South, a writer of fiction who had something important to offer about the region and the meaning of its past. The renowned southern historian C. Vann Woodward credited Faulkner with leading the literary attack on the stubborn myths that enshrouded the region's past, thereby helping clear the way for historians to take up the task of revising the traditional narratives that had dominated southern history since Reconstruction. More than that, Woodward tells us, it was Faulkner's fiction that framed his reading of that past. After reading Faulkner, Woodward asked, how could one write about the New South without thinking about Flem Snopes or Jason Compson? How could one discuss the planters without recalling such vivid characters as Thomas Sutpen or Old Carothers? How could a historian exploring the world of black people not have in mind Joe Christmas, Lucas Beauchamp, or Dilsey? When Woodward refers to the New South as the "age of the Snopes," it seems his emplotment of southern history, as well as his ironic and tragic tone, owes much to Faulkner's fictional rendering. Confessing himself to be a historian "dedicated to fact" but "inspired by fiction," Woodward speaks for many historians of the South who cite Faulkner or his characters alongside documented evidence as though Faulkner's people, his South are—if not real—historically "true."[3] This exchange between fiction and history began with Faulkner's absorption of local and regional history into his works of fiction, but at some point this fiction began seeping back into the narratives and plots historians employ to narrate the South's past.

As I waded into the historical materials that document Lafayette County's past, while at the same time immersing myself in Faulkner's fictional world, I found I was frequently confusing the fictional and historical worlds. Names of people, events, places, and countless little details that emerged from the historical record of Lafayette County began to blur with what I was learning about the fictional Yoknapatawpha County. It must have been the same for William Faulkner, surely more so, because local history and legend were in the very air he breathed and voices he heard every day.

Often I stumbled across things in the historical records that immediately triggered a reference to the fictional Yoknapatawpha. In the attic of the county courthouse, I opened a large, leather-bound ledger to find a copy of the land deed with the "X" by which Hoka, the Indian woman who briefly owned the land, signed it away to three white men. This became the town site of Oxford that now lay sprawling outside the courthouse below. I could only think of Faulkner's Mohataha, the Indian queen in her silk dress who signs her own "X" conceding the land to the whites and then heads her wagon west to Oklahoma.

Names and people continually provoked connections to Faulkner's characters. In church records I came across a slave named Dilsey who was admitted as a member of the white Baptist church, then ran away with the Yankees and was excommunicated. I found the name Snipes so often in local records and on tombstones in the hills east of Oxford to make me think that it probably inspired Faulkner's name for the Snopes clan. Tales of shrewd country traders and their complicated deals I came across evoked thoughts of the Snopeses' uncanny talent for trade. Other stories of country folk who come to town and rise to wealth and position, like Joe Parks, who is always pictured with his Snopes-like small black bow tie, trigger images of Flem on the rise. There are dozens of names — Varner, Littlejohn, Ratliff, Hightower, Carothers, Bundren, Houston, and McEachern — found in Faulkner's fiction and then in the old newspapers, maps, or census rolls until the two worlds of fiction and history become at times difficult to keep separate.

I heard many stories and legends while visiting this county, some of them verifiable, many not. Some tales speak of the Civil War era when families buried or hid silver and other valuables from the invading Union soldiers (or maybe from marauding Confederates and bushwhackers, though they are rarely acknowledged). One account tells of the old Price mansion, near the Yoknapatawpha River, not far from Faulkner's Frenchman's Bend, said to have family treasure buried by a slave or slaves just before the Yankees invaded the area. The slaves ran off with them, or the Yankees killed them; the accounts vary, but no one remained to tell where the treasure was buried. For years after the war, treasure hunters came to the now abandoned mansion to dig fruitless holes around the abandoned house, just as Faulkner's characters do in The Hamlet. There are other stories that bleed into the fiction Faulkner wrote. One is about a man who hid out in the attic to avoid Confederate provost marshals, something like Faulkner's Goodhue Coldfield holed up in his pacifist attic retreat, with his bitter daughter Rosa below scribbling odes to Confederate heroes. One afternoon Earl Truett, a local historian and genealogist, told me in a whispered voice that his grandfather once showed him the location of Toby Tubby's grave. According to legend, when Toby Tubby died his Chickasaw tribesmen tried to bury his African slave, along with some of his gold and silver, in the chief's tomb. To anyone familiar with Faulkner's Yoknapatawpha, these and dozens of other accounts in Lafayette County's past testify to the parallel and sometimes intertwining worlds of the actual and the apocryphal.

I passed part of one afternoon visiting Susie Marshall, granddaughter of a slave, sitting on the front porch of her home in Oxford's "Freedman Town," facing what is now Martin Luther King Drive. She told me stories of her family a century or more before and showed me a photograph of her great-grandfather Jerry Fox, posing proudly with his freedom papers in his coat pocket. She also recalled stories of her childhood when she worked with her family in the cotton fields, waiting at the end of the cotton rows ladling water for the workers as they picked their way down to her, long bags of cotton trailing behind them.

Among the long-settled families in this county the past is very much part of family history, and it never seems more than one or two degrees separated from the present. One warm summer afternoon I was digging through dusty old ledgers in the basement of the City Hall with the help of W. C. Hill, a member of the Skipwith Society. He was telling me stories of the area around Delay and "Old Dallas," the latter a notoriously violent community in the southern part of the county, near Faulkner's fictional Frenchman's Bend. When I mentioned my interest in the murder of Elizabeth Ragland by former slaves right after the Civil War, he looked up and said: "She was my great-grandmother." Like so much of the informal collection of stories that make up local history, the Ragland murder had filtered down to me in a variety of confusing, contradictory accounts, which left even the year of the murder uncertain. The next day W. C. and his wife, Sybil, led me to the Ragland family cemetery, and there Elizabeth Ragland's tombstone gave an eerie verification of the date of the murder: 1866. Later we went over to the old Ragland house where she had died, her throat slashed one winter night 130 years before, and where her bloodstained hand print was left on the doorjamb. Some of the people and stories I came across began to sound more like Faulkner than Faulkner.

Another time, while probing the history of Oxford's Second Baptist Church, among the first churches founded by former slaves, the Reverend Leroy Wadlington paused to tell me that some of the history of his church "reads like a novel." Much of the history of this place seems to read like a novel, or is it that the novels Faulkner wrote depicted so vividly the people and the history I was unearthing? Many local citizens thought Faulkner painted too bleak and gothic a picture of their community. They shunned him after the publication of *Sanctuary* (1931), which featured the sexual molestation of a young university coed by a depraved criminal. Some early admiring critics tried to distance Yoknapatawpha from the historical South and emphasized the more uplifting moral message they saw in Faulkner's writing. But the more I learned about the history of this place, with all its drama and violence and fascinating stories, I came to realize Faulkner hardly told the half of it.

By drawing so heavily from the world he knew, Faulkner gave Yoknapatawpha an undeniable historical and social authenticity. "The land, the people, and their history," one fellow southern writer, Robert Penn Warren, wrote, ". . . come to us at a realistic level, at the level of recognition. . . . No land in all fiction is more painstakingly analyzed from the sociological point of view."[4] Faulkner was fully conscious of using local history as a source for his fiction. When explaining the actions or motives of his characters, he often referred to the historical context within which he imagined them. "I discovered that my own little postage stamp of native soil was worth writing about," he told one interviewer, ". . . and by sublimating the actual into the apocryphal I would have complete liberty to use whatever talent I might have to its absolute top."[5]

If the actual corresponded to the apocryphal in so many of the details of the Yoknapatawpha saga, more caution is due before granting Faulkner authority as an interpreter of the larger meaning or plot of southern history. Precisely because Faulkner is so often convincingly realistic or plausible in parts, it becomes tempting to accept his credibility as an authoritative guide to the South. Realistic historical fiction, whether in writing or film or television, has a dangerous way of imprinting on our minds images that sometimes overpower the less vivid version of the past that comes to us from conventional historical narratives. Historians have kept busy in recent years trying to correct misrepresentations of history as presented in Hollywood films. It is not that they want to impose the same rules of evidence on fiction that are appropriate to historical scholarship. We all know that a writer or director will exercise a certain creative license and take liberties with what is well known to be the accepted truth. As the lines blur between fact and fiction, the historian who sets out to evaluate a fictional representation of history is thrust into two levels of response. One casts him as the defender of verifiable truth sorting out what is factually accurate and what is not. The other places him as an interpreter of the past in which facts and evidence of all kinds become the material with which one constructs a narrative or theory that explains the past. While the first role reduces the historian to a nitpicking researcher, the second moves the historian dangerously close to the writer's craft of inventing stories.

Historians are among the first to admit that the distinction between fact and fiction is hardly clear-cut. Even the most rigorous and objective empirical research rests on historical evidence created by humans and filtered through their social and cultural biases, whether conscious or not. The newspapers this book relies on, for example, were politically slanted and their coverage focused on the town elite. If the hard, cold facts of the past are tainted by our ancestors' human prejudices, the narratives historians construct to interpret the past are shaped by another level of complicated and sometimes unconscious human bias. Whether it is popular versions of local history or academic historical scholarship, interpreting, or even simply reporting, the past can never be an objective, impartial account of what happened, when, and why. Because the past includes everything that happened, historians must select what seem the most important events, actors, and themes, but this first step in deciding who and what *belongs* in history is often the most loaded with partiality. Not long ago most historical writing was limited overwhelmingly to the story of government, political leaders, and the major events of national history. In recent times the boundaries of history as a subject have expanded to include a wide range of ordinary people, including women and blacks, rich and poor, along with diverse realms of experience: work, family, sexuality, and religion. There has been an accompanying shift toward the intensive study of local society, as in this book, as a means of getting at the full range of experience in the past and the way people lived. While professional historians have consciously sought to include a wider range of experience in their studies, this only complicates the problem of deciding one's subject. The choice of focus, in the end, remains a very human, and therefore inevitably partial, decision.

Fully aware of the imperfections of historical data and influences that affect choice and interpretation, the historian has faith, nonetheless, that the past is something we can come to know and understand. Even if we could recover full and perfect knowledge of the past, no historian would claim that we could arrive at one true and final version of what happened, let alone its cause and meaning. On the contrary, most historians see their task as an ongoing obligation to reexamine the conventional wisdom or to tell the untold story. They seek to displace old myths or deliberate lies with what they see as a truer story.

It is not at all the purpose of this book to burden readers with nitpicking corrections of various historical "errors" or implausible stories found in Faulkner's fictional epic of Yoknapatawpha. To be sure, there are many dates and details in the Yoknapatawpha saga that are "wrong" insofar as they do not agree with the historical record. We know Faulkner sometimes deliberately changed things to keep history and fiction at a distance. Out of respect for his neighbors (or fear of lawsuits), he changed names (Ratliff was Suratt until Faulkner became aware someone with that name was upset with him). Beat Two became Beat Four, the hill country source of poor white racism, perhaps out of a similar sensitivity. Other discrepancies, along with many factual inconsistencies in events and biographies within and across his many stories, came from his indifference, even contempt, for research and facts as a source of truth. "As far as I know I have never done one page of historical research," he once boasted to a group of wide-eyed college students. "Also, I doubt if I've ever forgotten anything I ever read," he added.

"That what I research," he went on to explain, "I read exactly as I do fiction because it's people, man in motion, and the writer . . . never forgets that, he stores it away . . . and when he needs it he reaches out and drags it out, and if it don't quite fit what he wants to say he'll probably change it a little bit."[6] "I dont care much for facts," he complained to Malcolm Cowley, ". . . you can't stand a fact up, you've got to prop it up, and when you move to one side a little and look at it from that angle, it's not thick enough to cast a shadow in that direction."[7] Faulkner in the end was less concerned with "history as a factual record," Michael Millgate tell us, "than with the past, especially the past as viewed from the standpoint of the present."[8]

But Faulkner wrote about the past with unusual sensitivity and understanding, and having spent several years plumbing the "historical record" myself, I am not sure I believe Faulkner's protestations that he never engaged in historical research and did not care about factual details. But that depends on how we define research. I had to spend hundreds of hours over several years doing research in libraries and conducting interviews to retrieve just a portion of what Faulkner would have grown up knowing about the community. That kind of research was never Faulkner's style. Blessed with a spongelike memory and a fine ear for stories and expression, he apparently had little need for formal research to acquire a command of his historical material. He spent a lifetime surrounded by people who immersed themselves in the past, some of them deeply engaged in serious historical research and writing. Asked how he came to know southern history, Faulkner once replied: "When I was a boy there were a lot of people around who had lived through it, and I would pick it up—I was just saturated with it, but never read about it."[9]

From boyhood Faulkner surrounded himself with people obsessed by the past, some engaged in serious historical research, others in the telling of stories. They all became his unwitting research assistants. At home and with relatives, he spent countless hours listening to stories. His father told of his youthful exploits, and his Aunt Alabama told tales of his great-grandfather Colonel William C. Falkner (the traditional family spelling), a Civil War colonel, railroad builder, and novelist of local fame. The Falkner family servant, Caroline (Mammy Callie) Barr, told young Bill Falkner stories of slavery days, the "secesh times," and the Klan, all from her perspective as a former slave. When Faulkner was in grade school during the fiftieth anniversary of the Civil War, his teacher spent hours on the local history of the Civil War, while down at the courthouse aging veterans told their own war stories, while young Bill Falkner sat for hours and listened enraptured. His friend Phil Stone regaled him for hours on the Civil War and local history. Faulkner had several other friends and neighbors who were steeped in the local history. Maud Morrow Brown was writing a never-published but remarkably well-researched and thoughtful manuscript on Lafayette County and the Civil War, which bears striking similarity to the portrait Faulkner was sketching at the same time in his Civil War stories. Calvin Brown, her husband, an archaeologist at the university, published a widely respected book on Mississippi's Indians, an enthusiasm he and Faulkner shared. Faulkner's sister-in-law Dorothy Oldham wrote a master's thesis on Jacob Thompson, an important local political figure.

Out at the university historians Charles S. Sydnor and Franklin Riley, along with Percy Rainwater, who taught school in Oxford, were writing important works on slavery, Reconstruction, and secession. Professors Riley and Sydnor directed the work of dozens of graduate students researching state and local history. Some of this scholarship, along with popular accounts by local journalists, was immediately accessible in the local newspaper, the *Oxford Eagle*. The fiftieth anniversary of the Civil War, the Mississippi centennial in 1917, and the county centennial in 1936 all were occasions for the *Eagle* to offer extensive coverage of local history. Women in the community, notably Faulkner's maternal grandmother, played leading roles as keepers of the past. In addition to raising Confederate memorials, they often conducted historical research. The local chapter of the Daughters of the American Revolution did interviews and researched documents to produce an unpublished county history in the 1920s. By the late 1930s, the Works Progress Administration employed several women and men to conduct interviews of former slaves and old settlers and set down on paper much of the local folklore and history that pervaded the county.

No one knows how this historical knowledge surrounding Faulkner might have filtered into his consciousness. Suffice it to say it would have been difficult, especially for a man with Faulkner's curiosity about the past, to be alive in this environment and *not* become familiar with the past that enveloped him. "The pattern," Malcolm Cowley surmised, "was based on what he saw in Oxford or remembered from his childhood; on scraps of family tradition . . . on kitchen dialogues between the black cook and her amiable husband; on Saturday-afternoon gossip in Courthouse Square; on stories told by men in overalls squatting on their heels while they passed around a fruit jar full of white corn liquor; on all the sources familiar to a small-town Mississippi boy." [10]

Faulkner may be of greatest value to the historian trying to understand the Mississippi past when he is least like a historian. It is Faulkner's intuitive knowledge of his subject, not his "factual" accuracy, that offers the historian insights not accessible through conventional research. It is when Faulkner goes inside the minds of his characters and imagines dialogues and thoughts that he reveals layers of historical experience historians can never document. They can only envy the creative license a fiction writer enjoys in inventing characters, dialogue, and inner thoughts. No amount of archival research can ever yield the kind of insight Faulkner imagines in the mind of a Thomas Sutpen who as a poor white boy of fourteen suddenly becomes conscious of his inferior position in the hierarchy of class in the antebellum South. In Faulkner's fiction people who remain inarticulate to the historian are given a voice, a mind, and a point of view through which the reader can see the world from their perspective. He once explained that he wrote about things his subjects "could have done," or "would have done" when no one was "there to record the action." [11] Faulkner was recording not only the action but also the thoughts and unconscious feelings that compelled the action.

What was Faulkner attempting to "tell about the South"? What was he making of the larger historical drama in which his actors were playing parts? Faulkner's early admirers George Marion O'Donnell, Robert Penn Warren, Malcolm Cowley, and Cleanth Brooks all sought to identify the underlying theme and meaning of the Yoknapatawpha saga. None was more influential in shaping the popular understanding of Faulkner's historical framework than Malcolm Cowley, editor of *The Portable Faulkner* (1946), which marked a key turning point in Faulkner's reputation as a writer. Cowley set out to assemble the stories and excerpts he selected from Faulkner's work according to the coherent design he saw in them. All the stories and novels, Cowley wrote in the introduction, were "like blocks of marble from the same quarry." Cowley organized the blocks within a historical and thematic framework. He took pains, constantly querying Faulkner through his letters, to locate each story in time, to place them in some chronological order, and to organize them in sections dealing with distinct historical eras, social groups, and themes.[12]

As he demonstrated the remarkable historical scope and coherence of the Yoknapatawpha stories, at the same time Cowley disassociated them from their historical source. He told readers that Faulkner was using the "legend" of the South as a parable to illuminate universal moral themes. The legend of the South, Cowley explained, revolved around the dichotomy between Old South and New South and the distinctive social and moral order of each. The dominant class of the Old South was the "aristocratic" planters and slave masters, men like Colonel John Sartoris, who sought to establish in Mississippi a lasting social order. Based on a traditional code of honor, this way of life was to be inherited by their sons. The flaws in their "design" for the Old South, Cowley admitted, derived from their ruthless appropriation of the land from the Indians and by the "guilt" associated with slavery. They nonetheless "had the virtue of living single-mindedly by a fixed code." The Old South's ruling class gave way, after the Civil War, to a "new exploiting class descended from the landless whites" personified in the unscrupulous Flem Snopes. Beginning with Frenchman's Bend, then the town of Jefferson, the county was "infested by the tribe of Snopes . . . in the bank, in the power company, in politics, Snopeses everywhere gnawing like rats at the standards by which the South had lived." [13] Against the avaricious force of Snopesism the traditional values of honor and chivalry were no match. The decline of the old order and the ascendance of the modern are the main themes in an essentially tragic and pessimistic history. The "ultimate subject," as Cowley put it, was "not the South or its destiny . . . but rather the human situation as revealed in Southern terms." [14]

Old South against New South, Sartoris versus Snopes, declining aristocracy and ascending poor whites, the code of honor and unscrupulous greed, these are the dichotomies through which early Faulkner critics taught us to read meaning into his work. It was a romantic view of southern history and one that had become a familiar formula in both popular and scholarly interpretations of the South. The stereotypes, as they were fleshed out, drew heavily on stock images of Old and New South, some dusted-off versions of antebellum propaganda on Yankees and Cavaliers, some borrowed from the Vanderbilt Agrarians' view of a traditional South beleaguered by modern forces of industrialism. Still others came from popular culture, notably Margaret Mitchell's Gone With the Wind.

Whatever the source of this southern imagery, all did service in favor of romanticizing the Sartorises of the Old South and demonizing the Snopeses of the New South. Cleanth Brooks summarized much of the tone of this anti-Snopesian sentiment when he wrote: "The insidious horror of Snopesism is its lack of any kind of integrity—its pliability, its parasitic vitality as of some low-grade, thoroughly stubborn organism. . . . The difficulty of fighting Flem and Snopesism in general is that it is like fighting a kind of gangrene or some sort of loathsome mold. . . . Flem is a kind of monster who has betrayed everyone, first in his lust for pure money-power, and later in what Faulkner regards as a more loathsome lust, a desire for respectability." [15] Another early critic, Irving Howe, though writing at some distance from the agrarian romanticism that shaped Brooks's view of the South, nonetheless joined forces in his utter contempt for the reptilian Snopeses: "Let a world collapse, in the South or Russia, and there appear figures of coarse ambition driving their way up from beneath the social bottom. . . . Scavengers without inhibition, they need not believe in the code of their society; they need only learn to mimic its sounds." [16]

By the 1960s Brooks had completed his own more elaborate version of this agrarian romantic interpretation of Faulkner's Yoknapatawpha. His finely crafted essays made Faulkner accessible to a growing legion of professors and students as Faulkner became firmly ensconced in the academic canon. A new generation of Faulkner scholars would move beyond these early interpretations, often into social themes of race and gender, the interior realm of psychology, and the historical-intellectual context of Faulkner as a writer. In general, contemporary Faulkner scholars have more interest in the text and its author than in the historical context of the historical *subjects* he wrote about. Even those with a deep interest in historicizing Faulkner's fiction are understandably unlikely to do the kind of historical research required to retrieve more than a few pieces of the puzzle. Several probing studies have taken up the subjects of race and social class, themes that lie at the heart of Faulkner's historical interpretation of the South. Perhaps more out of neglect than agreement, however, the main structure of the Old South versus New South, Sartoris versus Snopes paradigm erected by Cowley and finished by Brooks remains intact, or at least unchallenged by some other framework for understanding the social history of Yoknapatawpha.

It is my hope that readers of this book will come away with a different reading both of the South's past and of Faulkner's fictional version of that past. Wisdom dictates that I leave the task of reinterpreting Faulkner to others more qualified than I and not risk practicing literary criticism without a license. I have profited enormously from several biographies and critical works on Faulkner, and my several sojourns to Oxford for the annual Faulkner conference have introduced me to a group of professional colleagues in literature who have generously guided my journey in Yoknapatawpha. I have enjoyed crossing the boundaries on the unfortified but sometimes formidable academic frontier that separates history and literature. I can think of no place better than Yoknapatawpha where the two disciplines can meet, communicate, and enrich one another's knowledge of this writer and his subject. But my travels in this realm of literature have also reminded me that I am a tourist in a country where the natives speak a different language and use different currency than historians are accustomed to using. Historians have their own special skills and modes of interpretation, and it has always seemed more fruitful that we use those rather than try to ape the language and approach of another discipline. While this book is in some ways an interdisciplinary adventure that joins literature and history, it is history not literary criticism.

As I immersed myself in Faulkner's historical-fictional world I came to admire his knack of setting his stories characters within a particular time and place in his Yoknapatawpha cosmos. Whether by references to larger events outside the county, or perhaps to the technology of mules or automobiles, Faulkner seemed attentive to placing his subject in time. He could not resist telling us the history of each character as well; even minor characters act as they do because of their personal and family background. The past bears down upon and shapes the present always. Faulkner also seemed keenly interested in how we come to know the past: whether by memory or record, through biased, vague "mouth to mouth tales" or through what we learn in written documents such as letters from "old trunks and boxes and drawers" written in a language that may sound to us "like Sanskrit or Choctaw." Part of Faulkner's obsession with the past had to do with his idea of time as a fluid entity in which the past and present flow into one another. The past was ever present in the here and now, he often repeated; everything we do, all that we believe, and all we think we know in the present and the future has been shaped by what came before. The "past is never dead," one of his characters says; "It's not even past." [17] These quotes and others are sometimes mistaken for a romantic southern traditionalism that reveres the past above the modern American cult of progress. But Faulkner's view of history was more tragic than nostalgic. He saw the southern past as a burden on his people, carrying with it sins so profound that the past constituted a curse that hung over the land, inherited by one generation after another.

In *Absalom, Absalom!*, William Faulkner's historical novel about Thomas Sutpen and his doomed plan to elevate himself in the society of the Old South, much of the story unfolds many years later in a setting familiar to most anyone who has gone off to college or anyplace away from home and shared stories about where they came from. It is 1909 and two Harvard freshmen are staying up late in their dormitory room, in the "iron cold" New England winter. They are in what C. Vann Woodward once called the "Deep North," a place and time that seems remote from the place and people they are talking about. One roommate, who is mostly listening to the story and helping piece it together, is Shreve McCannon. He is from Canada, a nation serenely sheltered from the traumas of revolution, civil war, and reconstruction, innocent of slavery and racism, all of which had left deep scars on its neighbor to the South. The other young man in the dorm room that winter is Quentin Compson, who comes from a small town named Jefferson in Yoknapatawpha County, Mississippi, a place his grandfather helped found in the 1830s. Unlike Shreve, Quentin has grown up with stories of the Civil War and all the calamities that befell the South. He is "a barracks filled with stubborn back-looking ghosts" who knows history has inflicted terrible pain on his people.

The story Quentin is sharing with Shreve has to do with a mysterious man, Thomas Sutpen, who came to Yoknapatawpha County "out of nowhere," established a grand plantation, and survived the Civil War only to die violently shortly afterward. Parts of Sutpen's story have been related to Quentin by different sources, each with very different points of view. One informant is an embittered elderly woman, Rosa Coldfield, who has carried a grudge against Sutpen for over forty years. Just before Quentin left for Harvard, this woman summoned him to her home one afternoon and regaled him with her diatribe against this "demon," as she calls him. The boys have other, more sympathetic, sources on Sutpen to consider. Sutpen told his story to Quentin's grandfather sometime in the 1830s, and this account filters through Quentin's father in ways that supplement and balance Rosa Coldfield's vindictive story. Far removed from any firsthand knowledge of the subject, with only some biased oral testimonies, along with a few letters and tombstone inscriptions as written documents, the two boys do exactly what historians do when interpreting the past. They piece the story together, they gather facts, they infer other events and thoughts, they imagine some things and research others, and they interpret motive and causation from the facts and evidence available to them. They construct a history, and they struggle to come to terms with its meaning.

For Quentin the story is a disturbing exploration of Sutpen's past, and by extension his own. It goes to the core of the South's tragic history, but it also impinges upon his own family's past. Quentin learns that he was probably summoned by Rosa Coldfield, so his father speculates, because of some inherited guilt she may think the Compson family bears for aiding Sutpen. Shreve, the Canadian, on the other hand, is personally innocent of this past and apparently unperturbed by any moral implications the story might have for him. Against Quentin's tormented probing of his people's past, Shreve plays the role of the objective historian, an outsider who is simply fascinated by the story for its intrinsic interest. Sheer curiosity and a desire to know about this exotic place, the American South, with all its folly and tragedy is what drives Shreve. He prods his tortured roommate to get on with the telling of the story, and provides witty, often sardonic, summaries of the plot as it unfolds. "Tell about the South," Shreve urges Quentin. "What's it like there. What do they do there. Why do they live there. Why do they live at all." [18] Faulkner's life work is in some degree or another a response to Shreve's questions.

As the two young men dig deeper into the story, the Mississippi native serving up more evidence, the Canadian helping make sense of it all, Quentin tells Shreve you can't understand all this if you are not part of it: "You would have to be born there." Shreve is unimpressed with this claim to subjective knowledge and replies: "Would I then?" "Do you understand it?" To which Quentin replies with honest confusion: "I dont know. . . . Yes, of course I understand it. . . . I dont know." Shreve: "Yes. You dont know."

I have thought often of this scene while working on this book. It speaks directly to the confused debate of our own day over whether we can understand people of different races, nationalities, or genders. It resonates even more with a historian who would claim he might know and understand the often strange people who inhabit that very foreign country, the past. One of the things I most admire in Faulkner is his attempt—even when it fails—to transcend his own time, his class, his gender, his race, his identity and to tell about the South in all its human diversity, to tell us about places, so to speak, where we were not born. Faulkner's durability as an author is explained in part by the capacity of readers and scholars to find in his work a remarkable range of human experience. Faulkner stayed close to home, close to what he knew well, and yet within that little "postage stamp of native soil" so bizarre, remote, and outlandish in many ways, he explored a vast human world. He is at his most impressive when he attempts to write outside his own personal experience, to render sympathetic sketches of poor whites or planters, women, and blacks, or to put the reader inside the mind of a retarded boy, a young child, a slave, a crazed killer, or an angry white racist. It is this same intuitive power to escape the confines of personal knowledge and experience that allows Faulkner to grasp historical time and be able to depict plausible people, motives, thoughts, and behavior. The creation and reading of both fiction and history depend on this desire to transcend the limits of personal knowledge, to learn something of human experience beyond the narrow compass of our own lives.

Though I have now lived in a neighboring state in the South for more than twenty-five years, I am an outsider to Mississippi. I was not "born there." Through research in old documents and occasional conversation, my goal has been to excavate and make sense out of the history of this place. In a sense, Shreve and Quentin's exchange speaks to most every reader of Faulkner, for his work invites us into a world that is strangely foreign to most of us now, even to those "born there" in more recent times. The South Faulkner wrote about has changed dramatically. Even the pictures taken by Martin Dain, the *Life* magazine photographer who documented Faulkner's contemporary world, with its gaunt men in overalls, unpainted cabins, and country stores, seem as though from another century. As I drive through this part of Mississippi most of the old sharecroppers' cabins, along with the barns Dain captured on film, are collapsing from neglect or engulfed by kudzu vines. There is still poverty here, but even the poor now live in double-wide trailers with all manner of appliances on the porch, and a car or two, maybe a boat, and always a satellite dish, out front. The simple boxlike country churches still are standing, though many now are prefabricated metal buildings and others have new asbestos or aluminum siding with bright green astroturf at the entrance. Service station convenient marts seem to have replaced the old general stores in the countryside, but most people make their way into Oxford to shop at the mall. In the age of air conditioning one rarely sees people sitting outside on the porches these days. With television, movies, computers, and travel, Oxford, and to some extent the whole county, is part of a national and international culture that seems to erode local and regional traditions.

For all the change that modern life has brought to this part of the world, the past remains, hanging over the place, shaping its daily life. As I drove south into Mississippi these past few years, I often thought of Faulkner's story of the blackened glass shard with the inscription that is part of his story "The Jail." As though anticipating the stream of scholars who would come to explore his world, he imagines a stranger "the outlander with a B.A. or (perhaps even) M.A. from Harvard or Northwestern [my alma mater, as it happens] or Stanford, passing through Jefferson" by chance. One of the local women, those mainly responsible for keeping the past, tells him the story of a "frail blonde girl" who, after the Civil War began, scratched her name and the date, "Celia Farmer, April 16th 1861," in the jailhouse window. The window becomes a proud display in the local museum, Faulkner imagined, apparently modeling this on the etched shard of blackened glass housed in the Mary Buie Museum in Oxford, which the curator brought out for me to admire during one of my visits. It is this window with its inscription from the past that becomes the "clear undistanced voice" of a long-dead frail girl who "across the vast instantaneous intervention, from the long long time ago" says, " 'Listen, stranger; this was myself: this was I.' "[19] It is voices like hers and others "performing their acts of simple passion and simple violence, impervious to time and inexplicable" that I have tried to listen to and animate in telling this story.

And as he talked about those old times and those dead and vanished men of another race from either that the boy knew, gradually to the boy those old times would cease to be old times and would become a part of the boy's present, not only as if they had happened yesterday but as if they were still happening, the men who walked through them actually walking in breath and air and casting an actual shadow on the earth they had not quitted. —WILLIAM FAULKNER, Go Down, Moses

one Yoknapatawpha

This is the story of a small parcel of land and the succession of people who inhabited it at different times in the past, all of them "casting an actual shadow on the earth" long after they passed through it. Even the land itself—at least the thick top layer of windblown soil—was migratory in the beginning. It arrived sometime after the last ice age in enormous dust storms, the windswept refuse of northern glaciers that blew across the plains and down into the Mississippi River Valley. There it settled like huge earthen snowdrifts above the bluffs on the eastern edge of the Delta, the river's broad alluvial plain. What would become, in William Faulkner's hands, the most southern of all places was covered in dust blown down from those cold northern plains thousands of years before.

Faulkner decided on calling the fictional county he created out of this place "Yoknapatawpha." It would surprise no one familiar with Faulkner to think he may have taken some perverse pleasure in forcing this unruly word into the mouths of readers and critics, millions of them in due course. But the name also rooted Faulkner's county in the geographical and historical reality of the world he knew firsthand and wanted to bring to life in fiction. Whether readers know it or not, the name is *real*, and so is much else about Yoknapatawpha County. The Chickasaw people apparently called the slow, winding river that flows through the southern portion of Lafayette County the Yoknapatawpha. When the whites took over, they adopted the names of those they dispossessed for the rivers, towns, counties, and the state itself. It was an ironic tribute anticipating modern suburban developers who name their places "Whispering Pines" or "Fairfield" after the habitat they destroy building them.[1]

The spelling, pronunciation, and meaning of Yoknapatawpha baffled the white people who took over the land from the Chickasaws in 1836. Because it was only a phonetic spelling, there was no set standard for writing the word, and even among local officials, map makers, newspaper reporters, and inhabitants there were a multitude of variations. There were probably even more variations in pronunciations (today it is pronounced YOK-na-pa-TAW-pha). This became comically evident during the Civil War when Union armies invading northern Mississippi moved back and forth across the river and often had to rely on local informants for its name. Their orders and field reports spelled the name of the river differently nearly every time. Even before the Civil War, one finds shortened and more manageable abbreviations used by local people in official county records and newspapers. The old Chickasaw word became shortened to "Yockney" and sometime later further abbreviated as "Yocona" (pronounced YOK-na), which today is the name borne by the river and a small community on the river near what Faulkner called Frenchman's Bend.[2]

According to local lore during Faulkner's time, Yoknapatawpha meant "land divided" or "split land," but there seems to have been no definitive agreement on exactly what kind of division this signified. Some thought the river was a hunting boundary between Chickasaw clans or possibly between the Chickasaws and Choctaws or some other Indians. One map seems to indicate different Indian peoples that had been absorbed by the Chickasaws on either side of the Yoknapatawpha River.[3] Others thought the divider was the "Old Trail," an Indian path that ran across the land from Pontotoc through Toccopola to Toby Tubby's ferry crossing on the Tallahatchie ("rocky river"). One pioneer described the trail as "a path not more than three feet wide, taking a course through the forest as straight as an arrow.

Not a twig nor bush obstructed the view as far as the eye could see."[4] The best available source on the Chickasaw language during Faulkner's time was Byington's *Dictionary of the Choctaw Language* (Choctaw and Chickasaw shared a common Muskhogean language). Originally compiled by Cyrus Byington, a missionary among the Choctaws in the 1820s, it was published by the Smithsonian Institution in 1915. As in English, "yakni" (land) had social and political meanings as well. Byington's dictionary tell us "yakni" could mean "the earth . . . the world; land; soil; ground; nation . . . country; empire; kingdom; province; state; a continent; district; dust; the globe; territory." "Patafa" comes from the verb "to split" and as a modifier it could mean "plowed, furrowed, tilled," or "split open." A modern Chickasaw dictionary tells us it also translates "to be ripped; to be cut open for disemboweling."[5]

Faulkner may not have been aware of these various levels of meaning, but, wittingly or not, he chose a word full of implications, many of them ominous, for the land and the people whose story he would tell. Perhaps none of the new inhabitants realized that the name Yoknapatawpha persisted as a rebuke to whites who dispossessed one race and imported another in order to break the land for cotton plantations ("Tore violently a plantation," in the memorable words of Faulkner's Miss Rosa Coldfield). The new occupants who took over this land would divide it into counties, townships, and sections for sale. They plowed the land to plant cotton and corn, and they watched as erosion rapidly tore apart the land. But the doom implied in the name Yoknapatawpha is also evident in its social meaning, for the land would soon see its new inhabitants divided and torn by war and racial conflict, all in ways their Chickasaw predecessors could not have imagined. The name Yoknapatawpha became a prophecy and a curse that would loom over the land and its new proprietors.

Land of the Chickaza

For close to a century and a half before their removal from Mississippi, the Chickasaws and other southern tribes underwent vast and complicated changes, some devastating and beyond their control, others deliberate responses to the challenges of their changing human and natural worlds. Sometime well before contact with the Europeans, the Chickasaws were themselves newcomers to northern Mississippi. The people known today only as the Mississippian culture that preceded the Chickasaws left behind large burial mounds that can still be seen in Lafayette County today. According to one version of their migration legend, the Chickasaws had undertaken a long and arduous trek from far west of the Mississippi River in flight from hostile northern Plains Indians. They were then one people with the Choctaws, sharing the same language and tribal identity and the same destiny east of the Mississippi. The legend tells of two brothers, Chicsa and Chacta, who, after crossing the Great River, agreed that Chicsa was to travel ahead with one group and locate a place to settle; Chacta and his band were to follow. But a heavy snow covered the trail, and the tribe became divided forever. As legend has it, this was a peaceful and lamentable separation, siblings separated by accidental family tragedy. The legend does not explain how or when a fierce enmity developed between the two groups, one exacerbated—if not created—by the intrusion of European rivalry in the Lower Mississippi Valley. In the Muskhogean language they shared "Chickasaw" meant "rebel"; it was a Choctaw epithet that their former brothers wore with pride.[6]

In their journey east, the Chickasaws were guided by an oracle pole, which the priests drove into the ground at the end of each day's trek. The next morning they would direct the tribe in whichever direction the gods had made the pole lean. It led them ever eastward, first to a settlement near the Tennessee River and then, sometime later, southward to the black prairie land at the headwaters of the Tombigbee River. The Chickasaws built a cluster of towns in what came to be known as the Chickasaw Old Fields, a few miles east of the Yoknapatawpha headwaters, on the other side of the Pontotoc Ridge near the present-day city of Tupelo. There they tilled the land, raising corn, squash, beans, and other crops supplemented by wild berries, nuts, and fruit from the forest. The black prairie land was fertile and the land was abundant. All around the towns the Chickasaws burned brush periodically to keep the land clear for defensive purposes and to encourage deer and other game to graze. The result was a light forest canopy and parklike glades of open meadow on which deer would roam almost like domesticated livestock. Though the villages in the Old Fields shifted locations over the years, this area was the permanent base from which parties of Chickasaw braves would depart to hunt and make war; it remained the center of the Chickasaw homeland until the 1830s.[7]

The Chickasaws were a small but formidable tribe feared by neighbors on all sides. Though at times bands of Chickasaws ranged from the edge of the Great Plains to the Atlantic and Gulf coasts, their main hunting grounds extended north to the Cumberland, Ohio, and Mississippi Rivers and only a few miles south of their towns to the land of the Choctaws. Their domain had been secured by a bloody tradition of war waged against neighboring tribes and intruding European forces. The Chickasaw warrior, his face dressed in red war paint, head shaved on the sides, a crest of black hair slicked with bear grease and decorated with eagle feathers, armed with bow, arrow, and tomahawk, was a fearsome presence in this part of the world long before and after the arrival of Europeans.[8] In conflicts with neighboring tribes several times their size, the Chickasaws were never defeated militarily, not even by whites with all their guns, armor, and horses. For three centuries the Chickasaws, the "Spartans of the Mississippi Valley," handily routed every European and Indian power that challenged them.

The first whites to encounter the Chickasaws were the Spanish with Hernando DeSoto, who arrived in the land of the "Chicaza" in December 1540. To a people living in a stone-age culture, deep in the interior of the continent, it must have been a remarkable spectacle: men with pale skin and beards, clattering through the forest in noisy metal armor, some mounted on strange-looking beasts, the first horses ever seen in this part of the world. The white men carried weapons unknown to the Indians: metal knives, swords, lances, and muskets. Along with this army of men, the Spanish brought hogs, cattle, and chickens as food supply to the expedition. All of these weapons and livestock and the strange people who brought them would eventually bring enormous change to the world of the Chickasaw, but this first encounter would involve only a brief, violent incident followed by more than a century of continued isolation from Europeans.

DeSoto was impressed with the Chickasaws' ample supplies of corn, and he hoped they would be willing to provide for his men and livestock, so he decided to establish a winter camp in an abandoned village called Chicasa. The Spanish worked on cultivating an alliance with their hosts, treating the chiefs to grand feasts and bestowing gifts upon them. The chiefs, in turn, brought gifts of food and clothes to their visitors. The Chickasaws had no domestic animals and had never before tasted anything like the pork the Spanish roasted for these feasts. They developed a strong appetite for this original southern barbecue and a few braves came back for more. A clash of cultures ensued. To Indians a chief's generosity with food and other material goods was a signifier of power. Furthermore, much of the tribe's food was regarded as a community resource, not the private property of individuals or families. To the Spanish, in contrast, the Indians were simply stealing their hogs. When they caught three braves in the act, they killed two of them, chopped off both hands of the third, and sent him back to his chiefs as an object lesson in how white men punished theft.[9]

Chickasaw distrust toward their brutal visitors grew when winter came to an end and DeSoto prepared to move on. He demanded that the chiefs supply his expedition with two hundred Chickasaw men to serve as porters. Having heard of the Spaniards' harsh treatment of other Indian tribes earlier in the expedition, the Chickasaws interpreted this request as an invitation to enslavement.[10] Before dawn one night in March 1541 several bands of

Chickasaw warriors struck without warning. They rushed the Spanish fortifications, screaming their war whoop and beating furiously on wooden drums. They set fire to the thatched roofs of the soldiers' quarters, and as the startled Spanish fled naked into the night, Chickasaw bowmen showered them with arrows. They could have annihilated the Spanish that night, but, inexplicably, the braves suddenly panicked and fled, leaving DeSoto and his men to escape. A dozen Spaniards, nearly sixty horses, and hundreds of pigs died at the hands of Chickasaw warriors that terrifying night (some pigs escaped to the wilds, progenitors of the renowned razorback hog). The Spanish gathered their surviving livestock and supplies and, after brief skirmishing, retreated westward, passing north of the Yoknapatawpha country, toward the "Great River," the Mississippi, which DeSoto would discover for the European world.[11]

A century and a half would pass before sustained contact with Europeans began for the Chickasaws in the 1690s. Then, during much of the century that followed, they were caught up in the struggle of European powers for control of the North American interior. The Chickasaws allied with the English in opposition to French incursions into the Lower Mississippi Valley. English traders, based in Charleston, South Carolina, cultivated a commercial and diplomatic alliance that was essential to the English struggle against the French for the Lower Mississippi Valley.

The French, in alliance with the Choctaws, launched in 1736 what was to be a war of annihilation against the Chickasaws. One force of several hundred French soldiers and Indian warriors under the command of Major Pierre D'Artaguette came south from Illinois. Another, led by French Louisiana's governor, Jean Baptiste Le Moyne D'Bienville, came north from Mobile with French and Choctaw troops. But when D'Artaguette's Indian allies saw the Chickasaw warriors descending upon them, shouting their fearsome war whoop, they fled in terror and watched the battle from a safe distance. Only twenty French soldiers escaped with their lives. The Chickasaw warriors captured D'Artaguette and other French and Indian prisoners. They drove small stakes of fat pine into their naked bodies and set them aflame and watched them burn to death slowly.[12] When Bienville's larger army arrived later at Ackia the Chickasaws triumphed over them. Bienville first ordered a charge led by a contingent of black slaves who carried large, heavy wooden shields, behind which the French soldiers marched, their flags flying and drums beating valiantly. When a massive volley of Chickasaw gunfire answered the French advance, the Choctaws also fled in terror and watched the slaughter of their French allies. The Battle of Ackia left Europeans and Indians with an unforgettable respect for the Chickasaw warriors. By 1763 the French challenge to English domination in the Mississippi Valley had been eliminated with the British victory in the French and Indian War. Chickasaw resistance to French rule had been instrumental to the British achievement.[13]

Trade, Not Treats

During the century that fell between the triumph at Ackia in 1736 and their removal from Mississippi in the 1830s, the Chickasaws remained in constant contact with Europeans. The Chickasaw way of life, their economy and population, their dress, food, and drink, their entire culture underwent tremendous change. A new system of exchange arose, primarily with English traders, followed by Americans. The Chickasaws had engaged in some trade with other Indian peoples, and a vast network of trails extending across the Southeast was one legacy of that commerce.[14] Now the Chickasaw Trail connecting all the way to Charleston would become a major artery of trade between the English based in Charleston and the Chickasaws in the borderland between English and French territory in the Lower Mississippi Valley. The Chickasaws quickly learned the white man's game of trade, how goods were assigned a particular value, how credit and debt could be kept in account for long periods, and how debts could be canceled by more exchange. The lessons were learned first with deerskins and guns, slaves and horses, calico dresses and liquor, and finally in land and money. The Indians were drawn in steps into the white world of the marketplace, but all the time they saw the whites joining their world.

The English established trade with the Indians for diplomatic purposes in their struggle against the French, and, more than the French, the English were motivated by commercial profit (hunger for Chickasaw land or religious concern for their salvation would not come until the American era). Successful trade relations depended on the wants of each party. In addition to Indian slaves, the English wanted animal skins, particularly deerskins for gloves, book binding, and other luxury articles, all in high demand in Europe. For a time, the abundance of game allowed the Chickasaws to harvest enormous quantities of pelts, which were loaded on pack horses or the backs of slaves for overland export across the Chickasaw Trail to Charleston.[15] A flourishing exchange economy emerged in the Lower Mississippi Valley. It built on earlier trade among different Indian peoples and grew as European goods whetted new consumer appetites, compelling various economic adaptations among the Indians. Many adapted with remarkable success, so that by the time of their removal from Mississippi, the more commercially oriented among the Chickasaws and Choctaws had developed the main features of the very same commercial economy of cotton and slaves white Americans would claim as their special province.[16]

The English saw their task as cultivating a market culture among the Chickasaws and supplanting traditional Indian notions of exchanging gifts with the concept of trade that placed a specific, accountable value on goods in exchange. "Trade not treats" was the slogan the English brought to the Chickasaw deerskin trade.[17] Of course, this concept was not entirely new to Indians who had exchanged goods across long distances long before the Europeans arrived, but now they had to learn the English terms of trade. A complementary strategy involved increasing Chickasaw consumer appetite, to encourage them to *want* more. Stimulation of some wants was easy, for many of the European imports—guns, horses, and knives—made the Chickasaws more productive at traditional skills of hunting and skinning animals. These weapons could also be put to use in wars and slave raids. The Chickasaw trade with whites fed upon itself, and they gradually moved away from a largely subsistence economy toward one of dependency on trade with the white world.

Deer had been a traditional source of food and clothing for the Chickasaws, and the supply was more than sufficient for their small numbers. But when deerskins became a commodity of trade with Europeans there was a virtually unlimited demand from outside their population. As hunting pressure intensified, the game population dwindled, and "the chase" required more effort, longer treks, and more conflict with competing tribes. At the same time, the usual imports of white goods were losing their power to stimulate the hunt. Guns, knives, pots, and other durable manufactured goods did not need to be replaced often. As for livestock, the Chickasaws began breeding their own; indeed, the Chickasaw pony became a prized breed among whites and Indians.

Imports from the European world shifted from utilitarian goods toward luxury consumer items. Clothing, jewelry, blankets, and other items gained favor among Chickasaw men and women, who became famous for their elaborate ornamentation. Among the men, one of the early favored items of clothing was breechcloths made in Britain, which soon replaced the traditional ones made of animal skins. One Chickasaw complained that the imported loincloths "don't cover our secret parts, and we are in danger of being deprived of our manhood by every hungry dog that approaches," but the edict of fashion overruled such practical concerns.[18] After decades of exchange with Europeans, the Chickasaws earned a reputation for sartorial splendor. One white described them "with showy shawls tied in turban fashion round their heads—dashing about on their horses, like Arabs, many of them presenting the finest countenances and figures that I ever saw." [19] Chickasaw women took to wearing large petticoats fastened with leather belts decorated with bright brass buckles.[20] Later, during the American era, the women began wearing imported calico dresses while the men adopted long pants, shirts, and shoes as standard attire. As buying power increased during the American era, some Chickasaws became lavish in their tastes. Men and women were "extravagantly ornamented," often laden with multiple necklaces and bracelets of silver. Chickasaw men adorned themselves with military uniforms, silver medals, swords, and other regalia, much of it acquired as presents from English and American agents. Wealthy Indians and chieftains took the trend to extremes. Wolf's Friend attended council meetings and negotiations with European powers dressed in a fantastic array of "scarlet and silver lace, and in the heat of day with a large crimson umbrella over him."[21]

Faulkner's Mohataha, regally adorned in a purple silk gown and plumed hat, followed by an African slave girl who holds a silver-handled Parisian parasol above her and carries her slippers while the Indian queen walks barefoot, becomes a more plausible image in light of these accounts. Other Indians in Faulkner's fiction wear artifacts from the white world and adopt names that are amalgams of English and Indian. Three Basket wears an enameled snuff box clamped through his ear. Other men wear the "formal regalia of the white man . . . broadcloth trousers and white shirts with boiled starch bosoms" and carry "New England–made shoes under their arms." These are the Indians Faulkner describes gathering at the Indian trading post, where they squat on the gallery munching cheese and crackers and peppermint candy, all bought at the trading post on credit.[22]

As the Indian trade evolved, by the late eighteenth century it was liquor, rather than clothing and ornaments, that became a major ingredient of exchange. Faulkner makes only passing mention of liquor and drunkenness in his sketches of the Indians, but it is one more sign of white contamination of Yoknapatawpha.[23] Before European contact, liquor was unknown to the Indians, who drank nothing more intoxicating than an occasional fermented ceremonial drink.[24] The liquor trade fit perfectly into the strategy whites had been pursuing all along in their trade with the Indians, for liquor was the ideal item of trade to supply a want created by white traders. It was, of course, intoxicating, temporary in effect, habituating, readily consumed, and easily replenished. Experts now believe that the Indian's vulnerability to alcohol had to do more with psychological demoralization than with any racially distinctive physiological weakness. Whatever the cause, alcohol arrived with devastating impact during a time of disturbing change in the Indian's world.[25]

English and, later, American officials decried the debauchery and demoralization that the liquor trade wrought among the Indians. British officials tried with limited success to regulate the number of white traders and ban the sale of liquor among the Chickasaws because it corrupted their "manners" and "rendered them ungovernable."[26] But, like the modern drug trade, efforts to repress liquor only increased its value and the profit to be made. An estimated four-fifths of the skins acquired from the Chickasaws in 1770 were paid for in rum.[27]

Though the liquor trade had initially been one of many imports intended to awaken wants among the Indians, its effect was to destroy instead of build the ethos of industry, sobriety, and thrift that whites claimed would come from wanting things. In the end, the baleful impact of alcohol on Indians became a common reference among those arguing for their removal from the encroaching white civilization. "Strong drink has long been the destroyer of this people," one American missionary to the Chickasaws wrote on the eve of removal. "Whiskey, that devouring foe, is the god they adore, and after it they heedless go."[28] Given their usefulness to the case for removal, the reports on the extent of Indian drunkenness and alcoholism may well have been exaggerated. In any case, it should be recalled this was an era of rampant drinking among white Americans, especially urban workers, and the temperance reform movement heightened awareness of the alcohol problem among Indians.

Mississippi Mélange

The exchange between whites and Indians was not only in goods. The most destructive imports from the white world were deadly germs, many of them airborne so that in their very breath, their speech, their touch, whites transmitted deadly diseases. Smallpox, measles, diphtheria, and other highly contagious diseases had scourged the population in Europe for generations and gradually built up immunities among the survivors. Among the hitherto untouched Native American population, these same diseases cut ghastly swaths of death.

Estimates of this biological catastrophe indicate that as many as 80 and 90 percent of the native population was decimated following contact with Europeans. The Chickasaws' location in the interior, away from river and oceangoing boats that carried epidemics quickly to other tribes to the south, ought to have protected them more than other tribes, but it did not. At the opening of the eighteenth century, just as sustained contact with Europeans began, estimates of the Chickasaw population put them at about 2,000 warriors and a total of about 10,000 people. Seventy-five years later,

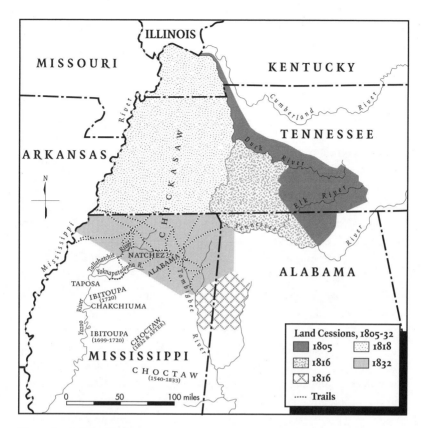

Map 3. Land of the Chickasaws

James Adair, who lived among the Indians and carefully documented their way of life, estimated there were no more than 450 Chickasaw warriors, or a total population of about 2,250, meaning a decline of about 80 percent. Much of this was due to disease, but warfare, slave raids, and famine took their incalculable toll as well.[29]

From the demographic low point Adair documented around the time of the American Revolution, the Chickasaws experienced a slow recovery rising to a total population of over 6,000 by the 1830s. But this population was a mélange of different ethnic groups.[30] The sources of repopulation indicate vast changes coursing through the Chickasaw way of life. Some came from the absorption of neighboring tribes who sought refuge from the French or other hostile Indians. The remnants of the Natchez Indians, whom the French nearly annihilated in 1730, came to live among the Chickasaw. Other small tribes, the Quinipissa (Napissa), Taposa, Ibitoupa, Chakchiumas, and some disaffected Choctaws were all absorbed into the Chickasaw nation during this period of turmoil.[31] Their numbers may have been small, but the combined effect was significant since they were added to a vastly reduced Chickasaw population. The admixture of neighboring refugees and captives did not radically upset the homogeneity of the Chickasaws, for they came for the most part from a common Muskhogean culture.[32]

More disturbing to the coherence of Chickasaw ethnic identity were the infusions of white and African blood. Together, the mixed-bloods and those of African origin would claim nearly half of the tribe's six thousand members by the time of removal.[33] The influx of whites into the Chickasaw nation began as early as the 1710s, when English traders based in Charleston entered into overland trade and began to marry Chickasaw women. Among the first whites to join the Chickasaw nation through marriage was a Scot named James Logan Colbert. He entered the Chickasaw trade in 1729 and married the first of three Indian wives who would bear a large number of offspring. During Colbert's forty-year stay among the Chickasaws he became a wealthy man with a "rich lodging" and 150 black slaves who worked his grand plantation, raising cotton, grain, and large herds of livestock.[34] The Colbert clan was the most prominent among a growing number of "mixed-blood" (meaning white and Indian) families.

For their part, the Chickasaws accepted white intermarriage as a means of solidifying their alliance with the English against the encroaching French and their Choctaw allies. The practice of marrying whites extended a custom of exogamous marriages that required everyone to marry outside their clan. Furthermore, marriage among the Chickasaws was not freighted with the kind of family and social obligations that characterized Christian marriages. "The matrimonial connection among the Chickasaws is slight," one chief explained to puzzled whites; "it is contracted without formality, and dissolved at the pleasure of either party." Depending on their wealth, men could take multiple wives, and the wives and children lived separately and to some degree independently of the man. The rights of women, especially married women, baffled whites: "It is an ancient and universal law among the Chickasaws that the wife has a separate estate in all her property, whether derived to her from her relations or acquired by her," one chief tried to explain to white officials.[35] (In 1838, on the basis of a claim by a Chickasaw woman to her own property, Mississippi became the first state to honor property rights for married women.)

White visitors regarded the Chickasaws as a strikingly handsome people. Chickasaw women became legendary for their beauty, and white visitors frequently admired the muscular physiques and athletic bearing of the men. They were also fascinated by the revealing dress and the guileless display of affection between men and women who embraced and kissed in public with no sign of shame.[36] George Rogers, an American missionary among the Chickasaws, was shocked by a public display of affection between a husband and wife who, after a week or two of separation, met unexpectedly—at the home of the woman's father no less: "they actually sprung from their horses, and were instantly enfolded in each other's arms, indulging in the most extravagant caresses, without seeming at all to heed the strange eyes which witnessed their conduct." Rogers and other whites looked away, thinking it "indelicate to witness such gross familiarity between the sexes."[37] Chickasaw customs of sex and marriage may have shocked Rogers, but they enticed others. For white traders, the Chickasaw domain offered a rare opportunity to indulge in beautiful women and polygamous marriages in a land remote from Christian moral constraints.

It was more likely avarice rather than lust that motivated white men to marry Chickasaw women, for with marriage came automatic adoption into the tribe and full access to a vast domain of land that was theirs without cost or tax. With shrewd calculation, on both sides, white traders married the daughters of the tribe's most powerful families. Polygamy multiplied the impact of whites whose mixed-blood progeny proliferated rapidly in the century before removal; by the 1830s one in four Chickasaws were identified as mixed white and Indian. Intermarriage, at the same time, blurred the lines between the races and obscured the insidious process by which the hosts became guests in their own land. White and mixed-blood knowledge of the language and ways of the English and Americans gave them advantages that helped them ascend in power within the tribe. By 1800 the mixed-blood minority effectively controlled the tribe's destiny and dominated the main sources of wealth.

As whites and their mixed-blood offspring rose in power within the tribe, the importation of African slaves, owned largely by the mixed-bloods, formed a new stratum at the bottom of Chickasaw society. Enslavement of captured tribal enemies (often Choctaws) had long been a tradition among the Chickasaws, and this increased following European contact. When kept for their own use as slaves, the Chickasaws would sever the muscles and nerves of the captive's foot to deter escape. Among the first articles of trade with Europeans were Indian slaves captured during raids on neighboring tribes and sold to the English who, in turn, exported them to the West Indies. The Indian slave trade became a New World counterpart to the vicious cycle of the African slave trade, with whites exchanging guns and liquor for captured slaves, forcing rival tribes to protect themselves from slave raids by capturing slaves to trade for guns. Chickasaws became both perpetrators and victims of these Indian slave raids, all of it fueled by the contest among European powers for control in the Lower Mississippi Valley.[38]

Sometime in the middle of the eighteenth century, the Indian slave trade began to reverse. Whites who had married into the Chickasaw tribe began to bring in African slaves to work the land, tend herds, and assist in the emerging commercial economy. Mixed-bloods, led by the Colberts, exhibited none of the puzzlement Faulkner's Indians display over how to use African slaves and fertile land. They exploited both at great profit. Indeed, the Colbert clan anticipated a certain Snopesian cunning in their knack for turning the advance of white civilization and the subjugation of their own people to their own advantage. No treaty negotiation could begin before the Colberts, along with other tribal leaders, received a host of bribes and favors, some petty, some of enormous value. Not least among the gratuities were family monopolies over ferry services, taverns, and trading posts along the Natchez Trace and other parts of the Chickasaw nation. "It was wondrous to behold," writes the historian Arrell Gibson, "the imagination, ingenuity, initiative, and unmitigated brass which this group of Chickasaws brought to the joyous business of integrating the nation's productive enterprises into a combine which they shrewdly managed." [39]

The mixed-blood clique also led the way for the expansion of the cotton plantation economy. Anticipating the white economy that would displace them, they learned quickly to buy more slaves to clear more land to raise more cotton to buy more slaves. It was the Chickasaw success at the white man's game, not their alleged incapacity to put the land to good use, that brought more pressure from whites to remove them. Cotton gins and gristmills began to dot the landscape, and Cotton Gin Port on the Tombigbee River became an active outlet for Chickasaw cotton exports to the Gulf. In 1830 Chickasaw cotton planters shipped more than a thousand bales along with large quantities of meat and livestock.[40]

The simultaneous growth of black slavery and commercial plantation agriculture among the mixed-blood sector of the Chickasaw people constituted the latter stage of a longer process of adaptation brought by the trade with Europeans. The biological impact of European germs on the Chickasaw people had threatened their very existence, but they survived and regenerated partly by amalgamating other Indians, whites, and African slaves. Adaptation to the new exchange economy with whites also disturbed and transformed their economy and culture. But the Chickasaws had endured and adapted to this as well, and some were seizing new opportunities offered by the cotton boom. It was not their inability to adapt to white civilization that doomed the Chickasaws in Mississippi—it was their success. As cotton prices were rising, as land hungry cotton farmers, and money hungry land speculators coveted the vast domain of the southern Indians, pressure mounted on them to trade the one commodity whites wanted most—the land itself.

From Reform to Removal

Removal was the last thing Europeans wanted when the Indian trade first developed, for, apart from their diplomatic and military importance in contesting rival powers, Indians were essential to harvesting deer and other products of the forest for commercial profit. All that had changed by the time the Americans took over. The heavy pressure the trade had brought on the population of wild game eventually depleted the area supply, forcing Chickasaw hunters to travel much farther for skins. For food, many were reduced to hunting small game once left for children.[41] "The buffalow and Bare are gone," the Chickasaw agent reported in 1830, "and there are but few Deer, not sufficient to Justify an Indian to depend upon for a support, more particularly those that have family." "Consequently," he concluded, "the Chickasaws are compelled to subsist by different means than that of the chase."[42]

As the economic value of the Chickasaw trade in skins and other forest products declined, their role as allies in the international struggle also waned in importance. After the defeat of the English, first in the American Revolution, then the War of 1812, and the withdrawal of the French from the Lower Mississippi Valley with the Louisiana Purchase of 1803, Americans had no further diplomatic need for Indian allies. What the Americans wanted instead was the land the Indians occupied. Before the Indian Removal Act of 1830, Americans debated two Indian policies. One sought to reform the Indian way of life and help them assimilate into white civilization. The other advocated removing Indians to the West, on the premise that Indians could not readily assimilate and, for their own protection, needed to be isolated from the corrupting effects of white contact.

To "civilize" Indians meant, above all, to transform them from hunters into farmers and to assimilate them within a Christian, English-speaking republic. As students of the Enlightenment, many reformers saw the natives not as innately inferior savages but instead as untutored children of nature, capable of reason and learning the best—and the worst—from their more advanced white neighbors. Evangelical Protestants joined the call for reform by insisting that the Indians were capable of conversion and salvation, and they led the crusade to "Americanize" the Indians. After the War of 1812 several denominations sent young clergy to "foreign missions" among the

Indians in the West where they raised churches, converted souls, taught school, and promoted temperance and Christian habits.[43]

Those who urged removal, on the other hand, countered optimistic theories of human evolution and capacity for progress with the argument that contact with a far superior European civilization had caused the American Indian to remain arrested in a primitive "hunter state." Instead of emulating the advancing civilization, they became vulnerable to its very worst influences, alcoholism chief among them. Some advocated removal because Indians were a dangerous threat to the safety of white settlers. But the case for removal more typically employed the same paternalistic humanitarian language adopted by reformers. Unable to resist the encroachments of white traders, swindlers, and liquor dealers, the Indians must be removed for their own good. Thus the line between compassionate calls for reform and removal blended together, each side agreeing the Indian way of life must end.

Within this debate over reform or removal there was substantial agreement on many other assumptions and goals. Among whites on both sides of the debate there was a conspicuous cultural arrogance that acknowledged little that was worth preserving, let alone imitating, in traditional Indian life. Each side characterized Indians as being in an inferior hunting and gathering stage of human development (despite their obvious reliance on horticulture). Implicit in their view of this primitive society was a critique of Indian sex roles, which gave women primary responsibility as cultivators of the soil while men hunted and made war.[44] What these "civilizers" wanted was to convert the men from hunters to farmers while turning women toward more exclusively domestic roles preparing food, making clothing, and raising children. In their missionary schools and churches and on model farms the reformers set up within the Chickasaw nation, they sought to teach the white man's agriculture and the family arrangements that went with them.

The goal of reforming the Chickasaws at first complemented the strategy of taking their land, insofar as the conversion from hunting to farming would require less land than the vast hunting grounds they had traditionally commanded. Once they were concentrated on farms, the unneeded hunting lands could be pried loose from the tribe and opened to white settlement. In the years before removal, this is exactly what was happening. As game was depleted and the hunting economy collapsed, many Chickasaws, especially the mixed-bloods, began to move away from the towns around Pontotoc and establish separate family farms. Toby Tubby, Chief Seely, and others who had located in the area between the Yoknapatawpha and Tallahatchie west of the Pontotoc Ridge were part of the recent dispersion of settlement that came with the transformation of the Chickasaw economy.[45] A growing number of men in the tribe now worked the fields exclusively, while the women turned to spinning and weaving and other domestic labor. Chickasaw culture had included no concept of private ownership of land as something that could be bought and sold, but there was a tradition of exclusive right to use of specific land, primarily for small vegetable gardens. With the mixed-bloods leading the conversion to commercial agriculture and livestock herding, each family claimed as much land as it could put to use, depending on the number of slaves and other laborers. They abandoned the traditional winter and summer wigwams in favor of log cabins, typically the same "dog-trot" cabins favored by white settlers. Indeed, they were living very much as the white settlers who were about to displace them.

For many full-blood Chickasaws these new values conflicted with traditional culture at a very basic level. Not least, the new ways challenged customary sex roles. Among Chickasaw males the manly virtues of a warrior culture were highly esteemed as were athletic prowess, hunting skills, and courage. Chickasaw braves were remarkable for being able to run incredible distances of one and two hundred miles through the forest. The Chickasaws lived by a code of honor and bravery that whites witnessed with amazement. Should a man commit some crime deemed worthy of the death penalty, he would face the consequences without protest or complaint and would never evade it by escaping, even when days and weeks passed between the sentence and the execution. One white witnessed an incident near Pontotoc in which one brave killed another by accident in some frolic. The brave presented himself to his victim's relatives and offered them the choice of executing him or having him kill himself. They chose the latter: "He loaded his rifle and discharged it into his breast by means of the ram-rod." [46]

Chickasaw men, more than their counterparts in other tribes, traditionally shared agricultural work with women. Men were responsible for clearing fields, and they assisted in farming the communal fields. Tilling the soil and gathering food, however, was primarily the work of women and, later, African slaves. White ideas of civilizing males by converting them from hunter-warriors to farmers went against these masculine ideals. Furthermore, Chickasaws valued security and stability, not change and material gain, and the insinuation of the latter values into their way of life was regarded by the more traditional full-blood Chickasaws as decline not progress.[47]

By 1830 the United States Chickasaw agent, John Allen, reported with obvious pleasure on the progress of civilization among the Chickasaw: "They have large herds of Cattle swine, sheep and goats, and poultry of every description. . . . The Country is well watered, and is well adapted to the culture of Cotton, corn, wheat oates, peas potatoes beans etc. Cotton Beef and pork are the principal articles for exportation." Not only had the Chickasaws advanced as producers but also as consumers, Allen reported. "The proceeds from the sales of Cotton, Horses, Beef Cattle Hogs etc after retaining a sufficiency for their home consumption is Generally applied to the purchase of nessaries and Luxuries of life; (towit) Slaves Shugar and Coffee, as well as dry goods of various description which are calculated to render them comfortable and ornament their persons." The economic "civilization" of the Chickasaws seemed to have been accomplished, Allen concluded. "The time has come when they no longer depend on the rifle for support, but it is used more for their recreation, and amusement than for the means of sustaniance. Every family cultivates the earth more or less, as his thirst for gain, or his imaginary or real wants increases." Along with their economic reform, Allen reported with pleasure that the new order had wrought a transformation of the family. "Much to the honor of the chickasaws, for the last eight years, the practice of the men requiring the woman to perform all the labour in the field is much changed—the men now (with a few exceptions) cultivate the earth themselves, while the female part of the family is ingaged in their household affairs. They spin weave make their own cloathing Milch Cows make butter Cheese etc." These "civilized" Chickasaws even adopted the appearance of whites, Allen noted approvingly: "They keep themselves decent and clean and in many instances particular attention is paid to fashions that are in use by the whites—It is their constant practice to appear in their best apparel at their public meetings, also when they visit the country villages in the white settlements."[48]

While Allen and the Chickasaw Agency brought economic reform to the Chickasaws, Protestant missionaries were working on their spiritual salvation. Joseph Bullen, a Yale educated Presbyterian minister, arrived among the Chickasaws in 1799. He baptized a few black slaves and drew a small following among Chickasaw women. Most of the Chickasaws remained faithful to their traditional gods, and Bullen left disappointed in 1803. It was not until 1819 that the missionaries returned, inspired by the religious enthusiasm of the Second Great Awakening and a remarkable collaboration between church and state. That year Congress passed an Indian Civilization Law, which provided federal subsidies to Christian missionaries. The missionaries were required to offer instruction in the "arts of civilization" as well as evangelize. The Methodists and Baptists entered the field, but it was the Presbyterians who had the most impact on the Chickasaw nation. With church and federal funds they set up Monroe Mission on the Natchez Trace near the Chickasaw Agency. The mission school drew fifty to sixty students, mostly young mixed-bloods. The students learned modern agricultural sci-

Chickasaw boy. (Courtesy of Smithsonian Institution)

ence at a demonstration farm near the school. All lessons were taught in English and were heavily laden with religious instruction. The mixed-bloods, eager for their children to adapt to the advancing white world, used their influence to see that the Chickasaw tribal council allotted $5,000 of its own money to support additional missionary schools. All of these schools were located far enough away from the tribal villages to ensure that students would be isolated "from the influence of their heathen brethren." Through the efforts of the missionaries some Chickasaw children were also placed in the homes of white settlers where they could learn English and "the habits of civilized life." [49]

While missionaries and other reformers issued heartening reports from the Chickasaw nation, most of the "civilizing" they took credit for was limited to the mixed-blood elite and African slaves, who proved the most receptive to Christian missionaries. There were more disturbing signs of demoralization among the mass of full-blooded Indians. Many Chickasaw men, once legendary for their athletic skill and physical prowess, had fallen into a pattern of daily drunkenness and fighting, while others passed the day playing ball or other games as though nothing else mattered. [50] Many still scorned farming as women's work and watched in dismay as the mixed-bloods adapted to the new ways, amassing wealth in plantations, slaves, and livestock, now all the exclusive property of individuals. Chief Piomingo, one of the last of the full-blood chiefs, called for a return to the old ways and sought to cleanse the tribe of white and mixed-blood influences, but it was a futile resistance movement. After 1800 the rule of the full-blood chiefs was mostly a guise behind which Levi Colbert and his clan, along with others among the wealthy mixed-blood elite, ascended to power. In treaty negotiations and other dealings with the white world, Colbert and his clique came to speak for the tribe. They knew the ways of the whites well because they had emulated them, and, wittingly or not, they collaborated in the demise of the people who had adopted them.

Land Divided

The American notion of "civilizing" the Chickasaws was an extension of the British effort to pull them into their market economy. It had begun with the British convincing the Indians that animals of the forest had value as items of trade in exchange for things the Indians learned to want, if not need. It continued with the Americans extending the logic of exchange to the land itself. Land, they taught the Chickasaws, was something they owned, a commodity with specific value that could be divided, bought, and sold.

This lesson began with Americans introducing the notion of land ownership as a collective, tribal claim. The Treaty of Hopewell in 1786 defined tribal boundaries for the first time and marked the beginnings of official relations between the United States and something it now defined as the "Chickasaw Nation." Its vast territory extended from an arbitrary diagonal line abutting the Choctaw domain to the south, west to the Mississippi, north to the Ohio River and east to a more complicated boundary delineated by the watersheds of the Cumberland, Tennessee, and Duck Rivers.[51] Having defined its boundaries and designated the "nation" that owned it, subsequent treaties would cede the Chickasaws' rights to the land to the United States, one chunk after another, until it was all gone.

In the Chickasaw treaty of 1801 the United States government awarded the tribe a paltry $700 in goods in exchange for a right of way to build the Natchez Trace. Though planned as a military road connecting Nashville to the American settlements in Natchez, the Trace became an important artery for white cultural influence and commercial activity that entered the heart of the Chickasaw and Choctaw nations. The Natchez Trace was also a crucial precedent, for the treaty established the idea of property rights as a salable commodity. Only four years later, in 1805, the tribe ceded all rights to its lands north of the Tennessee River, this time for the sum of $20,000, much of which went toward paying debts incurred in trade at white trading posts. As debts increased, the pressure to sell more land intensified, and as the trade in animal skins disappeared, land was all the Indians had left to sell. A few years later, in 1816, the Chickasaw nation ceded to the United States all its land between the Tennessee River and the west bank of the Tombigbee River, by now a proven artery for the burgeoning cotton trade. For this they received the sum of $12,000 a year in ten annual allotments. In 1818 the Chickasaws sold the rest of their land north of the Tennessee border, this time for $20,000 annually for fifteen years. Within just a few years, some twenty million acres had been ceded to the United States. The land was immediately thrown open to settlement by whites who poured westward following the War of 1812. The advance of white settlement only intensified pressure on the Chickasaws to cede their remaining land, now approximately 6.4 million acres in northern Mississippi and northwest Alabama. This, of course, was the heart of the Chickasaw homeland, the site of their towns, their ancestors' graves, and the place, according to the migration legend, the priests and the oracle pole had led them to centuries before.[52]

To the traditional Chickasaw full-bloods, their homeland was sacred; for the Colberts and the mixed-blood elite, it represented a prosperous investment in a nascent cotton plantation economy. They had been willing to cede undeveloped hunting lands, but both groups now joined in opposition to the sale of the Chickasaw homeland. "We never had a thought of exchanging our land for any other, as we think that we would not find a country that would suit us as well as this we now occupy, it being the land of our forefathers," Levi Colbert told the federal negotiators in 1826. Were they to move, he warned, it "may be similar to transplanting an old tree, which would wither and die away."[53]

Transplanting old trees was what the American government was about to undertake. The debate over reform or removal began to tilt strongly toward the latter during the 1820s. Pressure from encroaching white settlement was mounting, and in Andrew Jackson, a western land speculator and Indian fighter, these settlers found a powerful political voice advocating removal. Land in the West, across the Mississippi, was to be designated "Indian Territory," a giant reservation to which the Indians in the East would be removed. Chickasaw chiefs were invited to visit the nation's capital, where they were feted at banquets and treated to lavish gifts in what amounted to personal bribes. Delegations from Washington, in turn, came west to negotiate with the Chickasaws their removal to Indian Territory. The Chickasaws stood their ground.

Their resistance was broken by two events in 1830. One was the extension of Mississippi (and Alabama) state law over the Chickasaw nation. Tribal government and law and all authority of the chiefs were abolished in a stroke. The same year, Congress passed the Indian Removal Act, which formalized a procedure for removing the Indians to the West. When Chickasaw leaders realized that Andrew Jackson, now president, had no intention of protecting them from the intrusion of the Mississippi state government, they moved quickly to negotiate the best terms they could. In August 1830 the Chickasaw chiefs came to Franklin, Tennessee, where they met personally with President Jackson and negotiated a treaty by which they would cede their land and remove to Indian Territory. At a banquet at the Parker House hotel in Natchez Mississippi planters raised their glasses to Andrew Jackson: "He found one half of our territory occupied by a few wandering Indians. He will leave it in the cultivation of thousands of grateful freemen." [54]

Not quite yet, however. The Chickasaws took advantage of a clause in the Treaty of Franklin to stall removal. Even after 1832, when the Treaty of Pontotoc Creek set down new terms for removal, another two years would pass while the Chickasaw leaders, led by Levi Colbert, haggled over more favorable terms for the allotment of land to individual members of the tribe. Not until 1837 did the Chickasaw exodus begin, and it would continue over the next three years. Tribal delegations, in the meantime, traveled back and forth to Washington to negotiate amendments to the treaties, while others went west in search of new land. [55] Faulkner's story "Lo!" imagines one of these Indian delegations staging a sit-in at the White House while a befuddled president, modeled on Andrew Jackson, finally succumbs to their demands. [56] But whatever leverage the Chickasaw leaders were able to exert on federal officials eager to buy them out, their days in Mississippi were doomed to end.

During the interlude, when the Chickasaws were negotiating removal but had not yet migrated, white traders, squatters, land surveyors, and "land lookers" scouting land for settlers and speculators all swarmed into the Chickasaw domain. It was as though, Faulkner wrote, the property men were "setting up for the next scene and act before the curtain had even had time to fall." [57] These men were not like Faulkner's rather genial crowd of Indian traders and settlers, Alex Holston, Ratcliffe, Doctor Habershram, Louis Grenier (the "Old Frenchman"), and others. They were instead more akin to what Indian agent John Allen described as "gennerally men of the lowest grade and dregs of society, such men as are always unwilling to conform to the laws that govern the civilised world." The law was in the white man's hands now, and most of them ignored the feeble efforts to warn them against entering Chickasaw territory. [58]

The well-practiced methods of cheating the Indians at every turn were now given full license. One official in Pontotoc described the scene in 1835: "Immediately over the line, but off the Office section, a number of Shops have been established whither the Indians resort, and drink Spirits to an intoxication of almost unparalleled extent, presenting scenes of brutality revolting to every principle of humanity and consequences ultimately to the Indian truly appalling." [59] As the reality of their end in Mississippi took hold, the full-bloods fell further into despair. Chickasaw agent Benjamin Reynolds wrote in 1835: "No language which I am capable of commanding would carry a faithful picture of the scenes which are daily passing around here. For days together, hundreds of these unfortunate beings lie drunk around the [whiskey] shops and the evil increases daily, and in one year more, many of the men will be destroyed." [60]

Two categories of Chickasaw land came to market in the late 1830s: one was land allotted to individual heads of families, the other was collectively owned by the tribe. While most of the land was in the latter category, the best lands were often those controlled by individual Indians. Cheating Indians was an art by this time, and the full-bloods were most vulnerable. They often sold their land for a fraction of what the more astute mixed-blood Chickasaws received.[61] As a means of protecting unwary Indians, land sales were required by the treaty to have the signed approval of tribal officials, but this safeguard still left a good deal of room for bribery and cheating.

Hoka's "X"

In Lafayette County's local history the transfer of land from Chickasaws to whites became encapsulated in the story of Oxford's founding. Hoka (variously spelled Ho-ka or Ha-ka), a Chickasaw woman who had been allotted land under the terms of the removal treaties, signed her "X" on the deed, thereby transferring ownership to three white men. They, in turn, offered a portion of the land free of charge if the county's officials would make the site the county seat.[62] Hoka, apparently a family head and therefore eligible for her own allotment, sold her section of land to John Chisolm, John Martin, and John Craig for $800 and signed the deed with her "X." Below her mark James and George Colbert testified: "We the undersigned hereby certify that the above named Hoka is capable to take care of her own affairs this 13th day of June 1836." Chickasaw Agent Benjamin Reynolds also signed the deed.[63]

Hoka's "X" became a celebrated event in local history during the centennial in 1936. It served to legitimize white ownership, not only the acquisition of the parcel of land on which Oxford rose but, by implication, all the land that came to whites. It was transferred, not as spoils of war or conquest but by way of legal treaties, deed transfers, and allotments of money—all rational market exchanges fully in keeping with white rule of law. The crude

"X" at the bottom of the deed and the guarantee of tribal leaders at the same time underscored the incapacity of Hoka and the Chickasaws to comprehend fully the rules of white civilization.

A century and a half after those first land sales, suburban homes, farms, and business properties sold in Lafayette County, and all of northern Mississippi, entail a title search that traces back ownership of the land to similar deeds with the "X"s of other Chickasaw Indians who, like Hoka, signed away their allotted land. It is a persistent reminder of the historic origins of ownership and a poignant example of Faulkner's idea that the past lives in the present.

Hoka's memory is now memorialized in a movie theater and coffeehouse in Oxford that opened some years ago in an old metal Quonset hut, once part of a cotton gin. Probably few of the students and townspeople who frequent "Hoka" know much about the Chickasaw woman it honors. Fewer still know that her name, in the ancient language of her people, means "was," "since," or "because." Hoka's Faulknerian counterpart is an Indian queen, Mohataha, mother to Issetibbeha, who in her purple silk gown, and with a slave-borne parasol shading her, stops at the trading post to sign her own "X" to the document that relinquishes her people's claim to Yoknapatawpha. " 'Where is this Indian territory?' " she asks, climbing back into the wagon. "And they told her: West. 'Turn the mules west,' she said." The name "Mohataha" joins "moha," which meant "skimmed, peeled off," and "taha," which meant "done, gone, finished, completed, exhausted, used, passed." [64] Hoka and Mohataha, history, legend, and fiction fade one into the other.

Doom's World

Faulkner's interest in the "old people" who occupied Yoknapatawpha before the whites went well beyond the names they left for rivers and places. Though they remain one of the least worked veins of the vast mine of Faulkner critical studies, his Indian stories are of vital importance to the Yoknapatawpha saga. They provide more than simply an exotic prelude to the advance of whites and their slaves, for the fictional Indians of Yoknapatawpha reveal a larger moral judgment of all the human inhabitants of the land. The Indians are dispossessed of Yoknapatawpha only after they embrace the conceit that it is theirs to sell.[65]

Working against the stock romantic stereotypes of the noble savage, Faulkner offered instead a complex view of a society that may seem cruel and inhumane but never inhuman. His Indians are defined by their "otherness" in relation to white society, by their indifference or opposition to basic "taken for granted" values in white culture. Though they eagerly consume things brought in from the intruding white society, Faulkner's Indians have no ambition for material wealth or power before this European contamination. Faulkner simply omits the more acquisitive white-Indian mixed-blood element from this part of the story.[66] Even as the full-blood Chickasaws' traditional culture becomes corrupted by the importation of white clothing, food, ornamentation, African slaves, and other goods, they regard the culture these goods come from to be alien and inferior. In "Red Leaves," perhaps his best-known Indian story, Faulkner has the Indians talking nostalgically about the old days when work and wealth were scorned. He is taking readers to the other side of the white condemnation of Indian culture for its lack of a work ethic and spirit of improvement. When some of the Indians in Faulkner's fiction eagerly emulate white models of wealth and power, they offer an exaggerated burlesque of an aristocratic society that values not work but leisure, replete with African slaves fanning Indian chiefs in a landlocked steamboat palace.

Faulkner's Indian stories are all set in the early nineteenth century, the twilight of their time in Mississippi. It is a doomed race of natives who watch in amazement as their white "guests and then friends" invade their land with trading posts, grogshops, and plantations. The early white settlers exploit the naive Indians at every turn, swindling them out of their land, swapping horses or gold coin in exchange for enormous land holdings until the "Chickasaws were themselves the guests without being friends."[67]

Though in Faulkner's fictional accounts only a few whites enter the Indian domain, their corruptive influence is everywhere. The Indians are victims of the worst of white influence, but they are also willing students of European depravity. It is a Frenchman, Chevalier Soeur-Blonde de Vitry, who adopts Ikkemotubbe as his protégé in treachery and covetousness. Ikkemotubbe is one of those who often emerge among a subjugated people as an eager collaborator with the new rulers and their encroaching culture. He embraces icons of white power to pursue ascendancy within his tribe and, in the process, weakens any capacity his people might have had to resist. Ikkemotubbe is greatly impressed by a steamboat he sees plying the Tallahatchie, and he adopts the name of the captain, David Callicoat, who "told the steamboat where to swim." He then leaves Yoknapatawpha for New Orleans, where he makes money gambling and slave trading. It is there he meets de Vitry, a French nobleman in exile following the French Revolution, who cultivates in Ikkemotubbe a ruthless ambition for power. It is this French tutor in treachery who renames his pupil "the man." In Ikkemotubbe's crude French this Europeanized title evolves ominously from "de l'homme" to "Doom." Seven years after leaving, Doom returns to Yoknapatawpha with a small gold box filled with deadly white powder. He uses it to poison a young puppy in front of his cousin, the designated heir to his father's chiefdom; the cousin warily abdicates in favor of Doom. Doom now has his slaves drag an abandoned steamboat from the Tallahatchie through the forest and set it up as his royal palace. There he sits on his throne in the boat's ornate saloon, fanned by black slaves.[68]

In another story, Doom's son, Issetibbeha, goes to Paris and meets his father's aging mentor, de Vitry. Issetibbeha returns with an ornate, gilded Parisian bed (which he hangs from the ceiling of the steamboat and sleeps on a mat on the floor beneath it), a pair of girandoles (fancy French candle holders) he lashes to poles to use as torches, and a pair of red-heeled slippers that become icons of royal power in this Chickasaw kingdom.[69]

This image of regal decadence passes to the next generation with Moketubbe, Issetibbeha's son, who covets the red-heeled slippers and eventually poisons his father and takes over as chief. Moketubbe embodies the final stage of Chickasaw degeneracy. From his early childhood, Moketubbe becomes so fat he cannot walk, or so lazy he refuses to. He cannot even manage to get his bloated feet into the small slippers he killed his father to acquire, so they are left dangling from his toes. Servants have to tote him about in a litter on which he lies inert, dressed in a broadcloth coat with no shirt underneath, his huge belly swelling out above the bottom half of a suit of linen underwear, the slippers hanging on his toes or held in his lap, his arms, like flippers, extending from his corpulent flesh.[70]

To the Indians of Yoknapatawpha, African slaves are just another item of trade brought in from the white world, desired for whatever prestige they might confer on their owners but otherwise useless and often burdensome to their owners.[71] Faulkner's imaginary Indians are innocent of the market economy. While whites place a specific exchange value on slaves and land, the Indians do not comprehend why it is desirable to gain wealth in order to buy things they do not need or want. Left to their own, without any European influence, the Indians apparently have no avarice for material gain or power. They are avid consumers of things from the white world, but there is no linkage between their wants as consumers and any ethos of hard work, profit, and self-advancement. To the contrary, his Indian characters loathe work, and they embrace acquisitiveness and ambition for power only as a grotesque imitation of the invading whites. Faulkner represents this corruption of Indian culture as a parody of white efforts to "civilize" these "children of the forest."

More than any other characters in his Yoknapatawpha saga, Faulkner's Indians were the product of imagination, or of indirect knowledge. When asked how he developed his Indian characters, he once replied frankly: "I made them up."[72] There were Choctaw reservations in Mississippi, but the Chickasaws had long since left northern Mississippi. His knowledge of their history and culture, filtered through local lore, some reading, and the knowledge of his acquaintances, remained limited. As a boy, Faulkner had hunted for arrowheads and artifacts around the Indian mounds; some had been the target of treasure hunters. There in the mounds, Faulkner wrote, the Indians "would leave the skulls of their warriors and chiefs and babies and slain bears, and the shards of pots, and hammer- and arrow-heads and now and then a heavy silver Spanish spur." One of these mounds is featured in his story of a bear hunt, which deals with the relationship of whites and Indians to the wilderness: "Aboriginal, it rises proudly and darkly enigmatic" with "inferences of secret and violent blood, of savage and sudden destruction" still lurking there like some "dark and nameless beast lightly and lazily slumbering with bloody jaws."[73]

Toby Tubby's Land

The area that became Lafayette County had never been more than sparsely settled by the Chickasaws. It was only a small part of a vast tribal domain that once had teemed with deer, bear, bison, panther, and a great variety of small game. In the twilight of the Chickasaw era in Mississippi, some had moved westward across the Pontotoc Ridge to take up farming and other activities in the region. There was one small settlement, Toccopola, on the southeastern border of Lafayette, another nearby at Sarepta, and one around what would later become College Hill, north of Oxford. During the 1830s there were Chickasaws living in scattered settlements on the creeks flowing into the Tallahatchie.[74]

Local history often centers on Toby Tubby, who was chief or "mingo" to a clan that lived in the area. Whites often cast him with some affection as the last of the Chickasaws, a deferential collaborator with the new occupants. None seemed aware that his name translated to "white (or whitened) killer."[75] Toby Tubby stayed on for some time after the American takeover of northern Mississippi. He claimed three wives, as many different homes, and a number of African slaves. He operated a ferry across the Tallahatchie on the trail that went from Pontotoc through the new white settlements at Oxford and College Hill to Memphis (formerly Chickasaw Bluffs). It was a profitable enterprise, and together with his land and slaves, Toby Tubby enjoyed considerable wealth. He had learned to speak English and enjoyed considerable popularity and influence as a liaison between the encroaching white and lingering Indian populations. In local history Toby Tubby is depicted as a white man's Indian; it was said he took pleasure in bestowing gifts of Chickasaw ponies on white friends. Toby Tubby met a violent end after a trip to Holly Springs to acquire whiskey when some unidentified drunken assailant stabbed him. Bleeding badly, he made his way back to the cabin of Sam Rayburn, a white settler. Toby Tubby refused to take Rayburn's bed, saying "Indian no sleep in white man's bed," and he laid on the floor on a blanket. Sometime later, he died on the floor of Rayburn's log cabin. After his son came to retrieve the body, rumors began to fly that Toby Tubby was to be buried with one of his African slaves. According to local legend, white settlers intervened and "spirited the unhappy slave away." Toby Tubby's people buried him in secret, somewhere near the ferry and the creek that still bears his name. Soon more rumors told of his grave being laden with gold and other riches. Decades later, treasure hunters returned to search for the treasure locked away somewhere in this Chickasaw tomb, and even today, people in the county continue to talk about the secret of Toby Tubby's grave.[76]

Exodus

The official sale of the collectively owned Chickasaw lands (about 4 of the total 6.4 million acres) began at Pontotoc early in 1836 as the new counties were being formed and white settlers pouring in. There, a large crowd of white men gathered in what quickly became a teeming makeshift frontier town, with crude streets formed by the wagons, lean-tos, tents, and Indian huts. At the center were two log cabins, the Chickasaw Indian Agency and the United States Land Office. Advertisements of a public sale of lands were entered in all the major newspapers of America, and Pontotoc was thronged with speculators that winter. Many dressed in frock coats, beaver hats, and city-made boots. Big land companies in the East sent these men to Pontotoc with bags of gold and silver estimated at more than one million dollars.[77] Over three million dollars was realized from the sale, and more was to follow; "the Chickasaws are a rich people," one official wrote to Washington.[78] Deducted from these revenues, of course, were all of the expenses the government incurred in selling the land and moving the Chickasaws to the West. Among the bills for services rendered in the survey, sale, and migration were many that were both piddling and generously padded. Some bogus charges whites billed to the Chickasaw accounts amounted to a thinly disguised form of graft, not far from the one Faulkner's Yoknapatawpha pioneers contemplate in charging the cost of a lost padlock as an expense for "axle grease" for the wagons that would deport the Indians to the West.[79]

While the land sales were taking place in Pontotoc in 1836, Chickasaw leaders had worked out a treaty with the Choctaws to share land they had acquired in Indian Territory; the descendants of Chicsa and Chacta would be reunited following a westward trek that would reverse their legendary migration.[80]

The last days of the Chickasaws in Mississippi were a sad spectacle. Suspended between the world they had been dispossessed of and the strange new one they were headed for, many of them simply refused to accept their fate. Some fell into a demoralized pattern of drunkenness and violence while others played ball and frolicked, spending their land proceeds liberally, all to the chagrin of American officials and the delight of white traders. Some Indians withdrew into fatalistic silence and waited. Federal officials appointed Major A. M. M. Upshaw of the U.S. Army to supervise the migration. "You ought to move as soon as possible," Upshaw instructed the chiefs in May 1837, "as there are a great number of your people who are spending all their Money and making no crops, they get Drunk and lose their money and white men make them Drunk to cheat them of their property and their wives and children are suffering for something to eat. They should go soon so that they may have time to build houses before winter to keep the cold from their wives and children."[81] Even after all the treaties, the land surveys, sales, signing of deeds, the auction in Pontotoc, Upshaw's repeated pleas to the chiefs, and a commissary wagon train with supply rations mobilized, still the Chickasaws were slow to realize or to act upon the fate that had been decided for them. Some Indian leaders tried to arouse resistance, often with encouragement from white traders who wanted them to stay as long as their money held out. But the army applied stern pressure on the tribal leaders to prepare their people to leave.

The Chickasaws from Chief Seely's district, just north of Lafayette County, were among the first to leave in a small party of about 450 that began the Chickasaw exodus in July 1837.[82] Upshaw set out with the nucleus of his party traveling slowly through the Chickasaw nation: "The rattle and creaking of the wagons and carts, and the voices of the drivers of the approaching caravan were melancholy heralds of the sad journey they were about to begin. Giving a last look at the familiar hearth, home and dooryard, trees and fields, they turned towards the moving company and loaded their belongings into the wagons; their women and children mounted their ponies, and with heavy hearts the families joined the procession headed for a strange and distant country."[83] The main body of the tribe, a contingent of more than four thousand, did not leave until November 1837.

No one who witnessed the Chickasaw removal could ever believe the image of the "wandering Indians" in a primitive hunter state that had been so effectively promoted to justify their dispossession. Despite Major Upshaw's pleas that they sell all their belongings to white settlers, the Chickasaws insisted on traveling west in an enormous caravan of heavy wagons groaning with the weight of their possessions: household utensils, furnishings, farm implements, while behind them followed massive herds of horses and cattle along with swarms of dogs and cats. "I do not think that I have ever been a witness of so remarkable a scene as was formed by this immense column of moving Indians," one observer recorded; "several thousand, with the train of Gov[ernment] waggons, the multitude of horses; it is said three to each Indian and beside at least six dogs and cats to an Indian . . . a dense mass of animal life." [84]

The remaining five hundred or more Chickasaws in Mississippi continued to migrate, a few still arriving in Indian Territory as late as 1850. Some of the Choctaws chose to remain behind in reservations in Mississippi, but virtually all the Chickasaws left. The ancient people who had come East led by the oracle pole of their priests now returned to the West by the bayonets of the United States Army. Only the names of the rivers and some place names were left to remind whites of the former hosts, now unwelcome guests, they had dispossessed of the land. "Then they were gone," Faulkner wrote, as though Mohataha's scrawled "X" on the land deed had lit a fuse and set off an explosion so that "the single light touch of the pen in that brown illiterate hand, and the wagon did not vanish slowly and terrifically from the scene to the terrific sound of its ungreased wheels, but was swept, hurled, flung not only out of Yoknapatawpha County and Mississippi but the United States too." [85]

Out of quiet thunderclap he would abrupt (man-horse-demon) upon a scene peaceful and decorous as a schoolprize water color faint sulphur-reek still in hair clothes and beard, with grouped behind him his band of wild niggers like beasts half tamed to walk upright like men, in attitudes wild and reposed, and manacled among them the French architect with his air grim, haggard, and tatterran. Immobile, bearded and hand palm-lifted the horseman sat; behind him the wild blacks and the captive architect huddled quietly, carrying in bloodless paradox the shovels and picks and axes of peaceful conquest. Then in the long unamaze Quentin seemed to watch them overrun suddenly the hundred square miles of tranquil and astonished earth and drag house and formal gardens violently out of the soundless Nothing and clap them down like cards upon a table beneath the up-palm immobile and pontific, creating the Sutpen's Hundred, the Be Sutpen's Hundred like the oldentime Be Light.

—WILLIAM FAULKNER, Absalom, Absalom!

two Genesis

Hoka's "X" marked one of thousands of transactions by which the Chicka-saws gave up their allotted parcels of their ancestors' homeland to white speculators and settlers during the giant land grab of the late 1830s. The de-cade opened with a stream of white traders invading the Chickasaw domain as soon as the ink was dry on the Treaty of Franklin in 1830, more still after the Treaty of Pontotoc two years later. It ended with the last stragglers in the tribe's exodus leaving what overnight had become a full-blown extension of the American South's cotton kingdom. The Chickasaws, Faulkner wrote, were removed "like a float or a piece of stage property dragged rapidly into the wings across the very backdrop and amid the very bustle of the property-men setting up for the next scene and act before the curtain had even had time to fall."[1]

The main props for the next act were plantations with vast fields of cotton, others of corn, rustic mud-chinked "dog-trot" log cabins, followed in time with the white-columned mansions of the wealthy planters, their slave quarters, and the log or rough plank, dirt-floored cabins of the plain folk. There were new towns, public squares, and streets carved out of the forests, and soon a courthouse, jail, churches, and schools. Emanating from the town as spokes from a hub were crudely graded wagon roads that traversed the rivers and creeks on rough wood bridges. Ferries took goods, people, and livestock across the Tallahatchie, and by the end of the 1850s the Mississippi Central Railroad was belching steam as it ran through the former hunting grounds of the Chickasaw and Choctaw. Lafayette County was on the coarse western edge of America, but from the start, it was part of an emerging industrial economy feeding cotton to faraway factories.

There were thousands of new actors onstage taking the place of the departing Chickasaws: planters, yeomen, and townspeople who came west for land and opportunity. There were black slaves too, almost as many in number as the whites. They came with their masters or were sold and moved west in large coffles and sold to new masters in Mississippi. By 1840 as many people, free and slave, lived in Lafayette County alone as had lived in the entire Chickasaw domain of six million acres a few years earlier. Nine other counties also filled with new settlers and slaves, nearly 160,000 in all by 1840—over twenty-five times the size of the Chickasaw nation within less than four years and growing by the day. The human pressure on the land increased tremendously, and the land soon showed the strain.

More, More, More

The cotton frontier expanded rapidly westward, pushed by the exhaustion of soil in the old tobacco and cotton lands of the southeastern states and pulled by the lure of rich new land in the West. Southerners, much like their northern counterparts, moved west to improve their lives materially. Moving and starting over had been a central part of the American experience since the time of the Revolution, but in the early nineteenth century, migration became a defining characteristic of American society. Individuals plotted their lives with the expectation that they would move and move again as opportunities dictated, tearing themselves out of old ties of family and community they left behind and rebuilding new associations wherever they went. The reproduction of a western community, formed out of a migratory population of a diverse collection of strangers became a common experience for Americans in the nineteenth century. The recreation of American society in hundreds and thousands of communities became one of those commonplace features of life soon taken for granted. Yet each time a new county and town were founded and named, each time new government officials were elected for the first time, each time a new infrastructure of roads, bridges, and railroads was laid down, Americans defined their society anew.

Mississippi's hot climate, its booming cotton economy, and the centrality of African slave labor to the economy all made it quite different from states to the north, like Indiana or Illinois, being formed at the same time. But the process of community building, the way governments, towns, roads, schools, and churches were constructed in these new western communities, was similar in the North and South. So was much of the underlying culture of striving ambition and improvement that underlay American expansion in the West. The idea that the South was a fundamentally different society from the rest of America had its origins in both antislavery and prosouthern propaganda before the Civil War. Out of this would later emerge a popular historical image of the "Old South" as a traditional society, one encased within a stable hierarchy of class and race, ruled by an aristocratic plantation gentry who disdained the striving, money-grubbing ways of the Yankee. Like most myths, there was some historical reality to prop it up. The aristocratic "long-tailed" families of the Old South that lived in tidewater Virginia and the South Carolina lowcountry and their more freshly minted western replicas in Natchez enjoyed fabulous wealth and aristocratic grandeur. Northern Mississippi, however, was part of a raw, young cotton frontier full of men on the make. Some were from the old dynasties of the East trying to restore the wealth their fathers and grandfathers had amassed, but many more were just hopeful migrants who wanted to be among the rich parvenus of a promising new country.

Faulkner seems to have grasped this ambitious, striving quality of the Mississippi planters. In antebellum Yoknapatawpha the character Thomas Sutpen, the protagonist of *Absalom, Absalom!*, is sometimes seen as an outsider, a pretender who is alien to the class of gentlemen he is trying to penetrate in the antebellum South. We may better understand Faulkner—and southern history—if we see Thomas Sutpen instead as an exaggerated version of the typical rather than an anomaly. Early Mississippi had a strong attraction to men on the make, and Sutpen seems only an extreme example of the same grasping ambition that brought other Faulkner characters to the West, like Jason Compson. A Sutpen might have been regarded as extraordinary in the intensity of his obsession and the social distance he sought to traverse, from poor white to planter. But many were the men who sought

Buck Avant's Oxford mansion, later the home of the James Stone family.
(Courtesy of Special Collections, University of Mississippi)

to rise a rung or two on the social ladder, typically from a landowning yeoman farmer to a small planter with enough slaves and an overseer so he would not have to work in the fields. Whatever their ambition, for men on the make, Mississippi was the place to be.

Antebellum Mississippi was a socially fluid environment, and a man with new wealth could adopt the manners of a gentleman, perhaps disguise his family origins, even invent a genealogy, and who in this raw frontier environment was to say that he was *not* a gentleman. Tomlin "Buck" Avant arrived sometime in the late 1830s in Oxford from obscure origins but with all the trappings of wealthy planter. The second son of a Virginia planter, Buck Avant managed to borrow from his in-laws and wealthy neighbors all the money necessary to buy the land and build the house for his bride, the daughter of wealthy landowner James Brown. Avant filled the house with splendid furnishings and staged extravagant parties for Oxford's social elite. He treated his astonished neighbors to parties with music from orchestras imported from New Orleans and served the best of food and wine. He offered a level of hospitality that anyone would have considered elegant in eastern circles, but in the rustic environs of frontier Mississippi, it was positively ostentatious. It was only later that everyone learned his money was all borrowed and his display of wealth designed to extract more credit. When his wealthy creditors in Oxford approached him, he declared bankruptcy, fended off lawsuits, sold the house, moved into the overseer's cottage, and eventually died deeply in debt. His grand mansion stood for over a century as a reminder of the pretense that allowed a man of no substance to pose as a gentleman and of the innocence of those willing to believe he was. Then one night the Avant mansion went up in a burst of flames.[2]

The rapid western expansion of the American cotton frontier was both a symptom and a powerful stimulus to this striving pursuit of personal success that took hold of young males at all levels of white society. Daniel Jordan left his father's plantation in Washington County, North Carolina, and came to Mississippi full of hope and ambition—along with no small amount of apprehension and sadness about leaving his family behind and seeking his fortune alone. Jordan blamed a family trait for their lack of success, and he set out to overcome that curse in Mississippi: "Every Jordan that I have ever seen has the same failing but if it is possible in me the spell shall be broken. I shall make a desperate effort to do so and if it is possible that the family distemper can be broken I will brake it and change to Yankee shrewdness and perseverance." Western migrants, like Jordan, appeared torn by competing desires to improve their situation by moving west and maintaining ties to family and friends at home. Jordan begged his father and other family members to join him in Mississippi, enticing them with exaggerated claims of the riches the new land would offer. He scorned his relatives' lack of enterprise for refusing to join him in the West, but at the same time, he made clear his painful loneliness living apart from them. He had to make a cruel choice between the security of his family ties and his individual success—he chose personal ambition. Writing to his sister of his new resolve to stay in the West and seek wealth, he explained: "Here I can make *money money* and here could I be happy if my dear relations were with me." Jordan tried to reconcile the cruel choices he made by treating his Mississippi adventure as a means of returning home and improving his family's fortunes. "I think I can in this State make as much money in 5 years as [any] man should want and then I can return home to my friends with pleasure." But, he quickly added, he also feared he might "be like the rest of mankind, not satisfied with a sufficiency but wish to grasp after *more more more.*" [3]

Jordan needed no lessons in cupidity from Yankees, nor did most of the settlers, rich and poor, who came into the new country. It was a New Englander, George Rogers, who, touring Mississippi in the 1830s, was immediately struck by the avarice that drove the settlers: "The people are characterized by that restlessness of habit which makes them impatient of every thing which does not tend either to their pleasure or worldly interest. Pleasure and gain are the deities at whose shrines every knee bows, and every soul does homage."[4] The pursuit of new wealth, cheap land, high cotton, and the declining opportunities in the East pulled them west to Mississippi. "I know yu can make as much here in one year as you can make in three years where you live," John Fraser wrote back to South Carolina from his new home near Lafayette County.[5]

In the Southwest, as Mississippi and the other new Gulf States were then known, settlers joined their quest for individual success to a larger American conviction that the nation's destiny was to expand and spread its political and economic institutions across the continent. The opening of northern Mississippi to white settlement in the 1830s was also integral to the larger world economy that shaped the entire regime of King Cotton. That kingdom was driven by the advent of steam-powered mechanized production of cotton textiles in the industrial cities of the English Midlands and the mill towns of New England. The growing demand for cotton made prices soar by the time the Indian lands in northern Mississippi were thrown open.

Driving King Cotton's empire westward was also a voracious appetite for fresh land. In the older eastern states the repeated planting of cotton and the reckless disregard for erosion and soil depletion left behind a scarred swath of ruined, infertile fields as the cotton frontier advanced into the piedmont. "The successful cotton planter," a South Carolinian explained in 1828, "sits down in the choicest of his lands, slaughters the forest, and murders the soil." After ruining his own land, he "buys all that he can from his neighbors . . . and continues the work of destruction until he has created a desert of old fields around him, and when he thinks he can be no better, sells his lands for what he can get . . . and marches off to a new country to recommense the same process."[6] In Virginia and the other tobacco-growing states of the Chesapeake, the same pattern of repeated planting caused massive exhaustion of the soil. This brought deliberate efforts at economic diversification by the 1830s, which in turn gave rise to a surplus of slave labor. Slave owners would find a ready export market in the western cotton frontier. The major export of the eastern tobacco and cotton fields was people, land-hungry white settlers and slaves who came west with their masters or, more often, were sold and brought west in a massive exodus out of the East.

The opening of the West to American expansion offered a fresh field in which to start over, for individuals and for the entire cotton economy with its insatiable appetite for fresh land. For young sons of eastern planters, the West offered an opportunity to maintain or exceed the fortunes their fathers and grandfathers had accumulated in the first phase of the plantation economy. For middling yeomen and poor white families, so many of whom had been squeezed off the best lands by the expansion of the plantation system, the West offered cheap land to buy or free land to claim by squatters. For rich or poor, the underlying premise of this dynamic westward movement rested on just the opposite of a traditional, hierarchical society. The antebellum South, like all of America, was driven by a powerful new ideology that placed individual success on a high moral plane and celebrated social and geographic mobility. Enveloping and supporting this culture of individual striving was a national conviction that the westward expansion of American democracy, Christianity, and capitalism was beneficial to all and part of a divine plan to fulfill what they would call the republic's "manifest destiny." [7]

When the Indian lands of Mississippi and Alabama opened to American settlement in the 1830s, southern migrants joined with great gusto in a carnival of individual ambition and risky speculation. Joseph G. Baldwin, the most colorful chronicler of the "flush times," wrote: "Marvelous accounts had gone forth of the fertility of the virgin lands; and the productions of the soil were commanding a price remunerating to slave labor as it had never been remunerated before. Emigrants came flocking in from all quarters of the Union, especially from the slaveholding States. The new country seemed to be a reservoir, and every road leading to it a vagrant stream of enterprise and adventure.' " [8]

"The emigration to this country is incredible," one Mississippi migrant wrote back home: "I passed hundreds of Waggons on the Road and scarcely a day passes but you see more or less moving." [9] The population that flowed into Lafayette County came largely from the old southeastern states. It is not until the census of 1850 that we get our first clear view of these migratory streams, but the picture was probably similar in its outlines to what it had been before 1840. More than two in three of the white household heads in 1850 were born in the southeastern seaboard states: North Carolina (23 percent) and South Carolina (22 percent) led, while Georgia (15 percent) and Virginia (8 percent) contributed the rest. Their children's birthplaces indicate that many of these people came west in steps with parents born in South Carolina, for example, a child born in Georgia, another born two or three years later in Alabama, and subsequent children born in Mississippi.

One can trace a similar demographic trail from North Carolina or Virginia through Tennessee or Kentucky into Mississippi. A significant minority of Lafayette County's adult white population in 1850 was also born in the new states of the South, including many born in Tennessee (18 percent), Alabama (6 percent), and Kentucky (4 percent). Virtually the entire population was recruited from within the South and from outside Mississippi. A mere 28 of 1,384 white household heads in 1850 were born outside the South, and 11 of those were foreign born. [10]

The states of the Old Northwest (Ohio, Indiana, Illinois, Michigan, and Wisconsin) received massive streams of Irish, German, and other European immigrants, as well as migrants from the South and all parts of the North. The American settlement of the Old Northwest reflected the diversity of a rapidly growing urban, industrial society with a vast number of foreign-born immigrants. Northern Mississippi in the 1830s was something more than a mere transplant of society and culture in the Southeast; it was shaped in powerful ways by newness and western conditions. But in the origins of its population, its early commitment to cotton production, and its dependence on a large slave labor force, it was destined from the outset to be an extension of the South into a new country surrounded by southern people and institutions. No outside influences would challenge the steadfast commitment to cotton, slavery, and white supremacy.[11]

Land Divided for Sale

The Chickasaw cession threw more than six million acres of land on the market, and it gave white migrants, rich and poor, a sudden new chance for gain. The nature of land sales favored rich planters and large speculators. Those with a combination of money and cunning, together with a convenient lack of scruples in going after their main chance, gained advantage in what soon became a frenzied, speculative land grab.

The name Yoknapatawpha, land divided, became an augur of what would befall the whole area under the proprietorship of its new owners. Dividing land, marking it off by boundaries for sale and for government administration was the very essence of what white *settlement* meant. Before the Chickasaws even left for Indian Territory, much of their former nation had been surveyed, sold in pieces, settled, and the land broken for planting. Lines drawn across the land—lines only white men could see—defined counties and police beats within which newly minted governments would enforce the law. White settlers with their families, others with gangs of black slaves, cleared what land they could of trees, drained the swamps, cut down the canebrakes along the river bottoms, plowed the fields, and planted them with cotton and corn. Across the land the crude beginnings of cotton plantations, large and small, emerged, along with many more smaller farms, some raising just enough corn and hogs to feed a family. Roads replaced the Indian trails and connected plantations and farms to embryonic towns, with courthouses, churches, schools, log cabins, and, in time, a few grand homes. The property men had set the stage, as Faulkner put it, and the actors were already playing out the next act.

Shortly after the final negotiations of the cession in 1834, government surveyors mapped the Chickasaw lands in preparation for the giant land sale that began early in 1836. Nothing captures the white man's conception of land as a divisible, salable, usable commodity quite so succinctly as the map of the Chickasaw cession drawn by Henry Lusher for the United States government in 1835. In place of the natural boundaries of rivers, ridges, and forests, Lusher's map laid across the land a perfectly uniform grid. Within each six-mile-square township were thirty-six one-mile-square sections, 640 acres. Modeled after the Northwest Ordinance of 1787, this method of surveying land aimed at meeting the demands of land-hungry settlers and profit-hungry speculators who expected quick sales and rapid turnover in a dynamic real estate market.[12]

The Chickasaws had been dispossessed of their land allegedly to make room for an advancing tide of white settlers. Sturdy yeomen and aspiring planters of the Jacksonian republic, it was said, would put the hunting grounds of the "wandering Indians" to more productive use as farmlands dotted with towns, schools, and churches. But the lion's share of the Chickasaw lands, it soon became evident, was bought up by speculators, many of them large land companies owned by eastern capitalists who never set foot in Mississippi. Of the more than two million acres allotted to individual Chickasaws, less than twelve thousand acres, about one half percent, was sold to buyers of less than five hundred acres, and only one-fourth of all the Chickasaw lands sold went to buyers of less than ten thousand acres. A small group of about thirty-five land companies and individual speculators, some referred to bluntly as "gambling traders," were responsible for buying nearly 1.6 million of the first two million allotted acres sold.[13]

The same Jacksonians who spurred the Indians out of the land now tried to whip up popular resentment against the land speculator as a sinister capitalist who hoarded land for profit, drove prices up, and put all but the scrub land beyond reach of the common folk. It was not an unjustified attack. Land companies and individual speculators tried to turn a quick profit buying low and selling high. Their dominance of the market ensured that large planters with cash or credit would have an advantage over less wealthy farmers, many of whose income rested precariously on next year's crop. But the distinction between actual settlers and speculators was not always so neat. "Nearly every man was a speculator; at any rate, a trader," wrote Joseph Baldwin.[14] Small farmers squatted on homesteads they hoped to buy with next fall's crop while capitalists on Wall Street invested in north Mississippi land with the hope that rising land prices would bring them profits.[15]

A Time of Lawless Opportunity

Following the Chickasaw Treaty of Pontotoc Creek in 1832 and another in 1834 that modified the terms of removal, land speculators and their agents began swarming over the Chickasaw nation identifying the best farmland and negotiating what amounted to purchase options on land allotments of individual Indians. The Chickasaw treaties were unusual among those that governed the removal of the southeastern tribes. As a result of hard bargaining by Levi Colbert and the mixed-blood leaders, government negotiators agreed to allot land to individual family heads and then let it be sold in an open market that would fetch the best price.

Samuel McCorkle was one of many "land lookers" who, beginning in 1833, traveled through the area taking careful notes on each section as to the type of soil, topography, water supply, its potential for growing cotton or corn, and the availability of timber essential for fencing and building.[16] What McCorkle and other agents bought in the early stages of this land market were "floats," allotments of land that were promised to individual Chickasaws but were unfixed as to location. This practice allowed land buyers to purchase the allotment rights from the Indian and then work with the land office to determine the best possible location for the float. Often speculators would build a cabin for an Indian in order to secure the claim to a specific parcel of land, and this enhanced the value of the land in the bargain.[17]

The land sales operated on the fiction that Indians were free agents able to make their best deal in a competitive land market. The treaties, as we have seen, required that tribal leaders sign off on all contracts, and they did so precisely because most of the Chickasaws were assumed not legally competent to understand and negotiate contracts on their own. This provision was intended to protect the Chickasaws from being swindled by someone like a Jason Compson, one of Faulkner's Yoknapatawpha pioneers, who swapped his race horse for a vast estate from the Chickasaw chief named Ikkemottube; or a Thomas Sutpen, who traded a Spanish gold coin of dubious origin for one hundred square miles of prime land in the Tallahatchie bottom. Most of the individual Chickasaws who sold their allotted land early in the game got a fair price for their land allotments, at least $1.25 an acre, the initial minimum price, and up to $10 an acre for prime locations.

There was still plenty of room for unscrupulous traders to cheat the Indians. The payments were often advanced to the Chickasaws in the form of credit at the trading post, and Indian traders lost no time converting the proceeds from land sales into sales of watered down whiskey, jewelry, and clothing. If white traders took advantage of the Chickasaws, they also learned that the Indians' supposed innocence in the marketplace could cut both ways. Some Indians sold their allotments again and again, gladly accepting and spending the traders' earnest money before final contracts could be approved by the tribal council. "One Indian will sell his Reserve perhaps to 8 or 10 persons," Silas Caldwell complained to James Polk, the future president, who had hired Caldwell to buy plantation land in northern Mississippi.[18] What the white land buyers took to be ignorance or dishonesty seems to have been employed with no small degree of savvy by the Indians, who during the past century had learned about all there was to know about striking a deal with white traders.

Between the land and the abundance of speculative money with which to buy it there was a void of rational market mechanisms and legal sanctions by which land could be purchased, contracts honored, titles protected, and development secured. If all that law and order required were the presence of lawyers, the flush times of northern Mississippi might have been tidier. An ambitious corps of lawyers (their "mouths full of law," Faulkner wrote) arrived not far behind the land buyers, and their business flourished in the absence of a well-defined market and legal system. Joseph Baldwin remembered the flush times of Mississippi with a fondness only a lawyer could relish. It was, he wrote, "that sunny land of most cheering and exhilarating prospects of fussing, quarrelling, murdering, violation of contracts, and the whole catalogue of *crimen falsi*." "What country could boast more largely of its crimes?" he asked; "Swindling Indians by the nation! Stealing their land by the township!"[19]

The uncertainty of contracts, land locations, and titles all guaranteed that lawyers like Baldwin would have plenty of business, but what struck most observers was the absence of any legitimate authority. In theory, Mississippi law had been imposed since 1830 when Chickasaw tribal law was simultaneously abolished, but the nearest court or law enforcement official was over fifty miles from Pontotoc in Monroe County. "At this distance from the seat of justice, surrounded by the unbroken forest, few felt the restraints of law," one early Mississippi politician remembered. "As the Indians were daily receiving large amounts of money, and as they were, as a general rule, as improvident as children, money found its way into everybody's pocket. Every business prospered, and the greatest extravagance was everywhere practiced."[20] The result, in Faulkner's apt description, was "a country and time of lawless opportunity."[21]

The first auction held at Pontotoc early in 1836 sold a large block of land surrounding Pontotoc, while a second auction in the fall put more land up for sale, including all the nonallotted land in Lafayette County.[22] "Times are tolerable brisk here now," William Hack wrote from Pontotoc during the second auction in the fall of 1836; "our town is thronged with indians some drinking liquor some buying goods and others running their horses through the streets over stumps and against trees." [23] At the land office, auctioneers called out the numbers that identified each section of land by township, range, and section. Buyers in the crowd shouted their bids indicating the price they were willing to pay for the land. It summarized perfectly the commodification of land.

"Under this stimulating process," Joseph Baldwin later wrote of the land craze in northern Mississippi, "prices rose like smoke." "Lots in obscure villages were held at city prices; lands bought at the minimum cost of government, were sold at from thirty to forty dollars per acre, and considered cheap at that." If he exaggerated the inflation somewhat, he accurately captured the spirit of chicanery: "The old rules of business and the calculations of prudence were alike disregarded, and profligacy . . . held riotous carnival. . . . Swindling was raised to the dignity of the fine arts." Driving it all was a speculative enthusiasm, a contagious fever in which "avarice and hope joined partnership." [24] The raging bull market in Mississippi land fed on genuine optimism about new markets and wonderful profits to be had in land, cotton, and slaves. "Great negotiations for land and negroes among the newcomers," wrote a visiting Virginian. "The operations going on around me excite me, and I cannot help feeling the contagion, and want to be dealing in tens and hundreds of thousands." [25] "Knave or fool can now fill his pockets," David Hubbard wrote from Pontotoc during the boom. "Some must suffer or I am more mistaken than in most predictions as to future human actions." [26]

A Name for the County and the Town

Into this turbulent economic and social atmosphere, the state of Mississippi moved finally to extend its authority through local government, to quell the lawlessness and secure title to property. As land agents divided and sold the Chickasaw domain, the politicians met in Jackson, the new state capital, to draw other lines across the land, now for governance instead of sale. They designated ten new counties, all carved out of the Chickasaw cession in February 1836. Like the land grid, the county boundaries were arbitrarily drawn, not according to any natural barriers, such as hills or rivers, but as more or less square blocks about twenty-five to thirty miles across, all neatly stacked like cotton bales in two rows below the Tennessee border.[27]

Politicians in Jackson named Lafayette County in honor of the French hero of the American and French revolutions, the Marquis de Lafayette. He had become a cult figure in the early republic, and his popularity as a national idol soared during his American tour (which included Natchez) on the fiftieth anniversary of the Revolution in 1826. In Mississippi, the name is pronounced LaFAYette, and few would recognize the French pronunciation if they ever heard it. Initially the county was a large square about four and a half sections (twenty-seven miles) north and south with a stubby panhandle attached to its southeastern corner. Later, cessions to adjoining counties changed the northern and southern border, first gnawing off the northeastern corner above the Tallahatchie, then the southeastern panhandle, and finally a sliver along the southwestern border (see Map 1).[28] As the politicians in Jackson drew the county's boundaries, they also triggered the creation of county government by appointing four commissioners empowered to set in motion the democratic creation of the first county government.

Faulkner captured this moment of civic genesis in his story "The Courthouse (A Name for the City)," included in *Requiem for a Nun*. In its tone and humor the story has many of the marks of a frontier tall tale, and, beyond that, it contains any number of inconsistencies with the actual history of Lafayette County. In this story, however, Faulkner puts his finger squarely on the meaning of this protean moment in which white pioneers, adventurers in Indian country, became settlers and founders, recreating one small unit of an expanding nation. The story is told with a combination of irreverent humor and respect both for the achievement of the white founders and for the loss the exiled Indians suffered. The story is set in the summer of 1833 in a small settlement that had gathered around Alexander Holston's Indian trading post. Holston, the trader, along with Dr. Samuel Habersham, the Chickasaw agent, and Louis Grenier, a planter (remembered by later inhabitants as the "Old Frenchman"), arrive sometime around 1800 to form the nascent community's commercial, political, and agricultural taproots. During the next three decades others filter into the Yoknapatawpha country so that by 1833 the yet unnamed settlement clustered around Holston's store included a tavern, a jail, and "a meagre huddle of crude cabins set without order and every one a little awry to every other and all dwarfed to doll-houses by the vast loom of the woods which enclosed them."[29]

During their drunken Fourth of July muster, the local militia captures some outlaws suspected of being part of the infamous Harpe Brothers gang, or maybe John Murrell's. These marauders were among the "simple fraternity of rapine" who preyed on travelers along the Natchez Trace. After robbing and murdering their victims, the Harpe Brothers gang was known to slit their bellies and fill them with rocks so the corpses would sink in whatever river or swamp they were thrown.[30] After debating the option of lynching the outlaws, the law and order party prevails and decides to jail their captives. When the militia guard wakes from a drunken slumber the next morning, they discover the prisoners have dismantled the crude log jail and escaped. Worse yet, the monstrous iron padlock they had clamped on the jail door has disappeared. Some want to charge it off to the Chickasaw account, but Pettigrew, an officious little postman who delivers the mail from Nashville to Yoknapatawpha down the Natchez Trace, claims the padlock belongs to the United States government. He cites some ridiculous law to prove their liability, and he threatens dreadful penalties if the lock's value is not properly recompensed. It is to appease Pettigrew and resolve this "civic crisis" that the settlers determine to incorporate a town and name it "Jefferson" to honor, not the sage of Monticello, but Thomas Jefferson Pettigrew, the ethical postman who cannot be corrupted by money but is sufficiently flattered by this act of homage to relent in his impertinent honesty.[31]

The first courthouse in the fictional Yoknapatawpha County is a crude lean-to built as an annex to the jail, constructed in a joint effort by white settlers and black slaves. The Chickasaws, with Mohataha sitting regally in her wagon, watch while Ratcliffe [sic] consecrates this "new shrine" by installing an iron chest he had kept in the trading post to store assorted records. In this crude chest, Faulkner takes pains to explain, lies the origin of the courthouse as a keeper of legal records which document and legitimate the entire economic and social order that is being set down in the forests of northern Mississippi: a "minuscule of archive . . . a meagre, fading, dogeared, uncorrelated, at times illiterate sheaf of land grants and patents and transfers and deeds, and tax- and militia-rolls, and bills of sale for slaves, and counting-house lists of spurious currency and exchange rates, and liens and mortgages, and listed rewards for escaped or stolen Negroes and other livestock, and diary-like annotations of births and marriages and deaths and public hangings and land-auctions, accumulating slowly for those three decades in a sort of iron pirate's chest in the back room."[32]

The creation of Lafayette County's government and seat of justice had long since became a popular part of local lore by the time Faulkner wrote about it, especially after the county's centennial in 1936. Faulkner borrowed liberally from the actual history, at least as it was known to those who read the local newspaper or heard about it in school. His own great-grandfather, Charles G. Butler, had been there at the creation, so it would have been a special part of Faulkner's own family legacy.

Early in 1836, while the land office in Pontotoc was beginning its auction, the state appointed four commissioners to establish Lafayette County's new government. All were major landowners and developers in the area.[33] Their main duty was to set in motion a self-perpetuating system of democratically elected government by sponsoring an election for the county's first Board of Police, the chief executive body of county government in Mississippi. The Mississippi state constitution of 1832 allowed all white males twenty-one or older to vote, with only a loosely enforced residence requirement restricting the franchise. In March 1836 the five duly elected board members met at the log cabin of John P. Jones, a wealthy planter, who swore them into office. The first session of the government of Lafayette County, Mississippi, began within a month of the county's conception.[34]

According to state law, the Board of Police then took over the process of completing its own genesis. They began by drawing more lines across the land, marking out beats, political subdivisions for representation on the board and for the administration of justice. "Ordered by the court," the clerk scrawled in the fresh ledger of the board minutes that day, "that an Election be holden in sd. County on Saturday 2nd day of April next at the following precincts . . . for the purpose of Electing a Probate Judge a Circuit Clerk a Probate Clerk a Sheriff a assessor and collector a County Treasurer a County Surveyor a Ranger and a coroner officers for sd County."[35] By early June, a third election designated two justices of the peace and a constable in each of four beats (a fifth beat would be created later when population growth in the southern half of the county warranted it).[36] In Lafayette County, Mississippi, the American republic had replicated itself in microcosm, the county the offspring of the state, the state the creation of the Union. The social contract had been drafted anew in this small subunit of the nation.

All that remained was the designation of a seat of justice, a physical site and building to house the new government. The state required that it be within five miles of the geographical center of the county. In Mississippi, and across much of the new western country being opened to American settlement, there was little need to locate towns with an eye to defensive purposes, for any potential enemies among the native peoples or rival European powers had generally been vanquished or removed by this stage of settlement. The seat of government in Lafayette County was therefore simply designated by state fiat and set down in the center of the county. It was located there, of course, for the mutual convenience of all county inhabitants, some of whom would have to travel up to twenty miles from the far corners of the county to come to court. Instead of concentrating public expenditures in a likely commercial center, the county fathers were required to select a site whose only practical virtue was central access. Following two days of inspection, "the Court after mature deliberation Located the seat of Justice for the said County of Lafayette Miss. on fifty acres of Land donated to said Bord of Police for the benefit of sd County by John Chisholm John D. Martin and John J. Craig . . . Which site they do establish and declare it shall be known by the Town of Oxford."

The naming of Oxford may seem about as preposterous as Faulkner's tale of Jefferson. The name was born of what may have seemed at the time to be the wildly inflated ambition of this backwater burgh in the woods to become Mississippi's answer to England's Oxford as the home of the state university. It was young Thomas Dudley Isom, a relative of John Craig and clerk in the Indian trading post he operated, who proposed naming the new town after Oxford, England. What may have seemed like ridiculous conceit at the time this crude frontier outpost was being hacked out of the forest in 1836 was admired a few years later as shrewd foresight when the state legislature designated Oxford the home of the new university.

The site of the new town was in the section Hoka had signed over to Craig, Martin, and Chisholm earlier that month. They donated fifty acres to the county contingent on selection of the site as county seat. It was an act of generosity inspired not so much by civic spirit as by a well-calculated expectation that their remaining 590 acres in the section would soon be worth several times the $800 they paid Hoka. As the county's part of this bargain, it could sell off what it did not need of the fifty acres and use the proceeds to finance the building of a courthouse. Sheriff Charles Butler was ordered to stake off streets and town lots surrounding a courthouse square. Using a convenient hickory tree (or oak, by some accounts) as his base point, Butler took poles and chains and laid out a new town in the forest. That July the board called for bids on the construction of a temporary courthouse, a simple log cabin, probably little more than the crude structure Faulkner imagined.[37] No sooner did they commission this temporary shelter than they decided in September to request bids on two permanent buildings— a courthouse and a jail—both designed as imposing symbols of law and order on the Mississippi frontier. The courthouse would stand in the center of the town square and was planned as a grand edifice. It was to be two stories tall, fifty-two by forty feet at the outside, with thick stone foundations and walls, topped with a "cupilow" and rod and ball ornament, the building painted white with green shutters. Inside, the ceilings would rise fifteen feet, and the walls were to be covered with white plaster and two columns supporting the upper floors to be "neatly marbled." For a long time the courthouse would remain the only structure in the town not built of logs.[38]

The jail was to be no less permanent and impressive in its own grim way: "The dungeon or first story to be built of Post Oak hewn square 12 inches 2 walls one inside the other so that one wall will brake the joints of the other to the height of 8 feet Bars of Iron to be placed at right angles with the timber 3/8 thick and 3 inches wide fastened on the inside course of logs with a spike to each log 3 inches apart the floor of Post Oak timbers 12 inches square put close." The doors, the board specified, were to be "secured with strong prison Locks . . . a double bolt pad lock." On the second story, a "Debtors Room" rested on top of the dungeon.[39] This was the jail which, in Faulkner's imagination, would witness the whole town's history from its place off the square, standing through war and fire, its "old ineradicable bones . . . the old logs" encased behind the brick and whitewashed plaster which later generations would add.[40] Here, too, may have been the inspiration for the padlock in Faulkner's story, a symbol of law and order linked to the extension of national authority, a lock that, by chance, forced Faulkner's Yoknapatawpha pioneers to become founders of a new town. By October 1836, construction began on the county's new domiciles, and George Pullin was appointed "superentinder of the Public Buildings To wit the Court House and Jail."[41]

The Center, the Focus, the Hub

The stone for the courthouse was brought by steamboat from Cincinnati to Memphis and then hauled by wagon through the forests to where the new county was being laid out.[42] By 1840 the courthouse was complete, and already it was the hub of a whole new economic system laid out on the former Chickasaw hunting grounds. While the county government was busy housing itself, the board wasted no time in generating a network of roads, bridges, and ferries, a transportation infrastructure designed to serve the needs of a bustling commercial economy in the making. The roads radiated out from the courthouse rising in Oxford. The first and most vital road went northwest to the Tallahatchie, where plans were already afoot for a cotton port. Another would run due north to Holly Springs. Immediately, other roads were planned to connect to neighboring county seats: east to Pontotoc, south to Coffeeville, and west to Panola. The Board of Police soon approved the appointed juries' recommendations and appointed overseers for each road who were empowered to designate "hands" responsible for construction and repair. Simultaneously the county sponsored new bridges to span Hurricane Creek and what they called the "Yocknipatatpha" River. The board also licensed ferries to carry passengers, horses, and wagons across the Tallahatchie and fixed the fees the ferry operators could charge.[43]

Within a few months a county had been created and the rude beginnings of its urban center—the hub of a new economy integrated by a rough network of roads—was carved out of the land. It was a scene best documented through Faulkner's vivid imagination: "a Square, the courthouse in its grove the center . . . four broad diverging avenues straight as plumb-lines in the four directions, becoming the network of roads and by-roads until the whole county would be covered with it: the hands, the prehensile fingers clawing dragging lightward out of the disappearing wilderness year by year as up from the bottom of the receding sea, the broad rich fecund burgeoning fields . . . the veins, arteries, life- and pulse-stream along which would flow the aggrandisement of harvest: the gold: the cotton and the grain." The courthouse, "rising surging like the fixed blast of a rocket, not even finished yet but already looming, beacon focus and lodestar, already taller than anything else, out of the rapid and fading wilderness."[44]

At the center of this new creation was more than just a town; it was the county government, the legitimator of power and ownership, an instrument designed to secure title to land, slaves, and property of all kinds, an agency to record and enforce contracts and, when necessary, to supply the force on which all law rests. It would be a government that would serve as a referee responding to complaints and enforcing the contracts that were the essence of a free market economy. More than that, local and state government in this nascent economy were to serve in a more assertive way as a provider of roads, bridges, and other transportation and furthermore to act as regula-tor of the marketplace by licensing such businesses as ferries and taverns and even setting what they considered to be fair prices.

The role of government and law was something Faulkner understood as central to the social order that took form in Mississippi, and he was fascinated by its principal symbols, the courthouse and the jail, and by the trials and other court proceedings that appear in so many of his stories. "Above all, the courthouse: the center, the focus, the hub; sitting looming in the center of the county's circumference like a single cloud in its ring of horizon, laying the vast shadow to the uttermost rim of horizon, laying its brooding, symbolic and ponderable, tall as cloud, solid as rock, dominat-ing all: protector of the weak, judiciate and curb of the passions and lusts, repository and guardian of the aspirations and the hopes; rising course by brick course during that first summer."[45]

Faulkner's paean to this protector of the weak is tempered by the ac-knowledgment that the courthouse had been built by slaves and designed by a captive French architect whom Thomas Sutpen treats almost like a slave. Sutpen, and the whole community, conspire in exploiting the hap-less architect in order to advance the design that the "long invincible arm of Progress" had destined for this place.[46] Slave labor may well have been em-ployed in the construction of the actual courthouse and jail, but the captive French architect was only Faulkner's way of suggesting that this citadel of self-government in a free society was implicated in the contradictions of a society devoted simultaneously to slavery and democracy.

None of the white settlers of Lafayette County appear to have been disturbed by such contradictions. They were busy building a new economy and government; the air was full of the optimism of flush times in a new country. The prospects of Lafayette County looked bright, as even the rival editor in Holly Springs conceded in 1838: "It is fast 'growing' itself into importance, and if we are not greatly mistaken in our calculations, it is destined to become one of the most flourishing counties in the state of Mississippi."[47] A widely read survey of Mississippi published the same year praised Oxford for its precocious refinement: "It is only one year and a half since Oxford was laid out into town lots, and yet it now numbers 400 inhabitants. It is healthy, finely watered, and one of the most pleasant towns in all that region. Its public buildings are a courthouse . . . a jail . . . both of brick. There are as yet no churches, but arrangements are made for the erection of two. Oxford has two hotels, six stores, and two seminaries of education."[48]

It was still a crude little village designed to serve the minimal needs of the cotton frontier for government and other urban services. Churches would soon follow the buildings for law and order, business and education. Local boosters made the most of every school, church, and public edifice that went up in such places, but most early Mississippi villages, as one unimpressed traveler observed, were "forlorn, poverty-stricken collections of shops, groggeries, and lawyers' offices, mingled with unsightly and usually dilapidated dwelling houses."[49] Towns in this new country often had the coarse, masculine character of the frontier against which churches, schools, and the other marks of settled family life as yet had little influence. "There is something striking to the eye of a northerner, on entering one of these southwestern villages," one Mississippi traveler recorded. "He will find every third building occupied by a lawyer or a doctor, around whose open doors will be congregated knots of young men, *en deshabille*, smoking and conversing, . . . fashionably dressed, with sword canes dangling from their fingers. Wherever he turns his eyes he sees nothing but young fellows. . . . An old man, or a gray hair, scarcely relieves his vision."[50]

Little Memphis on the Tallahatchie

If the county's early town promoters had their way, Oxford would not have been the hub of transportation and economic activity in the county. It probably would have remained nothing more than a small hamlet huddled around the courthouse with a few taverns and hostelries to serve visiting country folk and officials. The real economic center of the county, and of all northern Mississippi, was expected to be on the banks of the Tallahatchie in the northwestern corner of Lafayette. There, at the navigable headwaters of the Tallahatchie, cotton could gather from miles around to be shipped downriver to the Yazoo and then Mississippi rivers en route to New Orleans.

To the north, there were no other navigable rivers below Memphis on the Mississippi. Far to the south of the Tallahatchie, and well below the shallow Yoknapatawpha, the Yalobusha River offered the only comparable outlet from the interior of northern Mississippi. The alternative was to haul cotton overland more than seventy miles from Oxford along rough, dusty, or muddy roads to Memphis, the former Chickasaw trading post that was fast becoming the major port for the new cotton lands of northern Mississippi. Instead, if Lafayette County partisans had their way, cotton from all over northern Mississippi would be funneled into the Tallahatchie.

The most ambitious Tallahatchie river town was promoted by Wyatt Mitchell, whose main vocation seems to have been boosting his own town, in partnership with Volney Peel, a government surveyor and engineer. They purchased a section of land on a bluff above the river near the ferry that Sloan Love, a mixed-blood Chickasaw, operated. Mitchell and Peel also bought up large parcels of land in the surrounding area anticipating a boom in urban real estate and surrounding plantation lands. Mitchell's Bluff was soon renamed "Wyatt" and nicknamed "Little Memphis." Its owners proclaimed it the chief cotton port in northern Mississippi, a homegrown rival to Memphis, located strategically at the highest point of navigation on the river.

In 1837 Mitchell and Peel laid out an elaborate town plan and offered lots for sale. Quickly, the town was incorporated, a bridge soon spanned the river, and the dirt streets of Wyatt were clogged with wagons brimming with cotton. Wyatt's gins and balers processed the cotton before shipping it on small stern-wheel steamboats that plied the shallow waters of the Tallahatchie below the bluffs. New stores, law offices, banks, warehouses, factories (including a cotton gin manufactory), lodge halls, academies, a hotel, and numerous residences—some two hundred structures in all, many of them in brick—all went up quickly in a boom-town atmosphere during the first few years of the town's life. Two men, Gillis and Allen, opened a real estate banking company, and during these flush times in northern Mississippi the "Wyatt money" they issued was the preferred coin of the realm. Mitchell and Peel had paid an unprecedented $10 an acre for the Wyatt site, but lots were now moving briskly at prices several times what they paid.[51]

Farther downriver at another ferry crossing along the road from Oxford west to Panola County, a second group of town promoters staked out a place they named Eaton, which they planned as a south bank, downriver rival to

Wyatt. Led by Dr. Corbin (or Corban), a planter and large landowner in the area, Eaton's boosters included other early land buyers who were diversifying their investments (among them Faulkner's great-grandfather, Charles Butler). Beginning sometime in 1836 they laid out streets, sold some town lots, and erected a few stores and other buildings. Wyatt and Eaton were momentary rivals for what town boosters expected to be a rich flow of cotton down the Tallahatchie to the markets of the world.[52]

Unfortunately, nature had not fully cooperated with the best-laid plans of Wyatt Mitchell, Dr. Corbin, and their enthusiastic band of town boosters. During the winter months when the cotton crop was brought to market, the water was often too low for navigation, and the river was obstructed by snags from below and overhanging tree branches above. Like American pioneers throughout the West, they quickly looked to the state for help. Early in January 1839 a mass meeting held at Wyatt passed resolutions begging the Mississippi legislature for appropriations to improve navigation on the Tallahatchie and clear the river for direct trade to Vicksburg. The alternative, they warned, was the shipment of cotton overland and—worse—over state borders to Memphis. The new citizens of northern Mississippi played heavily on state pride by pleading that it abolish the connection "with the inhabitants of a different state, who have not a single feeling in common with us." The "*narrow and grinding policy*" imposed by their Tennessee neighbors, they advised, would "impoverish the whole country." "And are we," they asked, "for want of a small sum of money to be appropriated to the river, to submit patiently, thus to be devoured by the *peddling population of a border state*?"[53]

When state aid failed to materialize, private funds helped clear the worst obstructions and allow navigation on the Tallahatchie to continue. "We believe the little town of Wyatt [is] destined yet to become a place of considerable commercial importance," local boosters prophesied.[54] Indeed, Wyatt seemed on its way to becoming the commercial center of the northern Mississippi cotton frontier.

Tore Violently a Plantation

Wyatt's ambitions as a trading and processing center and Oxford's as the local hub of government and transportation each rested on the wealth farmers could extract from the land. The towns, roads, and rivers were but pieces of an infrastructure designed to support the main game: cotton, supplemented by grain and other food production. The town would be servant to the country in northern Mississippi.

Elizabeth Hathaway traveled through parts of the county en route from

Holly Springs to Pontotoc in 1842 and described a landscape that "was the most undulating that I ever saw up and down all the way—scarcely 50 yrds of leval ground all the way, and to make matters worse we would have to pass a most horrible swamp nearly a mile thick." Heavy rains had washed out parts of the road, destroyed bridges, and left huge gullies "ever so near the road that one false step might precipitate us down 5 or 6 feet on a muddy dead stream overhung with . . . bushes." After being stranded on the road at night, surrounded by howling wolves and with a man she had only just met, Hathaway was delighted to find a more pleasing landscape as they continued the next day. "Beautiful forests, such as your eye never saw, with well cultivated farms now became frequent—cotton field as far as the eye could reach, with corn in the ear, and cultivated to perfection. . . . No more beautiful country could be imagined. Hundreds of fat cattle roam in these parts. . . . This portion of the country is well watered and very pleasant. The soil is red sandy loam bearing great corn. The timber large strait and beautiful—hickory, oak, some and different kinds of nuts—some fine pines—Wild Hyikory with luxurious Passion flowers, and other flowers, too numerous to mention, grow spontainiously." [55]

The lands of Lafayette County were the same mix of hills, forests, and open table lands and bottomlands. Solon Robinson visited northern Mississippi in 1845 and crossed the Tallahatchie River, noting, "I like these Indian names." When he came to the "Yokenatuffa," he mused, "a very pretty name when you get used to it." Robinson described the fertile river bottom lands and the hilly and sandy uplands covered with oak, hickory, and "a liberal sprinkle of the beautiful holly." [56]

The varied landscape shaped the social geography. The county contained in microcosm much of the diversity of the South, with the more fertile river bottom lands and level table lands, especially in the northern portion of the county, playing host to large plantations and sizable slave populations. In the eastern portion of the county, scrubby hills covered in pine and hardwood served as refuge for poor white farmers who raised hogs and corn and a little cotton on the side. Between these, scattered through the ridges and valleys across the county, were the majority of yeoman farmers, the plain folk, who enjoyed a modicum of prosperity and independence.

The county's eastern boundaries extended into Mississippi's North Central pine hills, the western slope of the Pontotoc Ridge, which ran like a hard straight spine down the back of northern Mississippi. These were rugged hills broken by numerous streams and gullies that laced through them and covered with scrub pine forests mixed with oak, hickory, and other hardwoods. The veneer of topsoil in this hilly part of the county was thin, less fertile, and, according to one survey, it "offered little inducement to cultivation." Nor did the Yoknapatawpha bottomland in the southeastern quarter of the county seem inviting to early settlers; spring floods drained slowly and the soil was described as "generally heavy and disposed to be 'cold.' "[57] Eugene Hilgard, the state geologist, identified the poorer pine hill and unattractive bottomlands of the county lying east of a diagonal line that extended along Puss Cuss Creek in the northeast quarter of the county down to the Yellow Leaf Creek to where it flowed into the Yoknapatawpha and from there due south. This would become the domain of mostly small farms cultivated by poor and middling white farmers; it encompassed the remote area Faulkner dubbed "Frenchman's Bend" in the southeast quadrant of the county.[58]

West of Hilgard's rough dividing line were the best farm lands in the county, undulating uplands with few pines, mostly mixed hardwoods— oak, hickory, and blackjack—and covered in places by two to four feet of rich brown loam topsoil. The best of these cotton lands were the high flat lands known as Woodson's Ridge and College Hill Ridge a few miles northeast and northwest respectively of Oxford. Two small hamlets, Abbeville and College Hill, became the trading centers serving these rich plantation districts.

The soft topsoil that covered the less hilly land of the county was the "loess" soil that was described earlier as the windblown dust from northern glaciers that had scoured the earth centuries before. Because this soil remained loosely packed and free of stones, it made the land remarkably easy to clear of trees and brush. It was as though this whole domain was made for King Cotton's expanding empire. Once the land was broken it became vulnerable to rapid erosion from rain and wind. Soon the land would be scarred by huge gullies they took to calling "Mississippi Canyons," deep lesions that exposed the reddish and yellow clay and sand below, cutting across the land like open ulcers. It was one of these gullies that so frightened Elizabeth Hathaway during her trek through the area as early as 1842. After a few seasons of cotton growing, as more new farms and plantations were laid out across the delicate soil, the land was riven with these gullies. But there was more land to be cleared and broken and in the meantime great profits to be made in "white gold."

In the northern half of the county, where the large planters and slaveholders concentrated, the level land was less subject to erosion than the hilly lands to the east. The proximity of transportation on the Tallahatchie River and the promise of Wyatt and Eaton also made this ideal plantation land. The river bottom lands, which flooded periodically and were covered with swampy canebrakes, offered some of the best cotton-growing land to any who would clear and drain it. It was in the northern part of the county that several of Faulkner's pioneer planters, Thomas Sutpen, Lucius Quintus Carothers McCaslin, and John Sartoris laid out their new estates, just like their historical counterparts.

One of the prime plantation areas was known as Woodson's Ridge around Abbeville, north of Oxford. It took its name from a mysterious early settler who died violently, a Sutpen-like figure whose story suggests something of the brutality of the Mississippi frontier. Woodson came to the area sometime in 1838 and apparently decided he would coerce his neighbor, a man named Hogue, to sell some additional land to him. Woodson, with three or four of his slaves, went over to Hogue's cabin one night, laid a gun on the table, and ordered Hogue to sign a deed of sale. Hogue jumped up, grabbed the gun, and shot Woodson dead. Woodson's slaves fled into the night. Hogue was never tried for the killing, and sometime later, he died of consumption. Woodson was a bachelor with no sons to take over his land. When his kin arrived soon after his death, they decided to sell his land, and they advertised it as "Woodson's Ridge." The name remained, paying honor to an ominous figure in the early history of the county.[59]

To the west, beyond College Hill, was where Faulkner's Thomas Sutpen built his plantation. Faulkner was fascinated with Sutpen's sudden creation of a plantation out of the wilds of the Mississippi swamps and forests. This determined man works diligently alongside his slaves, all of them stripped naked and covered in mud against the mosquitoes. Sutpen and his slaves "tore" a plantation from the land: from out of the mud came bricks fired in a kiln; out of the forest they drag timber and mill lumber. The swamps are drained and a formal garden laid out; the canebrake in the river bottom is cleared for the cotton fields. In young Quentin Compson's imagination Sutpen and his slaves "overrun suddenly the hundred square miles of tranquil and astonished earth and drag house and formal gardens violently out of the soundless Nothing." In two years Sutpen had completed the shell of his plantation mansion and, as his embittered censor Miss Rosa Coldfield repeatedly insists, he "tore violently a plantation," violating and exploiting the land, just as he did the people he used to advance the Sutpen design. Without knowing it perhaps, Faulkner was making use of one meaning of the Chickasaw word "Yoknapatawpha" to describe Sutpen and his slaves tearing, ripping, disemboweling the land.

Before it is finished Sutpen's mansion stands three years "unpainted and unfurnished, without a pane of glass or a doorknob or hinge in it . . . surrounded by its formal gardens and promenades, its slave quarters and stables and smokehouses." There he lived in "masculine solitude" in "the spartan shell of the largest edifice in the county" visited by neighbors who came for hunting parties, camping on the floors of "the naked rooms of his embryonic formal opulence," playing cards, and drinking. Then, mysteriously, Sutpen disappears and returns with four big ox wagons filled with chandeliers, carpets, drapes, and other furnishings to fill his bachelor quarters. Sutpen puts on a new hat and broadcloth coat as part of his reinvention as a gentleman-planter. Finally, to fulfill his design, to become a gentleman and commence a Sutpen dynasty, he arranges a marriage with the daughter of Goodhue Coldfield, a merchant whose upright Methodist propriety guarantees his daughter's purity.[60]

The Sutpen story is too magnificent to quibble about historical implausibility or exaggeration, but it is enough to say there is some of both. Perhaps the best way to balance Faulkner's story against its historical inspiration is to examine what we can know about Sutpen's counterparts in the planter class that took form in the county's early history. The wealthy planters of Lafayette County came not from the poor white class of the mountain South, as Sutpen did, but almost always from well-established if struggling slave-owning families that migrated from the Carolinas or Virginia or some other more western point along the way. Often these were younger sons who came west to set up their own plantations, perhaps bringing a portion of the slaves and capital from the home place with them. Typically a son or overseer came with a gang of slaves as an advance force for a planter family that stayed back home until the new plantation was ready. After scouting and buying land in Mississippi, once the crop in the old home place was taken in during the fall, a planter would send the slaves and someone to supervise construction of temporary housing and begin clearing land. The wagons were loaded with tools, farm implements, and supplies, and the slaves walked while the white men rode horseback.

At the new site they pitched tents or slept in the covered wagons until the first log cabins were constructed. No planters wasted time in these first vital years erecting ostentatious mansions. The first sawmill did not appear until 1838, when John Craig constructed one on Yellowleaf Creek. More sawmill operations would crop up along creeks throughout the county, but sawn lumber and bricks remained time-consuming, expensive options compared to log cabins. The strategy was to throw up adequate shelter, clear and plant the land, and begin making money, which would finance more commodious homes a few years later. In several instances planters built ostentatious, two-story mansions on top of an existing log cabin. Encased within a number of Lafayette County's large planter mansions with their high white columns and grand porticoes are the crude log rooms in which life in the new country began.

Rich and poor relied on the standard "dog-trot" cabin, which typically consisted of first one, then two cabins joined by an open breezeway, said to be for the dogs, hence the name. The walls were rough logs chinked with mud, the roof was thick split shingles, and the floor either rough-hewn wood floors or nothing more than the earth the cabin was built over. The slaves' quarters were not much different from their master's. Typically, they consisted of the same simple log structures arranged in a row behind the master's cabin. A kitchen and smokehouse, along with barns to house livestock, went up as outbuildings.[61]

Silas Caldwell came into the land he had bought in 1835 with eighteen slaves and went about building a base for a large new plantation in a fashion less opulent, but certainly no less expeditious, than Sutpen's: "I remained there Eighteen Days put up a house for Beanland [the overseer] four Houses for the negroes a Smokehouse and a kitchen and made a lot for out Stock," he added. "Mr. Beanland is very much pleased with his situation, the negroes only tolerably well satisfied."[62]

Solon Robinson, visiting a planter just south of Lafayette County, was struck by the humble living conditions even his prosperous host endured. This planter suffered to live in a "low log cabin, built on the universal, never-varying pattern of two rooms with a broad hall between." Nearby, Robinson visited a new plantation built by a rich Virginian who owned ninety slaves. This man, with his family, lived in log cabins on a plantation that was just emerging from the pioneer phase of development. Here too the "big house" was a rustic dog-trot cabin, and there were several others to accommodate children and guests. Meals were prepared in a separate log kitchen set off from the residences, and food was carried by servants, through the rain, to the planter's quarters. The slaves lived in a village of log cabins, Robinson noted, some "neatly furnished and provided with household matters and things, and . . . and look just like some white folks' houses."[63] After five or ten years, having brought the plantation into full production of cotton, improvements to the main house might include plank floors, rough planks nailed to the inside and outside of the log cabin, or perhaps a new frame structure and brick chimney.[64]

The Pegues clan, beginning with Alexander Hamilton Pegues and his father, Malachi, were among the largest slaveholders and biggest land-owners in the county. The Pegueses for generations had been wealthy planters of French Hugenot descent in the South Carolina lowcountry before their branch of the family migrated west, first to Tennessee in 1834, then to northern Mississippi in 1836. Alexander and his father bought large parcels of land on Woodson's Ridge, which came to be called "Quality Ridge," home to the "aristocratic Pegues, Bowles and Jones" families. The plantations along this ridge, as one local historian described them, "were the first in the county to attain that degree of satiety in land and slaves toward which

Dog-trot log cabin with plank addition, Lafayette County.
(Courtesy of the Mississippi Department of Archives and History)

every farmer was striving." But even on Quality Ridge, comforts were few in the early years. Alexander and his father must have shared quarters initially, for the 1840 census lists him and another white male along with eighty-seven slaves. They lived in "a rude bachelor affair of logs" surrounded by their slaves and land. Alexander hunted deer, wild turkeys, and birds and could be seen riding horseback about the county, his gun over his shoulder, followed by a large pack of hounds.

In 1844 Alexander Pegues brought a woman into this rustic masculine refuge. His bride, Rebecca Pegues, was his first cousin and childhood friend. Her branch of the family had moved from South Carolina to Dallas County, Alabama. After they married, Alexander and Rebecca continued to live out on Woodson's Ridge, but Rebecca transformed her husband's rude bachelor quarters into a country home surrounded with mock orange trees, flowering hedges of lilacs, honeysuckle, and other shrubbery and flowers.[65] They named it Orange Hill. Alexander built a separate cabin, fenced and flowerless, away from his now ornamented and feminized home. His new den was a place where he would entertain his hunting friends and political associates, a place for male camaraderie not unlike what Faulkner described in Thomas Sutpen's life. When Alexander Pegues's father died in 1847, he inherited another large estate in land and slaves; by 1860, with five thousand acres, he was the largest landowner in the county.[66] He and Rebecca continued to live at Orange Hill until after the Civil War.

Many of the wealthiest planters endured a prolonged period of Spartan privation, some for up to ten and fifteen years after arriving in the county. They aimed to stay, but they continued to live in what were originally constructed as temporary dwellings. John Peyton Jones was a very well-fixed neighbor of Alexander Pegues on Woodson's Ridge. He arrived with one hundred slaves and chests of gold, but he began life in northern Mississippi living in what was only a slightly grander version of the same crude dog-trot cabin chinked with mud that the poorest squatter inhabited. Jones was able to build on a much larger scale; his was an immense one-story house surrounded on all sides by broad verandas, and the house had a fireplace with a stone and mud-clay mortar chimney. His slaves' quarters behind the big house were a cluster of small log cabins, also built with stone chimneys and fireplaces.[67]

It was well after the opening of the land that these wealthy planters could begin to think about imitating the residential grandeur and refinement of their counterparts in the East. When M. J. Blackwell bragged to his brother in South Carolina about the cheap prices of land in northern Mississippi, he hastened to warn him about the rustic living conditions. "When I talk of improved places however you must not fancy a nice snug farm with a fine framed house painted white and every thing else in 'bon ton.' You must fancy from 50 to one or two hundred acres of cleared land with very homely log cabins of oak and blackjack logs, covered with oak clap boards—cracks pretty well daubed with clay."[68]

Plain Folk

The society that formed in northern Mississippi contained fine gradations of wealth, lifestyle, and status with rich eastern planters who inherited property, status, and manners forming an elite, along with upstarts striving to breach their ranks, especially notable among the newly rich "cotton snobs" of Mississippi and other parts of the western cotton frontier. Only a slim minority of those in Lafayette County could be considered planters. That status required at least twenty slaves, enough to allow the master to manage a plantation but not have to work in the fields himself. About 6 percent of all white family heads in 1840 claimed twenty or more slaves, 4 percent in 1850, and 7 percent in the 1860 census.

At the other extreme were the very poorest of white farmers who owned neither slaves nor land and often had little more than their clothing, a few household furnishings, a gun and ax, maybe an ox or mule and a plow. These poor whites scratched a living out the hills and backwoods where they usually squatted on land. The terms "poor white" and "white trash" were pejorative expressions that are often applied much too loosely to anyone who did not own slaves. But Lafayette County had a substantial population—about 30 percent of all white families in 1850 and 1860—who owned neither slaves nor land. Not all of these were necessarily in the dirt-poor lower strata, for some were younger men from families of means and others were in nonagricultural occupations.[69]

Between these parameters of poor white and planter were the vast majority of white southerners, the plain folk, mostly yeoman farmers who owned land and worked it themselves, typically with the aid of their families or with one or a few slaves. Most slave owners in the antebellum South worked alongside their slaves out in the fields. About half of all slave owners in Lafayette County claimed only one to four slaves. A majority of white families owned no slaves at all, and they usually worked their farms only with the help of their family members. Some in this yeoman category were largely self-sufficient, able to subsist on food and livestock they raised. But most were involved in raising small amounts of cotton, grain, or meat for the market or local trade to acquire the tools and other goods they needed. "They brought no slaves and no Phyfe and Chippendale highboys," Faulkner wrote of the plain folk who migrated to Yoknapatawpha County, "indeed, what they did bring most of them could (and did) carry in their hands." "They took up land and built one- and two-room cabins and never painted them, and married one another and produced children and added other rooms one by one to the original cabins and did not paint them either."[70]

Annie Fulmer and her people were just such people as Faulkner described. They came to Lafayette County from South Carolina with all they owned piled in a wagon drawn by an ox. Annie recalled that her mother rode with the household goods with her three daughters, and six boys took turns riding the one horse the family had while the others walked. Behind the wagon, a milk cow followed. When the ox died along the way, one of the brothers hitched the cow to the wagon, and the trek westward continued. The Snipes family also came from South Carolina in a wagon drawn by two mules filled with all their worldly possessions.[71] There were many more who came with less than the Fulmers or Snipeses, often squatters who had been squeezed off land in the East by the expansion of plantations and the general rise in land prices; they were drawn west by the prospect of acquiring fresh land.

Joseph Ingraham, a Yankee visitor in Mississippi, described the plain folk with condescension. "These small farmers form a peculiar class," he wrote in the mid-1830s, they have all the "awkwardness of the Yankee countryman" but "are destitute of his morals, education, and reverence for religion." "They are in general uneducated, and their apparel consists of a coarse linsey-woolsey, of a dingy yellow or blue, with broad-brimmed hats; though they usually follow their teams barefooted and bare-headed, with their long locks hanging over their eyes and shoulders, giving them a wild appearance." They worked hard, he admitted, and could be hospitable to travelers, offering whiskey "to the stranger with one hand, while they give him a chair with the other." [72]

Ingraham betrayed his own prejudices of class and region in his view of Mississippi common people. Most accounts of the poor and uneducated tend to be left to history by the privileged. An exception is the journal of Hugh and Margaret Coffey, who arrived in Lafayette County in January 1836 in a covered Jersey wagon pulled by oxen and packed with a few tools and household belongings. Five of their children rode inside the wagon, and their three grown sons rode horseback beside them. Ranging in age from three to twenty-four, the Coffey children would contribute to the family workforce in essential ways. At age fifty-one, this was Hugh's last chance at moving west to establish his own farm. His wife, Margie, forty-six, had given birth to eleven children and lived a hard life managing the family's meager resources. Six years before, the Coffeys had left their home in North Carolina near Waxhaw in Mecklenburg County. They settled temporarily near Selma, Alabama, in the heart of the black belt, where they farmed on shares before the encroachment of large planters drove up land prices and pushed them toward the new lands in the Chickasaw nation.

They left before Christmas 1835 and traveled two weeks up the eastern side of the Tombigbee before crossing the river at Aberdeen. Warned of drunken, dangerous Indians, they gave Pontotoc a wide berth to the south and camped in a pine forest just north of Toccopola, the Chickasaw village on Lafayette's eastern border. That night, as they slept among sounds of howling wolves and panthers, Hugh Coffey held a rifle at his side. The next day they traveled along the Indian trail that passed northward through the piney hills in the eastern part of Lafayette County where they saw no sign of habitation. They arrived at the Tallahatchie where the trail crossed at a rocky ford. Not far from there, in the northeast corner of the county near Wolf Creek, the Coffey family spied an ideal place for their farm, with a cabin site on a ridge above the river, with ample water supply from the nearby creek which could be tapped by a shallow well, and fertile fields in the Tallahatchie floodplain below.

The Coffeys were squatters. Before making any effort to secure title, they simply seized possession and commenced two months of hard work setting up shelter for themselves and their stock. They felled nearby timber and built a typical dog-trot cabin. After completing the cabin they put up a log corral for the livestock. The nearby canebrake proved ideal forage for their stock, and this allowed Hugh Coffey to preserve his limited supply of corn and hay. The canebrake also proved a prolific hunting ground for wild boar (hardy razorback descendants of DeSoto's hogs three centuries before), which provided a welcome source of meat for the family. That spring they plowed the fields and planted their first crop of corn and cotton.[73]

Panic

Lafayette County, along with all the new lands opened in northern and eastern Mississippi, was born amid a rising bubble of land speculation. For every dollar in gold or silver brought in to purchase the new Indian lands, there were hundreds more circulating in the form of banknotes. "Shinplasters," as some derisively called them, were nothing more than promissory notes, pieces of paper with a signature over an agreement to pay the bearer in hard currency upon presentation. In the absence of a system of banks in the West, land companies and "wildcat" banks issued these notes profligately. Their value was as good as the expectation that land prices would rise. With the expansion of paper money in circulation, the prices of land rose dramatically and a mad cycle of inflation and speculation took on a life of its own.

Then the bubble burst. President Andrew Jackson, whose Indian Removal Act had opened the land to whites, became concerned that speculators—not settlers—were buying up all the Indian lands. He was also alarmed by what people warned was a dangerous speculative bubble forming in the West. To remedy both problems Jackson issued the Specie Circular in 1836, which required that all future purchases of public land must be paid in hard currency, gold or silver, unless purchased by actual settlers. The settlers were required to take an oath that they intended to farm the land they bought. Speculators found ways to evade the law by hiring agents to pose as settlers and buy land for them, but Jackson's hard money policy brought a sudden end to Mississippi's flush times; the Panic of 1837 would now have its day.

People scrambled to redeem notes that had been backed by little more than speculative hot air, and debtors defaulted in droves. "Wyatt money," which had been accepted without question a year earlier, became worthless. "Money is extremely scarce, and I have never in my life witnessed 'such screwing and twisting' to get it," wrote a lawyer in January 1840. "But few men have money and those who have it, will be disposed to hold on with the expectation of buying negroes low for cash at sheriffs sales."[74] Banks suspended specie payments, wildcat banks folded by the dozens, and the financial panic that began in 1837 had severe economic aftershocks that sent Mississippi and the nation into a serious economic depression by 1839. The effects lingered into the mid-1840s.

A general decline in land prices was compounded by a steep decline in cotton prices, which plummeted from an average of more than 15 cents a pound in 1835 to below 8 cents in 1839, then continued downward to 5.5 cents by 1844. Not until the end of the 1840s would cotton rise above 10 cents again.[75] As Baldwin wrote: "The splendid lie of a false credit burst into fragments. . . . Men worth a million were insolvent for two millions: promising young cities marched back again into the wilderness. The ambitious town plat was re-annexed to the plantation, like a country girl taken home from the city. The frolic was ended, and what headaches, and feverish limbs the next morning!"[76]

The aspiring town of Eaton was one such disillusioned country girl whose history would be recalled as little more than an example of the preposterous ambition of the early settlers. Likewise, Wyatt, once so full of expectation, fell into a deep slump, recovered briefly after 1845, but by the time of the Civil War had become a ghost town of abandoned warehouses, empty lots, and disappointed dreams.[77] Sales of town lots in Oxford slowed dramatically, and land deals across the county fell apart as buyers defaulted. As the Mississippi land bubble deflated, speculators and settlers abandoned northern Mississippi for Louisiana, Arkansas, or the new Republic of Texas, which became a favorite resort of westerners in flight from trouble.[78] "GTT" became the familiar shorthand in land sales and church records for those gone to Texas.

Travelers in Mississippi observed abandoned plantations that remained like "bits of wreckage and flotsam marking the unseen graves of those who have perished there." People were stealing away in the night, one remarked, "all in a double-quick march to Texas," the new "stronghold of evil-doers."[79] "I don't feel myself settled here and have been trying to sell out but cant effect a trade yet," one northern Mississippi settler complained in 1840. "I don't see much prospect of a change for the better . . . if Van Buren is again elected we may make our calculations to go to digging and live upon what we produce out of the earth let it be little or much."[80]

The catastrophe for speculators was a windfall to the plain folk in northern Mississippi. Land suddenly became more affordable and more available. When speculators defaulted on their loans, their lands went back on the market in desperate sales that brought good bargains for ready buyers. The panic hit after the individual Chickasaw allotments had been mostly sold, but only one-third of the four million acres of land owned by the tribe collectively had sold at the Pontotoc auctions. The average price during the auction sales in 1836 had been $1.66 per acre. Prices fell dramatically as the effects of the panic were felt and also as poorer lands were put up for sale. By prior agreement with the Chickasaws, the minimum price was gradually lowered below $1.25 per acre. By 1842 the average price per acre sold at the Pontotoc land office was down to fourteen cents an acre.[81] "The old regime of Mississippi has passed away," one observer wrote a few years after the crash. "Our lands are now in the hands of earnest cultivators."[82]

The panic had other benefits for small white farmers in northern Mississippi. It worked, temporarily at least, to balance an economy that had focused single-mindedly on cotton to the neglect of vital food crops, and this was a niche small farmers filled readily. A shortage of pork in 1840 underscored the problem. Counties with easy access to the Mississippi and Yazoo Rivers were able to import pork and grain from the Midwest to make up deficits in the local food production during the 1830s. In the interior counties of northern Mississippi, where river transportation was problematic and imports of foodstuffs expensive, local farmers quickly filled the void. Many small farmers exploited the poor hilly lands the larger cotton planters bypassed as too poor or difficult to plow, land quite suitable for grazing hogs and cattle. In place of the wild razorback hogs that supplied the pioneer population, Mississippians began importing higher-quality stock from the East. The smokehouse became a standard feature on most farms. Farmers also began converting more newly cleared land to grain and vegetable production to feed their livestock as well as supply food to the local human population.[83] The 1840 census showed that farmers in Lafayette County raised nearly 271,000 bushels of corn the previous year, along with sizable crops of oats, wheat, rye, and market produce. The county also claimed close to 2,700 bales of cotton the same year. The commitment to food crops in relation to cotton would never be this strong again.[84]

The flush times of Mississippi during the great land grab of the late 1830s passed quickly into a sobering realization that the South, its economy and society, were not so easily rejuvenated simply by moving to the next fresh frontier. Southerners had recreated the slave and cotton economy in northern Mississippi with remarkable speed. Almost overnight the stage had been set for the next act: new lands were cleared, log houses thrown up, new towns and courthouses, churches and schools, and a cast of actors, free and slave, hurried onstage. The act began amid exaggerated hope, followed by depressing economic disaster. For those who stayed, and those who came later, the task remained to build a more enduring foundation for the new economy and society the pioneers had hastily erected.

That fast, that rapid: a commodity in the land now which until now had dealt first in Indians: then in acres and sections and boundaries: — an economy: Cotton: a king: omnipotent and omnipresent: . . . not the soaring cupola of the courthouse drawing people into the country, but that same white tide sweeping them in: that tender skim covering the winter's brown earth, burgeoning through spring and summer into September's white surf crashing against the flanks of gin and warehouse and ringing like bells on the marble counters of the banks: altering not just the face of the land but the complexion of the town too, creating its own parasitic aristocracy not only behind the columned porticoes of the plantation houses, but in the counting-rooms of merchants and bankers and sanctum of lawyers, and . . . the county offices too: of sheriff and tax-collector and bailiff and turnkey and clerk.

—WILLIAM FAULKNER, Requiem for a Nun

three Communities

Building a social community in antebellum Mississippi was no less challenging than laying down a new economic foundation. A community in such a young and volatile social environment could not rest on deep or lasting bonds of blood and face-to-face knowledge of one another. Among those with a deep stake in the county's future development was a community of mutual economic interest. This was largely the domain of wealthy white males, forged in a series of campaigns to boost new towns, railroads, schools, and the state university. Community also drew on less tangible notions of shared sentiments and values in religion, politics, education, and social improvement. Within the town, voluntary associations gave expression to a variety of shared interests and values among middle-class men and women. Across the county churches were of singular importance in pulling many isolated families and lonely individuals together in communities of faith. In their congregations and camp meetings men and women, masters and slaves found communion if not equality.

It took the better part of a decade before a more solid economic foundation formed and before the opportunistic atmosphere of Mississippi's flush times gave way to more sober plans for economic development and social organization. By then the "gambling traders" and speculators had either gone to Texas, or some other new frontier of expectations, or they had put down stakes in northern Mississippi. The small contingent that stayed from the pioneer generation would be joined by others—westward migrants still responding to the relentless pressures pushing them out of the worn-out lands of the East and pulling them to cheap land in Mississippi.

Land, slaves, and cotton were still the mainstays of the economy, but those who sought a future in Lafayette County now looked to other props on which to build prosperity. New schools and colleges became emblematic of the county's aspirations for the future. A more elaborate transportation network of improved wagon roads, stronger bridges, and a new railroad all smoothed the path between cotton fields and markets. Transportation also reinforced the centrality of the town in local affairs. The town both served and dominated the agrarian economy, and within it arose a class of merchants, lawyers, bankers, clerks, and planters whose way of life quickly distinguished itself from that of the countryside.

By the late 1840s signs of economic recovery were everywhere, most notably in Oxford. With the recovery, a spirit of expectation, even renewed confidence, took hold once more, now more grounded than in the heady days of speculative mania during Mississippi's flush times. Those who profited amid the renewed prosperity, especially the larger cotton planters and merchants and professionals in town, entered the 1850s imbued with a faith in progress and improvement and a not unrealistic sense of confidence in their capacity to shape their future.

King Cotton's Domain

As the cotton economy slowly recovered, the dominance of King Cotton intensified. The ratio of cotton to corn production nearly tripled between 1840 and 1860. Population growth continued at a slower pace in the 1850s, rising from about fourteen to sixteen thousand. Most of the growth came from an increase in the slave population, now over seven thousand (44 percent of the population). Corn, wheat, and other food crops kept pace with population growth, with corn production remaining steady at about forty bushels per person throughout this twenty-year period. Livestock production did not grow, and the number of hogs slaughtered actually declined markedly. But the land and labor devoted to cotton increased tremendously. In 1840, four years from its initial organization, the county's young cotton economy yielded a little under 2,700 bales. During the 1840s that nearly quadrupled to 10,400 bales, and in the 1850s cotton production nearly doubled again, rising to almost 19,300 bales in 1860.[1] Per capita cotton production rose over 60 percent from 0.74 to 1.20 bales during the 1850s. Total farm acreage expanded by over one-third during the 1850s. More striking was the dramatic increase in the dollar value of farms, which nearly tripled in the 1850s, rising to over three million dollars by 1860.[2]

King Cotton's court was dominated by large planters, but throngs of middling and small farmers now crowded in. In 1850 fully 80 percent of all farmers reported growing at least one bale of cotton. Ten years later almost 90 percent of the county's nine hundred farmers were growing some cotton. The wealthiest 10 percent of farmers, according to the value of their land, produced over 40 percent of the county's cotton in 1860. The least wealthy half grew less than 20 percent of the total bales. But farmers large and small had a stake in the future of cotton.

This intensified commitment to cotton was driven by an eagerness to take advantage of recovering prices fueled by the growing world demand for cotton as the industrial revolution gripped New England and the Northeast. Responding to the cotton mania that swept across the Deep South, farmers cleared more land to grow more cotton to buy more land and slaves to grow more cotton. They worked existing cotton lands more intensively, and when those wore out they cleared and broke more land and converted worn-out fields to pasture for livestock.

Mississippi cotton farmers eagerly embraced any new method that promised to increase yields and profits. Many began planting a new breed of Mexican cotton that brought significantly higher yield per acre. They also adopted new technology that promised greater efficiency. In place of crude hoes wielded by gangs of slaves the modern plantation adopted the tongue plow and a device called the "Mississippi scraper." Introduced about the time the cotton economy hit bottom in 1840, this device vastly enhanced the skimming of weeds between cotton rows and quickly became popular among planters in Mississippi.

The rapid clearing of new lands and the widespread use of new farm implements greatly accelerated the erosion of northern Mississippi's delicate loess soil. Solon Robinson, a northern agricultural reformer, while visiting a plantation just south of Lafayette County in the 1840s, saw in a single field some twenty plows "skinning the surface of this light, loose, fine, sandy soil, and sending it on a voyage of discovery to the gulf of Mexico."[3] Those who had "murdered the soil" in the East were well under way with the reckless destruction of Mississippi's fresh lands. "Even the present generation is rife with complaints about the exhaustion of the soils," state geologist Eugene Hilgard wrote in the 1850s, "in a region which, thirty years ago, had but just received the first scratch of the plowshare." Prime land that had sold as high as thirty dollars an acre, Hilgard reported, was going for ten dollars in 1860, and parts of Mississippi looked like Europe after the Thirty Years' War.[4]

The rapid destruction of farmland and the new methods of cotton growing required greater investments in land, equipment, and draft animals. The number of farms in the county actually declined during the 1850s, from a little over one thousand to just under nine hundred, but these farms now claimed much more land. Total farm acreage grew from nearly 275,000 acres in 1850 to more than 373,000 ten years later, and about 30 percent of this was actually improved, cultivated farmland. Those who could afford to were buying more land than they needed immediately in order to expand in the future. King Cotton, "omnipotent and omnipresent," as Faulkner characterized him, dictated the ruthless exploitation of his domain.

The forests receded rapidly in advance of King Cotton's expanding realm. Some of the timber was converted to lumber; by 1860 there were eight sawmills in the county, located along the creeks where they could harness the waterpower. The lumber now went into new homes, barns, and commercial buildings that replaced many of the rough log homes with their crude puncheon floors. Much of the timber, however, was simply set ablaze where it lay in the cleared fields to make way for cotton. It was, Faulkner wrote, "not plow and axe which had effaced the wilderness, but Cotton: petty globules of Motion weightless and myriad even in the hand of a child, incapable even of wadding a rifle, let alone of charging it, yet potent enough to sever the very taproots of oak and hickory and gum, leaving the acre-shading tops to wither and vanish in one single season beneath that fierce minted glare."[5]

Mississippi still offered promise to those coming from the East. Even as King Cotton devoured his own realm, there was more land available to clear and plant, for land was still sufficiently available and affordable to justify a strategy of continual clearing and exhaustion. "My land where I now live is so much worn that I am trying to make a purchase and probably may do so between this and laying by the crop," M. J. Blackwell wrote to his brother in the East in 1849. "Land of excellent quality can now be had at from 4 to 6 dollars in the woods or from 7 to 10 improved. You can get improved land at 7 to 8 dollars per acre which if you had them in So[uth] Carolina you would not be willing to sell for $20 per acre."[6] So long as land remained comparatively cheap and there was more to be claimed from the forests, the rewards of cotton planting in northern Mississippi continued to be more profitable than in the East. "This is a magnificent country for planters," Augustus Baldwin Longstreet boasted to his son-in-law, L. Q. C. Lamar, in 1850. "There are men here who left Newton County [Georgia] poor and in debt eight and ten years ago, who now have a good plantation and fifteen to twenty hands, and are buying more every year."[7] Even as antebellum Mississippi matured and its land eroded, it offered ambitious migrants a place of hope. The courthouse, Faulkner wrote, rising like a "lodestar and pole, drawing the people—the men and woman and children, the maidens, the marriageable girls and the young men, flowing, pouring in with their tools and goods and cattle and slaves and gold money."[8]

A Road to Prosperity

The growing commitment of Lafayette County farmers to King Cotton propelled the drive to improve transportation to market. Only yesterday, Faulkner wrote, "Pettigrew's pony express had been displaced by a stage-coach, yet already there was talk of a railroad less than a hundred miles to the north, to run all the way from Memphis to the Atlantic Ocean."[9] The campaign in the 1850s to bring a railroad through the county promised to transform a frontier outpost in backwoods Mississippi into a vital center of commerce just down the road from Memphis, New Orleans, or New York. Whatever cotton farming was doing to use up and wear out the land, there was a corps of forward-looking planters, farmers, and townspeople building new homes, farms, and towns, constructing new roads and bridges, and investing in a railroad, all toward creating an economy and society with a future. Even as the thin edge of the southern rights wedge entered Mississippi politics in 1850, local citizens were forging ahead, building a network of transportation and trade that linked them to distant national markets centered in the Northeast.[10]

Until the late 1850s, overland transportation was dependent on wagon roads radiating like spokes out of the Oxford hub to outlying hamlets and adjacent county seats. Along these rough roads wealthy planters rode in fancy carriages imported from the East and Europe while others rode in horse- or mule-drawn wagons, hauling cotton and other goods. Beginning sometime in the late 1830s, stagecoach service connected Oxford to Memphis, the capital in Jackson, and nearby Pontotoc. Travel was slow, especially when the roads turned to mud. Logs laid down crossways in boggy areas of the roads formed what were called corduroy roads, and they made for a teeth-rattling ride. The trip from Jackson took forty hours of miserable travel by horse or carriage. One traveler described the roads in the southern part of the county as the "worst roads, I'll wager, in Dixie." "Our Mules did finely, but poor creatures I know they are as much rejoiced as we are to be over those bad roads." [11] But these rough wagon roads provided the only regular access to the outside world. Stagecoaches heralded their arrival at each stop with the blowing of a bugle, a signal that brought townspeople scurrying to an eventful moment in a remote western community.[12]

With the recovery and expansion of the local cotton economy, what Lafayette County needed was a faster, more reliable method of getting the cotton to market. Once Wyatt's early promise as "Little Memphis on the Tallahatchie" faded, the dream of local boosters was to build a railroad connecting the county to the world beyond. Memphis, New Orleans, and the cities of the nation would be within reach in a fraction of the time it took by overland stage and wagon or by steamboat. The first signs of railroad fever surfaced in the spring of 1851, when a "large and enthusiastic meeting" took place at the courthouse. Faith in railroads and other internal improvements had been central to the Whig vision of western development. R. H. Buford and W. H. D. Wendel, two leading Whigs in the county, served as chair and secretary of the meeting that May. E. R. Belcher, a favorite Whig spokesman, urged, "concert of action is indispensable." To Democrat Jacob Thompson was given the task of proposing the resolutions for action. The railroad was promoted as a great boon to the entire community, and it won the bipartisan support of leading planters and townspeople.[13]

What became the Mississippi Central Railroad was already under way from Jackson northward as railroad fever rose in Lafayette County. The road had reached Canton, about 150 miles south of Oxford, by the summer of 1851. It was intended to connect with Holly Springs, so Oxford's destiny as a railroad town seemed certain if only local investors and political leaders would make it happen by buying stock and raising taxes to subsidize the road. "Every man who knows anything of the history of rail roads," one appeal went, "must be convinced of the incalculable advantages to all classes of citizens." [14]

A combination of public-spirited capitalism and a heavy dose of socialism brought Lafayette County its railroad. The Democrats, though averse to federal government intrusion in state and local affairs, seemed every bit as eager as the Whigs for public improvement at public expense. In May 1852 the citizens of Lafayette County were invited to purchase stock in the railroad. "We hope," the Democratic editor trumpeted before the public meeting, "there is no one in our community who will adopt the do nothing policy, and attempt to urge the impossibility of completing this important enterprise." Those "who oppose and retard (indirectly) all great enterprises, by urging the impossibility of their completion," he went on, ". . . are not the true friends of public enterprise but its enemies, and might properly be denominated drones." Let "the people en mass favor it" and those with means "take hold of it in harmony" and push it to completion.[15] When local patriotism failed to inspire the citizenry, rivalry and shame at the success of neighboring counties were brought on to prod reluctant investors. "If Marshall County can stand $250,000, Lafayette can go $100,000 easy." "Let not Lafayette County be behind any county on the line."[16]

Democratic Party leaders took prominent roles at the meeting to boost stock subscriptions. Colonel James Brown called the meeting to order and introduced a Mr. Clapp from Holly Springs, who urged people "to look around them, at the rapid strides making in Rail Road enterprises in other states—see the prosperity arising from them." Clapp went on to warn of dire consequences should the railroad not be built through Lafayette County. It would mean economic isolation and decline. "If the people do not wish this road—if they do not desire to be placed in railroad communication with every section of this Union, they have but to sit still and do nothing until this opportunity passes by, and they will be sure to not get it." The response of the crowd made it clear that Lafayette County people wanted to be part of a prosperous Union, not a backwoods frontier. When Colonel Brown opened the subscription book, "in a very short time about 500 shares were taken." But the otherwise ebullient reporter, William Delay, did not hesitate to carp that a "number of our citizens of wealth who we have heard express their intentions of taking stock, were not present." Ever the booster, Delay regained the spirit of optimism: "We have no doubt now, that the people of our county will come up nobly and manfully to the work."[17]

Private stock subscriptions were still going slow when H. W. Walters of Holly Springs spoke to those assembled at the county courthouse on a Saturday night in May: "The Road will be built, he had no doubt of that," the Democratic editor reported gravely, "but whether or not it would run through the counties of Lafayette and Marshall, depended upon the early action of the people of those counties." Walter warned of an amendment to the charter to change the route of the road through Panola and Desoto to Memphis, bypassing Lafayette. If each person would buy shares "in a very few years we would have the Iron Horse dashing through our town every day. Then, every man who had a bale of Cotton to sell, would find a purchaser in Oxford to give him as much as he could get in New Orleans."[18]

The advantages of a railroad were not so obvious to small farmers in the hilly eastern section of the county whose semisubsistence way of life involved only limited trade outside the county. They had reason to see the railroad as a benefit to large cotton producers at their expense, for the state had imposed a tax on all counties through which the new railroad would traverse. Instead of making landowners closest to the railroad shoulder the tax burden, Lafayette County's Board of Police decided to levy a general tax surcharge to raise the needed $50,000. This proposal went before the county's voters at the end of June 1852. Local railroad promoters began staging barbecues and speeches across the county, particularly in the piney hill country to the east where the yeomanry's support for railroads—and railroad taxes—was in doubt.[19] But a growing number of small farmers now saw themselves as players, or expectant participants at least, in the market economy, and they wanted a railroad. A "large majority" of voters approved the tax surcharge, but no sooner did they do so than the railroad promoters came back to the public trough, this time asking another $100,000. Private enterprise had failed to raise sufficient stock subscriptions, and they now wanted the county to take up the slack. Again, the voters gave their overwhelming approval to this venture in public enterprise.[20]

At the same time, plans were afloat for improved steamboat service on the Tallahatchie. The Agricultural Society has "determined to build a new Steamboat to run in the Tallahatchee River" by joint stock at $25 per share, the local newspaper announced. A long list of subscribers testified to the spirit of progress: "We have no doubt their laudable purpose will be accomplished before the next cotton crop is made." [21] What they did not foresee was that the speed and reliability of railroad transportation would soon bring the demise of the steamboat trade on the Tallahatchie. Wyatt was already on its way to becoming a ghost town of abandoned buildings and faded dreams.[22]

The Oxford of Mississippi

Lafayette County also looked to public funding for other props in its local economy. While the railroad was connecting the county to an expanding rail network, the state university added a vital stimulant to the local economy and a certain luster as the educational and cultural center of the state. The decision to locate the university at Oxford had been part of the rising sectional tension between the older settled parts of the Natchez area and the new counties of northern Mississippi during the 1840s. One of the selling points was that Oxford would be far more isolated, and therefore more healthy, both physically and morally, than the more crowded and sinful river cities of Natchez and Vicksburg. Though chartered in 1844, the University of Mississippi did not begin its first class until 1848, just as the cotton economy was flourishing anew.[23]

Beginning with the very naming of Oxford, local promoters had worked toward winning this rich and steady source of state largesse. They met with local competition when, in 1840, College Hill forged ahead by founding North Mississippi College with hopes that the legislature might take advantage of its presence and designate it the state university. They would become two of several sites considered by the state legislature that year. Oxford's citizens were "fully awake" to the benefits of the university and became very generous with gifts to influence the outcome. Local promoters raised $6,400 from private contributions to sweeten their bid. The money and the political influence of Oxford's leading men won the prize in the end. The coming of the university, one proud local editor later recounted, "sufficed to transform Oxford from an insignificant County site, with no prospect, reaching beyond the next Court week, to a thriving and prosperous town, which bids fair, at no distant day, to stand at the head of the list of inland towns in Mississippi."[24]

By the early 1850s the university enrolled more than 130 students from all sections of the state and a few from nearby states. Located a mile to the west of the town square and connected only by muddy pathways, the university even in its crude beginnings hastened the recovery of Oxford from the lingering doldrums of the depression. The construction of several new campus buildings gave Oxford's building trades a decided boost. New hotels and boardinghouses cropped up to serve students and visitors, and new stores took their place around the courthouse square. Several academies for young women and men suddenly appeared in and around Oxford, the latter to serve as feeder schools to the university.[25] Oxford Female Academy, Oxford Female Institute, Oxford Male Academy, College Hill Male Academy, College Hill Female Seminary, Union Female College, and North Mississippi College in College Hill were among the satellites that clustered in and around what the local paper dubbed "University City."[26]

The arrival of the university coincided with an architectural boom in new frame and brick mansions built for the house-proud merchants and planters of Oxford. The log cabin of the pioneers suddenly gave way to the two-story clapboard house, typically with its imposing columns and portico, Sutpenesque advertisements of their owners' prosperity. As more found prosperity during the recovery of cotton prices, it became the fashion among large planters to leave country estates to the daily management of overseers and move with their families into new town mansions. They came away from the isolation of the countryside to enjoy the lively social life that Oxford offered. From parties and shopping, to churches and schools, the town provided forms of community unknown to those isolated in the country. From the mid-1840s until the Civil War architects and builders were

Sheegog-Faulkner house. (Courtesy of University Museums, University of Mississippi)

busy putting up an impressive host of grand mansions in town for these planter families.

Jacob Thompson, a rising politician and son-in-law to one of the richest planters in the county, owned his own vast plantation lands including a 2,400-acre plantation on Woodson's Ridge. Thompson was among the first to build a large mansion in Oxford in 1841. The lumber had to be imported from Memphis and the bricks were made on site by Thompson's slaves. The house included twenty rooms filled with expensive art and elegant furnishings. Flanked by large verandas and surrounded by formal gardens and a tree-lined drive his gardener had planned, the Thompson mansion set an early standard for elegance in Oxford.[27]

More typical was the home built by Colonel Robert Sheegog in 1848. It was a large frame house just north of the Jacob Thompson mansion. Sheegog was born in Ireland and was described as "a man of large means in land, negroes" (though the census records show only nine slaves and 320 acres). He was a prominent citizen, in any case, and when he died in 1860 he was saluted as a pioneer of the county, a "good and true man" who would be remembered fondly by his many friends. The Sheegog home is the place William Faulkner would buy in 1930. Visitors to Rowan Oak, as Faulkner named it, can still see, behind the impressive columns and portico, the simple, unadorned functionality of a comfortable farmhouse. Though not a man of great wealth, Sheegog put the show up front, and his home still strikes a certain aristocratic pose set amid a formal garden and curving driveway lined with cedars.[28] The house was designed by William Turner, an untrained house designer who stood in great demand during the antebellum building boom in Lafayette County. No one knows how many mansions Turner put his hand to during the 1840s and 1850s, but his influence can be seen everywhere in the simple neoclassical designs with four columns in front rising two-stories to the portico and the otherwise rather simple ornamentation.[29]

The same proclivity to display to the street was very much the theme of the house Turner built on South Street in 1860 for William Thompson, Jacob's brother. A magnificent portico supported by four-square columns faced the street, but the house itself was only one room deep. Behind it were two small rustic log cabins erected by pioneer John Martin, one of Oxford's founders. The Civil War came before Thompson could complete the other half, so the two cabins remained attached to the shallow but ostentatious front. The Thompson-Chandler house, as it was later known, had an ornate iron fence in front and became the model for the Compson family home in Faulkner's *The Sound and the Fury*.[30]

One of the grandest Oxford mansions was built by Thomas E. B. Pegues, who, with his brother Nicholas, followed his sister, Rebecca, from Alabama to Lafayette County in 1850. Thomas Pegues was a rich planter in the Lafayette Springs area who owned over 2,400 acres and more than one hundred slaves. In 1856 he moved to Oxford, bought a lot of 100 acres for his home site, and began building what would be the costliest and most ostentatious mansion in the county. It was an enormous edifice built with bricks his slaves fired at the site. The house became a subject of local gossip because it was said to cost between fourteen and fifteen thousand dollars. The design of the house, an Italianate style quite unusual in antebellum Oxford, was attributed to a man with a strange-sounding French name, Calvert Vaux, a nationally well-known architect from New York. Vaux was actually born in England, and he never came to Oxford, but the local legend of Pegues' One Hundred must have inspired Faulkner's story of Sutpen's captive French architect. Thomas Pegues lined his driveway with magnolias, and along North Street, the main avenue that led from his mansion to the courthouse square, he had a row of oaks planted, making it one of the most elegant residential streets in town. He named his mansion Edgecomb and the local editor heralded it as "one of the ornaments of the town." "Pegues Folly," as the owner himself dubbed it, remained unfinished when the war came.[31] Lining North and South Street, out University Avenue, and in many of the streets around the square were many more grand new mansions, mostly built of clapboard with tall columns under broad porticos, all painted sparkling white and surrounded by spacious lawns. These new town mansions gave Oxford an impressive aura of wealth and permanency. They were houses built to last by people who aimed to stay.

With its new elegant mansions and university, the town began to take on a self-conscious image as a home of a culturally refined citizenry able to support a host of literary societies and social events equal to its station as Mississippi's educational capital. Several of the university's faculty helped formed new town and gown societies. "This is one among the most intelligent towns in North Mississippi," exclaimed a local editor.[32]

The annual examination of university and academy students became a prominent feature of Oxford's spring social calendar and attracted townspeople and planters along with prominent families from near and far. The "closing act of Session '52" received lavish coverage in the local press. "The Lafayette delegation as usual led the van," in an "imposing array [of] finery," followed by those from other counties and spectators standing to glimpse the show. This was a day for young, single women to make their presence known among the university men. "Upon every side you could look upon the 'fairest of the fair.' There was Miss B. . . . shining as a glittering star among the many, attracting as a magnet, many a gallant admirer of the beauty; and near by one could not fail to notice Mrs. C. of Oxford, whose captivating qualities many tongues have praised and from whose face description would recoil as unable to do justice to the task." [33]

None surpassed local editor Howard Falconer in his enthusiasm for the university and all that it promised in the way of material benefit and social improvement to the community. "How much, indeed, the town of Oxford depends," Falconer wrote, "upon the university might be, to some extent, apparent even to the passing stranger who should contrast the life and activity which prevail here, while the university is in session, with that utter stagnation which follows the departure of the students to their several homes." [34] The social and intellectual refinement might well make Oxford a rival to its namesake someday, another local admirer observed. Though "simple and unpretending as it may now seem," Oxford "may one day in the future become as notable a home of the arts and sciences as was ever the Athens of Greece, the Oxford of England." "The material is here in abundance with which to build a mighty mausoleum of learning as enduring as the eternal pyramids of the Nile." [35]

The two symbols of Lafayette County's progress, the railroad and the university, came together as the Mississippi Central was routed through Oxford to the front door of the campus. The triumphal union of education and commerce did not quite come about as hoped, however. College Hill, lying a few miles to the north and east, had persuaded (some said bribed) the board of directors to divert the line west from Abbeville to their settlement. It was only with the intervention of Oxford investors and university trustees that the railroad was brought through Oxford instead. James Brown and Thomas Isom led the movement to bring the railroad through Oxford in 1856, and they volunteered their own slaves to help with construction. Then, because the engines were thought to be insufficiently powerful to pull the trains up the hill to the campus, the road had to cut deep into the hillside to reduce the grade. Hilgard Cut, named in honor of Eugene Hilgard, a geologist at the university, took the road close to the university, but the gulch was so deep no passenger could see anything but its steep banks.[36]

"We are aware," Falconer reminded his fellow Oxonians in 1860, "that there are those who ascribe our present prosperous condition chiefly to the influence of the Mississippi Central Railroad." The university, he reminded people, was a major reason the railroad came into Oxford instead of taking the College Hill route to the west. Moreover, the university accounted for some "$100,000 every year that flowed into the local economy." It was, more than that, a magnet to "the intelligent and refined" who came to settle in Oxford, making it "to Mississippi, what Athens was to Greece . . . where wealth shall lavish her treasures, and Art adorn and fill with beauty every public edifice and private dwelling; where Eloquence shall achieve new triumphs, and Science daily lay her precious gifts upon the altar of Human Progress."[37]

Ours Is Emphatically a Moving Population

While the county's new settlers were erecting an economic foundation, they were also busy constructing a new social order. By the mid-nineteenth century the process of building new American communities in the West was becoming as routine as laying out a new town, setting up a government, or boosting a new railroad or university. Just as with local government, the plans for new social institutions were all in place waiting to be adapted to the new building site: churches, schools, clubs, and reform associations were all replicas borrowed from familiar eastern models.

But if the process of community building had become commonplace in antebellum America, it was also problematic. This was particularly true in northern Mississippi, where a volatile economic climate and a migratory population seemed in every way designed to work against the creation of a stable, integrated community life. Whatever they might have shared as southerners, Lafayette County's settlers arrived from a great variety of places, and they came together with few of the social bonds usually thought to define community. The rapid growth of the population in its early years meant most were newcomers. Adding to this continuing problem of fashioning a community out of new arrivals was the impermanence of the population. The county experienced a tremendous churning of its population as migrants passed into and out of the population. The social order had to be built upon a perpetually unstable demographic foundation. Far from being the kind of intimate community some Faulkner readers think they see in the fictional Yoknapatawpha, the historical model was a shifting assembly of passing strangers—strangers to the land and to one another.[38]

The central feature of Lafayette County's social history was the steady stream of temporary settlers passing through its borders. This migratory population meant that the community formed within what began and remained a river of movers. As we have seen, the 1840 population of more than sixty-five hundred had shot up to over fourteen thousand by 1850, despite hard times. By 1860 the population grew to a little over sixteen thousand, about nine thousand whites and seven thousand black slaves.

Though birth rates among slave and free were high, the population did not grow significantly by natural increase, nor did it grow simply by migratory additions to a stable base. Instead of a pile of stones that grew by birth and migration, the population appears more like Mississippi dust blowing in from the East, some settling in more permanent drifts, most blowing farther west as the winds of fortune dictated. The 1840 census recorded 628 household heads, most all of them adult white males. Less than four in ten (243) of these 1840 household heads could be found still living in the county a decade later. Having come so far to a land ripe with promise, why did these "settlers" not settle?

The panic and depression created tremendous turbulence in the population at the beginning of the decade, as we saw earlier. The Mexican War, 1845–48, brought more, not simply by pulling young men into a military adventure in the West but also by opening up a new frontier for American expansion that quickly drew Mississippi residents farther west. California's gold rush at the end of the decade was only the most dramatic episode in the ongoing lure of the West. Those who had already taken up stakes and moved to the Mississippi frontier in the 1830s were vulnerable to the siren call of the next frontier. John Bailey spoke of his young friends in Lafayette taking off for the California gold fields, "all stout harty young bucks bound for the gold diggings to make their fortunes." "I should like to be off with them if my business would admit . . . as I have considearable fever in that way."[39]

By the late 1840s, with cotton prices recovered, Lafayette County embarked on a robust period of prosperity that would last until the Civil War.

But this did nothing to settle the population. In 1850 only one in six whites had been in the county a decade. It was as though the frontier experience of unstable initial settlement was being perpetuated instead of surmounted. The economy of the 1850s was more solid than it ever had been (and ever would be for a century). This was truly Lafayette County's flush times. Despite the prosperity, about two-thirds of the 1850 population left the county before ten years were out. That meant less than 30 percent of the county's white household heads had lived in the county a decade or more by 1860. Other frontiers, fresher land, and new opportunities beckoned.

"Ours is emphatically a *moving* population," M. J. Blackwell wrote of his new neighbors in northern Mississippi. "It would surprise you to see how many persons in the west are willing to sell out and move." Men would sell Mississippi land for between seven and ten dollars an acre and buy fresh land across the river in Arkansas at one or two dollars. Clearing the land and laying out a farm on speculation "has become a kind of business with many," Blackwell noted. "They will buy a place, say at 4 or 5 dolls per acre clear 50 or 100 acres and put up something of an apology for a house and sell to some new comer for 8 or 10 dollars per acre, and off into the woods he goes again to improve some other place to sell again." [40]

Land, according to the kind of calculating mentality Blackwell described, was nothing more than a commodity, and one that shrewd westerners would buy, clear, plant, and improve, then sell and buy again someplace else. The so-called Old South was no tradition-bound society of landed gentry with deep ties to place; especially in its western regions, it was young, opportunistic, and forever moving.

This Lonely Land

Out in the country, where all but a few hundred lived, northern Mississippi was a lonely place to be. Whether they belonged to the core of established settlers or were birds of passage, the white inhabitants of rural Lafayette County lived much of their time in isolation from one another. The patterns of rural settlement in Mississippi came from long-established habits of extensive agriculture that placed each farm or plantation house at or near the center of each plot of land. None of the military, economic, or cultural forces that operated in more traditional agricultural societies to hold the farming population within a protective town from which they would go out to work in the fields ever prevailed for long among Americans. That lack of defensive need, together with abundant land and crops grown on an extensive scale, allowed them—compelled them—to spread out across the land.

In Mississippi the economies of scale in cotton production rewarded large expanses of land. Semisubsistence farmers raising corn and running hogs or cattle on the open range also required substantial parcels of land around them, even if it was common land for grazing and hunting. Because land was plentiful and cheap, and because it was quickly depleted, those who could afford it bought more land than they needed for immediate use.[41]

Though many large planters moved into Oxford where they enjoyed more comfort and social communion, most small farmers and many planters continued to live near their fields and work throughout the year at the many tasks farming demanded of them. Well past the initial stage of primitive dwellings, even well-off farmers in rural northern Mississippi for the most part lived in log cabins with crude furnishings. M. J. Blackwell noted in 1849 that "people in this county have but just commenced building fine houses, and even this matter now proceeds slowly owing to the unsettled state of the country."[42]

Dotting the landscape were a few small hamlets consisting of little more than a general store where farmers bought provisions and farm supplies, surrounded in rough proximity with a blacksmith shop, one or two plain wooden churches, perhaps a tavern, often with rooms for overnight guests, and maybe a school. Typically the store or tavern would serve as the seat of justice for the beat. There, amid barrels of goods and farm supplies, the justice of the peace would preside over court and mete out justice in his own fashion. The same store or tavern might also serve as a polling place where on election days men gathered to cast their ballots and where, before elections, office seekers would come to address their voting constituents.

A small hamlet might include a few dwellings for residents, but these micro-urban clusters were places that families in the vicinity came to by horse or foot when they wanted to trade, attend church, engage in political activities, take their children to school, or just visit and while away the time. Following these periodic episodes of sociability, they returned to their cabins and houses surrounded by fields and woods, isolated from one another and from most any daily social intercourse outside their families. More sophisticated visitors, like Belle Edmondson of Memphis, viewed these rural people through condescending urban eyes when she described the people of Sarepta as "dirty, miserable looking creatures—with no tastes and scarcely any civilization."[43] For most white farmers in rural Mississippi "civilization" or community of any kind was experienced as a place they visited, not an everyday part of life.

In 1850 the county's population averaged nineteen people per square mile; ten years earlier it had been only eight. By 1860 the population density thickened only slightly to over twenty-three persons per square mile.

Oxford probably had six to seven hundred people by 1860, but it remained too small to warrant an official population report in the census before 1880, when it reached one thousand.

The rural hamlets tended to coalesce along the roads that radiated from the Oxford hub beginning a few miles out. When the Mississippi Central railway came through the county in the 1850s new railway stations became the nuclei for market and shipping centers at Abbeville to the north of Oxford, Taylor's Depot and Springdale to the south. In the more remote and hilly portions of the county to the east and south of Oxford there were several small, scattered hamlets serving the mostly self-sufficient farmers in the hills. In clockwise order from Caswell northeast of Oxford were Liberty Hill, Lafayette Springs, Delay, Dallas, Paris, and Yocona in the Yoknapatawpha River valley southeast of Oxford. Toccopola, the former Chickasaw town, stood on the county border on the southeast while Sarepta, once in the remote panhandle of lower Lafayette, became part of a new county, Calhoun, formed in 1852.[44]

In Masculine Solitude

Mississippi was a frontier of promise and adventure for young white men aspiring to gain a place for themselves in a new country full of opportunity. But male ambition to move west often came at the expense of the domestic comforts and social ties women valued most. The West was often a lonely place for white women, cast amid a heavily masculine population and a society that offered little to compensate for the kinship and friendship they left behind.[45] The peripatetic people of Lafayette County sometimes appear as little more than an assembly of migrant strangers scattered across a remote land covered with woods and cotton fields. The mobility of the population suggests a people who rarely put down roots or congregated often enough to form what we think of as genuine communities.

Outside their families, including extended kin, many settlers in northern Mississippi would have enjoyed few lasting social bonds to the people around them. Moreover, among the white population of Lafayette County was a large surplus of males without female partners. Among whites twenty to fifty years of age there were no less than 144 men for every 100 women in 1840. Perhaps at this early stage of development it is not surprising that more men came west to perform the hard, dirty labor involved in clearing land, raising houses and barns, and breaking the land. Of necessity, they lived, as Faulkner's Sutpen had, "in masculine solitude." Those who were married might send for their wives and family after establishing their new farms and dwellings. Many boarded with other families or lived in hotels and taverns. The Holston House, where Faulkner's Thomas Sutpen stayed with other men when they first arrived in Yoknapatawpha, could have been modeled on the hotel known as the Oxford Inn operated by Charles and Burlina Butler, Faulkner's maternal great-grandparents. To transient men in a new country, the Butlers' hotel, and others like it, along with small boardinghouses in the countryside, served as a temporary home.[46]

Men who moved west also missed their families and friends back home. Letters from men in Mississippi referred sadly to the women they left behind and grumbled about the poor chances of finding a bride in the West. The Mississippi frontier was a rough, masculine domain, a lonely and forbidding place for women and all the more so for women without men to fend for them. For single women, in contrast, the uneven sex ratio of early Mississippi offered fine prospects for husbands. There were many young, unmarried women who came west with their parents, and those from well-to-do families were particularly sought after. William Faulkner's story of Thomas Sutpen's search for a new wife in frontier Yoknapatawpha reveals a calculating pursuit of a marriage partner that would further his design for a Sutpen dynasty. Ellen Coldfield, the daughter of a local merchant, was not particularly wealthy, but her father was an upstanding citizen, a steward in the Methodist church, and, at the same time, a man apparently willing to strike a deal exchanging permission to marry his daughter for some business advantage. Sutpen's determined pursuit of Ellen Coldfield likely had many parallels in Lafayette County's early history, for the story reflects the reality of choices that were both limited and absolutely critical to the ambitious schemes that brought so many men west.

Jacob Thompson was a young bachelor of twenty-six when he came to Mississippi. Soon after arriving in Lafayette County he began courting the daughter of Peyton Jones, one of the wealthiest planters in the county. Kate Jones was only fourteen, but on the Mississippi frontier her family wealth and her precocious beauty already had attracted the attention of several eager bachelors. Thompson was about to leave for Washington to take his seat in Congress when, fearful that some rival suitor would win Kate's hand, he persuaded the father to allow them to marry on condition that Kate would first go abroad to France for her education. It was not until she turned twenty and returned to America that they lived together as man and wife. Jacob Thompson had his bride—and a chest full of gold, a wedding present from the father.[47]

Thomas Dudley Isom arrived in 1835 when he was only nineteen. He clerked at the Indian trading post his brother-in-law John Craig had opened on the future site of Oxford, then returned to Tennessee for three years to study medicine. He was thirty before he found a bride. Sarah McGhehee of

Abbeville, South Carolina, was visiting her sister in College Hill when Isom met her and quickly proposed. They apparently returned to South Carolina to marry, for, according to local lore, the young bride brought the shoot of a magnolia tree in a cigar box, watering the roots each day as they traveled all the way from her home in South Carolina. The story appears in several accounts (including a mention by Faulkner), but in such inconsistent fashion as to make one wonder. Nonetheless, in front of the Isom house on Jefferson Street today stands Sarah Isom's giant magnolia as a symbol of the determination of all those Mississippi-bound women to transplant something of their eastern heritage of domesticity in the West. As a young bride, it was said, Sarah McGhehee sang a song that won Thomas Isom's heart: "The joys of childhood's happy hours, The home of riper years, The treasured scenes of early youth, In sunshine and in tears, The purest hopes her bosom know, When her young heart was free, All these, and more, she now resigns, To brave the world with thee."[48]

Many marriage-minded men looking for a woman to brave the Mississippi frontier with them sought mates within their own extended families, often at great distance. Alexander Pegues had lived for several years in his rustic bachelor retreat on Woodson's Ridge, with his horses and hunting dogs on a large plantation out in the country with dozens of slaves. During a visit with his relatives in Dallas County, Alabama, he proposed marriage to his cousin Rebecca Pegues. They had known each other since childhood in South Carolina. A wealthy planter like Alexander Pegues might have had good prospects of marrying well, even given the poor odds in northern Mississippi. But marrying a wealthy cousin had the additional advantage of consolidating wealth within the family. Rebecca did not give any answer until the night before he returned to Mississippi. She left a letter in his room. "To avoid an embarrassing interview I adopt this mode of conveying to you my sentiments," her letter began. Alexander must have expected what came next; it was in the time-honored formula of a letter answering unrequited love: "Although as I told you, I have the highest estimation and regard for you, my feelings are not such as you profess for me." She went on to write: "May I be permitted in conclusion my dear cousin, to beg that you will no longer cherish this delusion. Bid it in the strength of your manly character away from you."[49] Later, Rebecca confessed that, at the time, she had serious qualms about marrying a cousin, and it is clear from her diary that she was an extraordinarily serious-minded woman who was wrestling with questions about what she wanted in her own life.

Alexander went home to his Mississippi bachelor cabin and to solitude. They continued to correspond, and Alexander continued to hold out hope, but Rebecca repeatedly discouraged him.[50] More than two years later, Alexander visited her again in Alabama, and her sensibility began to get the better of her sense. "My feelings towards you," she wrote to him after his visit, "are not of recent origin either. I scarcely know their date. . . . But I believe now that a warmer sentiment has long been silently and mysteriously blending itself into my nature, until it has become a part of my existence and indissolubly united with it. And how has this event changed the whole colouring of my destiny!" [51] They married not long after, and Alexander brought his new bride to Mississippi.

The desperate shortage of marriageable women among the white population remained a chronic feature of Lafayette County well past the initial frontier stage. Among whites twenty to fifty years old there was still a large surplus of 123 men for every 100 women in 1850, and this same ratio held as late as 1860. For many white males, moving to northern Mississippi meant postponing if not permanently forsaking marriage and female companionship (at least of a conventional sort, for some would find clandestine liaisons with slave women).

The population that came west was young. In 1840 eight out of ten whites were under thirty years of age and half were less than fifteen years old. Women who came west were typically in their prime childbearing years, and because women were in such short supply, they commonly married young and soon began bearing children. [52] The result was a prolific population and an abundance of young children. Long after the county began, three in four whites were under thirty years of age in 1860, and 45 percent were under fifteen. The cabins of Lafayette County, like those Faulkner described in Sutpen's childhood mountain home, were "boiling with children."

The South that Lafayette County represented was young, mobile, and restless for more migration. The new lands of northern Mississippi had been cleared and planted, then laced with wagon roads connecting farms to hamlets and towns, and now a railroad connecting the town to Memphis and the markets of the world. Long after the county had passed through the primitive stages of settlement, however, the demography and social traits of the population continued to resemble those of a freshly settled frontier.

Family Ties

Though the white population appears remarkably volatile and rootless, there were also clear signs that many ties of family and kinship, neighborhood and social bonds, were transplanted in the West. The migratory streams into northern Mississippi flowed along the same overland and river routes settlers had followed since the new country opened up. The major contributors to Lafayette County's white population in 1860 were still

North Carolina (21 percent), Tennessee (20 percent), South Carolina (19 percent), Georgia (13 percent), and Alabama (10 percent); only a few came from Virginia (6 percent) and Kentucky (less than 3 percent). Though Lafayette County was now nearly twenty-five years old and the state of Mississippi had passed its fortieth anniversary, Mississippi-born residents constituted a mere 5 percent of the white population, despite a prolific birth rate. There were a sprinkling of migrants from New England and the Midwest, even a few foreign born, but in 1860 98 percent of all white household heads claimed the South as their birthplace. Northern Mississippi remained emphatically a society made up of southerners with almost no migration from outside the slave states.

Beneath all the movement of the population there existed, nonetheless, a web of intricate ties of family relation and neighborhood that made of this moving population something more than dust particles blowing across the land, strangers to one another. Many came to Lafayette County as part of a chain migration by which kin and neighbors in the East followed one another, a process that sometimes transplanted extended families and communities. The College Hill community north of Oxford began as a planned colony among Presbyterians who had lived together in Maury County, Tennessee. When the Chickasaw counties opened to settlement Goodloe Buford led some of the congregation first to land in Yalobusha County and then to the rich table lands north of Oxford. The same family names, like Buford and Tankersley, remained constant in the community's history over the next century. That was true of the rest of the county as well. Abbeville, on Woodson's Ridge, was named after the South Carolina town many of the early settlers came from, and the area became a magnet for migrants from the Palmetto State. The listing of people, their names and birthplaces in the census rolls, shows clusters of fellow North or South Carolinians, Virginians, and Tennesseans living next to one another. Some may have had ties of kinship, judging from the common surnames, others may have been friends and neighbors in their former settlements. In Mississippi, too, being a native of Virginia, or any of the other older eastern states, provided a kind of ethnic identity, and settlers found themselves most at home with people of their own origin.[53]

The family names listed in the census suggest that kinship groups were being transplanted, either at once or in stages, to the new lands of Mississippi. In 1850 a little over half of the white household heads shared the same last name with at least one other household head in the county, and there were many whose family names appear five and more times in the list of family names. Not all of these people were directly related, obviously, but we know from other genealogical information that many were. Apart from those who shared a family name, there were kinship ties bound by blood and marriage that become evident only in bits and pieces. Letters and diaries reveal brief glimpses of the vast undergrowth of siblings, cousins, and in-laws that existed beneath the moving population.[54] This is most evident among the literate elite whose intricate family connections were well recorded. Jacob Thompson, for example, was able to persuade his brothers William and John to follow him to Lafayette County. His two sisters also came with their husbands, Will Lewis and Yancey Wiley, both of whom were wealthy planters. When Rebecca Pegues married her cousin Alexander, both her brothers, Thomas and Nicholas Pegues, followed her to Lafayette County. These kinship networks among the elite were only the more visible of a much larger complex of relations that pulled kin and family across vast American distances to be with one another.

Communities of Faith

For the white folk of rural northern Mississippi only a few social institutions beyond the family drew people together in some concrete, organized expression of community life. Political organizations rarely reached beyond adult white males and only episodically at that. The town spawned a richer variety of social life, but for most rural people the most constant and important social institution beyond the family was the church and the various activities it sponsored. Protestant Christianity was a pervasive element in the popular culture of southerners, white and slave. Whatever doctrinal differences and liturgical styles might distinguish different denominations, the major churches in northern Mississippi, the Baptists, Presbyterians, and Methodists, shared a common language and a similar set of values.

The church was more than a place for worship once or twice each week; it was also a social group, a fellowship of believers, and one of the few associations that existed beyond the family. It provided a code of behavior as well as articles of faith. Religion gave people a way of interpreting events in their lives and in the world outside their families. More than any school or agency of government and law at this time, religion told people what was right and wrong. Active members of churches constituted a minority within the population, but it was a powerful one that exerted tremendous influence within and outside the fellowship.

No sooner did they clear the land and lay out new farms than whites of all ranks began forming new church congregations. In the new Chickasaw counties of Mississippi the Methodists and Baptists were the leading denominations. These and other churches thrived in Lafayette County. The 1850 census counted thirty-eight churches active in the county; the Methodists claimed twenty, the Baptists had eleven, and the Presbyterians seven. Church membership was estimated by the number of "accommodations" or pew seats, and in Lafayette County's population of sixteen thoussand there were nearly nine thousand pew seats; the Methodists accounted for almost half the pew spaces, the Baptists about one-third, and the Presbyterians one-fifth. These figures give us an idea of the relative strength of the denominations, but to use them as an indicator of church membership or attendance would be misleading. Historians estimate that only about one-fifth to one-third of the antebellum South was "churched." [55]

Baptist churches were the most congregational. Their churches were not ruled from above by church polity, nor were they led by an appointed clergy. They arose from the people who often found ministers in the lay congregation, drafted a constitution, put out the call for members, and only after organizing did they seek affiliation with the regional denominational organization. The rural Baptist churches normally found part-time preachers, typically farmers who knew enough of the Bible to command the respect and support of their flock but who were mostly uneducated if not illiterate. [56]

Among many in the rural churches of all denominations there was general suspicion of clergy who received formal education. "It was no unusual thing to hear 'book-larnin' of every kind publicly denounced from the pulpit as a species of infidelity . . . and a sinful exaltation of human wisdom against divine power and spiritual guidance in the ministry," one observer of Mississippi religious life remarked. "Even ability to read was, by some, considered *prima facie* evidence of heresy." [57] Church leaders elected Baptist preachers each year, and they served at the pleasure of their flock. Methodists relied primarily on itinerant circuit riders, at least until the more established congregations could supply their church with a permanent preacher.

Though rooted in degrees in the authority of the local congregational and only loosely supervised by any higher level of church governance, within (and to some extent across) denominations, small rural churches followed a consistent pattern of organization, worship, and discipline. The rules and procedures could be imitated easily from already organized churches, which provided a ready-made template for the new congregation. In 1841 a small group of settlers near Abbeville formed the Baptist Church at Hopewell and wrote out the constitution that defined their articles of faith. It was, with a few variations and some inventive spelling and phrasing, similar to other Baptist congregations founded nearby: "We whose names are hearunto subscribe Being desirous of living together in a Gospel Church State, in obedience to the command of the lord Jesus Christ . . . do Solemnly covenant with each other in The Strength of the lord to keep the faith as it was delivered unto the saints." The covenant included the specific beliefs to which all members had to adhere, including the "being of a God, . . . the Scriptures of the old and new Testament are the word of God." [58]

Though each denomination and congregation drew fine lines distinguishing the particular beliefs of their denomination, the standards for admission to membership rarely involved any thorough doctrinal examination or test of orthodoxy. They took the word of those who professed faith, and they opened the doors of the church as wide as possible to gather the largest flock they could. In a transient society, the letter of recommendation became the primary entry test. Before leaving their home church, departing members would ask for a "letter of dismissal," which they presented at their new church, usually without question. It became routine practice to accept new members "by letter." The letters of "dismissal," or "transfer," were form letters with no details as to the bearers' qualifications for membership and often with no specification of their destination. One typical letter of dismissal from a Cumberland Presbyterian Church said: "This certifies that H N Robinson a member of this church in good standing is hereby dismissed therefrom at his own request and is recommended to the favorable consideration of the people of God wherever he may be cast." [59]

Others, who were unchurched or affiliated with another church, often had to testify to their conversion experience before being welcomed into the fellowship. The Bethel Baptist Church in 1852 recorded that "Joseph Willson and wife Nancy Willson presented a letter from a sister church and was received. Sisters M. A. Daniel and Sarah Gullett came forward and related an experience of Grace was received and Baptised." "The Church opened the doore of the Church for the Reception of members when Sister Martha Pitter and Mitt Pitter came foward and was reseaved one a professoin of there faith." [60]

The flexibility of the Presbyterians on rules of admission and baptism were tested in revealing ways when a wealthy planter, Washington Price, asked for admission from his deathbed in 1855. Dr. Waddel, the session moderator, and Hugh A. Barr, one of the elders, explained to the session that they "were at the residence of Washington Price who was lying dangerously ill." "Mr. Prise expressed an anxious desire to become a member of the Pres. Church in Oxford and recive the ordinances of Baptism and the Lords Supper." But the rules of the church required examination by two church elders, and that presented a problem. There was no elder of the church within eleven miles of the Price plantation, located on the Yoknapatawpha River in the southern reaches of the county. Because "it being considered doubtful whether Mr. Price would retain the posession of his mental faculties until the presence of another Elder could be procured, it was . . . considered proper to proceed to examine Mr. Price . . . [who] gave very satisfactory evidence of Christian experience." On the spot, Mrs. Price also asked to be examined and received into the church. Washington Price died within a few days, his wife the next year; both passed into the next world full members of the Presbyterian Church.[61]

Just Believe

"All you need, all you have to do, is just believe," one of Faulkner's characters, Nancy Mannigoe, says. "Believe what?" her incredulous lawyer asks; "Just believe," she answers.[62] For many churchgoers in Mississippi, doctrine and practice mattered less than simple faith. Life was hard for people in northern Mississippi. Even for wealthy families, there were constant reminders of how tenuous their health and well-being was. Religion seemed to meet some basic needs for consolation in an uncertain world and brought people together in a community of faith.

Goodloe Buford, a devout founding member of the College Hill Presbyterian Church, was a prosperous cotton planter who owned thirty-three slaves and extensive landholdings. His diary entries for 1850 were filled mostly with notes on the practical matters that occupied each working day: the weather, the condition of the crops and livestock, loans, debts, and other financial matters, and the many illnesses that plagued his family, his slaves, and himself. The heavy rains that spring ruined much of the cotton and corn crops, and they had to be planted over; then a drought during the summer nearly destroyed them again. Buford, along with neighboring farmers great and small, was constantly at the mercy of nature and nature's God.

When the weather did not threaten their livelihood, disease and death menaced life itself. Several accounts report chronic problems of "sickliness" afflicting the area beginning in the late 1840s. M. J. Blackwell blamed it on man, not God. "North Miss is naturally a very healthy country," he advised his brother back east, "and yet owing to its rapid settlement, for years past, it has been a very sickly one, and no wonder; no country could be healthy with such immense forests of timber suddenly deadened."[63]

During 1850 Goodloe Buford recorded the ravaging effects of a smallpox plague that struck several people on his plantation. His wife and children all suffered from fevers, chills, and headaches that year. Buford himself had a bad spell of diarrhea, along with frequent fevers, boils, and sore throat. Then, adding to his miseries, in October his horse threw him and for days after he suffered a sore head and back and was spitting blood. The slaves were so frequently stricken with illness or injuries it became routine for him, instead of detailing the illnesses, to record in his diary how many hands were "up and well" and "in the fields" from day to day. Several neighbors and their slaves died within the year, and each death Buford took as a reminder of mortality. Buford's diary begins to read like the Book of Job. To add to the year's troubles, someone sued Buford in court, and in addition to losing several days in legal wrangling in Oxford that November, he lost the case. Buford was among the most prosperous and fortunate of people, but a year like this one might challenge anyone's faith.

Buford was a Calvinist who accepted these tragedies of everyday life with a certain stoic resolve. For him religion offered solace; at least, he did not seem anguished about his immortal soul. If his diary is any guide, he neither dwelled on his plight as a human being nor prayed that God might lighten his burdens. Buford was active in his church, belonged to the Bible Society, and was involved as well in the county Agricultural Association and other voluntary organizations whose purpose was to improve the world he lived in. But for Buford and many of his brethren, religion was more a means of coping with the world than it was a source of inspiration to improve it.

Each Sunday Goodloe Buford went to church, for one and often two sermons during the day and again in the evening for another sermon or discussion. No one appreciated a good sermon more than Buford. He often noted the subject of Reverend Gaston's text or Mr. Waddell's lecture and always complimented a "fine sermon" or "good lecture" when he heard one. He was critical of the congregation for not attending or showing respect while in church. "It is truly lamentable to see how careless parents are about the never dying souls of their children," he wrote after noting poor attendance one Sunday in May.[64] That September he was somewhat heartened after a Saturday of preaching with sermons in the morning and evening that the congregation showed "some little feeling, 10 or 12 came up to the anniocy [anxious] seat. Among them was my dear son, Warren."[65]

Rebecca Pegues, the cousin and reluctant bride of Alexander, joined her husband as a member of Lafayette County's planter elite. She and her husband owned 107 slaves by 1860 and landholdings of five thousand acres, including two plantations on Woodson's Ridge. But the comforts and privileges of her life did little to quiet the spiritual anxiety within her soul. While Alexander was away in Jackson or elsewhere engaged in politics, Rebecca remained at their home, Orange Hill, on Woodson's Ridge, surrounded by house servants, field hands, and her several children. Her days were filled with the tasks of mothering her many children, educating the young ones at home, and helping to supervise an elaborate domestic economy that included the production of cloth, clothing, and shoes for the slaves. Rebecca Pegues was an unusually intensive and intellectual woman; she read voraciously in literary classics, contemporary reviews, the Bible, and other religious writings. Her diaries include a detailed record of her activi-

Rebecca Pegues, plantation mistress and wife of Alexander Pegues. (Courtesy of Richard Stanley)

ties and reflections on what she was reading and thinking, as though she had no one else to share them with. She came from an old South Carolina family of Hugenot origin and was a devout Episcopalian. In Mississippi, Rebecca Pegues and her husband, Alexander, joined a small group of wealthy families who founded St. Peter's Episcopal Church in Oxford. Support was limited to a few prominent families, and it was not until 1851 that the church was organized and sometime after that when it began holding regular services. Though she attended other church services, usually in Oxford several miles away, much of Rebecca's religious life was pursued in private.[66]

Perhaps it was this isolation from coreligionists, her Calvinist Hugenot heritage, or just her own brooding personality that explains her spiritual anxiety. In any case, she exhibited little of the assurance one might associate with Episcopalians. The Pegues family did not fret about sending their children to dancing school or about the pleasures of good food and wine or a festive party. But on a deeper level Rebecca Pegues remained anxious about her life, and she worried constantly about her worthiness in God's eyes or perhaps in the eyes of others. She was a melancholy woman who, despite the good fortune of her position, complained about her lonely life and the burdens of her daily responsibilities for her children and her slaves. "I feel all a parent's anxiety about my children," she wrote in her diary one day "and oh! What responsibility I have — in educating and influencing these immortal souls."[67] "I am in a rather morbid mood today," she wrote in 1853; "stay here so much — live such an unsocial life — that my nature is becoming contracted — mind and feelings, from want of exercise and action. I am literally shut up here in the dull low walls of this log cabin."[68] When her baby boy died the next year, she could not stop thinking about death and took comfort in the faith that he had gone to a better world: "Who would recall the little spirit from its glorious [seat] above? — transplanted from this wicked, sorrowful world — this sinful existence to Heaven."[69] "I torture myself with anxiety about sickness," she wrote on her birthday in 1859. "How little am I calculated to bear losses and trials! Hitherto I have had almost uninterrupted prosperity — which I feel is not best for the soul's good. I need much chastisement, to make me a Christian. God may be sending it in mercy."[70] She seemed at times to resent the comforts her life had afforded her and in some perverse way welcomed the "visitation of sickness" and other calamities as a lesson. "I need chastisements as much as any one. I am as careless and forgetful of my high calling."[71]

Chastisements

Chastisements were one thing southern Protestant churches seemed designed to accommodate. The buildings rural congregations occupied were as simple and severe as the faith itself. After meeting in makeshift dwellings, often in log cabins, and sometimes in private homes, young congregations set about raising a more permanent church meetinghouse. The typical church was a rectangular clapboard building, one story topped with a low-pitched gable, painted white if the congregation could afford it but often left paintless, slowly weathering to a silvery gray. The churches were usually built without foundations and basements, propped up instead on log or stone pilings. Across the front was a shallow front porch, with two windows and two doors, one for men and one for women to enter the church and take their separate places on either side of the aisle. This gender segregation was often reinforced inside the church by a partition down the center. Slaves were also segregated either at the back of the church behind a partition or in a slave balcony above their white brethren. Beside the Baptist churches one would find a deep baptismal pool. Inside were simple pews, often nothing more than slabs of wood forming benches, and in the more prosperous churches, like the College Hill Presbyterian, enclosed pews for winter warmth.[72]

The severe architecture and sexual and racial segregation reflected a regimen of social discipline the church imposed on a community of believers. Once one was admitted within the fellowship of the church, conformity to the orthodox creed of the church did not seem to matter as much to church authorities as did the sins of everyday personal behavior. Much of their duties involved investigating and punishing such commonplace moral lapses as intemperance, dancing, gambling, and fighting, along with various infractions of sexual morality. The church also intruded occasionally in marketplace relationships to admonish debtors to pay their just debts or to investigate charges of cheating in business affairs.

Southern evangelical religion focused more on individual salvation through faith and piety than on social reform. It worked on saving souls more than on saving society and placed more importance on what one was *not* to do than on good works that might benefit society. The "reason for living," as one of Faulkner's characters summarized this way of thinking, "was to get ready to stay dead a long time." [73] Among northern Protestants, in contrast, the fervor of antebellum evangelical religion found expression in a multitude of social reforms from temperance and sabbitarianism to public education, women's rights, and antislavery. They often combined Christian morality with secular notions of republican virtue and sought to define individual sins as collective social problems that demanded an organized effort by Christians to redeem the nation. The antislavery crusade, to take one notable example, began from a Christian definition of enslavement of a fellow human being as a sin and extended that to an idea that all Americans were culpable for that sin. The reason for living, they might answer, is to improve this world and to be their brother's keeper. Temperance reform and other religiously rooted reform movements coursed through the antebellum South, to be sure, but the religious expression of social concern came up against a more traditional emphasis on human depravity and innate sinfulness, ideas that held a powerful grip on southern believers and their clergy. As the Baptists of Hopewell put it, they believed in "the Fall of Adam, the degeneracy of his Posterity, Corruption of human nature, And the inability of man to do that Which is spiritually good." [74]

Southern Protestants may not have embraced as fervently as their northern counterparts the gospel of social reform, but they were no less merciless on sinners for it. They upheld a Christian code of personal behavior that placed high value on self-restraint against the temptations of lust, anger, and greed. Church records reveal remarkably few cases of discipline or exclusion citing doctrinal heresy or theological disagreements about the true teachings of the faith. There were, nonetheless, several incidents of members being excluded for having associated with a church of a different denomination. When the Oxford Baptist Church learned that sister Cynthia Ann Lynum "had associated her self with the Episcopalians upon motion she was unanimously excluded from the fellowship of this church." [75] Likewise, Sister Robuck at Bethel Baptist "was excluded from the fellowship of the Church for joining another church." [76]

Several cases involved business disputes or disagreements over debts between congregation members. Bethel Baptist kept good records of disciplinary matters; its conference meeting in September 1852 noted that "brother Roderia [?] Williams inform church that brother A. Cantwell was indebted to him and had been for three years and he could not get Cantwell to pay him or give him any satisfaction." Brother Williams was willing to wait but only if Cantwell was willing to give him some form of security. The conference demanded that Williams "pay the debts or give brother William satisfaction by next meeting." [77]

Another case in the same church a few years later involved Brother Joseph Hollowell, "he being Acused of taking that which did not Bellong to him and then leaving Country with out giving Satisfaction to the Church." The "Church voted unanimously to exclude him from the fellowship of the Church." [78] Bethel Baptist also considered the charges against "brother Brithen Gordy and his wife for going of and leaving Maters unsetled and he was excluded from the Church." [79]

When brethren had some personal falling out, for whatever reason, that became the business of the church. This could extend to family squabbles, as in the case of Sister Mary Brown, who "refused to hold her Church letter on acount of a dificulty betwene here sellf and her brother Robert Davis." The nature of the dispute was never explained, but the fault seemed to lie with Brother Davis, who "refused to give the reason for his conduct toward his sister and it was moved and seconted that he be excluded from the felowship of the church which carried." [80]

Most church discipline involved personal lapses such as drinking, gambling, or dancing. Dancing was forbidden among Baptists, but, especially among town folk, it was becoming a fashionable temptation. The Baptists of Bethel charged Sister Knight with dancing in 1860 and reported she "would not make an acknowledgement." [81] The next year she repented and "made an acknowledgment and it was received," but another of her family, Sister Eunice Knights, "was excluded from the fellowship of the Church for dancing" in the same session.[82] Out at Abbeville, the Hopewell Baptist Church experienced a flurry of dancing infractions, and many members came forth and admitted their sins. Sister Arnold confessed she "had been dancing and was Sory for it and said if the Brethren and Sisters bare with her that she would try to live a different life." [83]

The dancing problem provoked the Oxford Baptists to issue a resolution "that partisipation in this amusement is a species of conformity to the world condemned by both the letter and the spirit of the word of God" and further "that it is the duty of the members of this church to abstain from this amusement and that if any do otherwise it is the duty of the church to rebuke them openly." It was undoubtedly William Faulkner's grandfather, Charles Butler, who had provoked this resolution by staging a lavish Christmas ball at a local hotel in 1873. The deacons upbraided Butler for his moral failings: "The pasture had called on bro B. to know the facts and was told that the report was true." It seemed that Brother Butler "did not feel that he was doing any harm by the act," adding that "if he had given any offince to the church . . . he hoped to be forgiven" and promised he "would do so no more." This act of contrition was apparently enough to win him reprieve.[84]

The Presbyterians in Oxford were less certain that dancing was ungodly when it came up before a session meeting in 1849. "An overture was presented to the Session inquiring whether it was compatable with Christian character of the rules of our Church for Church members to attend Balls or dancing parties or permit their children or those under their control to attend dancing parties." After some deliberation, the session concluded that dancing "is not compatible with Christian Character." "This answer was then ordered to be read publically from the pulpit."[85] The Presbyterians continued to be vexed by the dancing problem. Thomas Robinson held dancing parties at his house, and at the church session in 1854, "Mr. Robinson having appeared . . . the session held with him a long and friendly conference in reference to his past course and endeavored to induce him to abandon the practice of keeping his house open for dancings."[86] Robinson and several others in the congregation ran afoul of the Presbyterian sanctions against dancing a few years later. The church discovered "he had sent his daughter to Dancing School, did not think there was any Sin in so doing, and thought it probable he might do so again." He and others agreed to "apply for dismission from the Church" since they could not abide by the rules on dancing.[87]

Charges of intemperance were nearly as common as those involving dancing, and they sometimes provoked the same defiance among church members who resented the church elders defining Christian standards for drinking. The Presbyterians brought James Stockard, a prominent planter, before the session in 1847. He was "charged by common fame of the intemperate use of ardent Spirits at the camp meeting in August last and at various times in Oxford" and "Unchristian and improper conduct towards the Session on Sabbath the 19th last." Stockard also stood accused of issuing "false statements," and no less than ten witnesses were called forth to testify against him. Following what must have been lengthy testimony by the witnesses, the session admitted "although Seldom seen drunk in the common acceptation of the term, yet he does so indulge in the frequent free and public use of ardent Spirits as is altogether unbecoming a member of the Church of Jesus Christ, and in our opinion intemperate." Stockard was therefore "excluded from the Church privileges until he give Satisfactory evidence of repentance and reformation of life." [88]

In another case, H. L. Muldrow, whose drinking habits also displeased the Oxford Presbyterian Church, thumbed his nose at them when they tried to discipline him. "More than a year ago," he responded to the session in 1858, "I requested some of the Officers of your Church, to blot my name from your Church books, but I suppose from your note, (which is none of the most courteous) it has not been done. As far as I am now concerned you can do as you see fit, as I have no apology to make." The church leaders found "Muldrow charged of 'Intoxication' and Profanity" and he was ordered "excommunicated from the Church and that this sentence be made public." [89]

In their role as moral police, the churches validated character and reputation among those who submitted to the discipline of the fellowship. In a new, transient western community the churches provided one of the few moral restraints on a society that was sparsely settled, loosely governed, and remote from law enforcement. More than any other institution, the churches also brought people—rich and poor, man and woman, master and slave, powerful and weak—together in a more or less egalitarian community of faith in which all were expected to live by the same rules, believe the same creed, and be judged by the same God.[90]

I Never Saw So Many People

Religion in Mississippi involved far more than a code of moral precepts and chastisements for individuals; it was also a source of community. Church activities brought people together in a shared Christian culture and provided a welcome excuse for social gathering, a relief from the isolation that rural life imposed. At no time was this social function of religion more in evidence than in the periodic camp meetings and revivals that swept through the community.

"My sakes! I never saw so many people," recalled one woman of her first camp meeting at Spring Hill near Sarepta in 1845. It was the first of its kind in that part of the country, she recalled. Hundreds of people flocked to the Spring Hill revival, from Oxford, from Panola County, and from other parts twenty miles around. "The hillsides were covered with wagons, horses, mules, oxen, men, women and children, and now and then a dog. The arbor was a large shelter two hundred feet long and one hundred feet wide, rest-ing on posts set in the ground and covered with pine boards; the altar was about twenty by twenty, just in front of the pulpit." [91]

The camp meeting that year brought all classes together, it seemed; some were "dressed up in their best; some had on fine dresses, but most of them had on homespun; many had on store shoes, but some were barefooted." Rich and poor, slave and master, gathered before God at the camp meeting. They also brought different congregations and denominations together in ecumenical fellowship. Several clergy and lay members from different churches preached to the Spring Hill camp meeting, following one another in unspoken competition for the attention and enthusiasm of the audience.

After a day full of preaching, the night came and a powerful religious enthusiasm spread through the camp meeting. Following a "long sermon, full of fire and the holy spirit," by Reverend Miles Ford, "a long loud, sweet song of Zion started" and Reverend Miles "called up mourners." People came down to the altar, and it "was soon full of earnest seekers after salvation." As the singing continued, "the spirit seemed to catch like wild-fire, and they all rose up at once and began shouting and praising God; grasping hands and shouting." The woman recalled, "I soon felt like shouting myself." "The meeting, the shouting and singing were kept up until long after midnight, many fell at the altar in a sort of trance; some had the jerks; old Christians and new converts clasped each other and fell in the straw. All was confusion, all was happy." [92]

The Spring Hill revival was one of the more remarkable of its kind, but camp meetings in the countryside and protracted meetings in established churches became a common feature of religious life in Lafayette County. Reports of camp meeting revivals can be found in the very earliest newspapers, and they must have played an especially important role in the competition among new churches for converts. The local paper mentioned several revivals sponsored by the churches as early as 1843. The Methodists led off with a revival held at a campground north of Oxford in July of that year, and the Baptists proclaimed their own in September at Amaziah Church near Cornersville, followed the same month by the Cumberland Presbyterians, who held their revival at Clear Creek. A Baptist preacher named Campbell, who was visiting from Scotland, arrived that year and "got up a protracted meeting," the local editor reported. He "has been preaching here every night since and some of the days." "He is a sensible man," the editor observed, "his arguments are forcible and plain; he seems to be quite a radical, and makes the luke-warm Christian smart under the lash which he seems to ply without mercy." [93]

Revivals became annual events in the churches, usually in August or the late fall, before or after gathering time in the cotton fields, when there would be no time for anything but work. Even as they became customary, revivals continued to excite great interest, especially among young people who seem to have appreciated the social as much as the spiritual attractions they offered. "A glorious revival meeting has been in progress in the Cumberland Presbyterian Church of this place, since last Friday," wrote the local editor in November 1861. "Those who have gone to the 'anxious seat,' have been principally young ladies and boys—the youths of our town. May they all be convicted of their sins and become genuine Christians. . . . to day a Sermon adapted to Fast day will be preached. Of course the building will be filled to overflowing." [94]

Evangelical religion was a powerful egalitarian force that in several ways placed the high and low together on an equal footing as depraved sinners before a powerful God. At the same time, the churches reinforced the patriarchal values of duty and obedience that defined relations between God and humankind, man and woman, master and slave. But in both ways religion served as an important source of communal cohesion in an otherwise young, inchoate society.

On the perpetual frontier of migration and isolation that was Mississippi in the mid-nineteenth century, these communities of faith and communities of economic interest provided some sense of common identity and purpose. In the 1850s, a robust time of high cotton, a new railroad, a new state university, new churches and academies, and evidence of prosperity and improvement everywhere, it appeared that Lafayette County was something more than just a place through which people passed en route to the next frontier. The free men and women of Lafayette County had established what appeared to be a permanent economic foundation, and upon it they had fashioned a social order of family, church, and community. For the slaves of Lafayette County the task they faced in forging families and fellowship in the new world their masters had brought them into was more formidable.

There was in the land a sort of folk-tale: of the countryside all night long full of skulking McCaslin slaves dodging the moonlit roads and the Patrol-riders to visit other plantations, and of the unspoken gentlemen's agreement between the two white men and the two dozen black ones that, after the white man had counted them and driven the home-made nail into the front door at sundown, neither of the white men would go around behind the house and look at the back door, provided that all the Negroes were behind the front one when the brother who drove it drew out the nail again at daybreak. —WILLIAM FAULKNER, Go Down, Moses*

four **The Slaves**

Lafayette County was a slave society, not only because close to half the county was enslaved or just because nearly half the white families owned one or more slaves. It was a society organized around the institution of slavery and, beyond that, dedicated to the racial control of Africans by whites. The cotton economy rested on slave labor, and the system of government and law aimed at regulating slavery and protecting slave property. Increasingly slavery shaped political discourse and defined the relationship of Mississippi to the nation.

Our historical understanding of American slavery draws heavily on the older eastern states; less attention has been given to slavery and slave society as it formed anew on the western frontier. Most Mississippi slaves came west after being sold and traded. This meant that master and slave met in Mississippi as strangers, and it set the stage for a slave regime that was less inclined toward whatever paternalism derived from long-standing personal knowledge between master and slave. Many thought slavery in Mississippi was much harsher than in the East and that slaves were driven hard to wrest profit from new cotton plantations. It was also a slave regime that appears at times to be more rationalized and one that could offer economic incentives to slaves. The slaves of Lafayette County allow a glimpse into this world of a new slave society as it took form at the western edge of the Old South.

What Lucindy Saw

All her life Lucindy Hall Shaw, an elderly woman of eighty-six years, remembered what she saw that day when she was a young slave girl sitting on the porch with her mistress. Now, decades later, sitting on the porch of her own unpainted cabin in Freedman Town, the black quarter of Oxford, she told her story to Minnie Holt, an interviewer with the WPA. "One day Miss Sara wuz settin' on de po'ch sewin' an' I wuz settin' on de steps; dere wez a 'oman had done sumthin', I don't know whut; but de white overseer coched her an' tied her to a pos' an' whipped her 'till she drapped." Lucindy tried to arouse some response from her mistress. "I sed: 'Oh, Lord, Mist Sara dat overseer done kilt dat 'oman.' " But it was to no avail; "dey ontied her an' she wuz de'd."

Lucy told her interviewer how they disposed of the body: "dey jus' called an' old granpap slave 'round de place an' he bro't a shovel an' dug her grave rite dar; I sez grave, but hit wuzn't nuthin' but a hole in de groun'; he tok de shovel an' jus' rolled her in." She went on: "an' den he shoveled in sumthin' dat I tho't I saw move." She implored her mistress again: "I tol' Mist Sara, but she 'tend lak she didn't see nuthin'; she w'udn't tell me den but she tol' me atterwards, dat de overseer whipped her so hard she birfed a baby." [1]

Had Faulkner written such a scene we might dismiss it as macabre excess. What Lucindy reported seeing that day was by no means a common event. It made no sense to maim or kill one's slaves, and to beat, let alone kill, a pregnant slave was doubly insane. Whatever brought on this killing, it dramatized the brutal dehumanization that underlay slavery.

Slaves and slavery were frequent subjects of Faulkner's exploration of the history of Yoknapatawpha. Much of what he knew about the experience of slavery came from family servants, particularly Caroline Barr, known to the Falkner children as Mammy Callie. She had once been the slave of Colonel

Hugh A. Barr, a prominent lawyer and political leader in Oxford, who had come from Abbeville, South Carolina, in 1842 to join his brother James in Oxford. Barr was a Whig, but he became a strong supporter of southern rights. He eventually became a secessionist and later led Mississippi's resistance to Reconstruction.[2]

Mammy Callie and the Falkner family were never certain of her exact age. The headstone William Faulkner had placed on her grave when she died in 1940 gave her year of birth as 1840. The 1870 census has her born five years later, and she remembered being sixteen when she became free, which would put her birth about 1849. According to the 1870 census, Caroline Barr was born in North Carolina, so she must have been part of the great migration that brought slavery west into Mississippi. The confusion that surrounds her birth and early life suggests she might have been separated from her parents and kin while young. As a slave, Caroline did not appear in the census by name, and all we can surmise about her existence before 1870 was that she was one of six slaves owned by Colonel Barr. They apparently all lived in one slave house Barr had built near his home in Oxford. According to their ages, there was no one among the six who could have been Caroline's parent. The 1870 census marshal found Caroline Barr, twenty-five, and Jack Barr, thirty-five, living with three children, Mollie, fourteen (Caroline's younger sister), Fedrick, two, and Antonett, one. (Mollie Barr has a street named after her that runs through her former property in Freedman Town, not far from what is now Martin Luther King Drive.) Jack was one of four husbands Caroline would live with during her life. Not much is recorded about her life before she came to work for Murry and Maud Falkner in 1902. She served William Faulkner and his family, probably from the time he bought Rowan Oak in 1930 until her death in 1940. Caroline Barr was the model for Dilsey Gibson, the indomitable force in the Compson household featured in *The Sound and the Fury*.[3] We may never know all that Mammy Callie told young Bill Falkner in those endless hours of kitchen conversations or what she shared with William Faulkner as a grown man. But we can reconstruct some of the outlines of the world she and her people inhabited from the sources that survive.

The Slaves of Yoknapatawpha

The slaves of Faulkner's fictional world are present from the beginning, putting up the first courthouse of Yoknapatawpha, straightening the river near the Old Frenchman's place, laying out the plantation and raising the mansion at Sutpen's One Hundred. Indeed, African slaves arrive before the whites as slaves to the Indians. Some, like Sam Fathers, the mixed-race off-spring of a mulatto mother and Indian father, lives on in Yoknapatawpha after the Chickasaw exodus, first as a McCaslin slave and then as a freed-man, an Indian "inside a black man's skin."

One of Faulkner's stories about slavery is set in this Indian context, out-side the whites' Old South. "Red Leaves" may be one of the most haunting portrayals of slavery in American fiction, and it is poignant testimony of the power of fiction to imagine what historians can rarely document, the inner thoughts of a slave. It tells the story of a nameless African slave in flight. His owner is an Indian chief, Issetebeha (Doom's successor). In Faulkner's fictional interpretation, the Indian concept of slavery is a parody of white motives for profit and mastery. The Negro slaves they acquire from whites have little value as a source of labor. The Chickasaw chief, Doom, in imita-tion of the whites, had used black slaves to clear and cultivate land, but "he never had enough for them to do." Sometimes, for the entertainment of guests, Doom has his dogs chase his slaves for sport. "They are like horses and dogs," one of the Indians remarks of the Africans.

Faulkner's Indians take this bestialization of African slaves to the point of discussing them as a possible meat supply. Cannibalism, they quickly de-cide, is no solution to "the Negro question," which in their minds amounts to the oversupply of black slaves with no real work to do. "They are too valu-able to eat," one argues, ". . . when the white men will give horses for them." The Indians' slaves are "mated" and sold to acquire other material goods from the white world. Doom's son, Issetibbeha, we learn, has earlier sold "forty head" to a Memphis trader and with the proceeds has gone abroad to France, returning with the gilded bed, girandoles, and a pair of slippers with red heels. These, along with black slaves and a steamboat palace, serve as trappings of Indian royalty, which, in the forests of Mississippi, seem like mimicry of European decadence.

Now the slave's master, Issetebeha, has died, apparently poisoned by his treacherous son. The chief is to be buried with his dog, horse, and body ser-vant, the unnamed Guinea man who tries to escape his fate. Faulkner ven-tures into the mind of this slave, entering what he earlier described as "the thoughts sealed inscrutable behind faces like the death masks of apes." The frightened slave is a man of forty, captured in Africa as a boy of fourteen. He remembers being aboard the slave ship coming to America, a "drunken New England captain" roaring passages from the Bible on deck, while in the slave cargo hold below, desperate to survive, he managed to grab a live rat and eat it. Now he is a man marked for death but running for his life through the forests and swamps. He is hunted by the dead chief's son and his men, just as they hunt game, and with the same sense of sport. The chase is a ritual with an inescapable conclusion, the slave's "irrevocable doom." His determined pursuers agree it is "a good race," and they place bets on when their prey will be captured.

Against the cruel dehumanization of the chase, Faulkner evokes a fundamental human will simply to live. "It's that I do not wish to die," the fugitive contemplates, "in a quiet tone, of slow and low amaze, as though it were something that, until the words had said themselves, he found that he had not known, or had not known the depth and extent of his desire." Faulkner's fictional Indians live outside a culture that values human life for its own sake. They see nothing sinful about human enslavement or even human sacrifice. They find the slave's unwillingness to accept death as an odd sign of "a people without honor and decorum." [4]

Whatever is lost in this story to an accurate knowledge of the historical Indians of Mississippi, Faulkner has us look at slavery through what he portrays as an alien perspective devoid of Western, Christian humanitarian values, and it is those values that compel sympathy for the slave. The story was borrowed from the local legend of Toby Tubby, one of whose African slaves was rumored to be selected for sacrificial burial when whites intervened. The tale is suspect because human sacrifice and burial of servants was not part of Chickasaw burial practices (though sacrifice and burial of servants was a part of the Natchez Indians' culture, and refugees from that tribe had joined the Chickasaws following the French massacre). Whatever the ethnographic plausibility may have been, the power of the story turns on the shocking difference in basic values regarding human life and the duty of servants. [5] What at first appears to be a judgment against Indian barbarism, however, reflects back on the very slave society whites were bringing to Mississippi.

There is a similar device at play in Faulkner's study of antebellum southern society as depicted in *Absalom, Absalom!* Here it is Thomas Sutpen, the "beast," the "demon," in the eyes of some, who is cast as the violator of basic human decency. Sutpen, in trying to surmount his own humiliating experience of social inferiority as a poor white boy, comes to treat other humans as little more than instruments to advance his obsessive design for emulating his social superiors. This is particularly evident in his later years when, desperate to find a new mother for the son he is determined to have, Sutpen begins to regard prospective female partners as little more than breeding stock.

Sutpen, himself a savage man thinly disguised as a gentleman, is seen for the first time in Yoknapatawpha bearded, gaunt, unbathed, with a "sulphur-reek" in his hair, clothes, and beard. He arrives out of nowhere and with him is a band of twenty slaves, described as "a herd of wild beasts" huddled under his wagon cover "smelling like a wolfden." He has acquired them in Haiti, and they speak no English and no language any other humans in Yoknapatawpha can understand or even identify. Only Sutpen, who issues orders in "some dark and fatal tongue of their own," can communicate with them.

These slaves, Faulkner writes, are not like any humans, black or white, but more "like beasts half tamed to walk upright like men, in attitudes wild and reposed." Sutpen uses his slaves to hunt game like a "pack of wild hounds," running deer through the forest for Sutpen to shoot. These wild slaves have no blankets and no beds and "like a sleeping alligator" they cover themselves in the mud at night. When Sutpen's captive French architect, another victim of his inhumane mistreatment, tries to flee, Sutpen again uses his slaves like hounds, this time to track and capture the desperate white man. This depiction of white slavery reads as a condemnation of monstrous exploitation but one that is difficult to embrace without also condemning enslavement of Africans.[6]

Sutpen treats his men friends in the neighborhood to barbarous exhibitions of brutality in bare-knuckled, no-holds-barred fights between his slaves, which he stages appropriately enough out in the stables behind his new mansion. There, at night, a rough masculine democracy is drawn to these brutal spectacles. The crowd encompasses not only Sutpen's hunting and gambling companions from the local frontier gentry but also many of the poor white "riff raff" and slaves, all of whom form a ring surrounding the black gladiators doing battle. The events are akin to cock fights or dog fights, blood sports that were common forms of recreation on the southern frontier. The spectators placed wagers on the outcome and doubtless added bets as the fight progressed and the combatants wounded one another. The slaves, stripped naked in battle, fought, Faulkner tells us, "not like white men fight, with rules and weapons, but like negroes fight to hurt one another quick and bad."

When Sutpen's wife, Ellen, bursts into the crowd looking for her children, she is horrified to see in the ring her husband battling one of his slaves "both naked to the waist and gouging at one another's eyes as if their skins should not only have been the same color but should have been covered with fur too." The master's descent to this animal-like brutality with his slaves, we are told, came at the end of an evening's matches between the slaves and was his way of asserting "the retention of supremacy, domination." For Sutpen, too, this act of violent domination recalls his father's assaults on neighborhood slaves, whose balloon-like faces became the hapless targets of an "impotent rage" not against the slave but against his master and his class.[7]

Sutpen is regarded, at least by some of his detractors in the community, as an ogre, a demon, a beast, someone beyond the circle of civility within which people are expected to treat one another with respect and honor. Insofar as Sutpen is condemned by others for violating community norms, however, it is primarily for his dishonorable and inhuman treatment of women and the French architect, who is virtually a slave. If he also treats his slaves like subhuman beings, so does almost every slave owner in the South. Indeed, slavery, and all that went with it, from forced labor, trading, and whipping, to sexual exploitation and cruelty at its worst, were necessary, integral elements of the design whites had for the economic and social order of the slave society they built in northern Mississippi.

The Great Westward Migration

Mississippi slavery earned a reputation early on for being harsher than its eastern counterpart. It was a new cotton frontier, and the slaves were driven hard from the start to clear the fields and build the plantations and farms. The cotton fields of Mississippi demanded harder work than most had endured in the declining tobacco and cotton fields of the East. Slave gangs were often larger and they were worked by overseers who had no personal investment in the slaves.

Above all, what conditioned slavery in Mississippi was the massive relocation of large numbers of slaves brought primarily from the East to the West. For white people who came to Lafayette County, their journey was an adventure full of hope and expectation. It was often fraught with great hardship, risk, and frequent failure, to be sure, but they moved voluntarily seeking a better life. For the slaves of Lafayette County, the trek to Mississippi was more often a terribly wrenching dislocation in their lives. It was more than simply a forced migration that tore many of them away from long-standing ties to relatives, friends, and familiar surroundings. For the migration also frequently placed them under the power of new masters, sent them into a strange new land, and subjected them to what was often an entirely new, much harsher work regimen on the cotton frontier. The slaves of Mississippi and much of the southern frontier endured something like a second Middle Passage, an overland recapitulation of what their forebears had experienced in the voyage from Africa to the New World. The disruption and cultural adjustment involved in the migration to the West was perhaps less traumatic, but the population involved, approximately one million, was far greater than the number of Africans brought into North America.[8]

The sudden opening in the 1830s of the Chickasaw and Choctaw lands in Mississippi created a huge demand for slave labor in the West. While some of the slaves that came into northern Mississippi were imported from within Mississippi or from adjacent states, the main streams of slave migration came overland from the eastern seaboard. One flow of migration came out of Virginia and the other tobacco states of the Chesapeake over the mountains and through Kentucky and Tennessee; another flowed out of the Carolinas and Georgia across the Deep South. The slaves on the great westward trek would pass through Indian nations about the same time they were being forcibly removed to Indian Territory to make way for the cotton economy the slaves would help build. The slave coffles followed their own trail of tears.[9]

From scattered records, we know that some Lafayette County slaves arrived with their masters or overseers from the East or from adjacent western states, Tennessee and Kentucky primarily. These were a minority, for historians estimate that no more than one in three, and perhaps as few as one in five, slaves arrived with their former owners.[10] The majority were either brought in by traders and speculators or more often by new masters who had bought them in the East or in one of several western slave markets in Memphis, Nashville, and Natchez. There were smaller local slave markets set up in Mississippi, in defiance of state law, to serve the demand for slave labor. "Thir is a lot of negros to be sold in coffiville [Coffeeville] the first of August and for cash," one Mississippi overseer in nearby Yalobusha County wrote to his employer in 1839; "and i expect will be barganes to be bought and wish your assistance."[11] Polly Turner Cancer, a Lafayette County slave, remembered slave traders coming by her master's plantation frequently: "dere ust ter be a lot ov travelers cumin' thru sellin' hosses an' darkies, an' kinds ov things, dey'd just drap in on ole marster an' he'd feed dem; dey lived lak rich folks."[12]

Slave traders considered it best to bring slaves overland. Though sea and river routes were faster, the overland journey was cheaper and it allowed slow acclimation to the new environment during the seven to eight weeks the journey took. Joseph Ingraham observed the slave coffles arriving from the East: "This is done by forming them into a caravan at the place where they are purchased, and conducting them by land through the Indian nations to this state." The first week and more of the journey the slaves were chained and guarded carefully, lest they escape and run for home. One slave, Charles Ball, remembered the women lashed together with rope halters around their necks. On the men a "strong iron collar was closely fitted . . . round each of our necks. . . . In addition to this, we were handcuffed in pairs, with iron staples and bolts, with a short chain, a foot long, uniting the handcuffs and their wearers in pairs."[13] The slaves dreaded the journey, but after traveling too far to run for home, their fears turned to sullen resig-

Slave coffle moving west. (From Dummond, *Anti-slavery*)

nation. "Full of the impression . . . that the south is emphatically the grave of their race," Ingraham wrote, ". . . they leave home, as they proudly and affectionately term Virginia, with something of the feelings of the soldier, allotted to a 'forlorn hope.' " On a Sunday in Natchez Ingraham described a large slave coffle coming into town: a "long procession . . . slowly approaching like a troop of wearied pilgrims. . . . One sooty brown hue was cast over the whole horde, by the sombre colour of their tattered garments, which, combined with the slow pace and fatigued air of most of those who composed it, gave to the whole train a sad and funereal appearance." [14]

Some of Lafayette County's slaves recalled the migration they or their parents endured as slaves. Polly Turner Cancer's mother was among those who migrated with their master from the East. "My mother cum from S.C. from a place called Chinquapin; when she cum here dere wasn't many white folks, jus' indians; de country wuz full of wolves, an' deers, an' bears, an' foxes." During the trek overland from the East, she recalled, "Dey had tents to stay in at night. I'se heared my mammy say dat dere wuz a 'hole team ov dem cum togeder an' bro't dere slaves. Dey cum in wagons an' wud camp 'long de way." [15] Rebecca Woods came west from Virginia with a new master, Buck Avant, the one we met earlier whose mansion and parties were all bought on credit. He "bo't me off uv de slave block in Verginie; folks wu'd come up dar in droves to buy han's; my mother say dey bo't dem in car load lots." Rebecca was just a child when she arrived in Mississippi, and she remembered her early years toting water to the other slaves in the field: "wid so many mouths to feed in de quarter us hed to do sumthin' to make our sumpthin' to eat." [16]

Mattie Dillworth was eight years old "the night the stars fell" in 1833 when she stepped out on the back porch of her mistress's plantation in Kentucky to watch the sky. Four years later she would be traded to Mississippi, never to see any of her family again. Mattie had been a domestic servant to her mistress in a large plantation house in Kentucky. It was easy work, but her owner was a cruel woman who flailed her with a cowhide whip. When her mistress died, Mattie was put up for sale to settle the estate. She remembered being taken to the trader's yard "whar de visitors an' de speculators c'ud see us, an' dey set a day fer to sell us." She was on the back porch, where she had watched the stars falling a few years earlier, "when dey tol' me to cum to de block; de man puts me up on de block an' ses": " 'Here's a little girl 12 years old' she's got de scofula' [scrofula] but she's young an' will out gro' hit.' " No one offered to buy her. Mattie's mother had died and all she had left was her sister, who was put up on the block the same day and "dey sol' her in anudder direction, up de country, an' I aint never seen her to dis day." The slave trader took her to Mississippi, where the market for slaves was at its height. There she was sold to a striving white man who lost his house trying to pay for her.[17]

While Lafayette County's slave labor force was being assembled, the interstate slave trade was clouded with legal restrictions that stemmed from heightened fears about the influx of traded slaves. The Mississippi Constitution of 1832 went so far as to prohibit the importation of slaves for sale within its borders. This provision was not enforced because no penalties were specified in law, but the ban indicated a general distaste and suspicion toward slave trading, sentiments felt no less among the people whose very prosperity depended on this commerce. Images of human beings brought like so many cattle to the auction block, of children torn from their mothers' arms, of husbands and wives, sisters and brothers, sold apart and separated forever, had, in the meantime, become prime sources for abolitionist propaganda. North and South, the slave trade exposed slavery at its worst.

Mississippi's concern about the slave trade had more practical motives as well. Many regarded slave traders as unscrupulous businessmen capable of the very worst fraud and deceit. There were, for example, many cases of stolen slaves sold to unwitting buyers. The bandit John Murrell, who preyed on travelers along the Natchez Trace, had made a thriving business of this brand of slave trading. Even when the sales were legitimate, Mississippians feared their state might become a dumping ground for unwanted slaves who were diseased, mentally deranged, rebellious, or chronic runaways. Fears of slave insurrection heightened during the 1830s when news of the Nat Turner uprising in Virginia in 1831 brought the nightmare of every southern slave owner to frightening reality. In 1835 a hysterical panic swept through Mississippi following rumors of a slave insurrection in the Madison County. The slave trade, many feared, was an unwelcome source of dangerous slaves who might incite rebellion in Mississippi.[18]

Countering these fears was a soaring demand for slaves during the flush times of the 1830s. More than one hundred thousand slaves came into Mississippi that decade, nearly tripling the state's slave population. "The Fall of '36 is a time to be long remembered," one witness recalled. "All the public highways to Mississippi had become lined—yea literally crowded with slaves." Slave prices in Mississippi rose rapidly from an average of $700 to a high of $1,800. Most were bought on credit, and a speculative mania in slaves joined that in land sales. With the Panic of 1837 many slave buyers repudiated their debts employing the ingenious excuse that such sales were unconstitutional under Mississippi law. Meanwhile, the state legislature in 1837 passed a new law prohibiting the importation of "slaves as merchandise" into Mississippi, this time with penalties to enforce it. Slave migration slowed drastically as the depression descended.[19]

Once the panic subsided and the price of slaves began to recover, concerns about the evils of the slave trade and fears of slave insurrection began to give way to economic needs. Mississippi law, in theory at least, required slave buyers to cross state lines, usually to Memphis or across the river to Arkansas and Louisiana, to buy their slaves. Others went east where prices remained lower. Many of the latter became speculators in slave commerce, traveling to the eastern slave marts with huge amounts of cash to buy large coffles of slaves for resale in the West.[20] By 1845 Mississippi's pressing need for labor overcame qualms about the slave trade and the 1837 prohibition on slave trading in the state was rescinded.[21]

Accumulating Property

The widespread trade in human property that was essential to the expansion of the cotton economy into northern Mississippi stripped slavery down to its essentials. Slave trading required calculated assessment of the value of slaves, their economic skills, their health, and their reproductive capacity. At the slave markets potential buyers carefully inspected slaves, opening their mouths, poking their bodies, often stripping them naked to examine their genitalia and check for physical flaws.

Horatio J. Eden remembered vividly when he and his mother were brought into the slave markets of Memphis to be sold. The scene was Forrest's Trading Camp, the thriving business establishment of Nathan Bedford Forrest (later to become a prominent Confederate cavalry officer). Forrest's slave trading operation took place inside a large square stockade, lined with small rooms. Eden remembered that "when an auction was held or buyers came we were brought out and paraded two or three around a circular brick walk in the center of the stockade. They buyers would stand near by and inspect us as we went by, stop us and examine us. Our teeth, & limbs." In particular, they always "looked to see if there were any scars on our body from a whip as it indicated a vicious temper or as they said a 'bad nigger.'"[22] Not all slaves came to Lafayette County as a result of this dehumanizing process of trading, but it was a common experience for the majority who were brought west. Even those who came west with their masters remained subject to being sold later if economic hardship or death dictated.

L. Q. C. Lamar, preparing to leave Lafayette County and return to Georgia in 1852, revealed how slaves came to be treated as speculative investments by men with no real interest in slave labor as such. "I am somewhat embarrassed as to what disposition I shall make of my negroes," he wrote to a friend. "I have 15 and will have no place for them when I get to Georgia. A great many of them are young too. Some Lawyers get rich out here in this way. A firm invests all its surplus in negroes and hires a farm till they can buy one; and all they make goes to stocking their farm. Old Roger Barton told me that many fortunes are made this way. He says it gives them a *nest egg* and makes them economical and industrious and is a source of enjoyment and recreation. He says however, 'that *lawyers make damn poor farmers tho*','' but the property is there at least supporting itself, and accumulating."[23] When Lamar spoke of property "accumulating," he meant, of course, slaves reproducing: forming families and having children. The calculating mentality of the slave trader blended into that of the slave breeder; both were natural products of the trading and speculative mentality that sprang from the great westward expansion of a slave society.

I Had to Wurk Mity Hard

The slave population of northern Mississippi grew by migration and trade, more than by reproduction. In this setting the master-slave relationship was typically newly formed between strangers who knew nothing of one another's family relations and personality. In Mississippi most of the conditions shaping slavery were at odds with the mentality and practice of paternalism. The slave trade, the severe conditions of living, the demanding work regimen of the cotton frontier, the prevalence of absentee owners, the frequent use of overseers, and the comparatively larger size of Mississippi slaveholdings all tended toward a slave regime that was more impersonal and harsher than its eastern model. For many slaves coming from the declining tobacco and cotton fields of the East, Mississippi brought longer and harder days of work through the year. Frederick Law Olmsted and other observers remarked that slaves were driven harder and treated more harshly in the new cotton states of the Southwest.[24] Wherever profits made it expedient to drive slaves harder, so they were.

Lucindy Shaw remembered the cruelty of her masters in chilling detail. She was separated from her parents at such an early age she had no recollection of them nor of any family. "I don't kno' nuthin' bout whar I wuz born, an' I don't know nuthin' 'bout who wuz my mother an' father; I ain't ever seen dem." She was a young girl before the Civil War, the slave of Rueben Hall, a small farmer with only four slaves. They were "strainers," Lucindy recalled, "dey tried to be rich an' class demselves wid de rich white folks." They worked her hard to raise themselves up in society. "I don' kno' nuthin' but wurk," she remembered. "I had to wurk mity hard; I had to plow in de fiel's in de day an' den at nite when I wuz so tired I cu'dn't hardly stan' I had to spin my cut of cotton befo' I cu'd go to sleep; we had to card, spin, an' reel at nite; I wish I had a dollar fur evry yard ov cloth I has loomed thru dat ole slay." The Halls had no separate slave quarters, so at night Lucindy slept on their kitchen floor, "on one quilt an' kivver wid de udder one." "I ust to sot on de po'ch an' cry; 'spose I wuz cryin' 'cause I didn't hav' no mudder." Lucindy and her fellow slaves were subject to senseless cruelty: "dey ust to beat me lak I wuz a dog." [25]

Lucindy Shaw had witnessed the brutal killing of the slave mother and her aborted baby, and she was not the only one to witness the ruthless killing of a slave in Lafayette County. In what became a notorious case of slave killing, George W. Oliver, a wealthy planter with forty-eight slaves, in March 1859 struck and killed his slave John. The slaves were shelling corn, and John had taken over use of a long heavy "punch" used to push the corn into the mechanical sheller. Oliver commanded that he hand the tool over to Dick, another slave, but John resisted, whether out of resentment toward Dick or his master or some other cause the record does not make clear. Oliver contended in court that John had a history of being disobedient; the day before he had done something to provoke a whipping. After that John's "countenance," Oliver testified, was "vicious and savage." Oliver wrested the punch from him and struck him on the head with it, and he admitted striking at him twice again. His blows must have been powerful. John, described as a "very stout and strong man," had fallen dead. Killing a slave when resisting his master was not considered murder. Mississippi law allowed that "the master may use just such force as may be requisite to reduce his slave to obedience, even to the death of the slave, if that become necessary to preserve the master's life, or to maintain his lawful authority." But the overseer, a man named Bramwel, testified that Oliver had killed John "for nothing," simply because he "did not seem to work fast enough and Oliver told him to work faster and the negro didn't do it." Oliver claimed that John was mentally deranged and had a long history of vicious behavior and that he was "violent, turbulent, and rebellious." But the case against Oliver must have been persuasive, for district attorney James R. Chalmers prosecuted Oliver for the state and won a conviction for manslaughter. Some of the leading attorneys in the county had come to Oliver's defense, including Hugh A. Barr. They appealed the case and had it overturned by the Mississippi Supreme Court in October 1860.[26]

Slaves and owners often blamed overseers for the worst cruelties. As Polly Turner Cancer put it: "all overseers iz mean." She protested, as many slaves did, by running off, at least temporarily: "I'd run off an' hide in de thickets, an' de snakes wud run me out; we went to ole Marster an' tol' him how mean dat overseer wuz to us an' he turnt him off." [27] Some overseers enjoyed almost unregulated power over the slaves, and they had none of the financial investment and future interest that normally restrained owners from excessive brutality. "Managers are scarce," one planter warned James K. Polk, "good ones not to be had, and bad ones worse than none." Polk would know, since he went through several, and had to constantly deal with the consequences of his overseers' brutality or lack of care. Among the consequences were constant runaways and numerous deaths.[28]

Robert Stowers, an overseer for Jacob Thompson and an owner of many slaves in his own right, earned such a reputation for breaking unruly slaves that other planters sent their more troublesome ones to him. One former slave told the historian Charles S. Sydnor that Stowers often carried a shovel with him "to bury de niggers after he killed 'em!" Stowers was also known for less deadly punishment: "Mostly he whipped 'em and den rubbed in salt and pepper." [29] The practice of "salting," applying salt to the open wounds left from whipping, is mentioned so often in the records of slavery that it must have been a common practice. Salt both intensified the pain and supposedly aided in healing; the pepper only added to the pain.

Other overseers pushed the slaves hard, not out of cruelty but because they felt constant pressure to produce for their employers. One overseer boasted to his employer, "when I came here there was some three or fore lying up without a cause . . . it recuire a person to lern the disposition of a negrow to manage them." [30] Overseers and masters did their utmost to learn the disposition of their slaves.

Chunky Jack Is Gone

The hand that held the lash was not always in control. The master-slave relationship was constantly contested, and slaves and masters alike employed
a variety of strategies to accomplish their ends. For slaves one important
means of resistance was escape. Runaways were common across the South,
but the impulse to run must have been stronger among Mississippi slaves
who were more likely to be recently traded, separated from loved ones, and
exposed to a harsh new regimen of work under the command of a new
master or overseer. Most fugitive slaves were apprehended eventually, and
few were even attempting an escape from slavery to freedom. They were instead protesting and trying to manipulate things to their advantage. Once
caught or once they returned of their own volition, as they normally did,
truant slaves might expect more punishment. Escaping, even temporarily,
served to remind the master or overseer that punishment and severe treatment came at the risk of flight. Runaway slaves seemed also to understand
that running away might serve their ends, not only as a temporary respite
from fatiguing work or punishment but also as a means of manipulating
their master into some more permanent change to the slave's advantage.

Runaway slaves were always vexing overseers on the northern Mississippi plantation of future president James K. Polk, an absentee owner whose
main plantation operations remained in Tennessee. The record of Polk's
correspondence with his overseers in Mississippi, published in John Spencer Bassett's book *The Plantation Overseer*, is a rare picture of slavery on the
Mississippi cotton frontier. Polk's new plantation was in Yalobusha County,
just south of Lafayette, which began as a branch operation of his plantation
in Middle Tennessee. It was run by overseers and worked almost entirely
by male slaves who were sent from the home place in Tennessee and taken
some two hundred miles away from their wives, who remained in Tennessee. Unlike most slaves who came to Mississippi from Virginia or the Carolinas, Polk's slaves had both a special motive for running away and a place to
run to. One after another of Polk's Mississippi overseers became frustrated
by the constant irritation of runaways. "Jack and Ben had runaway from
your plantation," one of them wrote to Polk. "They say that Jack was very
badly whip'd indeed, that Beanland [the overseer] salted him four or five
times during the whipping, that Ben was also whip'd but not so badly." [31]
"Chunky Jack," as he was known, was finally tracked down to Helena, Arkansas, where he had been jailed, and he was returned to Beanland. But now
he was feared to be a subversive force among the other slaves, and he soon
ran off again, this time to Shawnee Town, a refuge for runaway slaves and
outlaws across the Mississippi River. [32]

The overseer, Beanland, begged Polk to see to it that another slave, Ben, who had fled back home to Tennessee, be returned to Mississippi immediately. For, Beanland remonstrated, "if he is not sent heare and maide [to] stay all the rest of the fellow had beter be sent to Maury [County, Tennessee, Polk's home place] for I will be damde if I can do anythinge with them."[33] Beanland's trials were only beginning. When he attempted to punish Chunky Jack, "to corect him . . . he curste me verry much and run alf before my face with in runninge 2 hundred yards I caught him and I did not now that he had a stick in his hande and he broke it over my head the 3 lick which I stabed him 2 with my nife and I brought him backe to the house and chainde him and I have him in chaines yet." Chunky Jack was incorrigible, and he continued to run away until Polk finally sold him.

One reason for so many runaways was the separation of slaves from their wives or husbands, some of whom were owned by others. Polk wrote to his own wife that he was busy trying to remedy this problem: "Today I have bought *Mariah's* husband, and have some expectations that I may be able to get *Ceasar's* wife. . . . I bought *Mariah's* husband, a very likely boy, about 22 years old, for $600." He warned also that the slaves he was sending to Mississippi "have no idea that they are going to be sent to the South, and I do not wish them to know it, and therefore it would be best to say nothing about it at home, for it might be carryed back to them."[34]

Several years and two overseers later, Polk was still receiving letters from his Mississippi plantation complaining about the runaways. Other slaves were seeking refuge with neighbors and complaining to them about the overseer's abuse: "I am pestered withe mareners conduct stroling over the contery and corect her she goes to sqr Mcneal for protection; with them exceptions we are dwoing wel."[35] "The Boy charls you sent down last spring run away some fore weeks agow witheout any cause whatever. I think he has goun back to tennessee where his wife is." Polk remained very concerned that the fugitive Charles be found and caught, and about two months after he fled, it was learned that Charles had "come in" to the Tennessee plantation where his wife lived. By this time Polk decided to give up trying to keep Charles down on the Mississippi plantation and made plans to sell him in Tennessee and let him remain near his wife. Charles had "beat" his master.[36]

Polk and his overseers may have faced unusual problems with runaways, but they were hardly alone. Bill Galleghy of Abbeville remembered the "nigger dogs" his family kept to track down runaway slaves. A steady stream of newspaper advertisements from masters offering rewards for escaped slaves can be found alongside notices from county sheriffs describing runaways who had been apprehended and jailed until claimed. "Committed

To the jail of Lafayette county, Miss.," one such notice appeared in 1838, signed by Charles G. Butler, Sheriff, "a Negro Man by the name of JO, who says he belongs to a man living in Louisiana, 30 miles below New Orleans by the name of Cobb. The boy is five feet six and a half inches high; heavy built rather yellow complexion; quick spoken when spoken to, and is about 25 years old. The owner is requested to come forward, prove property, pay charges, and take him away, or he will be dealt with according to law."[37]

The accounts of runaways indicate that they were typically rebelling against what they considered unduly harsh treatment. They seemed to understand that if they proved impossible to control they would be sold to a different—they hoped kinder—owner. Some overseers insisted the slaves were running away without cause and that the remedy was *more*, not less, whipping. Polk's overseer Isaac Dismukes begged him not to sell these troublesome slaves, lest it encourage the others to escape. When a slave named Gilbert fled in 1841 Dismukes learned from the other slaves that he planned to persuade Polk's partner in Tennessee to buy him, perhaps so he could be with his mate. Again Polk was rebuked by his stern slave manager, who offered instruction on how to discipline his own slaves: "Do not sell him if you wish to brake them from running away for they had reather bea sould twise than to bea whip once If hea getes back thare have him iron and send him to mea if you please I wil not inger him by whiping him I beleave that they believe that tennessee is a place of parridise and the all want to gow back to tennessee to stop them by ironing tham and send them back again and they wil soon stop cumming to tennessee."[38]

Apparently Polk listened this time, but Gilbert persisted. Years later, a notice from the Lafayette County jailer identified a slave named Gilbert said to be property of James K. Polk and asked that the owner or his overseer come to the jail and "prove his property."[39] Two years later, in 1851, it seemed Gilbert was giving another Polk overseer trouble: "Youre people are all well And behaving well at this tim," the overseer's report came back from Yalobusha; "Gilbert is still out of plase I got him home and he Ran of the next day."[40] Whether Gilbert was in place or not, there were other slaves at large almost every time the overseer reported to the absentee master. One wrote to Mrs. Polk, now a widow, in 1856, "your people are all well. But Wilson is not got hom Harbard and Manuel and fonser is got hom; iam in hops wilson will come home or imay her frome him; manuel and fonser sa Harbard was agoing to take them to Memphis to sey there oncle. But the got afird and come hom i have not whipped nary wone of them i will try them sey if the will dough without it. . . . But Harbard is a bad boy."[41]

The constant reports of runaways and the defensive explanations of the overseer tell us something about the contest that was frequently at play between the master or his agent and the slave. For the master or overseer the runaway dramatized the ongoing struggle between them and their slaves.

Faulkner's story about Tomey's Turl, a chronic runaway who gave his masters fits, may seem at first glance to be a ridiculous tall tale, an example of Faulkner's sense of humor getting the better of historical realism. Before writing the story, however, Faulkner mentions in a letter borrowing John Spencer Bassett's book on Polk's overseers, and whether or not he would call this researching the story, it was informed by the accounts of Chunky Jack, Gilbert, and the rest. The story, "Was," revolves around the irrepressible propensity of young slaves to find amorous partners and the adamant preference of two mature white bachelors to avoid any romantic involvement with women. On one level the story is a delightful tale about the foibles of Uncle Buck and Uncle Buddy McCaslin, two of Yoknapatawpha's more colorful characters. It is also a story that illuminates an understanding of slavery that was decades ahead of the conventional wisdom among historians of Faulkner's day. He penetrates to the heart of the master-slave relationship to illuminate a complex contest of will and manipulation on both sides. The masters in this story not only assume it is important for their slaves to find partners, but they also realize the choice of partner is not theirs to make. The slaves, for their part, use their power to run away to get what they want from their masters within something like a game of chase or cards.

Tomey's Turl, one of the McCaslin slaves, periodically runs off to the plantation of Hubert Beauchamp to pursue his sweetheart, Tennie. Tomey's Turl is the half-white offspring of "Old Carothers" McCaslin, Buck and Buddy's father (about whom, more later). This reminder of miscegenation bothers Mr. Beauchamp sufficiently that he refuses to buy Turl as Tennie's mate and bring to an end all this chasing about. Tomey's Turl manages to force the issue by repeatedly running off to the Beauchamp place with the McCaslins in hot pursuit, dogs, mules, and horses flying after the runaway slave. It is one of several manhunt stories in Faulkner where slaves and hunting dogs track the quarry, but the hunt takes on the character of a ritualistic game with the chasers and the chased all sporting participants.

Turl's passionate pursuit of Tennie is played off against the McCaslins' resolute aversion to women, particularly to Sophonsiba Beauchamp, Hubert's old-maid sister whose most striking feature is a large brown front tooth. Hubert is eager to marry her off to one of the very eligible McCaslin brothers, and he is offering a large dowry (some might say bribe) of land and slaves. Without the reader ever knowing exactly how, Sophonsiba and Hubert Beauchamp, apparently in collusion with Tomey's Turl, manipulate the McCaslins to their advantage. While still at large, Tomey's Turl muses: "just get the womenfolks to working at it. Then all you needs to do is set down and wait." In an elaborate series of bets, chases, and poker games (the last of which Tomey's Turl winds up dealing and apparently not always off the top of the deck), Uncle Buck McCaslin at first is left having to buy Tennie, bring her back to live with Tomey's Turl, and marry the spinster Sophonsiba. His brother intervenes and, after another hand of poker, the McCaslins get Tennie for nothing and Uncle Buck is rescued from his betrothal to Sophonsiba, at least for a time.[42]

Paterollers at Ever' Fork in de Road

Few masters could afford to treat running away as a sport, and for most slaves it was rarely a winning game. Apprehending and punishing runaway slaves, maintaining vigilance over any sign of slave rebellion, were all part of a slave society's struggle to control the movement and activities of slaves. After the Nat Turner uprising in 1831, new laws regulating slave patrols were enacted. Before, the job of policing slaves was given to local captains of the state militia, but beginning in 1831 Mississippi law handed the main responsibility to county government authorities. This became even more decentralized in 1833, when Mississippi allowed county Boards of Police to appoint patrol leaders. It was left to each beat representative on the board to decide whether and who to appoint patrol leader; the patrol leader, in turn, would appoint five or more men to serve, but only as he determined a patrol was needed.[43]

The patrols were intended more to intimidate the local slave population with symbolic display of power than to provide effective, constant vigilance over their activities or to apprehend fugitive slaves. The patrollers rode at night when the danger of slaves gathering or stealing away from their masters was at its highest. They patrolled infrequently, by law only twice a month but even less often in practice. They visited plantations and rode along the roads at night, apprehending slaves who were found away from their owners and breaking up illegal assemblies. A chronic source of danger to a slave society were towns, to which slaves flocked often to meet, drink, gamble, and mix with free society. Whenever a slave was apprehended without a pass, the patrol was instructed to inflict fifteen lashes. The purpose of the patrol system was also to discipline lax slave owners, for they were subject to fines and their slaves were exposed to whippings, which could inflict serious harm to valuable slave property.[44]

Anxiety over slave insurrection heightened after 1850. There were rumors of a slave uprising in or near Lafayette County circulating in 1850, coinciding with sudden political agitation over slavery. One planter just north of Lafayette County wrote: "The excitement relating to our Servants making some effort for their freedom has . . . subsided in this neighbourhood."[45] The turn toward greater vigilance came with the increasing tensions over slavery and the mounting paranoia in response to the antislavery movement in the 1850s.

In 1858 new efforts were made to tighten up and centralize the county slave patrol. This was aimed particularly at controlling the movement and gathering of slaves in and around Oxford. The County Board of Police required the patrol to ride "at least two nights in each month" in the southeast quadrant of Beat One surrounding Oxford. Other patrols were appointed for three-month periods to control the other parts of Beat One and "outlying beats, two, four, and five." Beat Three (the northeast quadrant of the county at this time), an area that included large slaveholdings surrounding College Hill, apparently went without any county patrol.[46]

The County Board was careful to define the powers of the patrol and especially to limit any punishment it might inflict on slaves it apprehended: "The aforesaid patroles Shall not abuse the property of any Person and shall whip any Slave that may be Caught off of his masters premises without Some token or pass from their overseer, Master or mistress, or some one that may have them under their controle but in no one case Shall Said patroles give any Slave more than thirty nine lashes for the Same offence."[47] Every three months, and later at six-month intervals, the Board of Police appointed new patrol captains and members. They were empowered to "whip each and every Slave out Side of their owners or Employers premises without a pass" up to thirty-nine lashes per offense.[48]

Many slaves recalled the "paddyrollers" as a terrifying constant presence in their lives. "Ef you tried to go off de place de paterollers wud meet you in de road an' wear you out rite dar in de road," Polly Turner Cancer recollected decades later. Rebecca Woods remembered "dey had paterollers at ever' fork in de road to keep de slaves frum runnin' away."[49] In the memory of former slaves the "paddyrollers" riding at night, whipping delinquent slaves, and inspecting slave quarters were a fearsome symbol of collective white power over them, one that in retrospect seemed to anticipate the night riders of the Ku Klux Klan and other white terrorist groups after emancipation. But the actual power of the patrol lay more in its capacity to strike fear into the minds of the slaves, for in practice the infrequency of the patrols and the general inefficiency of their surveillance allowed a good deal of illicit movement and congregation among slaves determined to evade them.

He'd Let Us Make Some Money

Public concerns about tightening slave surveillance coincided with a tendency evident among many owners to give their slaves more freedom over their lives as workers, consumers, church members, and social beings in the community. Slave owners and overseers made deliberate use of rewards as incentives to hard work and obedience. Many slaves, especially those on larger estates, it appears, cultivated their own gardens and cotton patches. That slaves were encouraged to raise a portion of their own food supply may not surprise anyone, but many were also raising cash crops of food, poultry, and even cotton for sale in local markets. The overseer on the Bowles plantation kept track of the corn the slaves had raised and then sold through him. They drew on the credit they earned throughout the year to buy things for themselves. Several were reported as having earned five dollars during the year.[50] "Marster used to let us raise our own chickens and sell dem at de tavern in Abbeville," Polly Turner Cancer remembered of her youth as a slave on Woodson's Ridge. She added that "we had to giv' dem to a man to sell fur us so de folks wud know dey wuzn't stolen." As this suggests, there was also a brisk business in stolen goods. One newspaper warned of a wave of thefts around Holly Springs and suggested that county officials require that "every negro that offers any article for sale in the county, without a written permit from his master, shall be subject to the lash."[51]

Polly found other ways to earn money as well, for her master took to paying them extra for what was literally "moonlighting." "He'd let us make some money too by pickin' cotton at nite by de moonlight; we didn't hav' to do hit, but he'd let us ef we wanted to." Her master encouraged other forms of slave enterprise as well: "Ole marster uster to let us gather chestnuts an' hazle-nuts on Sundays and den when de wagons wuz goin' to Memphis we wud put our sacks on dem an' dey wud sell dem fur us an' let us have de money."[52]

On the Polk plantation the slaves were allowed to raise cotton for their own profit during their spare time. In 1849 the slaves' crop amounted to some 8,400 pounds of cotton in all. One of the slaves also hired out as a blacksmith and apparently kept at least some of the money he earned. The slaves' cash crop had become part of the plantation routine by 1853, when the overseer wrote: "i have settled all the clam aganst the plantation that I nough of. I have collected a part of the blacksmith actcounts." The slaves' expectation of cash for their cotton must have seemed sufficiently important to the overseer that he put them in line in front of himself: "i have not anofe yet to pay the negrose but if you wish for them to have some mony i will let them have it; i can wate untwell your borther come down for mine wages." Two years later this arrangement was still in effect when the overseer explained to his absentee employer: "you wanted to know hough much you had to pay your negros you in ginerly pay them About 200 hundred dollars at a time." Whether this referred to annual or some other periodic payments is unclear. "Harry [the blacksmith] dous not git much work to dough the most of the planters has a back [black] smith and makes out with them." Again he offered to expedite pay day on the plantation: "if you wish I will pay them some of my oune mony." [53]

The Sabbath was the one day slaves had to themselves, and they used it to full advantage not only for religious and social purposes but also for making and spending money. This did not sit well with the elders of the First Presbyterian Church of Oxford. They learned of the slaves trading on Sunday during an investigation of one of their own elders, W. H. D. Wendel, whom they accused of desecrating the Sabbath. "He had been charged with the violating the sabbath by allowing his Servants to work for themselves on his Plantation on that day and paying them for such work." Wendel's apology revealed that this was common practice on neighboring plantations. "He acknowledged that he did allow them to do so, formerly, as was customary on the neighboring Plantation." He admitted to knowing better, "having felt it was exceedingly wrong . . . and assured the Session that he should never allow it to be repeated." [54]

But it *was repeated*, and what probably began as a rare privilege came to be claimed as a right among some slaves. Slave masters and overseers, for their part, understood the power of such a privilege not only as an immediate incentive but also because it gave them additional leverage over their slaves. Polk's neighbor John Townes Leigh had long encouraged his slaves to cultivate their own cotton patches. Leigh explained his liberal regime with apparent pride to visitor Solon Robinson. His slaves, he said, had hen houses and raised chickens, using the master's corn crib, which was always open. They also were allowed to raise cotton for their own use and sale and managed to put aside about $50 to $100 in cotton sales each year. Furthermore, slave women were weaving and making cotton and wool clothing for their use or sale.[55]

Leigh's son, Peter Randolph Leigh, took all of this much further after he inherited the plantation following the father's death in 1850. His story gives us some historical perspective on the plans of Faulkner's McCaslin twins, Uncle Buck and Uncle Buddy, to allow their slaves to earn their freedom and establish some kind of freedmen's commune in Yoknapatawpha. They apparently are motivated by an unspoken shame or sense of the guilt they have inherited from the outrageous sins of their father, Lucius Quintus Carothers

McCaslin (which we will visit momentarily). The twins, whose real names are Theophilus (Buck) and Amodeus (Buddy), grant the slaves they inherit virtual emancipation, leaving them to work for their freedom and live in the big house "Old Carothers" had built as the family mansion. The brothers, meanwhile, have chosen to live in a log cabin they build themselves in the style of a crude slave cabin. Each night they march their slaves into the big house and lock the door with a nail, but the slaves are perfectly free to leave out the back, restricted only by an unspoken "gentlemen's agreement" that they will return before daylight and maintain some semblance of enslavement. Faulkner's fanciful arrangement between master and slaves dramatizes the way many slave masters dealt with the autonomy slaves claimed for themselves, especially between sundown and sunup beyond their masters' eyes.[56] The McCaslin scheme of emancipation may well have been inspired by Frances Wright's radical experiment in gradual emancipation at Neshoba, Tennessee, which attracted attention among some Mississippi slave owners, like Peter Randolph Leigh.[57]

Leigh's willingness to experiment with new labor incentives effectively transformed slavery into something resembling free labor, or at least it was very much like the version of free labor that would later emerge with sharecropping in the postemancipation South. Leigh announced to all his slaves that they would be given a guaranteed allowance, a credit against which they could draw for plantation supplies, specified as "not necessary articles of support" but luxury items which, as consumers with free choice, they could buy for themselves. Leigh also introduced monetary fines for misbehavior and subtracted the amount fined, along with the debits for goods purchased, from the amount paid out to each slave. His careful notes indicate that he also implemented a system of cash bonuses and tips as further incentive. Notes of one such bonus indicated: "Pd. for best cotton picking during my absence on a trip to Virginia." Ten years later he was still practicing this system when he entered $109.50 as a "gratuity to negroes for year 1859."[58] Evidence from the 1850s points toward more slave masters indulging in this experimentation with incentives that gave their slaves access to cash or credit and to the things money could buy.

The idea of earning money by voluntary labor was no less radical than the concept that slaves could buy things they chose freely and even bargain with white merchants who were more than willing to compete for them as customers. How these consumers spent their money is only hinted at in a few of the former slave interviews and other sources. Their owners were expected to provide them with all they required in the way of housing, food, clothing, shoes, medicine, and other necessities. The slave, therefore, could spend money for discretionary purchases of luxury items, perhaps jewelry, fancy clothing, along with liquor and other consumer items the master might not have fully approved. At least two white men were ordered out of Oxford for selling liquor to slaves in 1860. This was during a time of heightened concern about slave insurrection, but there must have been many other incidences that went undetected or unpunished.[59] Polly Turner Cancer remembered how she spent some of her profits from selling chickens and nuts along the road to Memphis: "we wud generally spen hit fur lockets an' finger rings; I spec dey wuz brass, but we wuz jus' as proud ov dem as dey wuz pyor gol' [pure gold]."[60] Callie Gray, a slave on a nearby plantation, remembered: "Uv course sometimes the women wanted some fancy folderols they couldn't git on the plantation. Ef it was summertime they would pick blackberries, or wild grapes, or persimmons and sell 'em in town on Sadd'day afternoon."[61]

Foster Freeland, an Oxford merchant, did a brisk business in trade with slaves who flocked to his dry goods store on Sundays, the only day slaves were at liberty for shopping. He brought in from fifteen to fifty dollars from this trade, but his partner worried about defiling the Sabbath by doing business of any kind on that day. Freeland pardoned himself for this indiscretion by noting: "The enormity of the thing seems to be excusable in some degree from the fact that it is so common a thing here." Their correspondence also made it clear that they had to compete for the slaves' business. One partner lauded the other, who was "so clever with the boys and gives them such good bargains to which they would get anywhere else that he seems like an angel despensing blessings to children."[62]

Good Masters Don't Separate Families

"They endured" is how Faulkner once summarized the role of the Negro in the South's history. Uprooted, sold, brought west, and sold again, the slaves of Lafayette County, Mississippi, managed not only to endure but to build a new life in Mississippi, one that was supported by the most human of all props: family, religion, and community.[63] The great slave migration westward remains one of the most important and least understood aspects of American slavery. Much of the historical interest has revolved around estimates of the numbers of slaves traded to the West as opposed to those who migrated with their masters. But little has been done to illuminate the experience of the slaves, the impact of migration on their lives, and their adaptation to their new home in the West.[64]

The great westward migration that brought slaves into Lafayette County involved hundreds of sales and purchases by masters and traders, and these, together with the migration itself, wrought untold havoc on slave families. The hard work of laying out a new cotton plantation economy required the work of young slaves, especially males. The Mississippi frontier was no place for the aged slave. We can return to Joseph Holt Ingraham's keen observations for a detailed description of one slave caravan entering Mississippi, which suggests the pattern: "First came half a dozen boys and girls, with fragments of blankets and ragged pantaloons and frocks, hanging upon, but not covering their glossy limbs." Behind them were more young people, women with babies, whom Ingraham guessed had been born during the journey, followed by others riding in a wagon. Then, straggling behind the wagon, Ingraham described an elderly man, perhaps eighty years of age, "bent nearly double with the weight of years and infirmity. By his side moved an old negress, nearly coeval with him, who supported her decrepit form by a staff. They were the venerable progenitors of the children and grandchildren who preceded them." As Ingraham noted: "Old people are seldom seen in these 'droves.' The young and athletic usually compose them. But as in this instance, the old people are sometimes allowed to come with the younger portion of the families, as a favour; and if sold at all, they are sold with their children, who can take care of them in their old age." [65]

Many others left their parents behind. A letter from one slave to his father offers rare but poignant testimony to the experience. "I have been Separated from you so Long a time and that without Even Knowing where you were or whether dead or alive, untill very lately I chanced to hear that you were still in Existance and much nearer to me than I had Expected. For it has now been nearly Eight-years since I left my native country." [66] With literacy officially prohibited among slaves and with limited access to other means of communication, migration for most meant the end of all contact with distant loved ones.

If elderly relatives were, for the most part, left behind in the East, the Mississippi migration more often involved the transplanting rather than separation of the slave's nuclear family unit. The 1840 census offers strong evidence for this. Most convincing is the clear balance between the sexes for all age groups. In 1840 for every 100 slave women there were 99 men; ten years later there were still 98 men per 100 women among the slaves. Only in 1860 did the slave population develop a small male surplus; the ratio of men to 100 women rose to 103.

Why were so many women and young children brought into a raw new cotton frontier where the hard labor of clearing fields and putting up cabins demanded strong, young, male labor? Quite apart from any differences in physical strength, the productivity of female slaves in the fields was diminished over time because of pregnancy and child-rearing duties. The early presence of so many women and children suggests that more than labor productivity was being considered.

Many slave owners saw their roles as imparting Christian morality to their slaves, and they encouraged stable monogamous marriages. They also understood that bringing families west reduced the problem of runaways and rebellion. Married slaves, especially those with children, were less inclined to take flight and were generally more content. To that end, many masters arranged marriages, bought likely mates for their single slaves, or arranged for marriages on other plantations. Allowing slaves to find partners on neighboring plantations was rarely so complicated as it was in the case of Faulkner's McCaslin and Beauchamp plantations. Because slaveholdings in northern Mississippi were typically small and eligible mates limited, finding a partner among another master's slaves was common. Though Peter Randolph Leigh had some ninety slaves, he found it necessary to permit marriages with the slaves of his neighbor. "In buying and selling," he said, "good masters are always careful not to separate families. Two of my men have wives on President Polk's plantation which adjoins mine, and whom they are free to visit every Saturday night and remain with till Monday morning." [67] Some slave owners were exasperated when their slaves did not accept their own idea of a proper mate. August Baldwin Longstreet, president of the University of Mississippi, complained to his son-in-law L. Q. C. Lamar: "The creatures persistently refuse to live together as many [sic] and wife, even after I have mated them with all the wisdom I possess, and built them such desirable homes." [68] For some slaves, the only thing worse than forced separation from a beloved mate may have been forced union with one chosen by such a master.

Slave weddings were celebrated with the full support of the master. Ella Pegues remembered the weddings of her family's slaves with delight: "First came the candle holders, at the head of quite a procession, taking their places on either side of the bride and groom, the former wore a white dress, and colored sash, and the latter was attired in a neat suit." Afterward, she described a large barbecue supper "spread on wooden tables, or scaffolds, out in the ward." "Merry games and music on banjo and fiddle finished the evening." [69]

If slave buyers and owners saw to it that their slaves found marriage partners, those who sold slaves naturally had less reason to be concerned. At the death or financial ruin of a master slave families suddenly became vulnerable to separation. Polly Turner Cancer remembered when her owner, William Turner, died sometime before the Civil War: "Atter Ole Marster died dey put me on de block an' sol' me; dey stood me on a block on de porch an' here is how dey done hit; de man had a cane in hiz han' an' he wud hol' hit up an say, 'What am I bid? Goin'—Goin', Goin'; den he wud hit de side ov de house 'Blam' an' say 'Gone. . . . I sol' fur $1500." Apparently the sale was in violation of her master's will, which specified that none of his twenty-two slaves would be separated. "My ole marster aint never sol none ov his niggers from de family," Polly recalled, "but dey didn't 'no dat 'til dey red de will an' de will say dat we quzn't to be separated, an' we all had to go back an' be sol' over an' dis time I wuz bo't by Andy Turner," her former master's son.[70]

The interest masters took in seeing to it that their slaves married, had children, took good care of their children, and lived together as families in separate cabins all made good business sense. Slave reproduction guaranteed a future supply of labor at little additional cost. Moreover, clearing land and raising cotton was only one source of gain, for the fecundity of slave women, combined with the steady rise in slave prices, promised enormous profits to the slave owner. Slaves, as L. Q. C. Lamar noted, were an "accumulating" investment.[71]

Mississippi Mulatto

Sexual unions across the color line frequently abetted this "accumulation" of slave property. The white population, in striking contrast to the enslaved, was heavily masculine, especially in the age groups between twenty and fifty where, as we have seen, the ratio of males per 100 females ranged from 144 in 1840 to about 123 in 1850 and 1860. Approximately one-third to one-fifth of adult white males did not have a white female counterpart. This surplus of white men without women, combined with an abundance of slave women and the power that many white men had over female slaves, provided a situation ripe with temptation for sexual exploitation and clandestine interracial unions. The growth in numbers of those the census marshals identified as mulatto only hints at what must have been a frequent practice of white males crossing the boundaries of race and bondage to seek sexual partners.

Interracial sexual mixing was rarely admitted publicly among white southerners, but it was a theme Faulkner probed repeatedly in his novels. No white people in Yoknapatawpha are more haunted by their history of interracial transgressions than the McCaslin family, whom we met earlier. The sins of Uncle Buck and Uncle Buddy's father began with his illicit union with a slave girl he buys named Eunice. It was in dubious honor of Lucius Quintus Cincinnatus Lamar, the fire-eating hero of Oxford, that Faulkner named the father Lucius Quintus Carothers ("Old Carothers") McCaslin. To him and Eunice was born a daughter, Tomasina, or Tomey, as she was called. After Tomey comes of age, Old Carothers begins an incestuous relationship with her that begets a son named Terrel, known as Tomey's Turl. Eunice, in utter despair, drowns herself after learning that Tomey's father has impregnated her. Old Carothers McCaslin has perpetrated an outrageous offense compounded of miscegenation, sexual exploitation, and incest. His children, Buck and Buddy, in effect repudiate his legacy and, without ever explaining why, they set out to emancipate the family's slaves. His grandson, Ike, upon discovering this family secret, feels compelled to atone for the sins he has inherited by tracking down and compensating his grandfather's mulatto descendants. In the McCaslin story, and in many other references to mixed black-white blood in Yoknapatawpha, Faulkner was exploring what was historically a prevalent secret among his people. By 1860 there were 623 slaves, nearly one-tenth of the total, who were classified by the census marshal as "mulatto." Given all the secrecy and denial that surrounded the sexual liaisons across racial lines, this was undoubtedly an undercount.[72]

Racial identity was always open to interpretation, and more than one mixed-race offspring was able to pass into one race or the other without close scrutiny. An Oxford newspaper reported a story of a woman named Mary Ann who came to live in a small village identified only by its location, about thirty miles away on the road to Memphis (probably Holly Springs). She took up business sewing mantuas and told people she was the daughter of an early settler of Lafayette County who was partly Indian, apparently as a way of explaining her dark complexion. In the curious logic of racial thinking, Indian blood bore little stigma among white southerners. Indeed, females being in short supply, this woman soon found herself courted by a divorced man the newspaper reported discreetly as "Mr. M." Soon after they married, a handbill advertising a reward for a runaway slave arrived in town, and it described Mary Ann perfectly. Friends of Mr. M. showed him the handbill, and they all went together to pay a visit to the runaway's master. Everything they suspected was true, and Mr. M. returned home "much mortified . . . at the deception that had been practiced upon him." His wife was promptly returned to her master.[73] If Faulkner needed a historical inspiration for his story of Thomas Sutpen's marriage to his first wife, Eulalia Bon, whose racial impurity, once revealed, abruptly ends their marriage, this was only one of many that might have provided it.

There were other mixed-race inhabitants who won special status as freed people in Lafayette County. One, a woman "of Yellow complexion female of large stature aged about 20" named Mary Good, was designated free at birth by testimony of W. H. Smither, a prominent Oxford merchant, who may have been her mother's owner; her father remained anonymous. Another free Negro applying for license to remain in Lafayette was Roda Smith, apparently of mixed parentage, described as a "rather copper collour common size and about the age of Twenty nine years."[74]

Joel Williamson's study of Faulkner's great-grandfather Colonel William C. Falkner reveals that some mulatto descendants of a woman who once was his slave believed he was their ancestor. Whether this was true, and whether this was something the family even whispered about, is not known.[75] Given the prevalence of mulattoes in Mississippi, any white person (whether or not their family had once owned slaves) might wonder if someone across the color line might be kin. Faulkner also pondered whether, in addition to the blood of two races that intermingled and was passed down, there was also some guilt and responsibility that was inherited.

My Negroes Have Families

Most slave children came from slave parents, not interracial alliances. The most convincing evidence that slaves came to Mississippi in nuclear family units, in addition to the even sex ratios, is the early presence of large numbers of young children. Nearly four in ten (37 percent) slaves in the county were under the age of ten in the 1840 census, and more than half of those (20 percent of the total slave population) were under five. This abundance of young children points to the widespread existence of already formed procreative families being transplanted as units to the Mississippi frontier.

Slave housing reinforced the role of the family as the central social organization. Among the first buildings constructed on new plantations were houses for the slaves, and these were usually separate cabins designed for individual families, supplemented perhaps by single, unrelated slaves. If there were barracks to house groups of slaves, it was a temporary expedient. Even small slaveholders typically put up a separate dwelling for their slaves. The average number of slaves per slave house listed in the 1860 slave census was a little over four, and less than 2 percent of all the slaves lived under the same roof with ten or more other slaves. Ella Pegues, daughter to a family with large slaveholdings, remembered the quarters "with its rows of neat cabins on either side of a long lane or street, each cabin, had a garden attached, with palings around it. The 'overseer's' home stood a little apart, next to it was a meeting house."[76]

Frederick Law Olmsted, a northern visitor to northern Mississippi, described the slave quarters he saw in less flattering terms: "The negro cabins were small, dilapidated and dingy; the walls were not chinked, and there were no windows . . . the furniture in the cabins was of the simplest and rudest imaginable kind, two or three beds with dirty clothing upon them, a chest, a wooden stool or two, made with an ax, and some earthenware and cooking apparatus. Everything within the cabins was colored black by smoke. The chimneys . . . were built of splinters and clay." Olmsted found the cabins whites lived in, even wealthy planters, nearly as crude. The coarse conditions notwithstanding, Olmsted went on to describe a scene of domestic happiness in this north Mississippi slave cabin: "A man sat on the ground making a basket, a woman lounged on a chest in the chimney-corner smoking a pipe, and a boy and two girls sat in a bed which had been drawn up opposite to her, completing the fireside circle. They were talking and laughing cheerfully." [77]

Wise slave owners saw to it that their slaves were safely housed, for the health and well-being of valuable slaves was of paramount importance. On many plantations the log cabins erected at first were replaced, when time and building materials allowed, with framed buildings raised well off the ground, floored with wood planks, and equipped with fireplaces and brick chimneys, doors, and shuttered window openings, all designed to keep slaves warm in winter, cool in summer, and dry and comfortable at all times.[78] Peter Randolph Leigh proudly pointed out to visitor Solon Robinson how his ninety slaves lived in cabins that were "neatly furnished and provided with household matters and things . . . and look just like some white folks' houses." [79] On a nearby plantation, John Leigh boasted to Robinson of the care he gave to the housing and diet of his slaves. "The most of my negroes have families, and live as you see in very comfortable cabins, nearly as good as my own, with good fire places, good floors and doors, comfortable beds, plenty of cooking utensils and dishes, tables and chairs." [80] "We lived at the quarters," one former slave recalled. "They were good log houses, with dirt and stick chimneys." "We cooked, ate and slept in one room, no matter how big the family," another remembered.[81]

Not all plantations structured housing and dining around the slave family. At John Peyton Jones's large plantation on Woodson's Ridge the slaves were fed from a common kitchen. During the winter months they ate in a large dining room, and in warm weather they sat outside under the trees and were fed out of a large trough made from a long, hollowed-out log. Soup, milk, potlicker, and all the food was poured into the trough where the slaves ate with their hands and used hoecakes to sop up the liquid. Later these primitive conditions improved when adult slaves were given tin plates and eating utensils, while young slaves continued to eat from the trough.[82]

Other family functions were communal on some plantations. Those with large numbers of slaves, such as the Bowles family, built a separate cabin as a collective nursery for the slave babies. This was a double-size log cabin with fireplaces at each end, where the older slave women tended the infants and toddlers while their mothers worked in the fields. The mothers returned from the fields several times each day to breast-feed their babies and look after their children.[83]

Polly Turner Cancer was part of a slaveholding of twenty-two slaves, and they had a large nursery for her children. She remembered the care her master gave to the mothers. "De mothers wud cum to de house twice a day to suckle de babies—at 10 o'clock in de morning an' two o'clock in de evenin'; dey was taken good care of." "Dey had nurses fur de nigger chiluns sams as de whites." Her master made it well understood that he shared their interest in keeping their babies healthy: "Ole Marster wudn't let de wimmen do no heavy liftin' coz he wanted dem de have big fine babies; he always sed, 'I don't want no runts.' When we picked cotton he always made de men tote de sacks." Her master, William Turner, even played a role in selecting mates for his slaves; at least he discouraged matches he thought might degrade his slave stock: "one time a little nigger started to coutin' me an' marster tole him to git coz he didn't want no runts on his place."[84]

Generally, masters and overseers had reason to watch over the pregnant slave women out of concern for the health of mother and child, but they accepted death without emotion. "We are all wel with the exception of the girl matilda," James Polk's overseer wrote to him from northern Mississippi; "she had a child some ten days a gow and is grunting yet, nothing serious." Then he added matter-of-factly: "Her child died after some ten or twelve hours, from what cause I dont now she has not worked more than half her time cence you was here." The overseer was concerned to explain that the death of the baby was not his fault: "Her child died the next evening after born I believe caused from her one conduct not letting of mee now nothing of hit, until a few minets before the burth of the child. I cold not get the old woman [midwife?] there in time."[85]

William Turner assumed a more intrusive role in the domestic lives of his slaves than most owners. His slave Polly recalled: "rite in front ov hiz dinin' room wuz de place whar de slaves et' mother's didn't hav' to do dey own cookin' an' dey didn't hav' to feed dey own chilluns; dey had a cook to cook dey vittles; jes' bout sundown de mammies wud bring de chiluns an' set dem on a block 'long de table giv' dem dey supper 'fore de old folks; dey had plenty t' eat—sech as bread, an' molasses an' all de milk to drink dat dey wanted." Turner wanted all his slaves to eat well and stay healthy. "Ole Marster wud cum 'long an' say, 'Haz everybody got 'nuf t'eat 'cause I don't want nobody to go hongry at my hous'." Turner even got involved in parental discipline of children among his slaves, Polly recalled: "he wudn't let de mammies whip dey own chillun eder; ef he cum 'cross a woman wuppin' her chile he'd say, 'Git 'way woman; dats my buzness,' an' he'd giv' one or two little whacks and dat wuz all." [86] This was taking paternalism to a new level, with the master insinuating his authority between slave parent and child.

Whatever other intrusions slaves experienced in their family lives, and whatever they suffered through separation, migration, and trade, the slaves of Lafayette County brought to Mississippi a comparatively strong foundation of nuclear family units. While the white population remained heavily male, womanless, childless, and isolated from loved ones, the slaves of Lafayette County were living together in unions that brought forth an abundance of children.

A Slave Community

Once resettled in the West, the slave population was able to rebuild some basis for community social life that extended beyond nuclear family units. In many respects the social world most of Lafayette County's slaves shared was fuller, more accessible, and more constant than that available to whites. White people lived mostly in isolation from one another, spread out across a thinly settled rural landscape surrounded by their own farms and plantations. Most slaves, in contrast, lived among many of their own people, even in this part of Mississippi where few slaveholdings were large.

The basis for the slave community lay in the paradoxical mathematics of slaveholding: though most slave owners had few slaves, most slaves lived in large slaveholdings. The distribution of slave ownership varied only slightly between 1840 and 1860, even as the slave population grew and owners moved into and out of the county. Almost half the slave owners held four or fewer slaves, about the same average as the rest of the South. But this group owned only 10 percent of the county's slaves. That meant 90 percent of the county's slaves lived among five or more fellow slaves; 72 percent were owned by masters with ten or more slaves. Only a small minority of the white people in Lafayette County could claim twenty slaves, but 54 percent of the county's slaves lived in holdings at least this size.

Whereas isolated white families had to travel by foot or by horse, mule, or wagon for miles before visiting neighbors or going to town to do business or shop, most slaves lived cheek by jowl with their own people. On the larger plantations the slave cabins that typically housed one family would be arranged close together along a "street" facing one another. Polly Turner Cancer recalled of her master's slave quarters, "dere wuz a long row ov houses fur hiz black folks." [87]

The slaves of Lafayette County were also more settled than the whites who moved restlessly in and out of the county. The large planters who

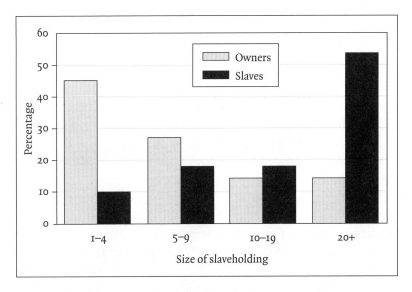

Figure 1. Percentage of Slaves and Slave Owners, by Size of Slaveholding, Lafayette County, 1860

owned most of the slaves tended to be more permanent, for the logical reason that they had invested more in land and buildings and were generally older men with families and kin in the region. Among those who survived the depression of the early 1840s, the return of prosperity and the success they had already achieved all gave them reason to stay on rather than leave.[88] Their slaves logically enjoyed more stability as well.

Our Colored Brothers and Sisters

Sunday was the most racially integrated and egalitarian day of the week in this slave society. Before emancipation blacks rarely had churches to call their own. They may have met in religious gatherings of their own, as slaves did in other parts of the South, but there is no record of such in Lafayette County. Early records of local churches show slaves present in the 1840s. The minutes of the Bethel Baptist Church of Christ, for example, list Jesse and Warren, identified as slaves of Washington Price, a large planter in the southeast quarter of the county. Price was the man who joined the Presbyterians on his deathbed, and we know he was not a member of Bethel Church. His slaves were joining on their own. Over the next few years more slaves joined Bethel Baptist: Tempy, Armsted, Penny, Ann, Nancy, Mariah, and Hester, and several other "colored members" were added to the books, sometimes with master's names, often not. There were several other slaves who were not listed but who must have belonged to the church because their names were recorded only upon leaving the church after emancipation.[89]

The slaves who joined Bethel were perhaps a dozen in all, among a congregation who numbered approximately 70 white males and 120 white females. But there they were among their white brethren for a few hours each week, being baptized, admitted, dismissed, disciplined, just like their white brethren. What did it mean for a slave to hear that "a couelered sister named Hester" was to be admitted to the fellowship? What did it mean to whites to have a slave "sister"? Slave members were held to the same strict standard of the whites, who were routinely disciplined or dismissed for various infractions of decorum or piety. When Jesse, one of the original slave members, was rumored to have violated the laws of God, a deputation of white brethren was sent to interrogate him and report. "Brother Wooten stated to the church that brother Henry couelered brother charged Jessie a couelered brother of being gilty of fornication the scriptoral steps being taken the folowing Brethren was apointed a comitte to see Brother Jessee Brother Wooten Hodg and Nabors who was to report the case at next conference ajorned." [90]

The Hopewell Baptist Church, in Abbeville on Woodson's Ridge, added several "colored" members when the names of Martha, Ann, and Dilsey were recorded in 1843. A few others joined in the coming years, and they appear to have done so independently of their masters and on the same terms as their white brethren. In June 1858, the minutes recorded, "After preaching by Bro Sawyer set in conference and opened the door for the reception of members where upon the follow in Bros and Sisters came forward and presented their letters and were received—to wit Jesse H. Awan [Avant?] and his wife Nancy Awan and Elizabeth Evetts and two Slaves of N. B. Pegues to wit Alexander and Deamer." The slaves were typically listed as "colored," a term rarely used in newspapers or private correspondence in these times but apparently adopted in all the churches as a polite term of respect. It was often coupled with "sister" or "brother," as in "our colored sister Dilsey." [91]

Town slaves had more opportunity than their country counterparts to attend the church of their choice. The most popular was the Baptist Church in Oxford, which claimed fifty-four "colored persons" as members by 1859, each one listed with the name of their master, though many of the latter were not Baptists. They were also accepted by the same procedures as whites, by letter of transfer issued by the congregation in their previous home, or by profession of faith and conversion. In the fall of 1861, with the war already under way, the Baptists of Oxford met and "bro W. Duprey proceeded to baptize Dilsey a servent of sister Sarah Howes who had been previously received by the Church." That same fall they admitted "Beckey

College Hill Presbyterian Church, with entrances to slave balcony remaining above the main entrances. (Photograph by author)

servent of W. H. Smither," who had apparently been "brought off with her owner" from Missouri when the war came, and she arrived without a proper letter of dismissal. Becky "was received under the watch care of the church untill she can procure a letter of dismission." Smither, her master, vouched for her, and explained that "owing to the now existing blockade there is no chance to procure her letter from the Church at Palmyra."

Early in the war several slaves were brought into Lafayette County from South Carolina, Georgia, and other parts of the South, their masters apparently thinking they would be safer in the interior. All were admitted with letters from their former congregations. Other new members were local slaves who came into the fold of the church by profession of faith. In July 1862, following preaching by Elder J. J. Sawyer, " 'Susan' and 'Lucy' servents of Mrs Mary Barr and 'Jane' servent of N. R. Prothgro were received into the fellowship of this church upon the relation of their experience of grace all of whom were baptised by brother Sawyer on the evening of the same day." Even following the Union invasion at the end of 1862 and the upheaval that came with the Emancipation Proclamation, still more came into the church.[92]

If slaves were accepted into the fellowship of these churches as equals in the eyes of God, they were not always treated as equals in the eyes of their white brethren. Of course, no slaves served as officers of the church in a position to judge whites, and they did not take seats in the church on an equal basis. As the churches brought the races together in one room on Sundays and for weekly prayer services and socials, it seemed imperative that the slave brethren be physically set apart within the church. In some churches this meant the colored members sat in the back, perhaps separated by a partition in the same way the sexes were in some congregations, but with a different connotation. At the Philadelphia Baptist Church founded in 1845 a "side room" was built to accommodate the slaves.[93] The Antioch Primitive Baptist Church added a room for its black members when it built a new church just south of Oxford in 1855.[94] In the Clear Creek Baptist Church a partition down the center of the church segregated the white men and women while on a balcony above them the slaves attended. All were united in one room and all separated in their respective compartments.[95]

The College Hill Presbyterian Church built a new brick structure in 1845 and about 1851 added a slave balcony or "gallery." This had the additional innovation of two outside entrances, for the men and women slaves who were separated in their pews as well, each with a stairway rising from the ground level outside. The enslaved brethren could enter the church but without coming inside the sanctuary reserved for whites on their level. Sometime after emancipation, when the former slaves abandoned their white brethren for a church of their own, the slave gallery at the College Hill Presbyterian Church was dismantled, as were most of those in other churches. The outside stairways rising to the two doors, high above the entrances used by whites, were also removed, but the doors themselves were left. They remain there even today more than a century and a half later, suspended about fifteen feet or more above and off to the side of the main doors. They serve as curious architectural survivors of the contradictions of a slave society, which on Sundays brought slaves and masters, blacks and whites together to hear the same sermons from the same book and sing the same hymns and learn to live by the same rules of life. Those rules came from a history of the Israelites who had been enslaved in Egypt and led to freedom by God's own Moses to a land of milk and honey. "Go down, Moses, Way down in Egypt's land," went the chorus of a slave spiritual their masters must have heard; "Tell ole Pharaoh, Let my people go." [96] The time would soon come when slaves would transform these biblical metaphors of emancipation into action. None would be more astonished than the people who thought they were the masters.

At which moment the destiny of the land, the nation, the South, the State,
the County, was already whirling into the plunge of its precipice, not that
the State and the South knew it, because the first seconds of fall always
seems like soar: a weightless deliberation preliminary to a rush not down-
ward but upward, the falling body reversed during that second by transub-
stantiation into the upward rush of earth; a soar, an apex, the South's own
apotheosis of its destiny and its pride, Mississippi and Yoknapatawpha
County not last in this, Mississippi among the first of the eleven to ratify
secession. —WILLIAM FAULKNER, Requiem for a Nun

five Revolution

On the Fourth of July 1844, the citizens of Lafayette County, Mississippi, organized a public day of celebration, prayer, speeches, and patriotic ritual all designed to instill a common sense of national identity in this tiny, far-flung corner of the Union. They celebrated the day with a zesty spirit of nationalism that cast their county and state as a community bound by prin-ciple, history, and destiny. "Our village was thronged with both sexes of all ages. All was peace harmony and good feeling," the *Oxford Observer* noted with satisfaction. The celebrants began the day in church with a prayer meeting. "After the benediction the prosession formed and marched to the grove where a sumptuous barbecue was prepared for the occasion. The number in the prosession was variously estimated at from 6 to 800; about 100 ladies partook of the barbecue."

The masculine spirit of partisan pugnacity that usually attended political gatherings of the day was coated with a thick syrup of patriotic sentiment that poured forth in speeches, prayers, and public toasts. The planning committee carefully orchestrated the first round of toasts to underscore the nonpartisan public spirit of the day. "The day we celebrate . . . May it never be palsied by partisan spirit—but like christians, may we in amity and good will commemorate its annual return." Other toasts paid homage to heroes of the Revolution: to the "memory of Washington," and, of course, to the hero for whom the county was named: "Lafayette—Whilst a sentiment of public virtue continues to acclimate the head and heart—the name of Lafayette will be honored as dear to liberty, true glory, virtue and humanity." Another toast celebrated the material prosperity now returning to the land: "Agriculture, Commerce and Manufactures—the brightest jewels in a nation's diadem—they are alike necessary to national independence and prosperity." The most robust patriotic sentiment toasted that day was to the Union and its inviolable integrity. "Our Federal Union—Formed into a perfect compact & hearty body by mutual concession and compromise—cemented by the blood and treasure of the nation's patriots and pure—and illuminated by the brightest constellations of geniuses that has sparkled in the political horizon—and the last hope of human freedom.—Palsied be the heart and withered the hand that shall contemplate its destruction." A. J. Buford, an ardent Whig, proposed a toast to "Our Union.—United by the purest blood of patriotism; preserved by the hand of God, and undivided devotion of a free people. —May the execrations of Heaven fall upon him who would sacrilegiously attempt to desolve the compact." William Mitchell offered another to "Union and liberty . . . and forever, one and inseparable." [1] American nationalism, it seemed, offered the broadest platform for community in this young, transient outpost on the nation's western edge.

Within a remarkably short time, this warm, heartfelt spirit of patriotism had turned sour and irreconcilable among many of Lafayette County's leading citizens. The same men who were swearing fidelity to the nation born in 1776 were plotting its dissolution by the 1850s and leading Mississippi, fast behind South Carolina, out of the Union in January 1861. In Lafayette County, and hundreds of counties like it across the South, a radical cadre of fire-eating southern separatists had begun to move the South toward their own revolution. They sought to forge a new identity as southern nationalists out of their former identity as Americans. They prepared also to defend

the sovereignty of that nation with the blood of their young men. The secessionists of Lafayette County plunged into revolution with exuberant confidence, thinking at first that they were soaring, as Faulkner wrote, never
recognizing they were falling, even after they hit the ground.

American Patriots

At the root of this shift from American patriotism to southern revolution
was the slavery question. By the end of the 1850s Mississippi's more moderate political leaders, men who held fast to the Union and who feared secession would mean war, destruction, and ruin for the South, found they had
precious little political ground on which to stand and advocate compromise
within the Union. It was instead the fire-eaters, the radical separatists, who
won the day. They were a group that found unusual strength and eloquent
leadership in the younger, smaller plantation districts of northern Mississippi. These fire-eaters came to dominate the political debate, and they did
so with such effectiveness that any who dissented were eventually reduced
to arguing not *whether*, but only *when* and *how* Mississippi ought to leave the
Union.

This radical strain of southern sectionalism emerged in the late 1840s
during a time of growing prosperity, with a future that appeared to promise endless prosperity within the Union. Cotton prices had recovered from
the disaster that had followed the Panic of 1837. More land was open to
cotton cultivation, and the plantation economy, with its slave labor system,
was continuing to expand across the South, with profitable increases in the
prices of slaves and land. The economic winds were at their backs.

Before this turn toward separatism, southern politics rarely focused on
truly divisive sectional issues for very long. In Mississippi a political culture
of fiercely competitive democracy took form during the 1830s and 1840s
around national and local issues that divided Democrats against Whigs. The
Whigs' main strength lay in the wealthy planters and townspeople, particularly in the counties that lay along the Yazoo and Mississippi Rivers in the
older sections of the state. The Democrats held sway in the predominantly
white hill country, especially in the new counties formed out of the Chickasaw and Choctaw cessions in the northern portions of the state. Lafayette
County, with widespread slave ownership and a diverse mix of planters, yeomen, and poor whites, lay between these two poles, and it presented something of a microcosm of Mississippi politics. Party politics in the 1830s
and 1840s revolved largely around intrastate sectional divisions and around
issues related to social class and economic policy. Banking laws, state debt

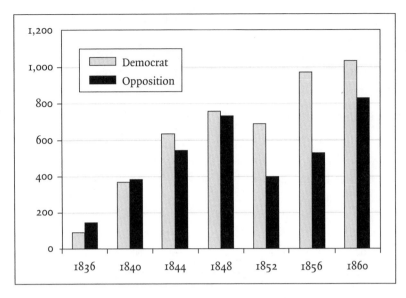

Figure 2. Voting by Party, Presidential Elections, Lafayette County, 1836–1860

repudiation, the location of the state university, state support for a new railroad—these were the bread-and-butter political issues that set Democrats and Whigs to scrapping in Mississippi. Politics were local and practical.

Like politicians everywhere in Jacksonian America, those in Mississippi vied to win the affection of the voter by presenting themselves as men of the people and excoriating their opponents as "aristocrats." They regularly resorted to attacks on character whenever their stand on issues did not appear sufficient to win. Partisan battles took on greater intensity in Mississippi because the once-dominant Whig Party, with its wealthy planter elite centered in the Natchez area, was losing power to the fast-growing counties of northern Mississippi. Not only did the weight of political representation in state politics suddenly tilt northward, but party allegiances also gravitated in favor of the rising Democracy in the northern Chickasaw counties. After a decade of rapid population growth in these new counties, the state in 1846 reapportioned representation and based it on the white population only. Down around Natchez in the older southwestern portion of the state there was talk of seceding from the state of Mississippi and joining Louisiana.[2]

Sectional politics in the state reinforced a vigorous two-party political climate. Even in the predominantly Democratic northern counties, the Whigs were serious challengers. Lafayette County's new electorate voted Whig in the 1836 presidential election and again in 1840. The Whigs had effectively blamed the Panic of 1837 on the Democratic president, Andrew Jackson. By this time, the Whigs had learned to imitate the populist style of Jacksonian politics. Their famous "log cabin campaign" of 1840 had an especially strong appeal among western voters. Whig strength in Lafayette County centered in the town of Oxford and in pockets of the rural countryside, particularly the wealthy plantation lands around College Hill and Abbeville. Though they were rarely able to beat the Democrats in an outright party contest, Whigs were able to win whenever the Democrats divided over candidates or issues, and southern secession became very divisive.

Whigs could also win what were supposed to be nonpartisan contests for county judgeships and other local government positions. This happened often enough that Whigs had managed to dominate county government simply by cloaking their partisan allegiance. Charles G. Butler, Democratic candidate for sheriff in 1843, tried to expose his opponent, J. J. Craig, as a Whig Party crony and complained vehemently that Craig was conducting a low campaign of personal attacks against him.[3] Butler's strategy apparently worked, but other Democrats were not successful. In 1850 "Crabstick" protested that the minority Whigs, by disguising themselves in a strategy of nonpartisan subterfuge, had managed to control most offices in the county. "When the elections are over," he carped to the local Democratic newspaper, "you can see this Whig Conclave winking and grinning at each other, at every corner of the street."[4]

The Lafayette County Democracy, nonetheless, had the advantage of an effective organization led by Jacob Thompson, congressional representative from Mississippi's first district, joined by L. Q. C. Lamar. Though the Democratic press in Lafayette County changed ownership and style frequently before 1860, the Whigs were not even able to sustain a newspaper from one election to the next.[5]

Newspapers of the day were blatantly partisan, and nearly every news item was laced with editorial political invective and personal slurs. One Whig stalwart, writing under the pseudonym "Lafayette," complained in 1844 to the Democratic press about the offensive remarks of "several 'distinguished democrats.' " Among them was Roger Barton, "who catered to the vulgar appetite by retailing one or two of his choice anecdotes . . . too obscene to be here repeated."[6] The Whigs could dish it out as well. One unidentified Whig denounced the Democrats' champion as "the mortal bonyface, lousy-headed, sleepy looking and soppy-mouth JAKE THOMPSON."[7]

Along with personal attacks came class appeals against "aristocratic" party leaders whose condescending attitudes toward the common folk marked them as unfit for rule in a democracy. This strategy played particularly well in the frontier environment of northern Mississippi, especially against the ostentatiously wealthy Natchez Whigs downstate. "It appears to this meeting," the Democrats in Oxford resolved in 1844, "that there are persons among us, whose conduct and bearing towards their less favored fellow citizens point them out, as more fit to be haughty subjects of an Aristocratical Government than humble citizens of a Republic of Freemen." The Democrats denounced a growing tendency among town folk to have exclusive social gatherings "gotten up to enliven the dull routine of village life," but which excluded the "wives, daughters, or sisters of plain, honest, industrious, republican citizens."[8]

The rhetoric of class politics might have played even better had the leaders of the Democratic Party not themselves been among the leading planters and slave owners of the county. Among the voters, Democrats appealed more to yeoman farmers and small slaveholders, while the Whigs drew support from large planters and the middle-class townspeople. Among party leaders, however, differences in social class, wealth, and social standing were not so noticeable.[9] Partisan rivalry, personal slurs, and demagoguery could all flourish within a political culture that took for granted Mississippi's happy membership in a Union that protected and promoted its interests.

From Mississippi to Mexico

During the mid-1840s whites in Mississippi had every reason to see themselves as a people favored and protected by the national government. Two Tennessee neighbors, Democrats Andrew Jackson and James K. Polk, had been elected to the highest office of the land. It was President Jackson who had thrown open the Chickasaw and Choctaw lands of Mississippi to American settlement. Now in 1844 President James K. Polk, whose Mississippi plantation lay a few miles from Oxford, embarked on an aggressive program of westward expansion. His ambition for America's "Manifest Destiny" encompassed not only the annexation of Texas into the Union but also a vast new western territory that extended United States claims all the way to California. For a time it seemed to open a new empire for slavery, a succession of new Mississippi-like frontiers, new cotton lands and new markets for the domestic slave trade. Equally important was the expectation of new political strength for the slave South—new states sending senators and congressmen to safeguard the future of slavery against any threats the emerging antislavery forces might pose.

When President Polk declared war against Mexico in 1846, Mississippians sprang enthusiastically to the call to arms. Polk called for one regiment from Mississippi, but more than enough for two full regiments clamored for a place in the Mississippi army, eager to prove their patriotism and honor. Eventually three Mississippi regiments saw duty in Mexico.

Lafayette County's men were at the forefront of the call to arms, and they contributed to no less than six companies, ninety-three men in all.[10] Captain William Delay, Democratic leader and editor of the *Oxford Observer*, led the Lafayette County men to war. Born in Kentucky and said to be of French origin (and a probable inspiration for Faulkner's "Old Frenchman"), Delay was a veteran of the Black Hawk War and had come to Mississippi only a few years earlier. Few local men were more suited for military leadership than Delay, and he was quickly elected captain of the Lafayette County Guards.

The new company gathered in the Cumberland Presbyterian Church, where the ladies of Oxford presented them with a banner they had made. The men marched off to Vicksburg, where they were mustered into service, and then on to Mexico. Twenty-eight of the more than ninety men who marched south that summer never returned. Mississippi soldiers were notable throughout the war for their courage and sacrifice. William Delay later recalled, "The survivors returned bringing with them the same banner, which had been presented them by the ladies of this place; though much tattered and torn, there was no stain of dishonor upon it."[11]

The war with Mexico brought a bracing self-assurance to the political and military leaders of the South. It was a stunning triumph in which southern officers, Mississippians Jefferson Davis and John Quitman not least among them, had played decisive roles. The triumph of 1848 presaged the confidence of 1861.

The war with Mexico also created two wedges that cut into the bonds between the South and the Union: the Wilmot Proviso and the Compromise of 1850. The first was the rallying point for northern Whigs and a disturbing number of northern Democrats who displayed their distaste for the expansion of slavery in the West by supporting David Wilmot's congressional provision that all territory gained in the war against Mexico would be prohibited to slavery. The Compromise of 1850 put into law new restrictions on slavery and set in place important elements of a national policy that boded ill for slavery.

Those who saw southern rights in peril witnessed the North rising in population and political power, and they saw it falling under the influence of a fanatical and willful band of abolitionists. "Our Northern brethren," the Democratic editor in Oxford wrote, "influenced by feelings of fanaticism or stimulated by unjust and ungenerous prejudices have in repeated instances for many years manifested, a settled hostility to the Southern States, and a growing disposition to intermeddle with the *relation between the master and his slave*."[12]

Southern Rights

The courthouse was crowded with men called to rally support for the Nashville Convention, which was about to convene to deliberate the South's response to antislavery measures in the Compromise of 1850. The resolutions they approved almost unanimously that evening warned that "a fearful and important crisis has arrived in the history of our country, . . . [brought on by] the continued attempts by the Freesoil and Abolition party of the North, to interfere with the institution of slavery in the South." A young man who had just arrived in town a year before, with the auspicious name of Lucius Quintus Cincinnatus Lamar, rose and spoke with stirring eloquence in support of the convention. In a display of bipartisan unity, Thomas Jefferson Word, a Whig from Pontotoc (and William Faulkner's ancestor), also spoke for bipartisan unity in defense of southern rights. In the summer of 1850, as politicians in Washington scrambled to find compromise positions and defuse the sectional crisis, many in Lafayette County were ready for revolution.[13]

The Compromise of 1850 defused the Nashville Convention, but in Lafayette County it only aggravated the feelings of hostility and suspicion toward the North. "The Clay compromise is a positive surrender of everything to the Abolitionists," the Democratic newspaper thundered, "and if it be accepted by the South, the fanatics have a plain and direct invitation to commence the crusade against slavery in the states, themselves." Support for the compromise was limited only to Whigs they claimed. Paul Barringer, a large planter and pro-Union Whig, worried that the provisions against slavery would give the secessionists a powerful weapon; "there are disunion men in this state that will use every effort to break up the Union."[14]

At this stage southern nationalism still remained nested within loyalty to the American nation. The strategy was to join a belligerent threat of secession to a demand for "southern rights" *within* the Union. Out of this came the essential materials of a southern nationalist ideology, one that emphasized the South's beleaguered status and exaggerated the abolitionist threat to slavery in the states where it existed. Above all, southern rights rhetoric made secession no longer an unthinkable option. Still, separatism remained a highly divisive issue that Democrats embraced at the peril of splitting their ranks and handing victory to the Whigs.

Led by the Democrats, Lafayette County's politicians joined the Southern Rights movement that sprang up in response to the compromise. Its aim was to bridge partisan divisions in defense of common regional interests. Even as they threatened southern separatism, they vilified the abolitionists as enemies of national harmony. The first Southern Rights assembly met in

Oxford in July 1850. It promised to bring both parties together on common platform "from which we may bid defiance to the abolitionists, and maintain the union." "Let us then try once more to unite like a band of brothers. Whig and Democrat, Ultra and Conservative, come up and participate in this family meeting."[15]

That same July the citizens of Lafayette greeted the Fourth with unusual seriousness, and no one was yet prepared to denounce the Union. The day was "handsomely and appropriately celebrated in Oxford, by the Sons of Temperance in connexion with the Sabbath Schools and the two Literary Societies of the University." The Oxford Brass Band, performing with "unusual skill and ability," led a large procession of town and country people to the Presbyterian Church for prayer and temperance addresses.[16]

The Southern Rights meeting that followed a few days later laid down the foundations for a new southern union of common interests, chief among them the shared interest in protecting slavery. A committee made up of three Whigs and three Democrats put forth resolutions the meeting roundly endorsed. "Whereas, we a portion of the people of Lafayette county without distinction of party, . . . believe the question of Slavery is one of such vital interest to the South that all party considerations and distinctions should be left out of view." Southern rights, they affirmed, were essential to—not subversive of—the ideal of union: "The preservation of the Federal Union of these states . . . is dear beyond price to every Southern patriot." They went on to promise "peace and harmony" in place of "discord and confusion" if the North would safeguard southern rights within the Union.[17]

The conflict was cast as a question of honor and respect as well as one of constitutional principles. The abolitionists in power seemed to be saying "in effect that we southern men are so corrupted and degraded by the institution of negro slavery, that we must not be permitted as slave-holders, to put our feet upon this country [California], conquered principally by our valor and prowess."[18]

The Southern Rights rhetoric now took on the familiar Lockean logic of the right to revolution, which proceeded from evidence that the South was being denied natural rights and was forced to choose between being "enslaved" by tyrannical antislavery forces or revolting. "The Ark of our safety has been sunk beneath the black billows of a cruel and unrelenting fanaticism. We have no hope from the Constitution or the Union, for the one has been totally disregarded while the other is used only to rivet our chains the more closely." They proclaimed their natural rights, "the rights of freemen! No government can take these natural rights away, for they are the gift of God. Let us, then, with one accord, with one heart and mind— as one man—in Union and harmony—strike for our rights, our property,

L. Q. C. Lamar, leading Democratic fire-eater, congressman, and later U.S. Supreme Court justice, in 1861. (Courtesy of Special Collections, University of Mississippi)

our domestic altars and firesides, and leave the consequences to that over-ruling Providence which giveth the victory to the Noble, the Brave, and the True." [19] "What Ought the South to Do?," a letter from "Senex" asked. "will the South . . . submit to these things, or will she resist and depend upon herself for the protection and preservation of her own rights." [20]

Submit or resist; that was exactly the choice radical Southern Rights advocates wanted to pose. What exactly did resistance mean? The answer remained vague, but the ultimate threat was separatism. They continued to advance the spirit of southern nationalism within a bipartisan spirit that placed region above party, but there were gaping divisions already.

The spirit of party and of Union soon pierced the veil of Southern Rights unity. A meeting in November 1851 witnessed open conflict over the question of disunion. Several of the county's Democratic leaders stood and spoke in favor of Southern Rights: Jacob Thompson, his brother, John W. Thompson, and Hugh R. Miller, judge of the circuit court. Then Colonel I. N. Davis gave an impassioned and lengthy speech appealing to pro-Union sentiment. The Democratic account ridiculed the "submissionists" and sneered at Davis's speech as one of those "bombastic Fourth of July orations." As Davis stepped down, people in the crowd began chanting for the eloquent fire-eater L. Q. C. Lamar to come forth and answer this "submissionist" pro-Union appeal.[21]

Lamar gave a vehement speech denouncing Davis and any who would encourage submission; then the meeting turned contentious. The Unionist faction complained that the Democrats tried to silence the opponents of disunion. The Democrats responded by explaining that the meeting was never intended to *debate* the issues; it was called by "the friends of 'Southern Rights and the Constitution' " and " 'Submissionists' came . . . without *any invitation.*" The Unionists saw the meeting as an opportunity to contest the Southern Rights movement's effort to dominate the debate, and they had packed the meeting with their friends. But the Southern Rights forces had the votes; they shut off debate and controlled the meeting. But any illusion of bipartisan unity in support of Southern Rights was dispelled by the factious character of this meeting.[22]

The Southern Rights advocates continued efforts to build bipartisan support, now with a permanent State Rights Association. "Friends of the downtrodden South — Men of Southern hearts" were invited to the organizational meeting.[23] The county's leading Democrats, B. F. Dill, James Brown, J. F. Cushman, and J. M. Howry, guided the meeting. They approved a constitution, appointed officers from each beat of the county, and planned monthly meetings with invited speakers. The county association was one of several that had sprung up that year, all reporting to a central association in Jackson.[24]

Beneath all the talk of bipartisan southern unity, political and personal dissension was seething. "The agitation of this slavery question at the South I fear is going to produce a great deal of mischief," Paul Barringer wrote to his brother. "You have but little idea the extent for the bad feeling between the parties here. It is becoming as bad as the day of Nullification in [South Carolina]."[25] The breach in ranks over the wisdom of secession had by now opened into a full-scale backlash against the fire-eaters. U.S. senator Henry Foote, a leading Democrat and former ally of the Southern Rights movement, broke with them, announced his support for the Compromise of 1850, and ran for governor in 1851 on the Union ticket, a bipartisan platform erected by pro-Union Democrats and their Whig allies.

The regular Democratic Party campaign that year was plagued by internal dissension, and Jefferson Davis, their candidate, lost to Henry Foote, setting the Southern Rights movement back.[26] In 1853 Governor Foote, together with a group of alienated northern Mississippi Democrats, staged what came to be known as the "Chickasaw Rebellion." Drawing support from the northern counties in the Chickasaw and Choctaw cessions, they rebelled against the dominance of the southwestern river counties and sent their candidate, Reuben Davis of Pontotoc County, to Congress.[27]

Instead of capitalizing on the disarray in the Mississippi Democratic Party, the Whigs were collapsing as a national political organization beginning in 1852. Sectional divisions tore the Whigs apart when the party's northern wing nominated General Winfield Scott as president. Scott was a Virginian but considered weak in defense of slavery. Lafayette County Whigs were disgusted with the nomination. Franc Duval, editor of the Whig's short-lived *Star of Union*, announced the newspaper's death; he sold the press and office to his Democratic rival and left town. Charles Fontaine, a leading Democrat in northern Mississippi, gloated, "We have broken the enthusiasm of the Whigs, and you know that much depends upon *enthusiasm*. It carries along the floating vote. Mississippi is safe for the Democracy." [28] It was, in effect, the end of the Whig Party and the end of any viable opposition to the Democratic Party in the South.[29]

Even as their opposition collapsed, many leading Democrats had come to realize that their continued success in Mississippi depended on their ability to retain the moderate center and not alienate pro-Union voters by bellicose talk of secession. Fire-eater L. Q. C. Lamar complained that his party tried to muzzle him because of his radical views on the issue. After two years of what appeared to be a brilliant political career in the making, Lamar left Oxford in 1852 to return home to Georgia. He left disgusted with the tendency of the party's elders to compromise southern rights for the sake of national unity. "My party has quit its principles," he wrote before departing for Georgia, "and is begging to get admission into a National party which we denounced as thoroughly corrupted on the slavery question. I cannot leave it but I will leave politics." [30] With voices like Lamar's stilled, it seemed for the moment that more moderate ones might be heard.

Not for long. By the mid-1850s the politics of sectionalism on the national stage had given new life to the Southern Rights movement following the imbroglio of Bleeding Kansas that ensued from the Kansas-Nebraska Act of 1854. L. Q. C. Lamar returned to Lafayette County in 1855 and soon rose to the fore as a leading voice for the resuscitated cause of secession. Only thirty years old, he was still struggling to establish a successful career in law and politics. His brief return to Georgia had brought disappointment in both endeavors. Back in Mississippi, he settled near Abbeville on some of the best cotton land in the county. Apparently with help from his father-in-law, Augustus B. Longstreet, Lamar purchased twenty-six slaves and a thousand-acre plantation he named Solitude. While the slaves began clearing and planting land, Lamar sought income by practicing law with a partner in Holly Springs. His fortunes were rising when the siren call of politics pulled him back into the arena and into the storm center of the secessionist revolution.[31]

After 1854, the rise of the new Republican Party, with its explicit antislavery stance, gave southern Democrats a new impetus to embrace the politics of sectionalism. Still, in northern Mississippi sentiment remained divided on secession, and the lessons of 1851 gave cautious men reason to worry that pro-Union Democrats would defect from an extremist position. Lamar's name was raised as a possible candidate for representative from Mississippi's first congressional district when the incumbent stepped down in 1857, but when party leaders met in Holly Springs to nominate candidates they spurned Lamar as too extreme and divisive. After fifty-six ballots, none of the leading candidates could secure a majority; Lamar's name was put before the convention and a few ballots later he was finally nominated. Lamar ran against James Lusk Alcorn, a former Whig and pro-Union man well known to northern Mississippi voters. Lamar, with his eloquence and with the support of Jacob Thompson, won with a handy majority. Lafayette County's fire-eating radical had been politically reborn and was on his way to Washington.

Abolitionists in Our Midst

The sectional crisis about to be acted out on the national stage took on an immediate and personal meaning within the local world of race and slavery in Lafayette County. During the 1850s the threat of abolitionism had become more than rhetoric and pamphlets emanating from distant organizations and political leaders in the North. It came to be seen as an insidious force whose agents were working within the South—indeed, within Lafayette County and neighboring counties. Its purpose was no longer simply to persuade whites of the immorality of slavery. The abolitionist campaign was now understood as a direct action underground movement, coordinated by something akin to a terrorist organization aimed at subverting slave loyalty, inciting slaves to rise in rebellion, to murder their masters, and inflict mayhem on any white person. It is only in this context of racial fear that we can understand the final triumph of the separatists.

Newspaper reports of furtive abolitionist agents and conspiracies of insurrectionary slaves often rested on frail evidence, but behind these were vivid memories of very real insurrections in Virginia, Jamaica, and Santo Domingo. Fears of such bloody uprisings lay at the very core of Mississippi's slave society. They were fears that went well beyond the material concerns slave owners had for protecting their property; in the minds of many Mississippi whites the specter of abolitionism now portended general racial chaos. According to this creed, all white people, whether or not they owned slaves, were besieged by enemies: treacherous abolitionists invading from without and murderous slaves rising from below.

Early signs of the abolitionist scare emerged during the Southern Rights campaign of 1851. One typical expression of concern focused on Yankee schoolteachers who might infect the southern mind with abolitionism: "We conscientiously believe that these yankee school-masters have done more than all other causes in combination, to familiarize the southern mind with the abolition of slavery, and to beget the feeling of pusillanimity, which is ready to concede away all our political and social rights." One advertisement for a school assured parents that the teacher was a "Southerner by birth, in feeling and education, an experienced teacher, and a complete gentleman."[32]

The hysteria over subversive abolitionists and rebellious slaves conveniently complemented the cause of the extreme secessionists. Any evidence of the abolitionist menace stood as proof of an antislavery conspiracy and brought the matter home to an immediate example of the enemy within. In the frenzy over abolitionist subversion was also found convenient justification to censor and intimidate political enemies and force conformity to the separatist party line. Mississippi, feeling besieged by northern enemies, was quickly becoming a closed society.[33]

Tolerance for even the most private debate over slavery was fast disappearing. William Hale, a Methodist minister and small farmer who lived in Liberty Hill, a small community in the hilly northeastern section of the county, had made some careless remarks one day in September questioning God's approval of slavery. Whatever he said was in private conversation with Thomas R. Williams, a man Hale must have considered a trustworthy friend. No one ever accused Hale of preaching antislavery sentiments from the pulpit or of voicing any public expression of antislavery. He was alleged to have said the Bible disapproved of slavery and that God was bringing the crisis over slavery to the nation as a means of working out his will to free the slaves. Williams managed to get Hale to acknowledge his remarks in front of several other men, and they, with Williams, signed a public letter denouncing Hale as an agent of abolitionism. "This is to certify that we have heard the Rev. Wm. Hale acknowledge to Thos. R. Williams, at Liberty Hill, on the 1st of Sept. 1851, that he (Hale) had said to him (Williams) in a previous conversation, 'that the thought had occasionally passed through his mind that may be the FINGER OF GOD was at work, in this matter of controversy between the Northern and Southern parts of the Confederacy, IN LIBERATING THE NEGROES FROM BONDAGE, as it did the Children of Israel from Egyptian Bondage.'" Hale tried to deny ever doubting the Bible's support of slavery, but he did acknowledge his comments about God's role in the sectional conflict. Hale was a pro-Union delegate to the state convention called to decide on Mississippi's response to the Compromise of 1850, so there were political motives in discrediting him.[34] Freedom of speech at

Liberty Hill and across the South was becoming a dangerous right to exercise for those who questioned slavery or secession—or God's approval of either.

This public denunciation must have had a chilling effect on speech of all kinds. Lafayette County, along with much of the South, was closing off serious debate. Slavery had become the centerpiece of a broader faith that now encompassed racial control and southern rights, and it was a faith no one could question without risk of expulsion from the community.

Fear of abolitionist designs to incite insurrection and destroy slavery had long been linked to intentions that went well beyond the goal of emancipating slaves. The more disturbing aim of abolitionists, some feared, was racial equality and amalgamation. In a lengthy series of articles in the local Democratic press on the antislavery movement, "Decius" took pains to distinguish between free soilers, who opposed the expansion of slavery because the presence of slavery and black people were detrimental to whites, and abolitionists, who wanted complete social equality between the races. "The bulk of the abolitionists religiously believe that the races of all colors are perfectly equal; and so they wish their widows, sisters and daughters to marry freely into all colors, so as eventually to wipe out what nature has given, and give a new and common color not yet pencilled or imagined!" [35]

Only slavery, its defenders argued, could protect white racial supremacy and purity. In an address before the Central Southern Rights Association of Mississippi, the honorable A. Hutchinson focused his attack on "those who propose equality and amalgamation," and he drew on the Bible and scientific evidence on the ethnography of races to support his plea to defend slavery against abolitionists.[36] Ideas that joined slavery to racial concerns had been around at least since Thomas Jefferson's time. They now helped thrust the defense of slavery beyond the narrow limits of the material interests of the slave owners into the broader platform of white racial supremacy, something all whites might have a stake in defending.

When secessionist agitation retreated following the setback of 1851, the frenzy that had arisen over antislavery conspiracies appears to have subsided temporarily. By the end of the 1850s, however, as sectional conflict peaked and the Mississippi secessionists sought to gain advantage over their opponents, the anxiety about subversion from within resurfaced with militant intensity. John Brown's raid on Harpers Ferry in 1859 compelled anxious slave masters in Lafayette County once again to see the intent of abolitionism not solely as a political movement aimed at regulating or limiting the expansion of slavery but also as a direct action incendiary movement of fanatics intent on inciting slaves to rise up and murder whites. White southerners responded with their own direct action. By 1858 the former

slave patrol no longer seemed adequate to the threat. Vigilance committees, militias, some calling themselves Minute Men, cropped up in several
Mississippi counties. They drew many men who were not formerly active in
politics into organized activities that transformed heretofore distant, abstract political issues into issues everyone could understand and none could
gainsay: the defense of home and family, women and children, all imperiled
by racial holocaust.

The agents of slave insurrection were found everywhere by 1860, and
any stranger that wandered into the county became suspect. One report described a "Dangerous Character," a man calling himself Lieutenant Henry
W. Paul, who showed up in Oxford offering fencing lessons. He had enlisted only two pupils and was charging expensive tuition and board. In
more rational times Lieutenant Paul's hapless business venture might have
passed without notice, but in the heightened tensions of 1860 "this gave
rise to suspicions, and a committee of the vigilance police of Oxford called
on the Lieutenant." They interrogated him about his origins and determined that Paul had not told the truth when he said he was from Virginia—
he was actually from Vermont. Further questioning revealed that he was related to the Cook family "of John Brown memory." He was promptly ordered
out of town, and the editor published a description of Paul in hopes of
warning other communities about this subversive agent.[37]

Another supposed abolitionist conspiracy came to light near Abbeville
sometime around 1859. A northerner, an unnamed mechanic who lived
in the neighborhood, was accused of "holding secret caucuses with the
negroes, and in a sneaking way informing them of the plans being laid by
the Abolition party for their freedom." The story "flew like fire through dry
stubble over the country." This man soon found himself arrested, put on
trial in Oxford, and thrown in jail. A mob entered the jail, took the prisoner
off to the woods north of town, gave him "the worst thrashing" of his life,
and ordered him to "make tracks for yankeedom."[38]

In May 1861 a suspicious band of men thought to be passing as wandering beggars were accused of abolitionist activities. "Last week a number
of beggars infested the suburbs of Oxford," the local newspaper reported.
"Some of them were, apparently, hale and hearty men, begging for food.
All such 'chaps' should be tied up to a sapling and just about thirty-nine
stripes administered by a deputized stout negro." Those intruders, the editor accused, were "spies from the enemy." "Let them be closely watched,
and, doubtless, ere long, they will be caught in some act entitling them to
hempen cravats stretched from the limbs of our forest trees." A western
community that from its beginnings had a steady stream of newcomers arriving was now warned to regard them as potential enemies. "The times

require that *all* strangers, of the least suspicious appearance, should be examined before vigilance committees and dealt with as their merits may justify." [39]

The mere suspicion of subversion became enough to lead authorities to expel citizens as well as strangers from the community. A brief article in the local paper in January 1861 reported that "a man named Simpson, and his son-in-law, together with their families, were ordered to leave this vicinity, for the utterance of abolition sentiments." The Simpsons reportedly stopped in Pontotoc, and the Oxford paper urged its neighbors to "pass them on," warning that "there is not the shadow of a doubt that Simpson and his son-in-law are abolitionists." [40]

Other cases involved less politically motivated but nonetheless dangerous subversion of the slave regime. Some accused a carpenter named Jones of selling liquor to Negroes, a common enough offense in the past but one that now required he be "escorted to the line" and warned out of the county. An unidentified Irishman was also thought to be selling liquor to slaves and ordered to leave the county. [41] The local newspaper urged vigilance over another local suspect in 1861: "Watch him," the article warned, without naming anyone, a "certain miller in this county is in the habit of going into the woods with negroes" and "delighting them by reading to them choice passages from the Memphis *Bulletin*" (a pro-Union newspaper). He might have "other incendiary documents," but that one "is surely bad enough." [42]

"It was now dangerous to utter a word in favour of the Union," one stubborn opponent of secession reported. "Many Suspected of Union sentiments were lynched" by "self-constituted vigilance committees." It was "a reign of terror" in which all who did not fall in line with the secessionist movement "were regarded as being tinctured with abolitionism." [43]

Along with reports of subversive abolitionists came rumors of slave conspiracies and incidences of defiant behavior among slaves in and around Lafayette County. In the town of Sardis, a few miles west in Panola County, local whites flogged a black mechanic until he confessed to an insurrectionary plot during the Christmas holidays in 1860. They organized a vigilance committee to "examine" the slaves, and that Christmas they were "never under better subjection." [44] There were several local reports of murder and arson, the latter often attributed to slaves or to parties unknown. One account of "An Incendiary" reported that the cotton gin belonging to J. M. Dooley was set on fire by a slave of Dudley Isom. "The fiendish fellow confessed that he had fired the house, and that he had done it 'for devilment.' " [45]

From a few miles north came the terrifying report in November 1860 of a slave named Dick, who killed his overseer the previous spring and now stood to suffer "the extreme penalty of the law, death by hanging." A crowd of "several thousand people" gathered in Holly Springs to witness the execution. What they were treated to was a defiant, brazenly remorseless slave who mocked his executioners from the gallows. "The wretch was profane and exultant," the newspaper reported. Instead of offering last words of denial or apology, Dick "urged the executioner to 'hurry up'; saying that he 'wanted to get to dinner in hell before the crowd down there had grabbed everything worth eating.' "[46]

There were other more frightening reports of collective slave insurrection nearby. The "excitement at Holly Springs" centered on "rumors reaching them of insubordination among the negroes." Whatever the reality, the people of Marshall County took it seriously and imposed a militant watch over their slaves. "A large extra police force was appointed, and citizens generally turned themselves into patrol clubs, who kept a vigilant watch all night, but no disturbance occurred." The press report gave every reason to take the threat with the utmost seriousness. "All things considered, there exists not the least doubt in our mind but that a deep laid scheme for general revolt exists in the South, and we suggest the great propriety of the citizens everywhere forming vigilant committees and keeping on the alert." With no hint of irony, the editor added the by now familiar allusion to an earlier revolution: " 'Eternal vigilance is the price of liberty.' "[47]

Rumors of "a contemplated rising of the darkies," together with stories of abolitionist agents and individual acts of slave rebellion, all fed on one another. There is, one editor asserted, "a determination on the part of the servile population of portions of our county, instigated by abolition emissaries in our midst, to make an attempt at insurrection." While the towns and rural beats deputized new police to patrol the slaves, "many citizens volunteered their services." Nothing less than "Sleepless vigilance is necessary—not so much over the deluded negro as over suspicious white men in our midst. The South is filled with abolition emissaries."[48]

The Paddyrollers Ride

Whites in Lafayette County suddenly saw themselves surrounded by a vast population of slaves who, they were now told, might rise and murder them in their beds at night. The alarm over insurrectionary slaves led the Lafayette County citizens to construct a whole new regimen of surveillance and discipline, one that took form outside the confines of local government. County-appointed slave patrols had been in operation, albeit with lax rigor, since the county's beginning. Efforts to strengthen the patrol in 1858 were followed the next year by several new measures. An August 1859 resolution issued that the patrols "are Commanded to wride at least four times in each month." By April 1861 the slave patrols of the county consisted of twenty-eight men, and they were now expected to "Patrole at least every two weeks and as often as they may think necessary, and report to this court, as the law directs."[49]

The county patrols were no longer deemed sufficient to the task of controlling the slaves. A rash of new citizens groups began turning to new measures, all supplementary to and outside of the authority of local government. The Agricultural Association, which had formerly concerned itself with transportation and economic progress, now turned its attention to suppressing the county's slave population. Its members met in the courthouse in October 1860 to draft "suitable rules for the more strict governance of negroes." The present patrol system, they determined was "inadequate to the prevention of mischiefs which are to be apprehended under the state of things now existing in the country."[50] They drafted an elaborate new slave code with a series of detailed rules intended to limit the freedom of slaves to move about and mingle with others but also to discourage whites from undermining slave subordination. One regulation insisted that "no negro be allowed, under any circumstances, to leave home without the written permission of his owner, employer, or overseer." Another aimed at repressing commerce with slaves providing that "no negro be allowed to buy or sell anything whatever, without a written permit." The code imposed a ten o'clock curfew and insisted that "the owner or manager on every plantation habitually visit each negro cabin, after ten o'clock at night, at least twice in every month, at irregular intervals, and oftener if necessary."[51] Several regulations indicate the new vigilantes were especially anxious about the dangers of slaves gathering in town. One specified that "no negro, under any circumstances, be allowed, at night or on Sunday, to visit Oxford, or any other place where goods are kept for sale, for the purpose of trading." They asked the town of Oxford to organize a "paid police or . . . a vigilant town patrol" to enforce order. Finally, they warned that "the practice of permitting negroes to attend barbecues" and other "political discussions" is "of pernicious tendency" and ought to be stopped.[52]

Other agencies for the control of slaves also cropped up suddenly in the form of new militia and vigilante groups. Ostensibly designed to enforce the new regimen of slave control, they often served as the armed terrorist wing of the secessionist political movement aimed at intimidating the opposition and silencing dissent among whites.

What was striking about the new militancy in Lafayette County was the suddenness and multiplicity of new armed militia groups that sprang into existence, especially between the fall of the 1860 presidential election and the beginning of war in 1861. In September 1860, General Bickley, the "father" of the KGC (Knights of the Golden Circle), came to Oxford and found an immediate following. Within a month, about thirty-five members in the Oxford Castle were reported to be meeting regularly.[53] In its secrecy and ceremony, its hierarchy of ranks and pompous medieval titles, and above all in its tactics of terror, the KGC foreshadowed the Ku Klux Klan. Its political purpose was soon made clear. It aimed at intimidating any whites involved in subverting slavery in any way. "Vigilance committees are being formed everywhere South," the approving Oxford editor reported, "and their duty undoubtedly is to hang up every white man convicted of insurrectionary movements."[54]

Soon after Lincoln's election, the citizens of Lafayette rushed to form a militia group, one of dozens that cropped up in the South calling itself the "Minute Men" in tribute to the spirit of 1776. The Democratic editor, Harold Falconer, called local men to the organizing meeting at the courthouse on Friday night with enthusiasm: "Speeches will be made. Let every man attend."[55] Even this seemed insufficient to the task of vigilance, for no sooner did the KGC and Minute Men begin than a Home Guard was proposed. The press cheered them on: "the older men of the community" propose to organize a military company "to defend their firesides and the dear household deities that circle round them."[56] Armed and ready for enemies within and without, vigilant men of Lafayette County prepared to defend their homeland.

The Closing of the Mississippi Mind

The arming of the citizenry and the implication of emergency these citizens' militias signified all helped to reify the perception of a people besieged by enemies. The secessionists were right, it all seemed to say; the threat to southern rights was real, and the alternative to armed vigilance was some unthinkable bloodbath of racial violence. For the men who joined these militia and vigilante groups, for the women and others who witnessed their activities, the abstract political issues surrounding the prolonged debate over slavery and states' rights were all neatly reduced to a basic fear. The real intent of the abolitionists, they could now see, was not to advance their cause by moral suasion or legislation but to incite slaves to rebel, to rise up against their masters.[57] The fire-eaters' political opponents accused them of whipping up hysterical fears as a political tactic, but if these fears were the product of propaganda, they were no less real.

The alarm over abolitionism proved useful in suppressing opposition to the rising separatist movement. One vigilance committee made this clear when it resolved to "take notice of, and punish all and every persons who may be guilty of any misdemeanor, or prove themselves untrue to the South, or southern Rights, in any way whatever." [58] One secessionist candidate in a nearby county bragged openly that "Seven tory-submissionists were hanged in one day," and the pro-Union candidate was intimidated into silence.[59] The distinction between loyal opposition to Southern Rights and abolitionist treachery had been obscured but was not yet obliterated.

The closing of the Mississippi mind to anything it perceived as an attack on slavery and southern rights was most evident in the public vilification of Frederick A. Barnard, president of the faculty of the University of Mississippi, in March 1860. One of Barnard's slaves (he owned two), a house servant named Jane, had been "cruelly outraged and beaten" by a university student named Humphreys. The beating, Humphreys claimed, was provoked by some display of disrespect by the slave toward him. Her injuries were severe and were still evident two months after her beating. Humphreys had earned a reputation for "bad character," and though there were no eyewitnesses, Barnard and his wife believed Jane, who said it was an unprovoked assault. Barnard demanded that the faculty dismiss the student. But the faculty refused, not because they believed Humphreys, they explained, but because this would be taking a slave's word over that of a white man. Barnard forced the student out over the faculty's objections, but one of Barnard's enemies (Dr. Henry Branham, an Oxford resident and relative of L. Q. C. Lamar) took the occasion to denounce him as "unsound on the slavery question" because he accepted "negro testimony" against a white man. Barnard reacted strongly and demanded a trial before the University Board of Trustees where he would face the accusations against him openly.

Behind the vendetta against Barnard were academic politics of the most venal order. Barnard was a northerner and an Episcopalian, both grounds for suspicion in Mississippi by this time. He had already been the target of attacks from enemies within and outside the university since he had been elected in 1856 to succeed Augustus B. Longstreet. He had won little affection by his efforts to impose discipline and academic rigor. Regarded by many as a reserve of aristocratic decadence, the university had won a reputation as a resort for wealthy planters' sons to drink, gamble, and carouse. Instead of tending to their studies, some students had become notorious for stealing chickens, accosting slaves, and "terrorizing" the good citizens of Oxford with their drinking and rowdy behavior.[60]

Though the Board of Trustees absolved Barnard, his trial became a public display of Mississippi's diminishing tolerance for any form of dissent on the slavery question. Barnard won whatever support he had only by repudiating any question about his loyalty to slavery and to southern rights. "I was born at the North," he pleaded before his accusers. "That I cannot help. I was not consulted in the matter. I am a slave-holder, and, if I know myself, I am 'sound on the slavery question.' " Indeed, Jacob Thompson (a trustee of the university) in a private letter praised Barnard's defense of his slave, Jane, as the highest example of slaveholder paternalism. "No man has a right to touch [my servant] without my consent," Thompson confided, "and he who would not do the same [as Barnard] would be despised by every man in Oxford." [61] But Thompson was conspicuously private with these thoughts, as were others who lamented Barnard's persecution but did nothing to defend him publicly. When Barnard left for a new post in New York later in 1860, it served as another example of the price men paid for any suspicion of nonconformity on the issues of slavery and race.

Triumph of the Fire-eaters

In the House of Representatives Lafayette County's congressman, L. Q. C. Lamar, rose to deliver his maiden speech in 1858. He made clear his absolute commitment to southern rights. "Others may boast of their . . . love of this Union. With me, I confess that the promotion of Southern interests is second in importance only to the preservation of Southern honor." [62] Lamar and the Mississippi delegation were notable for their aggressive defense of southern rights and their militant threats of secession and war. At times their zeal went beyond rhetorical sword rattling. In February 1858 a fistfight and general melee broke out on the floor of the House during debates over the Kansas question, and the honorable delegation from Mississippi was at the center of the brawl. Lamar was seen in a punching and shoving match with Owen Lovejoy, Republican congressman from Illinois. Meanwhile, his fellow Mississippian, the Honorable William Barksdale, was slugging it out with several foes when someone grabbed his hairpiece and flung it across the floor. Barksdale went scrambling on hands and knees to recover it, the sight of which suddenly sent the entire House into gales of laughter bringing the "shindy" to an end.[63]

There was no humor to the militant rhetoric of Lamar and his fellow Mississippians, however. If the protection of southern rights under the Constitution was to be violated, Lamar threatened in December 1859, "I war upon your government, I am against it. I raise then the banner of secession, and I will fight under it as long as the blood flows and ebbs in my veins." [64] His colleague Reuben Davis, also from northern Mississippi, warned Republicans that the attack on slavery was forcing the South into "revolution," one that would fail only after the South was "deluged with blood and made desolate with fire." The "South will resist with arms—resist to the dissevering of the last ties that bind these States together—resist to the pulling down of this grand political fabric of ours to its foundation."

On the eve of the 1860 election Reuben Davis issued another prescient warning of the coming violence: "We will resist . . . we will sacrifice our lives, . . . and convert our sunny South . . . into a wilderness waste." Before the South will be "driven one inch beyond where we now stand; we will be butchered first."[65] Both Lamar and Davis seemed to be warning their fellow Mississippians as much as their adversaries that the road they were taking was likely to be bloody, but none dared speak of the fearful consequences of war.

Back in Oxford, their constituents seemed all too ready for blood. In the fall of 1860 Mississippi governor John J. Pettus came to Oxford to address a large audience packed into the courthouse. E. A. Smith, a boy of fourteen, remembered the emotions Pettus stirred in the crowd that day. The governor's voice was "literally groaning like the roar of a volcano belching forth its angry fires." Pettus held his hands "as if in the act of firing a gun" and said: "The next compromise we offer, and the next demand we make, will be with our guns leveled at the breasts of the unfeeling tyrants and saying, we fight, we die, but we yield no more." The "wild thunders of applause that shook that building" that day, Smith recalled vividly. "Fists of vengeance were raised, loud yells of defiance were uttered, sinking down to a hoarseness that mean death and hurt to any one that dared at that dangerous moment to speak a word against the most determined resistance, quick, sure, and terrible to any and everything that smacked of further concessions."[66]

There remained a substantial bloc of voters in Lafayette County who still thought secession was rash, premature, and dangerous, but they no longer had a strong political organization or voice with which to combat the fire-eaters. The secessionists worked hard during the 1860 election to bridge divisions with these opponents by appealing to southern solidarity. They reached out to opposition leaders, invited them to joint meetings, appointed them to committees, and repeatedly reminded voters, as L. Q. C. Lamar put it at one political rally: "We have a common enemy, and must share a common fate."[67]

In November 1860, former Whigs and pro-Union Democrats nonetheless registered their opposition to the Southern Rights extremists by voting for John Bell of the Constitutional Union party (686 votes) and the Northern Democratic nominee, Stephen Douglas (144 votes). Together these 830 votes stood in opposition to the 1,034 votes supporting Breckinridge, the Southern Rights Democratic nominee. The long-standing campaign to muzzle the opposition notwithstanding, the election witnessed an unprecedented turnout on both sides, with the overall vote up nearly 25 percent from the previous presidential election. With their opposition divided and intimidated, Southern Rights Democrats delivered a majority of 55 percent in Lafayette County. Out at her plantation Rebecca Pegues wrote in her diary: "We are in the beginning of a revolution."[68]

Once the presidential election was decided, the revolutionaries had next to convince people that Republican victory dictated that the South secede. A short time after the election, on a cold, wet day late in November, a public meeting at the courthouse drew "a large attendance of citizens." The Democratic newspaper claimed an unprecedented solidarity: "Never before . . . since the first organization of our county, did such entire unanimity of sentiment prevail among our people at a public meeting."[69] "We trust that the ancient party lines are now entirely obliterated in Lafayette and throughout the South and not merely obliterated but forgotten." Where there was dissent, as in neighboring Holly Springs, the same editor roundly denounced any expression of pro-Union sentiment as outright disloyalty. Unionists were still trying to rally opposition to the coming of secession, but in Lafayette County the voice of Union had apparently been drowned by a chorus of southern solidarity, at least for now.[70]

The postelection meeting in Lafayette was a carefully orchestrated demonstration of bipartisan cooperation. It began with Democratic leader Alexander H. Pegues nominating Hugh A. Barr, a former Whig, to serve as chairman. Barr stated the purpose of the meeting in strictly neutral terms: "It was to give expression to the opinions and sentiments of the people of Lafayette County, in regard to the election of Lincoln and Hamlin." On a motion from the floor he then appointed a bipartisan committee of seven to draw up resolutions. Meanwhile, Sam Benton, a politician from Holly Springs, "delivered a powerful and effective speech against Lincoln's election as "an overt act" against the South. The resolutions laid similar sentiments before the meeting. "Whereas, the recent triumph of the Black Republican party . . . a Northern sectional party . . . elected because of their avowed opposition to the vital institutions of the South—indicates a settled and fixed hostility, on the part of the people of the Northern States, to the institution of slavery. . . . It is the imperative duty of the slaveholding States to resist and repel these threatened encroachments upon their constitutional rights, and, with this view, to devise measures for the preservation and perpetuity of their peculiar institutions, and the security and safety of the lives, property and just rights of their citizens." The meeting went on record in favor of a state convention "to determine action," but still the word "secession" was avoided.[71]

The southern revolutionaries now worked determinedly to undermine habitual loyalties to the Union and to absorb traditional American patriotism into a new conception of southern separatism. There was no better way to make this case than in the revolutionary origins of both nations and the tyranny each opposed. The American Spirit of '76 became the Southern Spirit of '61. The new southern revolutionaries were neither rebels nor traitors; according to this historical analogy, they were simply acting on the most exalted American principles. It was their patriotism, their loyalty to the founding principles of the very Union that had trampled on their rights and forced them, as England had forced its colonies, into a revolution for independence.[72]

Like their predecessors in '76, the revolutionaries of Mississippi made deliberate use of symbolic displays of sympathy for the southern independence movement in flags, badges, and other public signifiers of loyalty. The prosecessionist Democratic editor applauded "A Mississippi Flag" early in December: "There now floats from the top of the Masonic Hall, over the *Intelligencer* office, as handsome a flag, we venture to say, as can be found." The new banner captured the analogy of the southern revolution and the American Revolution: "It is a flag of fifteen stripes, and in place of the blue field with its galaxy of stars, there is substituted a single star, on the right and near the top; a magnolia tree, and a rattlesnake coiled, with the motto— *Noli'me tangere*—'do not tread on me.' " The editor went on to conclude that "we are willing to follow that flag to battle, to strike for our rights, and to return with it, wreathed in victory, or to return no more.

'Forever float that standard sheet,
Where breathes the foe but falls before us;
With freedom's soil beneath our feet,
And freedom's banner waving o'er us.' "[73]

Individual symbols of loyalty also were worn. Southern rebels wore "cockades," made of ornamental ribbons, on coats, dresses, or hats to signify their revolutionary sympathy. It was another practice borrowed from the American Revolution, and it had the effect of making people take a public stand for solidarity with the separatist movement. "A New Cockade," the Democratic editor proudly announced in early December, had been delivered to his office by an unnamed "young lady." This "Southern Rights Cockade" was described as a rosette surrounded with ribbons with an image of a half open boll of cotton, "king of the world," representing the eight cotton states of the anticipated "Cotton Republic" of Deep South states.[74] Opponents showed no such flags, ribbons, or other symbols of their opposition—silence and invisibility were their only means of protest for now.

While the revolution was campaigning to win the hearts and minds of

Lafayette County citizens, voters on December 20 had to choose two delegates to send to the state convention called in Jackson to decide on secession. This gave precious little time for the opposition to organize any effective alternative to the secessionists. Seeing that they were unlikely to win an outright contest with the secessionists, the opposition in Lafayette (and several other Mississippi counties) joined a coalition ticket. For the secessionists, this arrangement promised to muffle the voice of opposition in a smothering bipartisan embrace. For their part, those opposing secession hoped a coalition ticket would ensure at least one voice of moderation among the two in their delegation.

Before the election of delegates, several names were put forth in the press. The fire-eater L. Q. C. Lamar was the immediate favorite of the revolutionaries. With him on the coalition ticket was Dr. Thomas Dudley Isom, a former Whig with little political experience. Isom was nonetheless a well-known and respected pioneer citizen and physician who enjoyed widespread trust. Isom was a "cooperationist"; he urged caution and advocated secession only as a last resort, and then only in cooperation with other southern states. This was the only viable political ground opponents to the fire-eaters had left to stand on. Isom was a safe choice from the secessionist point of view. Following the election of Lincoln he had helped draft resolutions denouncing the victory of "Black Republicans" and calling for a state convention to determine action. Furthermore, as a prosperous property owner with twenty-nine slaves, Isom was safe on slavery.[75]

Only a week before the election, opposition forces tried to offer an alternative to this coalition ticket by proposing what they called a "Conservative ticket." A letter signed by "Many Farmers" proposed as delegates to the state convention two former Whigs, both opposed to immediate secession. One was Drury Robertson, a large farmer, sixty years old, and owner of eighteen slaves. The other was James S. Buford, a physician and partner with Dr. Thomas D. Isom, thirty-six years old, owner of ten slaves and part of the prosperous Buford College Hill family long identified with the Whig cause. "All conservative men are invited to aid us in electing said ticket."[76]

But one day before the election the local Democratic paper announced that both candidates had declined nomination in favor of the coalition ticket of Lamar and Isom. Robertson gave a suspicious explanation for his withdrawal, stating only that "under the present existing circumstances I think it expedient to decline the nomination." Many who opposed secession found it "expedient" to remain silent by this time. Despite their public renunciation of any nomination, in the election the next day Robertson and Buford polled small protest votes of 161 and 148 votes respectively. Most of these dissenting votes came out of Oxford and Abbeville, old Whig strongholds. There was another cluster of opposition votes from Dallas, a remote, mostly poor white section in the southeast corner of the county. The coalition ticket of Lamar and Isom won 815 and 834 votes respectively. The most significant vote in this plebiscite was silent. The turnout was about half what it had been for the presidential election the month before. With no real choice on the ballot, opponents of secession registered their protest in the only way left to them, by not voting.[77]

Revolution Is the Offspring of Enthusiasm

Though Lamar and Isom were sent to Jackson with no specific instructions regarding secession, the revolutionaries in Lafayette County were already mobilizing in the event of war before they even left. Within less than a week after the December 20 delegate election, the secessionists in Lafayette County called a "Military Meeting . . . to take into consideration the best manner of arming and equipping the military of the county." The local editor seemed convinced of the inevitability of secession and war before the convention had even convened. "In view of the prospect of war, by the Government upon the seceding States, . . . 'Let us keep our powder dry,' and have a sufficient supply handy." [78] The results of the census earlier that year had revealed the county had nearly 1,200 men of military age and ready to fight. Should conflict come, the editor of the *Intelligencer* opined, "Lafayette county would send to the wars a regiment of good men and true, who, inspired with a patriot's might, when his country's soil is polluted with hostile foes, would rush to battle like an avenging host." [79]

The mobilization effort in Mississippi was, to a remarkable degree, a community affair, with men, uniforms, arms, and supplies all furnished voluntarily by local effort. The state treasury was depleted, and there was no time to waste waiting for new tax revenues. The county's wealthy planters took the lead, with the Southern Rights Democrats most prominent. Before January was out the newly organized Lafayette Arms Supply Association began meeting at the courthouse to raise money to arm the Lamar Rifles, the first of several military companies organized in the county. Colonel Thomas E. B. Pegues, president of the association, announced that funds totaling $4,335 had already been raised, a good portion of which had already been given to Captain Francis M. Green to buy sixty Sharps rifles at thirty dollars apiece from arms dealers in St. Louis.[80] When Captain Green returned with the new rifles the following week the weapons of war were admired with glee: "They are beautiful and efficient weapons, with which, in the approaching Black Republican hunt, the 'game' can be brought down at a thousand yards." [81] If any thought was given to the likelihood that similar weapons would be used to cut down the sons of Lafayette County, it found no voice in this bold season of revolution.

As Lamar and Isom prepared to go to the convention in Jackson, the local paper mocked the death of Unionism in Mississippi: "Died. On the 6th of November last, at the ripe old age of 84 years, 4 months and two days, Uncle Sam, leaving a numerous and respectable set of friends and relatives to mourn his loss. The funeral will take place immediately, or, at least, as soon as decency permits. . . . The disease of which my uncle died was African Itch. . . . A great many Doctors worked on him from time to time, until finally, Dr. Buchanan took charge of the case." It was signed "Orphan Boy."[82]

Down in Jackson, Lamar played a decisive role in leading Mississippi out of the Union. Voters who thought they elected a balanced coalition delegation to represent Lafayette County may have felt disillusioned. Dr. Isom's voice of moderation never countered Lamar's, and the cause of the fire-eaters met only minor resistance from the delegates. "Our position is thoroughly identified with the institution of slavery," Lamar wrote in the declaration of causes for secession; "a blow at slavery is a blow at commerce and civilization. There was no choice left us but submission to the mandates of abolition, or a dissolution of the Union, whose principles had been subverted to work out our ruin." The declaration then submitted a long "train of abuses" proving the conspiracy against slavery. "Utter subjugation awaits us in the Union," Lamar continued. "We must either submit to degradation, and to the loss of property worth four billions of money, or we must secede from the Union framed by our fathers, to secure this as well as every other species of property. For far less cause than this, our fathers separated from the Crown of England. . . . We follow their footsteps. We embrace the alternative of separation."[83]

The vote for secession was received with great celebration in Oxford. "Mississippi is Out!," the Democratic newspaper proclaimed with glee. "We stop the press, at 8 P.M., to announce that a dispatch has just been received from Jackson, announcing that Mississippi has formally seceded from the Union. Oxford is brilliantly illuminated; bells are ringing, and guns are being fired. Three cheers for our gallant State."[84] One young boy remembered the scene that night: "All around the square, all up and down the thoroughfares, all along University street and around the campus, thousands upon thousands of candles were burning and 'hurrah for the Republic of Mississippi,' was heard ringing." "Far into the night the tempest raged, candlelights flashing, tar barrels burning, the plank walks going whack-a-lack, whack-a-lack, with a thousand feet, and the air reverberating and the walls resounding with a thousand voices yelling."[85]

Out on her Woodson Ridge plantation, Rebecca Pegues entered in her diary: "Mississippi seceded from the Union. . . . We are in the midst of stirring times." [86] On the university campus young Duncan McCollum jotted in his diary: "Wednesday 9. . . . Glorious day for Mississippi, seceded at 3 P.M. to-day. News came at sundown. Great demonstration at college and town illuminated. A salute fired. Boys parade a torchlight procession went to town and was joined by citizens. Several speeches. Fire balls on campus. Mrs. Lamar illuminated her dwelling. Immense excitement. Much music." That spring classes at the university came to a halt as students abandoned their studies in favor of drilling for the coming war. McCollum passed his time reading *The Last Days of Pompeii*, attending meetings of the literary society, keeping track of the news of seceding states, and watching the military spirit rise about him with no apparent anxiety as to how it would affect his life.[87]

Reuben Davis, on his way home from Congress, passed through northern Mississippi on the railroad. "I was scarcely out of the sound of cannon all the way." "Revolution is the offspring of enthusiasm," he mused. Davis determined to interrupt the blind enthusiasm with the sobering prediction that secession would bring war, and "the war would be protracted and desolating, and that emancipation would inevitably follow our defeat." [88] But that was not what the rebels of Mississippi wanted to hear in the winter of 1861. At that time they thought they were soaring toward independence, and there were now few voices left to tell them Mississippi was, as Faulkner put it, "whirling into the plunge of its precipice," plummeting into a bloody chasm. It would be a war that would expose their homeland to invasion and wanton destruction. Soon the war would evolve into a crusade that would destroy slavery and much of the economic and social order that rested on slavery. The revolution for independence that had begun with such enthusiasm in the winter and spring of 1861 would become revolution of another kind, one few people foresaw and fewer still dared warn against.

That noon, the regiment not even a regiment yet but merely a voluntary association of untried men who knew they were ignorant and hoped they were brave, the four sides of the Square lined with their fathers or grandfathers and their mothers and wives and sisters and sweethearts, . . . and then (the regiment) gone; and now not only the jail but the town too hung without motion, weightless and immobile upon the light pressure of invisible air . . . a town of old men and women and children and an occasional wounded soldier . . . static in quo, rumored, murmured of war only as from a great and incredible dreamy distance, like far summer thunder. —WILLIAM FAULKNER, Requiem for a Nun

six War

The revolutionary spirit of winter '61 flowed into spring as the county made ready for war. Most everyone knew it was coming now, and many were eager to be part of it when it came. Farmers cut back sharply on planting cotton that spring in favor of corn, wheat, and other food crops. Those still holding cotton from the previous fall were urged to sell it quickly before a Union blockade closed off the opportunity. Northern Mississippi had become the main food-producing region of the state, and Lafayette County farmers would be in a position to profit if wartime conditions cut off other supplies of grain and meat. War, they hoped, might bring more prosperity.[1]

In town the pace of life quickened with an unprecedented round of meetings, speeches, military parades, and flag presentation ceremonies. No enterprise had ever brought them together in such large numbers. Some tried to continue life as it had been and ignore or deny the coming war, but for most people all semblance of normality had been suspended in the crisis.

Out at the university many students now thought of nothing but the coming war. One of them, William Lowry, organized a military company among his fellow students, which they called the University Greys. As they drilled in their new uniforms, all thoughts of lectures and books were abandoned. Some faculty despaired at the situation and pleaded for more discipline. Already unpopular and suspect for his defense of his slave, President Barnard incurred more wrath from his enemies when he expelled Lowry for disobedience and tried to impose academic order against the martial enthusiasm of the day.

Barnard was not the only one exasperated with the students' neglect of their studies that spring. Hugh R. Miller scolded his son for getting mixed up with military excitement on campus and in the timeless voice of an exasperated father admonished him: "There is a very plain and obvious remedy for all this trouble in which you have involved yourself—and that is to attend punctually to all your college duties and not to be absent when it is so easy to be present. . . . You are there for the purpose of attending regularly all the College exercises and it is folly to suppose that you will be permitted to neglect them and to escape censure." Miller, who had been a leading advocate of secession, added optimistically that the "political news is all uncertain just at this time. It is most probable that we will have no war, though no reliable opinion can be formed for some days to come." [2] But this was only the wishful thinking of an anxious father. By April 1861, it was clear to most everyone that Mississippi's secession would be bought with blood.

Still, few foresaw a prolonged war with all its attendant suffering. Those who did found it wise to keep silent. Faulkner's Goodhue Coldfield not only forsook any personal support of the cause; he went so far as to refuse to sell goods to families who did. Behind his shuttered window, as Confederate soldiers marched past, he would roar passages from the Bible portending "violent vindictive" judgment on their cause. After some Confederate soldiers vandalized his store, he retreated to his attic, nailed the door shut, and withdrew completely from the community in the only form of protest left to him. [3]

There were many Goodhue Coldfields, less extreme or brave in their opposition, who withdrew from a community enthused with martial spirit. With such men silenced, there were none left to question openly the revolutionary illusion that a new southern nation was soaring into independence. There were none to tell them they were instead catapulting into an abyss of a long, cruel war in which distant battles would devour their sons and husbands, while at home massive armies would invade and wreak havoc on their homes and property. Nor could they foresee that a war intended to preserve slavery would in fact hasten its end. Few imagined that slaves, thought to be loyal if not contented, would, once given their chance, rise in rebellion and flee. Some would even return in the uniform of the enemy bearing arms and torches to set their town and homes ablaze. In the spring of '61 any such fears were silenced by revolutionary euphoria.

As the bold spirit of revolution faded and the awful reality of the war became clear, opposition broadened and found a whole new range of expression. For soldiers it might be expressed in desertion, shirking duty, or taking furlough without permission. For other men, opposition might involve draft dodging, blockade running and trading with the enemy, or bushwhacking against their own people. For men and women at the home front, private doubts about the wisdom of the cause came forth in a stream of letters to and from the front lines, complaining of hardships, reporting on Union invasion and destruction, or on men wounded and killed. Each letter, each lamentation, worked like solvent on the resolve to fight and endure, each time preparing them all, citizen and soldier, for defeat. It was a war that would destroy much of what the revolutionaries had claimed to be protecting, a war that left the county and much of the South destitute and humiliated in a way that makes Faulkner's words "the unvanquished" seem a cruel mockery of their actual fate. That ancient Chickasaw name, "Yoknapatawpha," land divided—and now people and nation divided, split, torn, ripped apart—in all its violent meanings, found its full significance in the ordeal of civil war.

Pro Altaris et Focis

"What the devil were you folks fighting about anyhow?" one of Faulkner's characters asks an old, one-armed Confederate veteran years after the war. He replies: "be damned ef I ever did know."[4] The fire-eaters had no difficulty answering that question in 1861. L. Q. C. Lamar made that emphatically clear in the Mississippi resolution for secession, and by early 1861 most southern rights advocates had embraced the secessionist view of what Lincoln's election meant to the South. Mississippi was fully committed to slavery as an essential system of labor and racial control. The North, and the Republican Party in particular, had fallen under the influence of fanatics who were determined to limit the westward expansion of slavery and eventually end it throughout the nation. Secession from the Union and independence from the Republican-controlled central government was the only recourse. The alternative, submission, meant loss of property and honor.

This reasoning seemed to play well among slaveholders in Mississippi who saw their interests, namely their slave property, clearly at risk. The secession convention delegates came overwhelmingly from the ranks of slaveholders. But in the hill counties of northern Mississippi, slaveholders were in a minority. In Lafayette County only about 40 percent of the white households owned any slaves, and half of those claimed less than five. Across the South, three in four white families owned no slaves in 1860. What stake did they have in this war? The new Confederacy was no longer simply asking for votes and consent to secede; it was asking families to send their sons to war, to take up arms and lay down their lives. These were sacrifices that demanded good cause. Whatever appeal Confederates made, it had to move beyond the usual masculine rhetoric employed in political discourse. Above all, the Confederates had to reach women, whom they would ask not only to urge their husbands and sons to war but also to provide continuing support for the war effort at home. No one could foresee it at the beginning, of course, but this would be a war that engaged enormous armies drawn from the civilian population, armies that suffered unprecedented casualties due largely to new weaponry. The war would also engage the civilian home front in massive mobilization efforts not only to recruit men but to supply the armies and tend to the wounded. It was also a war that would inflict its wrath on civilians at the home front. The success of the Confederate war effort would turn on its ability not only to mobilize a fighting army but also in its capacity to win the support of women and families in the white population.

What the devil *were* they about to fight for? In the winter and spring of 1861, the warriors of Lafayette County devised compelling responses to this question. Their appeal transcended both the narrow material interests of slavery and the more widely shared values of white racial supremacy to draw on more basic sources of identity rooted in masculine honor and the sanctity of white womanhood. This was to be a war fought by men in defense of their women, families, and homes.[5]

Southern patriotism began at home, and so did the mobilization effort. Lafayette County raised fourteen companies and sent over two thousand men into military service for the Confederacy (the numbers of refugee slaves and dissident whites who served in the Union army are not known). Companies were often raised in particular neighborhoods of the county, and the men joined and fought as friends and neighbors, often as family relations. Not only men but also the money to finance these companies, the rifles and ammunition to arm them, and the uniforms to clothe them, were all supplied locally. Several of the companies were organized or led by the leading planters and often named after them. The Thompson Cavalry, Avant

Southrons, and Pegues Defenders were among those named in honor of the wealthy planters who financed them. The Lamar Rifles honored the local hero who helped lead Mississippi out of the Union. The Lafayette Guards, Lafayette Farmers, and Lafayette Rebels all bore the name of their county with pride, while the Paris Rebels honored their community.

In the absence of state revenues, the expense of arming soldiers fell upon local voluntary resources. "There have been already nearly four thousand dollars raised by our citizens for the purpose of buying arms to equip the volunteer companies in Lafayette county," Oxford's local editor boasted in mid-January. More money would be needed to complete the job, he promptly added.[6] The Lafayette County Arms Society organized to lead the fund-raising effort. The state, it was supposed, would reimburse donors once it garnered the revenue, but people were encouraged to give out of patriotic duty and local pride: "Surely, when it is known that ten thousand could be usefully employed by the Association in furtherance of its objects, two or three hundred of our wealthy and prosperous citizens, will come forward, promptly, and supply the comparatively small amount that is yet required."[7] A group of "patriotic ladies of Oxford" determined to stage a charity event, a "public exhibition of tableaux" to raise funds for the Lamar Rifles. "When lovely women not only smiles upon our efforts to maintain our rights, but lends also a helping hand to the good work, who can doubt our conquering in the fight?"[8]

Women assumed an immensely important role in helping recruit young men, raising money, making uniforms, and in countless other ways equipping and comforting the young men being sent into war. "The women seem to vie with each other in doing every thing they can," Rebecca Pegues noted in her diary, proudly recording her own contribution in soldiers' clothing she had sewn and knitted. She often rebuked herself for not doing more, but she took pride in the number of men her family gave to the cause: "3 of my brave brothers and several nephews and relatives have gone off to the wars. . . . It gratifies me to have relations thus ready to do their duty; to sacrifice interest and leave their families." Her sister Catherine felt equally strong, saying she would "rather a thousand times her sons should go to war and be exposed to its dangers, than that they should stay at home when our country needs them."[9]

More important, women helped answer the question: what were the men fighting for? The role of women in defining the purpose of the war was articulated most clearly in the public rituals surrounding flag presentations to military companies. These became obligatory for every company, home guard unit, and cadet corps that organized in the county. It was a means by which women sanctified the cause and transformed the meaning of the war from a defense of slavery and political rights into a war to defend women, home, and family.

The first flag was presented in early February 1861 by a group of young women from Oxford's leading families to the Lafayette Guards. A large crowd of townspeople gathered in the Presbyterian Church to watch Miss Bruce Thompson, Jacob Thompson's daughter, escorted by First Lieutenant John Grace, march up the aisle before the pulpit. Following them was the "beautiful banner—its bright folds waving over her raven tresses. Her attire was simple, but very tasty—a snow-white dress, made whiter by contrast with her dark eyes and darker hair." Miss Thompson then spoke to the audience in what was described as a "very appropriate, well-delivered, brief address." She presented the banner to the Lafayette Guards and requested that they "guard it well on the battle-field—to preserve it from stain or dishonor—to bring it home unsullied, or 'come not at all.' " Captain William Delay, who had led the men of Lafayette into battle fifteen years earlier, received the banner with promises to defend it. The banner, hand-made by Miss Thompson herself, depicted a cotton plant and a motto in golden letters: "*Pro Altaris et focis*" (For altars and hearths).[10]

As the county mobilized for war that spring, these flag presentations became occasions of ever more elaborate ritual. In early March the women of Oxford consecrated the Lamar Rifles to war with grand ceremony. Two military companies from Holly Springs, along with a "large number of distinguished citizens," came down that afternoon by special train. The Lamar Rifles and Lafayette Guards formed ranks on the square and marched to fife and drum down to the Oxford depot to greet their guests. Hundreds of Oxford citizens, about half the town by one estimate, gathered at the depot where the Lafayette County troops fired a salute as the train arrived. The four companies marched back into town, around the square, and then went into a series of drills, "each striving hard to excel the other." "The gay plumage, the beautiful uniforms, and the enlivening music presented a scene more animated than had ever been witnessed since this was a town." Following supper at the University Hotel, the troops formed ranks again and marched to the Cumberland Presbyterian Church, which was brilliantly illuminated and filled with people who shouted as the men entered. This was the largest gathering ever in Oxford, one observer thought. Now the young women entered: Miss Sally Wiley, escorted by Captain Francis M. Green, followed by six other young women all "dressed in snowy white" with blue sashes, each indicating one of the seven states of the Confederacy. "The ladies of Oxford," the editor of the *Mercury* wrote, "have strewn the sweetest flowers in the pathway of the companies, and encouraged their brothers and sweethearts to join in the ranks." They had prepared a battle flag for the Lamar Rifles, a huge banner five by eight feet. On a background of white silk, fringed in red, was an image depicting symbols of Mississippi: a magnolia, a lone star in the blue sky, and an eagle clutching a cotton plant in one talon and a streamer in the other with the words: "Lamar Rifles, Always Ready." When the flag was unfurled, the crowd broke into a wild applause.

Sally Wiley, daughter to Yancey Wiley, a wealthy planter, then stood before the crowd and spoke. It was rare for women to speak in public, but the reports of this and other speeches that spring made it clear this exception to normal public decorum sprang from the very highest ideals of white southern womanhood. "For a few moments Miss Wiley betrayed a slight degree of embarrassment," one account noted, "but gathering confidence as she proceeded, she pronounced her address in a clear, distinct voice, and with a ladylike eloquence that charmed her every listener."

Sally Wiley adroitly underscored the conventional distinctions between the sexes and placed upon men the manly duty of defending their women in time of war. "In times of peace," she began, men focus on "their business relations" and the "pursuit of gain," and these pursuits "tend to effeminacy." Now Mississippi (pointedly referred to in the feminine) was threatened with dishonor if "she" submitted to the aggressions of the North. The allusion to fair Mississippi being ravaged by northern invaders took on a sexual meaning none could have missed. "Our noble State," Miss Wiley continued, "looking the danger full in the face, has resolved that she will submit to no inequality or denial of her rights." "Our safety is endangered, and our honor is at stake." The North, she predicted, "may attempt to invade our land and lay waste our fields, in order to constrain us to submit to degradation. When that hour comes, if come it should, we rely upon your strong arms and unquailing hearts to defend our rights, protect the mothers, shield the honor of the maidens of the land, and give security and peace to our firesides." The flag, she said, was a "memorial of our confidence and our approval." "As you gaze upon it you must remember that our eyes are upon you." She closed with a warning that in many ways summarized the sexual exchange between masculine chivalry and feminine devotion that was being communicated in these rituals: "As man can not love and cherish woman bereft of honor, so woman can not reverence and honor man devoid of courage." [11] Here, of course, was one good answer to those who asked: what were these young men fighting for? They were fighting not only to protect the honor of their women, but more than that, to win their love and avoid their scorn. Passing through the minds of the young men in the audience that day, the message must have been well understood in both sentimental and more carnal terms.

Accepting the flag for the company was Captain Francis Green, a former outspoken Unionist now eager to demonstrate his loyalty to the Confederate cause. He said he "could not promise . . . that it [the flag] should be returned as fresh and bright as it now appeared, for when it should be again laid before them it might be soiled by the smoke of war and rent by the bullets of the foe; but for this, at least, he would engage—that it should not be sullied by any stain of dishonor." Then, turning to his men, the captain implored them, when the flag unfurled above them in battle, to think always "of the dear ones who were its donors, and that thought would so nerve their hearts and strengthen their arms that they could never be defeated but by annihilation." [12] Through these community rituals the abstract cause of southern independence was fused into a defense of feminine virtue and community patriotism.

Once the first two companies were nearly filled, recruitment slowed for a time. Franc Duval, the local editor, explained that "if an actual war existed, there would be no difficulty in obtaining a regiment of volunteers in this County," but they are busy men who have no time "for the mere purpose of being drilled." "When the time for action comes," he predicted, "all these men will be 'thar.' " [13] A few days later more than 160 men volunteered for service in three new companies. "Oxford is the banner town of the State," Duval boasted.[14] The only concern now was whether war would come. "But, pshaw! Old Abe is about to spoil all our fun, by giving us no chance of a fight." If the North would not give the new Confederate nation a war, the bellicose editor looked forward to an invasion of Mexico "at no distant day." [15]

In early April the first Lafayette County troops, now mustered into service by the state, were dispatched to Pensacola, Florida, to take possession of Fort Pickens. The Lafayette Guards left at four in the morning, and a large crowd, including women and children, gathered at the depot in the darkness. In the crowd, men of the Lamar Rifles and University Greys, still without marching orders, felt dejected. As the train pulled out with more than one hundred Lafayette men, the soldiers left behind worried the war might be over before they had a chance for action. The local newspaper expressed hope it would all be over soon: "We trust we may welcome each one back, ere long, to Oxford. Peace is about to spread her wings, and wars 'loud alarums' will soon be hushed into peaceful repose." [16]

When war finally began that April at Fort Sumter in South Carolina, it was welcomed with exuberance in Oxford. "War, grim-visaged war, is now actually upon us," the *Intelligencer* reported, and local citizens were "greatly excited" notwithstanding fears that war might well bring death. To celebrate the occasion, a group of men fired a cannon on the square, a seven-shot salute to honor each Confederate state. The blasts shattered all the windows on the south side of the square, leaving it looking, the newspaper reported with unwitting prescience, "as if they had been 'through the wars.' "[17]

The defiant mood of the day was apparent in a private letter written not long after the war began: "Now nothing but annihilation will bring [the South] . . . into the old Union," Jacob Thompson wrote to James Buchanan, the former president he once served. "We have separated and our separation is perpetual. . . . As long as the northern states propose invasion, subjugation, so long will we fight, and when our ammunition is exhausted, we will fight with staves, pitchforks and scythe blades."[18] These were the brave words of a man who had staked his career on the success of the revolution, and to some degree they reflected the resolution of most whites in the county as they entered into war in that spring so full of courage.

A Town of Old Men and Women

Wartime mobilization reached deeper into the civilian population once the shooting began, and patriotic spirit soon ran up against a more measured reluctance to sacrifice for the cause. "I am sorry to see the ardor and enthusiasm of our people cooling off, we must wake them up," one man wrote privately in the fall of 1861 after the state's requisition for new troops had met with a significant shortfall.[19] A group of recruiters, known as "out pushers," exerted pressure on the remaining pool of men, many of whom had wives and children they were reluctant to leave behind, while others were either indifferent or quietly opposed to the cause.

John Robuck was a reluctant volunteer, and there were probably many like him who fought for the Confederacy less out of conviction than out of a desire to avoid dishonor and social embarrassment for themselves and their families. He opposed secession on principle and at first stoutly refused to join the stampede to enlist. Many, he commented cynically, wanted nothing more than to be officers and would join one company after another, stand for election, then quit unless they were elected. Robuck's family owned no slaves and operated a modest farm in the woods near the Yoknapatawpha River southeast of Oxford. By September 1861, he was still holding out, but pressure intensified, especially on young unmarried men like himself. The "out pushers," Robuck recalled, began using the threat of conscription to shame young men into joining. To those married men who worried about their families, their wealthy neighbors assured them of support. When a man Robuck called Frank Jones came to him, urging him to join Captain Delay's Lafayette Guards, Robuck claimed to have responded defiantly: "You own many negroes while I own none. Owning negroes will exempt you from our military service." Jones gave no response.[20]

When appeals to patriotism failed, the young women in Robuck's neighborhood tried humiliation. Sometime in September 1861, they sent a slave girl to deliver a present to him: inside the box was a hoop skirt, a sunbonnet, and a Mother Hubbard frock. Robuck retaliated by sending a thank you message back with the slave. He then sat for a formal portrait at the photographer's studio in Oxford, posing in his new feminine attire, skirt, bonnet, and frock, and gave a copy of the portrait to each of his feminine tormentors.[21] If Robuck's story is true, such defiance could not have come easily to many young men, and eventually he gave in to the social pressure that bore upon all young men in a time of war.

Several new military companies organized after war began in April 1861. The Avant Southrons, McClung Rifles, Thompson's Cavalry, and Mott Guards all raised volunteers for the war that spring. By the fall of 1861 there were eleven companies from Lafayette County in the field, and another five would be organized in early 1862. Estimates of the number recruited from Lafayette County into Confederate service range up to 2,220, a remarkable show when it is estimated that the white male population between ages eighteen and forty stood at a little under 1,600 in 1860.[22] Recruiters now encouraged men to enlist for the duration of the war with naive optimism: "Why not enlist for the war?" one editorial implored; "It may not last longer than six or twelve months. Should it be of longer or shorter duration, say three, four or five years, and there should not be a sufficient number of volunteers offering, a draft would be resorted to—and who among us would stand a draft?"[23]

By May 1861, most of Lafayette's military companies had left by train for battlefields in Kentucky, Tennessee, and Virginia. More companies formed late that summer: the Paris Rebels, Lafayette Farmers, Pegues Defenders, and Dave Rogers Rifles. All followed the others to distant battlefields by the early fall. Early the next year the last of the new companies would join them: the Lafayette Rebels, Smith Rifles (also referred to as the Abbeville Tigers), and one known only as Company H of the Mississippi Forty-First Infantry Regiment. Two others that organized early in 1862, the True Mississippians and Dixie Rebels, included many Lafayette County men.[24]

The scenes at the depot of departing soldiers and weeping family members had become a familiar part of life for the community by now. The festive air of martial pomp and ceremony that attended the military parades and flag presentations gave way to a more somber mood of wartime reality. As Ella Pegues remembered later, "After a while the glamour gradually wore off, and the war began to impress itself on my youthful mind, as much more serious than at first." One morning, she recalled, father "took us all to the depot—to see the departure of the 'Pegues Defenders,'" the company he had financed. "I was surprised to see strong men weeping like children, as they said good-bye to mothers, wives and sweethearts, and wondered what it all meant and if they did not expect to come back." [25]

The war effort also engaged large numbers of noncombatants: women, older men, even young boys and girls. A home guard had organized earlier, and now several new units formed in the county as a militia to protect the home front. As the fighting men went off to war, in May 1861 a large public meeting took place at Taylor's Depot to tend to the defense of "our homes and fire-sides against any invasion from the North" and the need to "suppress any servile insurrection in our midst." The Yocona Home Guards were formed among the older men of the area "for self-defense against any and all encroachments upon our rights, from whatever quarter." [26] By the end of April a countywide militia organized as the Home Guard of Lafayette County, with seven squads to serve each day of the week. Dedicated to "the protection of the lives and property of the citizens against foreign invasion and servile insurrection," their real purpose was vigilance over the enemy within, rebel slaves and dissident whites. [27]

As the older men formed home guard militia, boys too young to serve formed their own cadet companies, as though to prepare for a longer war that in time would enlist them. The Avent Cadets, with Robert Sheegog Jr. serving as captain, enlisted nearly three dozen boys between twelve and eighteen. They drilled in the smart new uniforms their mothers sewed for them: white pants with red stripes and yellow flannel jackets trimmed in blue. "We rejoice to see this military spirit manifested among the boys," the newspaper reported. With unusual prescience it went on to say: "Ere three years roll around they may be called upon to fill vacancies made by their fathers and brothers, slain in battle." [28] Within a short time the cadets were staging drills on the square and receiving their own flag from the young girls of Oxford. A Cadets Ball held in May drew "the youth and beauty of our town" where they enjoyed the "giddy mazes of the dance. . . . the lassies in their snow-white robes, and the lads in gay uniforms, all chatting and laughing, for the time forgetting the war-cloud hovering over our sunny South. . . . The Cadets know how to play the gallant, as well as soldier." [29]

The women of Lafayette County offered much more than flags and decorative displays. To a remarkable degree the fighting men of Lafayette County were supplied with uniforms, food, and provisions of all kinds through the efforts of local women. Once war came, some realized the existing voluntary groups that met to sew uniforms were insufficient, and they called for a more permanent organized effort. Franc Duval, the *Intelligencer* editor, used an anonymous letter, probably from a woman who felt any public role might be improper, to advocate and proffer male permission for their organization. "Let the ladies have a regularly organized society," Duval urged. "We earnestly request the ladies of Oxford to meet and organize a society determined and prepared to assist our troops, either with the needle, in making uniforms, etc., or, if the worst comes, to nurse and take care of the wounded soldiers." Women who "bid adieu to husbands, sons, brothers and lovers, and bid them go forth to their duty for our homes and country" were now saying that we "must do our duty, also." [30]

Citizens of Lafayette also prepared to take care of the soldiers' families by organizing a Military Relief Association. Through a combination of private donations, primarily from wealthy families, and public support from the county's coffers, they garnered money to supply the families of volunteers with needed provisions. Their "families will be exposed to want in the absence of those upon whom they are dependent" and "more money will be required for the companies newly organized and for the families of volunteers." [31]

With the troops gone, Oxford, like Faulkner's fictional Jefferson, had become "a town of old men and women and children and now and then a wounded soldier" that "hung without motion in a tideless backwash." [32] John Robuck, home on furlough in April 1862, noted that "nearly all the men had gone to the army. None were at home except very old men and boys under sixteen years of age, wealthy planters, millers, a few doctors and preachers." As for the women, he witnessed more than one who "had taken the place of her husband, . . . and was plowing or otherwise working the crop in person in order to support herself and little children." The Relief Association had promised donations of provisions, but what many soldiers' families lacked was labor. The spring of 1862, Robuck realized later, was only "the mere beginning of woman's war hardships." [33] Already the enthusiasm for war had tempered among the populace left behind once the parades and ceremonies were over. "I am very anxious about the war," Rebecca Pegues confided to her diary as the first reports of battles in the East reached Mississippi. [34] But these were still the distant sounds of cannon barely heard in northern Mississippi. "Whilst the enemy are ravaging the country and driving the inhabitants from their homes," she wrote toward the end of 1861; "we are insulated — secure thus far. We don't have even the sick and wounded to care for." [35] All that would change for her and everyone around her.

Strange Injured and Dead

For a full year, between Fort Sumter and the Battle of Shiloh, the community hung suspended, Faulkner wrote, as though having "lost all sense of motion . . . static in *quo*, rumored, murmured of war only as from a great and incredible distance, like far summer thunder."[36] The thunder presaged the coming storm, however. It was, in fact, about a year after that first revolutionary spring of 1861, full of patriotism and gallantry, a time when men rushed to enlist—afraid that the war would end too soon—that the first real storm of war came home.

From the battlefields of Shiloh (April 1862), later Corinth (October 1862) came trainloads of wounded soldiers, sick and dying, with limbs amputated and bodies mutilated. They arrived in Oxford at the same depot that, a year before, had witnessed townspeople cheering their own boys' departure. Some fifteen hundred wounded men (about the number the county had sent off to war at that point) were brought into Oxford to a makeshift hospital set up in the buildings of the university. Dr. Thomas Isom (who had cautioned against precipitous action that might lead to exactly this kind of carnage) was now serving as physician in charge of the Confederate hospital at the university. Care for the wounded depended heavily on voluntary aid from the women of the county. Women who a year earlier were sewing uniforms and flags now put their energies to tending the wounded and stripping homes of mattresses, blankets, linens, bandages, and cooking utensils on their behalf. There were already two to three hundred patients at the makeshift university hospital in the early spring of 1862. The wounded and dying coming in from the front lines overwhelmed the staff and facilities of the hospital. "The scene presented here is truely heart rending," wrote one attendant to Governor Pettus that May. "No room. Crowded 730 sick in the Hospital. 280 sick and wounded left here last night on the cars—against my earnest remonstrance." While Mississippi soldiers were off fighting and dying in Virginia and Tennessee, it seemed most of the Confederate soldiers lying in the hospital at Oxford were from other states.[37]

Almost half, seven hundred of the ailing men, would die at the Confederate hospital. The campus, recently the scene of youthful gaiety and martial gallantry, became a graveyard for young men. The magnetic observatory's "dead room" took on macabre new meaning by serving as a morgue. Initially the bodies were placed in pine coffins supplied by townspeople, but as the numbers of dead grew, a slave woman who worked at the hospital recalled, "they just buried them in bunches like dead chickens."[38] Most were not even identified before they were interred in their anonymous graves in a cemetery on campus. Aboveground were hundreds more who lost limbs or were otherwise maimed for life.

Those who survived the hospital were placed in homes of local citizens to convalesce. Many families already had wounded or ill sons and husbands to nurse and dead to bury. The women who served at home or at the university hospital, whether tending to the wounded and dying, bringing them food, or preparing bandages and clothing, saw before them the horrifying face of a war to which they had sent their own sons, husbands, and brothers. As Faulkner imagined Judith Sutpen and other women of Jefferson, there "in the improvised hospital where (the nurtured virgin, the supremely and traditionally idle) they cleaned and dressed the self-fouled bodies of strange injured and dead and made lint of the window curtains and sheets and linen of the houses in which they had been born." [39]

"After the Battle of Shiloh, many Confederate soldiers were sent out from the hospital to make room for the wounded," Ella Pegues recalled. "My father opened his country home to them and when they recovered and returned to their commands or were sent home on furlough he took others in their places. My sister at first arranged flowers for their room, thinking that among them might be some handsome young officers, but they were just plain emaciated soldiers, who did not seem to care for the flowers, at the same time they were very grateful for any kindness shown them." [40] For Rebecca Pegues, who had been so proud to have her brothers and other relatives enlist to defend the South, a new mood of anxiety descended once the carnage of the battlefield came before her eyes. "This terrible war keeps me so uneasy," she wrote. But she was emphatic in her support of the new conscription law and insisted that "we have now to use every effort against our merciless enemy." "This last battle of Shilow was not so great a victory as at first supposed," she added grimly.[41]

Not long after the massive carnage at Shiloh, the Confederacy instituted its long-awaited conscription policy. Every able-bodied man between the age of eighteen and thirty five not exempt from the draft was now a "must go." (Later, the Confederate draft widened to take men eighteen to forty-five, then seventeen to fifty.) Even John Robuck, who had defiantly stood up to the "out pushers" earlier, finally decided the "time had come at last when every man had to fight or hide." He joined the Lafayette Rifles. Not one man in the company owned a slave, Robuck noted with pride. Most of these late enlistees were married men who had joined only in the face of the conscription act. As the Rifles gathered at the depot to leave Oxford, several women from the wealthy families of the county sent them off with a ten-dollar gold piece and a promise to support the families they were leaving behind. Robuck proudly refused the gift, but a woman he called "Mrs. Davanport" insisted that he take it. As the train approached to take the men off, Robuck remembered "scores of husbands holding their wives in their arms, wives with their arms around their husbands' necks, sobbing bitterly, loth to give them up perhaps for always." He would also remember with bitter disappointment the promises his wealthy neighbors made to sustain those families.[42]

Grant's Army Cum Fitin'

It was not until the end of 1862 that Lafayette County experienced war first-hand. The Union army under General Ulysses S. Grant carried the assault on the South after Shiloh into northern Mississippi, laying siege to Corinth and driving the Confederate forces south to Tupelo. To the west, Memphis fell to Union forces that June. From Corinth Grant's forces advanced deeper into Mississippi, occupying Holly Springs by November 13. "Gloom hangs over us," Rebecca Pegues recorded in her diary. "I just realize how nearly we are upon the eve of invasion." "The army may leave us any day, then what is to be our fate?"[43] Another observer that November thought "matters *seem* a little more settled now, as our army *appears* to have takin a stand, south of the Tallahatchie near Abbeville." For now, he wrote, "we felt compara-tively safe; at the same time with the fearful apprehension preying upon us that our little army would be forced further south." "If the enemy spreads over the state ought we to flee before them with our negroes and families or remain at home? Hard question which no one here has yet decided."[44]

The invasion of northern Mississippi was part of a larger Union strategy aimed at gaining control of the Mississippi River, reopening it to trade from the Midwest, and, in the process, dividing the Confederacy. Vicksburg, Mis-sissippi, remained one of the last strongholds on the river, and from Oxford, Grant laid plans to deploy General William T. Sherman's forces in an over-land march on Vicksburg.

Grant and Sherman, chief among the architects of the new strategy of war that would emerge, met for a dress rehearsal in Lafayette County in December 1862. While Union General George B. McClellan was supervis-ing a stalemate in the eastern theater of war, Grant's forces won one victory after another in the West, and it was here, some historians argue, that the Civil War was won and lost. It was also here, in northern Mississippi, that a new strategy of warfare took form, one aimed at punishing and demoral-izing civilians through pillaging and destruction and disrupting the entire social order. Before this turn in policy, the Union army advanced into the South with a sword in one hand and an olive branch in the other. The "rose water" policy toward civilians operated on the assumption that a small elite of slave owners, led by the fire-eating fanatics, had dragged the South into secession and war, and support would vanish once the Yankees came and liberated the South from their control. The shift in Union civilian policy from conciliation toward punitive harshness evolved in a disjointed way beginning in late 1862. Grant's campaign in northern Mississippi, and the invasion of Lafayette County in particular, encapsulates all the contradictory policies and impulses at play in this dramatic turn toward total war.[45]

Lafayette County civilians were dismayed to see Confederate forces put up virtually no resistance to Grant's invasion of their homeland in early December 1862. News of Union advances down the Mississippi and a raid on the Mississippi Central Railroad south of him, at Coffeeville, panicked Confederate General John C. Pemberton into abandoning a strong and well-fortified line of defense on the south bank of the Tallahatchie near Abbeville and beating a hasty retreat southward. On a cold rainy day, December 1, the Confederates, some forty thousand troops, pulled out of Abbeville, setting fire to the Mississippi Central Railroad bridge, the train depot, and dozens of bales of cotton.

The Union invasion of Lafayette County followed quickly. Polly Turner Cancer remembered the day the Yankees came: "Grant's army cum fitin' an' skirmishin' rite thru here." It was exciting to watch: "dey wud draw dey swords an' de hosses wud rar' up on dey hin' feets an' dey didn't never break ranks neder; when does bombs began to fly an' de cannon bo 'Boom, boom.' "[46] Private Cyrus Boyd and his fellow Iowa infantrymen rode no gallant horses. He recorded the invasion from the perspective of the common foot soldier as he marched south toward the Tallahatchie on December 1. Rain and snow had turned the roads to deep mud, and the near freezing weather made progress difficult. That night Boyd and his comrades camped on the north side of the river and made a large fire with some split-rail fencing they tore down. They woke early the next morning and saw nothing but deserted Confederate forts and earthworks on the other side of the river. The Mississippi Central Railroad bridge across the Tallahatchie had been mostly destroyed by the fire the Confederates had set. As horses, wagons, and artillery were brought across on a temporary bridge, the federal army entered Abbeville in the midst of a heavy cold rain. Soldiers tore down more fencing for bonfires, and they ransacked the town for hogs, chickens, and other food. It was pandemonium: "Some were holding hogs by the tails and calling for help, and others skinning hogs." Boyd gorged himself on corn bread that was loaded with cobs and shells. He felt nauseous and recorded in his diary: "Don't know what the weather is outside, but inside of me it has been terrific."[47]

The Union army came south, down the rail line into Oxford, on December 2. Union colonel Lyle T. Dickey and his cavalry moved out ahead, harassing the rear guard of the retreating rebels, forcing them repeatedly to abandon defensive lines. The Confederates attempted to form a line just north of Oxford, and when that broke they reformed on the courthouse square. Civilian women and men watched from their windows as Union cavalry charged down North Street and then abruptly pulled back once they saw a solid line of Confederate infantry. But the Confederates did not take their stand in Oxford; instead of using the town as a defensive position, they broke ranks and retreated southward with Union troops pressing them every mile.

The Confederates left "a town of tearful women and weeping maids," one veteran later recalled. There was one young woman who was not crying; she stood on her porch excoriating the retreating soldiers as the "most cowardly aggregation of 'skedadling' cavalry in the whole Confederacy." Who was she, the soldiers wanted to know as they hastened out of town. "Miss Taylor Cook," one of them reported, and the name went down the line, repeated, it was said, "affectionately and most respectfully" by the men who admired her feistiness.[48] They nonetheless continued their retreat, though some were irritated with their officers for refusing to stand and fight.[49]

In panic, much of the white civilian population followed their army southward, packing what they could in wagons and moving down the roads in a hectic evacuation. Alexander Pegues, a Confederate political leader, had already escaped the county "in great haste" leaving his wife, Rebecca, feeling great "perplexity and confusion and terror." "It was right discouraging," she confided to her diary, "to see so many of them running off—fearful of arrest—deserting their homes, and leaving the women at the mercy of the invaders." After Grant's forces occupied the county, she and her children packed what they could in a wagon, left the plantation, and sought refuge in Oxford.[50] A Confederate officer described the exodus southward: "They are making their way South with their goods and chattles. . . . The road from this place to Okolona is literally crowded with families and stock of all kinds."[51] "The crop south of us has been almost an entire failure," one worried refugee wrote, "and to move south seems like entering the jaws of famine. We have here abundant crops, and it is hard to leave our bread."[52] But leave many of them did, in advance of the invading army.

Heavy rain and snow, together with the difficult terrain, slowed both the Confederate retreat and the Yankee pursuit. One correspondent from Chicago was astonished by the deep gullies that years of erosion had torn through the land in this part of Mississippi. Some, he reported, were "half a mile in length, and to a depth from four to twenty feet and varying in width from two to twenty feet." As cavalry advanced south into these chasms, "horses and riders went pell mell into the gorge, some never to come out, as they found their last ditch. Horses and men were much disabled."[53] Yoknapatawpha, the land split apart, slowed but did not deter the invasion from the North.

The Confederate rear guard formed another line of defense on what one Union correspondent described as a "small creek bearing the stunning name of Yockenapatopha."[54] That line also collapsed, and Union forces pressed their enemy farther south to Coffeeville. "How far south would you like me to go?" Grant asked General in Chief H. W. Halleck. "We are now at Yocony, and can go as far as supplies can be taken." But he later warned: "Roads have become too impassable to leave railroad any great distance. Streams are high." In fact, the bottomlands along the Yoknapatawpha were nearly impassable after the fall rains. On December 3 the Confederates dismantled a wooden bridge spanning the Yoknapatawpha and were setting it afire when the Union cavalry approached. Some Union cavalry tried to swim their horses across only to find the banks were too steep and muddy to ascend.[55] By December 8 Union forces ended their pursuit of the retreating Confederates and Grant reported that the "cavalry under colonel Dickey have now drawn off, having followed the enemy to Coffeeville."[56]

The primary Union goal at this point was not to seize control of the Mississippi interior but to stage an assault on Vicksburg, the last holdout against Union control of the Mississippi River. When the invasion halted below the Yoknapatawpha, Grant prepared to make Oxford his winter headquarters. The Confederates fell back south of the Yalobusha River using Grenada as General Pemberton's headquarters.[57] During the invasion of Lafayette County, the Union lost only nine killed and fifty-six wounded; another fifty-six were reported missing. Confederate casualties remained unknown, but hundreds had surrendered or deserted.[58]

The same day Grant's troops entered Oxford, to the west, another army under General William T. Sherman advanced into Wyatt "without the least opposition." Three days later, after constructing a temporary bridge, Sherman's men crossed the Tallahatchie and took up a position at College Hill. Union forces entered Oxford December 2; Grant arrived a few days later.[59] "We made quite a parade going through Oxford," one Union general recorded in his diary on December 5, "as it is a place of considerable importance. Flags were unfurled, bands struck up, bugles sounded, and men for the time being forgot their fatigue and marched in good order."[60] Private Boyd was impressed with Oxford, "a nice little town" with fine homes "many of them surrounded by fine lawns and the most beautiful shrubbery and evergreens." "The soldiers occupy all the nice places here."[61] General Grant took up headquarters near the railroad depot in a mansion belonging to wealthy planter James Brown. Union troops set up tents on the court-

Union forces occupy Oxford's Courthouse Square, 1862.
(Courtesy of Special Collections, University of Mississippi)

house square and in the front yards of large homes throughout Oxford.
Lafayette County, it appeared, had been restored to the Union.

Fiendish Yankees

The coming of war had forced separatists to translate formerly abstract
ideas about the conflict into a call to arms to defend home and family. Now
the invasion of Lafayette County by Union troops put a face on the Yankee
enemy, one people had only imagined before. In local memory stories of
Yankees stealing chickens, frolicking with slave women, burning houses,
and insulting white women would loom as large as those detailing military
operations in the area. Mary Smither remembered the day Colonel Dickey
and his troops descended on them: "The whole hillside was covered with
men and horses. . . . We were so helpless and frightened." She thought
Colonel Dickey, not unlike Faulkner's fictional Colonel Dick, was "an elegant gentleman" with "fine men" on his staff. Dickey assured her "he could
not fight and starve out women and children." [62]

If Colonel Dickey embodied the earlier "rose water" policy of conciliation, there were dozens of other Union soldiers and officers willing to show

Lafayette County civilians what Sherman called the "hard hand of war." Much of this was not part of any deliberate policy of punishing civilians, but simply young, undisciplined soldiers out of control. Some Union soldiers ran amuck in Oxford and particularly around College Hill. They looted deserted mansions and barged into others pushing frantic women and servants aside. They rummaged through houses looking for whiskey or wine to drink and stealing whatever they felt like in the way of food and souvenirs. Some destroyed personal property out of the sheer pleasure they apparently took in hearing the screams of women begging them not to.

Some of the most shameful incidents of this behavior involved Union soldiers stealing from slaves or using counterfeit Confederate money to cheat them. The slaves were the most eager to sell butter, eggs, and other luxury food items to soldiers, and many did a brisk trade with the invading army. But they, too, became victims of hungry and merciless soldiers: "Dey kilt all our chickens an' turkeys, an' cooked dem fer de soldiers," former slave Rebecca Wood remembered; "the whole yard wuz full uv chicken heads, but nary chicken." [63] Several slaves had their property taken, in part because, as Jane Wilburn later explained, the "yankees . . . wouldn't believe the cullud folks had anything uv their own; they jus' thought they wuz keeping them for their masters and mistresses." [64] One slave, Martin Mullins, lost his two most valuable possessions to the Union soldiers. "They rode up to me and I was commanded by the captain to alight and I did so and they took my mule, and a non commissioned officer took my watch." [65] Tamer Hewlett, a slave woman in her sixties, testified that her master "set me free" and "gave me the mule" which the soldiers took from her. An officer told her "he did not want take my mule . . . said he hated to do it but was compelled. . . . I suppose they would not have taken my mule unless they needed it. I ought to be paid for it was all I had." She signed the affidavit claiming compensation for her property with her "X." [66]

Reports on the extent and nature of the pillaging vary greatly depending on the source. A *Chicago Tribune* correspondent reported "but few outrages" from the troops quartered in Oxford. But others admitted to widespread pillaging: "They took corn and chickens and everything that could be eaten, and in a few instances I was sorry to learn that some of our men entered houses and committed depredations, stealing money and other valuables." [67] Some of what might have seemed like plain vandalism was purposeful foraging for food authorized by Union officers. Food supplies lagged behind the advancing army and were difficult to transport because of the destroyed track and bridges along the Mississippi Central line. Besides, given a choice between U.S. Army–issued food, tough dried meat or hardtack, and the chickens and hogs available in local farms, hungry soldiers chose to supplement their diet with fresh local food. Part of the motivation was nutritional, as one Union general explained; scurvy was "making its appearance in a slight form" and they had to forage for fresh vegetables.[68] There was also a good dose of vindictiveness toward the people who had supported rebellion. "To-morrow," one Illinois soldier wrote on December 3, "our rations run out and we shall begin to 'subsist upon the enemy.' Everything eatable will be taken by the army, and the people be left to look out for themselves. This is hard but just."[69]

The worst depredations were usually blamed on the notorious Kansas "Jayhawkers," and they no doubt earned their reputation for pillaging, but they were hardly alone. The soldiers were young men, many away from home for the first time, and not always closely supervised as the invading troops spread out through the countryside. The wine and liquor they drank during foraging raids did not help matters. One group of Illinois soldiers was reported terrorizing the countryside between Oxford and College Hill, plundering farmhouses for food and harassing the civilian population.[70] Much of this was undisciplined looting that took place in violation of orders. Some Union soldiers had become openly defiant of their commanding officers by this point in the war, and some sources note a surly tone of disrespect among the rank and file. On December 19, when Union troops were required to march by General Grant's new headquarters in Oxford and give three cheers for their commanding officer, Private Boyd recalled, "in our regiment only a scattered few cheered. But I could hear the men say in a low voice *damn Genl Grant*."[71]

If there was a lack of deference toward authority in their own army, there was more intense resentment toward the wealthy planters whose mansions Union soldiers pillaged in Lafayette County. Ever since the bloodbath at Shiloh, many soldiers had become hardened and embittered. For the first time in their campaign, Union soldiers were entering the richer slave plantation regions of the Deep South, and wartime propaganda had laid much of the blame for this awful war on the planter elite. Their homes in Oxford and the surrounding countryside became targets of vandalism and revenge.

One of the most conspicuous targets was the home of Jacob Thompson. A former cabinet officer under President Buchanan, now serving the Confederate army, Thompson was the epitome of treachery in the eyes of Union officers. From his rooftop, Thompson had watched Grant's army come toward Oxford and fled when it became clear the Confederates were not going to hold the town. Soldiers were already looting the Thompson mansion, destroying fine china and furniture, when Grant ordered that the home be converted to use as a temporary hospital for wounded Union soldiers. Any property in the house that was useful to that purpose was to be confiscated. Grant personally went through Thompson's correspondence to find incriminating evidence that showed his "treasonable" intentions before the war.[72]

Dey Swep' Ever Thing Clean in Dey Path

In local legend (and in Faulkner's fiction) Grant is often blamed for burning the town, but this is wrong; he planned to make Oxford his winter headquarters. He moved into the James Brown mansion while Union forces occupied Oxford and established camps up and down the Mississippi Central line. They had been in Lafayette County for about three weeks when a sudden blow at the main supply depot in Holly Springs not only forced a hasty retreat from Lafayette County but derailed the plan for Sherman's advance on Vicksburg. Confederate general Earl Van Dorn led a surprise raid on Holly Springs early on Sunday morning, December 20, and destroyed more than a million dollars worth of Union supplies. Grant had been notified of the movement of Van Dorn's troops flanking to the east through Pontotoc, but he was unable to intercept them. The Union commander in charge at Holly Springs, apparently taken by surprise, surrendered without resistance. He was later dismissed with charges of "cowardly and disgraceful conduct," but it was all too late, and Grant's plans to take Vicksburg were dealt a severe blow.[73]

The news of Van Dorn's raid "caused much rejoicing among the people in Oxford," Grant recorded in his memoirs. Oxford women who, a few days earlier, were weeping or remonstrating as the Confederates retreated, were now wearing what one Union private called "a look of joy and triumph." The slaves were not so joyous. Private Boyd observed: "Great crowds of Negroes stood along the side walks dressed in their best Sunday clothes and many of them looked frightened and disheartened that we were going *back*." Grant remembered the Oxford citizens who gathered outside his headquarters to gloat: "They came with broad smiles on their faces to ask what I was going to do now without anything for my soldiers to eat." Grant responded calmly (and not a little spitefully) that his army was going to confiscate from their farms all the food and forage it could find; "the smiles soon turned to dismay." "Countenances soon changed, and so did the inquiry. The next was, 'What are *we* to do?' " Grant must have been furious. One soldier's diary indicates that Grant considered razing the whole town of Oxford but thought better of it and rescinded his order.[74]

The turn toward a harsher policy of war waged against civilians drew on a new understanding of the widespread rebel sympathies among the southern people—exactly what Grant now witnessed in Oxford. At the beginning of the war, the assumption had been that a willful elite of aristocratic slave-holders had led the South into secession without respect to the will of the southern people. As the Union army pushed deeper into the South, Grant and others began to see enough hardened rebel sympathizers among soldiers and civilians to know better. When Grant's wife, Julia, visited him in Mississippi, she was astonished at the belligerence of the southern women she met. She, after all, was a native of the South who came attended by one of her slaves expecting to be welcomed by her people. Instead, a delegation of Holly Springs ladies treated her to a concert of rebel songs and berated her about the unconstitutional nature of the Union war against them. Other women took delight in telling her the news of Van Dorn's raid.[75]

Grant's embrace of a harsher civilian policy might well have been provoked by such displays as he and Julia saw in northern Mississippi, but it was also a response to the practical necessities of an army now penetrating deep into enemy territory and needing to "subsist off the rebel population." Confiscating local supplies of food became common practice during the Union advance into Mississippi. Now, however, Grant's orders took the practice of hand-to-mouth foraging to a whole new level of operation aimed at confiscating all food supplies that could be found, along with wagons and draft animals to transport them. They scoured the Mississippi countryside with astonishing Yankee thoroughness. Food for men and animals was the first order of the day, and this involved not only raiding pantries and smoke-houses but also emptying corn cribs and barns and slaughtering hundreds of hogs, beef cattle, and sheep. To carry away all their newly acquired provisions, every mule and horse that could walk, along with wagons, was appropriated as well. [76] "I didn't never see no fitin' durin' de war," Lucindy Hall Shaw remembered, "but I sho saw a lot of yankees; de hole regiments cum thru; dey swep' ever thing clean in dey path; dey didn't leave us bread."[77] Anything the army thought it might need was subject to confiscation, along with booty of all kinds: silverware, clothing, jewelry, china, crystal, even a church Bible. Some things were snatched for their value, but soldiers' diaries also admit they were looking for souvenirs of their wartime adventures.

"For 15 miles east and west of the Railroad, from Coffeeville to La Grange, nearly everything for the subsistence of man or beast has been appropriated for the use of our army," Grant boasted to his superiors in Washington.[78] "I was amazed at the quantity of supplies the country afforded," he later recorded in his memoirs. "It showed that we could have subsisted off the country for two months instead of two weeks. . . . This taught me a lesson which was taken advantage of later in the campaign." From Lafayette County to Sherman's March to the Sea, Grant, Sherman, and other Union generals were learning and applying these lessons in what became a new brand of warfare. "It should be remembered," Grant wrote, "that . . . it had not been demonstrated that an army could operate in an enemy's territory depending upon the country for supplies."[79] Lafayette County was a proving ground for a cruel new form of warfare.

Among the lessons Grant, Sherman, and Union soldiers were taking from the invasion of northern Mississippi was that this brand of warfare would also involve harsh punishment of the civilian population, including plundering their food supplies, destroying railroads, buildings, and other property, and encouraging slave rebellion and flight. The war had become more than just a military contest between two opposing armies. If it was not a full-blown "total war" in the sense the twentieth century would give to that expression, it was, nonetheless, a definite turn toward disrupting civilian life as a policy rather than as an incidental consequence of military conflict. The men and women at the southern home front would learn that the rebellion they were supporting, the war they had sent their sons and husbands off to fight, was going to be waged against them as well. A revolution is not a dinner party, one famous revolutionary once said. Few areas of the South learned the cruel lessons of war more painfully than Lafayette County, Mississippi.

Of course, southern civilians did not see soldiers pillaging their farms and inciting their slaves to rebel as part of a military strategy; they saw venal Yankees acting out of sheer malice. "I have not yet told you what those fiends in human form took from us," one angry victim wrote to his brother serving in Virginia that winter. "They took both of Lawrences fine horses . . . and two of our best mules . . . I hope it may never be my fate to witness such another scene."[80] Hundreds of such letters from the home front to the front lines ensured that the demoralization of civilians would have its effect on the morale of their men at war.

It may seem remarkable that along with what often appears to be wanton plundering of property, Union officers frequently issued vouchers to civilians acknowledging the food, meat, livestock, and equipment they were dragging away. Ordinary citizens of Mississippi, Union policy initially dictated, were to be presumed loyal citizens of the United States. Therefore, any property the U.S. Army confiscated from citizens could be reclaimed, or its value reimbursed, later. Many Lafayette County victims of foraging parties were, therefore, handed vouchers signed by Union officers as their corn, livestock, mules, and wagons were taken away. It may seem preposterous when Faulkner's Rosa "Granny" Millard in The Unvanquished requests an invading army to return the mules, silver, and other property it has appropriated from her, but the story dramatizes this principle of confiscation and redemption, which was supposed to be accorded to loyal southern citizens. In Faulkner's gallant Colonel Dick, he was documenting in slightly exaggerated manner the policy of conciliation toward civilians. Granny Millard is not only thoroughly charmed, she is also handsomely rewarded when confused Yankee soldiers, in a comical misunderstanding, hand over dozens of mules, chests of silver, and slaves. No wonder she scolds other southerners who assume the Yankees to be fiends.

Many in Lafayette County felt it their right to claim damages and compensation from the Southern Claims Commission, set up after the war to settle such cases. More than two hundred claimants from Lafayette County asked the government to recompense them for mules and wagons, corn, and other personal property given up to the invading army. Among them was Burlina Butler, William Faulkner's great-grandmother, who claimed losses that included confiscated horses, provisions, and forage worth nearly $1,200. Her claim was denied, as were most, because her loyalty to the Union was doubtful, but many did win compensation.[81]

Loyalty was the critical factor, and the invading Union army often had to make a judgment of civilian loyalty on the spot. Orders from Washington directed the occupying Union forces to "subsist off the *rebel* sympathizers," and those known to be Union sympathizers, or those who openly demonstrated support for the federal soldiers in their midst, often managed to win protection. Robert Cathey, who owned a farm near the Yocona River, secured a letter issued by General James B. McPherson, ordering, "All officers and Soldiers of this command are forbidden to forage upon or in any manner molest the property or person of R. F. Cathey a citizen La Fayette Co. Miss he having taken the oath of allegiance to the United States."[82]

In several other cases, however, Union sympathizers won no favor with the marauding army. Urcilla Fondren and her late husband had been ardent opponents of secession, but her large plantation near Taylor's Depot was too rich for the hungry Union army to resist. She reported later that "nearly all the ppy [property] on the plantation was taken for army use." Mrs. Fondren was left so destitute that "she had to ask for rations of Gen McPherson and he . . . gave her a horse . . . and a barrel of flour and promised that she should be paid for her property." She was repaid eventually.[83]

Other Union foragers made no apologies as they stripped the farms and homes over the protests of their owners. Jane Medders lay sick in bed when the army came and confiscated an enormous quantity of livestock, meat, fodder, and food. She could hear her daughters proclaiming the family's pro-Union allegiance and begging that their property be left alone. One soldier felt sympathy and tried to intervene, but the others only cursed the daughters and said the property "belonged to Uncle Sam."[84]

Albert Browning remembered the day the Yankee troops came and cleaned out his farm: "They came and took off the top of my crib and threw out the corn all around it and take baskets and blankets and filled them up and take them off. They killed the hogs and took them off. . . . They carried off the Fodder on their backs and on horses. They took the Bee gums off. . . . They took potatoes off. . . . They took the Poultry off." Browning complained to a Union officer, who intervened and placed a guard around the house.[85]

Sam Ragland was overseer at the plantation the late Washington Price had bequeathed to his minor son. Ragland tried to tell Union soldiers that the boy, Bem Price, was only sixteen, not of age to be regarded a rebel sympathizer. It did no good at the time, but later Bem Price would be one of the few to win his claim for compensation. "There was no cotton cultivated on the place this year," Ragland testified. "We were trying to make something to eat." Then the Yankees came: "after all of our crop was gathered" the soldiers arrived with "a very long train of wagons." Some loaded the wagons with corn while "another portion was killing and dressing hogs." "They continued to come every day with there wagons for about a week and haul away until everything was gone except a little corn that they left on the ground where loaded. . . . It was all I had left."[86] When they heard the "Yankees were coming," Sam, one of the Price plantation slaves, testified, he and others "took twenty three mules down into the bottom in the cane to hide them." But an "old mule named Dave would not go so we had to leave him behind." "The Yankees followed us right into the bottom and took the mules. . . . There were as good mules as you could find in the state."[87]

One unidentified wealthy woman thought that by inviting the Union soldiers to occupy her house and land, she might be protected. "The second night (the Jayhawkers or cavalry for I believe they are all jayhawkers) broke open the smokehouse and cellar and took or rather stole nearly all I had to eat that is sugar, meat, molasses, and potatoes." Like Granny Millard, she tried to appeal to the more gentlemanly Union officers: "I wrote a note to 'Headquarters' to Col Dickey, Chief of cavalry requesting protection from marauders and . . . Gen Grant sent two of his staff officers here and I boarded them." They suggested she turn her house over to some other officers as headquarters, "and I did acquiesce seeing and knowing that they were going to come if they wished and perhaps by treating them politely I would not be driven out of my own house." Several of the officers were every bit as courtly and polite as Faulkner's Colonel Dick, but she complained another was "the most bitter spiteful and I must say fiendish Yankee I ever heard of." He "took especial pains to annoy me in a thousand ways," and even "ordered my trees in the yard to be cut down for firewood."[88]

As Grant retreated northward that winter, the foraging and plundering continued with a fury. Farms for miles on either side of the Mississippi Central, the main line of march, were stripped bare. Not only was the food taken but most of the animals, wagons, and other things essential to operating farms and producing more food were taken as well. The war had come home with a vengeance. When Grant's army withdrew north of the Tallahatchie on a cold, wet December day, just before Christmas, "the country [was] literally devastated for ten miles in all directions around Oxford. The horrors of the situation at the university were unspeakable."[89] In Lafayette County that December the basic strategy of assaulting the Confederate home front had become clear. The purpose of all this pillaging went well beyond any need to feed the invading army, which, after all, was making a hasty retreat north toward supply lines in Tennessee. The motive was to deprive the Confederate military as well as the civilian population of food and undermine the morale of both. "There will be but little in North Mississippi to support guerrillas in a few weeks more," Grant reported to Washington after he pulled out of Oxford.[90]

More than just food, mules, and wagons were lost that winter. The invasion and plundering had shaken the pride and confidence of the civilian population and left a profound sense of humiliation and dishonor. This shame was seasoned with bitter anger not only toward the Yankee foe but also in growing measure toward those Confederate leaders who had abandoned them to the invaders.

"A melancholy gloom overhangs our beloved community," the Presbyterians of College Hill recorded in their church minutes. In language that was repeated in many letters and diaries, the minutes go on to detail some of the degrading examples of dishonor suffered at the hands of the "fiendish" Yankees: "They would enter dwellings at a late hour of the night, arouse the sleeping inmates and with the most profane and blasphemous language demand money and search ladies' trunks and private dressers and enraged at not finding nothing which they desired they would deface and destroy furniture with their sabers and bayonets. . . . They were regardless of the pleas of females and offered insults to the old helpless and inoffensive. . . . Thus from day to day . . . we were subjected to the insults and cruel treatment of our insolent unprincipalled foe."[91] But the agony of war was only beginning to be felt on the battlefields and at the home front. The "far summer thunder of war," as Faulkner put it, had now come home. They were falling not soaring, and "the once-vast fixed impalpable increaseless and threatless earth" below was fast becoming "one omnivorous roar of rock." When they hit the ground at the end of 1862 "the preliminary anesthetic of shock" was such "that the agony of bone and flesh will not even be felt."[92]

Then gone; that night the town was occupied by Federal troops; two nights later, it was on fire (the Square, the stores and shops and the professional offices), gutted (the courthouse too), the blackened jagged topless jumbles of brick wall enclosing like a ruined jaw the blackened shell of the courthouse between its two rows of topless columns, which (the columns) were only blackened and stained, being tougher than fire . . . and now the town was as though insulated by fire or perhaps cauterised by fire from fury and turmoil . . . and so in effect it was a whole year in advance of Appomattox (only the undefeated undefeatable women, vulnerable only to death, resisted, endured, irreconcilable).

—WILLIAM FAULKNER, Requiem for a Nun

seven The Vanquished

The war southerners sent their men to fight might have been enough to cope with, given the overwhelming odds of manpower, resources, industrial capacity, and commercial prowess all favoring the North. This war, however, had become more than just a military engagement between two armies. Coinciding with the invasion of Union forces into northern Mississippi, the war became a revolutionary upheaval that brought a breakdown of slave control combined with volatile shifts of loyalty among various elements of the white civilian population. The advance of the Union army into western Tennessee and, sporadically, into northern Mississippi left the people of Lafayette County in a no-man's-land between two armies, neither one capable of securing the area and protecting civilians. From within also, the pressure of war brought severe divisiveness. Not only did the war bring to the surface the massive fissure between slave and master, but there were also growing signs of white opposition to Confederate authority: draft dodging and desertion, blockade running, and banditry. Pervading all segments of white society was a war-weary spirit brought by hardship and deprivation, felt by grieving parents, wives, and children and by those who were no longer certain that the prize was worth the sacrifice. The Confederate frontier of northern Mississippi became a vacillating, contested field of guerrilla warfare with Nathan Bedford Forrest's Confederate cavalry harassing Union forces as they penetrated and retreated with indecisive effect. After 1862 it became a "ride and shoot" war of raiding and foraging that left the civilian population caught between two armies and subject to wanton pillaging by either side. On the field of battle, Forrest demonstrated that the Confederacy could hold out almost indefinitely, as long as the civilian population was willing to endure the hardships the war and blockade inflicted. The Confederate home front in Lafayette County also demonstrated it could endure the ravages of the Yankees. In the end, it was the opposition from within as much as the military defeats at the hands of the Union that undermined morale. The real wonder is not that southerners were vanquished but that they held out so long.[1]

Long before historians of the American Civil War began to turn their gaze from the battle fronts to the home front, from military leaders to soldiers and civilians, William Faulkner viewed the war through the eyes of the women and children, free and slave. Though not considered among his greatest literary achievements, *The Unvanquished* may stand as one of his more discerning interpretations of history. Young Bill Falkner grew up in a community immersed in the history and memory of the Civil War. For hours, day after day, he sat speechless and listened to aging Confederate veterans swapping war stories while they whittled and chewed tobacco on benches at Courthouse Square. His grandmother had been among the local women who led the campaign to raise funds for the Confederate memorial erected in front of the courthouse in 1907. There he stood, the marble soldier, facing South, back to the North, armed, erect, defiant even, the inscription below honoring the "just and holy cause" for which he had fought. Aging veterans whooped their rebel yells at the unveiling and some engaged in a sham battle afterward. The Civil War Faulkner depicted was less romantic than the one memorialized in local history. The women of wartime Yoknapatawpha were less patriotic in their support of the cause than their descendants who raised marble monuments in its honor, and the slaves Faulkner depicted are rebellious, quick to flee their bondage and strike out for freedom. Bushwhackers are shown preying on women left at home while others engage in trade with the enemy, and Confederate soldiers dressed in stolen Yankee uniforms are reduced to raiding and stealing horses in a war they no longer believe can be won. Faulkner told his own war stories, ones that were closer to the actual history of the war than to the romantic legends of the Lost Cause.[2]

Freedom War

The biggest blow to the Confederate home front came from within the very institution secession and war had intended to protect—slavery. In September 1862, during the Union invasion of northern Mississippi, Lincoln issued the Emancipation Proclamation, and the meaning of the war was transformed into a war against slavery. Lafayette County stood in the midst of an unrehearsed experiment in slave liberation, flight, and rebellion.

Fears of slave uprisings intensified with the advance of the Union invasion that fall. Apparently the home guard organized in 1861 had failed to provide sufficient security. On December 28, 1862, Major General W. W. Loring sent a telegram to General John C. Pemberton reporting that the "people of Lafayette County are anxious to organize themselves into a company of old men for the defence of their homes and to prevent servile insurrection which is threatened." These fears were not the product of paranoia or of political rhetoric such as had whipped up hysteria over slave insurrection on the eve of secession. The fear of slave rebellion was now grounded in the new reality of war. A new Union strategy, embodied in the Emancipation Proclamation, made the destruction of slavery part of a general assault on southern society at the home front.

But it was the slaves themselves who proclaimed their own emancipation, and they did so in the wake of Grant's hasty retreat in December 1862.[3] On January 17, 1863, another alarming telegram arrived from Major General Loring announcing that the "negroes have driven overseers from plantations in Lafayette Co. and taken possession of everything. I shall send a mounted Regt there at once." Pemberton responded the next day that he had an "Army with forty rounds of ammunition per gun boxed and ready to send to Lafayette County Miss." The story of Lafayette County's slave uprising that January is cloaked in silence. Loring reported only that a regiment had been sent to Lafayette County, but no details can be found in the Confederate records.

It was no false alarm. Rebecca Pegues wrote to her husband a few days before Loring's alarm to tell him: "All the negroes that remained in the country are all in a state of insubordination. No overseers scarcely on any plantations. They generally were compelled to leave. The negroes on many places are still armed." [4] A month later the slaves of Lafayette County remained rebellious, for another telegram reported they were "dividing the mules and other property of their masters among themselves." [5] Jane Wilburn, a town slave in Oxford, returning by railroad with her mistress during the turmoil that winter, recalled that "the negroes were all uprising and rioting." [6] "Wherever the yankies went," Eliza Pegues wrote to her brother that January, "they proclaimed freedom to the negroes, told them everything left belonged to them, use or sell it as they pleased. Charlotte writes they are in a state of insubordination and do and take what they please." [7]

The Union's dramatic turn toward a war of emancipation was part of the same logic of modern war that led the invading Union army to turn southern property to its own good. Indeed, slaves who flocked to the invading Union were treated initially as "contraband of war," enemy property that had fallen into the hands of the military. Until the fall of 1862, Lincoln held to his policy not to interfere with slavery, insisting that his goal was to restore the Union not to emancipate slaves. He came to realize that emancipating slaves might save the Union and destroy the cause of the rebellion. Responding to pressure in the North and abroad, in September 1862 President Lincoln issued the Preliminary Emancipation Proclamation. In brief, it declared slaves in those states and parts of states that remained in rebellion as of January 1, 1863, "forever free" by authority of the U.S. government. Moreover, in language full of ominous meaning to whites in the South, the proclamation specified that the federal government "will recognize and maintain the freedom of such persons, and will do no act or acts to repress such persons, or any of them, in any efforts they may make for their actual freedom." What this implied was that the invading Union army would not only allow but would also *encourage* slave rebellion. John Brown's revolutionary vision of slaves seizing their own freedom in armed insurrection had, it seemed, become official Union policy. More frightening still, the final version of the proclamation proposed to enlist refugee slaves in the United States Army and let them fight for their own freedom. Rebellious slaves with guns — the nightmare of every southern slave owner — was about to become reality.

The Union troops invading the South became an army of liberation. Everywhere they went that fall and winter they made sure the slaves understood they were free or about to be free. Many slaves seemed to know already, through the "grapevine telegraph" that quickly spread the news that the "blue men a'comin'" heralded the Day of Jubilee. Faulkner's Loosh, a slave of John Sartoris, is one who anticipates the invasion with dreams of freedom, and he seems to know more than the military officers do about the

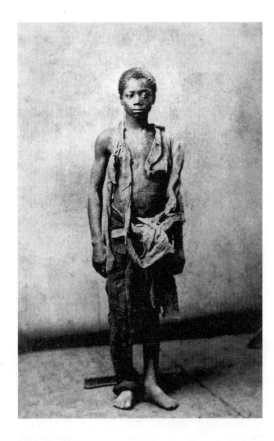

A refugee slave,
Corinth, Mississippi, 1863.
(Courtesy of the Mississippi
Department of Archives
and History)

course of the war as it comes nearer to his home in Yoknapatawpha County.
"Watch Loosh, because he knows," John Sartoris advises his family. What
Loosh knows is that "Ginral Sherman gonter sweep the earth and the Race
gonter all be free!"[8]

Many slaves did not wait for the Day of Jubilee. As the Union army drove
South, word went out ahead of them and large groups of refugee slaves
came north to the advancing line of bluecoats. "They seem to be intoxi-
cated with the idea of careless freedom held out to them," one slave owner
complained that fall. Slave masters were faced with a constant threat of
rebellion or flight. In early November, above Holly Springs, one Illinois soldier wrote in his diary: "Nothing to day worth note only occasionally we
see a drove of female negroes fleeing from Bondage." Again, the next day,
"we see large groups of negroes."[9] Another soldier described a scene near
Corinth in late September: "Negroes old and young crowded both sides of
the road and hung screaming and crying upon the rear of our retreating
forces." He found two slave children "whom their mother had dropped in
her scared and hasty flight and left to the tender mercies of the forest and

the rebellion." "We moved in a cloud of dust" toward the Union lines, he wrote.[10]

Grant was overwhelmed by the northward flight of slaves. For the first time in the war the Union army was entering the densely populated plantation region of the Deep South. "Citizens south of us are leaving their home, and negroes comin in by wagon loads. What will I do with them?" Grant asked his superiors in Washington. Orders came back to place refugee slaves in useful employment as teamsters and laborers, assisting in building forts and railroads and picking what was left of the cotton crop. "So far as possible," Halleck added, "subsist them and your army on the rebel inhabitants of Mississippi."[11]

In Grand Junction, Tennessee, just above the state line on the Memphis-Charleston rail line, the Union army organized a large "contraband camp" for the growing mass of slaves fleeing from bondage in Mississippi and western Tennessee. General Grant assigned John Eaton, a chaplain with the Union army, to supervise the camp. Grand Junction was the birthplace of what would later become the Freedmen's Bureau, a federal government agency charged with protecting the former slaves during their transition to freedom. Eaton, like most of the Union army and political leaders, had little clue as to what to do with the mass of slave refugees. The sudden, unexpected deluge of refugees was more than a nuisance to the army; it was regarded as a "menace" to the whole military operation.

John Eaton recalled the slave exodus into the contraband camp in language that expressed his despair and his admiration as he witnessed an enslaved people seeking freedom:

> Imagine, if you will, a slave population, springing from antecedent bondage, forsaking its local traditions and all the associations and attractions of the old plantation life, coming garbed in rags or in silks, with feet shod or bleeding, individually or in families, and larger groups—an army of slaves and fugitives, pushing its way irresistibly toward an army of fighting men. . . . The arrival among us of these hordes was like the oncoming of cities. There was no plan to this exodus, no Moses to lead it. Unlettered reason or the mere inarticulate decision of instinct brought them to us. . . . A blind terror stung them, an equally blind hope allured them, and to us they came. There were men, women, and children in every stage of disease or decrepitude, often nearly naked, with flesh torn by the terrible experiences of their escapes.[12]

Faulkner's own depiction of the exodus of slaves out of Mississippi bears a remarkable resemblance to Eaton's, particularly in its notion of a universal instinct for something called "freedom." In The Unvanquished the fleeing slaves are seen at first from a distance, a mass of people signified only by the huge clouds of dust they raise on the roads going north. They seem drawn like lemmings by religious faith to a river they call Jordan, across which is a promised land of freedom. Bayard Sartoris, a young white boy whose family owns slaves, is amazed at "the motion, the impulse to move which had already seethed to a head among his [Ringo, his slave friend] people, darker than themselves, reasonless, following and seeking a delusion, a dream, a bright shape which they could not know since there was nothing in their heritage, nothing in the memory even of the old men to tell the others." Faulkner describes this yearning for freedom as something that transcends memory and race. It is, he suggests, a basic human instinct: "one of those impulses inexplicable yet invincible which appear among races of people at intervals and drive them to pick up and leave all security and familiarity of earth and home and start out, they dont know where, empty handed, blind to everything but a hope and a doom." [13]

John Eaton confessed that Union soldiers, the supposed saviors of these slaves in flight, were frequently cruel and brutal. "Often the slaves met prejudices against their color more bitter than any they had left behind." Faulkner's description of Union soldiers beating back refugee slaves as they approach the "River Jordan" was not entirely fanciful. One Lafayette County plantation mistress wrote with undisguised pleasure that her runaway slaves were suffering at the hands of the Yankees. At Holly Springs, during the evacuation that followed Van Dorn's raid, refugee slaves were loaded on railroad cars. She wrote, "Several regiments of yankees had lain down their arms declaring that they would not fight to *free the negro* and that the negro *shouldn't go north* and so they run the train out of Holly Springs and detached the engine and run it back and after putting on a great power of stream reversed the steam running the engine with great power upon the cars of negroes killing them up awfully." Refugees who got to Memphis met other disasters: "I have just heard from Memphis it is a perfect reign of terror there. One hundred and ninety negroe children died there the day after the snow." [14]

"Their condition was appalling," Eaton later remarked of the refugees. "Sometimes they were intelligent and eager to help themselves; often they were bewildered or stupid or possessed by the wildest notions of what liberty might mean." [15] Faulkner's characters also have strange concepts of freedom. Bayard Sartoris, a white slave master's son, fears that the Yankees are "going to set us all free." In a dream he imagines freedom in the form of people wandering and lost "without any home to go to because we were forever free." When he and his young slave friend, Ringo, see what they think is General Sherman's army approaching, Bayard warns Ringo that the Yankees want to set them *both* free, and they dash off to ambush a Yankee soldier. Slaves like Loosh, on the other hand, take flight with a firm notion of the meaning of freedom as something God wants for his people. "I going," Loosh announces in a forceful summary of the meaning of emancipation. "I done been freed; God's own angel proclamated me free and gonter general me to Jordan. I don't belong to John Sartoris now; I belongs to me and God."[16]

Runaways had been a chronic feature of slavery, but what occurred in the winter of 1862–63 constituted something altogether different. Though many, like Loosh, returned to their masters eventually, the slave exodus that followed the Union retreat was much more than a short-term strategy of running off to bargain for better treatment within slavery; this was a flight *out of bondage*. Though the records indicate that a preponderance of men fled, the frequent reports of women and children fleeing northward also indicate many slaves saw this as an escape they would make as families. Before this exodus, the scattered advertisements and letters that document the runaways of Lafayette County rarely mention women running off. Women usually had primary responsibility for children, and they faced greater risks than men on the run. Now the roads leading north were thronged with women, children, and whole families heading for freedom. This, in Polly Turner Cancer's words, was the meaning of what she called the "Freedom War."[17]

Some slave owners and Confederate officials thought the answer was to relocate slaves in the interior, away from the advancing Union armies. Confederate president Jefferson Davis ordered that slaves be removed from the line of enemy advance, but Mississippi governor John Pettus replied that this would be "disastrous to the country" and calculated to "drive" the slaves into the hands of the enemy instead of protect them.[18] "When persons start with their negroes many of them run away," one slave owner complained. "I believe confidently they (all the negroes) are waiting for the arrival of the yankees and will leave en masse. *Now what ought we to do?*"[19] There were other pressures bearing on the slaves who stayed behind. The Confederate army was now impressing slaves at Vicksburg as laborers and teamsters. In early February 1863 the Confederate command issued an order for three hundred slave laborers and another one hundred teamsters to be filled with slaves from Lafayette and neighboring counties.[20] This gave slaves one more incentive to flee.

Long after the war, whites celebrated the legendary loyal slaves who stood by their masters during the war and refused to tell those "white trash" Yankees where the family silver was buried. They were loyal to their white masters and loyal to the South, and their image was often invoked in support of continuing paternalistic race relations.[21] There were many, no doubt, who did remain loyal. "Aunt" Johanna Isom, who survived to tell her story to the WPA interviewers in the 1930s, was a favorite reference for images of a slave "loyal to the nth degree to her 'white folks' " (the Jacob Thompson family). Yet even she admitted to fleeing during that winter of jubilee. She told of how "all her folks" took a mule and wagon and headed for Memphis after Grant left. A Yankee patrol intervened and threatened to take their mule and wagon unless they promised they would go back home go back home: "Sho wuz glad to get back home," she told the white woman interviewing her.[22] Rhoda Hunt was equally discreet when she told the white WPA interviewer, "yessum, I could tell you a heap about the Civil War and when the Yankees come but I'se been thinkin' 'bout it and my conscience tells me to keep my mouth shet, let de dead rest and don't bother trouble lessen trouble troubles you. No, mam, my mistress nebber would talk 'bout dem happenings enduring the Civil War and you ain't gonna get me to talk about nothin' my whitefolks wouldn't talk 'bout." [23]

One favorite piece of local lore told of "an old trusty slave negro" on the Price plantation who was left with the task of burying a large box filled with the family silver. The "Yankees came and took the old slave away," the story told, and "no one every knew what became of the box." Long after the war, the land surrounding the abandoned Price mansion (which Faulkner adopted as the Old Frenchman's place) became pockmarked with holes dug by local treasure hunters. The legend of the loyal slave who refused to betray the location of the box grew with each shovel full of dirt.[24] It was one of several such stories of abiding loyalty. "I remember when de yankees cum thru'," former slave Rebecca Wood told an interviewer years later. "Marster tol' us to git all de stock an' drive dem to de swamp' an' I remember us chilun wud ride on de cotton wagons when dey wuz drivin' hit to de swamp; we hid all the silver too, an' wu'd none uv us tell de yankees." [25]

Disloyal slaves were often said to be victims of deceiving Yankees who, according to one account in January 1863, "made close and constant companions of our servants exchanging hospitalities with them in the most social and familiar manner." "They used every act that deception falsehood and flattery could invent to induce them to leave their masters and homes and accompany them to the land of freedom." [26] Jane Wilburn recounted how Union soldiers would take hoop skirts and long gowns with long trains from the homes of wealthy white women in Oxford and dress up young slave women; "they took the white women's silk dresses an' give 'em to ther slave gals, an' den made 'em do their cookin'. It sho wuz funny to see them gals dressed up on them fine silk dresses wid hoop skirts, standin' over a big pot stirrin' ther soup for them yankees." They "wud be cookin' out in de yard wid dey trains hung over dey arms." [27] The dressing up of slave women in the silk gowns of their mistresses may have seemed like a humorous diversion, but it also had to be a deeply humiliating scene for whites to witness and an exhilarating one for slaves to behold.

The mention of "their slave gals" is one of several references to the personal, perhaps sexual, intimacy that developed between Union soldiers and slave women. Lucindy Hall Shaw, apparently referring to Union soldiers, remembered that "durin' de war de white mens wu'd run atter de cullud gals." She added, "I never did remire white mens an' I didn' thave nuthin' to do wid dem." One Lafayette County white woman whose slaves ran off with the Union soldiers learned that two slaves who opposed leaving were persuaded by their daughter Polly to flee. Polly had "become intimate with one of the staff officers, who professed to love her so devotedly and told her that her whole family mother and sisters, should live in splendor." [28] The census leaves us only meager clues about the degree of sexual collaboration between Union soldiers and slave women. There was a slight increase in the number of mulatto children who might have been conceived during the Union invasion, but the number of interracial conceptions appears generally low during the war when most local white men were away (mulatto births would surge after 1865). [29]

Slaves were taking sides in a war that was enveloping their world, and Confederate military officers found they could not count on them to help their cause. When a Confederate patrol discovered a group of Union soldiers ensconced in a plantation house near the Pontotoc County border, the officer "procured a negro to go and find out their strength and locality." The Union soldiers had taken over the plantation of a "Mr. Piggios" (possibly Thomas E. B. Pegues), "drove him and his family out of his house and armed his slaves." The soldiers told the slaves "they were no longer the slave, but the master" and to prepare for a "grand jubilee." The slaves and their emancipators then planned an elaborate supper, the soldiers bringing wine procured from Oxford and the slaves preparing a feast of turkey, pork, and other foods. When the Confederate patrol "charged upon the premises, surrounding the dwelling and quarters" they found that their spy, the "treacherous darky," had informed the Yankees. The Yankees fled, leaving behind a mule and "a splendid supper that their friends sambos had prepared for them." Though foiled in their surprise raid, the Confederates reported that "amidst our disappointment . . . we could not refrain from pitching into the served up turkey, pig, &c, &c." [30]

Slave owners were not prepared for the sudden defection of their slaves. One woman, told of how a Union officer had turned her house into a camp for "straggling negroes that come to him for protection." The soldiers fraternized with her slaves, and she suspected many would run off sooner or later. The slaves reassured her they would remain loyal to her, but when the Yankees suddenly left, she was astonished: "They took all of my negroes even Hester and Bet and Chapman an orphan boy in the kitchen." What truly bothered her was not so much that the soldiers "took" the slaves but that the slaves betrayed her. They "were so deceitful . . . they talked against the Yankees. . . . Old Harry assured me that they were none of them going to the yankees and they all deceived me very well for I was shocked as I had rang the bell several times and no answer or noise I hurried on my clothes and all were gone. . . . I kept thinking they would come in directly." [31] They never came, and the bell she was ringing to arouse the slaves became her own reveille to their betrayal.

Mary Smither awakened early one morning to someone shouting, "the negroes are leaving." She went outside and saw her father's two wagons, hitched to oxen, loaded with the family slaves' clothing and provisions and the "children dressed up white and clean." "Away they all went." [32] Long after Grant's army left, the slaves of Lafayette were continually running off to Memphis or somewhere behind Union lines. During 1863 and 1864 the Oxford Baptist Church alone excluded from its fellowship at least eighteen slave members because they had "all gone off with the Federal Armey." [33]

Among those slaves who remained, many, it seemed, no longer regarded themselves as slaves. Some simply refused to work, engaging in what the historian W. E. B. Du Bois called a "general strike" among slaves across the South.[34] "No one dares to threaten or correct a negro now," one dispirited slave owner complained; "if they do they leave forth with." [35] Numerous reports indicate that slaves were confiscating property to suit their own needs, extending the principle of self-emancipation to their masters' other property. "What the Yankees didn't take the negroes are taking or have taken," one woman complained in January 1863. "I understand that they took every thing in sis Julia's house and Fathers and broke up all their glass china etc." [36] Rebecca Pegues, stranded out at Orange Hill without her husband, related that she now feared her own slaves and had to seek refuge with her sister in town. "Our negro Evans has behaved very badly," she wrote to one relative in January 1863. "I wish I could have him taken and sent off to our army—or sold. Mr. Gist thinks him dangerous and is unwilling to go out there to live whilst he is there. . . . Oh! The anxiety they have given and still give me." [37]

The disloyalty of slaves provoked in whites a distrust and bitterness that sometimes spilled over into a generalized racial animosity. "I have learned a great deal about my servants since they left which makes me rejoice that they are gone, and I assure you I will never trust another darkie," one woman wrote after her slaves had run off. She wrote of the suffering the runaways had met at the hands of Yankee soldiers with some vindictive pleasure. Two of her father's slaves had returned saying they "were tired of the yankees but we found out they were fixing to get their families off soon." Out at her father's place, she went on, "his negroes have suffered for want of attention . . . and many of them were so mean they ought to die."[38]

The invasion upset the whole structure of dependence and authority that governed relations between master and slave. When J. F. Tankersley, a prominent member of the College Hill Presbyterian Church, was charged with killing a young female slave of his mother in the fall of 1864, he defended himself in terms that apparently every white slave owner could understand. All the slaves, he argued before the church session, had become "unmanageable, rude and insolent, setting at defiance all authority and insulting the female members of the family, breaking into the dwelling house, smoke house, and other houses and appropriating to their own use such articles as they desired, and also many other acts of rude and insulting conduct." When he went to administer a "correction" to this behavior, the "unfortunate girl" happened to be the first he confronted. She "not only rebelled but set his authority at perfect defiance, and attempted to make her escape." In anger, he shot her as she fled; she died a few days later. Tankersley expressed "deep sorrow for the offense as committed against God and the church" (though not against the dead slave, apparently). The church session deliberated over the case and decided the rebellious behavior of Tankersley's slaves was "intollerable, setting at defiance all family rule and government, disregarding the authority of the master." This kind of behavior, they feared, would "annihilate all family government" if it went unchecked. The judgment of the church session, "in view of the peculiar state of things in the country, and the demoralized condition of the servants, requiring the most absolute and rigid discipline," was that Tankersley ought be forgiven and allowed to remain in the fellowship of the church.[39]

War So Near Our Homes

Demoralization, by this time, may have better described whites than slaves, who were seizing their new freedom with astonishing boldness. In no other war before or since were American civilians exposed to the degree of invasion, destruction, and turmoil that white southerners suffered during the Civil War, and few parts of the South were more ravaged by prolonged invasions and raids than northern Mississippi. In a war that engaged so many of the civilian population, the morale of the home front remained critical to the success or failure of the Confederate cause. Northern Mississippi provides an especially vivid portrait of the Confederacy under the strains of war.[40] Dissension that had been drowned in a tide of martial gallantry and southern patriotism in the spring of 1861 soon resurfaced in the face of military defeats, conscription, invading Yankee armies, slave rebellion, and the grinding hardship of war and sacrifice on the home front. Fault lines of race, class, gender, and politics each divided the home front with varying force as the war continued. All whites — soldiers and civilians, men and women, fire-eating secessionists and Unionists, rich and poor — underwent a severe test of morale under the weight of invasion, destruction, slave rebellion, death, and defeat.

By early 1863, at the home front and the front lines, those who had supported a war to defend their homes, their women, and their slaves saw all three exposed to invasion, pillaging, and destruction at the hands of the enemy. Few of Lafayette County's military companies were left in Mississippi to defend their homeland, and letters from the front lines in Virginia, Tennessee, Georgia, and elsewhere were filled with anxious queries about the Union invasion back home. Charles Roberts was not far away in Tupelo when he wrote home to Oxford in June 1862: "My darling wife, . . . My great anxiety now is that Oxford will be left for awhile in the hands of the enemy." "I do not think they will in any way molest you. I would that I could be with you dear but you know that cannot and ought not to be in the present state of our Country." War, he added, "is a dreadful thing under the most favorable circumstances and more Especially when so near our homes."[41]

But as the war again drew ever nearer to his wife and family, Roberts's regiment was sent north to fight in Tennessee, and he, like most of Lafayette County's soldiers in the field, had to wait for whatever news they could get in letters from home. Thomas Goode Clark wrote to his wife from Richmond in December 1862: "It is a hard trial for I never wanted to see you all as bad in my life. We have understood that the yankies is all over our country and that our army has fell back to Grenada which has almost run some of our men crazy but I hope that it is not as bad as we have heard."[42] Isaac Duncan complained to his son fighting in Virginia that "in my opinion the chivalry of our state is in Virginia and I wish they were at home to infuse new life into our Western Army."[43]

Besides testing morale on the front lines and the home front, the Confederate obsession with the defense of Richmond and Virginia undermined Mississippi's objective of protecting the grain- and meat-producing northern counties that fed the rest of the state.[44] When more Mississippi troops were ordered to Virginia in the spring of 1862 some refused orders, and many deserted rather than abandon their families. One soldier wrote, "Quite a number of Goode Clark's com[pany] has deserted in consequence of being ordered to Virginia this is their excuse but really I think they don' want to fight anywhere." [45] For many of the men concerned, he may have been right, especially when fighting for the Confederacy meant abandoning home and family to marauding Union forces.

The spring planting season also brought tremendous pressure on farmers, especially those without slave labor, to return home to help their families put the crop in for the coming season. Some of the women John Robuck watched plowing and planting in the spring of 1862 "were wearing black calico frocks," mourning the men they lost at Shiloh and Corinth as they took their place in the fields.[46] Military discipline was altogether new to independent-minded white southern men, and few had any idea the war would last more than a few weeks or months when they joined. Confederate officers had great difficulty holding their regiments together as men deserted or failed to return from furlough. Under pressure, Confederate officers found they had to extend furloughs or risk outright desertion. They returned, in Faulkner's imagination, "actually almost sneaking home to spend two or three or seven days performing actions not only without glory (plowing land, repairing fences, killing meat for the smoke house)" that seemed "to emanate a kind of humility and apology." [47]

One solution that Confederate officers deployed was not to grant furloughs, especially when it meant a long trek home from the eastern front. Lieutenant Thomas Goode Clark begged for a furlough so he could return home in the winter of 1862–63, but his commanding officer, Colonel Miller, "thinks that every Boddy must stay in the army untill just such time as suits him. He is a hard master . . . it will do me good to tell him what I think of him for he is the most perfect tyrant that ever lived." The war, he added mournfully, "I hope will not last always." [48]

The Confederate conscription act passed in the aftermath of Shiloh brought a flood of new enlistees, many of them reluctant and resentful recruits coming into an army already shaken by defeat and invasion and often resentful of these stragglers.[49] Isaac Duncan wrote to his son in Virginia that "the Conscript law made quite a stampede among the malish [militia?] about Sarepta and more than two hundred and fifty volunteered in fact there are but 8 or 10 left between the ages of 18 and 35." [50] By the end of the war, nearly four thousand Mississippians claimed exemptions from the draft because of physical disability. Others were exempt because their work was deemed essential to the economy and government. Among the latter were several large planters exempted as "agriculturalists." [51]

The draft opened antagonisms between rich and poor, the most grating irritant being the so-called twenty-nigger law adopted in October 1862; it exempted from military duty one white man for every twenty slaves owned by one family. Though justified by concerns about controlling slaves, the effect of the law was to exempt draft-eligible planters and their sons. The conscription laws also exempted Confederate government officials, of which there were now legions, mostly from the upper ranks of society. In addition, those who could afford to, paid a substitute to take their place in the military.[52] One embittered dissenter in Lafayette County complained to neighbors in language that joined class and racial resentment: "It was the rich man's war and the poor man's fight. The poor man was fighting for the rich man's negroes."[53]

Questionable Loyalties

As the Union army drove deeper into northern Mississippi in late 1862, the morale of Confederate soldiers and civilians weakened dramatically.[54] Hundreds of Confederate soldiers voluntarily surrendered to Union forces or were captured with no resistance. Confederate records confirm widespread demoralization in the ranks. By December 9, Grant reported over twelve hundred enemy prisoners taken. "Besides these, many deserters come in daily to take the oath of allegiance and return home to the border States."[55] One report in a Memphis newspaper claimed that soon after the Union entered Oxford some sixteen hundred Confederate soldiers had deserted and "come in" to ask to be paroled. The deserters made "gloomy reports" on the demoralization of their forces. Another five hundred were reported captured, a third of them being paroled after taking the oath of loyalty.[56] Captured Confederate prisoners crowded into a makeshift prison in a large brick building in Oxford.[57] Private Cyrus Boyd witnessed more than one thousand Confederate prisoners brought up from south of Oxford. "The rank and file were the hardest looking set I have yet seen. Few of them had Knapsacks and they carried their spare clothes done up in an old quilt. They had no uniforms and were dressed in all colors and were dirty and filthy. . . . All of them looked haggard and worn out."[58] The "town was almost full of Rebel prisoners," another Iowa soldier wrote when he arrived in Oxford on December 6.[59]

From his headquarters in Oxford, General Grant invited loyal citizens as well as soldiers to receive amnesty and take the oath of loyalty to the United States. Here again we see Grant alternating, whether experimentally or indecisively, between a policy of conciliation and punishment. Mississippians, Grant wrote optimistically to General Halleck from Oxford on December 14, 1862, "show more signs of being subdued than any we have heretofore came across." Many were eager to surrender before the emancipation Proclamation went into effect.[60] A long line of men formed at the courthouse to sign the oath. Of the 226 men who signed the oath of amnesty that December nearly all were Lafayette County citizens, and more than three-quarters of them were over thirty years of age and therefore probably civilians. They may have been thinking the Confederate cause was lost and the Union army was there to stay. Certainly they were not thinking that the occupying forces might abandon them to the Confederacy they were forsaking.[61] Under the pressure of war and invasion, the loyalties of free people, as well as slaves, became flexible and calculating.

Unionist sentiment reemerged as the Union invasion advanced. In the Dallas neighborhood in the southeastern portion of Lafayette, Confederate spies reported that "caucuses" had appointed delegates to visit General Grant in Oxford and "make some arrangements with him . . . to see if they can't be protected and recognized under the 'old flag.' " "What the full intention of this people is I can't tell," the report continued, "but I am fearful there is a cat in the meal tub."[62]

The invading Union soldiers found many southern citizens welcoming them to Lafayette County. As the men in blue charged into Oxford in December 1862 one woman "rushed excitedly to the door of her dwelling, and, with arms akimbo and hair streaming in the wind, screamed out at the top of her voice, 'Go it Yanks! Give 'em hell! Shoot the dirty cowards! Thank God; I 'haint got no friends in the Southern army.' " (The description sounds remarkably like the feisty Taylor Cook, who had earlier chastised the Confederates as they retreated through Oxford.) Another account told of Dr. Simmonds, a planter living south of Oxford who had migrated to Mississippi from the North thirty years earlier, built a fortune from cotton and slaves, and married a southern woman. He was still regarded with suspicion by his southern neighbors—but rightly so, as it turned out. He told his houseguests he had been "privately a Union man" but had been "compelled to express himself otherwise." The retreating Confederates had burned his cotton, and his quiet disloyalty quickly turned to bitter resentment.[63]

Simmonds was one of many to come out of the closet and display Unionist sympathies once the invading Union army made it safe—not to say expedient—to do so. Private John Wilson of Illinois "took dinner with a good old Union Lady." While she was out gathering cabbage, some of his comrades stole her peaches, but Wilson apprehended them and returned the peaches to her. One woman set out the Stars and Stripes and waved to the passing Union troops from her porch, "whether from loyalty or to save her chickens I do not know," one cynical Union general wrote in his diary.[64] Whether saving their chickens or standing on Unionist principle, many white Mississippians embraced the invading army as their own.

Out in the field many Confederates soldiers were discovering doubts about the cause that they were fighting for, along with the war weariness and demoralization of a retreating army. "Our army have been discouraged," one Mississippian wrote in late December 1862. "Brother R. told me that he had heard several persons say that they knew whole reg[imen]ts that would lay down their arms if they were ordered to fall back again. They said that they could whip the federal army any day if they onely had a leader." [65] The numbers of desertions, surrenders, and self-administered furloughs surged in the wake of the Union invasion in December 1862. A Confederate officer reported massive disarray among Mississippi troops and asked General John C. Pemberton if he could move his forces "immediately to Okolona for the purpose of arresting stragglers and deserters from the army." He explained, "At that place and below I am informed that the number is enormous both of officers and men exhibiting a frightful demoralization and want of discipline." [66]

One diary of a Confederate private reveals the sagging spirits in the Confederate ranks and the blurred line in the minds of many soldiers between patriotic duty and loyalty to family. Henry Newton Faulkinbury had joined the Dixie Rebels organized near Sarepeta, on the border of Lafayette and Calhoun Counties (both claimed the company as their own). During the "great Corinth Retreat" many of his comrades "perished and dide on the road sides" and the rest "was all worn out and brooke down a marching by this time." "I had sorter Begain to expreance some of the hardships of the life of a soldier," he added ruefully. While in Vicksburg he was "taken sick" with the typhoid raging through the town. For four to five weeks, he wrote, he "sufferd agreat ameny a long lonsom summer night did I spend with lying in the old tent on my little bunk suffering with camp fevor no relatives ther of mine no company except som sick soldiers and a few friends left to nurs us." That summer Faulkinbury went home to recuperate and lingered through the fall "at home with my folks and in a very delicat state of helth." Then he heard on December 4, 1862, that "our country was being overpowerd by the federell troups as we had to retreat from Tallahatcha Station down the country." The next few days he "lay at home thinking of being cut off from our Command by the Fedrells." Faulkinbury alternated between squirrel hunting and preaching on Sundays before he finally resolved to return and "fixed up my things to start back to my company." [67]

The life of a Confederate soldier was hard and particularly demoralizing in Mississippi, where they were losing ground rapidly. They were poorly equipped with squirrel guns, muskets, and pistols brought from home, their own blankets and rough clothing, or stolen uniforms of the enemy, and exceedingly poor footwear. Sickness ravaged the troops. Faulkinbury recorded in his diary: "It was gest about as mutch as I could stand up to."[68]

If God Is Against Us

Faulkner's Brother Fortinbride took another fork in the same road Henry Faulkinberry faced. A casualty of battle wounds and starvation, Fortinbride leaves Colonel Sartoris's regiment and returns to Yoknapatawpha to take up preaching to his hill country neighbors. With the profits from Granny Millard's prosperous mule trading operation with the Yankees, he helps organize a relief program for the suffering poor left at the home front. He stands before his congregation in his faded frock coat, its origin betrayed by a large "USA" stencil, his "bones looking like they were coming right out through his face" and says to them: "I reckon there is a time when even preachers quit believing that God is going to change His plan and give victory where this is nothing left to hang victory on."[69]

A similar tone of defeat permeated the letters between the home front and battle fronts. They reflected a growing uncertainty not solely about the outcome of the war but especially about the heavy price it was exacting on their families and loved ones. News of fathers and sons killed and maimed in far-off battlefields arrived with every mail. "It seems like nearly all of my old associates are being either killed or wounded," R. M. Houston wrote to his mother from prison of war camp in Ohio. "It makes me feel very sad to think of the number that have either died from disease or been killed in our neighborhood since the war began."[70] Isaac Duncan had two sons in the war; he wrote to his son William in Virginia about the narrow escape from death his brother recently experienced. It seems, he went on, with "you and Jimmie being separated by this unholy war exposed to sickness and death continually that our family ties are being disolved and the only grate desire of our hearts should be to so love all of us that we may at last form an unbroken family in heaven." He told of the whole family weeping uncontrollably while reading a letter from William, which included a poetic farewell, apparently written in case he should die. The father wrote back that he could not bear "the thought of my darling boy who I trusted would have been a comfort to his parents in their declining years torn from us by the ruthless hand of this unholy war." Off in Virginia, young William was killed in battle before his father's letter arrived.[71]

Albert H. Clark, another local soldier, wrote to a friend after Shiloh: "The time is come when we will have to fight or die or be conquered . . . we can never be conquered, only by the ruling power of God but alas! if God is against us, we are ruined forever."[72] Many must have begun to ask whose side *was* God on in this "unholy war"? The Calvinists of College Hill Presbyterian Church dwelled on this very question in the winter of 1862. After recounting the depredations and humiliation they had suffered at the hands of the invading army, the church minutes recorded: "Such is a mere outline of the heavy calamity which God in his providence has seen fit to inflict upon our community." But they went on to speculate that "there were good reasons for this," for the Bible and "the dealings of God with nations and individuals teach us that the sin for which punishment is inflicted in this life is brought to our knowledge by the penalty inflicted upon us." The minutes do not reveal any probing of the exact nature of their sin, but there is no suggestion that slavery or secession was thought to be the cause of God's punishment. It must have been some failure to honor God, they concluded: "It is our duty, what ever may be our omission or commission [of] sins in sight of God to humble ourselves, repent in the dust, plead for His mercy." [73]

This uncertainty and pessimism, so in contrast to the revolutionary enthusiasm of '61, flowed back and forth between soldier and civilian, battle front and home front. Charles Roberts wrote to his wife from Tennessee after Grant's visit: "The news from Mississippi is anything but encouraging, at least, what little news we get and that comes in no reliable shape. I hope Oxford is not going to be again visited by the Yankees. I have not much fear of them making a permanent stay at our town, but they may pass through and commit many depredations." Later that spring he wrote again, full of worry after a month of no news: "When I don't hear from you for so long a time I become uneasy and anxious and everything looks dark and gloomy." [74]

It was looking dismal at home as well. "Some of the newspapers speak of our prospects being bright and brightening, but to me everything looks dark and gloomy," Eliza Pegues, a wealthy planter's wife, wrote to her son in the army following Grant's invasion.[75] "The citizens are weary of the war and ardently long for its conclusion," one northern observer commented in December 1862. "So far as Mississippi is concerned she is virtually conquered." [76] "Times are very hard," Isaac Duncan wrote to his son as early as June 1862, "everything is scarce and high. We are anxious for an honorable peace." "It is a task for me to write," his mother wrote a little later, "we are so discouraged I have no ambition. I feel that we are almost over run." These signs of demoralization and defeatism were apparent a full year before the fall of Vicksburg; after that disaster growing numbers in Mississippi wanted peace at any price.[77]

Faulkner portrayed the Sartoris family in *The Unvanquished* with the same mix of gritty perseverance and stoic resignation to defeat. Colonel John Sartoris, returning home briefly sometime after Shiloh and Corinth, evokes not the aura of "powder and glory" but "only the will to endure, a sardonic and even humorous declining of self-delusion."[78] For Lafayette County the "will to endure" sustained the people through the latter half of a war that no longer seemed possible to win or even survive *except* by stubborn endurance.

Treasonable Practices

The lines that separated loyal Confederates from Union collaborators were fast blurring under the pressure of war. When Faulkner cast Granny Millard and her family trading mules and horses with the invading Union army, he was acknowledging a widespread practice of trading with the enemy that was motivated both by the hardships of war and the enticing temptations for profit. In Granny's case, the charitable ends she and Brother Fortinbride put their earnings to left no doubt about their motives. But for others the distinction between war profiteering, treasonable trade with the enemy, and patriotic service on behalf of a deprived home front became a matter of interpretation.

Loyalties to the Confederate cause and to one's family came increasingly into conflict after 1862. The Union advance had left Memphis in its control, but northern Mississippi became a no-man's-land controlled by neither side, an undefined border patrolled by roving cavalry companies from both sides, advancing, raiding, and retreating.[79] Some Confederate forces were acting as independent raiders, often as rogue operations detached from the Confederate military chain of command. William C. Falkner, the author's famed great-grandfather, having been deposed as an officer in the regular Confederate army, like Colonel Sartoris, raised an independent cavalry company he called the First Mississippi Partisan Rangers. Falkner's Rangers were essentially privateers with a license to steal and plunder, for the troops were paid from the profits of booty garnered in raids against Union forces, stealing horses and munitions.[80]

Civilians in this uncontrolled zone found themselves between two predatory armies, neither able to provide protection. Northern Mississippi offered more grain and meat than other parts of the state. Nonetheless, the impact of the blockade, the disruption of slave labor, and the foraging of armies on both sides had left the region with food and other basic staples, notably salt, in chronic short supply, and their prices soaring. Clothing, footwear, medicines, and many other items were scarce or altogether impossible to come by at any price. The shortage of salt, vital to the preservation of meat, had created mutinous conditions among angry women in parts of the state. By 1863, Governor Pettus issued salt rations to the families of soldiers, and the county Board of Police was buying additional salt "for the use of families of Soldiers."[81]

What northern Mississippi still had in abundance was cotton, but the Confederacy had strictly forbidden trade with the enemy as part of its strategy of using King Cotton to bring pressure against the North. Rather than allow the invading armies to confiscate cotton, orders went out to burn every bale that was at risk of falling into the hands of the enemy. This was not a popular policy among hungry, suffering cotton growers, especially those in Lafayette County who were but a few miles from fabulous profits.

As Grant's forces entered the rich cotton lands of west Tennessee and northern Mississippi, a horde of cotton traders came in their wake, eager to buy up the cotton in the conquered territory. Grant became so exasperated with these traders and their interference in his campaign that he issued an order specifically banning Jewish cotton traders from further dealing. Grant's infamous order provoked strong protests from Jewish leaders across the North, and it was soon rescinded. But this episode drew attention to the enormous profits that lay waiting in the cotton trade across enemy lines.[82] Charles Dana reported from Memphis during January 1863 that the "mania for sudden fortunes made in cotton has to an alarming extent corrupted and demoralized the army. Every colonel, captain, or quartermaster is in secret partnership with some operator in cotton; every soldier dreams of adding a bale of cotton to his monthly pay."[83]

At night, along roads leading toward Memphis, with wagons and mules loaded with cotton, blockade runners made their way to Union lines in a clandestine trade of growing magnitude. One southern cotton trader in Memphis had a fleet of boats plying the Tallahatchie when the water was up.[84] Colonel Falkner, having resigned his command of the Partisan Rangers in the fall of 1862, turned to blockade running, smuggling cotton to Memphis or across the river to Arkansas. Cotton was bringing $2.50 a pound in Memphis by this time. With the money earned from cotton, he and other traders bought essential food supplies, such as salt, to sell in Mississippi at inflated wartime prices.[85] Faulkner's Granny Millard, with help from Ringo and Bayard, turn their profitable mule trading operation to great profit for the destitute poor white families of Yoknapatawpha. Granny's willingness to do business with the befuddled enemy is part of the cunning expediency that became a useful virtue in a war-torn society. The object at the home front was to survive, and dogmatic loyalties to one side or the other were only troublesome obstacles to that end.

There was furious popular reaction against wartime speculative activity, but it was typically condemned not because traders violated Confederate sanctions or profited by trade with the enemy. Blockade runners were instead condemned by consumers for price gouging. Confederate officials, on the other hand, saw it as treason. A circular they sent out in January 1863 announced a new clamp-down on "abolition speculators . . . actively engaged in endeavoring to supply the Federals with cotton contrary to the avowed policy of our Government." It announced a policy of ruthless repression of these "treasonable practices" and instructed Confederate scouts and pickets to burn all cotton "in danger of falling into the Enemy's power." Loyal citizens were invited to report names and residences of "all citizens who have been engaged with or without permission in these disloyal practices." [86] The enemy, or at least his collaborators, lay within.

Oxford's James Brown was among the more successful of many Oxford merchants who engaged in wartime trade in salt and other scarce items of trade. Brown's business may or may not have involved trade with the North, but it took advantage of the tremendous profits awarded those able to get essential provisions through the blockade to desperate consumers in the interior of Mississippi.[87] Charles Roberts wrote from the front line of battle in Tennessee to express disgust at his fellow Oxford merchants, Tom Wendel and Bob Cook, who were trading with the very enemy he and his comrades were sacrificing so much to defend against. "I can scarcely think it possible," he wrote to his wife. What bothered him more was the price gouging they were indulging in at home: "Two doll[ars] for a pound of sugar, one dollar for half a dozen Eggs and other things in proportion." "I don't know where this spirit of extortion is going to stop," Roberts complained, "it is not confined to any particular class or locality—the farmer wants an exorbitant price for what he has to sell and the soldier that is fortunate to procure anything that is in demand wants double what he paid for it. As for the suttlers and store Keepers that follow an army, they have no conscience at all." [88]

Not all trade with the enemy was motivated by speculative greed or disloyalty, but what exactly constituted loyalty was falling open to interpretation under the exigencies of scarcity at the home front. In a lengthy, defensive letter to his friend written late in 1863, Pat Willis, a small farmer and slave owner, explained the hardships that pressed him into trade with the Yankees. "From the opening of this war, to the 1st Instant, no man in the So. Confederacy was more bitterly hostile to furnishing the enemy with Cotton, than myself." Things had changed, he wrote, and while he still opposed on principle anything that seemed like "trade with the enemy for Speculation" the times demanded some desperate action. "Last Winter we fed and foraged, Van Dorn and Price's entire army, then followed Grant's immense force, which not only eat us entirely out, but have from that time to the present, Plundered us of Waggons, horses, mules, Oxen, hogs, Cereals, meat &c thus depriving our people of the means of making crops hauling from other points, raising meat, &c." Prices on all food had shot up because of scarcity and the withering value of Confederate money, but at least it was possible to find things to eat. But, he continued, "I have no Shoes, no sugar, coffee, candles, Bacon, lard, clothes, and a thousand things, actually necessary." Only out of dire necessity had he taken to trading with the Yankees. "I send a bale of Cotton to the accursed rascals, and they pay well for it, and furnish me with what finery? Luxurious? No, actually necessary for the subsistence of my family." It was not just civilians living off this trade, he pointed out. "Why my friend, the clothes, Boots, and thousands of other things that our army is supplied with have been smuggled out of yankeedom through the potent intervention of Cotton." [89]

When General James R. Chalmers, a native of Lafayette County, took command of the Confederate cavalry in Mississippi in 1863, he clamped down hard, confiscating all wagons and livestock, as well as cotton, captured in the illegal trade. Marthy Cragin, a hapless counterpart to the fictional Granny Millard, headed north from Oxford with an ox wagon full of cotton from the fall harvest in 1863, which she hoped to trade for salt and other necessities. But as soon as they crossed the Tallahatchie, she explained in a letter to the governor, a group of Confederate pickets overtook them, "burned our cotton, confiscated our drivers, wagons and teams." "I never would have attempted it if necessity had not have drove me to it, having been deprived of the necessaries of life for the last three years with a large and helpless family of girls, with no husband or son to assist in making them a support, and all but one old and decrepid servant, the one they confiscated." General Chalmers returned her elderly servant, but her pleas to give back her oxen and wagon fell on deaf ears. My oxen, she begged, are too "poor to eat for food," but they would help "alleviate the sufferings of a poor widow and helpless family." "I do not see where we are to get salt and cards," she added, "but we could better do without them then our team." Chalmers told the governor he had no recollection of Mrs. Cragin's case, but "it is only one of many such that have occurred." [90]

The only ones objecting to this nefarious trade with the enemy, Pat Willis insisted somewhat defensively, are men "who have either lost nothing, or those who have plenty to eat and to wear, and do not feel the urgent need of yankee aid." "Look at the prices in Middle or South Mississippi, where the Yankees have not had a fair sweep, and contrast them with North Miss, where the vandals have been constantly ravaging for over twelve months. North Mississippi, damned north Miss, trafficking and trading with Yankees &ccc." Prices had soared, he showed, and were triple price if paid in Confederate money. Union greenbacks were the "only money that will clothe and feed them." "We have fed both Yankees and confed troops for over twelve months, *constantly* but little is left in our section, and yet, where will you find *extortion* so little practiced as here." He admitted "while we *do* have *some* d——d men and women too, here, who traffic with the enemy *constantly for speculation only*, yet our people hold them in contempt."[91]

After the fall of Vicksburg in July 1863, Confederate officials in Mississippi generally turned a blind eye to trade with the enemy. Chalmers even lauded the border traders as "patriotic" and "liberal" in providing the Confederate army with badly needed supplies.[92] When the defending army, along with the civilian population, came to depend on an illegal cotton trade with the enemy, and when essential food and medicine were bought with U.S. greenbacks earned in this clandestine commerce, it seemed that terms like "patriotic" and even "enemy" had lost definite meaning.

Moss Backs and True Blues

There were others whose disloyalty to the Confederate cause was less ambiguous. Opposition to the war effort from within the South was expressed at great risk, and it took many forms, from draft resistance and desertion to aiding the invading enemy and even enlistment in the Union army. Many had opposed secession and the Confederate war effort out of principle rather than mere expediency or opportunism. It was this principled opposition that Faulkner captured neatly in Goodhue Coldfield, the adamant opponent of war who withdraws to his attic. There he stays, hiding from Confederate officials for three years, drawing food up in a basket that his daughter, Rosa, filled with food she scrounged from neighbors, all the time enduring public disgrace and poverty, doomed to spinsterhood by both. Her father stops eating the food and starves himself to death. "He was not a coward," Faulkner explains. "He was a man of uncompromising moral strength." For Coldfield, opposition to the Confederate war drew partly on a moral antipathy toward slavery but more emphatically on his practical abhorrence of the terrible waste of war.[93] That may explain much of sentiment that gave rise to the peace movement among the war weary in northern Mississippi.

There were many in Lafayette County who refused cooperation with the Confederate cause and many who, in some way, collaborated with the Yankees. As the Union armies invaded and retreated, on several occasions, the people of Lafayette had to make calculated decisions as to which side they were on. It would be misleading to suppose these decisions were always made out of deep and consistent ideological conviction of the type Faulkner depicted in Goodhue Coldfield. No doubt, many could identify with the Mississippi woman who, when questioned whether she was a Unionist or Secessionist, "merely allowed that she was a Baptist." [94] Some whose property was confiscated by Union forces had a material stake in maintaining their loyalty to the Union—or the appearance of same—if they were ever to win compensation later. There were many also who came to oppose the war out of practical acknowledgment that southern secession, whether just or wrong, was already a lost cause. They wanted an "honorable peace" before more lives and property were wasted.

In northern Mississippi the peace movement was strongest in the same counties where pro-Union sentiment had been strong before the war, generally among the small, slaveless, white farmers in the hill counties of the northeast.[95] In Lafayette County there remained a hard core of pro-Union sentiment rooted partly in the Whig tradition, motivated in some cases by deep political enmity, in others by class resentment, and sustained by a simple fear—now vindicated—that secession and war meant disaster. Rather than see the invasion and disruption of war demoralizing the southern home front, it may have simply given the long-standing opposition to the secessionist cause a new sense of conviction.

The clearest picture of this stubborn pro-Unionism is found in the files of the Southern Claims Commission, the federal agency that, after the war, reviewed claims by those southerners whose property was confiscated by the Union army and who claimed they were loyal Unionists.[96] A few of these loyalist claimants were among the wealthiest families in the county, prosperous old-line Whig planters, many with sizable slaveholdings, and many Oxford townspeople who had warned that the fire-eaters would bring ruin to the country.[97] Many also were nonslaveholding farmers who opposed, in varying degrees, secession, the war, the draft, and any number of other specific Confederate policies or leaders.

Jesse Sisk's opposition to the Confederacy surfaced when the draft forced his hand. A blacksmith and woodworker at Taylor's Depot, Sisk refused any cooperation with the Confederacy. When conscription officers came after him, he "laid out" in the woods and relied on friends for food and protection. Sisk was one of several "moss backs," so named because they hid out in the woods to evade the Confederate draft. After the war, Sisk won part of his claim for horses and other livestock taken by Union soldiers, and he stayed on in Taylor's Depot running a store.[98]

Elijah Cantwell, another successful claimant, was a yeoman farmer south of Oxford. He joined his neighbors in armed resistance to the draft when conscription officer W. P. Wilkins showed up to take some of them into service. Cantwell conducted relatives and neighbors along what amounted to an underground railroad of draft evaders going north to Memphis. With imagery reminiscent of antislavery propaganda, Cantwell described one party of men escaping northward toward Union lines "chased by dogs and torn by the dogs." "They came to my house," he testified, "torn and worn out and I kept them for three days and nights and then carried them through to Memphis where they joined the 1st Miss Cavalry USA." Confederate officials harassed and finally arrested Cantwell on numerous occasions, but he stubbornly refused to be intimidated and never took any oaths of loyalty they pressed upon him.[99]

Drummond Wheeler, a poor farmer opposed to secession, watched four sons conscripted into the Confederate army; every one of them deserted and joined the Union army. Confederate officers threatened to burn Wheeler's house and hang his sons before they arrested one, James, and took him away. "I was put under guard and kept there until the Evacuation of Corinth," James later testified; "when I got loose and came home, soon afterwards I was conscripted and served in the Cavalry." He defected that fall when "General Grant's Army came to Oxford and the Rebels fell back and I 'fell out' as my house was inside of the Federal lines." James Wheeler's loyalty was severely tested when Grant's army retreated to Tennessee a few days later. He followed the retreating army and "went away from this part of the country" but after two months in Memphis, he came back to protect his family. "I staid at home until the conscript officers got after me so close that I had to leave." The next stage in his defection from the Confederacy came when Wheeler enlisted in First Mississippi Rifles, U.S. Army, a regiment of Mississippi defectors that included several from Wheeler's neighborhood. After a year in service to the Union army, he came home on leave to see his sick brother. He was there only two weeks when Confederate conscript officers heard him shooting squirrels one day and caught him by surprise. Wheeler broke and ran through the woods taking a shot in his side as he fled for his life. A slave, Tobe Humphries, helped nurse his wound and protect him during a slow recovery. "I was extremely unpopular on account of my Union sentiments," James Wheeler testified.[100]

For every defiant James Wheeler, Elijah Cantwell, or Jesse Sisk there were dozens more, like John Robuck, who had little respect for the Confederate cause but joined the army reluctantly rather than shame his family or himself. In distant battlefields, with news of disaster and betrayal coming from home, these men had every reason to be asking, "What the devil are we fighting for?"[101]

Bushwhackers

There were other southern whites who operated without any cause but their own gain, bandits who took advantage of a war-torn society to prey on their own people. These were the criminal element often called bushwhackers. They were renegade southern men, typically deserters from the Confederate army, who scourged the countryside of northern Mississippi preying on defenseless women and families left unprotected at the home front. Here, too, the lines were not always so tidy. There were distinctions to be made between predatory bandits and those guerrilla bands operating as independent raiders, stealing horses or mules from the Union army or punishing Union sympathizers, just as there were between those trading with the enemy to bring salt and medicine to help sustain the Confederacy or for personal gain. The term "bushwhacker" might be used for those guerrilla bands that ambushed one side or the other, but in northern Mississippi it usually referred to southern white bandits who preyed on their own people.[102]

Faulkner appreciated the historical ambiguity surrounding these marauders when, in *The Unvanquished*, he portrayed his villainous Grumby as leader of a gang that called itself the "Independent Rangers."[103] But the distinction between Grumby's gang and the independent raiders Colonel John Sartoris leads are clear enough. Grumby and his gang represent the sort of amoral, predatory opportunists that emerge in most every war with no real partisan loyalties beyond their own rapacious greed. Grumby might have been based on any number of such bushwhackers operating during the war, but in Lafayette County the most notorious were two outlaws named Ross (or Raz) Boyd and Bill Winn. They operated out of the Caswell community in the hilly eastern part of the county. They were motivated partly by partisan opposition to the Confederacy; both dodged the draft by hiding out in the woods and proclaimed themselves "Tories," opponents of secession. But whatever their motives, they operated as bandits, their main enterprise being rustling and killing cattle, the meat from which they sold at high prices. They also stole horses and mules, typically from destitute older women left to fend for themselves during the war. Boyd and Winn constructed large pens in the woods to hold their stolen livestock and hired an old woman to tend and feed them while they were out pillaging. Once they demanded food from a woman, and when she refused they threatened to burn her baby with a shovel full of hot coals. They took every bit of her food. Like Grumby, Boyd and Winn wound up victims of their own brand of violent retribution; they were eventually caught and hanged.[104]

This type of banditry was often blamed on Unionists or anti-Confederates, as in the case of Boyd and Winn. "Nearly all the men gone from this country that could bare arms," Moses Hunt wrote from Paris, in the southern part of the county in May 1862; "there is a few half Yankees or half devils left to swindle and rob the wimmen and children out of what they have got."[105] Whether these bushwhackers were motivated by principle or avarice, their depredations acted as a constant menace to the home front with depressing impact on Confederate morale.

Not all this outlaw element preyed on fellow southerners. One of Lafayette County's renegades turned his wrath against the invading Union soldiers. This man, identified only as "Mr. L," was a Confederate deserter who "jest struck out 'freelance-like for hisself' " and hid in an attic of his house near Abbeville. According to local legend, he redeemed himself by killing Yankees. Watching Union foragers stealing chickens one day, he decided to go to a hen house and imitate a rooster crowing. When the Yankees came looking for chickens, he killed three or four of them and claimed to have killed eleven men in all using this ploy. You "just couldn't keep that feller in no army stall," one of his apologists explained later; "he had quaar idees 'bout army life; he jest done his fightin' when and where he found a Yankee."[106]

By August 1864, a Confederate officer in Oxford reported to Richmond that "the country is swarming with deserters, and without a force of regular troops I fear little can be done to break up these clans of tories." He went on to report, "Blockade-running and intercourse with the enemy has been quite common here, and the severest punishment will have to be meted out to these law-breakers to compel them to cease this corrupting practice."[107]

By this time the lines that separated law-abiding loyal citizens of the Confederacy and their enemies had become indistinct if not obliterated. In a territory left exposed to raids by both armies, citizens were left to switch their loyalties according to the expediency of the moment. Among the people of northern Mississippi the distinctions between a Union army ransacking its corn cribs, torching mansions, or encouraging slaves to rebel and a Confederate army foraging for food, confiscating and burning their cotton, or impressing their slaves may have been difficult to distinguish from bushwhackers who were preying on them without pretense of legitimacy.[108] That the Confederate army and government had proved unable to protect its people from these depredations further undermined loyalty to the cause. Whether principled Unionists of long standing or war-weary Confederates, growing numbers came to see the cause of southern independence as no longer their own.

Faulkner wrote that the burning of Jefferson brought its citizens to their own Appomattox, that is, to the realization of defeat and surrender, nearly a year before their men in arms gave up the cause. Many at the northern Mississippi home front, we have seen, were already seriously demoralized before Oxford was sacked by Union troops. In the summer of 1863 news came back of the disastrous defeat at Gettysburg and the fall of Vicksburg, both occurring on the same day in July 1863, one day before the Fourth when the rest of the Union would celebrate the anniversary of independence.

For some in Lafayette County the loss at Gettysburg and Vicksburg was a demoralizing blow to their hopes for the Confederacy; for others the losses were deeply personal. The young boys who had joined the University Greys were in the forefront of General George Pickett's disastrous charge on the third day of the Battle of Gettysburg; not one survived the day without being killed or wounded. What Margery Clark lost at Gettysburg left her heartsick the rest of her life. Throughout 1863 the letters from her husband and sons, Jonathan, Henry, and young Isaac had been full of depressing stories of starvation diets and shoddily dressed, barefoot soldiers. But nothing had prepared her for the news that came from Gettysburg that July. Her husband and two oldest sons all wound up in Pickett's charge. First her husband, Thomas Goode Clark, was slain while crossing the deadly wheat field that lay between them and the Union line. Then one of her sons, carrying the regimental colors, fell dead as the army marched into the bloodbath that day. His brother picked up the colors and, no sooner than he did, he, too, was shot dead, falling not far from his brother and father. When the news reached home, Mrs. Clark wailed and prayed aloud all night long. The rest of her life she would say to her surviving family that they "did not know what sorrow was." [109]

Too many of Lafayette County's families learned what sorrow was by this stage of the war. Over one-third of Mississippi's breadwinners were killed or died of disease.[110] There appears to be no exact count of how many of Lafayette County's men were killed and wounded during the war. If state level mortality rates held true, 35 percent or 770 of the approximately 2,200 men who served died from wounds or disease.[111] Countless others returned with missing limbs or scarred and mutilated bodies

Whether these soldiers were killed or survived at the front lines, many of their families were left without food and support and by 1863 were thrown to the mercy of public charity. A census conducted by county officials that year showed more than 450 destitute families of soldiers, 1,200 dependent children, and 1,664 in all—only a little less than the numbers of men en-listed in Confederate military service. Men who had taken up arms to defend hearth and home now learned of their women and children left behind to the uncertain fate of public charity.[112]

The pressures on the home front were soon felt at the front lines, and desertion became a contagious epidemic toward the end of the war. Large numbers of deserters and wayward conscripts had sought refuge in Jones County, in the central part of the state. By March 1864 the Confederates turned to fighting their own people in an armed invasion of the "free state of Jones."

There were little Jones Counties, pockets of deserters and draft resistors, all over the state by this time. General Forrest complained of "roving bands of deserters, stragglers, horse-thieves, and robbers, who consume the substance, and appropriate the property of the citizens." In Holly Springs, citizens complained that deserters infested the country, robbing friend and foe alike.[113] The apprehension of deserters and the repression of bushwhacking also proved a significant distraction for the Confederate forces that were supposed to be defending against Union raids. Private J. A. Bigger's diary in the fall of 1863 indicates that one of his major duties in the Lafayette County area was "hunting deserters," and it was not one he enjoyed.[114]

Confederate officers tried to deal harshly with the problem of desertion, but this carried a serious risk of exacerbating the problem. Earlier in the war, William Dillon wrote from Corinth about a fellow Mississippi soldier who, without permission, had gone home to help his family. His punishment resembled the discipline meted out to slaves; he "received 39 lashes, was branded on the left hip with a letter 'D' and had his head shaved and was then drummed out of the service." Dillon approved of the harsh discipline, but many others who witnessed this must have made certain that if they ever left service they would never return. By the end of the war Dillon reported that out of one Mississippi brigade of three thousand men, only eight hundred were doing duty at the time of surrender. The rest "were at home or lying in the woods." He added indignantly that "such a people do not deserve their liberty and a just God did not allow them to gain it."[115]

When General Nathan Bedford Forrest took command of the Confederate cavalry forces in northern Mississippi in the fall of 1863, he took severe measures to restore discipline. A severe freeze hit his Oxford headquarters that winter, and many of his men tried to leave for the warmth of their homes. When Forrest insisted they stay in camp, there was a virtual mutiny; nineteen men bolted camp and were captured. General Forrest sentenced all of them to be shot and ordered nineteen coffins be built and nineteen graves dug. Oxford's clergymen and leading citizens, along with several military officers, remonstrated against this draconian punishment, but Forrest did not waver. The soldiers were brought in wagons, sitting on their own coffins, down Pontotoc Street passing an astonished crowd of citizens and soldiers. The condemned soldiers stood by their open graves before the firing squad, blindfolded and ready for execution. At the last minute, on instructions from Forrest, the officer in charge announced a reprieve and shouts of hysterical joy went up from the soldiers and Oxford citizens who gathered at the scene. Forrest's concession may have been less a sign of gallant beneficence than an acknowledgment that many in his army were but one step away from mutiny and his efforts to force obedience might well backfire.[116]

Mississippi's governor Charles Clark also imposed harsh new policies against draft dodgers and deserters, but in November 1864, he issued a proclamation of amnesty to deserters and others absent without leave from the army. He sent out a circular to sheriffs of every county reminding them of their duty to arrest and turn in those who had not come in of their own accord. The governor organized a general court-martial to be held in December and demanded that sheriffs capture those still at large, "and if they resist they must be shot." This, he added, was a "disagreeable but essential duty."[117]

Finding little effective response to his amnesty offer, early in 1865 Governor Clark issued orders to convert the home guards into a militia to go after the deserters. Thomas Pegues wrote to him from Oxford in March 1865 a detailed letter that admitted tenuous local support for such an enterprise. While agreeing that it was "a great evil that there are so many [deserters] in the land," he cautioned, "it would be a still greater evil to call out the Militia to hunt them up." To impress the remaining boys and old men into service to round up deserters would mean "starvation and ruin for this county," because there would be no one left to provide for the families. They, too, would desert, Pegues warned, for "say what you will, men are not going to remain in service if their families have nothing to eat." Adding to the difficulty in this part of the country, Pegues went on, was that the slaves had run off or been removed south away from Union lines. Those who fled or were relocated were mostly males, Pegues explained. "Pretty nearly all the negro men are gone," and this left slave masters with the additional burden of feeding the slave women and children left behind. Furthermore, teams and wagons were in such short supply and the roads, bridges, and railroads were by now in such complete disarray that it was nearly impossible to bring in food from other regions.[118]

More was involved than practical problems of food production, for Pegues warned of a shaky morale problem among the populace. Local men simply could not be expected to go after deserters whom they saw as fellow citizens taking care of their families; "they will not get up deserters from fear of the consequences, as well as from a fellow feeling of the hardship of the case." Confederate soldiers seemed ready to abandon their companies in favor of their families given the opportunity. Pegues told the governor that a company of reserves had been stationed in Oxford for a month or six weeks supposedly trying to track down deserters. Pegues had to admit, "I do not honestly believe they returned five men to their commands who were worth the cost of their transportation."[119] Men who fought in defense of altars and hearths were now forsaking a war that had exposed both to devastation. "Pro Altaris et Focis" they went to war, and by the same inspiration, they were deserting and returning home.

The Town in Flames

By the summer of 1864 Confederate forces under Forrest were trying to restore control over northern Mississippi and set up a defensive line at the Tallahatchie River. That June Forrest had struck a decisive blow against Union efforts to penetrate the Mississippi interior in the Battle of Bryce's Crossroads. In August, Union forces under General Andrew Jackson Smith came out of Memphis by train and then marched from Grand Junction south toward Forrest's headquarters in Oxford determined to destroy his army. The Confederates, once again, took up a line of defense along the Tallahatchie, and on August 7–9 put up stiff resistance as Union forces approached and later crossed the river at Abbeville with heavy skirmishing on the south bank at Hurricane Creek (later fictionalized in Faulkner's story "My Grandmother Millard and the Battle of Harrykin Creek"). The Confederates retreated south again, back through Oxford as they had less than two years earlier. On August 9 Union cavalry entered Oxford against minor resistance and occupied the town. For a day, by one account, the soldiers occupied themselves "robbing and plundering indiscriminately men, women, children, and negroes." Again the home of Jacob Thompson was targeted and thoroughly ransacked; what furnishings were not destroyed were hauled away in a wagon. On learning that Confederate forces were approaching, Smith ordered a retreat to Abbeville the next day, and Forrest's troops returned to occupy Oxford again.[120]

Skirmishing continued on a daily basis north of Oxford, and by August 21, Union forces were advancing again on the town. "The Yanks are in large numbers," Belle Edmondson wrote in her diary, "yet we are confident of checking their wicked course before they go much farther."[121] Hard rains had raised the rivers that August, and Confederate general James Chalmers feared the Yoknapatawpha would rise and trap his forces. He ordered his troops to abandon Oxford and retreat south. Forrest in the meantime had decided, instead of trying to stop the invading army, to divide his forces in two and lead one on a diversionary raid into Memphis, the heart of the enemy's base of operations. After arriving in Memphis late at night, Forrest and his men rode on horseback into the lobby of the Gayoso Hotel, prompting one Union general to flee into the night in his nightclothes. One of Forrest's men signed the hotel guest book.

Union troops under General Andrew Jackson Smith advanced on Oxford on August 22 not knowing that Forrest had flanked them on the west. According to local legend, it was to avenge Forrest's humiliating foray into Memphis that General "Whiskey" Smith, drunk and enraged, ordered the sacking and burning of Oxford that infamous day in August. Perhaps that played a role, but by this time, Forrest had long been a thorn in the Union side. There is no record of Smith's explanation for his decision to torch Oxford, so we can only speculate. The destruction of civilian property, by this point in the war, had become a common Union tactic of demoralization. It is likely that the target of Smith's wrath was the civilian population. Oxford had been Forrest's headquarters, and Smith apparently decided to make the town pay a heavy price for supporting his operations in northern Mississippi.[122]

There were some sixteen thousand troops with Smith during the expedition that August, among them a contingent of African American soldiers recruited among the refugees that had fled north out of slavery following the invasion more than a year and a half earlier. They sang a popular marching song that captured the spirit of their transformation from slave to soldier:

But some ob dese days my time will come,
I'll year dat bugle, Ill year dat drum,
Ill see dem armies, marchin' along,
I'll lif my head and' jine der song.[123]

Now they came marching with Smith's troops, some, perhaps, to the homes of their former masters, rifles and bayonets in hand, and torches blazing. One imagines Faulkner's rebellious Loosh torching the Sartoris house.

Elizabeth "Zizzie" Pegues, who witnessed the sacking of Oxford, reported that the day began with deceptive calm, the Union soldiers entering around eight in the morning and posting guards to protect many of the mansions in town. Then about noon, when news of Forrest's Memphis raid reached town, the mood changed terribly; "the whole town was given up to the soldiers." "The Square is a horrid sight," she wrote to her family. "It would break your heart to look at it." [124] Smith ordered the courthouse burned along with all the buildings surrounding the Oxford town square. He also ordered that the homes of several prominent Confederate sympathizers, all wealthy citizens, be ransacked and razed. Chief among the targets was the home of Jacob Thompson, former federal cabinet officer and now Confederate government official, and the mansion of James Brown, where Grant had his headquarters during the first invasion. One Union soldier wrote home to Iowa that they had "made free with Oxford, burning all the fine brick blocks fronting on the public square, and also the Court House, in one grand conflagration." "The houses of some prominent official rebels were also fired," he explained. "The splendid mansion of Jacob Thompson, rebel Secretary of the Interior, with its gorgeous furniture, went up in crackling flames, a costly burnt offering to the 'Moloch of treason.'"[125]

William Faulkner's great-grandmother Burlina Butler, widowed proprietor of the Oxford Inn, begged General Smith to spare her only means of livelihood. But he "replied very sneeringly and insultingly and went on with the burning." Mrs. Butler was "not permitted to move anything out of her house but her clothing, one bed and some little furniture out of her private room. All was consumed."[126]

Holed up in the Thomas Pegues mansion, Edgecomb, on North Street, young Zizzie Pegues hoped that her family's own home might be spared. "We thought we were escaping finely for no Yankees came into our house till between four and five o'clock, then about 100 rushed into the back yard screaming for sugar." Between one and two hundred soldiers swarmed through the house, pillaged the pantry and smokehouse and then began taking off and destroying books, clothing, jewelry, and other property. Some tried to set fire to the upstairs, while other soldiers helped quench the flames.[127]

The destruction that took place that afternoon left the Oxford town square a scorched field of rubble. One surviving photograph of the ruins shows nothing but a few jagged brick chimneys and remnants of walls surviving in a scene of utter desolation. Some thirty-four stores and business houses, along with the courthouse, Mason Hall, two large hotels, and other businesses were all laid waste. Five dwellings, all belonging to prominent Confederate supporters, were also sacked and burned. General Smith seemed to take a certain satisfaction in the destruction and personally supervised the burning, acting "brutal in the extreme" and "mad with whiskey for the occasion," according to one bitter Confederate report. "He refused to allow the citizens to remove anything of value from their burning dwellings." "The soldiers were licensed for any crime, such as robbery, rapine, theft, and arson."[128]

Oxford in ruins, following the raid of General A. J. Smith, August 1864. This view
from the northeast shows the courthouse, whose chimneys still rise on the right;
the columns of the Cumberland Presbyterian Church can be seen on the left.
(Courtesy of Special Collections, University of Mississippi)

"After the town was in flames," another Confederate officer reported
later, "the soldiers dispersed all over town into private houses, some ran
into the churches and tolled the bells, others yelling like Indians, rushed
into private houses, throwing everything of value that they could convey
off; women and children ran screaming for help. This scene continued until
4 p.m., when the army withdrew in the direction of Memphis." [129] Where
"once stood a handsome little country town," the *Chicago Times* correspondent wrote, "now only remained the blackened skeletons of the houses, and
smouldering ruins." [130]

On August 24, 1864, William Humphries Young, a sergeant in the Mississippi cavalry, wrote home: "The Yanks have ruined this country, destroyed
the corn, killed all or nearly all the Stock, burned the Town of Oxford entirely up except a few dwellings." Chalmers and the Confederates were overwhelmed by the Union forces which "just drove him before them when they
chose to move." [131] "I am weary and sick," wrote one Confederate private
in his diary after witnessing the destruction in Oxford, "dispirited about my
country and this war." [132]

General Smith left the civilian population of Oxford and much of the
countryside to the north of town completely devastated. One plea from
Oxford to Confederate officials in Jackson described the local scene: "Private property of every description was almost universally destroyed, pillaged, or carried off, thus leaving a large majority of the citizens of the

place without the actual necessaries of life. Many being now, without even bedding, blankets or provisions of any kind, and unless these things can be procured from the Enemy much suffering must ensue the approaching winter, especialy among the poorer classes." The citizens of Oxford were asking for relief, not from their government officials but, in effect, from the Yankees. Apparently the Confederates had tightened the ban on trade again, for Oxford civic leaders now implored General Chalmers to permit them free trade with Memphis. "We know Genl the danger of opening communication with the Enemy," their petition read, "but at the same time we are cognizant of the suffering that must follow in case necessaries cannot be procured from the Enemy." They recommended that Felix R. Hardgrave and Asa R. Chilton be authorized to do the trading. The petition added: "It will require One hundred Bales of Cotton to supply the people with absolute necessaries for the winter." [133]

The news of the razing of Oxford must have had a devastating effect on the beleaguered Mississippi soldiers, many now fighting for their survival against the steady advance of the Union forces into the Deep South. Charles Roberts wrote home to his wife from Aberdeen, Mississippi, in January 1865: "Another year is past and gone; commenced and closed in war and bloodshed and its natural accompanyments of ruin and desolation to many a happy hearth. We have had much to mourn and yet very much to be thankful for. . . . Before another year has passed over I hope this terrible struggle will be ended and surrounded with those that are very dear to me I shall be pleasantly employed in making something for their comfort and support." [134]

As the soldiers of Lafayette County carried on through the last few months of war, their relatives and friends back home had all but surrendered to the inevitable. "Bad news from Va. and Mobile, Fort Morgan surrendered and we have been defeated at Fredericksburg," Belle Edmondson recorded in her diary that August. "God grant the days may brighten for our poor bleeding Confederacy." "Oh! God we have suffered, we have endured patiently thy chastenings, . . . let thy smile brighten the Sunny South with peace, soften the hearts of our enemies." [135] We are "a subjugated people," Rebecca Pegues recorded in her diary, "humiliated to the dust." [136]

For the remainder of the war, between August 1864 and the surrender at Appomattox in April 1865, the civilian population of Lafayette County did what they could to survive. There were no more major military engagements in the area and little left for foraging parties to pillage. Soon the soldiers were straggling back home, as Faulkner imagined, "afoot like tramps or on crowbait horses, in faded and patched (and at times obviously stolen) clothing, preceded by no flags nor drums and followed not even by two men to keep step with one another, in coats bearing no glitter of golden braid and with scabbards in which no sword reposed." [137] They returned to a home front that had already surrendered nearly a year in advance, "so that in the almost faded twilight of that land, the knell of Appomattox made no sound." [138]

"I aint a nigger anymore. I done been abolished," . . . Ringo said. "They aint no more niggers, in Jefferson nor nowhere else." Then he told me about the two Burdens from Missouri, with a patent from Washington to organise the niggers into Republicans, and how Father and the other men were trying to prevent it. "Naw, suh," he said. "This War aint over. Hit just started good." —WILLIAM FAULKNER, The Unvanquished

eight Another War

The war fought to win southern independence had been lost, the revolution defeated. Now there was another war. This was a genuine civil war that pitted the citizens of Lafayette County against one another in a violent struggle that lasted more than twice as long as the war for independence. The land divided now witnessed a race war between whites and blacks, a political struggle between Democrats and Republicans, and a labor struggle between landlord and tenant. This was a war with one side striving to maintain supremacy of the white race and the Democratic Party, the other to win civil rights for blacks and the survival of the Republican Party. Those who had led the revolution for independence now joined a counterrevolution against the freed slaves and against the Republicans who championed them. This was a cause they would not allow to be lost. The fruits of victory were a long reign of Democratic Party rule and a new regime of white supremacy marked in stages by political disfranchisement, lynching and other forms of violence, segregation in every quarter of daily life, and the wholesale denial of the rights of citizenship to former slaves.

William Faulkner rarely dealt with the history of Reconstruction in his Yoknapatawpha County. When he did, he never got beyond the stock caricatures of the Black Legend of Reconstruction, which vilified Republican misrule and glorified the redemption of the South by white Conservative Democrats. The leading characters in this scenario included venal, fanatical carpetbaggers ("Redmond . . . symbol of a blind rapacity almost like a biological instinct, destined to cover the South like a migration of locusts"); ignorant black voters (the "herd of niggers . . . with the Northern white men herding them together"); and heroic southern whites (Colonel Sartoris and his Confederate veterans) rising to combat black Republican misrule (Cassius Benbow, a runaway slave appointed county marshal).[1] The Black Legend of Reconstruction was an essential ideological cornerstone of Jim Crow's reign of white supremacy, for it illustrated the folly and danger of racial equality and black civil rights. It was more than just a popular version of the past; a large corps of professional historians, led by William A. Dunning of Columbia University, had grounded an interpretation of this "tragic era" in solid state-level studies. James Wilford Garner's study of Mississippi appeared in 1901 and quickly became incorporated into state school textbooks. Every southern school child (even a lackadaisical student like young Bill Falkner) could hardly avoid exposure to this version of Reconstruction. It was conventional wisdom, and with few exceptions, the Black Legend went unchallenged by most scholars and writers until the civil rights era. With other chapters of southern history, Faulkner was often ahead of the historians, but with Reconstruction he seemed unable or unwilling to question the orthodoxy of the day. If he probed the "dark and bloody ground" of Reconstruction in Lafayette County, as he had the war itself, he found a disturbing past.

This Defeated Land

The reminders of Lafayette County's suffering in the war remained visible for years. Oxford's courthouse, symbol of civic pride since its construction thirty years earlier, remained for several years, as Faulkner wrote, with its "blackened jagged topless jumbles of brick wall enclosing like a ruined jaw the blackened shell of the courthouse."[2] All but one of the stores and offices that faced the square were in the same ruined state. Oxford, visitors to the

South remarked at the end of 1865, "is the most completely demolished town they have seen anywhere."[3]

The process of rebuilding began not long after the war: new shops, offices, and a fine hotel slowly replaced the charred rubble surrounding the square. While the rest of the South "sat staring at the northeast horizon . . . like a family staring at the closed door to a sick-room," Faulkner wrote, "Yoknapatawpha County was already nine months gone in reconstruction."[4] That exaggerated the quickness and the spirit of what he called "reconstruction," or the physical rebuilding of the town. But once the war was over, the leading men of Lafayette County did summon a resolute determination to rebuild and transcend defeat. There was invigorating talk of building new cotton factories and railroads, of improved and diversified agriculture, and of public education as a means of social uplift and economic development.[5]

Overshadowing this optimistic spirit of progress, however, was a brooding sense of malaise, given more to grumbling about the abuses of northern carpetbaggers, the demoralized and lawless condition of the freedmen, and the gloomy prospects of the defeated South than to buoyant visions of the future. "The year 1867 will close upon all classes of our population more disheartened and despondent than they have ever been," the *Falcon* lamented, "the future before us is appalling and the prospect is that we have not seen the worst."[6] The ruins of the courthouse, surrounded by the "ragged" iron fence, remained for seven years in the center of the square, an ugly reminder of that August day of humiliation and destruction. Some suggested erecting a Confederate memorial on the site. For a time, the county considered abandoning this cruel admonition of defeat and turning the property over to the town for use as a park.[7]

Out in the countryside the marks of war could be seen everywhere. Farms torn up by foraging armies were now wasting from neglect: fences down, barns burned, corn cribs empty, and fields "turned out" and overtaken with rank weeds and brush. The livestock that survived looked like gaunt veterans of their own war after years of sharing forage with passing armies. Besides the loss of slave property, estimated at ten to fifteen million dollars, the value of farms fell drastically from over three million to fewer than two million dollars between 1860 and 1870. Cotton production that exceeded nineteen thousand bales in 1860 plummeted to nine thousand in 1870. Corn, wheat, and other crops fell in more or less similar patterns. In the newspapers, advertisements of large plantations for sale ran alongside lists of property forced into sale for taxes.[8]

The roads that linked plantation and farm to markets in Oxford, Memphis, and beyond were in severe disrepair after four years of war; most of the bridges had been burned, wrecked by invading armies, or washed out by swollen streams. The Mississippi Central Railroad, commercial lifeline to the county and all of central Mississippi, had suffered terribly during the war as first one army then the other burned trestles and bridges, tore up rails, and twisted them around trees in order to slow the other side's advance. Whitelaw Reid, a northern journalist touring the postwar South, recorded his ride on the rail line as a "dismal night of thumpings over broken rails, and lurches and contortions of the cars, as if we were really trying in our motion to imitate the course of the rails the Yankee raiders had twisted." The train had to stop at one burned bridge where the passengers walked to another train a half mile on the other side. Neglect had also taken its toll; railroad ties had rotted out, and bridges and trestles were in terrible repair. During the first year of operation after the war there were eleven accidents, mostly caused by the poor condition of the road and rolling stock. In 1872 the beleaguered Mississippi Central became affiliated with and, two years later, subsumed by the Illinois Central, which sought new routes into the Deep South.[9]

The people of Lafayette County looked worn and defeated as well. In one northern Mississippi community a traveler estimated that one-third of the men had lost an arm or leg and another third bore some physical wound.[10] One-fifth of the state's budget went to supplying artificial limbs for the thousands of amputees who returned from the war. Enterprising Yankees from northern cities flooded the state with advertisements of prosthetic arms and legs, all offered at discount postwar prices.[11] In a predominantly agricultural economy, a man without a leg or arm was not able to do much work, and his disability might throw an entire family on the meager resources of public charity.

In May 1866, William Delay, the old warrior, now county clerk, took a census of the county's disabled soldiers and destitute families, counting 304 in all. Pride played no small role in keeping this number low, for Delay advised that "quite a large number of disabled soldiers in this county [were] not reported" because "they possess such qualifications as enables them to support themselves" or "have friends who have provided for their support." Indeed, a more comprehensive census the next year turned up 1,664 destitute white people in the county, more than 70 percent of them children. About the same time, the Freedmen's Bureau estimated 500 destitute blacks in the county, bringing the total to somewhere near 2,200, about 13 percent of the population.[12] State law in 1865 required that the county "levy a tax in Kind of one half of one per cent on all corn, wheat, and Bacon Grown and produced" and "to enroll the indigent families of ther respective Beats." The county managed to raise $11,319, "being the distributive share of the fund for indigent families of Soldiers in Lafayette County." The Freedmen's Bureau was able to dispense its own rations of corn and pork to black and also to white families, but its supplies were extremely limited.[13]

The war also brought an intangible—but no less real or agonizing—loss of pride and honor. These injuries came as much from what took place at home as on the battlefield. In war Confederate soldiers had experienced victory and defeat and learned to accept the latter with a certain battle-hardened stoicism. At the home front women and families were left exposed to a series of invasions whose main purpose, it seemed, was vindictive destruction and humiliation.

The outrageous atrocities of "fiendish Yankees" and the insolence and disloyalty of slaves became inevitably linked. These two objects of wartime furor—meddlesome Yankees and unfaithful servants—remained powerfully joined during Reconstruction and the century that followed. Both had dishonored the white South, and it must have seemed that retribution against one was as good as vengeance against the other. In war, one veteran remarked, "you can strike back, in reconstruction we were unarmed and at the mercy of a merciless crew of carpet-baggers and for good measure, we were subjected to undescribable humiliation." [14] A people defeated and dishonored in war would find vindication in the assertion of supremacy over former slaves and in defiance of their Yankee protectors. They would win this war.

Yet Defiant

The recalcitrance that led the fire-eaters into secession and war four years earlier seemed unvanquished and as inflexible as ever. Soon after the war, in August 1865, delegates from all the counties met in Jackson to create a new state constitution and prepare for readmission to the Union. When the motion came to approve the Thirteenth Amendment, which abolished slavery, Hugh A. Barr, the Lafayette County delegate, offered an amendment stating that the United States—not Mississippi—had abolished slavery. The debate surrounding this proposal revealed that more was at stake than symbolic language, for some still held out hope the federal government might compensate slave owners for their losses. The convention finally settled on language acknowledging only that the "institution of slavery having been destroyed," it would cease to exist in Mississippi. (It would be 130 years later, in 1995, that the state of Mississippi ratified the Thirteenth Amendment abolishing slavery.) [15]

It soon became clear that Mississippi's legislators wanted to preserve all they could of the essence of slavery: forced labor and minimal civil rights.

Later the same year the legislature passed a series of laws aimed at controlling the labor of former slaves by requiring all freedmen to make contracts for the year by January 1 or be liable for arrest as vagrants. The Black Codes, as they were known, allowed heavy fines against laborers not under contract and against any employer who "enticed" a laborer already under contract with someone else to leave and work for him. The crime of vagrancy encompassed anyone deemed guilty of idle, disorderly behavior. Other offenses, if committed by blacks, included "insulting" gestures or language, "malicious mischief," and preaching without a proper license. Criminal laws that formerly applied to slaves and free blacks, the Mississippi lawmakers added, would remain "in full force." Perhaps the most draconian measure was the apprenticeship law, which gave the state power to declare former slaves under age sixteen orphans and bind them over to a "guardian," their former owners having first claim. The Negroes, Governor Benjamin Humphreys stated, had "been turned loose upon society, and the state must assume guardianship over them." [16]

The burden of enforcing the code fell on a newly devised county court system set up to decide an expected deluge of civil and petty criminal cases. [17] In Lafayette County the court was firmly in the hands of the old guard. Two of the three judges sitting on the Lafayette County Court, Andrew Peterson and William H. Smither, were members of prominent pioneer white families. The prosecuting attorney for the state was Robert W. Phipps, heir to a wealthy planter family, former Confederate colonel, delegate to the 1865 Constitutional Convention, a leader in the Conservative Democratic Party, who later served as Grand Cyclops of the local Ku Klux Klan. [18]

Remarkably few county court cases involved enforcement of the Black Codes. There were no cases of vagrancy and only three charges of enticing freedmen, two of them against freedmen themselves. (Caroline Barr, later servant to the Falkner family, was among those accused of being illegally enticed; she signed a contract without her husband, Jack's, consent.) Whatever force of law lay ready in the Black Code to control labor, the vagrancy and enticement laws were clubs not often used in Lafayette County. [19]

The new laws were being used to enforce a broader regimen of racial control. There were many convictions for petty criminal offenses, such as larceny, assault and battery, malicious mischief, and adultery, along with several civil cases, that were generally punished with fines and court costs. Dave, a freedman, found guilty of stealing meat from the smokehouse of Burlina Butler (Faulkner's great-grandmother), was fined five dollars and court costs. W. B. Bowen "assumes and agrees to pay fine," the court recorded. Bowen, like others who paid such fines or put up bond, put the convicted freedman to work for whatever time was necessary to work off the debt.[20] This was a means of reinventing slavery as debt peonage.

The county court also sentenced some freedmen to severe corporal punishment, public displays of the power of the state and a warning to all who witnessed. In three cases the court meted out a unique form of corporal punishment, in each case to freedmen convicted of petty crimes. In July 1866 freedman Sam McFadden pleaded guilty to charges of assault against a black woman named Willy. He was fined only one dollar and court costs, but, in addition, McFadden was ordered to be "suspended by the thumbs . . . on the Public Square in Oxford for five minutes and remain in the Custody of the Sheriff until the fine and cost is paid or give good and sufficient security therefor." James E. Markett, a white landowner of modest means who often procured cheap labor at the county court in this way, paid the fine.[21]

There were numerous convictions and penalties decided by the court against both whites and blacks, but no white person every suffered corporal punishment and public humiliation of the kind Sam McFadden and other freedmen endured.[22] Freedmen were often accused of stealing livestock and food from whites, a problem that had excited considerable consternation in the local press. In July 1866, the court convicted Noah (no last name given) for stealing a shoat (small hog) from the same James Markett. Noah was fined one dollar plus court costs and ordered to be "suspended on the Public Square in the town of Oxford for five minutes each day for two days and confined in chains during this time." It was the aggrieved, James Markett, who paid the fine and made Noah work off the debt, presumably after his thumb hanging. The brutal punishment inflicted on McFadden and Noah obviously did not benefit Markett or anyone else economically—to the contrary, given the physical injury these men risked.[23] In January 1867 a freedman named Peter Wilkins, convicted of "borrowing money without the permission of the owner" (a white man), suffered a fine of only one dollar and court costs. But he, too, was "sentenced to be suspended by the thumb" [sic] on the public square, and this time for "one hour each day for ten days."[24]

The image of this barbarous punishment captures the new relationship between the races. Instead of the master laying on the lash to enforce his authority, now the state, through local authorities, had taken over the role of punishing freedmen for violations of person and property. On full display in front of the courthouse—or the blackened ruins that had been left from that day of destruction and humiliation in 1864—these former slaves, grimacing in agony, suspended by their thumbs, served as dreadful warning to all freedmen of the punishment that awaited unruly behavior at the hands of their new master—the state of Mississippi. In two instances, this punishment was carried out on July 3, a day of special significance in Mississippi for it marked the anniversary of the fall of Vicksburg. The Fourth of July was shunned by most white families in Mississippi after the war, but it became a day of celebration for blacks and Republicans. This public display of power offered a pointed reminder to any freedmen inclined to celebrate Yankee victory or American liberty. "Both met the extreme penalty of the law with fortitude," the *Oxford Falcon* reported.[25] They and their people would need fortitude for the ordeal ahead.

They Will Not Work

Charles G. Austin was a stranger when he arrived in Oxford that first August after the war. He came to serve as subcommissioner of the Freedmen's Bureau post in Oxford. The local bureau began operations a short time before Austin arrived, but nothing had been done with the gigantic task of transforming a slave society into one based on free labor. The chief duty of the bureau was to supervise labor contracts between landlords and freedmen and instruct each party on their new rights under law. "Little has been done here," he reported to headquarters in Jackson that August. "The people both white and colored I find were generally ignorant . . . few or none knowing that it was necessary to form any written agreement to bind both parties."[26]

Austin was guardedly optimistic: "The planters and citizens of this town as far as I have been able to ascertain are generally well disposed and willing to do justice to their former slaves yet several complaints of abuse on the part of master to servant has been reported to this office." He went on to admit serious potential for distrust on both sides. "There are those who are loath to admit the freedom of the colored man. There is considerable complaint that the people (col) on the plantations will not work and are uncertain as to what they should do. They have no confidence in their former masters."[27]

It was a widespread assumption among former slave owners that, once free, blacks simply would not work unless coerced; they would not respond to the normal market laws of "work or starve." Mississippi's Democratic press was filled with complaints about freedmen loitering about the towns, waiting for handouts from the Freedmen's Bureau, and waiting, above all, for the "forty acres and a mule" freedmen believed had been promised them.

In the first flush of freedom, many former slaves left the plantations, came into town, and celebrated their emancipation by conspicuously enjoying their leisure and liberty. But what whites interpreted as an instinctive aversion to work was often a quite rational decision to negotiate the best deal they could in exchanging their labor for use of the white man's land. The 1870 census shows nearly all the black males eighteen or older reporting some occupation, over 60 percent as "farmers," another 27 percent as "laborers," and the rest in a variety of skilled occupations. Among adult black women, however, more than 70 percent reported themselves to be "housekeepers" or "at home." Most of those working were domestic servants; only 12 percent of adult black women worked in agriculture.[28] This meant a drastic reduction of the labor force from the time slave women worked in the fields. For the newly emancipated black family, freedom meant a major redefinition of gender roles along the lines of most white families. The choice black families made to withdraw women from the fields and the calculated reluctance of black men to sign contracts they feared might enslave them again were understood by white landlords as a stubborn refusal to work.[29]

Charles Austin saw his main task as Freedmen's Bureau agent as getting the freedmen to sign contracts and get to back to work. He distributed circulars and standard contracts among the planters and soon "business began to flow into this office." Austin was optimistic initially: "The people became enlightened as to their duties and for miles distant they come for information advice for circulars and blank contracts and to get contracts approved." His only problem was getting the information and contracts out into the countryside. The bureau was so poorly funded and understaffed it could not afford a horse or clerical support necessary for Austin to make his rounds. "Being entirely alone the good I might do is considerably restricted," he complained to headquarters. If only he could visit the plantations and talk directly with the freedmen, "a great deal of good might be done by instructing them of their duties the duties of their employers and to make them understand intelligibly their condition."[30]

While bureau agents tried to educate freedmen and their employers on their new rights and obligations, many planters determined to teach the freedmen their own cruel lessons in the principles of free labor. They threw off their land all but those who worked for them, leaving many elderly, young children, and disabled suddenly free to fend for themselves. Robert Stowers, who had earned a fearsome reputation for his harsh discipline of slaves, showed himself no less severe with freedmen. Now overseer and partner with Jacob Thompson, in the fall of 1865 Stowers ordered all hands on the plantation to either sign a contract for the next year or clear off the land. "Some Contracted at that time," the bureau agent reported, "and those that did not was to get out of his Quarters to enable him to furnish room for hands which he might employ in their stead." The freedmen protested, but

Stowers persisted in his work-or-leave policy until all but a few signed contracts with him for the coming year.[31]

For a time, Austin urged bureau headquarters in Jackson to provide a home for dispossessed former slaves. His plan was to confiscate two prime plantations owned by Jacob Thompson, who, suspected of involvement in the assassination of President Lincoln, had fled in exile to Europe after the war. The Freedmen's Bureau had been chartered in 1865 as the Bureau of Refugees, Freedmen, and Abandoned Lands, with authorization to take control of abandoned and confiscated lands. Thompson's Oxford mansion had been pillaged and razed during General Smith's 1864 expedition, but he owned two plantations in the county: the Home Place with 550 acres and Clear Creek plantation with over 2,700 acres. Both appeared to be ideal candidates for confiscation. The Thompson place (apparently Clear Creek), Austin wrote, "is one of the best in the country. It contains a mansion house and is well provided with other buildings. A fine place this would be for a colony and a colony will be needed by the first of next year." The alternative, Austin warned, was that evicted freedmen would wander "at large," congregate in town, and look to the government to provide rations. Unless "some provision is made for them hundreds must suffer." It was soon revealed that Thompson had transferred title to his son Mason in 1864, thus protecting the lands from confiscation and denying Lafayette County blacks what Austin had hoped would become their promised land.[32]

While some planters were throwing nonworking freedmen, sick or elderly dependents in particular, off their land, others were using the apprenticeship law in the Black Codes virtually to enslave those they deemed orphans or whose parents were considered unable to care for them. Assuming the law would be on their side, planters simply declared young freedmen subject to apprenticeship, drove their parents off the land, and had the court bind the children over to their custody. One eleven-year-old in Lafayette County was bound out against the tearful protestations of the mother. In some cases, the Freedmen's Bureau agent reported, the landlord "will not even allow the Parent to visit his or her child." [33] Despite pleas for protection, two years later the apprenticeship of minors was still common practice. A new bureau agent in Oxford, Thaddeus K. Pruess, reported in August 1867, "This system of binding children has been carried on last year to a great extent and is nothing more than slavery under a new name. Many parties have applied to me for relief. . . . I am satisfied that designing men have made a practice of binding children 14 and 16 years of age who were perfectly able to support themselves without their knowledge or consent. It is an evil therefor that should be looked into." [34]

Other cases showed it was as difficult for some freedmen to leave the plantation as it was for others to stay. George Oliver was furious when six or eight of the freedmen who had contracted with him for a year of work suddenly "absconded" in late spring 1866. We "suppose they concluded they were too free to work," the local editor observed. Oliver was the man charged with murdering his slave John in 1859. Now, following another labor dispute, he shot to death one of the departing freedman, Osborne Sherman.[35]

Most landlords and tenants were learning, slowly and painfully at times but better than Oliver apparently had, how to negotiate in a labor market without slavery. What was new was not just the freedman's choice *whether* to work or not work, it was also his choice as to *which* landlord. Suddenly there was competition for labor. For landlords, the problem was how to get the freedmen to work without driving them away to a rival employer.[36]

The Freedmen's Bureau reports give a picture of ongoing tension with constant violence and threats inflicted against freedmen. Agent Pruess reported on the situation in Lafayette in July 1867: "Complaints are daily made about the cultivation of the crops. Freedmen are threatened or ordered off by their employers accused of not working the crops properly and faithfully as per contract and disputes and difficulties are daily arising." One planter described a "a savage fellow going around the country calling himself captain Jo." Captain Jo hired his services out to planters, telling people "he is appointed by the bureau to thrash all refractory niggers and I tell you they catch it far and near around here." A neighbor "had the last chit and child save one no account woman leave in a great flurry yesterday morning" but Captain Jo "brought the last one back penitent and humble, well whipped." "Between you and I people believe every beat has its Capt. Jos. . . . it has the very happiest effect."[37]

Pruess did his best to be "extremely vigilant and watchful" of the freemen's interests, "with that single eye to justice to which they are so eminently entitled by the law of the land." He criticized local whites who refused justice to their former slaves but went on to note with his usual optimism: "There are on the other hand many parties who deal honestly fairly and humanely with the Colored man and he is under that mild and honorable treatment fast becoming a useful citizen and fulfilling that destiny for which God and nature designed him."[38]

Most freedmen, the *Falcon* editor, Sam Thompson, noted approvingly at the opening of 1867, had made contracts and were back at work; though some were still "luxuriating" and spending their money, "necessity" would soon end that. Planters, Thompson reported, had to pay more for laborers (either wages or crop shares) than last year because labor was scarce and competition was growing. Some landlords recruited black labor from Geor-

Black sharecroppers and white foreman in the cotton fields.
(Courtesy of the Mississippi Department of Archives and History)

gia and South Carolina, but it was not sufficient to the demand. One-third of the cleared land would lay idle because of the labor shortage. But it turned out better than expected in Thompson's view: "It was almost the universal impression that they would be idle and worthless. So far they have proved this idea wrong, and have shown that they could and would work as freemen."[39]

By 1868 this tone of guarded optimism had dissolved into despairing complaints of shiftless blacks who Thompson now believed had turned to stealing livestock and begging handouts from the Freedmen's Bureau in place of honest labor. Nearly every issue of the newspaper included a report of crime and disorder among the freedmen: murder, assault, drunkenness, and frequent accusations of theft. The only answer, it seemed, was to use the force of law and ultimately the military power of the government to coerce idle black laborers to work. Thompson cheered the state Freedmen's Bureau head, General Allen C. Gillem, when he ordered freedmen to secure jobs or risk arrest as vagrants.

That would not be enough, the *Falcon* editor believed. Courts and police powers had to be given over to the task of enforcing vagrancy laws and "compel those who are able to support themselves" to work at the point of a gun if necessary. Thompson referred to fears among local whites that freedmen were organizing militia companies and entertaining "illusions" that the state of Mississippi was going to be divided and given to them by U.S. authorities.[40] So long as freedmen had "illusions" of freedom to work as they chose or entertained dreams of land of their own, the planters' hopes of controlling their former slaves seemed doomed.

Whites Don't Need Their Services

Whites had their own illusions. If freedmen were dreaming of land and mules and bounty coming to them from the government, many whites were entertaining fantasies of a South without blacks—or at least with some alternative to black labor. Soon after the war, Mississippians organized several campaigns to recruit foreign immigrants from the North, from Europe, and even from Asia as a substitute for African Americans. If former slaves were not willing to work, the argument went, let them be replaced with willing immigrants, like those who had brought prosperity to the rest of America.

In 1867 the *Falcon* expressed enthusiastic support for the efforts of a labor recruiter named F. H. Rueff who promised to bring German workers to settle and work in Lafayette County. Germans, the editor wrote knowingly, are a "hardy and stout" people who are particularly well-suited to agriculture and perfect for the kind of "substantial, uniform, and permanent" laborers the county needed.[41] While antagonism and political tensions between blacks and whites mounted, enthusiasm for the white immigrant alternative grew apace. African labor is now "out of the question," an 1870 editorial argued; let us bring Germans, Norwegians, Danes, and Swedes, the "most thrifty and industrious people," to Mississippi.[42]

The dream of European immigrants flocking south to displace blacks had a moment of reality in 1870 when immigrant agents brought trainloads down from the North. Some two hundred immigrants, mostly Swedes and Germans, were brought to Lafayette County, thanks to the efforts of a Captain Nelms and Mr. Webber, who recruited them from Chicago. "Let them come and let them be well treated," the *Falcon* urged. This was the only way to show blacks that "whites don't need their services."[43] News of Chinese immigrants coming to work in cotton plantations in the Delta did not meet the same welcome. "The Chinamen possess no traits of character to recommend them," the *Falcon* pronounced; Mississippi should rely on northern European stock.[44]

When they arrived in Oxford by train in 1870, the immigrants "were all lined up, and each man was allowed to pick out those he wanted."[45] The scene bore a vague resemblance to the slave trade of earlier days, and one can almost imagine the poking of limbs and inspection of teeth. Many of these immigrant laborers found employment as house servants, and some planters put them to work in the fields. A group of local planters, led by Thomas E. B. Pegues, Paul Barringer, Thomas N. Buford, and others, formed a colonization company to sponsor more European immigration.[46] The census taken in 1870 found 263 foreign-born men, women, and young children in the county. More than half came from Sweden, the others from Germany, Switzerland, and other European countries. They worked as farm laborers, domestic servants, and skilled craftsmen, the latter often in building trades. Although they amounted to less than 2 percent of the population, the prospect of more white immigrants presented hope of a viable alternative to black labor.

Few white immigrants, however, saw fit to replace former slaves on terms their employers preferred. Plantation work was arduous and the Mississippi climate proved unbearably hot for northern Europeans. Some found their treatment at the hands of former slave masters more unpleasant than the heat. One group of imported laborers living near Clear Creek "did not like the treatment they received" and left the county. One English laborer brought his complaint to the British consulate, which provoked an investigation. Samuel Franklin, the English youth, allegedly gave his employer, a man named Henly, "trouble," and after a month of difficulty, Franklin ran away. Henly gave chase and caught him twenty-five miles away on the road to Memphis. Apprehended and dragged back to the farm, Franklin supposedly "behaved so badly and give so much insolence that [Henly] give him several licks with a stick." In Henly's defense, Thomas Buford hastened to add, the blows, "not more than three or Four did not break any bones." After his beating Franklin was apparently sent to Buford's plantation, where he would continue to "discharge his contract." Buford claimed Franklin was still "not disposed to do his duty." If this boy's experience is any indication of the way Mississippi employers treated white labor, it is not difficult to understand why freedmen were reluctant to work for former slave masters.[47]

It was another omen of doom for this scheme that a train filled with "forty or fifty" immigrants approaching Oxford just before planting season in 1870 plunged off a trestle, leaving twenty passengers dead and fifty others "mangled" or "slightly injured."[48] That unfortunate episode marked the final passing of any realistic hope for an alternative to black labor. Most of Lafayette County's immigrants left within the next few years. During the 1880s Mississippi's Board of Immigration and Agriculture continued printing handbooks in German, Swedish, and Italian extolling the opportunities for work in Mississippi, and they hired recruiters to go north and abroad, but there was little to show for their effort.[49] Locally, all talk of a foreign substitute for black labor had ceased. White landlords were left to deal with those they had brought into northern Mississippi to work the land a generation earlier.

The Landholders Oppose Schools for Freed People

The former slaves, in the meantime, sought whatever opportunities there were to fulfill their new promise of freedom and equality. They seized every chance for education as one of their first priorities. Young and old crowded into crude schoolrooms to learn basic skills that had been deliberately denied under slavery, skills that were essential to survival under freedom. Before 1870 Mississippi had no public school system for either race; now freedmen and their northern white allies took the lead in establishing their own schools several years in advance of the state system.

"The colored people of this town have done nobly towards raising a school fund to support schools for the instruction of the colored children here, already seven hundred thirteen and a half dollars have been subscribed," bureau agent Charles Austin reported in August 1865. "They are continually plying one with questions as to when the school will commence. What can I answer them." The next month the freedmen were moving forward on their own. "On the Jacob Thompson place stands the walls of a brick building," Austin reported. "The Freedmen think they can cover this and use it for a school house." "The harvest is abundant here," Austin implored his superiors in Jackson; "what we want are teachers. I feel for this people I would like to see them raised from their degradation."[50]

Austin's successor, Thaddeus Pruess, reported with pride the beginnings of the "First Freed School of Oxford" in 1867: "School commences at 8½ PM and closes at 5 PM. Holds five days in the week. The course of study is Grammer, Arithmetic, Geography, Spelling, Reading and Writing." The school is "doing much good amongst the Freed People of this vicinity." The "scholars are not very far advanced although they give every promise of rapid improvement."[51] Alexander Phillips, the teacher, was a black Methodist preacher and Republican Party organizer who came to Oxford from Holly Springs to become a champion of local freedmen.[52] "Mr. Phillips," another bureau agent, admitted, "is by no means an experienced teacher, his opportunities having been very limited, but what he lacks in scholastic lore he thoroughly supplies in indefatiguable energy and close application to the wants of his scholars."[53] By August 1867 another "colored school" announced itself, this one organized by former Freedmen's Bureau agent Captain Edward B. Rossiter, with his "lady" from New York joining him as assistant teacher. There "are a sufficient number of Negro children here to make two or three good schools," the Falcon noted.[54]

Depending on whether they saw schools as molders of well-disciplined workers or subversive agents of northern, Republican, radical ideas, whites alternately applauded and damned the efforts to educate the freedmen. In the end, their fears of educating former slaves overwhelmed whatever positive potential they saw in the project. A violent campaign against black education ensued, leaving school buildings burned and teachers harassed, assaulted, shot, and driven into exile.

As early as November 1865, the Reverend A. J. Yeater, a Presbyterian missionary working in cooperation with the Freedmen's Bureau in Oxford, wrote to headquarters in Jackson complaining of the "great difficulties in starting colored schools." Apparently no white property owner would rent space for a freedmen's school, so Yeater begged the bureau for funds to build a school. He thought "the people around Oxford are willing to have and to assist colored schools." That sunny illusion dimmed by January 1866, when he reported: "Oxford has returned to all its rebellious proclivities since the [U.S. Army] Garrison was removed." Yeater was physically accosted, robbed, insulted, and threatened by armed whites, especially the university students, who, according to Yeater, took a leading role in harassing anyone who sympathized with local freedmen. Yeater fled for his life.[55]

Daniel Perkins Borum, a white native of South Carolina, had lived in Lafayette for many years before he opened a school for freedmen ten miles east of Oxford in August 1867. "Mr. D. P. Borrum informs us that his colored school is in a flourishing condition," the Falcon reported. "About sixty scholars were expected to enter this week."[56] But whites were no more receptive to their white southern neighbor teaching freedmen than they were to northern missionaries. Now the opposition was rooted in concerns about labor control. White landlords in the neighborhood complained that field hands were leaving work to attend Borum's school. The log cabin that Borum used for his school was soon burned to the ground and beside the charred ruins someone posted a warning against starting any more such schools.[57]

Alexander Phillips also found his school under attack. Phillips proved a fearless advocate of black education and civil rights. He stood up to relentless harassment, threats, and violent assaults throughout his brief stay in Oxford. Students at the university threatened to "break up" his school as soon as it opened in 1867. When hostile whites forced Phillips out of his rented schoolroom later that year, no one else would dare rent space to him. Phillips resolutely "retired to the woods and constructed a temporary house of brush in which he has since been teaching," Pruess reported. In the summer of 1868, Phillips begged the Freedmen's Bureau for an assistant, saying he was deluged with scholars.[58]

Most planters wanted no schooling of any kind for freedmen, ostensibly because it interfered with their control of black labor. The "land holders are almost universally opposed to Freed Schools," bureau agent Pruess reported in October 1867. "There is no doubt but what Freed Schools could be established to advantage if land could be bought and teachers furnished but the planter will not assist in the establishment of such schools."[59]

White fears of educating blacks went much deeper than concerns about the time they might spend away from work; after all, most of the students were children too young to work. The objection stemmed from apprehension that northern missionaries and Republican sympathizers were going to be teaching the freedmen more than reading, writing, and arithmetic. "It is much better that our own people should teach the negroes," the Falcon editor explained, "than for the psalm-singing, puritanical, hypocritical importations from New England to do so."[60] Public schools for blacks, white conservatives argued, aimed at converting "loyal negroes" into Radical Republicans. A letter to the Democratic newspaper in March 1869 decried the subversive content of county school textbooks "filled with selections from the gilded infidelity and negro-equality rant of such ministers as Hall, such revered blackguards and scoundrels, as Beecher, Cheever, Bellows, Bacon, Tyng and Co., the very breath of whose lives is falsehood and slander."[61]

Fears of Yankee subversion through freedmen's schools was running high in Mississippi, but there were few instances of northern teachers actually operating in Lafayette County. John Robuck recorded one account of a northern woman who opened a school in the abandoned Price plantation in the southern part of the county. Robuck depicted the northern woman who came to teach school at the Price plantation as a "high-toned, philanthropic 'lady'" about thirty years old, "from the slums of some Northern city, who "suddenly ushered herself in among the negroes of our community." No white family would have anything to do with her, so she "boarded and associated exclusively with the negroes." By Robuck's account, she and other northerners were there to cheat the freedmen, to sell them textbooks they could not read and land titles that were not valid. When this woman opened her school, he wrote, the "negroes went wild" and all hands "quit work almost entirely" leaving the cotton in the field. This was in the fall of 1865 when cotton was bringing fifty cents a pound and hands earned one dollar for every hundred pounds they picked. With the school opened, they picked just enough cotton to be able to pay the school tuition. Labor was not the only issue. According to Robuck, she was teaching her pupils that white property belonged to them and that they were not only equal, they were superior to whites. It was this woman and her incendiary ideas that whites blamed for inciting freedmen to rob and assault Sam Ragland, their former overseer, and his wife, Elizabeth, early the next year. After three weeks of this school, local whites sent a written message threatening the woman with tar and feathering; she left the county the same day.[62]

"They hated us here," Faulkner's Joanna Burden says of her family, the carpetbaggers from Missouri who came to Yoknapatawpha to raise the freedmen from degradation and redeem their own race from the sin of slavery. "We were Yankees. Foreigners. Worse than foreigners: enemies. Carpetbaggers. . . . Stirring up the negroes to murder and rape. . . . Threatening white supremacy." None of it did any good, she went on, the "killing in uniform and with flags, and the killing without uniforms and flags."[63] Faulkner's Burden family embodied both the fanatical idealism of the Radical effort to raise up the former slave and its futility in the face of brutal white opposition.

While some whites were burning down schools and driving teachers from the county, some large landowners were offering their own paternalistic alternative to the freedmen's schools. In education, as in labor relations and politics, the white reaction to freedmen alternated experimentally between brutality and kindness, antagonism and cooperation. So long as blacks maintained some leverage as laborers and voters, self-interest and paternalism continued to condition white treatment of blacks.

White paternalism was never more pronounced than in the efforts by planters and other leading men of Lafayette to sponsor their own schools for freedmen. Proponents of a Sabbath school for freedmen in 1866 made a lengthy appeal for support from among their fellow white citizens. Opening with a grudging acknowledgment of abolition as an "accomplished fact," the appeal went on to elicit sympathy for their former slaves now abandoned to freedom. "This people are now thrown upon their own resources in a state of freedom, for which they are to a certain extent unprepared." It went on to claim that they "consider us, their former owners, to be *now* as we have *always been*, their natural guardians, and their best friends." Turning to the case for education, they continued: "If it was ever good policy to keep them ignorant it certainly is not longer so, but the very reverse. . . . If we do not teach them someone else will, and whoever thus benefits them will win an influence over them which will control their votes." Admitting the political motive behind their charity, they recast it as paternalistic duty: "But do we not owe it to them as a debt of gratitude? We remember how they, for our sakes, endured heat and cold, wet and dry, summer and winter, cultivating our fields, ministering to our comforts, promoting our wealth, improving the country, and actually advancing our civilization, by their physical labor; attending upon us at all stages of our lives, nursing our children, waiting upon the sick, going with us to the burial of our dead, and mingling their tears with ours in the open grave." The Sabbath school was designed "for the moral instruction of the colored people, as well as to teach them to read." "Regular preaching also is provided for them by the resident ministers of the different churches of Oxford." The advocates of this school claimed more than one hundred students, and twelve teachers were involved.[64]

A Sabbath school had the obvious advantages of not cutting into the workweek and keeping educational content to a minimum. Plans for a similar school received a warm welcome among the planters of the College Hill community. A "large Sunday School, designed for the manual as well as the moral culture of the negroes," the *Falcon* reported enthusiastically. "Some of the best citizens of the county are engaged in the enterprise and we heartily wish them success." The report also indicated a selective admissions policy: "Negroes who did not yield to the temptation to abandon their masters during the late war merit something at our hands."[65]

Limited education controlled by white conservatives was embraced as an alternative to the subversive education at the hands of northern teachers or Republicans. Whenever schools for freedmen emerged beyond conservative white control, they quickly became targets of violence and harassment. Though sometimes linked to labor control and more often to political concerns over Republican brainwashing, the assault on education for freedmen was rooted in deeper sources of racial antipathy and postwar white resentment toward former slaves. It was part of a broader program of white supremacy that aimed at keeping "niggers" from being "abolished," as Faulkner's Ringo so adroitly expressed it.

Praying for a Better Day

It was after the war that former slaves in Oxford began the first real church for freedmen in the county. They went to a place in the woods, on the "lower edge of the Old Pegues estate," the one-hundred-acre grounds that spread in back of Thomas E. B. Pegues's mansion on North Street. Their church was a bush arbor in the woods, a temporary shelter made with poles and brush. Later the congregation pitched tents to house their growing numbers of brethren. This church formed a nucleus for Freedman Town, the black neighborhood that filled the area northwest of the square beyond the railroad and depot. A group of black women in the Oxford Baptist Church transformed the congregation that worshiped at the bush arbor in Pegues's woods into Second Baptist Church. Led by Jane Wilburn and other women, they petitioned the white pastor of Oxford Baptist to transfer their membership. Several black members of the Oxford Methodist church also joined

Second Baptist. "Their voices blended in songs and their cries echoed to the heavens as they cast their aching and exhausted bodies on the ground in prayer; on bended knees they prayed for a better day," the church history tells.[66]

Five years after it began, the Second Baptist congregation was able to build a proper church of its own. They had apparently moved from the bush arbor and in 1873 were meeting on Sunday evenings in the back of the white church, by this time known as First Baptist. That same year, with aid from First Baptist's white parishioners, along with other whites in Oxford, Second Baptist purchased land for fifty dollars on Depot Street, near the bush arbor where the church began. Soon they constructed a permanent building for the church and a school.[67]

By the spring of 1868 Alexander Phillips announced the dedication of a new Methodist church, "to be known as the Colored Church at Oxford." Phillips cordially invited whites and assured them that "they shall have separate seats which will be provided for them." "We tender our thanks to the white portion of our population," his announcement stated, "for the liberal contributions which they have made and are making toward our Church."[68]

During slavery the churches were one of the few public spaces whites and blacks shared outside the plantation. Spiritually the churches they shared put them on an equal footing in the eyes of God, even if a partition or slave gallery separated them physically. Some integration continued after emancipation, for some former slaves remained in the congregations with their white brethren. As late as the 1920s whites attending Oxford's First Baptist Church recalled large numbers of blacks still crowding what had once been the slave balcony in the rear to join in services with whites.[69] But the general trend was toward separate congregations. In the decades following emancipation blacks organized some fifty churches in Lafayette County, and there were probably many ephemeral congregations in addition.[70] It was out of a desire for autonomy, it appears, that blacks began immediately to raise their own churches, hire their own preachers, and enjoy their own style of religious celebration in churches all their own. Sunday morning, which under slavery had been the most integrated time of the week, quickly became the most segregated, and largely by the choice of former slaves who found in their new churches a sacred sanctuary of freedom.

The Democratic press lauded the efforts of freedmen to organize their own churches. *Falcon* editor Sam Thompson gave his blessings in 1867 to one early effort to obtain land for a separate church and school, noting that as slaves they were "obedient, faithful, kind" and as freedmen they appear to be "honest, industrious, and humble" and deserve the help and friendship of their former masters. He called Oxford's generous citizens to give or sell at a good price a lot in the "suburbs" of the town for the church and school.[71]

The freedmen also organized self-help associations to dispense charity and provide burials for one another. The formation of the Freedmen's Benevolent Aid Society drew 150 members. After Christmas 1866 they had a public procession through Oxford and met in the Methodist church for singing and praying. White ministers Rev. S. G. Burney and Rev. C. A. Bell, along with Chancellor Waddel of the University of Mississippi, addressed the new society. Two of their own members, Austin Peterson and Lewis Boone, spoke as well. The group then marched in procession, accompanied by music and banners, to a building south of the square where they had dinner. All was approvingly noted by the *Falcon* editor: "Throughout the late war, and up to the present time, the negroes of Oxford and vicinity have conducted themselves in a manner that entitles them to the respect and sympathy of our people, and we are pleased to see that they are organizing associations for the relief of the needy of their race. — Their quiet and orderly conduct on the above occasion challenged the respect of all who witnessed their proceedings."[72]

The Freedmen's Benevolent Society made the Fourth of July a grand occasion for celebrating American liberty. They began the day marching around the square in procession with music and banners and later gathered in the Cumberland Presbyterian Church. There, several leading white citizens and "colored speakers" Jim Neilson and Gilburt Burney addressed the audience. All speakers noted "the identity of interest existing between the Southern man and the freedmen." "Our colored friends," the *Falcon* commented, "seemed to imbibe this doctrine freely and agree in the proposition." After the speeches, the crowd took part in a dinner prepared "for white and black," an occasion "beneficial to the morale of the colored community."[73]

In their churches and voluntary associations, former slaves seemed intent on establishing a degree of distance and autonomy from whites and often with white assistance. Nonetheless, there were frequent flurries of alarm over any gesture toward social integration between the races. When the civil rights bill was discussed in Congress in 1866, the *Falcon* editor railed against a law that would "allow the negro to eat with you, walk with you, ride with you, visit your parlor, intermarry with the whites, vote at the ballot box, to be appointed or elected to any office." The aim, he claimed, was "to force the white people of the South, to grant every right to negroes that white people enjoy."[74] Whenever they were free to choose, however, the freedmen of Lafayette County quietly pursued *autonomy from*, not *amalgamation with*, whites.

Organized into Republicans

Although freedmen withdrew peacefully from white religious institutions, when they entered the political arena there was a violent reaction. Politics was the most contested front in this "other war" known as Reconstruction. Largely in response to the defiance of Mississippi and other southern states, Radicals in Congress took decisive steps in 1866 to intervene on behalf of the freedmen. Radical Reconstruction joined the idealism of American democracy and humanitarianism to pragmatic political calculation. If states like Mississippi were to be readmitted to the Union, now with representation based on 100 percent instead of three-fifths of the black population, the losers in war might become the victors in peace. Democrats now tried to encompass their old-line Whig opponents in a coalition party they called "Conservative Democrat." For Republicans to establish a political base in the South, they had to extend the full rights of citizenship to the freedmen and use the power of the national government to grant and protect voting rights for blacks. What unfolded was a contest between Radical Republicans determined to use the power of the federal government to protect black political rights in order to survive against Conservative Democrats equally determined to maintain a "white man's government" by any means necessary.

The Reconstruction Act of 1867 placed Mississippi under rule by U.S. military forces, whose first duty was to see that all eligible voters were registered and delegates to a constitutional convention elected. By act of Congress freedmen were granted the right to vote, and the Fourteenth Amendment (ratified in 1867) guaranteed that all freedmen were citizens of the United States with equal protection under the law. The Fifteenth Amendment (1870) specified that the right of citizens to vote could not be denied by states on the basis of race, color, or previous condition of servitude. Republican Party organizers and politicians came south to mobilize their new constituency of freedmen and also to enlist as many Unionists, antisecessionists, and any other white southerners opposed to the Conservative Democrats as they could into their ranks. As Ringo put it so succinctly, the "niggers" were being "organized into Republicans"—slaves transformed into citizens, voters, candidates, even officeholders, and, above all, equal citizens under the law.

In July 1866, a voter registration drive began across the state. Isaac Duncan (the despondent father whose son William was killed in the war) served as president of the county's Board of Registration; he was eager to have the income. He and the board circulated handbills and enlisted people at precincts all over the county. The final tally in September 1867 showed 2,413 voters registered: 1,464 whites and 949 blacks, giving an advantage of 515 votes to the whites.[75] When the prospect of black suffrage was first raised, the *Falcon* opposed it, even though the editor claimed no freedmen would dare vote for the Radicals: "Negroes have at least sense enough to know who their best friends are." Southern whites, he went on, "know the negroes are a weak and dependent race, and are not competent, and but very few of them ever could be qualified to exercise the right of suffrage. The Southern people will never consent to thus raise the negro to an equality with the white race."[76]

In November 1867 blacks went to the polls for the first time in Lafayette County. The *Falcon* continued to strike a pose of confidence that blacks would vote with their former masters and not let Radicals "use them for their own selfish purposes."[77] Conservative Democrats boycotted the election; only half of the county's registered voters turned out, and Republicans won approval of the constitutional convention by a comfortable majority. They also managed to elect one of the two delegates, Colonel W. G. Vaughn, a white Republican, who beat out Thomas E. B. Pegues, the Conservative Democrat nominee, by a mere nine votes.[78] Across the state Republicans swept eighty-one of one hundred delegate seats. Seventeen of these were black delegates, and Democrats quickly dubbed it the "Black and Tan" convention. Whatever came out of this convention Conservative Democrats were going to attack. To them the most odious provision in the new state constitution was the "test oath," which required all voters to qualify by swearing they never had taken up arms against the Union and that they believed in the "civil and political equality of all men." Both of Lafayette County's delegates, according to the *Falcon*, resigned their seats "in disgust" and came home. Colonel Vaughn reportedly quit the Republican Party and joined ranks with the Conservatives (if he did quit, he returned to the fold, for he ran successfully as a Republican for the state senate in 1869).[79] The election to ratify the "Black and Tan" constitution in the summer of 1868 was the first real contest between the parties, and in Lafayette County, it was a hard-fought, violent election.

Republicans could win fair elections in Lafayette County only by reaching beyond the black minority to enlist white voters, "scalawags," as they were known, who came largely from the Democrats' old opposition. These native white Republicans could play an important role in counties like Lafayette, divided as it had been by secession and war. An odd assortment of old-line Whigs, Unionists, moss backs, blockade runners, even Tory bushwhackers were ready to be assembled into a loose coalition with Republicans to challenge the Democratic regime. The lines of dissension ran through the electorate at different angles, but each offered a crack in the wall of white solidarity sufficient to encourage Republicans in their effort to win white voters. Now, of course, this required an interracial alliance with the newly enfranchised freedmen, but enough might join, not in support of black equality so much as in common opposition to old enemies.

In Lafayette County the old opposition to the Democratic Party found a new home as scalawags in the Republican Party, and their support of the Republicans gave the party the margin it needed to win in a racially balanced county.[80] But the scalawags of Lafayette County did so at great risk. "Our sort had to be very careful," Thomas Garrett told the Southern Claims Commission, "or we would pull rope." A decade after the war, Jesse Sisk and others who had opposed the Confederacy remained blood enemies of the Democrats. The commission's special agent reported that Sisk was "true blue" and that he "was indiscreetly loyal during the war and has been since. His unionism will yet cost him his life or he will move."[81]

Republicans worked diligently mobilizing their new black constituents and building a biracial alliance with dissident whites. The Loyal League (or Union League, as it was sometimes called) was the principal organization through which Republican leaders sought to bring black voters into the political process and forge an identity with a party and leadership that was vilified by local white landlords. Local Conservative Democrats scoffed at the first effort by Nelson G. Gill, Republican leader of Holly Springs, to organize a local Loyal League in August 1867. According to the Falcon, local blacks decided to have nothing to do with the organization. "The freedmen of this community have conducted themselves in a manner since the war which entitles them to the respect and confidence of the white citizens, and we warn them against such creatures as this man Gill."[82] When the Loyal League nonetheless formed, the same editor denounced it as an insidious presence, a secret cabal led by outsiders intent on undermining the loyalty of freedmen to their former masters.[83] The Loyal League organized festive social gatherings, barbecue suppers with dancing, games, and a full compliment of political toasts, speeches, and discussion. The Democratic paper never failed to point out the preponderance of blacks at these events, but in doing so it acknowledged the interracial alliance local Republicans had forged.

Some Republican leaders were newcomers to the county, but very few would qualify as "carpetbaggers" from the North; most were white southern "scalawags" who came from other southern states. Among the most radical advocates of black civil rights and equality in the region was Robert Flournoy of Pontotoc. A former slave owner and native southerner, Flournoy came to his courageous stance as a racial egalitarian out of nothing more than Christian humanitarian conviction. Republicans also recruited

Jerry Fox, Republican leader and former slave from Virginia, posing with his "freedom papers" in his pocket. (Courtesy of Susie Marshall)

local freedmen and whites into the party leadership. The Republican strategy was to use the power of patronage to give party leaders a local base. The problem was that, wherever they came from, Conservative whites saw them as outlanders stirring up trouble between the races. Adelbert Ames, the carpetbag Republican governor from Massachusetts, had appointed Judge DeWitt Stearns of Pennsylvania probate judge in Lafayette County. Major S. V. W. Whiting from Arkansas was another Republican appointed by Ames to local office. Two Republican leaders came from Tishomingo County, a Unionist stronghold in the northeast hill country of Mississippi: A. Worley Patterson, who served as U.S. marshal with the federal district court, and Robert A. Hill, who served as federal district judge. Captain James H. Pierce also was with the U.S. marshal's office. Daniel Perkins Borum, the freedman's school teacher, was one of the few identifiable native Mississippi scalawags among the Republican leadership, along with James Wheeler, Jesse Sisk, and W. G. Vaughn. Black Republican leaders included Alexander Phillips, of Holly Springs, and Tobe Humphries, Bob Stockard, and Mack Avent, all former slaves of Lafayette County. Jerry Fox, another former slave, had arrived from Virginia during the war.[84] Governor Adelbert Ames had appointed most of the Republican officeholders in county government (like Faulkner's character, Cassius Q. Benbow, who was appointed marshal of Yoknapatawpha County). Contrary to the Black Legend, the overwhelming majority of Republican officeholders were white. Republicans did manage to win local offices, and sometimes with black candidates, but that was the exception, not the rule.[85]

Politics was more than just a matter of getting voters to the polls; on the local level it meant building a community of like-minded supporters who came together with a sense of belonging. Republicans put on a good show for their new troops. They staged magnificent torchlight parades. The newly enfranchised freedmen wore red oilcloth caps festooned with bright red feathers and wrapped themselves in large blue and red sashes. They pinned badges with long flowing ribbons on their breasts and marched en masse to the exhilarating sound of African drumming as they lofted torches, banners, and transparencies. In such moments every freedman must have felt himself a citizen belonging to something larger than his family or church. They had also joined in common cause with a movement that defined itself in opposition to their former masters. They did so in an unprecedented alliance with whites who begged for their votes, rewarded a few of them with offices, and expressed, above all, a spirit of shared interest.[86] This was a heady experience for anyone barely three years out of bondage.

The Loyal League also provided security and party discipline, particularly on election days, when black voters traveled to and from the polls in large groups, drums beating, marching on occasion through a gauntlet of armed and angry whites. Faulkner's description of Republican organizers "herding niggers" to the polls described what whites saw on these occasions. Only in such large groups did black voters feel safe. Even then, the threat of violence was often brazen. "There is not a foot square in this state where a meeting of white and black persons would be permitted to organize a Republican Party," Robert Flournoy of Pontotoc complained. "Mobs and murder would certainly be the result."[87] Flournoy exaggerated, but only slightly, the threat to his party in Mississippi. In 1872 Republican leader James Pierce led a group of some four hundred black voters, four abreast, down North Street about noon going toward the courthouse polls. On the square a group of Democrats lined up a cannon, pretended to load it with cut-up chain, and fired into the crowd of Republicans. Though it was actually a blank charge, it had the desired effect of frightening the black voters into hasty retreat.[88] Against all odds, the Republicans nonetheless could deliver the vote and manage on rare occasions to extend a black minority into a narrow Republican majority in state and local elections. But in the summer of 1868, as Republicans prepared to vote on the new constitution, they met resistance that no amount of party spirit alone could overcome.

This Is a White Man's Government

Democrats mobilized their own followers and reached out in two directions: one, to all whites with an appeal to bipartisan racial solidarity; the other, to "loyal" blacks with an appeal to interracial paternalism. They adopted the label "Conservative" or "Conservative Democrat" to soften old partisan enmities with former Whigs and Unionists and bring them into an alliance against new enemies. A call to an "anti-Radical" rally early in 1868, made an emphatic appeal to white solidarity: "Let every decent white man attend. A white man that does not do his duty is a traitor to his race. Come forthe, then, one and all, and combine to defeat a party which has sworn to degrade and ruin your race."[89] Their appeals to white solidarity usually aimed at stirring resentment toward black pretensions to social equality and political power under Radical Reconstruction. A typical piece in the *Falcon* told of "Uncle Dick," a freedman who supposedly spoke to a black audience about his dream of racial revenge. "I will never be satisfied until the white man is forced to serve the black man, as we were forced to serve them." The new state constitution, the same editor argued, would license "NEGRO SUPREMACY in the administration of government, and NEGRO EQUALITY in the schools, in the militia, and in the jury box" and invite "MISCEGENATION."[90] Justified by the notion that Black Republicans aimed at depriving whites of their liberty and honor, while elevating blacks to supremacy, not mere equality, the Conservatives treated Reconstruction as a life-or-death struggle for racial survival. "This is a White Man's Government," they proclaimed after the election of 1868, "and trusting in our firm purpose our good right arms and God of Right, we will maintain it so."[91]

At the same time, Conservative Democrats sought to divide black voters through a combination of paternalistic appeals to "loyal" blacks and strong doses of intimidation. Democrats invited blacks to lavish barbecues and political rallies, which featured "loyal" black speakers testifying to their suspicions of the Radicals and their fidelity to the Democrats. Jim Neilson (variously spelled Nelson), former slave to William S. Neilson, a wealthy Oxford merchant, was a prominent speaker at the Democrats' 1867 Fourth of July barbecue. William Neilson owned nine slaves before the war, and he was said to have rewarded each of those who remained loyal to his family with a twenty-dollar gold piece. Jim Neilson was one of them, and he was grateful. Described as "highly respected by both white and black for his faithfulness, honesty, industry, and practical good sense," Neilson rose to address his racially mixed audience at the Cumberland Presbyterian Church in Oxford. He began with "a very low bow, which drew great applause, especially from the colored portion of the audience," the *Falcon* reported. Conceding that the Yankees may be responsible for setting the blacks free ("although it made many of us a heap worse off than we were before"), Neilson argued it was their former masters who had provided for the freedmen in their hour of need. "We all know where our true friends are; the interests of white folks in the South are our interests; they are the proper ones for us to go to, to advise with about our interests."[92] "There is no county in the United States," the *Falcon* added, "in which a better feeling exists between whites and blacks."[93]

As one hand opened in a gesture of welcome to "loyal" blacks, another presented a clenched fist of intimidation. Some of this appeared in the form of favoritism to "loyal" blacks, who were issued Democratic badges, large tin stars, to wear on their shirts. These emblems, whites assured them, were a guarantee of secure employment, higher wages, and good treatment at the hands of whites. Those without the Democratic star could expect the opposite. Balloting was not secret at this time, and on election days white Democrats surrounded the polls and made a great show of taking down names of blacks voting with the Republicans. The names of both Radical and Conservative blacks were then published in the *Falcon*, explicitly as a guide for white employers.[94]

The Democratic Club of Caswell Precinct, in the eastern part of the county, met at Pegues' Mill on the Fourth of July to adopt a series of resolutions that made this carrot-and-stick strategy absolutely clear. Noting the organization of the Loyal League, designed to "oppose the liberty of the South," it resolved not "to employ, countenance, or support" anyone who was a member. Further, it resolved to "protect" those men who rejected the "overtures" of the Radicals and "denounce and discountenance, as an enemy, every colored or white man" who supports them.[95]

Deadly Enemies

Large landowners depended on black labor to produce their cotton crops, and they could not afford a harsh program that risked alienating workers. Many small white farmers, on the other hand, had reason to see blacks as both economic and political rivals, and their racial animosity was unchecked by any dependence on black labor. Conservative strategies vacillated between these two poles accordingly. Whether wooing or intimidating black voters, the goal of both strategies was to defeat the Radicals and maintain a "white man's government." But excessive political violence had potentially detrimental economic consequences for those wealthy land-owners whose fortunes depended on black workers now free to choose their employers.[96]

Both strategies went on full display in the summer of 1868 when Mississippi voted on the new "Black and Tan" state constitution. Alexander Phillips described the scene at the Oxford precinct: "Whiskey and money went freely on that day. I suppose every black man who voted the democratic ticket got a drink of whiskey or something else." The Democrats put on a dinner "for the democratic colored voters and all good conservatives," and the blacks wore their "democratic stars" to display their loyalty. There was also intimidation aimed at "radicals that would not repent." Out at Alexander Pegues's plantation three freshly dug graves gave the clear implication that freedmen who voted Republican would find a place in them. Open graves with unnamed tombstones became a forceful means of intimidating black voters on several plantations that summer.[97]

There was real as well as threatened violence. Republican election commissioners riding out to the eastern district of the county "were fired on by a band of ruffians, at which time they lost their horses, bridles, and saddles." On more than one occasion, white men entered Phillips's church during services and political meetings. One time they rode their horses right into the church, threatened to shoot into the crowd, and demanded that Phillips cease speaking. "There has been several men shot at since the election began," Phillips wrote to bureau headquarters in Jackson. "I am not afraid of rebels," he added, "although they may kill me. Give me liberty or give me death." Judge John McRae, on hand to supervise the election, reported violence and intimidation of Republicans in every corner of the county. Near Springdale in the eastern part of the county a "band of rebel cutthroats" shot into the house where he was staying. At Taylor's Depot white men, "inflamed" by black voters, made "severe threats." One promised: "You shall not work my lands; you shall not live in my cabins; you shall not have any employment." The local doctor added: "You shall not have another drop of my medicine." At Hull's Precinct, on the other hand, whites "got many votes from the colored people with sweet talk and false promises." Jo Bates, in Abbeville, "threatened that the colored people would be shot in their fields and on the road, and their houses would be burned down, saying we will not suffer you to vote against us and then let you live among us."[98]

Democrats refuted every charge of election improprieties. Isaac Duncan, in his official capacity on the Board of Registration, swore that "there were no threats or intimidation, or fraud, violence, or any obstruction to a free exercise of the elective franchise" and the election was "conducted with as good feelings as any other election I have ever known" in Lafayette County.

A group of freedmen, including Jim Neilson, Newton Chilton, Jack Barr, and other "loyal" blacks, signed with their "X" a statement reassuring government authorities that "no one was kept from voting . . . no force or violence was used or threatened." [99]

The 1868 vote in Lafayette County was an overwhelming Conservative victory against the state constitution: 1,895 to 298. Across the state the new constitution was defeated; without a new constitution, Mississippi would remain out of the Union. Republicans challenged the election, and a congressional investigation ensued. During the hearings Lafayette County was one of several Mississippi counties Republicans singled out for its flagrant election fraud and intimidation.[100]

In the meantime, in July 1868, Conservative Democrats threw a lavish barbecue in Oxford for the loyal blacks who helped them defeat the constitution. All freedmen were invited to attend, including those who wished to "redeem" themselves after voting with the Radicals. An estimated 2,500 to 4,000 "colored" attended what the *Falcon* described as the "most extensive affair in the way of a barbecue ever given in the County." Watching the crowd was an "ample police force and strict order was maintained during the day." A large procession arrived at the ground where Professor Stewart's Brass Band played "stirring music." Loyal voters were treated to "immense supplies of meats and bread" that had been "furnished by the white people" from every quarter of the county. Colonel R. W. Phipps rose "amid deafning cheers" and spoke, followed by other white Democratic Party leaders, Captain O. F. Bledsoe, and state senator elect Dr. Gabbert. Newton Chilton was delegated by the "colored committee" to follow with his own address. After dinner several prepared toasts defined the party's position against Radical Reconstruction and celebrated the shared interests of Conservative whites and their "loyal colored" allies. They raised one toast to the "White and Black Races of the South": "In slavery, which was fastened on them by the North, they gave to each other protection and fidelity. In freedom, which has resulted from the war, they will give to each other justice, friendship and mutual support." The "Colored Committee" offered their own toasts, one denouncing the Freedmen's Bureau for its attempt to "organize our people into oath-bound Leagues, in deadly hostility against our old masters, with whom we have been raised and for whom we have the greatest respect." [101]

Skeletons Rising in the Yoknapatawpha

The "deadly hostility" of which they spoke had been in evidence in Lafayette County for some time already. Early in 1866, probably a January night, a group of blacks entered the home of Sam and Elizabeth Ragland. Ragland was an overseer on the late Washington Price's plantation in the southern part of the county, and according to one account, these were Price's former slaves. There may have been bad blood between them and Ragland. After the war Ragland told of how when the Union soldiers came to the plantation in 1862 he "had hid the mules out so that I did not think that they could find them but the niggers told them and went and showed them where they were." Local whites regarded the Price slaves as the "most vicious slaves in the county." Now they came looking for money, for food, or perhaps for the treasure that, according to local tales, one of Price's slaves hid during the war. They attacked Elizabeth Ragland in bed where she lay sleeping and slit her throat. She stumbled outside the door and died beside the house, her neck nearly severed all the way through. One of the intruders hit Sam Ragland on the head with an ax, but he survived.

Ragland was unable to identify any of the intruders. One account says that the Freedmen's Bureau investigated the murder, but there is not even a mention of the incident in its official correspondence. A vigilante group of some three hundred whites met at Ragland's house in a "blood heat." A contingent of them began carrying out their own interrogation of local blacks. One freedman, "Old Jess," nearly seventy years old and an unlikely suspect, was reportedly found with Sam Ragland's derringer pistols in his possession and confessed to being leader of the murderous gang. He gave up the names of some twenty accomplices before his interrogators murdered him.

Now a deadly vendetta began against those Old Jess had named as Elizabeth Ragland's killers. An unidentified group of white vigilantes executed twenty or more men and women, one by one. The accounts of the reign of terror that took place in the southern portion of the county that winter are inconsistent, vague, and cloaked in secrecy. Some accounts refer to lynchings, and one describes a group of suspects, bound by chains and vines, being pushed into the Yoknapatawpha River to drown. Most of the victims simply disappeared while away from their homes. Some reported seeing skeletons rising to the surface of the Yoknapatawpha, and others spoke of skeletons found in one of the holes below the water.[102] This was the violent and lawless southeast corner of the county Faulkner called Frenchman's Bend, described as remote from law, "straddling into two counties and owning allegiance to neither," where the inhabitants "were their own courts judges and executioners." It was also a place Faulkner described as having "not one negro landowner in the entire section" and so dangerous that "strange negroes would absolutely refuse to pass through it after dark."[103]

The Ku Klux Terror

The Ku Klux Klan was first organized just north of the state line in Tennessee, allegedly by Nathan Bedford Forrest, the former Confederate general. A Klan was organized in Oxford sometime in the spring of 1868, before the election that fall; people later said Forrest himself came down to organize the first den in Lafayette County. The men met in a small brick house off the square (where Faulkner's friend Phil Stone and his father later had their law offices). Sam Thompson, secretly one of the Klan organizers, announced the Klan's presence in his newspaper, the *Oxford Falcon*: "It is the popular impression that they [the Klan] are the spirits of our heroes who fell upon the battle-fields in the late war, and that they are now revisiting the earth for the purpose of aiding us in the great struggle now impending." [104]

Several Klan members later interviewed by Julia Kendel, daughter of a prominent Democratic family in Oxford, freely shared with her their exploits during Reconstruction. The Klan established five dens, one in Oxford with seventy members and others in each beat of the county totaling another eighty or more in membership. Its leadership included Grand Cyclops, Colonel R. W. Phipps, an Oxford lawyer and chair of the County Democratic Party executive committee, and Sam Thompson, Cyclops of the Oxford den and editor of the Democratic *Falcon*. Those identified as heads of the rural dens also served as leaders in local Democratic clubs. The Klansmen Kendel identified represented a mix of small and middling landowners, most of them young men in their twenties and thirties, typically married with children. Many had been born outside Mississippi, but they were well established in Lafayette County and many had many kinship ties within their neighborhoods. Whatever else they had in common, the members of the Klan were white, they were Democrats, and they were native southerners.[105]

The Ku Klux Klan operated as the paramilitary wing of the Conservative Democrat political party. Its campaign of intimidation and violence targeted Republican leaders, white and black. As the election for the constitution approached in May 1868, Alexander Phillips wrote a letter describing the campaign of terror the Klan had launched: "Sir I seat myself to write you a few lines to let you know of our troubles here. Their is not a week that passes over our head but som of our people have their houses brok in to by the Ku K.K. and whiped taked and hung until all most dead. . . . I hear deeds perpetrated weekly and the white pepole say that if they black men vote the Radickle ticket and they shall suffer." This violence, he wrote later, is "very degrading to any comunity claming to be civilised." [106]

By the time the 1868 election arrived, the Democratic press was prophesying "race war" and "extermination" if freedmen voted in support of the

Radicals. An open letter signed by several "loyal" freedmen begged their people not to support the constitution lest it "make the white people in this county, the deadly enemies of all the colored people who so vote, which may terminate in the extermination of the colored race in the South." In response to Klan violence and other white harassment Phillips had reported in the county, the U.S. Army sent a garrison of soldiers to Oxford on June 23, 1868, to try to keep peace during the election. Republicans had been subjected to an onslaught of assaults, and Phillips along with others had been begging for military protection during the polling in June.[107] Soon after the garrison arrived, a night of violence broke out in Oxford. A white man named Rupe, a painter from Water Valley who was drunk and enraged, shot his gun into Alexander Phillips's house, and when Phillips came out of the house Rupe shot him in the face. The incident nearly set off a riot. Several blacks in the vicinity fell on Rupe and gave him a thrashing. That night over one hundred armed black men gathered in Oxford at a Radical protest rally held near the garrison. Only the presence of federal soldiers prevented a general melee.[108]

While the garrison provided protection for Radicals in Oxford, in outlying rural areas Republican sympathizers were exposed to a reign of terror perpetrated by the Klan and by random acts of white ruffians. Much of the violence against blacks appears to have been concentrated in the eastern hill country and in the southern portion of the county. In these areas the racial hatred of small white farmers raged unchecked by the moderating effects of the planters' need to attract and hold black labor. The freedmen of Lafayette County prepared to defend themselves.

It was near Denmark, southeast of Oxford, that a group of blacks, with a freedman named Jake Watson as their captain, organized their own militia company to defend against white violence. The Klan den of Lafayette Springs, a notoriously rough neighborhood in the eastern hills, issued a warning to Watson to disband, but he ignored them. The Klan rode out to Watson's and demanded that he come out. They set fire to a bundle of straw outside the house, and as it went up in flames, Watson and some other black men came out "fighting with anything they could get their hands on." The Klansmen fired on them with buckshot, wounding Watson and two others; a fourth escaped. That same night, the Klan rode over to the cabin of Sandy Newberry, the first lieutenant of the militia. Newberry hid out and when they found him the next morning, they gave him a severe beating, two hundred lashes with a leather stirrup. Then they rode over to the cabin of Jake Boone, another black militia leader, and gave him a whipping. The Klan threatened Watson and the other officers with death if they dared to call their militia to another drill.[109]

The county remained tense with violence. In the spring of 1869, there were new reports from east of Oxford of armed blacks assembling to drill at night, yelling loudly, shooting off guns "which naturally alarmed the white portion of the community." The Klan rode at night, called the unidentified militia captain out of his cabin, and inflicted a painful whipping. They burned a second militia officer's cabin down and left him injured. The next day a large band of blacks had their revenge, reportedly burning white houses and murdering several whites. A band of some three hundred whites confronted them before both sides backed off.[110] "We regret to see the growing tendency of the negroes of this community to take the law in their own hands," lamented Sam Thompson in 1870. "The law," he went on, "is now in full force and administered to all alike, and this species of mobery must have an end."[111]

The army garrison sent to Oxford to maintain peace during the 1868 election returned in August 1869 and maintained a presence off and on until 1875, when Mississippi's Republican regime came to an end.[112] Conservative whites were challenging the very legitimacy of Republican government and the foundation it rested on: black citizenship. In the end, the Klan and the Democratic Party demonstrated that the *only* way Republicans could rule Mississippi was at the point of a bayonet. Even then, it proved no easy task, for beyond the eye of the military, violence erupted across the country.

In Oxford, in the protective shadow of the army garrison, Republicans staged Loyal League rallies and torchlight parades, which helped steel the black voters to turn out to vote a second time for the new state constitution and for Republican candidates in the election of November 1869. Before the election, most local government officials were turned out of office by order of Governor Adelbert Ames, the provisional governor appointed by President Grant. All vacant offices would be filled with Republicans appointed by Governor Ames, which meant that Republican election officials would be able to secure the polls. In November Republican voters turned out in legion and managed to carry the county by a narrow margin. Across the state, Republicans were able to convert the black majority into electoral victory. The constitution, now with the test oath provision removed in order to mollify Conservatives, was finally approved. Mississippi reentered the Union shortly afterward.[113]

Again, in the presidential election of 1872, Lafayette County Republicans were able to forge a winning coalition of black and white voters to edge out the opposition by eighty-five votes.[114] When local offices fell open to election the year before, Republicans managed to hold onto seats on the Board of Supervisors. Two freedmen, Jerry Fox and Mack Avent, won election in their beats, Fox in Oxford, and Avent in Beat Four in the southwest corner of the county. They won even as Democrats began to take back most offices in county government.[115]

The Oxford Klan Trial

Republican victory and political domination only heightened the tension and violence in Lafayette County and across Mississippi. Northern Mississippi became notorious for white terrorism, which had become so pervasive that it seemed beyond the power of state law enforcement to quell. Congress passed the Ku Klux Klan Act in 1871 making violations of civil rights a federal crime. Gideon Wiley Wells, United States district attorney for northern Mississippi, set out to vigorously prosecute and convict whites under the powers of the new act. The first case to be brought to trial under the new act opened in Oxford in June 1871, with L. Q. C. Lamar, former champion of secession, serving as lawyer for the defense of the accused Klansmen.

The Klan trial was under way in the U.S. federal district court's temporary quarters in Oxford when Lamar caused a terrific stir in the courtroom one afternoon. He stood and claimed that a man in the courtroom had been stalking and threatening him. Judge Robert Hill ordered Lamar to sit down and be silent, but Lamar continued to speak and when a court deputy came toward him, Lamar picked up a chair and threatened to hit the deputy. Judge Hill grabbed the chair, and when U.S. marshal James Pierce approached Lamar to calm him down, Lamar struck Pierce in the face, giving him "a pretty hard lick with his fist." The blow knocked Pierce down and fractured his cheekbone. Lamar defied the court to arrest and imprison him. People in the courtroom, including a crowd of University of Mississippi students, began to applaud Lamar. One report said the Klansmen on trial stood and cheered, stamped their feet, and let out rebel yells in uproarious approval of Lamar's defiance. District Attorney Wells ordered one of the disorderly students arrested, but the student "did not move" and appeared as though "he intended to fight . . . nobody attempted to arrest him." U.S. soldiers guarding the prisoners drew their guns. Someone went to call more soldiers. One raised his rifle, and one observer said he "thought [the soldier] probably would shoot. . . . Everybody got still."[116]

There in the Oxford courtroom—Lamar defying the court to arrest him, the crowd of prisoners and spectators cheering lustily, black and white U.S. soldiers armed and prepared to shoot—was a scene that encapsulated the whole story of Reconstruction. Laws and constitutional amendments devised to equalize the legal status of former slaves, to make them citizens, like all laws, relied on the coercive power of the state and nation, and ultimately on the state's force of arms. In a democracy no government or military could rule for long at the point of a gun if there was insufficient public support for laws of any kind. The Oxford Klan trial was the first court test of the U.S. government's determination to use the force of federal law in defense of blacks' rights as citizens. Now the very violence the law intended to curb had invaded the courtroom. So had the Conservative white defiance of federal authority and the defiance by men like Lamar and the men in the gallery toward the very legitimacy of the proceedings. "The excitement is intense," one observer wrote from Oxford that summer, "public opinion of course sets with 'our boys' [the Klansmen] . . . we have 50 U.S. soldiers here but we need 500." [117] Perhaps five thousand or maybe fifty thousand— how many soldiers, how many guns, for how long? The willingness of white southerners to oppose Republican power with intimidation and violence and their readiness to defy federal military and judicial authority put the problem of Republican rule squarely on the trigger finger of those soldiers in the courtroom. For the Republicans to govern required in the end the consent of the governed. What white southerners had demonstrated was that they would not consent and that it would require the violence of the national government to enforce the law.[118]

It was in that same Oxford courtroom that Judge Hill framed a compromise between the Klansmen and the federal government. The defendants pled guilty, their sentences were suspended, and the convicted men were subject to probation. Gideon Wiley Wells prosecuted nearly seven hundred cases against the Klan in northern Mississippi, and its days of organized terror came to an end within a year or two after the trial. Some three hundred Klansmen took off for Texas to avoid prosecution. One of Wells and Pierce's last operations in Lafayette County was in 1872 against a number of white men accused of "wholesale killing of Negroes" in the area around Yocona. This was a delayed response to the mass killings that followed the Ragland murder six years earlier.[119]

The threat and use of violence and the use of other forms of intimidation continued after the demise of the Klan, just as violence had preceded it. But the Conservatives increasingly turned to election fraud, stuffing ballot boxes or removing Republican votes, instead of violence. It was easier and less risky to "count them out instead of shoot them out," they determined. The scattered precincts of the county, the inexperience and lack of education among so many black Republicans, and the lack of effective supervision of elections all offered ample opportunities to rig an election. Democrats later bragged that they had managed to hide one of their men in the courthouse vault; when the election official placed ballot boxes inside for safekeeping, he would simply replace Republican with Democratic ballots.[120]

The rebuilt courthouse, Oxford. (Courtesy of University Museums, University of Mississippi)

L. Q. C. Lamar, a hero all over again for his defense of southern white rights at the Klan trial, won election to Congress the next year. In 1874 the Democrats swept back into power in Mississippi, and the state legislature elected Lamar to the United States Senate. The fire-eating author of Mississippi's secession ordinance was now the spokesman for the unvanquished voice of southern states' rights within the Union. Lamar seized the opportunity to plot a course of conciliation between the South and North in his famous eulogy of Charles Graham Sumner, late abolitionist and architect of Radical Reconstruction. There was Lamar, one hand, figuratively, open, palm up, pleading in his eloquent southern voice for mutual forgiveness and reconciliation, asking only that the South be left alone. His other hand, the same that felled the U.S. marshall in the Klan trials, was still clenched in defiant resistance against black equality.[121]

Lamar's eulogy worked magically on northern public opinion, which had never been as fervent as Sumner and the Radicals about spending the blood and treasure of the nation on behalf of black equality. President Grant spoke for many when he responded to Governor Ames, begging for U.S. troops to safeguard a fair election against an army of white militia, that "the whole public are tired out with these annual autumnal outbreaks in the South." Ames summarized what was happening in Mississippi: "A *revolution* has taken place—by force of arms—and a race are disfranchised—they are to be returned to a condition of serfdom—an era of second slavery."[122] Without U.S. troops to protect them, the Republicans were doomed. In 1875 Mississippi had been "redeemed" by the Conservatives. In this other war, for home rule and white supremacy, the vanquished in one war survived to be victors in the other.

In Oxford the ruins of the old courthouse were being cleared and a new structure going up during the Klan trial in the summer of 1871. The reconstruction of the courthouse was funded partly with money borrowed from the Chickasaw school fund and partly with money begged from the federal government. As the new site of the U.S. federal district court for northern Mississippi after the war, Oxford was eager to provide adequate housing for the court. This was one form of federal occupation Oxford was glad to have. Republican judge Robert Hill had gone to Washington with the blessings of local businessmen and planters to secure congressional funding to replace the facilities General A. J. Smith had burned down a few years before.[123] By August 1871, seven years after the fires had consumed its antecedent, the new courthouse was nearing completion. This reincarnation was notably grander that its ruined predecessor and topped with the handsome addition of clocks on each face of the cupola. "Our people are indebted to General A. J. Smith for the brilliant illumination, during the 'late unpleasantness,' of the old courthouse and almost the entire town of Oxford," the *Falcon* noted wryly.[124]

Each hour the bell in the clock tower on the new courthouse would strike, Faulkner wrote, and the pigeons and sparrows would explode from the belfry every time "as though, the hour, instead of merely adding one puny infinitesimal more to the long weary increment since Genesis, had shattered the virgin pristine air with the first loud ding-dong of time and doom." Time, it seemed, was repeating itself for the human inhabitants of Mississippi as well. Except for the clock tower and some other architectural flourishes, the new courthouse—like the society—was reconstructed essentially as it was before the war. The courthouse, Faulkner wrote, was "restored, exactly as it had been, between the two columned porticoes, one north and one south."[125]

You got me, you'll wear me out because you are stronger than me since I'm jest bone and flesh. I can't leave you because I cant afford to, and you know it. Me and what used to be the passion and excitement of my youth until you wore out the youth and I forgot the passion, will be here next year with the children of our passion for you to wear that much nearer the grave, and you know it; and the year after that, and the year after that, and you know that too. And not just me, but all my tenant and cropper kind that have immolated youth and hope on thirty or forty or fifty acres of dirt that wouldn't nobody but our kind work because you're all our kind have. But we can burn you. Every late February or March we can set fire to the surface of you until all of you in sight is scorched and black, and there aint one god-damn thing you can do about it. You can wear out our bodies and dull our dreams and wreck our stomachs with the sowbelly and corn meal and molasses which is all you afford us to eat but every spring we can set you afire again and you know that too.

—WILLIAM FAULKNER, The Mansion

nine Rednecks

"Vardaman! Vardaman! Vardaman!" The crowd at the Oxford depot shouted in a deafening roar interspersed with rebel yells as their hero, James K. Vardaman, the "Great White Chief," descended from the train. Dressed in his white linen suit, he doffed his broad-brimmed black Stetson to the throng, revealing his long, dark hair combed back behind his ears and falling in curls to his neck. The Oxford Brass Band played "Dixie" while leading a procession slowly toward the square. Some five thousand people, almost three times the population of the town, most of them country people, turned out to see their champion. Young boys climbed up trees to catch a glimpse of their famous visitor. Others crowded close to touch him and just to see him better. Country people all over the white hill counties named their children after him and his disciple, Theodore Bilbo. The "Great White Chief" often rode to the hustings in a large lumber wagon hauled by a team of ten white oxen, a symbolic retort to the adversary who called his followers voting "cattle." Vardaman's supporters also wore red neckties, turning another insult — "rednecks" — into a emblem of defiant pride in answer to the condescending "Bourbon" planters and business elites, whose rule they challenged.

Among the speakers preceding James Vardaman in Oxford that day was Lee Russell, native son of Lafayette County, who hailed from the Dallas neighborhood in the southeastern quarter of the county. Russell, the son of a hardworking farm family, had raised himself from the poverty of that neighborhood to become a prominent lawyer and legislator. Lee Russell was already among the richest and most powerful men in Oxford. But he could stand before these men who were dressed in overalls and wool hats — he in his lawyer's coat and tie — and say, "I'm one of you," and they knew he was, or at least had been. Introducing Vardaman that afternoon was Colonel John W. T. Falkner, Russell's law partner, one of the Oxford gentry who was *not* one of them and never had been. But Falkner, seeing the political winds blowing in Vardaman's direction, had positioned himself as the local leader of Vardaman Democrats a few years earlier. His grandson Bill, then thirteen years old, could have been among the boys climbing the trees to gawk at the spectacle that day. In later elections Bill would drive his grandfather and Uncle John, and sometimes Lee Russell, to political rallies. That day his grandfather gave a "beautiful and eloquent speech," and then Vardaman rose and began his address.[1]

By this time in his career Vardaman had his campaign speech perfected, from the opening sentimental tributes to the Confederate dead and syrupy flattery of local women, down to the last racial epithet against the black men who would defile them. His speech that afternoon went on two hours, Vardaman's long, curly hair now loose and flying about his face as he spoke and gesticulated with emotion, the crowd roaring its approval as each political button was pushed. Warming to the task, Vardaman turned his rhetorical cannons against the enemies of the people before him. There were demons above: the aristocratic Bourbons, the Delta planters and moneyed interests in the banks and railroads who had run the state in their own selfish interest. Their other enemy, Vardaman told them, threatened them from below: the blacks whose very existence gave the Delta planters their political power in the statehouse and whose aspirations to freedom and independence since emancipation mocked the white man's descent into poverty and dependence. The resentment against the rich and powerful joined hatred of the lowly and powerless. The "revolt of the rednecks" would seize the power of the state from the Bourbons and use it to elevate the poor whites, through better schools, free textbooks, good country roads, and public health. White folks would get a larger share of the public resources, and that would come at the expense of blacks. This potent combination of class and racial resentment was a proven formula for populist success. Vardaman and his successors, Theodore "The Man" Bilbo and Lee Russell, learned how to appeal to the resentments—and also to the aspirations—of Mississippi's "forgotten man."

Snopeses and Rednecks

The rise of Vardaman and his successors was part of a larger social movement that fascinated William Faulkner. He made common country folk and the ascendance of the Snopes family major social themes of his Yoknapatawpha saga. Faulkner's treatment of these people has often been misunderstood simply as condescension and ridicule, but it is far more subtle and sympathetic than that. These poor white county people were the first subjects he explored when he began writing about Yoknapatawpha County, and he returned to them again and again. He explored their inner psychology of class and racial resentment and the social and historical context that gave rise to their "impotent rage." Faulkner seemed most interested in the alternative responses to poor white resentment, some choosing violent acts of revenge, others a dogged ambition to escape the plight of their class, to rise and emulate their social superiors.

Faulkner's Snopes family exhibited both these strategies of revenge and redemption. The Snopes trilogy (The Hamlet, The Town, and The Mansion) is the story of the rise of Flem Snopes, whose father, Abner Snopes, had been a bushwhacker with Grumby's Independent Rangers during the Civil War. The father apparently enlisted as a Confederate private but fell in with Grumby stealing horses from Confederate and Union forces as opportunity allowed. In The Unvanquished Faulkner casts Ab Snopes as a collaborator with Granny Millard and the boys in their mule stealing operation. Snopes betrays Granny, and Grumby murders her, and we leave Ab Snopes tied to a tree being whipped by the slave boy Ringo. When he reappears in the short story "Barn Burning" Ab Snopes carries with him a bitter reminder of his bushwhacking days: a bad limp from a gunshot wound inflicted when he was caught stealing horses from Confederates—shot by Colonel John Sartoris himself, according to one account. Now Ab Snopes is an embittered, itinerant sharecropper with a large family, two sons, twin daughters, his wife, and her sister. He has turned sour, Ratliff explains at the beginning of The Hamlet, not solely because of the stigma of his wartime past but also because of his humiliation at the hands of a cunning horse trader named Pat Stamper. But it is his maimed leg, his poverty, and his irascible wrath toward all those who "beat" him that seem to fire his anger. He takes out his class resentment in fruitless lawsuits against rich neighbors. When those fail, he burns their barns in the dark of night, a spineless act of revenge by an otherwise powerless and incompetent man. One of the many Snopes relations, Mink Snopes, is also resentful toward his better-off neighbors and kin; he carries out his revenge with a gun instead of kerosene and a match.

Against this pattern of poor white rage and revenge, Faulkner explored the alternative path of what we might call social revenge through self-improvement—this is the road Flem takes. Ab and Mink settle their scores with violence and destruction. But while Ab or Mink Snopes get mad, Flem gets even—and then some. He often gets the better of his rivals by beating them in the county's favorite sport—deal making and trading—the stakes of which are both profit and honor.

Flem Snopes is the New South counterpart to Thomas Sutpen, who came of age in the antebellum South. Young Sutpen feels humiliated by the slave butler of the rich planter, Pettibone, who employs his father as a lowly laborer of some kind. After contemplating murder and violence either against the black butler or his master, young Sutpen finally reasons that the only satisfaction, the only genuine retribution, is to become a Pettibone himself, to have land and slaves and a mansion, to beat his social superiors at their own game. That is exactly what Flem Snopes sets out to do as well. Instead of becoming a wealthy planter with slaves, according to the antebellum standard of success, Flem seeks to emulate and surpass the big man of Frenchman's Bend, Will Varner. Flem never resents Varner's wealth or position and does not aim to bring him down. Instead Flem becomes his protégé, learns the ways of trade, and manages to "pass" Jody Varner, the lackadaisical son, as the main inheritor of Varner's status and business savvy. Varner is primarily a merchant and moneylender who became a major landowner usually by extending credit to local farmers and foreclosing on their land when they fail to pay their debts. Flem Snopes shrewdly perceives there "aint no benefit in farming," and he tells Varner's son, Jody, "I figure on getting out of it soon as possible." What Flem figures to do instead is to get into business as a clerk in Varner's store, and from that he extends operations lending money as usurious rates, acquiring the local blacksmith shop, and picking up the Old Frenchman's place, the dowry he received for marrying Varner's daughter, who is pregnant by a man who absconded to Texas. He swaps the worthless Frenchman's place for a share of a restaurant in Jefferson, and the first volume of the Snopes trilogy closes with Flem moving to town where his ambitions find a grander field for expansion.

Flem is one of several Faulkner characters among poor country people whose ambitions are to leave farming and go into business, law, or politics—anything to escape the endless cycle of poverty and dependency that is the lot of most small farmers in Mississippi by the end of the nineteenth century. Labove, the law student Varner hires to teach school at Frenchman's Bend, is the son of a prosperous farmer, but he is no less determined to leave the farm for a career in politics. Labove's father owns his own farm free and clear and is, therefore, all the more perplexed that his son would forsake such a legacy in favor of law and politics. Young Labove apparently agrees with Flem that there "ain't no benefit in farming."

Some see in Faulkner's Flem Snopes and his clan the embodiment of modern greed and corruption invading a traditional agrarian community. Cleanth Brooks went so far as to say that Snopesism represents some form of Yankee plague, a calculating money lust that contaminates the New South with values outside the traditional agrarian folk culture. Faulkner seemed to understand, however, that Flem Snopes was imitating trading skills and embracing values that were deeply embedded and widely shared in this society. Whatever deeper motivations of pride and social ambition drive Flem Snopes, his success in getting ahead usually turns on his ability to take advantage of the greed and lust of *other* men. His own material ambitions seem to be always calculated and controlled, and he feels no other lust or passion of any kind that we know of. Flem Snopes may not offer a very sympathetic figure (any more than Thomas Sutpen did a generation or two earlier), but he is a pure southern type—indeed, a very American type—a man born to poverty and driven by ambition to rise in society. We never see into Flem Snopes's soul because, as the Prince of Darkness discovers, he has no soul; "is that my fault?" asks Flem! As a result, we are left without the sympathetic understanding of Flem's background and psychology that Faulkner provides for us in Thomas Sutpen, whose humiliating childhood experience at the front door of Pettibone's mansion explains his life.

It does not take much imagination, though, to understand what a person like Flem Snopes would have suffered as a boy, moving every year from one seedy, unpainted sharecropper's shack to the next, feeling scorned by his social superiors, perhaps self-conscious about his shabby clothing, and lacking cash for the things in country stores that others could buy, gazing at the "tin cans whose labels his stomach read." [2] Flem has also seen his father humiliated and enraged, trying to wreak vengeance on people richer, more powerful, and better educated than he can ever be, while every time they beat him at law or horse trading. Ab Snopes has told his boys of his heroic service in the Civil War, and he has even named Flem's younger brother

"Colonel Sartoris" Snopes in honor of the local hero. A savvy youth like Flem had to know the truth: that his father was, in fact, wounded in the foot while stealing horses, and his career as a Confederate private was superseded by one as a bushwhacker, preying on old women left to defend themselves. Ab Snopes, seething with resentment against the class of landlords that now "own me body and soul" as a lowly tenant farmer, sees no better way to settle his score with them than with cowardly, anonymous acts of arson executed in the dark of night. It is revenge that only brings more dishonor to the Snopes family in the end.

Flem turns his back on all that and goes to the hamlet to begin a career in trade, and from Frenchman's Bend he heads into town to build a fortune and buy a mansion of his own, in fact the mansion of his father's nemesis, Major Manfred De Spain. We never see Ab Snopes again, and it is not unimaginable that Flem would simply have no further dealings with the father whose legacy of poverty and revenge he has now risen above. Flem Snopes is not meant to be an admirable or lovable figure, but nothing he does is illegal, violent, racist, or even mean-spirited. If he is acquisitive and cunning, so are his adversaries; he learns quickly and beats them at their own game. Flem Snopes's social ambition is born of a humiliation and pride Faulkner leaves us only to imagine, but his is a life driven by some need for vindication. The story of Flem Snopes is one of personal struggle for redemption. Mississippi's "revolt of the rednecks," on the other hand, is a story of the collective politicization of class resentment and racial anger. In this chapter, we explore the rural world Flem escaped; the next will deal with the new life in town he and many of his kind pursued.

This Ruined Land

Following the travails of Reconstruction, the people of Lafayette County had little cause to celebrate the promise of a "New South." In the rising cities of the South that slogan bespoke an optimistic spirit of progress, the rebirth of a reformed and prosperous South rising from the ruins of war. New industries, railroads, and skyscrapers were all material expressions of a robust South that had put past defeats behind. For the small farmers, black and white, who lived in the older cotton-growing regions of the Deep South, the rhetoric of progress and optimism seemed a cruel mockery of their own miserable situation, for theirs instead was a world of defeated hopes, poverty, and class and racial strife that festered throughout the century following the Civil War.

The decline of what had only recently been a frontier of fresh land and hope in northern Mississippi was palpable in the ruined countryside itself.

Much of the verdant forest and open fields the Chickasaws had left a generation earlier was, by the 1870s, a wasteland of eroded fields, deep gullies, and
silt-filled creeks. Eugene Hilgard, state geologist and professor at the University of Mississippi, surveyed Mississippi's ravaged land after the war with
particular attention to the north central loess hill region that encompassed
Lafayette County. The tragic devastation of the land, Hilgard lamented, was
not the consequence of nature or war, though each contributed; it was more
the product of the rapacious, shortsighted strategy of its migratory inhabitants. White settlers entered a fresh, nearly virgin land and stripped it of
much of its vegetation. Then, by growing the same crops of cotton and corn
year after year, they wore out the soil and exposed it to drastic erosion. Most
settlers saw the land as an expendable resource, which they willingly exploited before moving on to Texas or the next frontier, leaving behind an
exhausted, ruined land.

These nomadic habits, apart from the damage they wrought on the soil,
Hilgard warned, also shaped the "moral and intellectual life of a community" making it difficult to cultivate the spirit of improvement, beginning
with the "improvement of our homes." Hilgard was German-born, and he
looked at these American habits of waste and constant movement with
a critical European eye. Looking over the ravaged land their forefathers
had left, he wrote, "well might the Chickasaws and Choctaws question the
moral right of the act by which their beautiful, park-like hunting grounds
were turned over to another race, on the plea that they did not put them to
the uses for which the Creator intended them."[3]

As a result of a shortage of labor and the general disarray of the economy during the war, many cultivated fields had been "turned out," meaning left unplanted and laid bare to the destructive effects of sun, rain, and
wind. The exposed land, Hilgard explained, soon formed a hard-pan surface that sloughed off water, creating torrents that carved deep gullies into
the hilly land. The soft loam topsoil washed away in enormous quantity,
leaving massive gullies ten to twenty feet deep. Inside these "Mississippi
canyons" the red sand that lay a few feet beneath the topsoil gave the gullies the appearance of enormous bleeding sores across the land. These
ravines widened rapidly as the channeled water undermined the banks,
which then caved in and washed away. During heavy rains these gashes
in the land became rivers full of a "tumbling, gruel-like mass of sand and
water" which glutted the stream beds causing damaging floods over adjacent farmland. The otherwise fertile Yoknapatawpha River bottomland was
subject to chronic flooding that made planting risky. Before the war, plantation owners had countered this problem by putting slave gangs to work
straightening and channeling the stream beds, but now the "sand scourge"

overwhelmed any such feeble efforts to counter this destructive cycle of erosion. The rivers and streams that had so abundantly watered Lafayette County now became veins "draining away the lifeblood of the land," another observer wrote.[4]

One traveler coming through Lafayette on the Mississippi Central Railroad sometime after the war remarked that "the whole country along that railroad looks like a turkey gobbler that has been pulled through a briar bush by the tail." Land that once produced grain and cotton was now overrun by broom sedge: "the hills denuded of soil and even subsoil, and the fertile valleys overrun with a flood of arid sand, where but a few years ago we had lively streams running between high banks all the year round — through fields waving with corn and cotton." [5] A northern reporter visiting in 1881 noted: "Much damage has been done to the agricultural interests of the country by washing away of the surface soil. Over thousands of acres this process has gone on so long that nothing is left but the inert and unproductive clay, and this is cut up by gullies and chasms so wide and deep that they often have to be bridged like rivers." The exposed and eroded land was also subject to leaching of nutrients, which, together with the repeated planting of cotton and corn each year, left the fields more desolate every year.[6]

Some efforts were made to reclaim the land and protect it from further erosion. State geologists, beginning with Hilgard, pleaded with farmers to straighten and channel creeks and gullies to control erosion, to diversify crops and land use, and to use winter cover on exposed fields. Others explored new ways of using the land. Before his death in 1893, L. Q. C. Lamar operated large plantations near Abbeville and Taylor. He brought in an English overseer to conduct experiments in new agricultural practices and stock breeding with the idea that ruined cotton lands might be profitably turned to pasture.[7]

The same transient nature of the farm population Hilgard had noted in the pioneer generation continued to thwart agricultural reform. Now, the culprit was tenant farming not frontier opportunism. Most farmers in Lafayette County worked land they did not own. Because they moved frequently from one tenant farm to another every year or two, they exploited the land without regard to the future.

Faulkner described the slovenly appearance of the tenant farm the Varners rented to Ab Snopes: "The gate itself or what remained of it lay unhinged to one side, the interstices of the rotten palings choked with grass and weed like the ribs of a forgotten skeleton. . . . The sagging brokenbacked cabin set in its inevitable treeless and grassless plot and weathered to the color of an old bee-hive . . . the sagging and stepless porch of the perfectly blank house . . . the barren yard littered with the rubbish—the ashes, the shards of pottery and tin cans—of its last tenants." "The house aint fitten for hawgs," Ab Snopes snorts in disgust to his new landlord, Jody Varner. Ab Snopes and his family have moved so many times his children have lost count. In another scene Mink Snopes contemplates his shabby sharecropper's hovel, a "paintless two-room cabin with its open hallway between and a lean-to kitchen, which was not his, on which he paid rent but not taxes, paying almost as much in rent in one year as the house had cost to build; . . . and which was just like the one he had been born in, which had not belonged to his father either, and just like the one he would die in if he died indoors . . . just like the more than six others he had lived in since his marriage and like the twice that many more he knew he would live in before he died." If the sharecroppers' cabins were neglected and left a little worse than each tenant found it the year or two before, the land they worked was even more run down. Neither landlord nor tenant had any incentive to make things one bit better.[8]

The pressure on Lafayette County's land intensified after Reconstruction. At first, because of the labor problems after emancipation, the number of improved acres fell from over 100,000 in 1860 to under 90,000 in 1880. This happened despite a substantial increase in the population, which rose from 16,000 in 1860 to nearly 22,000 by 1880. After 1880 the population stayed about the same for the next eighty years. The number of acres under till, however, climbed nearly 50 percent between 1880 and 1910, from less than 90,000 to over 133,000 acres. At the same time, farms were breaking up into smaller parcels for sharecroppers. Between 1860 and 1900, the total number of farms in Lafayette County quadrupled (913 to 3,817). More than half the farms were now less than fifty acres, and the average farm had only thirty-three acres under cultivation. The plantation economy survived in several large estates located in the best land in the county, around Abbeville and College Hill, and in the Yoknapatawpha bottomlands. Most of the county's agricultural production, however, was now in the hands of poor "dirt farmers" who scratched out a living on small plots of worn-out land they rented for a share of the crop.[9]

The final desecration of the land came during William Faulkner's early life, when lumber companies came into the hills of Lafayette County and cut huge swaths through the hardwood forests. Small farmers in the hilly woodlands had long regarded the trees as little more than a nuisance; now they were an unexpected source of income. White oak trees were valued as staves for whiskey barrels, and a Mississippi company brought in Yugoslavian woodworkers in 1915 to manufacture staves. When state prohibition came in 1918, and national prohibition two years later, the whiskey

Sawmill on Kittle Creek near Tula, ca. 1910. (Courtesy of Special Collections, University of Mississippi)

barrel industry gave way to the lumbering of red oak and post oak for railroad ties. Once all the oak was harvested, lumber operations cut down hundreds of acres of scrubby pine trees. Small mobile "peckerwood sawmills" were hastily set up in the hills to gnaw away at the last of what, less than a century before, had been the Chickasaws' wilderness.[10]

By the time Faulkner began writing about his native land in the 1920s, the evidence of destruction was everywhere to be seen. He grew up in a land torn apart by gullies that ran down the hillsides, with creeks and rivers clogged by quicksand sludge, a landscape also of denuded fields pocked with stumps left by the lumbermen who had cut their way through the woods like locusts.[11] "Chickasaw Indians had owned it," Faulkner wrote in one of several eulogies over the devastated landscape, "but after the Indians it had been cleared where possible for cultivation, and after the Civil War, forgotten save by small peripatetic sawmills which had vanished too now, their sites marked only the mounds of rotting sawdust which were not only their gravestones but the monuments of a people's heedless greed. Now it was a region of scrubby second-growth pine and oak among which dogwood bloomed until it too was cut to make cotton spindles, and old fields where not even a trace of furrow showed any more, gutted and gullied by forty years of rain and frost and heat into plateaus choked with rank sedge and briers loved of rabbits and quail coveys, and crumbling ravines striated red and white with alternate sand and clay." [12]

Exodus

The nomadic traits of Mississippi's population that Eugene Hilgard had decried continued to undermine long-term commitment to improvement. Beneath what appeared to be a stagnant population after 1880 was continuous churning. Given the hardships Lafayette County offered and the bleak prospects of improvement, it is not difficult to understand the forces pushing people off the land. The incoming population was attracted by unusually cheap land, which averaged a little over seven dollars an acre in 1910, among the least expensive in the South. Many came out of desperation from lands that were equal or worse elsewhere in the South.

The editor of the *Oxford Eagle* in 1883 complained about the drainage of the county's "best" people: "The stubborn fact stares us in the face that many of Oxford's very best citizens have moved away from this place within the past twelve months, and others are going and still others want to go."[13] Many of the white families followed the path to Texas, still the favorite refuge for those escaping bad luck in Mississippi. "GTT" remained a familiar shorthand for Mississippians who had left for their next chance. As early as 1870 the local newspaper reported: "Several of the oldest citizens of LaFayette county have sold out within the past few weeks and removed to Texas."[14] Groups of families formed migrant expeditions to Texas, and a well-established chain of kin and neighbors made the trek all the easier to follow. By the 1880s and continuing into the early twentieth century "Texas letters" from former Lafayette County dwellers became a routine item of local news. Sometimes they expressed sadness at the friends and neighbors migrants left behind in Mississippi, but they often included glowing reports of agricultural prospects in their new homes, boasts that must have convinced more to follow their neighbors westward.[15]

The black exodus out of Lafayette County had to do with more than worn-out land and bleak economic prospects. After Reconstruction the plight of blacks in northern Mississippi grew worse than ever as they endured political disfranchisement, segregation, and violence. But the only recourse black Mississippians had was to suffer where they were or leave. Susie Marshall, born in the early twentieth century to a family of black sharecroppers, recalled that "when folks wanted to leave they just stole away in the middle of the night." Those caught were beaten as an example to others, but that treatment also served as an incentive to the braver ones among them to leave. From time to time, the editor of the *Oxford Eagle* lamented the black exodus for what it meant to the local labor supply but never expressed the slightest remorse about the treatment that compelled it.[16]

Beginning in the 1880s the main magnet pulling blacks out of the hills

Black sharecroppers, Lafayette County. (Courtesy of University Museums, University of Mississippi)

of Mississippi was the Delta, only a few miles to the west and just beginning to open up to rapid development. Until then, the upper Delta remained an almost uninhabited floodplain covered with cypress forests. Northern lumber companies, having cut over most of the North Woods of the Upper Midwest, now came South to take advantage of cheap land, cheap labor, and abundant timber. New railroad lines were built through the Delta opening up this area to large-scale lumbering operations for the first time. But the rich, flat, alluvial land of the Delta was useless for agriculture unless the floods could be controlled. Under pressure from timber and railroad interests, the state of Mississippi undertook massive levee construction to protect the land from flooding and, as the forests were cleared, this fertile land now became ideal for cotton planting. "Now the land lay open," Faulkner wrote of the Delta, "from the cradling hills on the East to the rampart of the levee on the West, standing horseman-tall with cotton for the world's looms—the rich black land, imponderable and vast, fecund up to the very doorsteps of the negroes who worked it and of the white men who owned it."[17]

Good wages offered by the lumber and railroad companies, then new farming opportunities on fresh land drew blacks out of the hills and into the Delta, draining the hill counties of the youngest and most productive elements of the black population. Nothing suggests that whites did anything to discourage black emigration. "The colored population continue to 'exo-

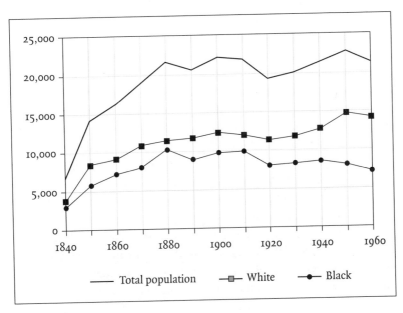

Figure 3. Population, by Race, Lafayette County, 1840–1960

dust' to the Mississippi Delta," the *Oxford Eagle* noted in 1888.[18] Some were also moving into Memphis. Both were local moves, but they set the stage for the Great Migration out of the South that World War I set in motion. The Great Migration continued through the 1920s, then surged during World War II as blacks moved north and west. During the Great Migration the Illinois Central that came through Oxford played a major role in recruiting and transporting black southern labor into Chicago. What once was a commercial artery for the local cotton crop now became an enormous siphon taking off the labor that the local cotton economy had depended on for over three-quarters of a century. White landowners who had complained for decades about black labor now watched in dismay as their black tenant farmers left forever.[19]

"Stay where you are," the editor of the *Eagle* pleaded. "Help rebuild the waste places; be encouraged by the happy prospects and prepare yourselves for the participation in the bountiful and sure harvests. You are living in one of the fairest, if not the fairest, countries on the globe. A land good to be born in, is good to live in and die in. Stay where you are." [20]

Pestilence

Northern Mississippi became a notorious place to die in during the late nineteenth century. A series of yellow fever epidemics cut deadly swaths through the population, the first in 1878 and 1879 and then again in 1897 and 1898. Following so soon after Reconstruction, this first scourge of pestilence seemed like some biblical visitation of punishment on the land. Yellow jack, as it was known, was a horrible disease that struck with little warning and killed rapidly, ending in convulsions with vile heaves of black vomit, the color coming from the dried blood that had hemorrhaged inside the stomach, a repulsive-looking spew some likened to coffee grounds. The disease had African origins, and blacks, therefore, brought with them to America sufficient immunities to avoid the worst effects of the disease. The plague ravaged whites, however. They died in vast numbers, quickly and violently, and with a blackened vomit that must have caused some to wonder what sins this affliction was punishing.[21]

Yellow fever concentrated almost entirely in urban areas and spread quickly along the avenues of trade, up the Mississippi River from New Orleans to Memphis and along the railroad lines that emanated from both cities. Oxford was easily within range of contagion, and the Illinois Central line became a dangerous conduit of disease. In the end, fear—more than disease—afflicted the town during the first scourge of yellow jack. Before Walter Reed's discovery of the mosquito-borne origins of yellow fever in 1901, some refused to acknowledge its contagious nature, thinking instead that prevention was simply a matter of pure air and virtuous living. Holly Springs, which local boosters had been promoting as a health resort, graciously invited refugees from the fever-stricken city of Memphis and nearby Grenada to enjoy its high elevation and fresh air. But when it became clear that the fever did its deadly work just as well in Holly Springs's clean air, its citizens panicked and fled the city, leaving it, one witness noted, a "quiet, deserted, funeral, to the dying and the dead." Only thirty miles from Oxford, Holly Springs witnessed 1,400 people struck by yellow jack; 314 died. Before it was over, some fifteen thousand Americans died from yellow jack in 1878. All that slowed the scourge in its deadly path was the quick death it brought and the superstition, or unwitting knowledge, that the dead must be buried before nightfall. Below ground, the afflicted were beyond reach of the mosquitoes that spread the plague.[22]

The city fathers of Oxford accepted the theory that yellow fever was highly contagious; in early August 1878, they imposed a strict quarantine, first on all trains coming north or south into town, then on all travelers entering the city. They quickly established a new board of health and formed a patrol of two dozen men assigned to guard the roads coming into town warding off all who attempted to enter. Many townspeople fled, and, to protect their property, the town board organized an armed guard with orders to shoot to kill. Yellow jack came again the next year, working its deadly way up the

Mississippi Valley and into Memphis. The fever struck Oxford, but it passed quickly, leaving seven dead.[23] J. E. Bundren remembered when yellow jack raged through Taylor's Depot that year. A camp meeting revival was in full swing when a woman "became hysterical and started screaming to the top of her voice." Everyone thought it was the spirit moving her, until they heard her yelling that a man near her was in convulsions from yellow fever. People scattered from the meeting, and the next morning they pulled their belongings onto wagons and evacuated, leaving but a few brave souls to look after the sick and dying.[24]

It would be almost twenty years before yellow fever returned to threaten the county. In 1897 news of infections in Memphis instantly led to a quarantine of Oxford, enforced by an armed guard along a perimeter five miles from the main square. All trains were forbidden to stop, and no one was allowed to enter the town. All public assemblies were banned, and a curfew was imposed. The threat passed without incident in Oxford that year, but the next August, 1898, yellow jack reappeared, and the city government immediately passed measures to ensure that the town was "strictly quarantined against the world." This time the fever invaded Lafayette County. Whites fled in panic, leaving the town by special trains while many black residents were sequestered in a detention camp, evidently to safeguard the property of whites in flight. The fever took thirty-two lives in Lafayette County that August.[25]

As yellow jack faded from the scene, other forms of pestilence entered Mississippi, striking not people but the main source of wealth: cotton and cattle. The boll weevil first appeared in Mississippi in 1907, eating its way through one cotton field after another in its relentless march across the South, arriving in northern Mississippi by 1914. Many of the worn-out cotton lands in Lafayette County and across the state had already been converted to pasture to support a growing cattle and dairy industry. The boll weevil hastened the shift from cotton to cattle. Just as livestock and dairy farming were being promoted as the salvation of Mississippi's distraught cotton farmers, a plague of ticks infested the state's cattle. Efforts by the state to impose dipping laws met with angry resistance from many livestock raisers.[26] A land once so bountiful and generous had turned inhospitable to its human tenants.

White Sweat

The land eroded and ravaged, people migrating in desperation, pestilence sweeping through in frightening scourges; these biblical visions of blight and suffering need no exaggeration for us to understand the plight of Mississippi's poor farmers. The tinder underlying the redneck revolt built up slowly beginning in the 1870s, long before a new breed of political leader so artfully ignited it in the early twentieth century. The farmers' discontent had its origins in the traumatic economic changes that affected class and race relations in the decades after the Civil War and Reconstruction. Large numbers of poor and mostly self-sufficient white farmers were pulled, lured, and sometimes coerced into the production of cash crops, chiefly cotton.[27]

Before the Civil War, the South's white yeomen sustained their families by producing all that they could for themselves, limiting their dependence on the marketplace to selling a small cash crop and buying a few store-bought essentials. None could be totally self-sufficient, but they operated within a semisubsistence economy raising a mix of grain and vegetable crops and some livestock. If land and labor allowed, they raised enough cotton to sell a bale or two, or they sold surplus grain and livestock. These small market crops might be exchanged for tools, guns, coffee, sugar, tobacco, candy, ribbons, sewing items, and other products they could not produce for themselves. In Lafayette County, those farmers living near the Tallahatchie or the Mississippi Central Railroad were generally more oriented to this production for external markets. Most of the poor hill country farmers in the eastern and southern sections of the county limited their economic exchanges to barter with neighbors or occasional forays to an isolated country store where they could buy what they needed. On some Saturdays, especially court days, when the circuit court held sessions, many farmers and their families flocked to town to shop and visit. But Oxford was a long way for those in the more remote corners of the county. Faulkner's Anse Bundren of *As I Lay Dying* had not been to town in twelve years when his wife, Addie, died. Only her request that she be buried with her people in the town cemetery forced Anse and his children on the long and arduous trek, traversing the swollen Yoknapatawpha River and miles of hot, dusty roads by horse and wagon. Anse, not incidentally, was also eager, at long last, to get a new set of false teeth in town.[28]

By 1900 most farmers were fully involved in producing for the market rather than food for their families. Immediately after the war, farmers across the South committed more of their land and labor to the production of cotton and corn for the external marketplace. Cotton prices had soared during the war and were still as high as fifty cents a pound before production resumed. Farmers jumped in with both feet to take advantage of the boom and later found it was difficult to turn back to their more self-sufficient habits. Cotton prices declined after that and with little relief, reaching their lowest point in thirty years during the depression of the 1890s. The financial centers of the cotton market lay far beyond Oxford and Memphis, in

New York City and Liverpool where speculators sent prices up or down in ways that to farmers in Mississippi seemed totally disconnected from the amount of labor they put into producing the cotton. The market could be a cruel instructor when it came to the elementary but painful lessons of supply and demand. The county's cotton production was rising close to its prewar levels by 1880, but prices slumped as supply increased from about ten cents a pound down to eight cents during the 1880s, then plummeted below five cents in the depression years of the mid-1890s. At the same time, the costs of farming, especially fertilizer for worn-out lands, along with the costs of bringing cotton to market and sustaining a household, were all rising, at least in the retail prices farmers paid at the country store. Taxes also bore heavily on poor farmers. Before the Civil War the tax base had rested on slave property and luxury items such as watches and carriages. After emancipation the tax base shifted almost exclusively to land, and the small landowners were burdened as never before.[29]

Once independent white yeomen now descended into debt and dependency as sharecroppers. As the price of cotton fell below the cost of production, they mortgaged their farms hoping for better times ahead. But when they did not come, many landowners, large and small, forfeited their land to creditors. Many joined the ranks of the landless, reduced to renting from landlords.[30]

Poverty can be a social equalizer, and in a biracial society with nearly half the population recently emancipated from slavery this brought violent repercussions. Under the pressure of market forces the condition of black and white farmers was converging as blacks rose and whites fell to a common status as sharecroppers. Sharecropping was the most common form of tenancy; it allowed farmers to rent land paying a share of the crop instead of cash. In Lafayette County, by 1910 almost two-thirds of all farmers were tilling land owned by someone else. Among blacks, sharecropping had been the norm since the end of slavery. Nearly eight out of ten black farmers in Lafayette County were sharecroppers in 1910. For many of these black sharecroppers their lives were hardly better than under slavery, but for the other two out of ten black farmers who managed to gain full or partial ownership of some land by 1910, they were on the rise. White farmers, at the same time, were sinking from economic autonomy into tenancy and dependency. Farming someone else's land and paying rent to a landlord had been virtually unknown to whites until the late nineteenth century. By 1910, over half (54 percent) of all white farmers in the county had fallen into sharecropping. Except for the color of their skin, they occupied the same social and economic plane as most of the county's sharecroppers.[31]

Lucas Quintus Carothers McCaslin Beauchamp, a proud, independent, landowning black farmer in Faulkner's Yoknapatawpha County, incited anger among his white neighbors just by walking into a country store wearing his black broadcloth suit, with his heavy gold watch chain, his hat at a rake, and a gold toothpick. Lucas Beauchamp is the son of Tomey's Turl, the slave we met earlier manipulating Uncle Buck and Uncle Buddy into letting him marry Lucas's mother, Tennie. His grandfather Old Carothers McCaslin was a wealthy white planter, and though his white descendants feel shame for his miscegenation and incest, Lucas Beauchamp is proud of his white ancestry. Lucas acted just as though he was as good as or better than the white men in the store, and he was.[32]

This degradation of white farmers to the level of freedmen also meant subordination to white landlords. This is exactly what Ab Snopes so bitterly resents when he snarls to his wife that he plans to have a word with his landlord, Major De Spain, "the man that aims to begin tomorrow owning me body and soul for the next eight months."[33] Returning from De Spain's tall white mansion, "bigger than a courthouse" to his young son's amazed eyes, on their way back to their rented cabin, which "aint fitten for hawgs," Ab Snopes stops and glares back at the large white plantation house. He says to his son, Sarty: "Pretty and white, ain't it?" "That's sweat. Nigger sweat." Then he adds: "Maybe it ain't white enough yet to suit him. Maybe he wants to mix some white sweat with it." His bitter remark summarizes the entangled emotions involving racial and class resentment and the transfer of one to the other.[34]

Varner's New Domain

"What do you rent for?" Ab Snopes asks Jody Varner about a tenant farm out at the Old Frenchman's place that he has heard the Varners have available. "Third and fourth. . . . Furnish out of the store here. No Cash," Jody replied. "I see," Snopes says, "Furnish in six-bit dollars." "That's right," Varner responds. "I'll take it," says Ab Snopes.

In this abbreviated exchange Ab Snopes and his new landlord have agreed to a contract, a complex set of economic arrangements that will bind them over the next year. The conversation is brief and the language cryptic; it is clear they are dealing in terms that were negotiated so routinely that little needed to be explained. To decode the contract: Ab Snopes agreed to pay one-third of the corn and one-fourth of the cotton he raised in exchange for use of the farm. He would supply his own mule and tools, while the Varners provided the land and house. Snopes also agreed to buy all his family's supplies, food, clothing, and other basic needs for the season out of Varner's store. It would be on credit, and for every seventy-five cents (six bits) worth of goods at their cash price, he would owe one dollar, a 33 percent premium that amounted to interest on the store credit account.[35]

Sharecropping required the tenant to yield independence to a landlord or merchant whose control of land and credit gave him great leverage over the lives of the tenants. Depending on whether the landlord furnished only the land and cabin or supplied in addition the stock and tools necessary to farm, the rent typically amounted to a quarter or half of the crop produced. Many poor tenant farmers owned little more than the clothes on their backs and had to farm "on halves," paying half the crop in return for use of the land, house, stock, and tools. Whatever their share of the crop, both landlord and tenant had a mutual interest in producing the largest crop possible. Because he shared the risks as well as the rewards of his tenants' farming, the landlord also felt compelled to supervise their work habits and intrude on their private lives. Sharecroppers were expected to maximize productivity by putting all family members to work in the fields—men, women, and children. While negotiating their agreement, Jody Varner wanted to know how many "hands" Ab Snopes could put into the field because the more productive a labor force, the more land could be planted and the greater the potential harvest. The practice of women and children working in the fields, though not unknown among white families during harvest time, for example, had traditionally been regarded as the lot of black slaves. Following emancipation, black families were willing to forgo productivity in favor of keeping the women and young children at home away from hot, heavy work in the fields. For them this was the mark of freedom and one they exercised willingly and at considerable sacrifice.[36] Now white croppers like Ab Snopes were being pressed to put their women into the fields. Major De Spain sees it as his prerogative to question when his tenants worked as well; he chides Ab Snopes for not being in the fields the day he moves in. Snopes replies defiantly: "I figger I'll start tomorrow. I dont never move and start to work the same day."[37]

One reason for sharecropping was because cash was scarce in the rural South. The war had left the credit and banking system shattered, and, particularly away from urban centers, credit was a personal arrangement. Faulkner's characters make elaborate deals exchanging things often with no money ever changing hands; mules, land, notes, and goats all pass from one person to another in a cash-poor country economy. Mink Snopes pays for the sewing machine he buys from Ratliff with a creased and worn note he has carried around in his pocket for years and which he claims is good for money from his cousin Flem. Because most poor farmers rarely had any cash on hand, they had to have credit at the local store. They needed to furnish their family with food and supplies and the farm they were cropping with fertilizer and seed, all between spring when they planted and fall when cotton was gathered, ginned, and sold. T. L. Avent, a white farmer in the eastern part of the county, began his account with P. B. Parks in February 1893 with the purchase of a pound of borax, nails, and coffee, all items entered as debits in the account book. Every month the charges were entered for cloth, soothing syrup, gun shot, ribbons, bridles, socks, and every variety of food and goods. The debt was reduced from time to time with payments in chickens and eggs, and sometimes cash, but the debt ran through the year until harvest time.[38]

It was within this niche of credit and furnishing that a new class of merchant-creditor emerged to become a major force in the southern rural economy and rival to the planter class, which controlled land but was often unable to supply credit. The lines between merchant and planter often became blurred. Sometimes the planters would fill the need for credit and furnishing supplies by setting up a plantation commissary, like the store Faulkner's Wash Jones ran for Thomas Sutpen. Sutpen was unusually ambitious about recouping his lost fortune, but there were not many planters in Lafayette County with the capital or the business experience necessary to move into this kind of operation. The new merchant-creditor class was coming from the other direction, like Faulkner's Will Varner, who began as country store owner and extended his activities into new roles as mortgage creditor and landlord. New country stores of this type began appearing in every corner of Lafayette County in the decades following the Civil War. In 1867 the Mercantile Agency listed only 6 stores for all of Lafayette Count, all of them in Oxford; by 1925 there were 114 stores listed for the county, 89 of them in Oxford. From Abbeville, College Hill, and Taylor's Depot to Lafayette Springs, Dallas, and Denmark, country merchants were establishing footholds even in the most remote reaches of the county.[39]

Merchants became landowners by extending credit to farmers who put up their land as collateral. When the cotton crop failed or when prices were down and the debtor failed to repay, the merchant foreclosed on the mortgage. The merchants then typically became landlords renting out the land to tenants. It was country merchants of the Will Varner model who were ascending in the new economic order, building from their base as furnishing agents and creditors into new roles as landlords, cotton gin owners, and other ventures, consolidating what often became powerful local monopolies. "He owned most of the good land in the country," Faulkner wrote of Will Varner, "and held mortgages on most of the rest. He owned the store and the cotton gin and the combined grist mill and blacksmith shop in the village proper and it was considered, to put it mildly, bad luck for a man of the neighborhood to do his trading or gin his cotton or grind his meal or shoe his stock anywhere else." [40]

Land, wealth, and power were all tilting in favor of the new merchants. Under the terms of Mississippi's 1876 agricultural lien law, farmers pledged not only their crop but also their farm implements, livestock, and land, if they owned any, to secure credit for the coming season. Wesley Pickens was one of thousands who signed a "Chattel Deed of Trust on a Crop to be Made," in February 1877; in it he pledged "the entire crop of cotton, corn, and other produce made by me, my family and tenants during the year 1877 on the plantation of Dr. J. B. McEwen or elsewhere: also one sorrel horse and one bay horse and all other stock of every kind together with one spring wagon." He already was indebted for $251.80 and interest and would be advanced $150 in supplies to begin planting. He signed the deed with his "X." [41]

Many planters did not have sufficient cash reserves to supply their tenants, and they, too, sought credit at banks, like the one John W. T. Falkner ran in Oxford. The planters often turned to local merchants to furnish their tenants, and the crop lien was assigned to the merchant. The credit agreements between merchant and landlord were considered ironclad and incontestable. Through his control of credit the merchant could dictate that the tenant buy supplies only from him, that he plant only cotton, that he gin the cotton at a specified gin and sell it to the merchant. Even the tenant's decision to buy shoes for his children was subject to approval. Whatever they purchased at the store, goods bought on credit cost between 25 and 50 percent over the cash price. Often prices were deliberately obscured from farmers who knew only that their purchase would be entered in the account books and tallied after harvest. [42]

In the fall at gathering time the cropper's cotton was ginned and weighed at facilities owned or designated by his creditor, and the accuracy of the scales or the fairness of the ginning charges were generally not matters open to dispute, however questionable. Typically uneducated and illiterate, most tenant farmers were in no position to challenge complicated accounts by which the merchant entered charges over the span of eight months or more, for it was only after all the cotton was gathered, ginned, and sold that the store account would be settled. If the weather had been kind and the crop was good, if cotton prices in the world market had not fallen too low, even a poor dirt farmer could come out ahead. If he and his family had kept a tight lid on their appetites for all but the bare necessities in food and clothing, they might "cash out" and even have enough money left to tide them over until next spring's planting when new contracts would be made.

If not, if the crops were poor, prices low, or if the family's consumption exceeded what his share of the crop was worth, then the debt might be carried over until the next season and the tenant could be bound to his creditor another year. Sharecropping was not slavery, but neither was it altogether free labor.

Hogs, Cows, and Fences

Poor farmers with no land could no longer fall back on their traditional habits of self-sufficiency to supply food and clothing for their families. New fence or stock laws introduced in the 1870s required that hogs and other livestock be fenced once planting began in the spring to protect the crops of others. This challenged the long-standing custom that allowed landless farmers to graze their stock on open land. It imposed additional expenses, not only to build fences but also to buy feed, and without their own meat supply they were even more dependent on local merchants. It was as though the poor farmer and his livestock were themselves being fenced in.[43]

Snopeses were forever running afoul of the fence laws. Ab Snopes gets into trouble with Mr. Harris because he ignores and even defies the law and lets his hog run into Mr. Harris's corn field and feed there. "He had no fence that would hold it," Harris explained to the justice of the peace. Harris even gave Snopes some wire to patch his pen, but Snopes, either out of laziness or, more likely, just incorrigible orneriness, refused to tend to it. When Harris caught his hog the next time, he kept it and charged Snopes one dollar "impoundment fee." Snopes paid his dollar, retrieved his hog, then burned Harris's barn. Mink Snopes, also a poor white tenant farmer in The Hamlet, has a similar run-in with his landowning neighbor, Jack Houston. Mink lets his cow wander into Houston's pasture and deliberately leaves her to graze all winter on another man's land. Houston goes to court and forces Mink to work off the impoundment fee of several dollars. Ironically, Mink is required to build fences on Houston's property, which he does with stubborn determination working hard into the night. It is only after he settles this account that he evens the score by ambushing Houston, shooting him dead.[44]

If the fence laws made it hard for poor farmers to raise their own meat, their opportunities for growing food crops also became severely limited by the new conditions of tenancy and credit. Most tenant farmers were required to plant all the land in cotton and corn and not in vegetable crops for their own consumption. The landlords and merchants who imposed these rules wanted to maximize their tenants' production of cash crops. More than that, the purpose was to intensify the tenants' dependence on food bought on credit at the store, which was often the source of greater profit to the merchants than the cotton crop itself.[45]

After cotton prices fell to five cents a pound in the 1890s, most farmers could no longer cover the cost of production, which was about seven cents per pound. As merchants foreclosed on mortgages, poor farmers lost their crops, tools, and farm animals, and they fell deeper into debt, often bound from year to year to their creditor and to another man's land. Among the farmers who owned land, many had to mortgage it to cover what they hoped was just one or two bad years. In 1910 about 70 percent of farms in the county operated by owners were encumbered with a mortgage of some amount.[46] Many formerly independent freeholders saw their farms pass into the hands of banks and merchants. Dispossessed farmers, having no other skills and few other opportunities, slipped into the ranks of tenancy, perhaps "cropping" the very farm they had owned. Or, worse, they might be evicted in favor of other tenants, often blacks who were preferred by the new landlords.[47] All of this added to the volatile tinder of race and class resentment just waiting to be ignited.

Barn Burning

No wonder it appeared to Ab Snopes and his kind that white farmers were descending into the conditions of black servitude while former slaves were rising to the status of white tenant farmers. Though blacks suffered a harsh system of discrimination, one already embedded in Mississippi law and custom, since emancipation they had become competitors in the same marketplace as whites, able to negotiate contracts similar to the white man's and sell the fruits of their labor as white farmers did. To be sure, black tenant farmers were not the full equals of whites; for one thing they did not have — or dared not use — the same recourse to law that whites like Ab Snopes resorted to so readily to settle grievances against landlords. But precisely because black tenants proved more tractable and might be more easily bossed and cheated, many landlords preferred blacks over whites.

As whites descended and blacks rose to a comparable economic plane, a combustible brew of racial hatred and class resentment simmered, ready to blow up from time to time. White farmers' rage could explode in two directions: above them against the landlords and merchants, the bankers and railroads, or below them, at blacks.

Arson, murder, and other forms of personal revenge were only a small part of a broader pattern of violence that marked class and racial strife in the South following Reconstruction. The pattern of feuding and violence was by no means always related to class hostility. The area south of the Yoknapatawpha, particularly around Dallas, was a mostly poor white and yeoman domain of small farms. Corresponding roughly to Faulkner's Frenchman's Bend, the neighborhood developed a sinister reputation for "bitter feuds, violence and bloodshed" that "caused it to be shunned by law-abiding citizens." Remote from law and order and straddling Lafayette and Calhoun Counties, this was a neighborhood that officers of the law, including federal revenue agents looking for moonshine stills, put their lives at risk entering.[48]

The same spirit of lawlessness could be channeled into collective, political acts of protest or revenge. White farmers formed vigilante organizations that owed their inspiration to the Ku Klux Klan and probably drew on the same rough element of men the Klan had recruited for its dirty work. Their brand of terrorism became known as "whitecapping," a reference to the Klan's regalia, even though they did not don the white robes and hoods. Their targets were usually black tenant farmers, but they also attacked the new merchant class that rented to black tenants. Whitecap violence erupted during hard times when white farmers forfeited their land to creditors, were evicted from it, and then were replaced by black tenants. Merchants often preferred new black tenants because they were willing to work harder and demand less. Blacks, for their part, preferred cropping for merchants because they were usually less intrusive than planters, accustomed as they were to bossing slaves.[49]

The outbreaks of whitecap violence were episodic and local, and they concentrated more in the southwest corner of the state below the Delta than in the north central hills. Beginning in 1877–78, again in the early 1890s, and then between 1902 and 1906 (coinciding with Vardaman's rise to power) waves of whitecap violence surged in local epidemics up and down the state. The whitecap gangs usually rode at night and inflicted whippings, mutilations, rape, and occasionally murder on their victims; they shot into houses and burned down the shacks of black tenant farmers. In these and other heinous acts of terror, the goal was to "bulldoze" blacks off the land and teach the new merchant-landlords a firm lesson in white solidarity.

The hatred toward merchants often took a sinister anti-Semitic tone. Some of the merchant-creditor class were Jewish immigrants who had come South after the war, filling a niche within the new cotton-sharecropping economy. The Dun and Company credit reports identified several merchants in Lafayette County as Jews or "Hebrews."[50] Jewish merchants must have seemed particularly well-suited to the role of villain in the eyes of some southern farmers. Outsiders to the prevailing Protestant religious culture, they were usually alien to the South as well.

The merchant class, whatever its ethnic or regional identity, introduced unfamiliar business practices which many Mississippi farmers found odious. The merchants were often accumulating wealth at a time of agonizing distress among the farmers, who saw themselves as the ones actually tilling the land and producing the true sources of wealth. Beneath all of this explosive resentment lay the outrage that these new merchants, perhaps especially the newcomers, were willing to flout the customs that sustained white supremacy.[51] These sentiments would eventually find a political voice and organization, something to collectivize and politicize the "impotent rage" that, hitherto, was being vented in acts of violence and revenge.

Revolt of the Rednecks

Whitecapping, bulldozing, barn burning—these were the violent and vindictive expressions of a people lacking any effective means of changing their world. In the years between Reconstruction and World War I new spokesmen emerged who sought to transform this agrarian discontent into a coherent political movement.[52] Between the 1870s and the 1890s the Grange, the Farmers Alliance, and the Populist Party all sought to organize farmers and advance their causes. In Mississippi, these third-party movements failed to win real power for poor whites. The triumph of agrarian protest in Mississippi, in the end, came from within the Democratic Party. It was not until the Democrats adopted a primary election scheme in 1902 that the rednecks' revolt found its leader. The following year James K. Vardaman, the "Great White Chief," rode to victory as governor on a tide of white dirt farmer resentment against the Bourbon planters and industrialists, and against blacks.

Before Vardaman's victory, Mississippi politics was controlled by a group of wealthy Delta planters and a constellation of railroad and business interests. The Bourbons, as they were called (referring to the reactionary landed aristocracy that ruled postrevolutionary France), controlled politics and state government through the Democratic Party. Their leaders were typically conservative Confederate veterans, the "Brigadier Generals," who served as symbols of the Lost Cause and Redemption. All nominations were decided by the Democratic Party's state conventions where each county's delegation was based on the number of representatives in the legislature. Representation, of course, was based on the total population, even though blacks were effectively disfranchised and were Republican in allegiance anyway. Democrats in the mostly white hill counties resented this system because it gave to a small white elite in the heavily black counties of the Delta the power to dominate the party, name its nominees, and control the entire political agenda.[53]

Out of the hills of Mississippi white voters began to voice their discontent, calling for reform of the Democratic Party or raising the rallying cry for third-party movements. Though Lafayette County remained more solidly Democratic than other white hill counties, it was situated in the center of some of the most fiercely contested political ground in the state.[54]

Agrarian politics found its first organized expression in the Grange movement during the 1870s. In Lafayette County, Grange leadership came mostly from the wealthy planters north of Oxford, but local chapters in each beat enlisted small farmers and always included at least one woman among the officers. The Grange educated farmers about the collective problems they confronted and thereby laid the seedbed for agrarian political consciousness.[55]

The first real political expression of farmers' discontent came with the Greenback Labor Party, which galvanized farmers in the South and West around the cry for free and unlimited issue of cheap paper money (greenbacks), something indebted farmers desperately wanted. The Greenback Party organized rapidly in northern Mississippi beginning in 1878. It forged alliances among dissident Democrats and old-line Whigs and reached out to Republican voters, including blacks who shared with white dirt farmers a set of common economic grievances. The threat of an interracial alliance against the Bourbons was a specter that terrified them. Greenback or "fusion" (Greenback-Republican) candidates won striking victories. Tate, Panola, Yalobusha, and Calhoun Counties in the state elections of 1879 all went to the Greenback Party. Lafayette County, however, elected a solid Democratic ticket, as it would repeatedly, despite vigorous opposition from the dissident Greenbackers.[56]

The Democrats' stronghold in Lafayette County was maintained only by an ongoing campaign of violence, intimidation, and fraud, a tradition that continued long after Reconstruction. U.S. marshal James Pierce described a typical election scene in Oxford in 1876: "The Sheriff a democrat, placed bout the box quit a number of very active obnoxious democrats as deputy sheriffs" and through their "persuasion, threats intimidation etc. they are enabled to prevent many voters from casting their votes as they would desire." "Colored men are too timid to pass up and vote the republican ticket alone," Pierce explained, "if they have to be pulled around by a lot of fierce young democrats, whose business in life is to over awe the colored republicans."[57] It often went beyond intimidation to blatant use of violence at the polls. The congressional election of 1880 was hotly contested by Democrats, Republicans, and Greenbackers. U.S. marshal B. P. Scruggs was in Oxford to observe polling at the courthouse when, to his astonishment, he witnessed a group of Democrats loading a cannon and firing it into the line of opposition voters, mostly blacks, who stood not twenty feet away. Several Republican voters were injured by flying debris from the cannon, two men's trousers were set afire by the shot, while inside the blasting brought large chunks of plaster down from the courthouse ceiling, injuring at least one Republican precinct officer. Town officials, all Democrats, refused to put a halt to this "demonstration."[58]

Democratic rule depended on this kind of violence and fraud. With a "fare vote and honest count the election of the fusion ticket will be a fact," A. H. Kennedy, one of Lafayette County's white Republican Party stalwarts wrote in 1881. So long as Democrats controlled the polling, they "invariably appoint sharp shrewd partisans to represent them at the ballot box . . . [and] they appoint ignorant dupes to represent the Republicans . . . and a good many times appoint negros that can't count so much less read and write their own names." The federal court in Oxford tried several hundred cases of alleged election violations in the district, but Judge Robert Hill handed out the same weak penalties he had issued earlier against the Klan. "My liberty and life is continuously in danger," Kennedy wrote; "last Saturday just as the court adjourned . . . I was actacked by a rable of 10 young bloods who spoke very roughly to me said I was an avowed enemy of thers as well as the entire South and that a man born and raised in the South that would turn stranger to his people deserved to be tared feathered and burned . . . finely they approached me with drawn knives seemingly determined to take my life." A deputy sheriff intervened and arrested the attackers, only to turn them loose within five minutes on the promise they would behave.[59] The Democracy of Lafayette County, having redeemed the state from "bayonet rule" by Republicans, was now ruling by violence of its own.

Fusion candidates were convinced they could win Lafayette County against the Democrats in a fair contest. The only way to guarantee fair elections, their followers insisted, was to bring in federal election poll watchers. After a carnival of violence and fraud during the state elections of 1881, the Republican administration in Washington sent in a strong force of election supervisors for the congressional elections of 1882. The result was a stunning victory for the fusion "Independent People's Party" whose candidate was former Confederate general James R. Chalmers, a Greenback partisan.[60]

By 1890 Bourbon planters from the heavily black Delta counties and hill farmers from the predominantly white counties converged on a plan to eliminate altogether the remaining black voters from the polls with a new state constitution. One group feared biracial fusion alliances against them, the other resented the black votes that Delta planters used to control the state; each joined in white solidarity against black political power in Mississippi. Agrarian dissidents in the white counties initiated the crusade to replace the 1868 "Black and Tan" state constitution, which they denounced as a "putrid reminiscence" of Reconstruction.[61] Though they hoped for a greater voice for white farmers, the agrarians soon found that the focus of the 1890 constitutional convention was the elimination of "unqualified" voters—aimed against blacks but including many of their own people. Working carefully within the confines of the U.S. Constitution, which prohibited outright disfranchisement by race, Mississippi's new constitution delineated a set of literacy and tax requirements. One stipulated that voters be able to read or demonstrate "understanding" of the Constitution, a test easily used by Democratic registrars to screen voters. The real barrier for poor people, regardless of their color or literacy, was the annual poll tax of two dollars, which they had to pay for the previous two years in order to vote. Among poor farmers whose total cash income might be fifty dollars a year, four dollars was a prohibitive tax, so most chose not to pay and therefore not to vote.

Black voter registration, already low, fell to about 11 percent of all eligible blacks in Mississippi by 1892. In Lafayette County, where blacks claimed over 43 percent of the total population, their share of the registered voters fell to 325, or about 19 percent of the total registered voters. Overall, turnouts at elections plummeted under the new voting laws. Less that 17 percent of Mississippi's voting-age males turned out to vote after 1890; this was the lowest rate in the nation, which averaged over 73 percent in 1900.[62] The 1890 constitutional convention, in brief, had disfranchised many whites along with blacks. The voting qualifications in the new constitution had aroused a storm of opposition up and down the state, and the delegates at the convention decided it was "unnecessary and inexpedient" that the electorate ratify the constitution. It was fitting that Mississippi's 1890 constitution, which would disfranchise so many citizens, was simply proclaimed law without a popular referendum. In Lafayette County and throughout Mississippi, agrarian protest against Bourbon rule had been yet another exercise of "impotent rage."[63]

The Great White Chief

From within the Democratic Party, calls for political reform from the white hill counties began to focus on the party's convention system that allowed the "rings" or "dictators" of the Bourbon oligarchy to dominate the nomination process. Since the 1880s reformers had urged direct primary elections to let the people decide nominations.[64] Because political parties were private organizations and, therefore, not subject to constitutional law for-

James K. Vardaman rally, 1911. Vardaman is standing on the wagon. (From Richard Aubrey McLemore, ed., *A History of Mississippi* [1973], vol. 2)

bidding racial discrimination, the Democrats' "all white primary" would effectively eliminate the last vestige of black political power at the same time. The Bourbons, secure in their dominance, finally gave into the call from the hills for a primary election system in 1902, never realizing, until after the explosion left them stunned, that they were lighting the fuse to a powder keg of agrarian populist revolt.

The primary election gave a direct voice to white voters, and it placed a premium on the candidate who could move a crowd with his charisma. People who for years sat out politics now came out to witness tremendous demonstrations complete with processions of citizens, brass bands, singing choruses, ladies presenting flowers, and children climbing trees to view long, eloquent speeches and debates by men standing on cotton bales or wagons. These extravaganzas went on for hours in a full day of marvelous political theater. This direct appeal to the voters also gave advantage to the candidate who promised government policies that offered practical benefit to the lives of the common folk. Good schools, free textbooks, good roads, public health, prison reform, and other progressive reform programs were all geared to win favor with a newly empowered electorate.

No one mastered the new democratic style of Mississippi politics more successfully than James K. Vardaman, a newspaper editor from Greenville. He was raised next door to Lafayette County, in Yalobusha County. The Vardamans had suffered hard luck and migrated to Texas before the Civil

War and lost most of what they had at the end of the war before returning to Mississippi. Though raised in poverty and at ease mingling with the
common folk, Vardaman also appealed to them with his calculated appearance of social superiority. He dressed in a white linen suit, white shirt, tie,
white boots, and a broad-brimmed black Stetson hat over his long dark hair.
He was tall and imposing and carried himself with a certain courtly elegance, full of confidence. Even the poorest white dirt farmers who flocked
to see him could feel at once that he was their champion, their "Great
White Chief," a man who could stand up and do battle with the Bourbon
aristocrats. He was a gregarious politician who loved working the crowds
at rallies, barbecues, and church suppers, shaking hands with "legions
of men," bowing "gracefully to noble women," and kissing "car-loads of
babies." [65]

Vardaman delivered an astounding seven hundred formal campaign
speeches in his campaign for governor in 1903. Families would come by
wagon, mule, and foot from miles around to hear him. Local businesses
would close and courts adjourn on "Vardaman Day." Even his enemies mar-
veled at his speaking skills. His typical campaign speech went a full two
hours and began with gracious flattery of the virtue of southern women,
only a few of whom dared attend these masculine affairs, for Vardaman also
delighted his male audience with coarse, vulgar humor. He never failed to
offer tribute to Confederate heroes and pay homage to Mississippi pride.
Vardaman then took out after the enemies of his people and offered reme-
dies to their suffering. He was a strong advocate of free public education
for poor whites. He wanted to see school tax revenues reallocated from
the populous black counties to the white counties. He wanted the state to
issue free school textbooks because the cost of books was prohibitive for
many poor families. Beyond that, he advocated good roads, prohibition,
or at least a local option liquor law, and an end to convict leasing. He attacked the money interests, the trusts and corporations, and particularly
the railroads; it was they, and the wealthy Delta planter aristocracy, Vardaman charged, who had established corrupt "ring rule" in Mississippi. There
were few political leaders more progressive than Vardaman, but it was progressivism for whites only.

Having pilloried the powers above his people, the cause of their misery, Vardaman turned their wrath toward those below them, or those they
wanted to keep beneath them — the blacks. The most serious threat to white
people in Mississippi, to white women in particular, he told his audience,
was the Negro and those whites, particularly northerners, who would raise
him to a level of equality. In 1903 the chief villain was Republican president
Theodore Roosevelt, who had tried to force a black woman postmaster on

the citizens of Indianola, Mississippi. "A vote for Vardaman is a vote for White Supremacy," his campaign advised, "a vote for the quelling of the arrogant spirit that has been aroused in the blacks by Roosevelt and his henchmen, a vote for the better education of white children, a vote for the safety of the Home and the protection of our women and children." Vardaman openly supported lynchings, promising that if he were a private citizen and a "negro fiend" (rapist) had been apprehended, he would "head the mob to string the brute up," and, he added, "I haven't much respect for a white man who wouldn't." Education for blacks, Vardaman argued, would only "spoil a good field hand and make an insolent cook." While governor, he eliminated the small budget allocated to the state Negro Normal School attached to Rust University in Holly Springs. Vardaman justified this by arguing that education for the Negro only serves to "sharpen his cunning, breeds hopes that cannot be fulfilled, inspires aspirations that cannot be gratified, creates an inclination to avoid honest labor, promotes indolence and in turn leads to crime." The legislature gave up any hopes of overriding the governor's will.[66] He advocated repeal of the Fourteenth and Fifteenth Amendments to the U.S. Constitution and openly rejected the concept of equality between the races. The Negro, he argued, was "a lazy, lying, lustful animal which no conceivable amount of training can transform into a tolerable citizen." [67]

Racial politics were hardly new in Mississippi, but never had the state witnessed an aspirant to public office willing to voice such blatant racist rhetoric. Vardaman's appeal to white supremacy and his demonization of blacks constituted a "permission to hate" extended from the highest office in the state. In his racism, Vardaman was surpassed only by his disciple, Theodore "The Man" Bilbo, elected as governor in 1916 and again in 1928. Bilbo dominated Mississippi politics with a strangely appealing combination of rascality and racism. "Bilbonic plague," as some called it, enlarged upon the Vardaman tradition of Negrophobia with appeals to anti-Semitism and proposals for deportation of blacks to Africa.[68]

September Lynching

Vardaman and Bilbo did not initiate the "dark journey" blacks would endure in Mississippi, but their regimes encouraged drastic hardening of race relations. The most palpable expression of this was a tightening system of law and custom regulating segregation of the races, but physical separation was the least of the problems Mississippi blacks faced now. Indeed, many blacks might have wished for more segregation if only to protect themselves from the violence and insults whites inflicted on their race. In both the quantity and the quality of their brutality, white Mississippians led the South in the wave of savagery that rose between Reconstruction and World War I.[69]

The new strain of racism that emanated from Vardaman, Bilbo, and their agrarian followers dwelled on the Negro's capacity for evil of all kinds, but most particularly on the black male's instinctive lust for white women. Vardaman always offered the most exalted praise of southern white womanhood, which he imbued with particular moral virtue and sexual purity. The natural passions of all men might endanger their chastity, but lust gave in to animalistic licentiousness in black males, Vardaman warned. Left unprotected, all white women stood in danger, and unless subject to the terror of lynch law, black males would molest and rape them. This thinking was common throughout much of the Deep South, but it took an especially mean turn in Mississippi.[70]

Lynchings were often elaborate public events, at times hideous rituals of prolonged torture and mutilation. They were typically conducted in broad daylight, sometimes announced in advance, and often attended by large crowds, which on occasion included women and children. The leaders of lynch parties were often well-known, respected members of the community, not poor white rednecks, though they may have been members of the mob. Often the victim of lynching had already been apprehended by legal authorities, imprisoned in a local jail, facing what was almost certain to be a swift trial, conviction by an all-white jury, and with the sentence almost assuredly to be death by hanging. Lynching denied the victim the dignity of a legal process intended to acknowledge his equality under the law and his citizenship as a member of the civic community.

The incidences of lynching in Mississippi became so common that many seem to have barely rated notice. Newspaper accounts, often the only source that identified lynchings, were sometimes remarkably scanty in their treatment of these events. "Four negroes were lynched in Grenada last week;" one brief entry in an 1885 newspaper reported, "also one at Oxford."[71] A careful gleaning of Mississippi's newspapers reveals reports on ten lynchings in Lafayette County (along with four legal hangings) between 1865 and 1935. The accounts are incomplete and sometimes do not even name the person lynched or the victims of his crime. All but one of those lynched were reported to be black males. Most were accused of rape, murder, or assault, usually with a white female identified as victim. There were several lynchings in remote parts of the county that apparently went unreported. Two black men near Paris, in the notoriously violent southeast corner of the county, were lynched after being accused of peeping into the windows of white houses. "Their relatives refused to come cut them down," according to one account, "because negroes were not allowed in Paris."[72]

The lynching of Nelse Patton took place in September 1908. "Dry September," as Faulkner called it in his short story of that title, seemed to be a favorite month for lynching. It was just before gathering time when accounts were due and an enormous burst of labor required. Nelse Patton had been in trouble with the law frequently, usually for "retailing," meaning bootlegging illegal liquor. The previous September Patton had been arraigned three times for bootlegging, each time represented by attorney William V. Sullivan, a prominent Oxford attorney who had served as U.S. senator.[73]

The next fall, Patton was serving a sentence for another conviction of bootlegging and was allowed to serve his sentence out of jail as a trustee. As one of his duties Patton was sent to deliver a written message from a jail inmate, a white man named McMillan, to his wife, Mattie. McMillan was from another county and was serving a term for a federal offense. Mattie McMillan and their three children, one a daughter of seventeen and two very young ones, had moved in with another family in a house about a mile north of town so she could be near her husband. Since McMillan's sentence in June, Patton had delivered numerous messages to Mattie McMillan without incident, but this time something terrible happened.

Apparently Patton showed up at the house drunk. By one account he entered the house without knocking and took a seat. "Seeing the woman apparently alone and without protection," the report in one newspaper said, "his animal passion was aroused and he made insulting remarks to her." Mattie McMillan ordered him from the house, they shouted angrily at each other, then she went for a pistol in a bureau drawer. He rushed her from behind, grabbed her, and slashed her throat from ear to ear with a razor blade he carried in his back pocket. She ran from the house spewing blood, trying no doubt to scream but unable to make any sound through her lacerated throat. When they found her dead some seventy-five yards from the house her head was nearly severed from her neck. Meanwhile the seventeen-year old daughter rushed into the house, Patton grabbed her, but she managed to escape and ran to her mother, who lay dead outside. Newspaper reporters speculated it was the young girl Patton was after, and he had killed the mother just to have his way with the daughter.[74] But Patton fled the scene.

A citizen posse quickly formed to chase down the killer. Nelse Patton was on the run. He could hear behind him men shouting, guns shooting, and dogs barking. He fled three or four miles through the fields, over fences, and through briers, all the time hearing hundreds of gunshots behind him fired by the oncoming posse. John Cullen, a white boy of fourteen, had heard the alarm and, armed with his shotgun, he saw the large black man running for his life crossing the railroad tracks. Cullen and his brother ran after him and followed him into a vine-covered ditch leading into Toby Tubby Bottom, a creek valley north of town. Patton threatened the boy with his razor, still covered with Mattie McMillan's blood. Patton then broke and tried to run past the boy, but young John Cullen raised his shotgun and blasted him in the back. When Patton kept running, Cullen let go with another barrel.[75] The second shot finally stopped Patton, and Sheriff J. G. Hartsfield and his posse brought him on horseback to the jail. "The negro presented a bestial appearance when being brought through the streets," the newspaper reported. "He was bloody from his wounds and unsteady in the saddle, either from whisky or the effects of his wounds. . . . His copper-colored skin shone in the sunlight with great red splotches of blood."[76] The prisoner was locked up in the county jail.

By half-past eight that evening a crowd of about one hundred "men and boys" formed and headed toward the jail. At the jail Judge W. A. Roane, a respected and popular jurist, stood before the mob and spoke bravely for justice and decency. He pleaded with the men to let the legal system take its course, promising there would be a speedy trial the following Monday, where he would preside. Mob rule would only bring shame on the community, Judge Roane implored. Sheriff Hartsfield and other county officials also spoke for law and order that evening. With other lynch mobs, a show of legal authority, an appeal to Christian compassion, or to local pride and decency could often turn a crowd back home, but not this night.

Following these pleas, none other than Mississippi's former U.S. senator William V. Sullivan, Patton's erstwhile champion in court, rose before the mob and inflamed the men to do their duty. Senator Sullivan later boasted to a newspaper reporter: "I led the mob which lynched Nelse Patton and I am proud of it. I directed every movement of the mob, and I did everything I could to see that he was lynched."[77]

The mob surged forward, now determined to enter and pull Nelse Patton out of the jail, out of the legal system that was surely going to sentence him to death, and out of the civic community that, by law, granted him basic human rights. The point of this lynching was not only to punish Nelse Patton, it was to show that this man's heinous crime could not be treated just as a crime. It was a violation of white womanhood that did not deserve the justice and dignity of the law.

The crowd broke down the front door of the jail, but Sheriff Hartsfield bravely refused to yield the keys that would allow them through the inner doorway that led to the prisoners' cells. The crowd now determined to break their way into the jail by destroying the interior doors. This was the jail originally built in 1836 with thick logs and strap iron and then rebuilt after the

Civil War, when it had been burned, and now covered in a more genteel Victorian facade of brick and wood trim. This remarkably sturdy old building, designed to keep outlaws inside, now proved a formidable obstacle to the mob's wrath. It presented a kind of contest between the tradition of law and order that had led to the jail's immediate construction when the county was founded back in 1836 and the bloodthirsty rage that now, more than seventy years later, drove those determined white men to storm the jail. They worked for the next four to five hours, deep into the night, pounding, chopping, and cutting away at the walls of the jail to pull a terrified black man out of its protection. They got sledge hammers and cold chisels from hardware stores on the square and set about their work with furious determination.

Meanwhile, Nelse Patton inside his cell on the second floor must have heard his former defender, Sullivan, outside inciting the crowd to lynch him. During the next few hours he "could hear every stroke of the men, as brawny arms wielded the sledge and could measure his span of life by the ringing strokes of the frenzied men just without the barrier erected to keep him confined." Before long, large throngs of men from throughout the county had joined the mob at the jail, coming in by foot and mule to watch and participate in the task. Two hours passed before the men broke through the first inside door and a "great shout of exultation went up from the part of the mob inside," which was quickly "taken up by hundreds on the outside of the jail." The scene, one reporter noted, "presented the appearance of a lawn party, where the guests were all male and in their shirt sleeves." Out on the square a wagon bearing the corpse of Mattie McMillan passed the jail on the way to the depot. The mob continued its work to avenge the death of this woman, a prisoner's wife whom few if any of them knew or would have cared about, except for what a black man upstairs in the jail had done to her.

Beyond the first door to the cells the men discovered another steel door, and they now decided to give up on that entry and move to the outside front wall. Climbing up on ladders to break through the wall to the cells upstairs, the men pulled away the brick facing. By this time reinforcements arrived on the railroad, men coming from adjoining counties north and south. The work resumed, now with relays of men wielding the sledge hammers and pick axes. Behind the brick facing they found twelve-inch-thick logs and behind them an iron lining four inches thick, the "old ineradicable bones" of the jail, as Faulkner once described them. This last barrier required a battering ram to remove. "There could be no more dismal sound to a criminal than the constant dull thud of crowbar and pick eating their way into his cell, and yet there came no sound from within the jail." The sheriff and his deputies had gone home. Some local preachers had tried to calm the mob's wrath, but they also left as the mob reached the final violent moment that was now almost at hand. Finally, they broke through the wall and found Nelse Patton "crouched and cringing in a dark corner of the cell with the gleam of murder in his eye." He soon turned into "a wild man with an iron bed post and a spade handle as weapons" flailing away at his assailants and wounding three men before a fusillade of bullets cut him down. They quickly hauled the lifeless body downstairs to the crowd outside. They threw the body out of the jail. Someone, John Cullen remembered, "cut his ears off, scalped him, cut his testicles out, tied a rope around his neck, tied him to a car, and dragged his body around the streets." The newspaper account said only that the men placed a hangman's noose around the neck of the corpse and "a hundred willing hands pulled his remains through the public square" and strung the body up on a tree in front of the courthouse, mocking the rule of law that building was meant to uphold. "The mob then dispersed quietly, at half-past twelve." [78]

The memory of that long September night must have stayed with the people of Lafayette County throughout their lives. William Faulkner was eleven years old and lived just two blocks from the public square where the body remained hanging the next day. Faulkner later told a publisher he had never witnessed a lynching and could not describe one, but the killing of Nelse Patton had to have made an impression, whether or not he saw it or saw the body the next day. Elements of this and perhaps other true crime stories of the area were brought into his short story "Dry September" and the novel Light in August. In the latter Joe Christmas, thought by some to be partly black, slashes the throat of his white lover, Joanna Burden, and flees for his life. He is apprehended but breaks free and is chased by a posse before he is shot dead and sexually mutilated by Percy Grimm, who revels in his role as defender of white womanhood against the evils of the black race. Faulkner did not have to witness any lynchings to know their power over both races in Mississippi. They were the ultimate expression of the white rage that wanted not only to desecrate the black victim but also to demonstrate the supremacy of their own white brotherhood.

The hill flattened away into the plateau on which the town proper had been built these hundred years and more ago, and the street became definitely urban presently with garages and small shops with merchants in shirt sleeves, and customers; the picture show with its lobby plastered with life episodic in colored lithographed mutations. Then the square, with its unbroken low skyline of old weathered brick and fading dead names stubborn yet beneath scaling paint, and drifting Negroes in casual and careless O.D. garments worn by both sexes, and country people in occasional khaki too; and the brisker urbanites weaving among their placid chewing unhaste and among the men in tilted chairs before the stores. The courthouse was of brick too, with stone arches rising amid elms, and among the trees the monument of the Confederate soldier stood, his musket at order arms, shading his carven eyes with his stone hand. Beneath the porticoes of the courthouse and on benches about the green, the city fathers sat and talked and drowsed, in uniform here and there.

—WILLIAM FAULKNER, Sartoris

ten The Town

The town was the world Faulkner knew best. His ancestors, the Falkners and Butlers, had always been part of the Mississippi small-town bourgeoisie of lawyers, hotelkeepers, bankers, and businessmen. It was from his perspective as a townsman that Faulkner witnessed the advent of rural people coming in from the country, leaving behind the drudgery of farm life, to make their way in town. Typically set in the early twentieth century, coinciding with the rise of Vardaman and the modernization of town life, the path from the rural countryside of Yoknapatawpha County and Jefferson measured the distance from an older, traditional society to the dynamic, modern environment of the town.

The urban atmosphere of Oxford, barely over two thousand people in 1910, may not have impressed visitors from Memphis or any other American city, but to country people in Mississippi the town presented an altogether different world from the one they inhabited. Though from personal experience Faulkner knew the town far better, he seemed fascinated by country people and country ways. Earlier he had watched them from the perspective of a town youth who, with his friend Phil Stone, enjoyed laughing at ridiculous stories they would swap about the country people they called Snopeses. He observed them a little later in life with more understanding and from a different perspective as a neighbor out on Puss Cuss Creek in Beat Two, where he bought a farm in 1936. At times, Faulkner seemed to invite readers to view country folk through the eyes of townspeople, with a combination of ridicule of their rustic ways and condescension toward their striving to transcend those ways. While Vardaman, Bilbo, and Russell were rising to political power, it was the economic and social ascendance of the country people that Faulkner studied. Their transition from country to town, from farming to trading, and their ambition for getting ahead provided Faulkner one of the major themes of his Yoknapatawpha saga in the early twentieth century.

Oxford Town

To a boy of ten, coming to town from the country was an experience to be remembered a lifetime. Rush Allen remembered lying awake much of the night and rising early the next morning full of excitement. It was fall, about 1898; the cotton had been gathered and it was time for his father to make the annual trek into "Oxford Town" to sell his crop and buy things that could only be found at stores in town. That morning Rush was busy running down chickens and pulling them from their roosts in the trees. His mother collected eggs and packed some butter she had churned. The Allens would sell these farm products from the back of their wagon on the town square. Rush Allen had been born in the family's log house ten years before. The countryside they traveled through on their way to Oxford that morning was in many ways only a more ragged version of the place his grandfather had arrived in two generations before him. Like most country roads in northern Mississippi, the one they took to town in 1898 was deeply rutted by wagon wheels; that morning it was covered with a "stiff mud" that was knee deep in places. They traveled through a landscape of "cottoned out" farms, hillsides denuded by timber cutting, and the earth clawed by years of erosion.

As Rush and his father approached Oxford, he could hear the train whistle blowing in the distance and smell the coal smoke wafting over the trees.

Country folk coming into Oxford Town on Delay Road, over the Yocona River covered bridge, 1903. (Courtesy of Special Collections, University of Mississippi)

Then they would see the courthouse clock and the new water tower rising above all the other buildings and trees. Placards advertising tobacco and other products were tacked up on the fences that lined the road to town. The boy was too excited to eat that morning, but his mind now turned to food as they approached town. The stores lining the square in Oxford offered an array of goods one normally could not get in the country. Heavy bunches of bright yellow bananas could be seen hanging in front of the grocery stores. The town stores had many of the same candies, pickles, crackers, and canned goods that country stores offered, but always in far greater profusion. There were also restaurants, like George Buffaloe's on the square, where one could sit down, choose from a menu, and for fifteen cents be served a plate of meat and vegetables and a large piece of pie with ice cream. Dry goods stores, like Neilson's, were stocked with an array of ready-made shirts, dresses, and other clothing in all sizes and colors. The Allen family sold their cotton, chicken, eggs, and butter and returned home with full stomachs, a supply of town-bought foods, perhaps some new shoes and clothing, and, for young Rush Allen, lifelong memories of the day they went to town.[1]

"'Why aint I a town boy, pa?'" Vardaman Bundren implores in Faulkner's famous story of a rustic family's trip to town; "God made me, I did not said to God to made me in the country.'" "Wouldn't you rather have bananas?" his father replies.[2]

The town of Oxford had always been a special place for country people to gather, particularly on Saturdays and court days, when men gathered to swap livestock and stories, and women met to shop and talk with distant neighbors. They came to town to trade, to sell cotton or produce, buy clothing and provisions, trade mules or horses, get a bank loan, attend a political rally, or meet a train. The town was a place where men and boys found temptations of the flesh that were unavailable if not unknown in the countryside. It was also the place many nearby country families came to attend church on Sundays. To country visitors the town looked different and town people acted different. The town was all laid out in neat, well-ordered blocks and wide, straight streets. Those surrounding the square and going up to the university were lined with plank sidewalks so that pedestrians did not have to share the streets with animals and wagons.[3] Faulkner's Mink Snopes, a poor white sharecropper who lives in a barren unpainted cabin, enters Jefferson through "an ordered overarch of sunshot trees, between the clipped and tended lawns where children shrieked and played in bright small garments in the sunset and the ladies sat rocking in the fresh dresses of afternoon and the men coming home from work turned into the neat painted gates, toward plates of food and cups of coffee in the long beginnings of twilight."[4]

Oxford had been the center of wealth in the county since antebellum times. Beginning in the late 1840s, wealthy planter families began moving into town and built fine mansions. The town boasted large, handsome churches built of brick with high steeples and bells, some with fancy pews and carpets inside. Around the square, two-story buildings with plank walks and galleries above, all built since General Smith's visit in 1864, formed the commercial heart of the town. The new courthouse stood proudly in the center with its clock tower rising far above the other buildings on the square, a beacon to approaching visitors. On the eastern side of the square was a large, handsome brick building built in 1885 to house the federal district court and post office.

Another notable feature was added to the square in 1907, when the Confederate monument was unveiled, a soldier standing at rest atop a high pedestal overlooking the south side of the square. There had been quite a debate over where to locate the statue. A majority faction in the United Daughters of the Confederacy, Albert Sidney Johnston Chapter, insisted that the monument be erected on the university campus as a special tribute to the University Greys who had fallen in Pickett's Charge at Gettysburg. Sally Murry Falkner, the author's grandmother, led the dissenting faction that wanted to memorialize all the county's Confederates with a monument on the square. When they lost, Sally Falkner resigned from the chapter and

Confederate veterans reunion, Lamar Rifles. (Courtesy of University Museums, University of Mississippi)

led a fund-raising campaign on behalf of the United Confederate Veterans, Camp 752, to erect the monument that stood in front of the courthouse. After the money was raised and the statue ready to install, Sally Falkner had to do battle again. This time she fought a group that wanted the statue placed on the north side of the courthouse and facing north. She and her faction insisted that the marble Confederate soldier stand at the south side of the courthouse, armed, with his back defiantly to the north.

Sally Falkner prevailed, and in the fall of 1907 the last of the Confederate veterans in Lafayette attended the unveiling ceremony. The old comrades in their uniforms and hats listened to a long tribute by a state official. Afterward they fired a three-gun salute, and Miss Ada Pettis unveiled the statue. The veterans gathered after that for a sham battle at the old field west of the university. They did not reenact the hasty retreats the Confederates had made from Oxford in 1862 and 1864 but instead the famous victory at the Battle of Chickamauga, which the men in gray won again on this day of homage.[5] Now the Confederate statue stood on its tall marble shaft, facing south, armed, defiant in asserting he had fought for what the inscription below proclaimed to be a "just and holy cause."[6] Faulkner would place the university statue on the Jefferson town square, just as his grandmother had wanted. He described him standing with his hand shading his eyes, looking out for the advancing enemy—or was he looking for his retreating comrades, or perhaps deserters seeking safe haven, Faulkner could not resist musing. It would become in Faulkner's fiction a symbol of the enduring past in the present and a symbol of romantic memory's triumph over historical reality. But it was also "epilogue and epitaph," he wrote, "because that old war was dead."[7]

Along North and South Street (renamed Lamar Street around 1930 in another bow to a Confederate hero) were among the most imposing houses in town, some antebellum survivors, others newly built in Victorian splendor. Many town mansions imitated the neoclassical standard of antebellum architecture, large, square, two-story houses, wood clapboard siding, painted white, fronted with porticoes and white columns rising all the way to the second story. To a young country boy who had rarely seen anything but crude log and unpainted plank cabins and small, wooden churches, Oxford must have seemed incredibly busy, exciting, prosperous, and grand. During the early twentieth century the distinctions between town and country became much sharper, and so did the distinctions between town and country people.

The Oxford the Falkner family came to in the fall of 1902 was an urban center of sufficient size and importance that it was filled with things the young Falkner boys had never seen in Ripley, the small north Mississippi town where they had lived. "Bill and I were speechless with wonder," younger brother Murray remembered; "never had we seen so many people, so many horses and carriages, and so much movement everywhere. And the lights—arc lights! The first we had ever seen." They also saw plank sidewalks filled with people who were out walking as late as nine in the evening.[8] In their lifetime the Falkner boys would witness the coming of remarkable changes that further set Oxford apart from the country as never before: electric lights and appliances, telephones, indoor plumbing with flush toilets, window screens, automobiles and paved roads, motion pictures, photographs, minstrel shows and vaudeville, circuses, airplane shows, college football, and jazz bands. The world was changing in the twentieth century, and in towns like Oxford those changes were being felt far more dramatically than in the rural hinterland.[9]

The New Age Entered Town

In 1896 a new symbol of modernity appeared above the Oxford skyline—a water tower that rose 140 feet with a tank able to hold sixty thousand gallons. Not only did the tower feed pure water into homes all over town, it also promised more reliable fire protection. Alongside the courthouse cupola, the water tower became a town landmark people could see from miles away. In his novel The Town, Faulkner records the water tower as an emblem of progress, "standing against the sky above the Jefferson roof-line." It is also a signifier of Flem Snopes's progress in taking over the town — "not a monument" but "a footprint" that marked where he had been before he moved to the next goal.[10]

Basic utilities like telephones, electricity, gas, indoor toilets, bathtubs, sinks, washing machines, and sewerage service became common features of town life at least for most business and professional families in Oxford between the late 1890s and the 1920s.[11] White and black working-class families by the 1920s were also beginning to enjoy some of these modern conveniences. Kitchens and privies that had been kept in outbuildings in the back yard were now brought inside the modern home. Indoor flush toilets and bathrooms with hot water on tap, bathtubs, sinks, washing machines, gas stoves, and dozens of other modern appliances brought with them new standards of convenience and sanitation to town life that would be unknown to most country people for years to come. In the country, outdoor privies (or, as often, a latrine in the corner of the barn), wood stoves, kerosene lanterns, and most domestic technology had changed but little during the previous century compared to the changes townspeople witnessed between the 1890s and 1920s.

For town women, a wide array of new household conveniences were mechanizing domestic chores that once took days to perform. Their kitchens now had hot and cold water on tap, gas stoves to cook on, and daily deliveries of ice to keep food cold. Many Oxford families continued to keep milk cows and chickens in their back yards, but commercial dairies were now making that unnecessary. Laundry day was far easier when washing machines replaced the tubs of water and lye set out back over open fires. By the 1920s electricity was powering refrigerators, washing machines, irons, vacuum cleaners, and an array of other domestic appliances. Reasonably well-off families, such as the Falkners, had always had household servants to help with domestic chores and child rearing. Like Caroline ("Mammy Callie") Barr, they were usually blacks who worked as live-in servants in a room upstairs or in a small dwelling in the back. But not all families could afford full-time house servants, and whether or not they had servants, the coming of household conveniences, like running water and milk and ice delivery services, brought an enormous change for the better to the daily routines of housewives and servants.

Outside the home, the town offered exciting new forms of entertainment. The Opera House near the square put on minstrel shows and other vaudeville acts that toured the South. The town became a center of popular recreation as circus troops, balloon shows, theater troupes, and art shows came to northern Mississippi. During the 1890s the university launched an intercollegiate football team, and its games attracted spectators from all around. As early as 1898 the town government found it necessary to establish a licensing system for the profusion of entertainment being offered to the public. Circuses, animal shows, and other exhibitions "not devoted exclusively to religious, benevolent, or educational purposes" were required to pay a heavy daily tax when they came to town. Other forms of entertainment, "magic lantern shows" and photographic galleries, whether in "open air or tent gallery" or traveling exhibits in railroad cars, were required to pay the town for their license. Shooting galleries, skating and bicycle rinks, dance halls, soda fountains, and restaurants were among the other new lines of business now taxed.[12] In *The Town* Faulkner has Montgomery Ward Snopes open a photographic gallery, with a back-room peep show of pornographic images brought back from France after World War I. More wholesome, but no less modern and sensational, spectacles came to town in the form of movies. The Falkner boys were among the dozens who paid a nickel to crowd into the Lyric Opera House to watch "Bronco Billy" on film. When the lights were turned off a hand-cranked projector threw a brilliant cone of light up on a screen where shadows of ladies' hats and heads of tall men sometimes could be seen against miraculous scenes of cowboys and Indians. On summer evenings they went to the Air Drome, an outdoor nickelodeon, where they sat on planks eating popcorn and watching movies.[13]

One day in 1905 the people of Oxford lined the road leading to the square to watch the first automobile coming into town. It had come all the way from Jackson, Mississippi, and in ten days had arrived in Water Valley, less than twenty miles away. Two days later the front porches and sidewalks were filled with people waiting for their first view of a horseless carriage. Darkness fell and the crowd finally saw the headlights approaching. The Falkner boys remembered that night as the car passed beneath the arc light in front of their house on South Street and a "thick dust billowed from beneath the tremendous rubber-tired wheels, and we were all enveloped in a choking, swirling cloud of it." [14]

For some, the horseless carriage quickly turned from novelty to nuisance. The cars frightened horses and proved "a menace to the safety of the citizens . . . [and] destructive to private property." An ordinance passed in 1908 by Mayor R. S. Adams and the Town Board banned automobiles from the streets of Oxford. In Faulkner's Yoknapatawpha, this was the edict insisted on by the "old mossback" Colonel Sartoris. The new, young leaders of the town, instead of rescinding the law, framed a copy of it and hung it outside the town hall where people as far away as Chicago would come by to laugh at it. The law remained on the books only until 1910, when it was repealed, but a speed limit of twelve miles per hour was imposed. Within a short time over one hundred cars were running through the streets of Oxford. Colonel John W. T. Falkner was among the first automobile owners; his 1909 Buick touring car was the pride of the family.[15]

The town was embracing progress, just as the "new age had entered Jefferson," Faulkner wrote. "Not only a new century and a new way of thinking, but of acting and behaving too." [16] A long-standing element of American faith, the ideal of progress took on new significance in the early twentieth century. The achievements of science and technology and the improvement they brought to everyday life helped sustain new ideas about effecting progress in all realms of human existence. In the American South this progressive notion of human agency empowered to improve human existence challenged, and in some respects overcame, the legacy of defeat that had hung over the land since the Civil War. As evidence of material progress became more concentrated in the town, at the same time, rural decay seemed to continue unabated, leaving the progressive town standing apart from the backward country as never before.

"Not long ago," the *Lafayette County Press* observed in 1908, the "self-satisfied air of her people and the utter non-progressiveness" of Oxford was the theme of jokes. The children of Oxford, it had been said, had grown up never hearing the sound of a hammer. Some of the finest antebellum homes had fallen into decay, paint peeling, shutters hanging awry, and clapboards missing. The streets, especially around the square, were pocked with deep holes that filled with mud during rains. Potholes on the town square were so large that pranksters would place signs in them warning "No Fishing Allowed." Now it seemed Oxford was "on the eve of a general shaking up of dry bones in a business way" and would soon become a "model and progressive town." A new waterworks system, an "up-to-date" electric light plant, new construction at the university, new church buildings, and other improvements all were signs of "a keener and better educated civic consciousness." [17] Faulkner recalled the spirit of awakening that gripped the town of his youth: "Overnight it would become a town without having been a village; one day . . . it would wake frantically from its communal slumber into a rash of Rotary and Lions Clubs and Chambers of Commerce and City Beautifuls." [18]

"Oxford is at last on a real, substantial boom," another local editor boasted in 1919. "The people are waking up to the trend of the times. After many years of sleep and slumber the cover [of] apathy is being flung in every direction and a spirit of civic pride and activity is in evidence on every hand. Buildings are being remodeled and painted, and life is being injected in all lines of business. The hammer and saws can be heard in every direction from early morning to late in the evening, and the carpenters and workmen of the town are kept busy." [19] Ed Thompson, owner of the Colonial Hotel, announced in 1922 that "more houses have been painted in this town in the last twelve months than in a whole generation before." Looking back, the *Oxford Eagle* editor, George Price, wrote in 1924, the Civil War had "blighting effects" on the town spirit. "A pall settled over this section that was as deadly as the sleeping sickness." Now, he exclaimed, "the spirit of 'I Will' has returned to Lafayette county. With it will come the disposition of her citizens to pull together." [20]

Women from the town's prominent families took a leading role in shaping the new civic consciousness, particularly in their efforts to beautify and purify the town. They joined with their male counterparts, the leading businessmen and professionals in the Civic League, which in 1908 launched a campaign to clean up the town. It publicly urged town government to trim trees and maintain the streets while encouraging private property owners to clean up their yards and take down the high fences used to control livestock. Prizes were offered for the best-kept yards. [21]

Well into the 1920s and 1930s country ways of living continued to pervade the town as much as town ways penetrated the country. Behind even the more ostentatious mansions one could find small barns and pens containing milk cows, hogs, chickens, horses, and mules. Not all the animals were penned; cows, hogs, chickens, and other livestock often roamed freely through the streets and back alleys of the town. Country life infiltrated the heart of town in other ways. On Saturdays the square was the favored place for trading mules, horses, and other livestock, as well as selling watermelons and other produce. In 1909 the city government enacted a new stock law making it unlawful to graze horses, mules, cows, goats, or hogs on the streets, sidewalks, or alleys within the corporate limits, punishable by a fine of up to twenty-five dollars. Another ordinance required licensing of all dogs owned in town. [22] In these and other ways, progressive elements in Oxford were struggling to delineate the boundary between town and country.

Many reforms were the inspiration of health concerns as much as the pursuit of urban refinement and beauty. The concentration of people in the town made it a dangerous place for contagious diseases. Yellow fever, smallpox, and other epidemics had ravaged the town since Reconstruction. After yellow fever paid its last mortal visit to Oxford in 1898, there were new cries to clean up the town. As the origin of diseases in germs became more fully understood, health reformers attacked the causes of disease in the slovenly sanitation they now associated with backwardness and lack of civic consciousness. Outdoor privies leached into underground wells contaminating the water, while garbage and animal manure littered public thoroughfares and private yards. A public meeting issued resolutions calling for the town to "be speedily put in first class sanitary condition and kept so"; in addition, the assembled citizens called for a "complete system of sewerage" to be installed throughout the town.[23] Although yellow fever disappeared, there continued to be other deadly diseases, notably typhoid fever, which often came from contaminated milk, and the deadly Spanish influenza, which swept through Oxford in 1918. The new awareness of germs and preventive sanitation gave birth to a stronger sense of civic responsibility for the community's health, ideas that ran parallel to those guiding social reform and city beautification.

Several improvements of sidewalks and streets and of major public utilities, light, water, and sewerage exceeded annual tax revenues, and the city fathers asked the public to approve special bond issues. With support from local civic improvement groups, they garnered support by appealing to urban pride and drew on invidious distinctions between town and country. Not all Oxonians joined this chorus of progress, particularly when it came at public expense. There had always been a hostile aversion to paying taxes, particularly for abstract notions of public benefit, and some objected to the intrusiveness of "progressive" reforms. The enforcement of stock laws and the removal of livestock from the square, for example, was denounced as a dictatorial edict from the town's do-gooders. Other new crusades to ban public spitting, out of concern for tuberculosis and general sanitation, created fierce resistance from some obstinate tobacco-chewing men. When one pastor gently urged his parishioners not to spit on the church floor, several men quit the congregation in protest.[24] But the drumbeats of progress drowned out the sound of these dissenting voices for the most part.

"Oxford is no rural hamlet," one editor appealed to voters, it "is a city set on a hill." "Brother voter, down in your heart you are ashamed to carry your friends from a distance over some of our plank walks."[25] Every "friend to progress and seeker of prosperity" ought to see the public benefit and economy of improving the town's main streets with their "mudholes and mires." In a similar appeal in 1909, one editorial argued that Oxford "is now in a transitional stage, from a small country town, with wells and cisterns for her water supply, oil lamps for her source of light, dirt roads for her streets, and no sewerage system at all, to the status of a little city, seeking to enjoy all the modern facilities of the best equipped cities in the country." Naturally, the editor surmised, the expenses for such amenities will be "far greater than they were when Oxford was a mere country town." At the end of that year the town had spent some $100,000 on improvements to the

The new Oxford waterworks, with Joe Parks on the left, 1920s.
(Courtesy of University Museums, University of Mississippi)

waterworks, electric power plant, sewerage system, sidewalks, and street paving. The women and men of the Civic League had played a critical role in defining goals of improvement and garnering public support for their vision of progressive Oxford.[26]

Oil Oozing from Oxford Streets

Oxford also promoted economic development as never before. Formerly satisfied with its traditional role as county seat and home to the university, by the late 1890s the "Athens of Mississippi" now boasted ambitions of becoming a center of industry and enterprise. "We Need Factories," one headline pleaded. At least two cotton factories ought to find support in Lafayette County, the *Oxford Eagle* argued in 1898. A gristmill, a steam-driven cotton gin and compress, and a steam laundry, were already established "industries" in Oxford. But where, the editor implored, is the capitalist who will invest in a cotton factory? We "are in the midst of the great cotton belt . . . yet not a yard of cloth is woven within a radius of hundreds of miles." An ice manufacturing plant, furniture factory, and canning plant were among the other enterprises he envisioned for industrial Oxford. The town has the potential of "winning as high a commercial reputation, as we have educational, and we need only the capital and enterprise to succeed."[27]

These dreams of commercial and industrial prowess reached their heights soon after World War I, when an oil and iron ore boom appeared to have struck Oxford. A man named W. J. Hixson came into town from Tennessee in the heat of summer 1919 and proclaimed that his extensive explorations of the county had revealed rich deposits of high-grade iron ore and, better yet, vast lakes of oil lying underneath the land. Hixson had all the charm of a smooth-tongued traveling salesman, and he lit the fuse of public enthusiasm at a mass meeting at the courthouse that August. "Hear me!," he pleaded; "When time was young and the earth was new, Almighty God built great vaults in the earth and placed within their walls, precious metals, minerals and petroleum—and then placed upon the surface many indications and earmarkings of these materials to guide the prospector." Hixson played the crowd beautifully, casting himself as one of them, a country boy "with courageous aspirations to achieve the attainments and successes of a country boy's ideals of city life." Through his learning he had "discovered the combinations to these locks or safe-guards with which the petroleum has been sealed all these years." He went on to describe "iron ore deposits of great magnitude" traversing the county in a broad belt seven miles wide, exclaiming as well the vast acreage of "merchantable timber" sitting on top of the "mineralized belt." George Price, the Oxford Eagle publisher, though expressing some skepticism about Hixson's grandiloquent rhetoric, seemed unable to resist the illusion of the area on the verge of a fabulous oil boom. "Oil Has Been Discovered in Lafayette County," the Eagle's headlines screamed. "Leachings and Seepages of Oil Form Great Films on Water." Before the state geologist, E. N. Lowe, could examine this belt of minerals and oil, landowners and speculators were already doing a brisk trade selling mineral rights to the land. Lowe's sobering report, however, advised that Hixson's signs of oil were only "escapes of bubbles of gas of vegetable origin in pools of stagnant waste." Furthermore, the iron ore Lowe found was of such low quality and so isolated from railroad transportation that it was worthless to mine.[28]

The hot air emanating from the oil boomers was not about to be discouraged by mere scientific facts. Dreams of vast riches lying beneath worn-out cotton fields and eroded land were simply too alluring. Besides, as Hixson argued persuasively, the naysayers were only the "devil minded aristocracy knocking, or the ignoramus howls of the lower class."[29] By January 1920 the Eagle proudly announced the organization of the North Mississippi Oil and Development Company, with headquarters in Oxford, Mississippi. The company's major stockholders came from the town's leading men of enterprise. This time a Texas oil man named Edgar P. Haney, described in the local press as "a very fluent speaker" well versed in developing oil fields, addressed the eager crowd at the courthouse. Haney prophesied a boom in land prices and population following the discovery of oil.[30]

People were eager to believe in the oil boom. In the automobile age, oil had suddenly become the key to riches in the modern economy. Stock in the new company sold quickly, as did leases on mineral rights as anxious farmers and oil speculators rushed to make their deal, but it was two long years before any drilling took place. *Eagle* publisher George Price had taken on all the printing and publicity for the oil company and was left holding a large unpaid bill. Nonetheless, he remained irrepressibly optimistic about the coming oil bonanza. At the end of 1921 Price announced that a derrick site was being staked off about six miles west of town. The drilling at "Oil City," as he christened it, would continue "until oil is spouting skyward, or," he added more soberly, "the hole is found to be a dry one."[31]

"Oxford will take on new life," Price promised his readers; "property values will go skyward by leaps and bounds." The "great moral dream in which Oxford has slumbered for these many years will be turned into a nightmare of turmoil and excitement . . . Oxford will become a great city." The city was already thronged with newcomers crowding into town, according to enthusiastic newspaper reports. He printed a letter from one oil investor who predicted the coming of a massive change from cotton to oil "that is going to make the boll weevil starve." Soon Price's headlines were reporting "Oil Oozing from Oxford Streets" within three hundred yards of the *Eagle* office. There is, he exclaimed, "an immence lake of oil beneath the streets of the city." "Let every one rally, boost and push the movement along," he urged his fellow citizens; "we should all stand together and all boost." Crowds of people gathered around the derrick to watch the drilling begin that spring of 1922. "No one knows how long it will take to strike oil," Price warned, but he left no doubt: "There is oil in North Mississippi. This is a certain fact." He printed a photograph of the derrick, Lafayette No. 1, as it was now being called, rising above the trees.[32]

By that summer, even George Price's optimism had withered. The drilling had ceased sometime in May. Not only had no oil been struck, but the oil developers had also incurred enormous expenses for construction costs and disappeared, supposedly to secure more funds outside the county. Local contractors were busy dismantling Lafayette No. 1 and hauling off the lumber and hardware they had provided the company. "It seems," Price finally admitted dolefully, "that the game was a great big bluff."[33] Faulkner could hardly have invented a richer tale of greed and gullibility, one made all the more delicious for being told at the expense of smart, modern townspeople rather than their rustic country counterparts.

Oxford's hopes for industrial salvation from agricultural decline died hard; there would be other efforts to promote manufacturing plants and other enterprises. The lack of waterpower and other sources of cheap fuel made these plans for industrial development little more than fruitless dreams. Oxford's growth would rest instead on its traditional role as a market town for the county's rural population, a government center, and a university town.

The New "Ole Miss"

The University of Mississippi had long been an important part of Oxford's public image, but until the early twentieth century it remained only a small part of the town's economy. In the two decades following 1886 the student body grew from a little over 200 to over 360; a growing minority were women. The growth in students, faculty, and staff all fueled the town's businesses while expansion of the campus brought new construction. The students continued to come almost entirely from within Mississippi, including many from Oxford, some of whose families had moved there while their children attended the university. By the turn of the century, a provincial backwoods college had become a modern American university modeled along the lines of the "new American university" developed at Johns Hopkins and Michigan. Earlier about one in five students had been very young, mostly under fifteen. They were actually doing preparatory work before entering university studies, having studied in one of Mississippi's rudimentary schools or at home. Preparatory courses were discontinued, and most students now came to the university with an education from one of the state's new high schools or private academies. The classical curriculum that focused on Greek and Latin was deemphasized, and students could now study new fields in science, mathematics, and a variety of other subjects. By the early 1900s about one-third of the students were attending professional schools: law, engineering, medicine, education, and graduate study. The faculty stood at twenty-two professors and most had doctorates from one of the nation's leading universities. Research and publication became the hallmark of the modern university. Several professors and administrators and their spouses and children became respected figures in Oxford social circles. "Ole Miss," the affectionate nickname it came to be known by, was now setting a certain tone for the "Athens of Mississippi."[34]

Outside the classroom the university experienced other dramatic changes. The growing presence of women at the university brought changes to student social life. The traditional male student preoccupations with shooting, drinking, and gambling gave ground to more sophisticated and glittering festivities: dress-up balls, jazz bands, and elegant banquets. The advent of fraternities and sororities also enlivened the social life of the university by the turn of the century, and the Opera House in town was the scene of many stylish dances they sponsored. By the 1910s students were bringing bands in from Memphis, including one led by W. C. Handy, the "Father of the Blues." At the same time, college football, organized at Ole Miss in 1893 by Professor Alexander Bondurant, became a popular focus of student culture and part of a strong bond between town and gown.[35]

That bond was imperiled when state officials threatened to remove the university to Jackson. It was, ironically, Lafayette County's native son, Governor Lee M. Russell, who first proposed to relocate the university in 1920 in retaliation against enemies in Oxford. That threat continued as late as 1927, when Governor Theodore Bilbo launched another attack on Oxford. The Oxford press and business community responded passionately. Oxford's defenders staged mass meetings in town and solicited support from townspeople and alumni across the state. Alfred Hume, the new university chancellor, made an impassioned speech in 1927 appealing to the deep sentimental ties so many alumni had to the university in Oxford. His speech was widely credited with swaying the legislature to desist in attacking Oxford.[36]

Oxford Is on a Boom

Oxford's role as market center to the county also confronted challenges in the early twentieth century. The expansion of the cotton economy after the Civil War and the dispersion of crossroads merchants and cotton gins throughout the countryside meant that the local cotton crop no longer funneled automatically into Oxford. Abbeville to the north and Taylor's Depot to the south, both on the Illinois Central rail line, became rivals to Oxford for the cotton market, while small gins and compresses scattered across the county also took a share. "Toccopola and Como often boast of a better market for cotton" than Oxford, one editorial chided.[37] In the face of growing competition, Oxford's cotton merchants and town boosters worked to regain their share of the cotton market. One major cotton broker set up a tent camp on the edge of town each fall and invited farm families to stay free while they sold their cotton and bought supplies in town. In 1907 the new Farmers' Union began a campaign for a large new cotton warehouse in Oxford. Local businessmen had to be persuaded to support this improvement with the threat that rival towns with modern warehouses would otherwise capture trade that ought to flow to Oxford. Oxford "has always had a pretty hard name as a market" for cotton, one *Eagle* editorial complained. Now cotton merchants had to compete with "several hustling towns on the railroads" and offer better prices if they wanted the farmers' trade. To lose a thousand bales of cotton meant that merchants throughout the town lost

Oxford cotton market, 1909. (Courtesy of University Museums, University of Mississippi)

thousands of dollars in trade.[38] In other ways, Oxford merchants began catering to the country trade. Porter-Sisk Hardware expressed concern for visiting ladies from the country "who spend several hours in town without any place to rest." The store offered rest rooms for their convenience and provided free gifts to women who came to "demonstration days" presented by visiting sales representatives. "An entirely new and progressive spirit is beginning to animate our business men," one editor boasted.[39]

The prosperity of the 1920s brought a flurry of energetic organization among the town's business leaders. A Business Mens' League and the town's first "real" Chamber of Commerce sought to unify and galvanize business progressivism. Earlier efforts to form a commercial body had failed, apparently because of political and personal factionalism, but a new spirit of civic progress was said to have taken hold among Oxford's business leaders. "There is a future for Oxford and Lafayette county," the *Eagle* proudly exclaimed. "Let us make it a bright future; . . . let's get some industries located in Oxford to give employment to our boys; let's find a way out of the rut and quagmire into which we have gotten." [40] By 1924 Oxford also boasted a Rotary Club, the signal embodiment of the urban civic ethos in towns and cities across America. The Rotarians, meeting each week over lunch at the Colonial Hotel, took the lead in promoting such improvements as paving the square and promoting health and education.[41]

The Shipp plantation house, built in the 1850s, was abandoned by the time of this photograph in the 1930s. (Courtesy of the Mississippi Department of Archives and History)

Good Roads

The same progressive spirit fueled campaigns to bring some of the benefits of modern life to the countryside. "Good Roads" and "Good Schools" were the mottoes of the day, the panaceas reformers envisioned alleviating the misery of rural life. For country people in Lafayette County the rural economy offered little hope of advancement. Neither Vardaman nor any of the new populist political leaders could do much about the basic problems that afflicted Mississippi dirt farmers. The price of cotton, the worn-out land, and the boll weevil, the chronic cycle of indebtedness and poverty were simply the irremediable facts of rural life for most farmers in the early twentieth-century South. Reformers wanted farmers to shift from cotton to cattle, or to other crops, and they wanted to improve the conditions of rural life. "Too many boys leave the farm where they would have made good substantial citizens," one editor complained, "and go to the city where only one in a thousand succeed in life's battle. There are some farmers who fairly drive their sons from the farm by teaching them that there are easier ways of earning a living." [42] They knew, as Flem Snopes said, "there ain't no benefit in farming."

Progressive reformers often had a romantic view of a bucolic rural community lost to depressing economic conditions, some beyond the control of farmers but others the result of public neglect of reforms and improvements that could reverse the decline of rural life. Their object was to keep the rural population on the farms by revitalizing the farm economy and bringing more of the amenities of town—good roads, good schools, churches, mail delivery, electricity, and telephones—to the country.

One editorial in 1910 lamented the ruin of the old home place for many country people who had abandoned their farms and come to town. Once the scene where the "happiest days of your life were spent . . . home of prosperity and thrift with happiness and hope in the ascendency." Now, the old home place was described with its "yard in weed, and fences falling down, garden almost gone, and the old house . . . now going to wreck and occupied by strangers, probably by negroes." What had once been a countryside "dotted with neat and prosperous little homes" was now being taken over by "negro settlements often the nurseries of degradation and crime." At the bottom of this process of "ruinous decay" in the countryside, the editor concluded, was its lack of access to church and school because of the horrible conditions of the roads.[43] Good roads and good schools for country people became the standard cures progressive reformers offered to the ills of rural life.

Roads in Lafayette County and across most of Mississippi had always been crudely constructed, poorly maintained, and lacking any overall plan. Roads typically zigzagged from one prominent property owner to another, eventually feeding into arteries to the county seat. Over the years, the expansion of the market economy brought heavier traffic along all the major roads. The soft loess soil that eroded so readily in the fields was far more exposed to rain and wind in the road cuts. Mississippi roads were described as a "bottomless hole of red mud" in the winter and a "blinding cloud of dust blown from chuck holes" in the summer.[44]

With rivers near its northern and southern borders and many smaller creeks feeding into each of them, transportation in Lafayette County was also especially vulnerable to flooding and bridge damage. A torrential storm in 1906 brought an estimated fifteen inches of rain and washed out bridges and railroad beds up and down the county. For people living south of the Yoknapatawpha River, like Faulkner's Bundren family, periodic floods swamped the bottomlands, covering roads and washing out bridges, leaving them stranded. The heaviest traveled roads leading into Oxford were in desperately poor condition by the turn of the century. One low spot at the crossing of Hurricane Creek just six miles north of town on the main road north to Abbeville and Holly Springs had become notorious. Horses and cattle coming into this crossing after heavy rains would get stuck in the mud holes and had to be dragged out by rope and a team of oxen. When Colonel Falkner, en route to Memphis with his grandchildren, came to this crossing in his famous Buick, he found a pair of black men with ropes and mules who had set up a small business rescuing bogged down vehicles.[45] "It must be admitted," one editorial on behalf of good roads in 1911 admonished, "that the roads leading into Oxford, the county seat of Lafayette county do not reflect credit upon the 20th century civilization, of which we are so fond of boasting, nor upon this county administration."[46]

Road maintenance in Mississippi had traditionally relied on men who lived along the public roads and made use of them. They either worked off the tax by giving a certain number of days as road hands, or they paid the road tax if they could. By 1912 that tax was $5 a year, a substantial amount for most farmers. As farms shifted from owner to tenant, this road tax fell on the poorer tenants who farmed the land rather than the wealthier landowners, who moved into town and rented out their farms. In 1912, the total budget for road improvement was a little over $18,000 for the year, and nearly $16,000 came from the road tax.[47] The goal of the good roads movement was to equalize the tax burden and greatly increase the money going to road improvement and maintenance by turning from individual taxes to bond issues. The goal was to enlist public support for what reformers envisioned as a public good that would benefit the entire community. This went against a deeply embedded southern tradition of limited taxation based on individual benefit.[48]

Vardaman and Bilbo made good roads part of their platform, and both called for a state highway agency and tax reform to fund a modern system of state roads. In 1916 Governor Bilbo finally secured the first state highway commission, which brought new federal dollars to the state. Any hopes for a state system of road construction continued to run up against fierce opposition to taxation, especially state taxes, which had been ingrained in many voters and politicians since Reconstruction. It was not until 1922, when Governor Lee Russell introduced the tax on gasoline and a revenue sharing program, that Mississippi could move forward with its state highway program.[49] A reform that had begun out of concern for the animal-powered wagons of country folk had by this time become the crusade of automobile-driving townspeople.

Good Schools

Along with good roads, progressive era reformers saw the improvement of public schools as a basic remedy for rural decay. Vardaman made the improvement of education for white children a central feature of his appeal, and as governor he allocated funds to increase the budget for teachers' salaries and school buildings, and he attempted to lower costs for textbooks, which parents were responsible for purchasing. Other Mississippi governors in the progressive era continued to make public education a major part of their campaign. Good schools were popular among many rural whites, but there was deep public resistance to school tax increases, underscored by white resentment that their tax dollars were going to support black schools. White property owners, the argument went, paid nine-tenths of the county's school taxes but accounted for only about half the student population. Furthermore, many poor white families could not afford to send their children to school because of the additional expenses of buying textbooks, crayons, other incidental fees for heating and cleaning the schoolroom. In any case, the children of the poor could attend school only for a short time in the winter when they were not needed in the fields.[50]

Apart from the question of cost, many country people were suspicious of the very idea of public school education as a means of personal betterment. The schools were not teaching farmers' sons and daughters what they needed to know to make a living on the farm; that had always been passed down from father to son and mother to daughter. "Why was it necessary to go to school anyway?" young Walker Coffey asked himself. His classmates who grew up in town "didn't know a buggy shaft from a wagon tongue from the tongue of a plow."[51] What the schools were teaching was reading and writing, mathematics and history, all knowledge and skills that seemed irrelevant or—worse—subversive to the futures these children were to follow. The schoolroom door opened on the path to town, away from the farm and away from the family. The schools, one state superintendent admitted, "are educating our boys out of sympathy with their environments and making them dissatisfied with their surroundings . . . our boys are manifesting more and more a disinclination to remain in the country."[52] The progressives instead saw the school as the agent of progress, a means of improving the lives of rural children, whether by opening young minds to scientific agriculture or preparing them for lives in town.[53]

Faulkner carefully sketched a typical one-room school in Frenchman's Bend with its new "professor," Labove, who plays football and studies law at the university in Oxford. Labove's father explains to Varner that his son does not want to take over the family farm; "He says he wants to be Governor." Labove is a young man driven by some inner ambition to transcend his family's humble status. He lives a Spartan life of deprivation, sleeping in a heatless lean-to attached to the school. Among his few possessions are his law books and a brilliant nickel lantern, the light from which beams out of the windows of his cold lean-to late into the night. His pupils, a motley

Rural school, Woodson's Ridge. (Courtesy of University Museums, University of Mississippi)

mix of country children, share nothing of his penchant to learn and raise themselves from their rural life. "They called him Professor too even though he looked what he was—twenty-one—and even though the school was a single room in which pupils ranging in age from six to the men of nineteen whom he had had to meet with his fists to establish his professorship, and classes ranging from bald abc's to the rudiments of common fractions were jumbled together. He taught them all and everything."

A survey of Lafayette County schools in 1908 reveals that Varner's country school was quite typical. In rich and poor neighborhoods the pattern was one of primitive one-room schoolhouses in poor repair, limited supplies of books and other equipment, typically one teacher coping with children of diverse ages, and a school term squeezed between gathering time and planting time (November through March). "Antioch had 55 pupils in house valued at 'something like $100,' no repairs this session, no school library and 'parents take little interest in building up school,'" the survey reported. College Hill, one of the richest rural neighborhoods in the county, had twenty-eight pupils in a "house worth $1500, no books in library and public sentiment wholly indifferent."[54]

Not all country people were indifferent to schooling. Many parents moved the entire family, changed jobs, and sacrificed in countless ways to get their children educated. Several private and semiprivate high schools and normal schools were founded in the late nineteenth and early twentieth centuries designed to educate rural youth. Private funding through gifts and tuition gave white pupils a better education without sharing tax revenues with blacks. One prime example was the Tula community in the remote southern part of the county. During the 1890s this isolated country hamlet became home to the Tula Normal Institute and Business School in the 1890s. In 1921 the same community raised $10,000 to build a new consolidated schoolhouse to replace the shabby one-room schools scattered about the area. The new school was the pride of the community until it was destroyed by fire one night. In a story redolent of Faulknernian gothic, a young man from Water Valley named Carl Blackwell was said to be distraught over rejection by his sweetheart, who left him to teach at the Tula school. He sent vile, threatening letters to school officials, and one night, in a hopeless act of vengeance, he set fire to the school. The proud symbol of Tula's ambition burned completely to the ground, along with the old school building, a church, and a blacksmith shop. Having spent their last dollars on construction of the school, the school board had deferred buying fire insurance. Over the next twenty years, in resolute defiance of their fate, the people of Tula paid off the debt for the burned school, and with volunteer labor and contributions they rebuilt the school, board by board, exactly as it had been before.[55]

By the late 1930s, the WPA guide to Mississippi described Lafayette County as one drove along the highway through "a once prosperous farming area now having its existence threatened by erosion and a one-crop economy." A century after the arrival of the cotton frontier, now all one saw was "farm houses weathering or abandoned, raw red gullies gnawing at the vitals of the swelling hills, fields reverting to forest growths, and villages with only the schoolhouse and gasoline station new."[56]

The Old Order Passes and Adapts

As rural life decayed, Oxford Town was vibrant and growing. Underlying its progress was a slow shift in power and wealth away from the declining old families and toward a new enterprising breed, many of whom were coming in from the county to make their way in town. Beginning in the 1840s, as we saw earlier, the town's most prominent families had been drawn mostly from the class of large planters who had moved into town, leaving daily management of their plantations to overseers. They built grand mansions in town so their families could enjoy proximity to churches, schools, shops, and all the amenities of small town society. By the early twentieth century Oxford's leading citizens were genuine townspeople—bankers, merchants, lawyers, doctors, university administrators, and professors—with economic foundations firmly planted in town. These new townspeople, the Falkners not least among them, were the harbingers of the new age that entered Oxford.

The quickening of town life in the early twentieth century is reflected in Faulkner's depiction of the new order in Jefferson. "Until then, Jefferson was like all the other little Southern towns: nothing had happened in it since the last carpetbagger had given up and gone home or been assimilated into another unregenerate Mississippian. We had the usual mayor and board of aldermen who seemed to the young people to have been in perpetuity since the Ark or certainly since the last Chickasaw departed for Oklahoma . . . old Mr Adams the mayor with a long patriarchal white beard, who probably seemed to young people . . . older than God Himself, until he might actually have been the first man." Major De Spain, veteran of the Spanish American War, deposes Adams as mayor and ushers the progressive era into town: "The new age had entered Jefferson; he was merely its champion." Oxford, in fact, had an R. S. Adams serve as mayor; first elected in 1900, he was reelected five more times before he resigned in 1916. But the actual Adams, instead of a hoary patriarch of old, was very much in the forefront of progressive Oxford in these years. Behind this transition into the progressive era is the ascendance of a new generation, whom Faulkner portrayed as young people "who were not yet store- and gin-owners and already settled lawyers and doctors, but were only the clerks and bookkeepers in the stores and gins and offices, trying to save enough to get married on, who all went to work to get De Spain elected mayor." [57]

It is the same shift toward a new order that Colonel John Sartoris anticipates at the end of Reconstruction when he tells his son, Bayard, "I acted as the land and the time demanded . . . now the land and the time too are changing; what will follow will be a matter of consolidation, of pettifogging and doubtless chicanery in which I would be a babe in arms but in which you, trained in the law, can hold your own—our own." [58] The shift of power and status from plantation to town, from landed gentry to bankers and lawyers, witnessed some children of the old elite adapting to the new order, like Bayard Sartoris or Jason Compson, while young, ambitious men, like Flem Snopes, ascend from below.

Oxford's Bem Price, thought to be the wealthiest man in town during the early twentieth century, offers one illustration of the gravitation of wealth and the sources of wealth from country to town. Bem Price was the son of Washington Price, proprietor of a large plantation near the Yoknapatawpha River and master to more than seventy slaves. When Washington Price died in 1855, young Bem was sent off to live with his uncle in North Carolina, where he attended school. Because he was only eleven when the war broke

Colonel John W. T. Falkner,
William Faulkner's
grandfather, was a lawyer,
banker, and political leader.
(From *Oxford Eagle*)

out, Bem Price was able to successfully press his claim for compensation
from the Southern Claims Commission.[59] The old plantation continued to
supply income, but Bem Price moved to town and shifted his wealth to new
urban enterprises. By 1871, he was partner with Paul Barringer, a former
planter and Unionist who had also been able to win a handsome claim of
$32,000 for his wartime losses. They opened a general grocery business,
which thrived as farmers shifted from self-sufficiency to cotton production.
When Barringer died in 1878 his young partner had moved into banking.
The postwar South had a desperate need for capital to finance the economic
reconstruction of the region, and banking could be extremely profitable.
Many of the leading merchants, lawyers, and other wealthy professionals
(including Colonel John W. T. Falkner) became involved in this money-
making field in postwar Oxford. In partnership with Charles Roberts, an
Englishman and Civil War veteran who operated a bookstore on the square,
Price opened the Southern Bank of Oxford sometime before 1877. The Bank
of Oxford bought them out in 1877, moved into their offices on the south
side of the square, and continued with Bem Price as the bank's cashier.
Creditors estimated his net worth to be between twenty-five and thirty thousand dollars by 1876, and his fortune grew from there. Price bought the old

Thomas E. B. Pegues mansion, Edgecomb, on North Street from his former partner, Charles Roberts, and renamed it Ammadele in honor of his sister, Amma, and his wife, Delle Bowles, daughter of another wealthy planter family. The children of the old planter elite had reestablished themselves in the trappings of antebellum opulence, but now with economic foundations, as well as mansions, firmly ensconced in the town.[60]

Others among the town's upper strata had origins from within the old Mississippi bourgeoisie. William Faulkner's own family illustrates as well as any the different paths Mississippi's established town elite took into the New South. On both sides of Faulkner's family tree, the Falkner and Butler families for three generations had been tied to the economy of the Mississippi town, not land and agriculture unless as a sideline speculation. Colonel John W. T. Falkner, like his father, made his primary occupation as lawyer the base for a remarkable array of business and political enterprises. After selling his father's railroad in 1885, Falkner left Ripley and moved to Oxford that year when he was thirty-seven years old. He had already lived there when he studied law at the university, and he knew that Oxford, home to the federal district court and state university and an important center of Democratic politics in northern Mississippi, offered him opportunities his former home, Ripley, could never provide.

By 1892 Colonel Falkner was serving Lafayette County in the state legislature, first as representative and then for three successive terms as state senator. During Democratic president Grover Cleveland's administration Falkner won appointment as assistant U.S. district attorney, and he served as treasurer of the university for many years. Though remembered in his waning years as an old man with an ear trumpet snoozing in a chair outside his bank, completely out of synch with the times, Colonel Falkner had been a leading force in the modernization of Oxford. He led the move to establish the new waterworks, the electric power company, a modern sewerage system, asphalt road paving, and many other progressive civic improvements.

Colonel Falkner was also heavily involved in a variety of local businesses as well: a cottonseed oil mill, a transportation company, a hardware store, and the new Opera House. In 1910 Falkner organized the First National Bank of Oxford, which he served as president over the next ten years. During the 1890s he had built what the family called the "Big Place," a large home done up in grand Victorian style with cupolas and gingerbread trim, at the corner of South Street and University, one of the best addresses in town. The Big Place was a magnificent billboard advertising his new wealth and position in town. The "Young Colonel" (as he was sometimes called to distinguish him from his father) dressed in a straw Panama hat and linen suit, with an imposing gold watch chain and an ornate gold-headed cane.

He was often seen sitting in front of his bank on the square talking with passersby or touring the town in his gleaming Buick driven by his chauffeur, a black man named Chess.[61]

The Falkner family's affinity for business and politics all but died out with the passing of Colonel Falkner in 1922. His son John Jr. lived in Oxford, was active in Democratic Party politics, continued in the family law practice, and won a post as judge. His other son, Murry (William Faulkner's father), followed his father to Oxford in 1902. Murry never demonstrated any serious business acumen, though his father would set him up with one business or appointed position after another. He operated a livery stable that hired out carriages and provided passenger service primarily to and from the railroad station. But with the coming of the automobile, the livery service was doomed; Murry moved into selling hardware. That business failed too, and thanks to his father's connections with Lee Russell, Murry found a job in the administration of the university.

After the Young Colonel's death, the decline of the house of Falkner seemed to continue with Murry's oldest son, Bill, whose only ambition was to be a writer, like his great grandfather and namesake, Colonel William C. Falkner. An unmotivated, not to say lazy, student, Bill was kept back in school and finally dropped out without even a high school education. He failed to find or hold on to any respectable work. For a time he did menial work at his grandfather's bank, but he was more interested in nipping whiskey from the Colonel's desk drawer and quit. He left Oxford and picked up odd jobs in the Northeast. When World War I came, the American armed forces rejected him for being too short, so he went to Canada to enlist for pilot training. He returned with an RAF uniform, affecting a British accent, carrying a cane, and limping from what he told people was a near fatal airplane crash during combat over France. He attended the University of Mississippi briefly with uninspiring results. His job at the university post office, arranged through political connections, ended with him being fired for willful refusal of duty. ("I reckon I'll be at the beck and call of folks with money all my life," he told a friend as he walked away from the post office, "but thank God I won't ever again have to be at the beck and call of every son of a bitch who's got two cents to buy a stamp.") People in town referred to him as "Count No Account," a sardonic tribute to the illustrious family name now borne by what appeared to many as a pretentious n'er-do-well given to tall tales, excessive drinking, and little sign of ambition for gainful employment. Whatever talents he would later demonstrate as a writer, in business affairs William Faulkner was generally a disaster. He was, in fact, a highly disciplined worker and by no means was he physically lazy. But much of his life was haunted by a chronic lack of money, which he spent as quickly as he made it on airplanes, a country farm, and horses, along with household and family expenses. In fairness, much of his money was spent on a large retinue of relatives and dependents, many of them also struggling economically. All of this helps us understand how even prominent and financially strong families could fall into decline in rural Mississippi; it also illuminates Faulkner the writer. His view of the striving and often successful country boys who came to Oxford and made their way in the modern town economy was from the vantage point of a town boy, successor to a once ascendant, now declining family.

Faulkner's identity with the town elite in decline is reinforced by evidence from his mother's side of the family. Maud Butler Falkner had roots in the Oxford business class that stretched back to the town's founding. She and Murry had met in Oxford, and it was her family ties in part that pulled the young family back to Oxford in 1902. Maud's grandfather Charles Butler we met earlier as the first county sheriff and the man who had laid out the town lots back in 1836. For years he and his wife, Burlina, operated the town's leading hotel.

Their son Charles Butler Jr. followed in his father's footsteps serving as town marshal and tax collector, but in the 1880s he brought disgrace on the family name. First in 1883, for dubious reasons, he shot and killed Sam Thompson, editor of the *Oxford Eagle*, who was drunk and disorderly and resisting arrest, or at least so Marshal Butler claimed. When Thompson's widow, Elizabeth, took over the paper, she did her best to heap shame on her husband's killer, insisting that it was an unjustifiable grudge-motivated killing of an elderly, inebriated man who posed no real threat to Butler. Butler was tried and acquitted but never entirely redeemed in the public eye.

Then, sometime around Christmas 1887, Charlie Butler vanished from Oxford and was never seen again. He absconded with several thousand dollars in tax receipts he had collected for the town. Charles Butler, age thirty-nine, suddenly and without explanation, abandoned his wife, Leila, and their two children, Sherwood, eighteen, and Maud, sixteen. Some said he was facing ruin and was desperate for money, but this was not true; he left behind a small estate inherited from his parents. There were rumors that he had problems getting along with his wife and that he ran off with another woman. There was speculation that the other woman was Mrs. Jacob Thompson's servant, described as a "beautiful octoroon" woman, who was said to have disappeared at the same time. Whatever the truth was —and no one ever found out—the abandoned Butler women were forced to sell whatever property was left in the family estate and live in straitened circumstances. Friends helped pay off debts, and town officials agreed to reduce her property taxes.

The Butler women Charles Butler left behind must have felt embarrassed in every sense. For a time, they left Oxford to live in Jackson, Tennessee, but they returned by 1893. Whatever disgrace and hardship the father had brought to the family six years earlier, his wife and children apparently continued to enjoy the respect and friendship, perhaps sympathy, of society in Oxford. The son, Sherwood, married the daughter of merchant and restaurant owner George Buffaloe, who helped launch him in business. In 1896 Maud Butler also married well it appeared; one could hardly do better than to marry the oldest son of so prominent a man as Colonel John W. T. Falkner.[62]

The Falkners and Butlers were not alone among many prominent families in Oxford sliding into genteel poverty. One of Bill Falkner's youthful companions, Phil Stone, descended from a family that reflected a similar mix of fading glory and troubled adjustment to the new order. "General" James Stone (the title, like so many in the South, was purely honorific) owned a large plantation in the Tallahatchie bottom in Panola County, east of Oxford in the Delta. The land had belonged to his wife's forebear, a Methodist minister named Potts who acquired one hundred square miles around 1836. Potts and his sons, Theophilus and Amodeus (known in the family as Buck and Buddy), opened some of the land to cotton farming, but much of it remained a wilderness that served as a hunting camp for General Stone and his friends. James Stone's forebears were also Delta planters in Panola, though of more modest means. But just as Colonel Sartoris had prepared his son Bayard for the new order, James Stone's father sent him to military school in Kentucky and then to law school at the University of Mississippi. From his father and through his marriage to Rose Alston, James Stone came into an enormous amount of Delta property. But he turned from farming to his law practice in Batesville, a few miles east of Oxford in Panola County.

In 1892 the Stones left Batesville and moved to Oxford. The Delta was a sickly place, and two of the Stones' children had already died. Mrs. Stone had been pushing her husband to move the family to Oxford, which was higher in altitude and regarded as healthier. Besides, two of their sons were about to go off to the university in Oxford; this way, they could live at home. Furthermore, Stone's legal practice would prosper in Oxford, where the federal district court and the Illinois Central Railroad, which Stone would serve as general counsel, offered far greater opportunities.[63]

The Stones bought the old mansion of Tomlin "Buck" Avant, the imposter "aristocrat" from Virginia, who had built it with borrowed money on the northwest edge of Oxford in the 1840s before he declared bankruptcy and died. It had once been a grand, lavishly furnished mansion, painted white with six tall columns rising in front a full two stories. Now the dark mansion survived as a legendary haunted house in Oxford. By the time the Stones bought it in the 1890s it had been abandoned and neglected for years.

Their new town home in Oxford became the "big house" to an urban version of the Delta plantation they left behind. The Stones' mansion was surrounded by fifteen hundred acres, including several parcels rented out to tenants, pastures for livestock, a barn for horses, a bull house, smokehouse, and a large vegetable garden. General Stone's Oxford "plantation" also included a large staff of black servants, whom he treated to gifts of liquor each Christmas. Stone's position as local counsel to the Illinois Central Railroad afforded a very comfortable income, which he spent lavishly entertaining family and friends, very much in the spirit of Buck Avant.

Stone invested in the Bank of Oxford and by 1908 had been elected its president. He used the bank to promote agricultural reform in the county and extended a great deal of loan money to an agricultural economy that seemed impervious to reform and unable to prosper. When the banking crisis came in 1930, the Bank of Oxford failed, and the Stone family fortunes suddenly collapsed. They lost most of the property in Panola and some of the land surrounding their house in Oxford to tax collectors. General Stone had never fully adapted to life in town. Well before his financial problems, he frequently went off to his Delta hunting camp with male companions and occasionally escaped into alcoholic "toots" followed by "dry out" stints at a nearby sanitarium. He died at the hunting camp in 1936 leaving the family nearly destitute.

The Stone sons had attended the university and followed their father into legal careers. Phil Stone, young William Faulkner's friend, was more interested in literature than law, and while he continued after his father's death to practice law in his father's old firm, his debts increased. None of the family ever recovered from the blow of 1930. By the early 1940s the Stones converted one hundred acres of the remaining land surrounding their Oxford mansion into small lots for modest suburban homes financed through the Federal Housing Authority. The Stone Subdivision, laid out in the shadow of the old antebellum mansion, was Oxford's first suburban development of its kind. The house itself, dark and weathered from neglect, and rumored to be haunted with ghosts, went up in a massive blaze in 1942.[64]

Even in a prosperous economic environment, American life offers few guarantees even to the most prominent families who try passing on the rewards of one generation to the next. But in this part of the American South the economy no longer offered many chances for easy wealth, not in the way the early cotton frontier had to antebellum planters. Some wealthy families surviving from the old order watched their sons carve out a foothold in the New South, and they saw their daughters marry successful "new men" and their sons marry into money. But others witnessed, sooner or later, a decline of fortune, often eased by a legacy of family money and connections, but in the end a relentless downward slope. Oxford offered examples of each. Alongside smart new Victorian houses and refurbished antebellum mansions, with new Buicks parked out front, were symbols of faded grandeur, the once opulent mansions whose decaying beauty was marked by peeling paint and weathered wood, yards grown over with vines and grass, and, inside, shabby furnishings, threadbare carpets, and dust. Faulkner's Compson family lived on in its old mansion, selling off their land in parcels to finance a wedding or tuition at Harvard, a strategy that might slow their social descent, if not their economic decline. But for every case of an old established town family with wealth and energy waning, there were others on the make, in town or coming in from the country. These new people, these "outlanders" as Faulkner sometimes refers to them, were hungry for success and bristling with ambition, eager to absorb the savvy of the New South instead of merely imitating the manners of the old.

Lee Russell's Revenge

As a boy Lee Russell and his brother rode their horse for miles every day, first to the public school near his family's farm, and then to the normal school at Toccopola. His family had lived near Dallas in the southeast corner of Lafayette County for generations. His father, a Confederate veteran, had married Louisa Jane Mackey, the daughter of a local physician, after the war. Their son Lee, the first of six children, was born in 1875. The Russell family was well above the status of poor whites, though many lived in their neighborhood. They owned a farm they called Mucaloon, after the creek that ran through it and rented out in parcels to tenant farmers raising cotton while the Russell family lived in a modest house on a ridge overlooking their land.

The Dallas community where the Russells lived was known as a lawless area. Stranded several miles south of the Yoknapatawpha River, the area festered with feuds among the white families in the neighborhood, some likely stemming from hostilities during the Civil War, when the area became known for anti-Confederate resistance. Whatever their cause, there were more than twenty murders in the Dallas area recorded after Reconstruction, and local people told of many more that went unreported. The land was hilly and the soil poor, and as the cotton fields wore out and the woods lumbered over, the cemeteries filled and the population dwindled. By

Lee Russell, law partner
in Falkner, Russell, and
Falkner and governor of
Mississippi. (Courtesy of
the Mississippi Department
of Archives and History)

1935 "Old Dallas" would become extinct, leaving behind only the cemetery
with the tombstones of its murdered sons and their kin.

Lee Russell's mother, Louisa, wanted a better life for her son, and the
path to that was a good education. It was Louisa Russell's ambition that
got young Lee up early each morning and spurred him to stay the course at
Toccopola. He graduated in 1897 and promptly went on to the University of
Mississippi to study law. People later told of how young Lee Russell, now
twenty-two, walked all the way along the dusty, rutted roads from Dallas to
Oxford, every step taking him away from the country and toward a new life
in town. He worked his way through law school, waiting on tables and doing
odd jobs, and he graduated in 1901. By this time his mother, now widowed,
moved the entire family into town, rented a house near the university, and
worked hard putting each of her children through the university. All found
successful careers in town and none returned to the family farm. Within
a few years of graduating Lee Russell had launched a promising political
career and was on his way to the governor's mansion. Faulkner's hardworking student and schoolteacher, Labove, might easily have found some inspiration in the Lee Russell story, but there were many that emulated his
ambition for learning and self-advancement.[65]

University students in Oxford were still predominantly the sons of wealthy Delta planters and prosperous townspeople throughout the state. The Grange and others had pushed for a state college that would serve the needs of the state's farmers, and this led to the creation of Mississippi Agricultural and Mechanical College (later Mississippi State University) in Starkville in 1878. The university in Oxford retained its traditional role as the home of Mississippi's white elite, training them in liberal arts and professional education. The election of Governor Vardaman challenged that; he wanted to democratize the university, to open it to common white folk. He would begin by appointing his people to the Board of Trustees.[66]

Lee Russell came to the university just before the Vardaman revolt, and he cut his political teeth doing battle against privilege at Ole Miss. While at the university he had attempted to join Sigma Alpha Epsilon, one of several fraternities that had become an important part of the social life on campus. They blackballed Russell, he said because the rich kids scorned a poor country boy who had to work his way through school waiting tables. To add insult to injury, one day some of the fraternity boys doused Lee Russell with a pail of water from an upstairs window. He was humiliated and angry, and he would never forget it. He quickly transformed his seething wrath into a political attack against what he denounced as aristocratic, secret societies. He and another student went to Jackson and succeeded in persuading the university's Board of Trustees to regulate fraternities beginning with a ban on all pledging of new members in 1902–3. This was only the start; he made a promise he would ultimately ban fraternities at the university. At the core of his political ambition was his undying urge for revenge against the fraternities and all the unearned privilege and snobbery they represented.

Two years after Russell graduated from law school in 1903, Colonel John W. T. Falkner invited him to join his firm, which soon became Falkner, Russell, and Falkner, with the addition of the Colonel's son John Jr. Colonel Falkner was a member of the university Board of Trustees Russell had petitioned the previous year, and he had his eye on this young man as a potentially useful ally in the new political order emerging with the Vardaman revolution. Having won election as Lafayette County's representative in the state legislature, then two terms as state senator, the Colonel was rudely awakened to the strong winds of populist unrest blowing through Mississippi when he stood for a third term in 1903. His opponent, G. R. Hightower, a minor county official, swept to victory, and Colonel Falkner came in an embarrassing third in the race.

Colonel Falkner was only fifty-five years old in 1903, and he wanted to regain his position of leadership in the local Democratic Party. Bringing Lee Russell into his law firm was part of Colonel Falkner's effort to align with the emerging Vardaman faction, whose appeal in the hill counties was already powerful. Lee Russell soon gathered a following, particularly among the white farmers in Lafayette County. He served as county attorney and in 1907 ran for office as a state representative. Russell canvassed the county, speaking about good roads, flood control, better public schools, and public health, and he won the first primary.[67] The election of 1907 continued to bring great changes in local and state politics. The old crowd of officeholders in the county courthouse and the statehouse were being thrown out, and the new men of the Vardaman faction were taking over.

Together with his growing popularity as a lawyer and politician, Russell was beginning to make money in a variety of business ventures in Oxford, several of them in partnership with Colonel Falkner. The Falkners and Lee Russell had become close allies in business and politics. This was not just a calculated expedient move by the established Falkner family to align itself with a rising star in the Vardaman movement; the Falkner and Russell families enjoyed numerous friendly social ties as well. One oft-repeated story (with shades of Sutpen at Pettibone's door) tells of Colonel Falkner slamming his front door on Lee Russell when he came to pay a social visit sometime after his election as lieutenant governor in 1915. But the origin of this story is suspect, and there is too much countervailing evidence to indicate that, once Lee Russell had proven his talent for politics and business, he became accepted by Colonel Falkner. The old guard in Oxford who opposed the Vardaman movement, on the other hand, resented Lee Russell, and it took on a personal animosity. But outside these political enemies, he became a respected member of Oxford society welcome to mix socially with the Falkners and other established families. Indeed, Russell was now in a position to do favors for the Falkners, including finding Murry Falkner his job at the university. Lee Russell was prospering in business and law. Soon he could be seen driving about in an elegant touring car, the first of its kind in town and a notable sign that this country boy, shunned by the rich kids at the university, had come to town and made it. He moved into a large house on North Street, right next to Bem Price's grand mansion, Ammadele.[68]

Russell ran for office again, this time for the state senate, in 1911, the year of Vardaman's famous victory against Leroy Percy and the "secret caucus crowd." Vardaman took Lafayette County with almost 70 percent of the vote, while Russell beat his opponent, W. P. Shinault, nearly two to one.[69] With his political base secure, Russell now set out to have his revenge against the fraternities, just as he had vowed ten years earlier. He launched an all-out attack on the fraternities at Ole Miss. These exclusive societies, he argued passionately, did nothing but waste money and encourage dissipation, gambling, and harassment of women. Furthermore, he accused fraternities of undermining scholarship, overshadowing the traditional literary societies, and poisoning college spirit by encouraging cliques. Above all, Russell charged, the fraternities permitted the "social ostracism" of non-fraternity men from the social life of Oxford. He wanted all fraternities at the university and every university in Mississippi banned completely and forever.[70]

Russell's antifraternity crusade was an attack on aristocratic privilege, snobbery, and exclusion, one proclaimed in a voice fully in tune with Vardaman's assault on the Delta Bourbons, the "aristocrats" who had run the state for so long. Lee Russell had become the champion of the Vardaman movement in his part of the state, but his choice of fraternities as a target generated a hard core of enemies, especially in Oxford. Fraternity membership had become an important mark of distinction among many of the Mississippi elite by this time. Fraternity dances and banquets were a prominent feature of the smart set in Oxford, whether or not they attended the university. All the Falkner men who attended the university had been fraternity members and in fact had belonged to the same fraternity that had rejected and demeaned Lee Russell. Many other citizens in Oxford saw the attack on the fraternities as an attack on their university and their town's whole society. They sent petitions down to Jackson refuting Russell's charges of "dissipation" and immoral conduct. The bill passed in 1912 nonetheless, and the fraternities now had to dissolve or go underground—they went underground and waited more than a decade for repeal.[71]

The next year, Russell's enemies in Oxford struck back by seeking to disbar him. The charge was that Russell had defended a university student accused of a number of assaults, but it was clear that any excuse would serve for those who wanted to destroy Russell and end his career in politics. Leading the attack was James Stone, lawyer and bank president and ardent opponent of the Vardaman-Bilbo faction. Russell was exonerated and the charges dismissed as "groundless and maliciously designed," but the enmity of his Oxford adversaries was far from over.[72]

Russell was not through either. In 1915 he ran for lieutenant governor on the ticket with Theodore Bilbo and won. It was a vicious campaign of mudslinging, much of it concentrated in Russell's home county. Russell put it down to the ruthless maneuvers of the old Bourbon "secret caucus crowd" that was being moved out of power. He ran ahead of Bilbo in Lafayette County, taking 60 percent of the vote, but the vicious personal attacks during the campaign suggest that local opinion on Russell had further polarized.[73] Late in 1914 Russell's enemies in Oxford financed a newspaper, the *Independent*, to counter what they thought was the *Eagle*'s overly favorable treatment of "Russell the Rascal," as they dubbed him. The *Eagle* stood firmly behind him, and its publisher, George Price, bought out the anti-Russell paper before the election of 1916.[74]

In 1919 Russell launched his campaign for governor of Mississippi. John Falkner Jr. the "Young Colonel's" son, headed the Russell campaign in Lafayette County, and his nephew Bill served as chauffeur to the candidate as he addressed rural voters that summer. Russell, the heir apparent of the Vardaman-Bilbo faction, was regarded as the favorite going into a four-way race in the primaries. Russell won endorsement from both Bilbo and Vardaman, the latter arguing that Lee Russell's childhood poverty was his strongest qualification: "No man who has not known the hardships of the poor people is able to sympathize with them." His opponents destroyed one another, and their followers could not unite in an anti-Russell vote. Lafayette County's native son took 75 percent of a record county vote in the first primary and 80 percent in the second primary.[75] In September 1919, Russell arrived at the Oxford depot in triumph with a brass band leading a torchlight parade with hundreds of supporters to the courthouse square, where a crowd of two thousand cheered their champion. Colonel John W. T. Falkner introduced his victorious candidate. The "redneck" from Dallas, the reject from the fraternity at Ole Miss, was the hero of the town and county. He was the first Lafayette County native elected governor.[76]

The hard-core anti-Russell crowd back in Oxford held deep resentment toward him, and they took every opportunity to let him know it. The political atmosphere of Mississippi at this time was severely polarized, and political discourse was rampant with invective. The anti-Russell press called him a "common little bounder and character assassin," a "shameful liar and contemptible slanderer." Before the presidential election of 1920 the anti-Russell ring in Oxford managed to exclude him from a place in the state delegation going to the National Democratic Party Convention. This was an unprecedented slap in the face to a sitting governor. Russell soon struck back. As governor, Russell declared that the 1920 census had been in error and that the population of Oxford fell short of the two thousand required for city status. The city government, which had been reorganized on the commission model in 1914, was therefore illegitimate, he proclaimed. He ousted all local government officials from city offices and quickly appointed his own people. There was a flurry of debate, legal actions, petitions, and editorials surrounding "the Oxford matter," and it left bitter feelings on both sides.[77]

Out at the university the resentment toward Governor Russell's anti-fraternity edict was boiling in the fall of 1920, when a group of students threw a rope over a tree limb and lynched an effigy labeled "Lee M. Russell" and set it afire. Russell was furious. This incident must have recalled his humiliation and rage when he first came to the university. He personally came up from Jackson to conduct an investigation of fraternities on campus. He interrogated one student about one of the exclusive clubs organized as a front for the fraternities: if he, the governor, were a student, would he be invited to join the Red and Blue club? The student answered defiantly: "I imagine it would be just as it was when you were here, Governor, you wouldn't get in." Russell reacted with vengeance. He ordered four students dismissed from the university and required that all students register every organization they belonged to; any false reports would be punished with immediate dismissal. Many students left the university rather than submit (including William Faulkner, a member of SAE fraternity). In trying to democratize the university and settle an old score, Russell had taken on the alumni and elite of Oxford and Mississippi.[78]

Russell's enemies had their turn to gloat the next year when his former secretary, Frances Birkhead, brought embarrassing charges against the governor. She claimed he had seduced and impregnated her, then forced her to have an abortion. She was suing Governor Russell for $100,000 as compensation for her physical suffering. The charges were sensational and profoundly disturbing to Russell both politically and personally, but numerous circumstances made the charges look suspicious. Because Birkhead had moved to Louisiana and brought charges from there, the case was regarded as a federal offense. This, not by chance, forced Governor Russell back to federal district court in Oxford to be humiliated in front of his enemies. The Birkhead case, many believed, was a frame-up designed by his former ally Theodore "The Man" Bilbo and intended to end any hopes Russell had of going on to the U.S. Senate. Russell and Bilbo already had a vicious falling-out that came to physical blows. Bilbo had sworn vengeance against Lee Russell, and insiders believed Bilbo paid Birkhead to make the accusations. Russell's side apparently found incriminating evidence of this plot, and Bilbo, knowing that, fled to avoid a subpoena that would force him to testify and possibly expose his plot. He was eventually found hiding in a barn behind a frightened calf and was dragged to court in Oxford. But Bilbo steadfastly refused to testify, claiming that whatever he knew about the case was privileged information acquired as Russell's legal counsel. The jury, meanwhile, acquitted Russell after less than half an hour of deliberation. Russell had denounced the suit as "the most damnable blackmail conspiracy in the history of Mississippi" and blamed it on the "malicious attempts of enemies to blacken my character." The scandal ruined Russell nonetheless. He left Oxford, never to return. The young man who had come to town and been humiliated twenty years earlier must have left feeling some of the same rage. The Russell-Birkhead affair "left a nauseating stench in the nostrils of many Mississippians," whether they suspected the charges were true or that it was a frame-up. Lee Russell finished out his term and returned to private law practice in Jackson. His brother Albert bought his house in Oxford, but other family members also left Oxford after the Birkhead scandal. When Lee Russell died in 1943, the *Oxford Eagle* barely mentioned the county's only native son to serve as governor.[79]

The court later found Bilbo in contempt and sentenced him to thirty days in the Oxford jail. After serving ten of the thirty days of his sentence in the Oxford jail, Bilbo staged his release as the kickoff to his next political campaign. He arranged in advance for a grandstand on the courthouse square where a large crowd gathered. Holding up a brick in one hand and a school textbook in the other, Bilbo promised to run for governor again and pave every main road in Mississippi with bricks manufactured in Parchman Prison and provide free textbooks to every schoolchild. There were ten planks in his platform—one for each day he served of his jail sentence. He did not win that election, but he went on to serve Mississippi as governor from 1928 to 1932 and U.S. senator for three terms beginning in 1934. During his last term the Bilbonic Plague found a whole new life in his virulent opposition to the emerging civil rights movement.[80]

Country Boys Come to Town

Lee Russell was only the more notable of many ambitious country people aspiring to wealth and position in town during the early twentieth century. Few were more notable for their success than the Avent family, whom many think inspired aspects of Faulkner's Snopes saga. There were several families in the county with the name Avent or Avant. The Avents we are concerned with here came from a pioneer family from North Carolina that settled in the eastern part of Lafayette County around 1839. Benjamin Avent, the family patriarch, fathered fourteen children with his first wife and four more with his second wife, the last when he was seventy-six years of age. Though this part of the county was comparatively hilly and less fertile, land was cheap and plentiful. Benjamin Avent farmed the land and garnered considerable property; by 1860 he claimed ownership of eleven slaves and $19,000 in real estate and personal property. The Avent clan remained numerous, most of them still farming the land at the turn of the century.

It was Benjamin Avent's grandson Thomas Wesley Avent, born in 1859, who in midlife began the migration from the hill country into Oxford Town. He had been farming land in the area around Liberty Hill, a small rural church in the northeastern quarter of the county. Judging from his holdings, T. W. Avent was more Varner than Snopes. He owned some two thousand acres and operated a cotton gin. In 1883 Avent married Sidney Parks, the daughter of another large and resourceful family in Beat Two. Their union was prolific. Thomas and Sidney Avent had fifteen children, but nine died during birth or infancy.

It was the tragic loss of their daughter that compelled them to forsake the country for town. Somehow during cotton ginning time, September 1900, Etta, almost four years old, wandered into the gin and was mangled by the machinery. Thomas and Sidney were deeply distraught and decided to sell the gin and the farm and move to town. They wanted their remaining five sons to acquire better schooling in Oxford so that they would have a chance to escape rural life. Thomas, now over forty, sold the property in Liberty Hill and moved his family into Oxford to start their new life. The Avents, in fact, had swapped their land for a store in Oxford, but it was only after they arrived that they discovered they were duped. The business was heavily encumbered, and the Avents would face some difficult times getting on their feet again. While Thomas worked at the store, Sidney ran a boardinghouse at their home on Madison and North Fourteenth. Despite their shaky beginning, Thomas Avent rose in wealth and position. In 1910, in partnership with Colonel Falkner, he became one of the founders and directors of the First National Bank.[81]

The Avent family rapidly became a prominent feature of Oxford business, government, church, and social affairs. All five sons established prominent positions in banking, farming, medicine, and business. The Avent children "evidenced a marked degree of ambition," it was said, because of their father's early business reversals in Oxford. They "had to make their own way and with some assistance to each other were quite successful in achieving their goals in the quest of an education and establishing themselves as influential business and professional men in their communities." Together they established a kind of Snopesian conglomerate of enterprise and power in the community. John Edward Avent was an officer in the bank with his father and Colonel Falkner, and he became a leading merchant and civic booster who was constantly involved in campaigns to promote Oxford's growth. John, alas, had been one of the more enthusiastic promoters of Oxford's oil boom in 1920. Willie Avent was a large farmer in the southern part of the county. James Kirl Avent became a physician and was elected president of the Mississippi Medical Association. Audley Avent had large farming interests and owned Avent Gin and a retail grocery in Oxford. He also acquired "extensive" real estate holdings, joined his brother as director of the bank, was elected city alderman, served as deacon of First Baptist Church, and became a major benefactor of the church. All the Avents were successful, prosperous, and upstanding members of the community their parents had come to around 1900 with their boardinghouse and an encumbered store.

None of the Avent children was more notable for success than Thomas Edison "T. E." Avent. Born in 1891, he studied pharmacy at the university and opened Avent's Drug Store on the square after graduating in 1914. He married in 1919 and the next year expanded his operations by launching a dairy business. The threat of typhoid and other diseases from contaminated milk had been a constant problem for Oxford residents, and consequently people were beginning to prefer milk provided by commercial dairies instead of taking chances with their milk cow in the back yard. T. E. Avent began with one cow at the end of 1920 and soon had a herd of more than three hundred. When more farmers began shifting from cotton production to cattle raising, Avent sold off his herd and concentrated on processing the milk he now bought from local producers. Avent Dairy grew rapidly at its plant on North Street.

Beyond the drugstore and dairy were an array of real estate and farming operations that made T. E. Avent one of the richest men in the county. Among his real estate developments was Avent Acres, a subdivision in the northeast quarter of town constructed after World War II. It was Oxford's version of Levittown, tract houses, all similar, on small lots, designed to be affordable for returning veterans and other first-time home buyers. Avent had been an active city alderman, and he donated to the city a park adjacent to his subdivision, which was named in honor of him and his wife. This subdivision was surely a model for Faulkner's Eula Acres, one of Flem Snopes's many enterprises. Faulkner scorned this kind of modern housing, "a subdivision of standardized Veterans' Housing matchboxes" with their "minute glass-walled houses set as neat and orderly and antiseptic as cribs in a nursery ward, in new subdivisions . . . which had once been the lawn or back yard of kitchen garden of the old residencies." [82] But for young families coming to town and GIs returning from service, these new homes, often financed by government loans, were the American dream.

T. E. Avent's philanthropy extended in other directions as well, as a benefactor of the university and the town. When he bought up a lot with an antebellum home named Cedar Oaks on North Lamar, he donated land elsewhere in town to which the house was moved. It became the Heritage House, a club for Oxford women. Shortly before his death, out at Liberty Hill T. E. Avent, returned some of his philanthropy to his country birthplace by donating money for a new church. Made of metal so it "would not burn down or rot down," the church was dedicated by T. E. Avent at a large and well-publicized ceremony attended by an array of dignitaries, including the university chancellor, a senator, and Oxford's mayor and aldermen.

It was a poignant reminder of the country origins of one of Oxford's new men of wealth. When he died two years later, T. E. Avent was heralded as "an unselfish and much-loved philanthropist." [83]

Joe Parks, also thought by many to be a partial model for Faulkner's Flem Snopes, was another ambitious new man who came into Oxford from the country and rose to prominence in Oxford. He always wore a small black bow tie, one of Flem Snopes's affectations, and he was an extraordinarily shrewd and successful trader and deal maker. Joe Parks had been on the board of directors of Colonel Falkner's First National Bank since 1911 and was involved in a movement to oust Colonel Falkner as president in 1920; he became the next president. About the same time, Parks got involved in the bogus Oxford oil boom and was reported organizing the oil company and buying stock. It is not altogether clear whether he and his fellow promoters were victims or perpetrators of this scheme.

Parks came from Beat Two, the same northeastern quarter of the county where the Avent clan had originated. He was born on a farm in 1867 and continued farming and operating a mill in the country until 1919, when he moved to Oxford, immediately before his rise to the bank presidency. He had long since been involved in business and politics in town. In 1907 he was elected beat supervisor, part of the Vardaman revolution that swept much of the old guard out of office. He served for sixteen years on the Board of Supervisors and also did duty on both the county and city school boards where he was an ardent advocate of good schools. Parks built a strong reputation as a successful businessman as well. When he took over as president of the bank, the *Eagle* confirmed that "he is a fine businessman, and until recently one of the most successful farmers and mill men in this county." Parks, the editor added, has now moved to Oxford "and the people welcome him and his family." Many locals credited his leadership when the bank weathered the Great Depression. Parks and his first wife, Lillian, had twelve children before she died. He married Sally Houston in 1919, the year he moved to town. Parks served as elder in the Presbyterian Church and continued as president of the bank until his death in 1951. Parks and Avent may have supplied some of the physical characteristics and business shrewdness that Faulkner attributed to Flem Snopes and his clan, but both were exemplary and beloved citizens of the town they had adopted.[84]

The Parks and Avents were among the more prominent of the country people who made good in town; there were many others who in more modest ways reflected the same theme. Walker Coffey was only nine when his father finally moved the family into "Oxford Town" to stay in 1915. The Coffeys were descendants of Lafayette County pioneer Hugh Coffey, whom we met earlier as one of the plain folk migrating west to Mississippi in 1836.

They had lived in the northeastern section of the county for generations, a long line of farmers and country people who fought for the Confederacy, worked hard, had large families, voted Democratic, and attended the Baptist church. A country school was named in Hugh Coffey's honor near the old family homestead. Walker Coffey's father fought in the Spanish-American War, married, and began life farming in Bay Springs near the Caswell community east of Oxford. He worked hard all his life farming, raising cattle, running a sawmill, a gristmill, and one year working in Memphis as a streetcar conductor.

In the fall of 1915, the Coffey family sold the house and mill at Bay Springs and moved to Oxford, where they hoped their son, Walker, and his two sisters could "get a good education and be somebody in the world." They moved into a rented four-room house on Second North Street (now North 14th) that had one water faucet and an outdoor privy. They kept a milk cow, some chickens, and a kitchen garden in the back yard. The father found a job delivering mail in a mule-drawn buggy to Tula and Delay in the southern part of the county.

Walker, nine years old in 1915, went to school starting in the fourth grade that fall. The teacher called him to the board and asked him to do the multiplication tables. Walker stood in front of the board, chalk in hand, utterly frozen in humiliation. He had only a few months of schooling before this and had no idea what four times two even meant. "This was the biggest disappointment and the most embarrassment that I have ever experienced as I had a fierce sense of pride," he remembered decades later. They put him back into the third grade, and, for a time, he resented school. But his parents told him education was important to him, so he studied mightily, learned his times tables, and within three years he was number one in his class.

Walker Coffey worked most of the time he was growing up. Beginning at age nine or ten he worked after school at Stone's dairy driving cows to pasture for three dollars a month and a gallon of skimmed milk. Later he delivered newspapers for twenty-five dollars a month. The job left him only five hours of sleep a night, but he now could buy the things other boys had: a baseball and glove, some nice clothes, candy, and all his school supplies, which took a burden off his father. He took other jobs helping his father buying cross ties and delivering ice for the Bagget Ice Plant. "I loved making money," he recalled. Some of his "uptown" friends would see him dirty and wet but he "felt proud . . . doing honest work." "You are just as good as any boy in this town," his mother told him hundreds of times; "you have good blood in you."[85] It was that same "fierce sense of pride," as Walker Coffey put it, that drove him to work hard and succeed in competition with the town boys.

The Coffeys' material progress could be measured in the houses they lived in, the clothes they wore, and the cars they drove. They moved every year or two to a newer, slightly larger and nicer home. They rented until 1921, when they bought a small five-room house on North Seventh Street for $1,200. Three years later they added indoor plumbing once city sewers were brought out to their neighborhood. By 1925 the Coffeys bought a Dodge touring car and the family went on an unforgettable camping vacation in Florida. Later that year Walker Coffey's "daddy" drove him to Starkville, where he entered Mississippi A & M College to study engineering. He did well in college, joined a fraternity (Lee Russell's ban had been repealed), and four years later took his first job in Atlanta.[86] Walker Coffey, now twenty-three, had fulfilled the dream that brought his family to Oxford fourteen years earlier.

Snopesism Reconsidered

These sketches of country boys making good in town cast a different light on the sinister image some have of subhuman Snopeses who are seen crawling in from the country like locusts to invade the town and topple its traditional leaders. Faulkner's tale of the Snopes clan is no Horatio Alger story of American success through pluck and luck, but neither is it the dark legend of villainous usurpers destroying the agrarian Arcadia of Yoknapatawpha that some find in these stories. The social phenomenon of sharp trading and ambition was pervasive in Yoknapatawpha; Flem Snopes was just a quick learner and a skillful player. Faulkner's treatment of Flem Snopes and the whole phenomenon of Snopesism was less moralistic and outraged than it was a mix of awe, ridicule, and no small amount of snobbery. Several Faulkner scholars have made these points in reading the fictional Snopeses, but their historical counterparts, the poor whites and "rednecks", deserve a more discerning and compassionate review.[87]

John Falkner, the author's brother, remembered vividly country people like the Russells, Avents, Parks, Coffeys, and others who were coming into Oxford to make their way during his youth. Many were poor white sharecroppers with "a little more 'git up and git'" than their neighbors who stayed behind on the farms. "They came to town for a better living for themselves and better education for their children, and by their initiative they secured both." At first they might live in "jerry-built frame houses that rented for only a few dollars a month," jamming large families full of

Lafayette County Courthouse and Confederate Memorial, 1930s.
(Courtesy of the Mississippi Department of Archives and History)

children and assorted kin into small two-bedroom houses. They picked up menial jobs, then opened businesses of their own, often cafes and small grocery stores. Finally, the more successful among them "moved onto our Square and became merchants and town clerks and aldermen." "Before you actually knew they were coming, to your surprise they were already there." John Falkner admitted that the children of these newly arrived country people often "studied harder than we did and most of them made better grades." They had the "same driving urge their parents had. They took advantage of every opportunity. They were persistent and insistent."[88]

Established families in town, John Falkner conceded, had "coasted along in the same old rut that we considered good enough for us all," and the arrival of these "Snopeses" came as a rude wake-up alarm. When the "new blood" took over the banks, shops, and town government "we didn't like it," he admitted, but "it was probably good for us, for it made us hump along more lively than we had before in order to keep ahead or even to hold onto what we had."[89]

This probably exaggerated the differences between the old town "aristocracy" and the rustic arrivistes coming in from the countryside, but it captures the mix of grudging admiration and condescension many townspeople must have felt toward their more successful neighbors who climbed into the upper reaches of the town's economy, government, and social circles. For young William Faulkner, "Count No Account," the presence of these ambitious country people provoked the kind of derision that often veils jealousy or insecurity. With his friend Phil Stone, Faulkner concocted the Snopes characters out of a mix of local anecdotes and exaggerated black humor. Stone saw the "rise of the redneck" as a major social challenge to the old order, and it was Stone who guided early Faulkner critics to see this struggle between Old South aristocracy and Snopesian perfidy as a major theme in Faulkner's work.[90]

But Phil Stone's view of the rise of the "rednecks" was that of an embattled opponent, a descendant of the Delta planter class who was politically opposed to the Vardaman faction. The Falkners and Butlers, we have seen, were always town people who had always been part of the commercial culture of trade. The Falkners were also firmly aligned with Vardaman and his followers, and they had many business ties to those ambitious country people who served as models for Flem Snopes. Faulkner delighted in ridiculing the rustic vulgarity of the Snopeses and in detailing the cunning talent of Flem Snopes, but his point of view was more subtle than Stone and others would have it. Faulkner seemed to understand that these country people were imitating, not subverting, the society they were trying to rise within. Moreover, they were agents of change, modernizing forces challenging the old guard and old ways.[91]

Whatever critics and readers make of the fiction, if we turn to the historical counterparts of the Snopeses with any degree of compassion, we can see a very familiar American story of migratory country people striving to improve their lives. Along with the successful Russells, Avents, Parks, and Coffeys came hundreds of farm families escaping the grinding poverty, worn-out land, and weevil-infested cotton fields to seek whatever opportunity for work and education they could find in town. What is clear from their stories, especially in Walker Coffey's autobiography, is that their ambitions for education, wealth, and social improvement were motivated by a strong sense of pride and family honor. They sought respect, not just wealth, and they deserved respect as much as their antecedents in town.

The town's established families, like the Falkners and Stones, may have looked down their noses at these country people who were taking over the town's economy and positions of influence. They no doubt ridiculed their rustic manners, dress, and ways of living. At school the town kids shunned the "country children" no matter how good they were in school or sports.[92] Some of the old guard in town may also have despised the new political demagogues who appealed with great success to the racism and class resentment of poor whites. But in the end, these new people from the country were not so different in their goals and values from the old elite. Faulkner understood this at some level, and he created in Flem Snopes not a demon with alien values but a pure distillation of common traits. Instead of looking through a microscope at some parasitic species, Faulkner was holding up a mirror in which we may see values and behavior pervasive in the town and the countryside.

Not only a new century and a new way of thinking, but of acting and
behaving too: now you could go to bed in a train in Jefferson and wake up
tomorrow morning in New Orleans or Chicago; there were electric lights
and running water in almost every house in town except the cabins of
Negroes; and now the town . . . paved the entire street between the depot
and the hotel . . . every morning a wagon came to your very door with
artificial ice and put it in your icebox on the back gallery for you . . . a
new time, a new age: there were screens in windows now; . . . Moving
faster and faster: from the speed of two horses on either side of a polished
tongue, to that of thirty then fifty then a hundred under a tin bonnet no
bigger than a wash-tub."

—WILLIAM FAULKNER, Requiem for a Nun

epilogue What Was, Is

It was within the dynamic context of Oxford Town that William Faulkner
came of age in the early twentieth century, and it was from the vantage
point of the town that he observed the native land he wrote about. Many
readers and critics, especially those outside the South, found in Faulkner's
Yoknapatawpha a colorful, somewhat bizarre rendering of a remote enclave
of a folk society that seemed frozen in time and almost immune to the
dynamics of change transforming the rest of modern America. Faulkner,
however, was very conscious of the massive forces of change that had swept
through his part of the world, and that is what his Yoknapatawpha saga
chronicles.

Toward the end of his writing career, Faulkner took several occasions to review the story he had told about Yoknapatawpha. "And now at last, I have some perspective on all I have done," he wrote in 1953. "I realize for the first time what an amazing gift I had: uneducated in every formal sense, without even very literate, let alone literary, companions, yet to have made the things I made. I don't know where it came from." [1] Where it came from lay within Faulkner's own genius as a writer but also from deep within the history of the place where he lived.

If we look back on that history, the most salient feature of the past is the constant motion of people through the land and the motion of time and change. One imagines a compressed version of this story, like a preview to a movie, as a succession of people moving across the stage. First, the ancient Chickasaws in some unrecorded long ago, well before Europeans even dreamed of a New World, move eastward across the land following the oracle pole of their priests. They finally settled in the towns just east of Yoknapatawpha, the land divided, which served as hunting grounds and eventually the site of a few small Indian settlements. Then, centuries later, coming northwest into the Land of the Chicaza in 1540, DeSoto with his expedition of Spanish soldiers come clattering through the forest to find their winter camp. Men in armor, mounted on strange-looking beasts bring with them other exotic animals the Chickasaws had never seen. Weapons of metal, guns and swords, knives, and lances all introduced a technology that would change the world as they knew it forever. Then a brief, violent encounter followed by a hundred years of relative stillness, prelude to the massive storm about to come. Then a century or more of movement and exchange, back and forth: English traders bringing things from the white world—guns and knives, hides and technology, liquor and African slaves, blood and genes—leaving the world of the Chickasaws a part of the European world as much as the Europeans had become a part of their world. Full-bloods and whites, mixed-bloods and Africans, and every conceivable combination of the three races produced a mix of genes and cultures that whites nonetheless classified as Indian, uncivilized, and unfit to be part of the American nation. Having persuaded the Chickasaws they were, themselves, a "nation" that "owned" the lands they inhabited, it stood to reason they also possessed the right to sell their land. Piece by piece, they ceded their lands, down to the homelands of northern Mississippi. Then, President Jackson and his land-hungry supporters forced all the southern Indians to move west so the Americans could put their land to "better use."

More movement of people: the Chickasaws move west in long wagon trains, with droves of ponies, cattle, dogs, and chickens, their wagons brimming with artifacts whites had brought into their world. White settlers move west to take their place, arriving in covered wagons or on horseback.

Others come west in large coffles, chained together, slaves driven overland from Virginia, the Carolinas, and down from Tennessee and Kentucky into the new country of northern Mississippi. One lured by hope and greed, the other driven by the lash, two migratory streams pour, free and slave, into the newly formed Lafayette County, Mississippi. The newcomers come in only slightly faster than other settlers move out, farther west, to Texas or some other frontier. That churning population all the time growing, bringing by 1860 over three times the number of the entire Chickasaw nation within Lafayette County alone.

Then war came to the land divided. It began with a revolutionary movement led by fire-eaters who wanted to separate Mississippi from the nation that had given birth to it just a short time before. Four chaotic years of war follow with armies, civilians, and slaves moving across the land. Young men, mostly simple farmers, become soldiers, forming military companies, and gathering down at the depot where trains take them off to distant camps and battlefields—and graves. They go to war to defend their homes, their women, their families, and (some of them) their slaves, but they left all of them exposed to invasion, vandalism, and emancipation. Four years of armies moving across the land, some invading, others retreating, raiding, both sides foraging and pillaging the land in a war that turned against the people themselves. Slaves, who before had run away for a few days to see a spouse or lover, or protest a whipping before returning, now flee in mass out of bondage. Moving in large crowds, slave men, women, and children, north to Holly Springs and Grand Junction, acting on a knowledge that they were escaping something terrible called slavery and on a blind faith that they were going to something better called freedom. The "blue men" tell them what they somehow seem to know already—that they are slaves no more. More armies move back and forth, through and around Lafayette County, General Forrest striking the Union adroitly, but neither side able to secure control. Then the Union's last unforgettable visit in August 1864, which in a few hours leaves the town square a charred pile of rubble, the pride of Lafayette County, the courthouse, a blackened shell, which stands for years as a humiliating reminder of their defeat. Another civil war ensues lasting a decade; the war between North and South now imploding to become an internal, fratricidal war between races and political parties. Reconstruction was a war fought not against "foreign" carpetbaggers but between Lafayette County citizens over the most basic issues of racial supremacy and control of labor. Those who lost the revolution for independence won a counterrevolution that established white supremacy for the next century.

Both sides of that other war lost in the end. A long ordeal of racial repression coincided with chronic economic depression across much of the Deep South. In the countryside stagnation and depression fed on itself: one-crop agriculture, sharecropping, debt, grinding poverty, all intertwined with racial competition, violence, and subjugation.

Again, change would appear foremost in the movement of people, some escaping the countryside for town, others out of the South altogether. Blacks who had been responding to nearby opportunities for higher wages in the developing Delta or in Memphis, by World War I were poised to join the Great Migration northward. World War I shut off the flow of European immigrants to the industrial cities of the North precisely as it intensified world demand for American manufactured products. They turned to the most available source of labor, America's own black peasantry in the South. Northern manufacturers send labor agents south to recruit. None were more active than the Illinois Central Railroad, which came right through Lafayette County and into the Delta to pull thousands of blacks out of the cotton fields "up North" to Chicago, Detroit, and other northern cities. It was an exodus out of Jim Crow's reign of subordination and degradation that recalled the flight to freedom in 1863 their parents and grandparents had taken up in that time of Jubilee. Soon a vast network of family, kin, and neighbors stretches from Chicago and Detroit down to Mississippi sending news of a better life, making it easier for the next wave to leave.

There is migration within Lafayette County too: people moving from farm to town, first by wagon or mule, then by truck or automobile, along newly graded roads that smoothed the path between the two worlds. Soon more and more country people make permanent moves forsaking the county for the comforts of town life. Like immigrants coming into small houses in town, they gain a toehold at the edges of the urban economy and, in time, some climb its peaks. The town's population swelled by almost 50 percent in the 1920s alone, rising from two to nearly three thousand in 1930 and nearly four thousand twenty years later. In the early twentieth century, the whole society was shifting away from the countryside and toward town. Oxford had become the center of a new consumer culture powered by electricity and gasoline and offering a cornucopia of radios and movies, cars and washing machines, flush toilets and ready-made clothes, bananas, moon pies, ice cream sodas, and cold Coca-Cola at the fountain.[2]

These gadgets and consumer items, along with the paved streets and water tower, electric lights and gas, were more than just modern conveniences that made material life more comfortable for those who came to town. Along with these new technologies the town also fostered a progressive spirit that gave new life to the simple idea that progress was both desirable and within the competence of a new generation of leaders to effect.

Brimming with confidence and full of self-congratulatory bombast, these progressive townspeople were the harbingers of a spirit of hope that had all but died in the Civil War. Vardaman, Bilbo, and Russell also gave political expression to this progressive spirit. Though limited to their white constituents, their programs for better schools, good roads, and other social reforms spoke to a new hope for improvement and advancement. African Americans heading to the urban North and white country people moving into town, both pursuing a better life, were corresponding signs of movement and self-improvement that came alive in the early twentieth century.

When the Great Depression descended in the 1930s there were those in the rural South who might not have noticed, having suffered their own protracted depression for the last several decades. It hit the rural countryside hard, nonetheless, and it came just at the time when the South was beginning to enjoy some of the prosperity that had spread out from the cities during the 1920s. Convinced that southern poverty and backwardness was a burden to the entire American economy, the federal government in 1936 defined the South as the "Nation's Number One Economic Problem." The New Deal channeled federal revenues and labor into programs to rehabilitate the South and its economy. Out around Abbeville a Civilian Conservation Corps camp employed hundreds of young unemployed workers who helped heal the ravaged land. They planted thousands of pine trees and kudzu plants, a rapidly growing vine imported from Japan. Within a short time, the kudzu had grown over the gaping "Mississippi canyons" and road cuts, forming a thick green gauze that covered, even if it would never heal, the ulcerous lesions left from a century of reckless land use. Under the hot Mississippi sun the kudzu rapidly grew into the trees, soon devouring forests, abandoned cars, old mule barns, and sharecropper shacks, as though this exotic agent of the modern world were determined to obliterate the obsolete countryside.

Again, war set off a massive movement of people within and out of Mississippi. The Great Migration, slowed by the economic depression of the 1930s, resumes with double the force during and after World War II. The development of the mechanical cotton picker finally offered an alternative to cheap black labor, and just in time. The main pull was still north to Chicago and other midwestern industrial cities, but many also move out west to war industries in California. Before the Great Migration about nine in ten African Americans lived in the former slave states; only half remained before it finished.[3]

The black exodus out of the Deep South was more than just a response to new opportunities in the North and West; it was a delayed response to the long ordeal of racial subjugation that had descended in Mississippi after

Oxford on the Hill, painting by John McCready, 1939.
(Courtesy of the University of Mississippi)

Reconstruction. Their loss of voting rights left them without any political leverage and exposed them to a regimen of exploitation with little recourse to justice. The withdrawal of federal protection and the wholesale repression of any white dissent against the rule of white supremacy left blacks in Mississippi alone to face a reign of oppression and terror. Though lynchings were no longer the public rituals they had been at the time Nelse Patton was mutilated and hanged in front of the Oxford courthouse in 1908, brutal violence remained the ultimate expression of white supremacy. In 1935, another fatal September, Oxford witnessed one more lynching. A black male named Ellwood Higginbotham stood trial for killing a white man he claimed had entered his house at night with a drawn pistol. Higginbotham's defense was plausible, but he knew he was doomed and he fled after the shooting. A large posse with dogs swarmed over the countryside in search of him, finally apprehended him, and brought him to trial in Oxford. While the all-white jury deliberated his fate, a mob outside the courthouse feared they might acquit on grounds of self-defense; two jurors, in fact, were holding out for that. Before a verdict could be decided, the mob broke into the jail, dragged Higginbotham out, and hanged him from a tree outside of town. Between 1880 and 1945 Mississippi had witnessed nearly six hundred lynchings, most all of them black males, including many very young adolescents. Mississippi led the South in its reign of violence and in the severity of black subjugation. No white jury would ever convict whites guilty of such crimes, and the press routinely attributed the lynchings to "parties unknown."[4]

To black people in Mississippi the reminders of white supremacy were evident in less dramatic form every day of their lives. From the wretched schools their children attended to the segregated rest rooms and drinking fountains at the courthouse, the pattern of exclusion and inferiority was both symbolic and purposeful. The political advantage in excluding black voters may have been obvious, but the economic and social benefits of white supremacy lay more in the intangible psychology of race. The ultimate purpose of the system of segregation, subjugation, and intimidation was to remind blacks that they were not full citizens, not the equal of white people, and that there was nothing they could do about it—except leave.

William Faulkner had been wrestling with Mississippi's legacy of racial inequity beginning with *Light in August* (1932), and he continued to do so in *Absalom, Absalom!* (1936), *Go Down, Moses* (1941), and numerous short stories and parts of other novels. But it was not until *Intruder in the Dust* (1948) that he confronted directly the injustice of contemporary race relations in the South. The story centers on Lucas Beauchamp, grandson of "Old Carothers" McCaslin and Tomasina, his slave and daughter. Lucas Beauchamp refuses to act like a victim of white racism. He is a proud, independent, landowning man who carries himself with great dignity and depends on no favors from white people to maintain his independence. He is one of Faulkner's strongest African American characters, but the story is more about the responsibility of white people to deliver racial justice to the likes of Lucas Beauchamp than it is about what blacks might do to win it. Faulkner resorted to familiar stereotypes when he cast the rural, racist "rednecks" against the decent, paternalistic, upper-class townspeople. The Gowries are a family of rural poor whites with a reputation for crime who live in a rough area in the hills of Beat 4. They despise Lucas Beauchamp because he acts proud and independent, and one of the Gowries frames him for murder and then leads the mob to lynch him. Chick Mallison is the son of a well-to-do town family who becomes indebted to Lucas Beauchamp when he rescues him from an icy creek one winter day. Chick is frustrated that Lucas will not play the "nigger" in response to his paternalistic bestowing of gifts, which he gives in order to cancel his debt to a Negro. Finally, Chick is able to do that by coming to the rescue and solving the crime while Lucas Beauchamp is in jail. Chick enlists Miss Eunice Habersham, an elderly woman from a once aristocratic old family in decline. Her parents owned Molly Beauchamp, Lucas's wife, during slavery times. Though her family's wealth has faded, Miss Habersham acts out of a tradition of upper-class paternalism and her instinctive trust and respect for Lucas Beauchamp. Chick's young black friend, Aleck Sander, helps the other two, and Lucas guides them from his cell, but it is the young white boy and the old white woman who are the real heroes of the story. Along with solving the mystery, Chick and Miss Habersham have to persuade lawyer Gavin Stevens to overcome his racist assumptions and serve justice. Faulkner has Stevens speak for white moderates, like himself, who become burdened by guilt once they realize the injustice done to Lucas and all his race. It is they, the decent white people of the South, who must give justice to "Sambo," he explains. If they fail to do so, then the North, the federal government, will once again feel obliged to intervene and do it for them, only to fail as they had before. "I'm defending Sambo from the North and East and West—the outlanders who will fling him decades back not merely into injustice but into grief and agony and violence too by forcing on us laws based on the idea that man's injustice to man can be abolished overnight by police." [5]

The publication of Intruder in the Dust in 1948 coincided with the emerging challenge to racial subjugation in Mississippi and America. That year the civil rights plank introduced by northern liberals split apart the Democratic Party. When the novel was turned into a movie the next year, Hollywood came to Yoknapatawpha and filled the cast with local people. Suddenly the author who had scandalized the community ever since the publication of Sanctuary (1930) became a local hero. At the same time, the novel and film exposed to national scrutiny painful aspects of racial injustice most white Mississippians preferred not to have in the limelight.

While the filming of Intruder took place, a black man named Nathan Cohran was arrested for allegedly raping a white woman. Cohran was a partner with the woman's husband and had been a frequent guest of theirs when he would come over and drink beer with them in the kitchen. Then her husband went away to Birmingham for work, and Cohran continued his evening visits with his partner's wife drinking beer in the kitchen. She was probably afraid that the neighbors had seen him coming and going, so she told her husband and accused Cohran of raping her. Cohran was in the jail when the film was being shot and the film crew and local officials became concerned that the extras recruited for the movie might get art and life confused as they gathered about the jail to lynch Lucas Beauchamp. The remains of the holes in the jail's walls were still there from the night forty years earlier when another mob had lynched Nelse Patton. Nathan Cohran was removed to the safety of the Holly Springs jail, while Miss Habersham turned back the fictional mob with nothing more than her moral resolution.[6]

The statement *Intruder in the Dust* made against racial injustice, moderate though it was, positioned Faulkner in a more favorable light among northern literary critics. Faulkner had already won literary acclaim in France, Italy, and other parts of Europe and Asia. The publication of Cowley's *Portable Faulkner* in 1946 helped rescue his work from obscurity in America, and *Intruder in the Dust* now strengthened his bid for recognition as a major American writer. In 1949 Faulkner won the Nobel Prize for literature and suddenly was thrust into the limelight as a spokesman not only for American literature but also for democracy and peace in the Cold War cultural battles of the 1950s.[7] Faulkner stepped uncomfortably onto the world stage, precisely as the civil rights movement was beginning to expose racial injustice in the South. In 1955, a year after the U.S. Supreme Court had ruled segregated schools unconstitutional, James Silver, a historian at the University of Mississippi, managed to persuade Faulkner to speak at the Southern Historical Association meeting in Memphis. Faulkner made one of his strongest statements against segregation when he urged white moderates in the South to accept the inevitable and take the lead in desegregating the South and ensuring racial justice before the federal government intervened. We "will not sit quietly by and see our native land, the South, . . . wreck and ruin itself twice in less than a hundred years, over the Negro question," Faulkner implored. "We speak now against the day when our Southern people who will resist to the last these inevitable changes in social relations . . . will say, 'Why didn't someone tell us this before?' "[8]

Most white people in Oxford and Lafayette County did not want to "be told" now or anytime, and not by a fellow southerner, that things would have to change. Faulkner's family and neighbors denounced his statements, and anonymous enemies made threatening telephone calls. The forces for change in Mississippi came not from Faulkner's idealized white moderates but instead from its own black citizens. Together with young black and white civil rights workers from outside the state and from the legal and political forces of the federal government, they led a revolution against Jim Crow's rule in the South. Some called it the Second Reconstruction, and, in many respects, the civil rights era resembled the events of a century earlier.

At home in Oxford, the civil rights movement had only recently begun to stir. Nathan Hodges Jr. was a disabled army veteran from Meridian who came out of World War II with the conviction that "we were citizens as good as our white brothers." During an investigation of the senatorial election of 1946 Hodges testified against Senator Bilbo and took pride in opposing the "Bilbonic Plague" in Mississippi. Hodges headed north to Chicago to study the trade of mortician and afterward returned to Mississippi, arriving in Oxford in 1951 to establish a funeral home. There was virtually no organized voice for black civil rights in Oxford, so he and others in 1952 established a local branch of the NAACP, which went under the discreet name of the Lafayette County Improvement Association. They met in churches where no whites would disturb them. They paid their dues in money orders of $50, which did not need to be filled out at the post office and could therefore not be traced locally. Between two and three hundred local blacks joined the organization. Arthur Herod, a sawmill laborer, had lost some of his fingers in an accident at the mill and could not work. Once he became active in the NAACP no white employer would hire him anyway. Later Herod went into the ministry and became active in the civil rights movement. Herod and Hodges became the leaders in Lafayette County's nascent civil rights movement. They attended meetings throughout the state, while the Oxford organization limited itself to quiet meetings and paying dues. When Hodges left for Aberdeen in 1956 the organization discontinued, but he returned to reorganize a local NAACP chapter in 1962, this time with no disguised name. By then, Oxford had developed a corps of black educators, clergy, and business owners whose aspirations provided the foundation for the local civil rights movement. The Reverend W. R. Redmond Jr. and the Reverend Wayne Johnson both brought concern for education to their role as black church leaders. Della R. Davidson and Susie Marshall were educated at Rust College in Holly Springs and served as teachers and school administrators in Oxford and Lafayette County. Mabel McCune, co-owner of Oxford's Colored Funeral Home, served as the first president of the NAACP. For blacks in Lafayette County, the town was the incubator of change and the base for a new cadre of community leaders.[9]

Meanwhile, from outside Mississippi, the U.S. Supreme Court had shaken the pillars of Jim Crow's regime in 1954 with its decision that segregated schools were unconstitutional. The *Brown* decision was a constitutional blow to Jim Crow that energized the civil rights movement to challenge other forms of racial discrimination with direct action protest and civil disobedience.

Whites in Mississippi experienced significant changes in many aspects of their lives in the twentieth century, but any threat to the racial order met with fierce resistance. The Mississippi legislature answered the *Brown* decision with new laws to stymie integration. It set up the State Sovereignty Commission, whose purpose was to monitor and disrupt the civil rights movement.

It may have been fortunate for Faulkner that he died in July 1962, just before the day of reckoning he had prophesied. James Meredith, a black veteran of the U.S. Air Force, won admittance to the University of Mississippi, and he arrived in late September to register. The campus was filled with hundreds of federal marshals who were there to protect Meredith. In a publicly broadcast speech from the White House, President John F. Kennedy pleaded with white Mississippians to uphold the law and the honor of Mississippi, which had been proven on the battlefield and gridiron. He even invoked the name of former senator L. Q. C. Lamar, paragon of southern patriotism and reconciliation. But as Kennedy spoke, a full-scale riot was breaking out around the Lyceum, the university administration building where Meredith had gone to register. Waving Confederate flags and shouting racial epithets and insults against Kennedy and the federal marshals, a mob of angry whites had gathered at the university to protest this black man's violation of Ole Miss. They began hurling stones, bricks, bottles, and pipes at the federal marshals, who fought back by launching tear gas into the crowd. President Kennedy insisted that Governor Ross Barnett, an outspoken opponent of desegregation, order the Mississippi Highway Patrol to campus to restore order, but nothing happened. Finally, Kennedy ordered the National Guard to intervene.

The battle that raged in Oxford that fall of 1962 took place almost exactly one century after General Grant's invasion during the Civil war.[10] Again, whites in Mississippi plunged into a rebellion against change. Again, extremist politicians led them, while the most fanatical proponents of white supremacy and states' rights made it dangerous for moderate whites to speak against the day Faulkner had warned them about. The violence and hatred that exploded in Oxford that fall was the past living on in the present, determining every thought and gesture. "Maybe nothing ever happens once and is finished," Faulkner wrote. "Maybe happen is never once." [11] Lying in his fresh grave on the other side of town, he had written of what he knew and what he imagined happening in the past—and happening again—in the place he called Yoknapatawpha, the land divided.

Abbreviations

AmS   George P. Rawick, ed., *The American Slave: A Composite Autobiography*, supplement, series 1, vol. 10, Mississippi Narratives

FB   Freedman's Bureau Records, NARA

LCC   Lafayette County Courthouse, Oxford, Mississippi

LCDA   Lafayette County Database, Aggregate—county-level data on demographic and economic statistics compiled from a multitude of published U.S. census reports, 1840–1960, spreadsheets

LCDI   Lafayette County Database, Individual-level—data compiled from U.S. census manuscripts, 1840–70, in SPSS files

MDAH   Mississippi Department of Archives and History, Jackson, Mississippi

mf   microform

ms   manuscript

NARA   National Archives and Records Administration, Washington, D.C.

OR   Official Records, *The War of the Rebellion: A Compilation of the Official Records of the Union and Confederate Armies* (Washington, D.C.: Government Printing Office, 1886)

PMHS   *Publications of the Mississippi Historical Society*

SCC   Southern Claims Commission Records, Mississippi, RG 217, NARA

SHC   Southern Historical Collection, University of North Carolina, Chapel Hill

SHGSC   Skipwith Historical and Genealogical Society Collection, Oxford-Lafayette County Public Library

UM   University of Mississippi

UMSC   University of Mississippi, Special Collections, John Williams Library

WPA   Works Progress Administration, Source Material, Lafayette County, microfilm and typescript, MDAH

Introduction

1. Harry Runyan, *A Faulkner Glossary* (New York: Citadel Press, 1964), is helpful in dating the historical focus of Faulkner's novels and short stories.

2. Ward L. Miner, *The World of William Faulkner* (New York: Grove Press, 1952); Joseph Blotner, *Faulkner: A Biography*, 2 vols. (New York: Random House, 1974). Other excellent explorations of the parallels and links between the actual and apocryphal worlds of Faulkner's fiction and history include *Faulkner's Mississippi: Land*

into *Legend*, video, directed by Robert Oesterling, script by Evans Harrington, 1965; Arthur F. Kinney, ed., *Critical Essays on William Faulkner: The Compson Family* (Boston: G. K. Hall, 1982); *Critical Essays on William Faulkner: The Sartoris Family* (Boston: G. K. Hall, 1985); *Critical Essays on William Faulkner: The McCaslin Family*, (Boston: G. K. Hall, 1990); Charles S. Aiken, "Faulkner's Yoknapatawpha County: Geographical Fact Into Fiction," *Geographical Review* 67 (Jan. 1977): 1–21; Aiken, "Faulkner's Yoknapatawpha County: A Place in the American South," *Geographical Review* 69 (July 1979): 331–48; Gabriele Gutting, *Yoknapatawpha: The Function of Geographical and Historical Facts in William Faulkner's Fictional Picture of the Deep South* (Frankfurt am Main: Peter Lang, 1992); Elmo Howell, *Mississippi Scenes: Notes on Literature and History* (Memphis: E. Howell, 1992). Thomas S. Hines, *William Faulkner and the Tangible Past: The Architecture of Yoknapatawpha* (Berkeley: University of California Press, 1996), and Martin J. Dain, *Faulkner's County: Yoknapatawpha*, (New York: Random House, 1964), offer visual portraits of the world Faulkner wrote about. See also Tom Rankin, ed., *Faulkner's World: The Photographs of Martin J. Dain* (Jackson: University Press of Mississippi, 1997). John B. Cullen and Floyd C. Watkins, *Old Times in the Faulkner Country* (Chapel Hill: University of North Carolina Press, 1961), is an early example of what are now numerous accounts by contemporaries and relatives of Faulkner that illuminate parallels between the factual and fictional; some are more reliable than others. Joel Williamson, *William Faulkner and Southern History* (New York: Oxford University Press, 1993), is a fascinating exploration of the Falkner and Butler families in their Mississippi historical setting. Final quote from William Faulkner to Malcolm Cowley, [Hollywood, Calif., Aug. 16, 1945], in Joseph Blotner, ed., *Selected Letters of William Faulkner* (New York: Random House, 1977), 197.

3. C. Vann Woodward, *The Burden of Southern History*, rev. ed., (Baton Rouge: Louisiana State University Press, 1968), 38; Woodward, *Thinking Back: The Perils of Writing History* (Baton Rouge: Louisiana State University Press, 1986), 109, 145.

4. Robert Penn Warren, "William Faulkner," in *William Faulkner: Four Decades of Criticism* ([East Lansing]: Michigan State University Press, 1973), 96.

5. Interview with Jean Stein, quoted in Blotner, *Faulkner*, 1595.

6. Frederick L. Gwynn and Joseph L. Blotner, *Faulkner in the University* (1959; rpt. Charlottesville: University Press of Virginia, 1995), 251.

7. Blotner, *Faulkner*, 1205.

8. Michael Millgate, "Faulkner and History," in *The South and Faulkner's Yoknapatawpha: The Actual and the Apocryphal*, ed. Evans Harrington and Ann J. Abadie (Jackson: University Press of Mississippi, 1977), 38. Millgate, Cowley, Brooks, and others see Faulkner using the local and historical only as a means of studying what they see as a more universal and timeless "human condition."

9. Robert Cantwell, "The Faulkners: Recollections of a Gifted Family," in *New World Writing: Second Mentor Selection* (New York, 1952), 306, quoted in Michael Millgate, *The Achievement of William Faulkner* (New York: Random House, 1966), 25.

10. Malcolm Cowley, ed., *The Portable Faulkner* (1946; rev. ed. New York: Viking Penguin, 1967), viii.

11. David Minter, *William Faulkner: His Life and Work* (Baltimore: Johns Hopkins University Press, 1980), 78, paraphrasing Gwynn and Blotner, *Faulkner in the University*, 59–60.

12. Malcolm Cowley, *The Faulkner-Cowley File: Letters and Memories, 1944–1962* (New York: Viking Press, 1966).

13. Cowley, ed., *Portable*, 389.

14. Ibid., xxxii.

15. Cleanth Brooks, *William Faulkner: The Yoknapatawpha Country* (Baton Rouge: Louisiana State University Press, 1963), 222.

16. Irving Howe, *William Faulkner: A Critical Study*, 3d ed. (Chicago: University of Chicago Press, 1975), 80. The first edition of this work appeared in 1951, and Howe, a disillusioned communist, was referring to Stalin's Russia, not today's.

17. William Faulkner, *Requiem for a Nun* (1951; rpt. New York: Vintage Books, 1975), 80.

18. William Faulkner, *Absalom, Absalom!* (1936; rpt. New York: Vintage International, 1990), 142. Original italicized; otherwise, punctuation as in the original.

19. Faulkner, *Requiem*, 225. Original italicized.

Chapter One

1. My thanks to David Carlton, quoting Tom Connelley.

2. Faulkner seemed only vaguely aware of the meaning of his fictional county's name. More than once he told people that it meant "water runs slow through flatland," which described the Yoknapatawpha River well enough, but that was not at all what the word meant to the Chickasaws. This mistaken translation, which by now has been repeated so often it has taken on a truth all its own, is puzzling because the word and its meaning were well known among his contemporaries. Faulkner's understanding of the word is documented in Frederick L. Gwynn and Joseph L. Blotner, *Faulkner in the University* (1959; rpt. Charlottesville: University Press of Virginia, 1995), 74. Faulkner's mistaken translation of the word may be explained by a similar Chickasaw word, "Yaknipatassa," which means "flat land," according to the Byington dictionary cited below (n. 64). The confusion over the meaning of the word continues; an otherwise reliable local history published by the Skipwith Historical and Genealogical Society, *The Heritage of Lafayette County, Mississippi* (Dallas: Curtis Media Co., 1986), 195, defines Yoknapatawpha as "water passing through the air."

3. John K. Bettersworth, *Mississippi: A History* (Austin, Tex.: Steck, 1959), 25, map of Indian peoples in Mississippi. See also John Swanton, *Indians of the Southeastern United States*, Smithsonian Institution, Bureau of American Ethnology, *Bulletin* 137 (Washington D.C.: U.S. Government Printing Office, 1946), map 11, after p. 34, for a more detailed map.

4. Yates, essay in "Formation," WPA.

5. Pamela Munro and Catherine Willmond, *Chickasaw: An Analytical Dictionary* (Norman: University of Oklahoma Press, 1994), see pp. 359, 299 for entries for "yaakni' " and "patafa." An earlier source, *A Chickasaw Dictionary*, compiled by Jesse Humes and Vinnie May Humes (The Chickasaw Nation, n.d.), confirms that "yockona," meant land, but it offers no satisfactory translation of "patawpha."

6. Arrell M. Gibson, *The Chickasaws* (Norman: University of Oklahoma Press, 1971), 10–11; Patricia Galloway, *Choctaw Genesis, 1500–1700, Indians of the Southeast* (Lincoln: University of Nebraska Press, 1995), 330–31, analyzes variations on the Chickasaw migration legend.

7. Gibson, *Chickasaws*, 10–11; James H. Malone, *The Chickasaw Nation: A Short Sketch of a Noble People* (Louisville: John P. Morton, 1922), 19–21. The Choctaws had a similar migration legend, though it had the Chickasaws deliberately departing to the

North. Swanton, *Indians*, 777–78, cited in Richard White, *The Roots of Dependency: Subsistence, Environment, and Social Change among the Choctaws, Pawnees, and Navajos* (Lincoln: University of Nebraska Press, 1983), 2, 328 n. 4; Department of the Interior, Census Office, Extra Census Bulletin, *The Five Civilized Tribes in Indian Territory* . . . (Washington D.C.: U.S. Census Printing Office, 1894), 29–30.

8. Gibson, *Chickasaws*, 7.

9. Malone, *Chickasaw Nation*, 42, 40–51 passim; Gibson, *Chickasaws*, 31–32. For full treatment of the DeSoto expedition, see Patricia Galloway, ed., *The Hernando De Soto Expedition: History, Historiography, and "Discovery" in the Southeast* (Lincoln: University of Nebraska Press, 1997).

10. Jonathan Daniels, *The Devil's Backbone: The Story of the Natchez Trace* (1962; rpt. New York: McGraw-Hill, 1989), 5.

11. Gibson, *Chickasaws*, 31–32, 42; Malone, *Chickasaw Nation*, 43–44, 48–49; Charles Hudson, "The Hernando DeSoto Expedition, 1539–1543," in *The Forgotten Centuries: Indians and Europeans in the American South, 1521–1704*, ed. Charles Hudson and Carmen Chave Tesser (Athens: University of Georgia Press, 1994), 89–90.

12. H. B. Cushman, *History of the Choctaw, Chickasaw, and Natchez Indians* (1899; rpt. Norman: University of Oklahoma Press, 1999), 371–74; Daniels, *Devil's Backbone*, 22; Gibson, *Chickasaws*, 51; Daniel H. Usner Jr., *Indians, Settlers and Slaves in a Frontier Exchange Economy: The Lower Mississippi Valley before 1783* (Chapel Hill: University of North Carolina Press, 1992), 82–83.

13. Gibson, *Chickasaws*, 51–54; Malone, *Chickasaw Nation*, 251–63.

14. William Edward Myer, "Indian Trails of the Southeast," Smithsonian Institution, Bureau of American Ethnology, *Bulletin* 42 (Washington D.C.: U.S. Government Printing Office, 1928), 727–857; Malone, *Chickasaw Nation*, 57–78. I am grateful to Christopher Everett for helping me better understand this subject and providing these citations.

15. White, *Roots of Dependency*, 10–11, 32. White focuses on the neighboring Choctaws, but the general outlines of his story fit the Chickasaw experience also. Florette Henri, *The Southern Indians and Benjamin Hawkins, 1796–1816* (Norman: University of Oklahoma Press, 1986), chap. 5 and passim.

16. Usner, *Indians, Settlers and Slaves*, passim.

17. White, *Roots of Dependency*, 57–58; Henri, *Southern Indians*.

18. Quoted in Gibson, *Chickasaws*, 68.

19. John E. Parsons, ed., "Letters on the Chickasaw Removal of 1837," *New York Historical Society Quarterly* 37 (July 1953): 280.

20. Gibson, *Chickasaws*, 8.

21. Ibid., 144, 86, 80.

22. William Faulkner, "Red Leaves," in Malcolm Cowley, ed., *The Portable Faulkner* (1946; rev. ed. New York: Penguin Viking, 1967), 57; "The Jail (Nor Even Yet Quite Relinquish—)" ibid., 671; "The Courthouse, (A Name for the City)," ibid., 42.

23. William Faulkner, *Requiem for a Nun* (1951; rpt. New York: Vintage Books, 1975), 193, 188.

24. Anthony F. C. Wallace, *The Long, Bitter Trail: Andrew Jackson and the Indians* (New York: Hill and Wang, 1993), 23; Henri, *Southern Indians*, 124.

25. White, *Roots of Dependency*, 58–59, 69–96; Henri, *Southern Indians*, 122–25; Peter C. Mancall, *Deadly Medicine: Indians and Alcohol in Early America* (Ithaca: Cornell University Press, 1995).

26. Gibson, *Chickasaws*, 68.

27. Ibid., 70.

28. "Extract from a letter of Mr. Anson Gleason, Tokish, Sept. 28th, 1830," *Missionary Herald* 26 (1830): 383.

29. White, *Roots of Dependency*, 354 n. 25; Swanton, *Indians*, 118–19; James Adair, *Adair's History of the American Indians*, ed. Samuel Cole Williams (1775; New York: Promontory Press, 1930), 378. Swanton provides other estimates, which vary, but all support the notion that there was a drastic decline at the early incursions of the French and English about 1700 and a partial recovery after the American Revolution and the end of serious colonial rivalry.

30. Gibson, *Chickasaws*, 142, 179. Peter H. Wood, "The Changing Population of the Colonial South: An Overview of Race and Region, 1685–1790," in *Powhatan's Mantle: Indians of the Colonial South*, ed. Peter H. Wood, Gregory A. Wasilkov, and M. Thomas Haltey (Lincoln: University of Nebraska Press, 1989), 38, 66–68. Daniel Usner's careful estimates of eighteenth-century Indian populations indicate there were 7,000 Chickasaws in 1700, 3,500 in 1725, 2,000 in 1750, and 2,300 by 1775. He estimates a less devastating Choctaw decline from 17,500 in 1700 to a low of 12,500 in 1750, recovering to 13,400 by 1775. Daniel H. Usner Jr., *American Indians in the Lower Mississippi Valley: Social and Economic Histories*, Indians of the Southeast (Lincoln: University of Nebraska Press, 1998), 35.

31. Gibson, *Chickasaws*, 48, 64; White, *Roots of Dependency*, 50, 52, 60–61, 65–66. Swanton, *Indians*, map 11, after p. 34, suggests the remaining Natchez lived between the Yoknapatawpha and Tallahatchie Rivers after 1733.

32. Swanton, *Indians*, table 1, p. 10, classifies all the major and minor tribes of the Southeast. According to Swanton, among the Indians of other tribes who joined the Chickasaws, only the Natchez were outside the "Muskhogean division," though they, too, originated from "Muskhogean stock."

33. Of 6,070 total population counted in the preremoval census of the Chickasaws, 1,156 (19 percent) were African slaves and roughly one quarter, 1,229, of the remaining 4,914 were designated mixed-blood, making a total of 44 percent who were of African or mixed white-Indian origin. The remaining 56 percent were called "full-blood" Chickasaw, but by this time, many were of mixed tribal origins. Gibson, *Chickasaws*, 142, 179.

34. Ibid., 65.

35. Ishtahotopa, King, et al., to Andrew Jackson, [1835], Letters Received by the Office of Indian Affairs, Chickasaw Agency, 830–1835, mf M234, roll 136, NARA. At issue was the question of whether allotments were due Chickasaw women heads of families, which the United States finally allowed. This rule was the basis by which Hoka received the land patent she sold to the founders of Oxford. See also Gibson, *Chickasaws*, 19–20; Swanton, *Indians*, 705–6; Adair, *History*, 145–53.

36. Cushman, *History*, 113, 395.

37. [George Rogers], *Memoranda of the Experience, Labors, and Travels of a Universalist Preacher* (Cincinnati: John A. Gurley, 1845), 206.

38. Gibson, *Chickasaws*, 40, 41–42, 64–65; White, *Roots of Dependency*, 35–36; Usner, *Indians, Settlers and Slaves*, 56–59, 65.

39. Gibson, *Chickasaws*, 150.

40. Ibid., 124; Daniel H. Usner Jr., "American Indians on the Cotton Frontier: Changing Economic Relations with Citizens and Slaves in the Mississippi Territory,"

Journal of American History 72 (Sept. 1985): 297–317; Jesse D. Jennings, ed., "Nutt's Trip to the Chickasaw Country," Journal of Mississippi History 9 (Jan. 1947): 40–45, 60–61.

41. Gibson, Chickasaws, 144.

42. John L. Allen, "Report of the Chickasaws, on the Scope of Civilization," Feb. 7, 1830, Letters Received by the Office of Indian Affairs, Chickasaw Agency, 1830–35, mf M234, roll 136, NARA. Early white settlers in northern Mississippi, in contrast, recalled the abundance of game with deer providing a readily accessible food supply. This theme of abundant game is one Faulkner also alluded to frequently in descriptions of pioneer Yoknapatawpha County, e.g., Absalom, Absalom!, and Requiem for a Nun. In attempting to square these conflicting reports of scarce and abundant game, it should be remembered that it was in the interest of American Indian policy to stress the obsoleteness of a hunter culture in a land without game. It is also likely that the depleted game supply had recovered as trade in skins slackened in the years preceding removal.

43. See Willam H. Barr to John C. Calhoun, Secretary of War, Abbeville, S.C., June 18, 1824, Letters Received by the Office of Indian Affairs, 1824–81, Chickasaw Agency, 1824–70, 1824–29, mf M234, roll 135, NARA.

44. Wallace, Long, Bitter Trail, 48, 30–49, 58.

45. One report indicates that settlement was concentrated in the Chickasaw towns east of Pontotoc at least until 1789; G. W. Long, acting Sub Agent, to Office of Indian Affairs, Nov. 5, 1824, Miss., Letters Received by the Office of Indian Affairs, 1824–81, Chickasaw Agency, 1824–70, 1824–29, mf M234, roll 135, NARA. The Treaty of Pontotoc Creek, 1832, allotted temporary homesteads to individual Indians, and many took up residence on them during this interlude before removal in 1837. The origin and location of all the Chickasaw settlements in the Yoknapatawpha area is not clear from the records. Gibson, Chickasaws, 146.

46. Rogers, Memoranda, 207.

47. White, Roots of Dependency, 34, 41–46, 59.

48. Allen, "Report of the Chickasaws."

49. Missionary Herald, 37 (1831), 352; quoted in Gibson, Chickasaws, 113.

50. Gibson, Chickasaws, 129–30.

51. Ibid., 79, summarizes the boundaries.

52. Ibid., 103–5.

53. Quoted ibid., 164.

54. Quoted ibid., 173.

55. Ibid, 172–78, outlines the main terms and some of the details of these treaties. Allotments were made to individuals and to families based on family size and slaves owned. The proceeds from the sale of these allotments were controlled by a tribal commission, which could transfer funds to the individual, but only if the commission judged them competent. Proceeds from the public land sales would go into a common tribal fund. Ibid., 177–78, 179–80.

56. "Lo!" focuses on a mixed-blood chief, Francis Weddel, a fictional but plausible example of mixed-blood wealth and influence. See Elmo Howell, "President Jackson and William Faulkner's Choctaws," Chronicles of Oklahoma 45 (1967): 252–58.

57. Faulkner, "The Jail (Nor Even Yet Quite Relinquish—)," in Portable, 672.

58. Allen, "Report of the Chickasaws"; John L. Allen, Sub Agent, to Elbert Her-

ring, Indian Bureau, Washington City, Jan. 4, 1834, Pontotoc, Letters Received by the Office of Indian Affairs, Chickasaw Agency, mf M234, roll 136, NARA.

59. The register and receiver of the land office at Pontotoc to Secretary Lewis Cass, May 29, 1835, quoted in Grant Foreman, *Indian Removal: The Emigration of the Five Civilized Tribes of Indians* (1932; rev. ed. Norman: University of Oklahoma Press, 1953), 202.

60. Benj Reynolds, Agent, Chickasaw Agency to Lewis Cass, Apr. 29, 1835, quoted in Monte Ross Lewis, "Chickasaw Removal: Betrayal of the Beloved Warriors, 1794–1844" (Ph.D. diss., North Texas State University, 1981), 122.

61. "A Friend to the Indian" to Indian Office, n.p., Oct. 1835; Letters Received by the Office of Indian Affairs, Chickasaw Agency, mf M234, roll 136, NARA, testifies that "half breeds and whites living with Indians are selling for $10 per acre, while the other indians are selling to speculators for $.75 or $1.50 and then the speculator is turning around and selling for $5 to $10."

62. *Oxford Eagle*, Dec. 10, 1936, p. 1.

63. Deed Records, Book A, p. 125, third floor storage, LCC.

64. Faulkner, *Requiem*, 187; Cyrus Byington, *A Dictionary of the Choctaw Language*, ed. John R. Swanton and Henry S. Halbert (Washington, D.C.: U.S. Government Printing Office, 1915), 155, 262, 337. Other Indian names and words in Faulkner's fiction either have a plausible translation or sound authentic.

65. Howard C. Horsford, "Faulkner's (Mostly) Unreal Indians in Early Mississippi History," *American Literature* 64 (June 1992): 311–30; Elmo Howell, "William Faulkner and the Mississippi Indians," *Georgia Review* 21 (1967): 386–96; Howell, "The Chickasaw Queen: In William Faulkner's Story," *Chronicles of Oklahoma* 49 (1971): 334–39; Lewis M. Dabney, *The Indians of Yoknapatawpha: A Study in Literature and History* (Baton Rouge, Louisiana State University Press, 1974), all deal with historical parallels and discrepancies in Faulkner's Indian stories.

66. Sam Had Two Fathers, is a mix of Indian, African, and white races; Boon Hogenback, is a descendant of a Chickasaw queen. In his story "Mountain Victory," Waddel resembles the prominent Choctaw planter Greenwood LeFlore, who stayed on in Mississippi near Greenwood, Mississippi, named in his honor.

67. "The Jail (Nor Even Yet Quite Relinquish—)," in *Portable*, 670. Faulkner's Indian stories include "Red Leaves" (first published in 1930), "A Justice" (1931), "Lo!" (1934), "A Courtship" (1948), all of which are included in *Collected Stories of William Faulkner* (New York: Vintage Press, 1987), 313–406. "Red Leaves" and "A Justice" are included in *Portable*. Significant portions of *Go Down Moses* (1942), particularly chapters entitled "The Old People" (originally published in 1940) and "The Bear"; Faulkner, *Requiem*, 185–91. "Mountain Victory" (1932), is the story of a Chickasaw man, but it takes place after the Civil War and outside of Yoknapatawpha.

68. Faulkner, "A Justice," in *Portable*, 6. Dabney, *Indians*, 72–89, offers a perceptive interpretation of "A Justice."

69. Dabney, *Indians*, 94–95. A Choctaw chief, Red Shoes, an ally of the French, may have inspired this. Gibson, *Chickasaws*, 50. Red slippers were also a symbol of royalty in France.

70. "Red Leaves," *Portable*.

71. Ibid., 62–63.

72. Dabney, *Indians*, 11n.

73. Faulkner, "Mississippi," *Holiday*, Apr. 1954, 35; Faulkner, "A Bear Hunt,"

(originally published 1934) in *Collected Short Stories of William Faulkner* (New York: Random House, 1950), 65. See also Thomas S. Hines, *William Faulkner and the Tangible Past: The Architecture of Yoknapatawpha* (Berkeley: University of California Press, 1996), 21–23.

74. "Chickasaws," WPA; Skipwith, *Heritage*, 170.

75. "Tohbi" translates "whitened, bleached; blanched, made white," according to Byington. "Tubbe" was a common suffix to male names indicating "killer." Horsford, "Faulkner's (Mostly) Unreal Indians," 316. The WPA source materials indicate that the local understanding of the name was that it meant "old and bent and walks with a cane." "Tobbona" translates to "bent over; stooping; bowed down," but nothing in the physical description of Toby Tubby supports this as a plausible interpretation.

76. "Chickasaws," WPA. See also Skipwith, *Heritage*, 170, 188; Gutting, *Yoknapatawpha*, 195–96. Faulkner, "Fire in the Hearth," refers also to this legend. During my 1990 conversation with Earl Truett, a local historian and genealogist, he confided to me in a hushed voice that as a child he had learned the location of Toby Tubby's grave but was determined to keep it a secret.

77. Mary Young, *Rednecks, Ruffleshirts, and Redskins: Indian Allotments in Alabama and Mississippi, 1830–1860* (Norman: University of Oklahoma Press, 1961), 114–37. See also Gibson, *Chickasaws*, 179–80. William Carroll to C. A. Harris, Pontotoc, Miss., Nov. 11, 1836, Letters Received by the Office of Indian Affairs, 1824–81, Chickasaw Agency, mf M234, roll 137, NARA, discusses gold and silver brought to Pontotoc.

78. Carroll to Harris, Pontotoc, Miss., Nov. 11, 1836.

79. *Expenditures from the Chickasaw Fund. Letter from the Secretary of War, . . . 1843*, 1982 reprint, Doc. 65, House of Representatives, War Department, 27th Cong., 3d sess.; Faulkner, "The Courthouse, (A Name for the City)," in *Portable*, 35.

80. Gibson, *Chickasaws*, 178. In 1855 the two tribes separated again; ibid., 254–55.

81. "Major Upshaw's Speech to the Chickasaw Chiefs," May 12, 1837, Letters Received by the Office of Indian Affairs, Chickasaw Agency Emigration, 1837–50, mf M234, roll 143, NARA.

82. Gibson, *Chickasaws*, 183; Map, "The Chickasaw Country in 1796–1800," in G. H. V. Collot, Bureau of American Ethnology, *Bulletin 73*, Plate 10, MDAH; this map identifies Chief Seely's District just north of present-day Lafayette County.

83. Foreman, *Indian Removal*, 205.

84. B. R. McIlvaine, quoted in John E. Parsons, ed., "Letters on the Chickasaw Removal of 1837," *New York Historical Society Quarterly* 37 (July 1953): 280. See also Foreman, *Removal*, 214; Gibson, *Chickasaws*, 186–88.

85. Faulkner, "The Jail (Nor Even Yet Quite Relinquish—)," in *Portable*, 672.

Chapter Two

1. William Faulkner, *Requiem for a Nun* (1951; rpt. New York: Vintage Books, 1975), 191.

2. Buck Avant's mansion was later occupied by Augustus Baldwin Longstreet, president of the University of Mississippi, and, later still, by the family of Phil Stone, William Faulkner's friend and early mentor. It burned in 1942, several years after Faulkner wrote of the Sutpen mansion meeting a similar fate. Susan Snell, *Phil Stone of Oxford: A Vicarious Life* (Athens: University of Georgia Press, 1991), 23–26, 218–21,

236, 246–47, 250–51; Thomas S. Hines, *William Faulkner and the Tangible Past: The Architecture of Yoknapatawpha* (Berkeley: University of California Press, 1996), 59; Charles B. Cramer, "A History of Selected Examples of Ante-bellum Architecture in Lafayette County Mississippi," paper for UM Art Department, 1965, pp. 14–15, typescript, UMSC.

3. Daniel W. Jordan to Malvina [Jordan], Plymouth [Lowndes County, Miss.] Aug. 3, 1833, in Daniel W. Jordan Papers, 1827–66, ms, Duke University Library, mf "Records of Ante-Bellum Southern Plantations," Kenneth M. Stampp, ed., (Frederick, Md., 1986), Series F, Part 2, Reel 10; punctuation added.

4. [George Rogers], *Memoranda of the Experiences, Labors, and Travels of a Universalist Preacher* (Cincinnati, 1845), 269. Rogers's observations of Mississippi took place about 1838.

5. Margaret B. DesChamps, ed., "Some Miss Letters to Robert Fraser, 1841–1844," *Journal of Mississippi History* 15 (1953): 181–89, quoted in John Hebron Moore, *The Emergence of the Cotton Kingdom in the Old Southwest: Mississippi, 1770–1860* (Baton Rouge: Louisiana State University Press, 1988), 133.

6. *South Carolina State Gazette and Columbia Advertiser*, Sept. 27, 1828, quoted in Lacy K. Ford Jr., *Origins of Southern Radicalism: The South Carolina Upcountry, 1800–1860* (New York: Oxford University Press, 1988), 38.

7. James Oakes, *The Ruling Race: A History of American Slaveholders* (New York: Vintage Books, 1982), 69–95. For an excellent study of another county on the western cotton frontier, see Daniel S. Dupree, *Transforming the Cotton Frontier: Madison County, Alabama, 1800–1840* (Baton Rouge: Louisiana State University Press, 1997).

8. Baldwin, *Flush Times*, quoted in Malcolm J. Rohrbough, *The Land Office Business: The Settlement and Administration of American Public Lands, 1789–1837* (1968; rpt. Belmont, Calif.: Wadsworth, 1990), 185.

9. James Winfield to Daniel W. Jordan, Brownsville, Tenn., Oct. 6, 1829, in Jordan Papers.

10. LCDI. A published version of the early county censuses may be found in Catherine E. Eatman and Earl A. Truett Jr., *1850 U.S. Federal Census, Lafayette County, Mississippi* (Oxford, Miss.: Eatman and Truett, 1979); Earl A. Truett Jr. and Catherine E., Mrs. G. L. Eatman, comp., *1840 U.S. Federal Census, Lafayette County and Yalobusha County, Mississippi: Also Index to 1850 U.S. Census, Lafayette Co., MS*. (Oxford, Miss.: Truett, 1981). See also Skipwith Historical and Genealogical Society, *The Heritage of Lafayette County, Mississippi* (Dallas: Curtis Media Corp., 1986), 1–18.

11. Christopher Morris, *Becoming Southern: The Evolution of a Way of Life, Warren County and Vicksburg, Mississippi, 1770–1860* (New York: Oxford University Press, 1995).

12. On the Northwest Ordinance, see Andrew R. L. Cayton and Peter S. Onuf, *The Midwest and the Nation: Rethinking the History of an American Region* (Bloomington: Indiana University Press, 1990).

13. Mary Elizabeth Young, *Redskins, Ruffleshirts and Rednecks: Indian Allotments in Alabama and Mississippi, 1830–1860* (Norman: University of Oklahoma Press, 1961), 131–32. Sales of land in northern Mississippi, the historian Roy Robbins writes, "were attended by gambling traders from all parts of the United States, and bona fide settlers had little chance to secure land. Consequently much of the rich loam fell into the hands of a few wealthy proprietors." Roy M. Robbins, *Our Landed Heritage: The Public Domain, 1776–1936* (Princeton: Princeton University Press, 1942), 61. See also *De Bow's Commercial Review* 4 (1847): 86–87.

14. Joseph G. Baldwin, *The Flush Times of Alabama and Mississippi* (1853; rpt. Baton Rouge: Louisiana State University Press, 1987), 236.

15. Dennis East, "Land Speculation in the Chickasaw Cession: A Study of the New York and Mississippi Land Company, 1835–1889" (M.S. thesis, University of Wisconsin, 1964).

16. McCorkle (Samuel) Papers, MDAH; Samuel McCorkle Papers, 1834–54, UMSC, photocopy of original in Holly Springs Historical Society; East, "Land Speculation," 16–17, describes the work of David Hubbard, another land looker with the New York and Mississippi Land Company.

17. East, "Land Speculation," 17, 18.

18. John Spencer Bassett, *The Plantation Overseer: As Revealed in His Letters* (1925; rpt. New York: Negro Universities Press, 1968), 46; East, "Land Speculation."

19. Baldwin, *Flush Times*, 47.

20. J. F. H. Claiborne, *Mississippi: As a Province, Territory, and State with Biographical Notices of Eminent Citizens* (1880; rpt. Spartanburg, Reprint Company, 1978), 447.

21. William Faulkner, *Absalom, Absalom!* (1936; rpt. New York: Vintage International, 1990), 49.

22. See map indicating public land sales in Mississippi in Young, *Redskins*, 183.

23. Dorothy Oldham, "Life of Jacob Thompson" (M.A. thesis, UM, 1930), 24–26. Quotes from William Hack to Bro[ther], Pontotoc, Miss., Oct. 13, 1836; William Hack to C. A. Hack, Pontotoc, Miss., Nov. 21, 1836, William Hack Letters, MDAH. I am grateful to Bruce McTavish for leading me to these letters.

24. Baldwin, *Flush Times*, 83–84, 87, 85.

25. William F. Gray, *From Virginia to Texas, 1835* (Houston, 1909), 52, quoted in Rohrbough, *Land Office Business*, 185.

26. David Hubbard to John Bolton, [Pontotoc, Miss.], Jan. 11, 1836, quoted in East, "Land Speculation," 51.

27. Population growth and political pressures eventually led to the addition of several counties, all added after the Civil War. Presently there are eighteen Mississippi counties in the former Chickasaw cession. William Thorndale and William Dollarhide, *Map Guide to the U.S. Federal Censuses, 1790–1920* (Baltimore: Genealogical Publishing Co., 1987), 183f, shows the county outlines for each decennial census.

28. John H. Long and Peggy Tuck Sinko, eds., *Mississippi: Atlas of Historical County Boundaries* (New York: Simon and Schuster, 1993), 111–12.

29. "The Courthouse (A Name for the City)," in Malcolm Cowly, ed., *The Portable Faulkner* (1946; rev. ed. New York: Viking Penguin, 1967), 44.

30. Jonathan Daniels, *The Devil's Backbone: The Story of the Natchez Trace* (1962; rpt. Gretna, La.: Pelican, 1989); Robert M. Coates, *The Outlaw Years: The History of the Land Pirates of the Natchez Trace* (New York: McCauley, 1930); John D. W. Guice, "A Trace of Violence," *Southern Quarterly* 29 (1991): 123–43.

31. Elmo H. Howell, "A Name for Faulkner's City," *Names* 16 (1968): 415–21.

32. "Courthouse," 21, 46.

33. John Cooper Hathorn, *Early Settlers of Lafayette Co., Mississippi: A Period Study of Lafayette County from 1836–1860 with Emphasis on Population Groups* (1938; rpt. Columbia, Tenn.: Skipwith, 1980), 14–15.

34. "Minutes, Board of Police, 1836–46," Chancery Clerk's Office, LCC; Hathorn, *Early Settlers*, 16.

35. "Minutes, Board of Police, 1836–46," Mar. 21, 1836.

36. Ibid., June 11, 1836.

37. Ibid., Oct. 24, 1836. The temporary courthouse cost only $43.05 for lumber. One pioneer described the first courthouse as "a log cabin, just at the brow of the hill on the left, on Pontotoc Street" (now University); see "Early Recollections of Oxford," *Oxford Eagle*, Feb. 17, 1910.

38. "Minutes, Board of Police, 1836–46," Oct. 24, July 7, 8, Sept. 23, 1836; Moore, *Emergence*, 183.

39. "Minutes, Board of Police, 1836–46," July 7, 8, Sept. 23, 1836.

40. Faulkner, "The Jail (Nor Even Yet Quite Relinquish —)" in *Requiem*, 193. When the city fathers finally decided to replace the old jail (sometime after Faulkner's death), locals remember how it stood impervious to the bulldozers and wrecker balls before finally surrendering to destruction.

41. "Minutes, Board of Police, 1836–46," Oct. 22, 24, 1836.

42. *Natchez Free Trader*, Aug. 8, 1837, quoted in Moore, *Emergence*, 183.

43. "Minutes, Board of Police, 1836–1846," passim. Morris, *Becoming Southern*, 132–37, provides an excellent account of early road building in a new Mississippi county reaching out to external markets through collective improvements.

44. Faulkner, *Requiem*, 34–35, 192.

45. Ibid., 50.

46. Faulkner, *Absalom, Absalom!*, offers the original account of the French architect, and the story is repeated in *Requiem*, 32–33, 193.

47. *Marshall County Republican* (Holly Springs, Miss.), Oct. 27, 1838.

48. *Besancon's Annual Register*, quoted in *Marshall County Republican* (Holly Springs, Miss.), Oct. 27, 1838. A report the previous year claimed three hundred persons had homes in Oxford and that in addition the town had six stores, two hotels, and a church, all built with logs. *Natchez Free Trader*, July?, 1837. The next year two schools and a second church were constructed. *Natchez Free Trader*, Aug. 8, 1837, both quoted in Moore, *Emergence*, 183.

49. Quoted in Moore, *Emergence*, 181.

50. [Joseph Holt Ingraham], *The South-West, by a Yankee*, 2 vols. (1835; rpt. New York: Negro Universities Press, 1968), 2:168.

51. Franklin L. Riley, "Extinct Towns and Villages of Mississippi," PMHS 5 (1902): 311, 348–50; Moore, *Emergence*, 181–82.

52. Riley, "Extinct Towns," 311, 348–50; Skipwith, *Heritage*, 192–94; C. John Sobotka Jr., *A History of Lafayette County, Mississippi* (Oxford: Rebel Press, [1976], 30–32; Hathorn, *Early Settlers*, 30–31. A map of Wyatt is in Earl A. Truett Jr., *William Hardin Cain: His Descendants and the Founders of Northwest Lafayette County, Mississippi*, vol. 1, (Oxford, Miss.: Earl A. Truett Jr., 1978), 16.

53. *Marshall County Republican* (Holly Springs, Miss.), Jan. 5, 1839.

54. *Guard* (Holly Springs), Jan. 26, 1842; see also *Marshall County Republican* (Holly Springs, Miss.), Aug. 3, 1839. In 1840 Memphis shipped 35,000 bales of cotton. Lewis Cecil Gray, *History of Agriculture in the Southern United States to 1860*, 2 vols. (Washington, D.C.: Carnegie Institution, 1933), 2:900. Wyatt claimed 10,000 bales in 1842, so its boast as "Little Memphis" was not so far-fetched.

55. Elizabeth Hathaway to Jay Hathaway, Pontotoc, Miss., July 9, 1842, Larrabee (Elizabeth Hathaway) Letters, MDAH.

56. Herbert Anthony Kellar, ed., *Solon Robinson, Pioneer and Agriculturist: Selected Writings*, 2 vols. (Indianapolis: Indiana Historical Bureau, 1936), 1:449.

57. Eugene W. Hilgard, *Report on the Geology and Agriculture of the State of Mississippi* (Jackson: E. Barksdale, 1860), 307. "Cold" soil meant poorly drained and therefore not productive.

58. Ibid., 296; Charles S. Aiken, "Faulkner's Yoknapatawpha County: Geographical Fact into Fiction," *Geographical Review* 67 (Jan. 1977): 4–5.

59. "Outlaws," WPA.

60. This summary and the quotes, in order, are from Faulkner, *Absalom*, 36, 46, 5, 6, 44, 50–51, 54–56, 53.

61. Skipwith, *Heritage*, 17.

62. Bassett, *Plantation Overseer*, 49.

63. Kellar, *Solon Robinson*, 1:451, 458, quoted in Moore, *Emergence*, 135.

64. Moore, *Emergence*, 87.

65. "Diary of Rebecca Ann Evans Pegues, 1840–1882," Pegues Diaries and Letters, typescript; Mattie Pegues Wood, "The History of My Father's Family," typescript. I am grateful to Guy Turnbow of Oxford for making this valuable material available to me. For further scraps of information on the Pegues family, see James Durwood Cole, "Origin of the White Population of Lafayette County" (M.A. thesis, UM, 1935), 18; David Reese Chapter, D.A.R., "Some Early History of Lafayette County Mississippi," typescript, 1922, UMSC, unpaginated, clipping on Alexander H. Pegues; *Oxford Eagle*, Mar. 27, 1969; on Thomas E. B. Pegues, see subject file "Lafayette Springs" MDAH; Mrs. Calvin S. Brown, "Some Pioneer Women of Mississippi," typescript in Mrs. Calvin S. Brown Papers, MDAH.

66. *Oxford Eagle*, Apr. 21, 1926, account by Ella Pegues, his daughter. Various biographical accounts claim Alexander Pegues owned 150 or more slaves, but, if he did, they were not accounted in the census or tax records. LCDI.

67. "Woodson Ridge," WPA; Oldham, "Jacob Thompson," 35–36.

68. M. J. Blackwell to Edmund B. Blackwell, Esq., Lamar, Miss., Feb. 15, 1849, Charles Stubblefield Collection, file 4, M. J. Blackwell Letters, UMSC.

69. LCDI. Charles C. Bolton, *Poor Whites of the Antebellum South: Tenants and Laborers in Central North Carolina and Northeast Mississippi* (Durham: Duke University Press, 1994), 5, 192 n. 9, refers to numerous local studies of different parts of the South which show the range was between one-third and one-half of southern white families who claimed no land and no slaves. Bolton's study of Pontotoc County, on Lafayette's eastern border, shows figures slightly higher than in Lafayette County: 37 percent farmers with no land or slaves in 1850. Ibid., 85. On Faulkner's treatment of this class, see Elmo Howell, *Mississippi Scenes: Notes on Literature and History* (Memphis: E. Howell, 1992).

70. William Faulkner, *The Hamlet* (1940; rpt. New York: Vintage International, 1990), 5. Steven Hahn, *The Roots of Southern Populism: Yeoman Farmers and the Transformation of the Georgia Upcountry, 1850–1890* (New York: Oxford University Press, 1987), provides a portrait of yeomen in northern Georgia that would apply generally to northern Mississippi in the 1850s. Bolton, *Poor Whites*, describes their north Mississippi counterparts.

71. Cole, "Origin of the White Population," 13–14, 19.

72. [Joseph Holt Ingraham], *The South-West, by a Yankee*, 2 vols. (1835; rpt. New York: Negro Universities Press, 1968), 171–72.

73. Skipwith, *Heritage*, 3–12; see also Vernon Larry Walters, "Migration into Mississippi, 1798–1837" (M.A. thesis, Mississippi State University, 1969); Cole, "Ori-

gin of the White Population." Moore, *Emergence*, 1, 23, confirms the persistence of DeSoto's hogs, called "alligators" by the settlers.

74. Albert T. McNeal to James K. Polk, Coffeeville, Miss., Jan. 15, 1840, quoted in Bassett, *Plantation Overseer*, 135–36.

75. The most reliable source on cotton prices is Gray, *History of Agriculture*, 2:697, 1027. See also John Hebron Moore, *Agriculture in Ante-bellum Mississippi* (New York, Bookman Associates, 1958), 67–69; Moore, *Emergence*, 20; Walters, "Migration into Mississippi," 139–40.

76. Baldwin, *Flush Times*, 90.

77. Moore, *Emergence*, 182–83, suggests that Wyatt resumed as an important cotton port after 1845; most local history accounts assume Wyatt and Eaton faded immediately. Steamboat freight, though expensive and problematic because of low water and obstructions, was still less than overland freight before the coming of the Mississippi Central Railroad.

78. Robbins, *Our Landed Heritage*, 132.

79. Bradley G. Bond, *Political Culture in the Nineteenth-Century South: Mississippi, 1830–1900* (Baton Rouge: Louisiana State University Press, 1995), 63–64, quoting Jehu Amaziah Orr, 1845; J. A. Orr, "A Trip from Houston to Jackson, Mississippi, in 1845," *PMHS* 9 (1906): 173–78.

80. William Hack to C. A. Hack, Pontotoc, Miss., Jan 26, 1840, William Hack Letters, MDAH.

81. Senate Documents, 31st Cong., 2d sess., II, no. 2, recapitulated in table in Bruce Duncan McTavish, "With Strangers United in Kindred Relation: Education, Religion and Community in Northern Mississippi, 1836–1880" (Ph.D. dissertation, UM, 1993), 27. When the last of the Chickasaw lands were sold in 1854 some were going as low as $0.02 per acre. See also, Gibson, *Chickasaws*, 179n.

82. D. C. Glen, "Mississippi," *De Bow's Commercial Review* 7 (1849): 38–39, quoted in Robbins, *Our Landed Heritage*, 132.

83. Moore, *Emergence*, 22, 23, 24, 121.

84. The ratio of pounds of cotton (bales X 400) to bushels of corn was 3.93 in 1840, 7.39 in 1850, and 11.97 in 1860; from LCDA.

Chapter Three

1. LCDA.

2. LCDA.

3. Herbert Anthony Kellar, ed., *Solon Robinson, Pioneer and Agriculturist: Selected Writings*, 2 vols. (Indianapolis: Indiana Historical Bureau, 1936), 1:449, quoted in John Hebron Moore, *The Emergence of the Cotton Kingdom in the Old Southwest: Mississippi, 1770–1860* (Baton Rouge: Louisiana State University Press, 1988) 44; also 27, 30, 31, 36, 85; Lewis Cecil Gray, *History of Agriculture in the Southern United States to 1860* (Washington, D.C.: Carnegie Institution, 1933), 797, 701.

4. Eugene W. Hilgard, *Report on the Geology and Agriculture of the State of Mississippi* (Jackson, 1860), 239, quoted in Robert Frank Futrell, "Economic Readjustment in Mississippi during Reconstruction, 1865–1875" (M.A. thesis, UM, 1939), 95.

5. William Faulkner, *Requiem for a Nun* (1951; rpt. New York: Vintage, 1975), 195.

6. M. J. Blackwell to Edmund B. Blackwell, Esq., Lamar, Miss., Feb. 15, 1849, Charles Stubblefield Collection, folder 4, M. J. Blackwell Letters, UMSC.

7. Lamar to Mr. Chappell, [Oxford, Miss.], May 14, 1850, quoted in Edward Mayes, *Lucius Q. C. Lamar: His Life, Times, and Speeches, 1825–1893*, 2d ed. (Nashville: Publishing House of the Methodist Episcopal Church, South, 1896), 45.

8. Faulkner, *Requiem*, 192.

9. Ibid., 192–93.

10. David M. Potter, *The Impending Crisis, 1848–1861* (New York: Harper Torchbooks, 1976), chaps. 1, 7, examines the paradox of nationalism and integration through railroad development in a time of rising sectional tensions.

11. Belle Edmondson Diary, Oct. 17, 1864, in Loretta Galbraith and William Galbraith, eds., *A Lost Heroine of the Confederacy: The Diaries and Letters of Belle Edmondson* (Jackson: University Press of Mississippi, 1990), 185.

12. "Transportation, Old Roads," WPA.

13. *Constitution* (Oxford), May 10, 1851. Among the major investors and supporters mentioned in the newspaper accounts were James Brown, Washington Price, A. J. Buford, D. Robertson, R. H. Buford, W. G. Vaughan, W. S. McKee, D. M. Nelson, and C. G. Butler (Faulkner's mother's grandfather). A larger group that led the campaign to educate voters is found in the *Democratic Flag* (Oxford), June 22, 1852. Wendel, variously spelled Wendell.

14. *Constitution* (Oxford), June 7, 1851. At this moment, the road was known as the New Orleans and Holly Springs Rail Road. Moore, *Emergence*, 175.

15. *Democratic Flag* (Oxford), Aug. 11, Sept. 1, 1852.

16. Ibid., Aug. 11, Sept. 1, 1852.

17. Ibid., May 5, 1852. The local leaders in the Mississippi Central campaign were W. H. Lawshee, Springdale; Robert Sheegog, James Brown, Thos. Wendell, Hugh A. Barr, Dr. Jno. Thompson, all from Oxford; A. J. Buford and Reverend Mr. Gaston, College Hill; Mr. [Alexander] Pegues, Capt. H. M. Lee, Abbeville; Dr. Robinson and Moses Church, Sarepta.

18. Ibid., May 19, Dec. [n.d.], 1852.

19. Ibid., Mar. 10, May 19, June 9, 16, 1852.

20. Ibid., Aug. 18, 1852. The vote was ten to one in favor on the second vote.

21. Ibid., Apr. 21, 1852.

22. Moore, *Emergence*, 181, 183–84; Franklin L. Riley, "Extinct Towns and Villages of Mississippi," MHSP 5 (1902): 311–83.

23. James Allen Cabaniss, *A History of the University of Mississippi* (University, Miss.: UM Press, 1950), 5; Frances R. Huff, "The Relationship of Oxford and the UM, 1848–1947" (M.A. thesis, UM, 1947), chap. 1.

24. *Oxford Intelligencer* (Oxford), Nov. 14, 1860.

25. *Constitution* (Oxford), June 14, 1851, reported 134 students enrolled at the university; all but 12 from Mississippi, and hailing from 27 counties in all different sections within the state. See also Cabaniss, *A History of the University of Mississippi*, 5; Moore, *Emergence*, 184.

26. *Democratic Flag*, Dec. 15, 1852. The 1860 census listed the following schools for Lafayette County: common schools 29, with 900 pupils; O.S. Presbyterian College, 50 pupils; Cum. Pres. Female College, 50 pupils; Male Academy, 60 pupils; State University, 216 pupils; total 33 schools, 1276 pupils. Census data printed in *Oxford Intelligencer*, Jan. 2, 1861.

27. Jack Case Wilson, *Faulkners, Fortunes and Flames* (Nashville: Annandale Press, 1984), 12. Dorothy Oldham, "Life of Jacob Thompson" (M.A. thesis, UM, 1930),

42–43; Joel Williamson, *William Faulkner and Southern History* (New York: Oxford University Press, 1993), 126–27. Oldham and Wilson confirm that this mansion went up in 1841, not 1851 as Williamson appears to have it.

28. Thomas S. Hines, *William Faulkner and the Tangible Past: The Architecture of Yoknapatawpha* (Berkeley: University of California Press, 1997), 56–59; Wilson, *Faulkners*, 12; *Oxford Intelligencer*, Aug. 29, 1860. Sheegog was sometimes spelled Shegog, but the former was the most common contemporary spelling in local newspapers.

29. Hines, *Tangible Past*, 52, estimates Turner designed more than a dozen houses in this four-column mode and that he built or influenced many more in the area.

30. Hines, *Tangible Past*, 54–55. The name Compson is thought to come from an amalgam of Thompson and Chandler.

31. Wilson, *Faulkners*, 108–11; Hines, *Tangible Past*, 83–87; "Antebellum homes," WPA. Quote from the *Oxford Intelligencer*, June 6, 1860. Ward L. Miner, *The World of William Faulkner* (New York: Grove Press Books, 1952), 33, 43, repeats the common error of confusing Alexander and Thomas Pegues, but his suggestion that Thomas (and/or Alexander) Pegues inspired Faulkner's Thomas Sutpen is nonetheless plausible.

32. Mary Ruth Dunlap, "The *Oxford Observer*, Oxford, Mississippi: 1843–1844" (M.A. thesis, UM, 1973), 9; quote from *Observer*, Mar. 30, 1844; from *Southern Reformer*.

33. *Democratic Flag* (Oxford), July 28, 1852.

34. *Oxford Intelligencer* (Oxford), Nov. 14, 1860. On Falconer, see Emelda Villacortes Capati, "*Oxford Intelligencer*: 1860–1861" (M.A. thesis, UM, 1961).

35. *The Democratic Flag* (Oxford), Apr. 14, 1852, quoting letter from "The Cumberland Girl," "a young lady in our village," who wrote to the *Watchman and Evangelist* (Mar. 12, 1852).

36. "Railroads," WPA.

37. *Oxford Intelligencer* (Oxford), Nov. 21, 28, 1860.

38. Don Harrison Doyle, *The Social Order of a Frontier Community: Jacksonville, Illinois, 1825–1870* (Urbana: University of Illinois Press, 1978), examines similar problems of social organization in an equally volatile society in the Midwest.

39. John J. Bailey to Wm. L. Treadwell, Lamar, Miss., Nov. 26, 1849, Aldrich Collection, UMSC.

40. M. J. Blackwell to Edmund B. Blackwell, Esq, Lamar, Miss., Feb. 15, 1849, Blackwell Letters.

41. See Don H. Doyle, *New Men, New Cities, New South: Atlanta, Nashville, Charleston, Mobile, 1860–1910* (Chapel Hill: University of North Carolina Press, 1990), chap. 1, for an overview of southern urbanization.

42. M. J. Blackwell to Edmund B. Blackwell, Esq, Lamar, Miss., Feb. 15, 1849.

43. Belle Edmondson Diary, Oct. 17, 1864, in Galbraith, *Lost Heroine*, 185.

44. Maps varied widely in their choice of which places to include, and several of the early ones are inaccurate. J. H. Colton, *Mississippi*, 1864, is one of the more detailed and reliable; it included Oxford, and, in clockwise order, College Hill, Wyatt, Abbeville, Melton?, Rocky Ford, Liberty Hill, Toccopola (on Pontotoc County border), Dallas, Sarepta (annexed to Calhoun County), Springdale, Yocona (where Taylor's ought to have been indicated and is not), and Mt. Sylvan on the road west from Oxford to Panola.

45. For a fuller treatment of gender differences among western migrants, see Joan Cashin, *A Family Venture: Men and Women on the Southern Frontier* (Baltimore: Johns Hop-

kins University Press, 1991). She begins with an apt contrast between the experience of Thomas Sutpen and Ellen Coldfield.

46. "And here is the large brick mansion, the 'Oxford Inn' by Capt. Butler; a magnificent building, it too—well suited for the purpose for which it was intended; elegantly furnished, and will compete with most of your city 'soire' Hotel's." *Oxford Observer*, Sept. 16, 1843. The census of 1850 counted thirty-three men residing in the Oxford Inn.

47. Oldham, "Jacob Thompson," 37–38.

48. Accounts of the Isom courtship and the magnolia can be found in *Oxford Eagle*, Mar. 27,1969; "Homes," WPA; Skipwith Historical and Genealogical Society, *The Heritage of Lafayette County, Mississippi* (Dallas: Curtis Media Co., 1986), 387. McGhehee is variously spelled MGhee, McGhee.

49. Rebecca Pegues to Alexander Pegues, June 24, 1841, in Pegues Diaries and Letters, photocopy of typescript in author's possession.

50. Rebecca Pegues to Alexander Pegues, Feb. 9, 1943, ibid.

51. Rebecca Pegues to Alexander Pegues, June 24, 1841, May 10, 1844, ibid.

52. For every white woman between ages fifteen and forty-five there were 1.37 children five years or younger in 1840 (922/671). Children under the age of five were about one-fifth the white population in 1840; LCDA.

53. Robert C. Kenzer, *Kinship and Neighborhood in a Southern Community: Orange County, North Carolina, 1849–1881* (Knoxville: University of Tennessee Press, 1987), offers a close and revealing examination of kinship ties in an eastern community.

54. The estimate of the 1850 population sharing a common surname with one or more others is based on a random sample of two hundred household heads from census manuscript entries; LCDI.

55. LCDA. By 1860 the total number of churches in the county had declined from 38 to 32, with 12,300 accommodations or seats; this was probably a result of consolidation. They included 12 Methodists with 3,700 seats, 8 Baptist with 3,200 seats, 6 Presbyterian with 2,900; 5 Cumberland Presbyterian with 2,200. The value of church property had soared from $15,260 to $69,850. The estimates of church seats are not precise, most historians agree. For an excellent view of religion in Mississippi, see Randy J. Sparks, *On Jordan's Stormy Banks: Evangelicalism in Mississippi, 1773–1876* (Athens: University of Georgia Press, 1994), and Edward Nelson Akin, "Mississippi," in Samuel S. Hill, ed., *Religion in the Southern States: A Historical Study* (Macon, Ga.: Mercer University Press, 1983), 177–98. On church membership estimates, see Sparks, *Jordan's Stormy Banks*, 149.

56. Sparks, *Jordan's Stormy Banks*, chap. 2.

57. F. D. Srygley, *Seventy Five Years in Dixie: Recollections and Sayings of T. W. Caskey and Others* (Nashville: Gospel Advocate Publishing Co., 1893), 191–92.

58. "Minute Book of the Baptist Church at Hopewell," Constitution, [July 17, 1841], Hopewell Baptist Church, also known as First Baptist Church, Abbeville, Miss. (Lafayette County), Records, 1841–1969, reel 10, Lafayette County Baptist Records, in SHGSC.

59. Letter dated May 27, 1889, Holden Cumberland Presbyterian Church, in George Hill Papers, MDAH.

60. "A Record of the Proceedings of the Baptist Church of Christ at Bethel, Lafayette County, Mississippi," Nov. 13, 1852, Sept. 29, 1867, Lafayette County Baptist Records, in SHGSC.

61. "Records of the Session of the Presbyterian Church in Oxford, Miss." Oct. 8, 1855, ms., First Presbyterian Church, Oxford. Spelling and punctuation as in the original.

62. Faulkner, *Requiem*, 234.

63. M. J. Blackwell to Edmund B. Blackwell, Esq, Lamar, Miss., Feb. 15, 1849.

64. Goodloe Warren Buford, "Diary," May 12, 1850, typescript, UMSC.

65. Ibid., Sept. 28, 1850.

66. On St. Peter's Episcopal Church, see Skipwith, *Heritage*, 72–73; Rev. William Asger, "A History of Saint Peter's Episcopal Church" (n.p., 1951).

67. Rebecca Pegues, "Diary," Apr. 6, 1860 (Good Friday), Pegues Diaries and Letters.

68. Ibid., May 14, 1853.

69. Ibid., Nov. 25, 1854.

70. Ibid., Jan. 14, 1859.

71. Ibid., Apr. 12, 1861.

72. On women and gender and racial segregation in the churches, see Sparks, *Jordan's Stormy Banks*, chaps. 3, 8, and pp. 107, 116. There are numerous mentions of partitions separating the sexes; see Skipwith, *Heritage*, 144–99, passim.

73. William Faulkner, *As I Lay Dying* (1930; rpt. New York: Vintage International, 1990), 169; the words are from Addie Bundren quoting her father.

74. "Minute Book of the Baptist Church at Hopewell," Constitution, [July 17, 1841]; Sparks, *Jordan's Stormy Banks*, 1–4.

75. "Minutes of Oxford Baptist Church," Mar. 1, 1874, First Baptist Church, Oxford, Miss., (Lafayette County) Records, 1858–1979, reel 10, Lafayette County Baptist Records, SHGSC.

76. Records, Bethel Baptist, May 25, 1861.

77. Ibid., Sept. 1852.

78. Ibid., Dec. 1868.

79. Ibid., May 25, 1861.

80. Ibid., May 23, 1857.

81. Ibid., Jan. 26, 1860.

82. Ibid., May 25, 1861.

83. "Minute Book of the Baptist Church at Hopewell," Nov. 1869.

84. "Minutes of Oxford Baptist Church," Feb., Mar., Apr. 1874.

85. "Records, Presbyterian Church, Oxford," Aug. 15, 1846.

86. Ibid., Sept. 18, 1853, Apr. 2, 6, 20, 22, 1854.

87. Ibid., June 13, Nov. 1, 1857.

88. Ibid., Nov. 6, 1847.

89. Ibid., Feb. 5, 1858.

90. Sparks, *Jordan's Stormy Banks*, chap. 9, and passim, stresses the egalitarian impulse of the churches and the contradictions of slavery and race.

91. Gene Ramsey Miller, *A History of North Mississippi Methodism, 1820–1900* (Nashville: Parthenon Press, 1966), 43, citing WPA, "History of Calhoun County," 148–51. This account was recorded by someone identified only as "Rambler" in 1857.

92. Ibid.; Sparks, *Jordan's Stormy Banks*, 108–9.

93. *Oxford Observer*, Oct. 21, 1843, quoted in Mary Ruth Dunlap, "The Oxford Observer, Oxford, Mississippi: 1843–1844" (M.A. thesis, UM, 1973), 38. Cornersville was in the northeast corner of the county, which became annexed to Marshall in

January 1846, as indicated in John H. Long and Peggy Tuck Sinko, eds., *Mississippi: Atlas of Historical County Boundaries* (New York: Simon and Schuster, 1993), 111.

94. *Oxford Intelligencer*, Nov. 15, 1861.

Chapter Four

1. Lucindy Hall Shaw interview, in *AmS*, part 5, pp. 1927, 1925, 1931. References to the following interviews of former slaves from Lafayette County are all from *AmS*: Ernest Branon, vol. 6, part 1, 198–99; Polly Turner Cancer, vol. 7, part 2, 336–52; Rena Clark, vol. 7, part 2, 408–11; Rhoda Hunt, vol. 8, part 3, 1074–77; Joanna Thompson Isom, vol. 8, part 5, 1091–1106; Lucindy Hall Shaw, vol. 10, part 5, 1925–31; Andrew Smith, vol. 10, part 6, 174–75; Jane McLeod Wilburn, vol. 10, part 5, 2283–96; Rebecca Woods, vol. 10, part 5, 2392–94.

2. *Biographical and Historical Memoirs of Mississippi*, 2 vols. (Chicago: Goodspeed, 1891), 1:346–47.

3. Caroline Barr is one of the most important and least known of Faulkner's historical sources. Bits and pieces of information on her can be found in the following sources: Joseph Blotner, *Faulkner: A Biography*, 2 vols. (New York: Random House, 1974), 76, 1035. Blotner refers to Colonel Barr as a major planter and landowner, and John Faulkner, the author's brother, also describes "Old Colonel Barr" as living in Oxford across the street from where he lived (on University Avenue) and owning "nearly all the land from here to Burgess" (in the western part of the county). John Faulkner also places Caroline Barr's birth date at about 1849. John Faulkner, *My Brother Bill: An Affectionate Reminiscence* (Oxford: Yoknapatawpha Press, 1975), 48. The only Barr of any prominence in antebellum Lafayette County was Hugh A. Barr, who, according to the census, owned some land and a few slaves, lived in Oxford, and worked primarily as a lawyer. He was also an active member of the Oxford First Presbyterian Church. On Hugh A. Barr, see "The Bar," "Miscellaneous Interviews," WPA. The census data on Hugh A. Barr are found in U.S. Census, Slave Schedules, 1860, Miss., Lafayette County. No slave names are given, but the six slaves Barr owned included a black male age thirty-two, a mulatto male twenty-five, a black female twenty-eight, two black females sixteen and fifteen, and a black male ten (?); LCDI. On Caroline Barr, see also Walter Taylor, *Faulkner's Search for a South* (Urbana: University of Illinois Press, 1983), 20–21; Joel Williamson, *William Faulkner and Southern History* (New York: Oxford University Press, 1993), 153–54. Williamson has Callie Barr's birthdate as 1855, but I do not find any evidence to support this. Malcolm Franklin, Faulkner's stepson, reports that she was born the "night the stars fell" (1833) in South Carolina near Barr's Landing, married a South Carolina Barr slave, and came west after the Civil War, working her way from Arkansas to the Delta to Tippah County, where she met the Falkner family. Franklin, *Bitterweeds: Life with William Faulkner at Rowan Oak* (Irving, Tex.: Society for the Study of Traditional Culture, 1977), 109f. Murry C. Falkner, *The Falkners of Mississippi: A Memoir* (Baton Rouge: Louisiana State University Press, 1967),12–15, confirms that Caroline Barr was a marvelous storyteller and that her knowledge of Mississippi before and during the Civil War must have informed William Faulkner's fiction. He also mentions her tales of adventures in Arkansas and the Delta.

4. William Faulkner, "Red Leaves," in Malcolm Cowley, ed., *The Portable Faulkner*

(1946; rev. ed. New York: Viking Penguin, 1967), 57–84; "Red Leaves" originally appeared in the *Saturday Evening Post*, Oct. 25, 1930.

5. Minnie S. Holt, "Lafayette County—General History and Points of Interest," WPA.

6. William Faulkner, *Absalom, Absalom!* (New York: Vintage International, 1990), 4, 27.

7. Ibid., 20–21.

8. Michael Tadman, *Speculators and Slaves: Masters, Traders, and Slaves in the Old South* (Madison: University of Wisconsin Press, 1989), 5, 12; Allan Kulikoff, *The Agrarian Origins of American Capitalism* (Charlottesville: University Press of Virginia, 1992), 263; Peter Kolchin, *American Slavery, 1619–1877* (New York: Hill and Wang, 1993), 96–97.

9. For a fuller treatment of the westward slave migration, see Kulikoff, *Agrarian Origins*; Tadman, *Speculators and Slaves*; Steven Deyle, "The Domestic Slave Trade in America" (Ph.D. dissertation, Columbia University, 1995); Deyle, "The Domestic Slave Trade In America: The Lifeblood of the Southern Slave System," paper given at conference on "Domestic Passages: Internal Slave Trades in the Americas, 1808–1888," Gilder Lehrman Center for the Study of Slavery, Resistance, and Abolition at Yale University, Oct. 22–24, 1999. I am grateful to Professor Deyle for sending me a copy of his paper.

10. Tadman, *Speculators and Slaves*, estimates that one in three or four arrived with their masters from the East. Charles Sackett Sydnor, *Slavery in Mississippi* (1933; rpt. Gloucester, Mass.: Peter Smith, 1965), 147. Sydnor draws on research by Frederic Bancroft, *Slave-Trading in the Old South* (Baltimore: J. H. Furst, 1931), to estimate approximately 30 percent of slaves from the East and 50 percent of slaves from states adjacent to Mississippi were brought in by migrating masters or overseers, the rest as a result of slave trading. Bruce McTavish has tallied the interviews of former slaves in northern Mississippi from the Rawick, ed., *American Slave*, collection and found 20 percent arrived with their masters. Bruce Duncan McTavish, "With Strangers United in Kindred Relation: Education, Religion and Community in Northern Mississippi, 1836–1880" (Ph.D. dissertation, UM, 1993); his findings on slave migration were presented in "Strangers to One Another: Slaves and Community on the Cotton Frontiers of Northern Mississippi," paper presented at the Southwestern Historical Association—Southwestern Social Science Association Annual Meeting, Dallas, Tex., Mar., 1995. The calculation of all these figures is fraught with complications, and they can be used only as rough estimates. The main point that slave migration did not usually involve transplanting whole slaveholdings from East to West seems to be supported. Whether this meant the frequent breakup of nuclear families is another issue, and the evidence from Lafayette County argues against that.

11. John Spencer Bassett, *The Southern Plantation Overseer, as Revealed in His Letters* (1925; rpt. New York: Negro Universities Press, 1968), 119, quoting May 31, 1839, letter to James K. Polk from his Mississippi plantation. The sale of these slaves may well have been due to the collapse of cotton prices and bankruptcy of many slaveholders who were liquidating their estates at this time.

12. Polly Turner Cancer, AmS, 340.

13. Kulikoff, *Agrarian Origins*, 249, quoting Ball, *Fifty Years in Chains* (1837).

14. [Joseph Holt Ingraham], *The South-West, by a Yankee*, 2 vols. (1835; rpt. New York: Negro Universities Press, 1968), 235–40.

15. Polly Turner Cancer, AmS, 339.

16. Rebecca Woods, AmS, 2392.

17. Mattie Dillworth, AmS, 612–15.

18. Christopher Morris, "An Event in Community Organization: The Mississippi Slave Insurrection Scare of 1835," *Journal of Southern History* 22 (Fall 1988): 93–111; Sydnor, *Slavery*, 157–64.

19. Sydnor, *Slavery*, 164–66.

20. References to several different ventures involving northern Mississippians going east to speculate in slave trading may be found in T. G. Treadwell to Wm L. Treadwell, Lamar, Miss., May 10, 1849; A. B. Treadwell to Wm L. Treadwell, Lamar, Miss., June 23, 1849, A. B. Treadwell to W. Lowndes Treadwell, Lamar, Miss., Mar. 1850, Aldrich Collection, UMSC.

21. Sydnor, *Slavery*, 147, 171. Sydnor cites Bancroft, *Slave-Trading*, 387, when estimating that Mississippi imported over 102,000 slaves during the 1830s, and roughly 58,000 and 57,000 during the 1840s and 1850s respectively.

22. Horatio J. Eden, quoted in John W. Blassingame, *Slave Testimony: Two Centuries of Letters, Speeches, Interviews, and Autobiographies* (Baton Rouge: Louisiana State University Press, 1977), 631–32 (punctuation added).

23. L. Q. C. Lamar to Robert [Harper], Oxford Miss, Feb 8, 1852, Lamar (L. Q. C.) and Edward Mayes Papers, 1854–1918, MDAH (typescript of letter in Lamar-Harper Letters of the A. C. Lunsford Collection, GDAH, Atlanta).

24. Sydnor, *Slavery*, 13.

25. Lucindy Hall Shaw, AmS, 1929

26. Helen Tunncliff Catterall, ed., *Judicial Cases Concerning American Slavery and the Negro*, vol. 3 (Washington, D.C.: Carnegie Institution, 1932), 371–72. The Supreme Court ruling is found in 39, *Mississippi Reports*, 526–40, George W. Oliver v. The State. See also E. A. Smith, "Early Recollections of Oxford," *Oxford Eagle*, Mar. 3, 1910, who remembered the case being appealed and lost, another example of the unreliability of memory and local history.

27. Polly Turner Cancer, AmS, 340.

28. Bassett, *Overseer*, 120, quoting letter to James K. Polk, July 2, 1839.

29. Sydnor, *Slavery*, 70n; Stowers is identified as the overseer in J. W. Pancoast to Bonner (?), Dec 13, 1865, "Registered Letters Received, July 1865–Mar. 1866, Jackson, Miss., Acting Assistant Commissioner of the Northern District of Mississippi," entry 2188, RG 105, FB, NARA.

30. Bassett, *Overseer*, 126, quoting letter to James K. Polk, Sept. 10, 1839 (punctuation added).

31. Ibid., 55–56.

32. Ibid., 78–79.

33. Ibid., 64–65.

34. Ibid., 77–78.

35. Ibid., 129, quoting letter to Polk, Nov. 3, 1839 (punctuation added).

36. Ibid., 136, quoting letter to Polk, Jan. 15, 1840 (punctuation added).

37. Galleghy [variously spelled Gallegly] interview in Skipwith Historical and Genealogical Society, *The Heritage of Lafayette County, Mississippi* (Dallas: Curtis Media Co., 1986), 146; *Marshall Co. Republican* (Holly Springs, Miss.), Dec. 1, 1838. For other typical ads see *Organizer* (Oxford), Apr. 7, 1849, Apr. 20, 1850; *Democratic Flag* (Oxford), June 16, 1852; *Marshall Co. Republican* (Holly Springs, Miss.), Nov. 3, 1838.

38. Bassett, *Overseer*, 159, quoting letter to Polk, Sept. 1, 1841 (period added).

39. *Organizer* (Oxford), Apr. 7, 1849.

40. Bassett, *Overseer*, 192–93, quoting a letter to Polk, Apr. 16, 1851.

41. Ibid., 216–17, quoting a letter to Mrs. Polk, Sept. 14, 1856 (punctuation added).

42. Faulkner, "Was," in Cowley, ed., *Portable Faulkner*, 85–108; originally published in Faulkner, *Go Down, Moses* (New York: Random House, 1942).

43. Sydnor, *Slavery*, 78–79. Unfortunately, there is little mention of slave patrol activities in surviving local records. J. Michael Crane, "Controlling the Night: Perceptions of the Slave Patrol System in Mississippi," *Journal at Mississippi History* 61 (Summer 1999): 119–36. Crane offers an informative overview of the slave patrol; I am grateful to him for making his work available to me.

44. Sydnor, *Slavery*, 78–79, 83, 118.

45. Unidentified to Hon. C. L. Thomas, Lamar, Miss., Jan. 26, 1850, Aldrich Collection, UMSC.

46. "Minutes, Board of Supervisors, 1855–65," Jan. 6, 1858, Lafayette County, WPA transcript, RG 60, MDAH. The original volume of minutes for these years could not be located in the Lafayette County Courthouse; fortunately, a handwritten version prepared by the WPA could be found at MDAH. Beat numbers changed over time, but the central beat surrounding Oxford remained Beat One. Before the Civil War Beat Two was in the northeast quadrant, Beat Three in the northwest. Beat Four, originally the two southern quadrants combined, became the southwest quadrant, while Beat Five became the southeastern quadrant.

47. "Minutes, Board of Supervisors, 1855–65," Jan. 6, 1858, Lafayette County, WPA transcript, RG 60, MDAH.

48. Ibid., Oct. 11, 1858; see also Ibid., Oct. 16, 1860, Jan. 7, 1861.

49. Andrew Smith, *AmS*, 174; Rebecca Woods, *AmS*, 2393.

50. Sydnor, *Slavery*, 97–98. Ted Ownby graciously shared an early version of his work on slaves as consumers, now part of his book *American Dreams in Mississippi: Consumers, Poverty, and Culture, 1830–1998* (Chapel Hill: University of North Carolina Press, 1999).

51. *Marshall County Republican* (Holly Springs, Miss.), Sept. 15, 1838.

52. Polly Turner Cancer, *AmS*, 351.

53. Bassett, *Overseer*, 187, 203, 210–11, quoting letters to Polk, Nov. 5, 1850, Apr. 18, 1853, June 17, 1855 (punctuation added). Sydnor, *Slavery*, 99 n. 74 seems to think the cash payments made to Polk's slaves were made as a substitute for their private production of cotton and that the money was raised by hiring out Harry the blacksmith. He notes the private cotton patches are not mentioned after 1850. But in light of his comment about Harry's diminishing profits, it seems more likely that a sum of $200 would have come from the production of cotton, about five bales at ten cents a pound.

54. "Records of the Session of the Presbyterian Church in Oxford, Miss." Jan. 17, 1858, First Presbyterian Church, Oxford.

55. Herbert Anthony Kellar, ed., *Solon Robinson Pioneer and Agriculturalist: Selected Writings*, 2 vols. (Indianapolis: Indiana Historical Bureau, 1936), 291; Sydnor, *Slavery*, 99.

56. On the slave community, see George P. Rawick, *From Sundown to Sunup: The Making of the Black Community*, vol. 1, series 1, *The American Slave: A Composite Autobiog-*

raphy, ed., George P. Rawick (Westport, Conn.: Greenwood, 1972); John W. Blassingame, *The Slave Community: Plantation Life in the Antebellum South*, rev. ed. (New York: Oxford University Press, 1979).

57. Janet Sharp Hermann, *The Pursuit of a Dream* (New York: Oxford University Press, 1981), examines Frances Wright's Neshoba experiment, which aimed at gradual emancipation of slaves who would earn the price of their freedom. Several eminent Mississippi planters became enthused about the possibilities this plan offered, including Joseph E. Davis, brother of the Confederate president. I am grateful to Christopher Morris for suggesting this connection.

58. Sydnor, *Slavery*, 99–101. The Leigh manuscript was in the private hands of Armistead Claiborne Leigh, of Los Angeles, California, at the time Sydnor did his research and could not be located for this study, but Sydnor included extensive passages from this source.

59. *Oxford Intelligencer*, Nov. 21, Dec. 5, 1860. These incidents occurred during a period of extreme apprehension regarding anyone inciting slave rebellion or misbehavior of any kind, as described in the next chapter of this book.

60. Polly Turner Cancer, AmS, 351.

61. John Hebron Moore, *The Emergence of the Cotton Kingdom in the Old Southwest: Mississippi, 1770–1860* (Baton Rouge: Louisiana State University Press, 1988), 102–3, referring to Callie Gray, a slave of James Fant in neighboring Marshall County.

62. Foster Freeland to Mrs. James Freeland, Oxford, Miss., Dec. 20, 1847, in Freeland (Foster and Freeman) Papers, MDAH.

63. These subjects are treated at greater length in Eugene D. Genovese, *Roll, Jordan, Roll: The World the Slaves Made* (New York: Pantheon Books, 1974).

64. See the references above to works by Tadman, Kulikoff, and Deyle. See also Peter Kolchin, *American Slavery, 1619–1877* (New York: Hill and Wang, 1993), 96–97.

65. [Joseph Holt Ingraham], *The South-West, by a Yankee*, 2 vols. (1835; rpt. New York: Negro Universities Press, 1968), 238–40.

66. Rossel Green to Dear Father (addressed to Mr. Tom, Boy Servant of Mr. T. L. Treadwell, care of Mrs. Blackwell, Lamar, Miss.), near Durhamville, Apr. 4, 1846, typescript, box C-9, Aldrich Collection, UMSC. Thanks to Bruce McTavish for bringing this letter to my attention.

67. Kellar, ed., *Solon Robinson*, 2:291.

68. Quoted in "Antebellum Homes," WPA.

69. *Oxford Eagle*, Apr. 21, 1926.

70. Polly Turner Cancer, AmS, 345–46.

71. A fuller discussion of the mutual incentives slaves and masters shared in family formation and reproduction is found in Christopher Morris, *Becoming Southern: The Evolution of a Way of Life, Warren County and Vicksburg, Mississippi, 1770–1860* (New York: Oxford University Press, 1995), 69–74.

72. LCDA; John Cooper Hathorn, *Early Settlers of Lafayette Co., Mississippi: A Period Study of Lafayette County from 1836–1860 with Emphasis on Population Groups* (1938; rpt. Oxford: Skipwith, 1980), 41, 83.

73. *Democratic Flag* (Oxford), Dec. 22 [?], 1852.

74. "Probate Court Record, 1836–1846," Mar. term 1839, Chancery Court Clerk's Office, LCC.

75. Joel Williamson, *William Faulkner and Southern History* (New York: Random

House, 1994), examines what might have been interracial branches in the Falkner family tree.

76. *Oxford Eagle*, Apr. 21, 1926; data on slave housing from slave census, 1860, LCDI.

77. Frederick Law Olmsted, *A Journey in the Back Country* (New York, 1863), 140, 142, quoted in Sydnor, *Slavery*, 40.

78. Moore, *Emergence*, 85, 87.

79. Quoted Ibid., 135.

80. Kellar, ed., *Solon Robinson*, 2:290.

81. Quoted in Moore, *Emergence*, 90.

82. Oldham, "Jacob Thompson," 35–36.

83. Sydnor, *Slavery*, 64; the Bowles plantation books cover operations of one of the larger plantations in Lafayette County for the year 1851. The diary and account books were in the private possession of Mrs. Bem Price at the time Sydnor did his research. While they could not be located for my own research, Sydnor appears to have included much of the important information from these records in his book.

84. Polly Turner Cancer, AmS, 340.

85. Bassett, *Overseer*, 139, 141, quoting letters to Polk, May 3, June 7, 1840 (punctuation added).

86. Polly Turner Cancer, AmS, 340–41.

87. Ibid., 340. On slave housing, see John Michael Vlach, *Back of the Big House: The Architecture of Plantation Slavery* (Chapel Hill: University of North Carolina Press, 1993).

88. Moore, *Emergence*, 36, discusses the more permanent improvements that took place on plantations between 1845 and 1860.

89. Records, Bethel Baptist. A fuller treatment of religion and slavery in Mississippi is found in Randy Sparks, *On Jordan's Stormy Banks: Evangelicalism in Mississippi, 1773–1876* (Athens: University of Georgia Press, 1994), 132–45. See also John B. Boles, *Black Southerners, 1619–1869* (Lexington: University Press of Kentucky, 1984); Albert J. Raboteau, *Slave Religion: The "Invisible Institution" in the Antebellum South* (New York: Oxford University Press, 1978); Eugene D. Genovese, *Roll, Jordan, Roll: The World the Slaves Made* (New York: Pantheon Books, 1976).

90. Records, Bethel Baptist, May 21, 1859.

91. Hopewell Baptist Church, aka First Baptist Church, Abbeville, Miss. (Lafayette County), Records, 1841–1969, Nov. 25, 1843, reel 10, Lafayette County Baptist Records, SHGSC.

92. First Baptist Church, Oxford, Miss., (Lafayette County) Records 1858–1979, September 1861, October 1861, reel 10, SHGSC.

93. "Church Erected in 1845," *Oxford Eagle*, Mar. 27, 1969.

94. "Antioch Primitive Baptist Church," *Oxford Eagle*, May 7, 1987.

95. "Clear Creek Baptist Church," *Oxford Eagle*, Mar. 27, 1969; See also the account of the Clear Creek Baptist Church of Burgess, which also had a slave balcony in "Good ole days oft recalled," *Oxford Eagle*, Mar. 27, 1969.

96. "Minutes," College Hill Presbyterian Church, Nov. 1, 1836–Jan. 11, 1864, mf, SHGSC; the entry for Jan. 3, 1851, suggests that the stairway to the gallery was not completed until sometime after this date. *College Hill Presbyterian Church, Oxford, Mis-*

sissippi, *Sesquicentennial Celebration, June 22, 23, 1996*, [n.p., 1996], [4], confirms that the slave gallery was not added until the early 1850s.

Chapter Five

1. *Oxford Observer*, July 13, 1844; Bradley G. Bond, *Political Culture in the Nineteenth-Century South: Mississippi, 1830–1900* (Baton Rouge: Louisiana State University Press, 1995), 95. Part One of Bond's book provides an excellent overview of antebellum Mississippi politics.

2. Percy Lee Rainwater, *Mississippi: Storm Center of Secession, 1856–1861* (Baton Rouge: Otto Claitor, 1938), 9, 10.

3. Letter from "B" of Oxford, dated Oct. 23, 1843, printed in *Holly Springs Gazette*, Nov. 3, 1843.

4. Letter from "Q in the corner," in response to letters from "Crabstick" in Whig paper, *Star of Union*, quoted in *Organizer* (Oxford), Apr. 20, 1850.

5. *Dollar Democrat* (Oxford), edited by Percy Howe, 1841–43; *Oxford Observer*, edited by William Delay and J. T. Stockard, 1843–; *Organizer* (Oxford), published by William Delay, 1849; *Constitution* (Oxford), by Benjamin F. Dill; *Democratic Flag* (Oxford), William Delay, 1852; *Oxford Signal*, 1856; *Oxford Intelligencer*, edited by Howard Falconer, 1860; *Oxford Mercury*, 1861. Unfortunately, no Whig newspapers survive.

6. *Holly Springs Gazette*, May 23, 1844.

7. *Oxford Observer*, Aug. 19, 1843.

8. *Dollar Democrat* (Oxford), July 7, 1843.

9. David Nathaniel Young, "The Mississippi Whigs, 1834–1860" (Ph.D. dissertation, University of Alabama, 1968), chap. 4, compares party leadership across the state, 1834–61, and shows no significant differences in social and economic characteristics. Based on profiles of party leaders, this appears to hold true for Lafayette County as well.

10. Mary Ruth Dunlap, "The Oxford Observer, Oxford, Mississippi: 1843–1844" (M.A. thesis, UM, 1973), 16.

11. Dunlap, "Observer," 17.

12. *Organizer* (Oxford), June 9, 1849.

13. Ibid., June 9, 1849. Joel Williamson, *William Faulkner and Southern History* (New York: Oxford University Press, 1993), 38–39. Thomas Jefferson Word was the uncle of William C. Falkner, the author's great-grandfather. Bond, *Political Culture*, 95f., argues that the compromise galvanized Mississippi anti-Unionism, "which led to the elimination of dissent and eventually to secession."

14. *Organizer* (Oxford), June 15, 1850; Paul Barringer to Daniel M. Barringer, Oxford, Miss., Nov. 18, 1850, D. M. Barringer Papers, SHC. I am grateful to Bruce McTavish for bringing this collection to my attention and to Louis Kyriakoudes for providing photocopies of this letter.

15. *Organizer* (Oxford), July 6, 1850. Emphasis added.

16. Ibid., July 6, 1850.

17. Ibid., July 13, 1850.

18. On the central importance of honor in southern culture, see Bertram Wyatt-Brown, *Southern Honor: Ethics and Behavior in the Old South* (New York: Oxford University Press, 1982).

19. *Organizer* (Oxford), Sept. 28, 1850.

20. Ibid., Sept. 28, 1850.

21. Ibid., Nov. 16, 1851. The account of this meeting comes from the Democratic press. No copies of the Whig *Star of Union*, published in Oxford, survive, and its views are revealed only in the rejoinders of the rival Democratic paper. Another local Whig paper, the *Mississippi Journal*, is mentioned in *Democratic Flag* (Oxford), Nov. 10, Dec. 15, 1852. This is the paper whose press and office the *Democratic Flag* took over following the election of 1852.

22. *Organizer* (Oxford), Nov. 16, 1851.

23. *Constitution* (Oxford), Mar. 22, 1851.

24. Ibid., Apr. 5, 1851.

25. Paul Barringer to Daniel M. Barringer, Oxford, Miss., July 24, 1851, Barringer Papers, SHC.

26. William C. Davis, *Jefferson Davis: The Man and His Hour* (New York: Harper Collins, 1991), 207–9, examines the evolution of Davis as a Southern Rights spokesman; see also Paul Barringer to Daniel M. Barringer, Oxford, Miss., July 24, 1851, Barringer Papers, SHC.

27. Rainwater, *Mississippi*, 18–19; Bond, *Political Culture*, 9–101, 107–8; Reuben Davis, *Recollections of Mississippi and Missipians* (Boston: Houghton Mifflin, 1890), 331–33.

28. B. F. Dill to Colonel C. D. Fontaine, Oxford, Miss., July 6, 1852, Fontaine (Charles D. and Family) Papers, MDAH.

29. Quoted in the *Democratic Flag* (Oxford), Aug. 4, Dec. 15, 1852. On Duval, see Emelda Villacortes Capati, "The *Oxford Intelligencer*: 1860–1861" (M.A. thesis, UM, 1961), 10–11. After editing pro-Union newspapers in Pontotoc and Holly Springs, Duval returned to Oxford in 1861 to join Howard Falconer as editor of the *Oxford Intelligencer*. The American Party, known as the Know Nothings, attempted to build an opposition party but found little support in Lafayette County.

30. *Democratic Flag* (Oxford), May 5, 1852; L. Q. C. Lamar to Robert [Harper], Oxford Miss, Feb 8, 1852 (typescript of letter in Lamar-Harper Letters of the A. C. Lunsford Collection, Georgia Department of Archives and History, Atlanta), in Lamar (L. Q. C.) and Edward Mayes Papers, 1854–1918, MDAH.

31. On Lamar, see Edward Mayes, *Lucius Q. C. Lamar: His Life, Times, and Speeches, 1825–1893*, 2d ed. (Nashville: Methodist Episcopal Church, South, 1896), and James B. Murphy, *L. Q. C. Lamar: Pragmatic Patriot* (Baton Rouge: Louisiana State University Press, 1973).

32. *Constitution* (Oxford), June 14, 1851.

33. James Silver, *Mississippi: The Closed Society* (1963; rpt. New York: Harcourt, Brace and World, 1966), traces the narrowing of the debate over racial segregation in modern Mississippi back to the antebellum defense of slavery and secession.

34. *Constitution* (Oxford), Sept. 27, 1851. The letter was signed by H. D. McIntosh, A. G. Patton, J. A. Hunt, R. A. Redding, H. Redding, L. Redding, D. Singletary, John Gardner, and J. A. Hickman.

35. Ibid., July 12, 1851.

36. Ibid., July 12, 1851.

37. *Oxford Intelligencer*, Dec. 5, 1860.

38. E. A. Smith, "Confederate Column," *Oxford Eagle*, May 19, 1910.

39. *Oxford Intelligencer*, May 15, 1861.

40. Ibid., Jan. 9, 1861.

41. Ibid., Dec. 5, Nov. 21, 1860.

42. Ibid., Apr. 10, 1861.

43. Reverend John H. Aughey, *The Iron Furnace: or, Slavery and Secession* (Philadelphia: William S. and Alfred Martien, 1863), 51–52. Aughey, a "refugee from Mississippi," fled the state after being tried for his pro-Union sentiments.

44. William L. Barney, *The Secessionist Impulse: Alabama and Mississippi in 1860* (Princeton: Princeton University Press, 1974), 210, quoting *Weekly Panola Star*, Dec. 27, 1860, Jan. 10, 1861. Political supporters of John Bell and the Constitutional Union ticket claimed the entire affair was trumped up to give advantage to the secessionists.

45. *Oxford Intelligencer*, May 29, 1861.

46. Ibid., Nov. 14, 1860.

47. Ibid., Sept. 26, 1860, quoting the *Holly Springs Star*, Sept. 19, 1860.

48. *Oxford Intelligencer*, Sept. 26, 1860.

49. "Minutes, Board of Supervisors, 1855–65," August, Apr. 18, 1859, WPA transcript, RG 60, MDAH.

50. *Oxford Intelligencer*, Oct. 24, 1860.

51. Ibid., Oct. 24, 1860.

52. Ibid., Oct. 24, 1860.

53. Ibid., Sept. 26, Oct. 24, 1860.

54. Ibid., Sept. 26, 1860, quoting *Holly Springs Union*, Sept. 17, 1860.

55. *Oxford Intelligencer*, Nov. 14, 1860.

56. Ibid., Nov. 21, 1860.

57. Winthrop Jordan, *Tumult and Silence at Second Creek: An Inquiry into a Civil War Slave Conspiracy*, rev. ed. (Baton Rouge: Louisiana State University Press, 1995), offers a fascinating glimpse of the community reaction to a slave insurrection plot.

58. Barney, *Secessionist Impulse*, 210, quoting *Weekly Panola Star*, Dec. 27, 1860, Jan. 10, 1861.

59. *Independent Monitor*, Nov. 16, 1860, quoted in *Eastern Clarion* (Paulding), Dec. 26, 1860, cited in Barney, *Secessionist Impulse*, 213. Barney includes several other accounts of vigilante violence in northern Mississippi and stresses the political motives behind this campaign of terror.

60. Frances R. Huff, "The Relationship of Oxford and the University of Mississippi, 1848–1947" (M.A. thesis, UM, 1947), chap. 2.

61. William J. Chute, *Damn Yankee!: The First Career of Frederick A. P. Barnard, Educator, Scientist, Idealist* (Port Washington, N.Y.: Kennikat Press, 1978), 159–60, 168–73. For a complete record of the trial, see *Record of the Testimony and Proceedings, in the Matter of the Investigation, by the Trustees of the University of Mississippi, on the 1st and 2nd of March, 1860, of the Charges Made by H. R. Branham, against the Chancellor of the University* (Jackson: Mississippian, 1860).

62. Murphy, *Lamar*, 38.

63. Mayes, *Lamar*; Murphy, *Lamar*, 41–42.

64. Murphy, *Lamar*, 49.

65. Rainwater, *Mississippi*, 53, 94.

66. Smith, "Confederate Column," *Oxford Eagle*, May 19, 1910. The Pettus speech apparently took place sometime in late 1859.

67. *Oxford Intelligencer*, Oct. 3, 1860; for accounts of the election and Democratic Party efforts at reconciliation with the opposition, see ibid., Aug. 8, 22, 1860.

68. Rebecca Pegues, "Diary," Nov. 28, 1860, Pegues Diaries and Letters, typescript in private possession of Guy Turnbow, Oxford, Mississippi.

69. *Oxford Intelligencer*, Nov. 28, 1860.

70. Ibid., Nov. 28, 1860.

71. Ibid., Nov. 28, 1860.

72. Ibid., Dec. 5, 1860, May 15, 1861, for examples of the historical comparisons of the American and Southern revolutions.

73. Ibid., Dec. 5, 1860.

74. Ibid., Dec. 12, 1860

75. Ibid., Dec. 5, 1860; Thomas D. Isom, see Robert Lowry and William H. McCardle, *A History of Mississippi* (Jackson, Miss.: R. H. Henry, 1891), 511; *Biographical and Historical Memoirs of Mississippi* (Chicago, Goodspeed, 1891), 1:1006.

76. *Oxford Intelligencer*, Dec. 12, 1860. Rainwater, *Mississippi*, 179, explains the political strategies behind the coalition ticket and the separate "extreme cooperationist" ticket in Lafayette County. Robertson was sometimes identified as Robinson, in the census and in other sources, including the 1860 census, but the prevailing spelling was Robertson.

77. *Oxford Intelligencer*, Dec. 19, 1860; Charles C. Bolton, *Poor Whites of the Antebellum South: Tenants and Laborers in Central North Carolina and Northeast Mississippi* (Durham: Duke University Press, 1994), 169. For the vote by precinct, see *Oxford Intelligencer*, Jan. 2, 1861.

78. *Oxford Intelligencer*, Dec. 26, 1860.

79. Ibid., Dec. 26, 1860.

80. Ibid., Jan. 23, 1861.

81. Ibid., Jan. 30, 1861.

82. Ibid., Jan. 2, 1861.

83. *Journal of the State Convention*, (Jackson: E. Barksdale, State Printer, 1861), 86–88.

84. *Oxford Intelligencer*, Jan. 9, 1861.

85. E. A. Smith, "Secession in Lafayette County," *Oxford Eagle*, May 26, 1910. Smith wrote a series of articles based on his reminiscences of secession and the war.

86. Rebecca Pegues, "Diary," Jan. 9, 1861, Pegues Diaries and Letters.

87. "The Diary of Duncan McCullom, 1861," typescript, J. Kinlock McCullom, ed., 1963 [1969], UMSC.

88. Davis, *Recollections*, 402, 412. Political allies tried to warn Davis against predicting war and hardship, but he insisted on doing so. For another amusing reaction, see Barlow (Treadwell?) to father, Cedar Grove, Jan. 22, 1861, Aldrich Collection, UMSC: "I was on my way to Jackson to see, among other things, the 'Republic of Mississippi' draw its first breath . . . although when I arrived at Jackson the New Republic had been breathing Kicking and Squealing for seven long hours still the rejoicing of the Juveniles at the idea of being out of the United States added to the Commotion and perplexity caused the 100 fathers of the New born nation to decide what to do next in order to save the tender infant."

Chapter Six

1. *Oxford Intelligencer*, Jan. 16, Apr. 3, May 8, 1861; in the last account the editor estimated Lafayette's commitment to cotton had been cut back by 25 percent, while corn was up by one-third.

2. H. R. Miller to George Miller, Pontotoc, Miss., Mar. 14, 1861, Miller Family Papers, UMSC.

3. William Faulkner, *Absalom, Absalom!* (1936; New York: Vintage International, 1990), 64–65.

4. William Faulkner, *Sartoris*, 199; quoted in Douglas T. Miller, "Faulkner and the Civil War: Myth and Reality," *American Quarterly* 15 (1963): 202.

5. James M. McPherson, *For Cause and Comrades: Why Men Fought in the Civil War* (New York: Oxford University Press, 1997), emphasizes the ideological convictions among common soldiers on both sides. I stress domestic and gender concerns because they appear most prominently during the initial stage of local mobilization.

6. *Oxford Intelligencer*, Jan. 16, 1861.

7. Ibid., Jan. 23, 1861.

8. Ibid., Jan. 30, 1861; quoted as written.

9. Rebecca Pegues, "Diary," Aug. 13, May 16, 1861; May 24, 1862, Pegues Diaries and Journals.

10. *Oxford Intelligencer*, Feb. 6, 1861.

11. Accounts of this event are taken from *Mercury* (Oxford), Mar. 9, 1861, reprinted in *Lamar Rifles: A History of Company G, Eleventh Mississippi Regiment, C.S.A.* (1901; rpt. Topeka, Kan.: Bonnie Blue Press, 1992), 52–57; *Oxford Intelligencer*, Mar. 20, 1861. Transcripts of the speech differ slightly in the two accounts.

12. *Oxford Intelligencer*, Mar. 20, 1861.

13. Ibid., Feb. 13, 1861.

14. Ibid., Feb. 27, 1861.

15. Ibid., Apr. 3, 1861.

16. Ibid.

17. Ibid., Apr. 17, 1861.

18. Jacob Thompson to former president Buchanan, Oxford, Miss., June 7, 1861, reprinted in Jack Case Wilson, *Faulkners, Fortunes and Flames* (Nashville: Annandale Press: 1984), 1. This was one of several Thompson letters confiscated by the occupying Union forces in December 1862 and published by the *New York Daily Tribune* as incriminating evidence of Thompson's disloyalty to the government he had served as a cabinet officer.

19. Pat A. Willis to Lt. H. W. Walter, Holly Springs, Miss., Nov. 11, 1861, in H. W. Walter Papers, Holly Springs Historical Society, photocopy in Walter Letters, UMSC.

20. J. E. Robuck, *My Own Personal Experience and Observation as a Soldier in the Confederate Army during the Civil War, 1861–1865, also during the Period of Reconstruction* (Birmingham: Leslie Printing and Publishing Company, 1911), 7, 12, 13–15. Robuck may have the chronology confused here, and he may have been just telling a good story. The Confederate draft law did not go into effect until the middle of 1862 and the provision exempting one white man for every twenty slaves came later, in October 1862.

21. Ibid., 13–15. On the role of women in recruiting and sometimes resisting the call to arms, see George C. Rable, *Civil Wars: Women and the Crisis of Southern Nationalism* (Urbana: University of Illinois, 1991), chap. 4.

22. Walker Coffey, *Confederate Soldiers: Lafayette County, Mississippi* (N.p., 1990). Coffey's compilation of company histories and individual Confederate military records is the most thorough record of the county's military contribution to the Civil War, but it may omit some companies that included men from Lafayette and neighboring counties. There is no similar account for the white and black soldiers from Lafayette who served the Union Army. Coffey counts 1,785 Lafayette County Confederate soldiers; the census for 1860 indicates there were 1,583 white males between eighteen and forty; LCDA. At the end of the war, estimates sent to state officials stated that 2,220 men had served from Lafayette County; see William Delay, Clerk, to A. J. Gillespie, Oxford, telegram, May 30, 1864, in Confederate Records, Indigent and Disabled Soldiers and Dependents, MDAH. An earlier list indicates that 1,845 men enlisted by July 1863: "A list of Soldiers that have went from Lafayette County, Mississippi Into the Confederate and State Service Since the commencement of the present war to Mar. 1st, 1863," in RG 151, MDAH. E. A. Smith, "Confederate Column," *Oxford Eagle*, July 21, 1910, estimates that 2,000 Lafayette men served and adds that if Mississippi and the South had contributed with the same zeal, the Confederacy would have had 1.3 million in service.

23. *Oxford Intelligencer*, May 22, 1861.

24. Coffey, *Confederate Soldiers*, lists fourteen companies. Maud Morrow Brown, a knowledgeable local historian, claims these fourteen and mentions two others, the True Mississippians and Dixie Rebels. C. John Sobotka Jr., *A History of Lafayette County, Mississippi* (Oxford: Rebel Press, 1976), 33, 106 n. 2, also lists sixteen companies, but some that differ from Brown and Coffey, including the Lafayette Dragoons, Webb's Rangers, Lafayette Defenders, Company A, Fourth Regiment, and Lafayette Cavalry. Some of this confusion may be explained by a number of companies that recruited men across county borders and by changes in company names.

25. Ella F. Pegues, "Recollections of the Civil War in Lafayette County," Maud Morrow (Mrs. Calvin S.) Brown Papers, MDAH.

26. *Oxford Intelligencer*, May 1, 1861.

27. Ibid., May 1, 1861.

28. Ibid., May 8, 1861.

29. Ibid., May 22, 1861.

30. Ibid., May 8, 1861.

31. Ibid., May 29, 1861.

32. William Faulkner, *Requiem for a Nun* (1951; rpt. New York: Vintage, 1975), 198.

33. Robuck, *My Own Personal Experience*, 18

34. Rebecca Pegues, "Diary," Aug. 1, 1861, Pegues Diaries and Letters.

35. Ibid., Nov. 15, 1861.

36. Malcolm Cowley, ed., *The Portable Faulkner* (1946; rev. ed. New York: Viking Penguin, 1967), 679.

37. W. T. Caskey to Governor Pettus, Oxford, Miss., May 3, 1862, in Willie D. Halsell, ed., "The Oxford Hospital, 1862," *Journal of Mississippi History*, 8 (1946): 43–44.

38. Maud Morrow Brown, "At Home in Lafayette County, Mississippi, 1860–1865," 54, Maud Morrow Brown Manuscript, MDAH.

39. Faulkner, *Absalom*, 155–56; Matthew C. O'Brien, "William Faulkner and the Civil War in Oxford, Mississippi," *Journal of Mississippi History* 35 (May 1973): 167–74; *Oxford Eagle*, Mar. 27, 1969; Pegues, "Recollections"; Brown, "At Home in Lafayette County," 54–57. See also Jemmy Grant Johnson, "The University War Hospital,"

PMHS 7 (1912): 94–106. On Confederate women as nurses, see Rable, *Civil Wars*, 121–28.

40. Pegues, "Recollections."

41. Rebecca Pegues, "Diary," Apr. 24, 1862, Pegues Diaries and Letters.

42. Robuck, *My Own Personal Experience*, 16–18. Robuck says he joined in March 1862, but his dates may not be reliable because the Battle of Shiloh took place in April and the draft law followed this. He probably made up the name Davanport, perhaps to protect the identity of a local family.

43. Rebecca Pegues, "Diary," Nov. 16, 1862, Pegues Diaries and Letters.

44. John H. Miller to Col. Hugh R. Miller, Pontotoc, Miss., Nov. 14, 1862, Miller Family Papers, UMSC.

45. On the importance of the western theater of war, see William L. Barney, *Flawed Victory: A New Perspective on the Civil War* (New York: Praeger, 1975). On the shift in Union policy toward Confederate civilians, see Stephen V. Ash, *When the Yankees Came: Conflict and Chaos in the Occupied South, 1861–1865* (Chapel Hill: University of North Carolina Press, 1995), chaps. 1, 2.

46. Polly Turner Cancer, AmS, 346.

47. Mildred Throne, ed., *The Civil War Diary of Cyrus F. Boyd, Fifteenth Iowa Infantry, 1861–1863* (Millwood, N.Y.: Kraus Reprint, 1977), 88–90; this diary is reprinted from four issues of *Iowa Journal of History* 50 (1952).

48. J. M. Hubbard to *Commercial Appeal*, [n.d.] quoted in J. G. Deupree, "The Noxubee Squadron of the First Mississippi Cavalry, C.S.A., 1861–1865" PMHS 2 (1918): 56. Miss Taylor Cook, according to local lore, later married the only son of Nathan Bedford Forrest. This story may have inspired Faulkner's quite different account of Celia Cook [also referred to as Celia Farmer] in *Requiem for a Nun*. On the Celia Cook/Farmer story, see also E. O. Hawkins, "Jane Cook and Cecilia Farmer," *Mississippi Quarterly* 18 (Fall 1965); Joseph Blotner, *Faulkner: A Biography*, 2 vols. (New York: Random House, 1974), 138; Gabriele Gutting, *Yoknapatawpha: The Function of Geographical and Historical Facts in William Faulkner's Fictional Picture of the Deep South* (Frankfurt am Main: Peter Lang, 1992), 69–70. Gutting explains that Jane Taylor Cook was the woman involved and that the story was well known to Faulkner's loquacious friend Phil Stone.

49. M. C. Miller to Col. Hugh R. Miller, Pontotoc, Miss., Dec. 31, 1862, Miller Family Papers, UMSC.

50. Rebecca Pegues, "Diary," June 20, 1862; Apr. 8, 1863, Pegues Diaries and Letters.

51. First Lieutenant S. F. Kendrick to Colonel John Adams, Pontotoc, Miss., Dec. 11, 1862, Pemberton Papers, NARA. Kendrick was describing the exodus from Pontotoc, thirty miles east of Oxford.

52. John H. Miller to Col. Hugh R. Miller, Pontotoc, Miss., Nov. 14, 1862, Miller Family Papers, UMSC.

53. *Chicago Tribune*, Dec. 12, 1862, report dated Dec. 2.

54. Ibid., Dec. 13, 1862.

55. Ibid., Dec. 12, 1862, report dated Dec. 3.

56. *OR*, ser. 1, vol. 17, pt. 1, reports, 472–73. Grant's correspondence indicates he remained in Abbeville December 3–7 and only by December 8 did his correspondence originate from Oxford.

57. William T. Sherman, *Memoirs of General William T. Sherman* (1875; rpt. West-

port, Conn.: Greenwood Press, 1972), 280–81, explains that exaggerated reports of Union progress at Helena, Arkansas, and a raid on the Mississippi Railroad at Coffeeville had panicked Pemberton to abandon what was a strong line of defense at the Tallahatchie.

58. OR, ser. 1, vol. 17, pt. 1, 472–73.

59. Sherman, Memoirs, 280; Chicago Tribune, Dec. 10, 1862, correspondence from Oxford, Dec. 5, 1862.

60. General Joseph Stockton, Diary, Dec. 5, 1862, excerpts printed in Oxford Eagle, Nov. 3, 1960; original diary in Chicago Historical Society.

61. Throne, ed., Civil War Diary of Boyd, 94.

62. Mary L. Smither, "Reminiscences of Mary L. Smither," 19, (1913–25), typescript, SHGSC. Smither says Dickey resigned after the northern Mississippi campaign, apparently because of his disgust with the Union treatment of civilians.

63. Rebecca Wood, AmS, 2993.

64. Jane McLeod Wilburn, AmS, 2295.

65. Martin Mullins, case 9958, SCC.

66. Tamer Hewlett, case 9948, SCC.

67. Chicago Tribune, Dec. 12, 1862, from report of Dec. 3.

68. Joseph Stockton, Diary, Dec. 12, 1862, Oxford Eagle, Nov. 3, 1960.

69. Chicago Tribune, Dec. 12, 1862, report dated Dec. 3.

70. Wilson, Faulkners, 4.

71. Throne, ed., Civil War Diary of Boyd, 94; entry for Dec. 19, 1862.

72. Wilson, Faulkners, 1, 3, 13.

73. OR, ser. I, vol. 17, part 1, 516; Ulysses S. Grant, Personal Memoirs of U. S. Grant, 2 vols, (New York: C. L. Webster, 1885–86), 1:432–33.

74. Grant, Memoirs, 1:435; J. V. Frederick, "An Illinois Soldier in North Mississippi: Diary of John Wilson, Feb. 15–Dec. 30, 1862," Journal of Mississippi History 1 (1939): 193, diary entry for Dec. 21, 1862: "Gen. Grant orders the town burned but reconsiders the thing and counter mands [sic] the order." In local lore, and in Faulkner's occasional references to the Civil War, Grant, and sometimes Sherman, are blamed for the burning of Oxford. The burning of Oxford did not take place until much later.

75. Julia Dent Grant, The Personal Memoirs of Julia Dent Grant (New York: G. P. Putnam's Sons, 1975), 104–9; Ash, Yankees, chap. 2.

76. Rebecca Wood, AmS, 2993.

77. Lucindy Hall Shaw, AmS, 1928.

78. U. S. Grant to Col. J. C. Kelton, Holly Springs, Miss., Dec. 25, 1862, OR, ser. 1, vol. 1, pt. 1, 478, 480.

79. Grant, Memoirs, 1:435–36, 432. See also James W. Silver, ed, Mississippi in the Confederacy as Seen in Retrospect (Baton Rouge: Louisiana State University Press, 1961), 267; Throne, ed., Civil War Diary of Boyd, 95–96.

80. M. C. Miller to Col. Hugh R. Miller, Pontotoc, Miss., Dec. 31, 1862. Miller Family Papers, UMSC.

81. Burlina Butler, case 18278, SCC. Her losses occurred in December 1862 and August 1864. Burlina Butler was acting as executrix to her deceased husband's estate, which might have been a way of evading questions about her own loyalties. She would have had difficulty establishing her claim to Union loyalty; she was listed as an active member in the Ladies Military Aid Society in 1861. Oxford Intelligencer, May 22,

1861. There were two other Butlers who made claims to the Commission: Branch and Margaret.

82. Robert F. Cathey, case 8542, SCC; letter dated Dec. 17, 1862.

83. Urcilla Fondren, case 8581, SCC.

84. Jane Medders [or Medors or Meadows?], case 9957, SCC.

85. Albert G. Browning, case 0272, SCC.

86. Bem Price, case 20490, SCC.

87. Ibid.; William Faulkner, *The Unvanquished* (1938; rpt. New York: Vintage International, 1991), 11–12.

88. Unsigned to sister Dona, Oxford, Miss., Jan. 27, 1863, H. W. Walter Papers, UMSC, identified as photocopy of original in Holly Springs Historical Society, though it could not be located there during my visits.

89. Brown, "At Home in Lafayette County," 100.

90. Grant to Kelton, OR, ser. 1, vol. 17, pt. 1, 478, 480.

91. Skipwith Historical and Genealogical Society, *The Heritage of Lafayette County, Mississippi* (Dallas: Curtis Media Corporation, 1986), 163.

92. Faulkner, *Requiem*, 199.

Chapter Seven

1. Much of the new social history of the Confederacy stresses the division and demoralization at work on the southern home front, particularly among women and slaves. On the role of women, Catherine Clinton and Nina Silber, eds., *Divided Houses: Gender and the Civil War* (New York: Oxford University Press, 1992), brings together much of the new scholarship. See also Drew Faust, *Mothers of Invention: Women of the Slaveholding South in the American Civil War* (Chapel Hill: University of North Carolina Press, 1996); LeeAnn Whites, *The Civil War as a Crisis in Gender: Augusta, Georgia, 1860–1890* (Athens: University of Georgia Press, 1995). On the role of slaves in the Civil War, a superb source is Armstead Robinson, "Day of Jubilo: Civil War and the Demise of Slavery in the Mississippi Valley, 1861–1865" (Ph.D. dissertation, University of Rochester, 1976). Ira Berlin et al., *Slaves No More: Three Essays on Emancipation and the Civil War* (New York: Cambridge University Press, 1992), summarizes many of the findings of the Freedmen and Southern Society Project. In response to these and other recent works that emphasize the collapse of the Confederacy at the home front and the failure of its will to win, see Gary W. Gallagher, *The Confederate War* (Cambridge, Mass.: Harvard University Press, 1997), who demonstrates the tenacity and will to win of the Confederacy at home and in the field. My evidence for Lafayette County reveals great internal dissension and demoralization but also the tremendous sacrifice and perseverance. Moreover, as the next chapter demonstrates, the will to fight continued for the next decade as the war for independence turned to a struggle over white supremacy.

2. William Faulkner, *The Unvanquished* (1938; New York: Vintage International, 1991). For an excellent guide to this novel, and one with reliable historical references, see James C. Hinkle and Robert McCoy, *Reading Faulkner: The Unvanquished, Glossary and Commentary* (Jackson: University Press of Mississippi, 1995).

3. For a fuller treatment of the end of slavery, see the excellent series produced by the Freedmen and Southern Society Project under the general title *Freedom: A Documentary History of Emancipation*, including ser. 1, vol. 3, *The Wartime Genesis of Free Labor:*

The Lower South, ed. Ira Berlin, Thavolia Glymph, Steven F. Miller, Joseph P. Reidy, Leslie S. Rowland, and Julie Saville (New York: New Press, 1990). See also Berlin et al., eds., Free at Last: A Documentary History of Slavery, Freedom, and the Civil War (New York: New Press, 1992). Eric Foner, Reconstruction: America's Unfinished Revolution, 1863–1877 (New York: Harper and Row, 1988), 1–17 and passim, sets emancipation in the context of Reconstruction policies that would unfold later. See also Clarence L. Mohr, On the Threshold of Freedom: Masters and Slaves in Civil War Georgia (Athens: University of Georgia Press, 1986).

4. Rebecca H. Pegues to Alexander H. Pegues, Oxford, Jan. 12, 1863, Pegues Diaries and Letters, typescript in private possession of Guy Turnbow, Oxford, Mississippi.

5. Major General W. W. Loring to Lt. General J. C. Pemberton, Grenada, Miss., Dec. 28, 1862; Loring to Colonel J. R. Waddy, Grenada, Jan. 17, 1863; Loring to Waddy, Grenada, Miss., Jan. 18, 1863,; T. C. Tupper to Waddy, [no place cited], Feb. 14, 1863; Letters and Telegrams Received, Papers of General John C. Pemberton, War Department Collection of Confederate Records, RG 109, NARA. See also John K. Bettersworth, Mississippi in the Confederacy: As They Saw It (Baton Rouge: Louisiana State University Press, 1961), 163–64, who quotes both telegrams. The second telegram could not be located in the Pemberton Papers.

6. Jane McLeod Wilburn, AmS, 2290.

7. Eliza Evans Pegues to Capt. Josiah J. Pegues, The Cedars [Dallas County, Alabama], Jan. 18, 1863, Pegues Diaries and Letters.

8. Faulkner, Unvanquished, 23; Robinson, "Day of Jubilo."

9. J. V. Frederick, "An Illinois Soldier in North Mississippi: Diary of John Wilson, Feb. 15–Dec. 30, 1862," Journal of Mississippi History 1 (1939): 92, Nov. 7, 8, 1862.

10. C. Carpenter to Emmett, Sept. 20, 1862, quoted in Robinson, "Jubilo," 470.

11. U. S. Grant to H. W. Halleck, La Grange, [Tennessee], Nov. 15, 1862, OR, ser. 1, vol. 17, pt. 1, 470.

12. John Eaton, Grant, Lincoln and the Freedmen: Reminiscences of the Civil War (1907; rpt. New York: Negro Universities Press, 1969), 2.

13. Faulkner, Unvanquished, 81.

14. Ibid., 92, 29, 228.

15. Eaton, Grant, 2.

16. Faulkner, Unvanquished, 24–25, 26, 74–75.

17. Polly Turner Cancer, AmS, 346.

18. James Wilford Garner, Reconstruction in Mississippi (1901; rpt. Gloucester, Mass.: Peter Smith, 1964), 27.

19. John H. Miller to Col. Hugh R. Miller, Pontotoc, Miss., Nov. 14, 1862, Miller Papers, UMSC.

20. [Governor] Jno. J. Pettus to Lt. General Pemberton, Jackson, Miss., Feb. 3, 1863, in Pemberton Papers, telegrams, February 1863, NARA.

21. Maud Morrow Brown, "At Home in Lafayette County, Mississippi, 1860–1865," 92; typescript, box 1, Mrs. Calvin S. Brown Papers, MDAH.

22. Brown, "At Home in Lafayette County," 92; in her WPA interview Isom reported having taken refuge in Pittsboro for a year and a half, returning to Oxford after it was burned.

23. Rhoda Hunt, AmS, 1075. She was former slave to the McGlauns in Lafayette Springs.

24. By another account, Union soldiers poisoned the well on the Price plantation, and the only slaves who knew the secret of the silver box died before they could tell anyone. "Homes," WPA.

25. Rebecca Wood, AmS, 2993.

26. College Hill Presbyterian Church Minutes, Jan. 5, 1863, quoted in Brown, "At Home in Lafayette County," 107.

27. Jane McLeod Wilburn, AmS, 2287, 2295.

28. Lucindy Hall Shaw, AmS, 1929; Unsigned letter to sister Dona, Oxford, Jan. 27, 1863, H. W. Walter Papers, UMSC.

29. LCDI. By 1870 the mulatto population stood at 357, down from 623 in 1860. Only 26 mulatto children in the 1870 census could have been born between 1862 and 1864, when white men were away. In 1870 nearly one-quarter of the county's mulattoes were born since 1865. Reporting on race or color left a great deal of discretion both to the census taker and to those they were classifying.

30. First Lieutenant S. F. Kendrick to Colonel Jon Adams, Pontotoc, Miss., Dec. 11, 1862, Dec. 14, 1862, near Water Valley, Pemberton Papers, NARA.

31. Unsigned letter to sister Dona, Oxford, Miss., Jan. 27, 1863.

32. Mary L. Smither, "Reminiscences of Mary L. Smither," 20, typescript (1913–25), SHGSC. Smither's account goes on to say that some or all of the slaves returned in ten days begging forgiveness and were accepted with paternalistic compassion.

33. "Minutes of Oxford Baptist Church," Mar. 1863, November, 1864, vol. 1, mf, SHGSC.

34. W. E. B. Du Bois, Black Reconstruction (New York: Harcourt, Brace, 1935). Eric Foner, Reconstruction: America's Unfinished Revolution, 1863–1877 (New York: Harper and Row, 1988), 3–4.

35. S. G. Miller to George Miller, Pontotoc, Miss., Oct. 31, 1862, Miller Family Papers, UMSC.

36. Unsigned letter to sister Dona, Oxford, Miss., Jan. 27, 1863.

37. Rebecca H. Pegues to Alexander H. Pegues, Oxford, Miss., Jan. 12, 1863, Pegues Diaries and Letters.

38. Unsigned letter to sister Dona, Oxford, Miss., Jan. 27, 1863.

39. "Minutes, College Hill Presbyterian Church," mf, SHGSC; Brown, "At Home in Lafayette County," 220–22.

40. Cf. Wayne K. Durrill, War of Another Kind: A Southern Community in the Great Rebellion (New York, 1990); Orville Vernon Burton, "On the Confederate Home Front: The Transformation of Values from Community to Nation in Edgefield, South Carolina," unpublished paper. My thanks to Professor Burton for making this available.

41. Charles Roberts to his wife, camp near Tupelo, Miss., June 14, 1862, Charles Roberts Letters, UMSC.

42. T. Goode Clark to Margery Clark, Camp Liddell, near Richmond, Dec. 12, 1862, Clark Family Papers, 1837–68, UMSC; "Letters written to Mrs. Margery B. Rogers Clark, wife of G(oode) Clark, by her husband and her two sons, Jonathan and. A. H(enry) Clark, Dec. 7, 1861–June, 1863," Mrs. Calvin S. Brown Papers, MDAH; punctuation added.

43. Isaac Duncan to William E. Duncan, Sarepta, Miss., June 19, 1862, quoted in Brown, "At Home in Lafayette County," 126.

44. John K. Bettersworth, Confederate Mississippi: The People and Policies of a Cotton State in Wartime (Baton Rouge: Louisiana State University Press, 1945), 49, 67.

45. Isaac Duncan to W. E. Duncan, Sarepta, Miss., June 19, 27, 1862, quoted in Brown, "At Home in Lafayette County," 64, 67.

46. J. E. Robuck, *My Own Personal Experience and Observation as a Soldier in the Confederate Army during the Civil War, 1861–1865, also during the Period of Reconstruction* (Birmingham: Leslie Printing and Publishing Company, 1911), 18.

47. Faulkner, *Unvanquished*, 95. In this and other passages, Faulkner describes a demoralized Confederacy, at the front lines as well as the home front. On furlough extensions, see *Lafayette County Heritage News* 16 (Winter 1994): 22–23, for a list of furlough extensions with dates.

48. T. G. Clark to Margery [Clark], camp near Goldsboro, North Carolina, Jan. 15, 1863.

49. Isaac Duncan to W. E. Duncan, Sarepta, Miss., June 10, 1862, quoted in Brown, "At Home in Lafayette County," 60, 147; William Sylvester Dillon, "Typescript of Civil War Diary, Apr. 12, 1861, to June 25, 1865," Apr. 26, 1861, UMSC. On Confederate conscription, see James M. McPherson, *Battle Cry of Freedom: The Civil War Era*, (New York: Oxford University Press, 1988), 430f.

50. Isaac Duncan to W. E. Duncan, Sarepta, Miss., 1862, Mrs. Calvin S. Brown Papers, file 2, MDAH.

51. "Records of Exemptions, Mississippi, 1864–65," Conscription Records, RG 109, Chap. 1, vol. 253, NARA.

52. Bettersworth, *Confederate Mississippi*, 191.

53. Elizabeth Turnage, case 8586, SCC.

54. For a fuller treatment of the impact of Union invasion on civilian morale, see Stephen V. Ash, *When the Yankees Came: Conflict and Chaos in the Occupied South, 1861–1865* (Chapel Hill: University of North Carolina Press, 1995).

55. *OR*, ser. 1, vol. 17, pt. 1, 475. An earlier report from Colonel Lyle T. Dickey to Colonel John A. Rawlins, Camp near Yocknapatalfa [sic] River, Dec. 7, 1862, noted that "near 200 horses and mules" were captured, along with various supplies and Confederate money. He also reported 10 Union soldiers killed, 63 wounded, and 41 captured; for the Confederates he reported 70 killed, 250 wounded, and 750 taken prisoner.

56. *Memphis Bulletin*, Dec. 19, 1862.

57. Mildred Throne, ed., *The Civil War Diary of Cyrus F. Boyd, Fifteenth Iowa Infantry, 1861–1863* (Millwood, N.Y.: Kraus Reprint, 1977), 94, 95

58. Ibid., 91.

59. Frederick, "Illinois Soldier," 193.

60. Grant to Halleck, Oxford, Miss., Dec. 14, 1862, quoted in Brooks D. Simpson, *Let Us All Have Peace: Ulysses S. Grant and the Politics of War and Reconstruction, 1861–1868* (Chapel Hill: University of North Carolina Press, 1991), 33.

61. "List of Citizens Taking the Oath of Allegiance to the U.S. Government at Oxford Mississippi, Dec. 1862," RG 393, pt. 4, entry 1706, NARA. One example of the animosity that surrounded such shifts in loyalty can be found in W. C. Taylor to Thomas N. Wendel, Pontotoc, Mar. 11, 1863, file 15, Longstreet-Hinton Collection, UMSC. Wendel felt falsely accused of shifting allegiance to the Union, probably because of trade with the enemy. Taylor assured him he and Slater, his partner, were still considered a "true and loyal southerners."

62. Unknown to Colonel John Adams, near Water Valley, Dec. 14, 1862, Pemberton Papers, NARA.

63. *Chicago Tribune*, Dec. 13, 1862, report dated Dec. 6, 1862.

64. Frederick, "Illinois Soldier," 193, Dec. 20, 1862; Joseph Stockton, Diary, Dec. 27, 1862, reprinted in *Oxford Eagle*, Nov. 3, 1960.

65. M. C. Miller to Col. Hugh R. Miller, Pontotoc, Miss., Dec. 31, 1862, Miller Papers, UMSC.

66. Lt. Colonel C. R. Barteau to Gen. Pemberton, Saltillo, Miss., Dec. 7, 1862, Letters and Telegrams Received, Pemberton Papers, NARA.

67. H. N. Faulkinbury, "Diary," typescript, MDAH. This family is not listed in the 1860 census for Lafayette County, so he may have lived in Calhoun County, which in 1852 was created out of parts of other counties, including the area surrounding Sarepta, which had been the southeastern panhandle of Lafayette County.

68. H. N. Faulkinbury, "Diary."

69. Faulkner, *Unvanquished*, 136.

70. R. M. Houston to M. E. Houston, Johnsons Island, Ohio, Nov. 27, 1864, reprinted in *Lafayette County Heritage News* 20 (Fall 1997): 10.

71. Isaac Duncan to W. E. Duncan, Sarepta, Miss., June 1862, typescript, box 1, Mrs. Calvin S. Brown Papers, MDAH.

72. Brown, "At Home in Lafayette County," 58.

73. Quoted Ibid., 105–8; cf. *Heritage*, 163, quoted in slightly different form.

74. Roberts to his wife, Shelbyville, Tennessee, Jan. 30, 1863, Charles Roberts Letters, UMSC.

75. Elizabeth H. Pegues to Captain Josiah J. Pegues, The Cedars [Dallas County, Alabama], Jan. 18, 1863, Pegues Diaries and Letters; also quoted in Brown, "At Home in Lafayette County," 91–92.

76. *Chicago Tribune*, Dec. 12, 1862, report dated Dec. 3.

77. Isaac Duncan to William, Sarepta, Miss., June 19, 27, 1862, quoted in Brown, "At Home in Lafayette County," 26, 27; James Wilford Garner, *Reconstruction in Mississippi* (1901; rpt. Gloucester, Mass.: Peter Smith, 1964), 51–52, 55.

78. Faulkner, *Unvanquished*, 10.

79. Ash, *When the Yankees Came*, provides a fuller treatment of the chaotic character of this no-man's-land between the Confederate frontier and Union-controlled garrison sites.

80. Joel Williamson, *William Faulkner and Southern History* (New York: Oxford University Press, 1993), 42–45.

81. Bettersworth, *Confederate Mississippi*, 150–51, 154; "Minutes, Board of Supervisors, 1855–65," Apr., Nov. 1863, WPA transcript, RG 60, MDAH.

82. Later Mississippi's Confederate government would impose similar restrictions on "alien enemies" in their midst, confiscating their property or forcing them to serve in the Confederacy. Garner, *Reconstruction*, 27.

83. Quoted in James M. McPherson, *Battle Cry of Freedom: The Civil War Era* (New York: Oxford University Press, 1988), 620, 621.

84. Harold D. Woodman, *King Cotton and His Retainers: Financing and Marketing the Cotton Crop of the South, 1800–1925* (1968; rpt. Columbia: University of South Carolina Press, 1990), 217–24.

85. Williamson, *William Faulkner*, 44–45.

86. Assistant Adjutant General R. M. Hove (?), Circular, Columbus, Miss., Jan. 20, 1863, Pemberton Papers, NARA.

87. Brown (James) Papers, MDAH; see in particular letters: Dodd and Owen to

James Brown Esq, Jackson, Miss., Jan. 5, 1865; D. Helacker (?) to James Brown, Mobile, Ala., Jan. 30, 1865.

88. Charles Roberts to wife, Camp near Shelbyville Tennessee, Feb. 12, March, 9, 1863, Roberts Letters.

89. Pat A. Willis to Samuel E. Carey, Holly Springs, Miss., Nov. 22, 1863, in H. W. Walter Papers, Holly Springs Historical Society, photocopy in Walter Letters, UMSC. The census of 1860 lists a Patterson Willis, age forty-nine, born in Tennessee, owning 240 acres worth $1,500 and claiming personal property worth $15,000, including seven slaves; LCDI.

90. Bettersworth, *Confederate Mississippi*, 176–77; Marthy [Martha?] Cragin to Governor Clark, Oxford, Miss., Nov. 28, 1863, and Chalmers's response, Jan. 11, 1864, Governor's Records, Administration of Governor Charles Clark, vol. 56, RG 27, MDAH.

91. Pat A. Willis to Samuel E. Carey, Holly Springs, Miss., Nov. 22, 1863.

92. Bettersworth, *Confederate Mississippi*, 177.

93. William Faulkner, *Absalom, Absalom!* (1936; rpt. New York: Vintage International, 1990), 99–100; also, 71, 79, 81, 211–12; "his conscience may have objected. . . . not so much to the idea of pouring out human blood and life, but at the idea of waste: of wearing out and eating up and shooting away material in any cause whatever." *Absalom*, 100. Coldfield refused to own slaves and immediately freed two slaves he had received as compensation for a debt, keeping careful account of the labor each owed him as they paid him back at their fair market value. Among the few white critics of slavery in Yoknapatawpha are the elderly McCaslin brothers, who are ardent supporters of the Confederacy and have to settle which one got to go off to war with a game of poker—the loser to stay home and look after the slaves.

94. Bettersworth, *Confederate Mississippi*, 202.

95. Ibid., 204–8.

96. Beginning in 1871, more than 220 citizens came forward and publicly declared to this commission that they had lost property to the Union army and were loyal Unionists, therefore deserving compensation. Not only was this a time when it was very risky to acknowledge one's anti-Confederate sentiments, the commission imposed a very rigorous and public test of loyalty and an equally demanding proof of loss. We can assume, therefore, many more might have proven loyalty, but had no losses to claim, and that many others were simply intimidated by the whole process. See Frank W. Klingberg, *The Southern Claims Commission* (Berkeley: University of California Press, 1955); Sarah Larson, "Records of the Southern Claims Commission," *Prologue* 12 (Winter 1980): 207–18.

97. The widow Urcilla Fondren lived on a plantation of seventeen hundred acres and claimed over $33,000 in losses when the Union army camped there and the widow Fondren generously offered all that they needed. Several of the family's former slaves testified to her patriotism and loyalty. Urcilla Fondren, case 8581, SCC.

98. Jesse Sisk, case 4696, SCC.

99. Elijah Cantwell, case 20828, SCC.

100. James Wheeler, case 17459, SCC.

101. For a fuller treatment of morale and motivation among Union and Confederate soldiers, see James M. McPherson, *For Cause and Comrade: Why Men Fought in the Civil War* (New York: Oxford University Press, 1997).

102. Stephen V. Ash, *Middle Tennessee Society Transformed, 1860–1870: War and Peace in the Upper South* (Baton Rouge: Louisiana State University Press, 1988), chap. 7, "Lamentations," includes a fuller description of this bandit element and distinguishes them from more partisan and principled guerrillas.

103. Faulkner, *Unvanquished*, 170.

104. "Outlaw Days," WPA.

105. Moses Hunt to H. J. Hunt, Paris, Miss., May 30, 1862, reprinted in *Lafayette County Heritage News* 13 (Summer 1991): 38.

106. Interview with Bill Galleghy, "Outlaw Days," WPA.

107. Charles T. Biser to General S. Cooper, Oxford, Miss., Aug. 31, 1864, OR, ser 1, vol. 39, pt. 1, 400.

108. Bettersworth, *Confederate Mississippi*, 198–99, explains that the Confederate cavalry earned a reputation similar to that of the Kansas Jayhawkers for pillaging, typically through illegal impressment of property and slaves.

109. Kate Barnes, obituary of Mrs. Margery Rogers Clark, n.d., newspaper clipping in, Thomas G. Clark Civil War Letters, UMSC. See also Brown, "At Home in Lafayette County," 141–42.

110. Garner, *Reconstruction*, 122, 123; see also David Macrae, *The Americans at Home* (Glasgow: Horn and Connel, 1885), 218, for his observation of a town meeting in Aberdeen, Miss.

111. Approximately 15 percent of Mississippi's Confederate soldiers died from wounds incurred in combat, and another 20 percent died of disease. We can get an idea of local casualties by the few company records that survive. At the end of 1864, only 7 of the original 125 in the Lafayette Rebels were still fit for duty. Among the 139 men enlisted in the Lamar Rifles, 14 were killed in action, 17 died after battle from wounds, 8 more died of diseases, and 68 were wounded in action. Only 20, less than 15 percent, escaped without any combat wounds, and many suffered multiple wounds during the thirty battles the company endured. Casualty rates among the Lamar Rifles were a little higher than among Mississippi's Confederate forces. See Brown, "At Home in Lafayette County," 219; Thomas P. Buford et al., *Lamar Rifles: A History of Company G, Eleventh Mississippi Regiment, CSA* . . . (1901; rpt. Marble Hill, Mo. Steward Printing and Publishing, 1992), 51, 15; "List of names of Destitute families of Soldiers in Lafayette Co., Mississippi," in Confederate Records, Indigent and Disabled Soldiers and Dependents, 1863–68, RG151, MDAH. Estimates of Mississippi casualties are found in Dunbar Rowland, *Encyclopedia of Mississippi History*, vol. 1 (Madison, Wisc.: S. A. Brant, 1907), 141.

112. On public support of destitute after the war, see "Minutes of the Board of Police, beginning Oct. 10, 1859 through 1863," Apr. 3, 1865, WPA typescript, vol. 3, p. 243, RG 60, vol. 583, MDAH. State law in 1865 required that the county "levy a tax in Kind of one half of one per cent on all corn, wheat, and Bacon Grown and produced" and "to enroll the indigent families of ther respective Beats according to the provisions of the same det [sic]." Some $11,319 was raised, "being the distributive share of the fund for indigent families of Soldiers in Lafayette County." The estimate of 2,220 Lafayette County soldiers is made in William Delay, Clerk, to A. J. Gillespie, Oxford, Miss., telegram, May 30, 1864, in Confederate Records, Indigent and Disabled Soldiers and Dependents, MDAH. An earlier list indicates 1,845 men enlisted by July 1863: "A list of Soldiers that have went from Lafayette County, Mississippi

Into the Confederate and State Service Since the commencement of the present war to Mar. 1st, 1863," in RG 151, MDAH.

113. *OR*, ser. 1, vol. 52, pt. 2, p. 950, quoted in Garner, *Reconstruction*, 24–25.

114. J. A. Bigger, "Diary, Apr. 30, 1862–May 12, 1865," Aug. 15, Sept. 15, Nov. 1, 1863, Jan. 1, 1864, typescript, UMSC.

115. William Sylvester Dillon, "Typescript of Civil War Diary, Apr. 12, 1861, to June 25, 1865," Corinth, Miss., May 27, 1862, UMSC.

116. Brown, "At Home in Lafayette County," 162.

117. Broadside, *Circular to Sheriffs*, Governor Charles Clark, Nov. 16, 1864, Governor's Records, MDAH. See also "List of Deserters and Conscripts arrested by Sheriff of Chickasaw Co, in 1864," Confederate Records, Substitution and Desertion Records, 1863–64, RG 151, MDAH.

118. T. E. B. Pegues to Governor C. Clark, Oxford, Miss., Mar. 30, 1865, Governor's Records, MDAH.

119. Ibid.

120. Biser, to Cooper, Aug. 31, 1864; Wilson, *Faulkners*, 13–14. On the Battle of Hurricane Creek, see Elmo H. Howell, "William Faulkner's General Forrest and the Uses of History," *Tennessee Historical Quarterly* 29 (1970): 287–94.

121. Aug. 11, 1864 entry, Belle Edmondson Diary, Loretta Galbraith and William Galbraith, eds., *A Lost Heroine of the Confederacy: The Diaries and Letters of Belle Edmondson*, (Jackson: University Press of Mississippi, 1990), 171.

122. Howard T. Dimick, "Motives for the Burning of Oxford, Mississippi," *Journal of Mississippi History* 8 (July 1946), suggests that Smith's actions were in response to the Fort Pillow massacre in which Forrest's men slaughtered black Union troops who had surrendered.

123. Vernon Lane Wharton, *The Negro in Mississippi, 1865–1890* (1947; rpt. Westport Conn., Greenwood Press, 1984).

124. Zizzie [Elizabeth] Pegues to Bettie, Oxford, Miss., Aug. 26, [1864], Pegues Diaries and Letters.

125. Correspondent of the *Dubuque Times*, in *New York Times*, Sept. 10, 1864, quoted in Garner, *Reconstruction*, 17.

126. *Oxford Falcon*, Nov. 23, 1865, reprinted in *Lafayette County Heritage News* 11 (Fall 1988): 5–6.

127. Zizzie [Elizabeth] Pegues to Bettie, Oxford, Miss., Aug. 26, [1864], Pegues Diaries and Letters.

128. Biser to Cooper, Aug. 31, 1864.

129. Brown, "At Home in Lafayette County," 211.

130. Dimick, "Motives for the Burning of Oxford," 120; Joseph Blotner, *Faulkner: A Biography*, 2 vols. (New York: Random House, 1974), 31.

131. William Humphries Young to [unknown], n.p., Aug. 24, 1864, Young Letters, Special Collections, Gettysburg College. I am grateful to David Hedrick, Special Collections Librarian, who kindly responded to my query in the H-Civil War discussion group.

132. J. M. Love, "Civil War Diary," p. 78, Feb. 25, 1865, ms, UMSC.

133. To Maj. General J. R. Chalmers, from R. F. Looney Col. P.A.C.S, and 69 signatures, Oxford, Miss., Sept. 26, 1864, Confederate Records, Adjutant General's Office, Incoming Correspondence, 1861–64, file 12, RG151, MDAH.

134. Charles Roberts to his wife, Aberdeen, Miss., Jan. 1, 1865, Charles Roberts Letters, UMSC.

135. Belle Edmondson Diary, Aug. 25, June 17, 1864, in Galbraith and Galbraith, eds., *Lost Heroine*, 172, 145.

136. Rebecca Pegues, "Diary," June 17, 1865.

137. Faulkner, *Unvanquished*, 95.

138. William Faulkner, *Requiem for a Nun* (1951; rpt. New York: Vintage Books, 1975), 201.

Chapter Eight

1. William Faulkner, *Requiem for a Nun* (1951; New York: Vintage Books, 1975), 205; William Faulkner, *The Unvanquished* (1938; New York: Vintage International, 1991), 207.

2. Faulkner, *Requiem*, 200, 40.

3. *Oxford Falcon*, Nov. 23, 1865.

4. Faulkner, *Requiem*, 204.

5. The *Oxford Falcon* reported numerous new enterprises and organizations that were apparently proposed and even launched during this period, but there is little evidence of any real signs of economic development.

6. *Oxford Falcon*, Dec. 21, 1867.

7. Ibid., Aug. 10 1867.

8. LCDA.

9. Whitelaw Reid, *After the War: A Southern Tour, May 1, 1865, to May 1, 1866* (Cincinnati: Moore, Wilstach and Baldwin, 1866), 423, quoted in Robert Frank Futrell, "Economic Readjustment in Mississippi during Reconstruction, 1865–1875" (M.A. thesis, UM, 1939), 211. See also Ross H. Moore, "Social and Economic Conditions in Mississippi during Reconstruction" (M.A. thesis, UM, 1937), 132–34.

10. James Wilford Garner, *Reconstruction in Mississippi* (1901; rpt. Gloucester, Mass.: Peter Smith, 1964), 122, 123. See also David Macrae, *The Americans at Home* (Glasgow: Horn and Connel, 1885), 218, for his observation of amputees and wounded at a town meeting in Aberdeen, Miss.

11. Garner, *Reconstruction*, 203; "Correspondence and Circulars Pertaining to Artificial Limbs, 1863–1868," RG 9, vol. 56, Confederate Records, series 402, MDAH.

12. Both censuses are found in Confederate Records, "Indigent and Disabled Soldiers and Dependents, 1863–1868," MDAH. Edward Rossiter, Sub-agent, to Major A. W. Preston, Oxford, Miss., May 2, 1867; vol. 239, p. 2; "Letters Sent, Apr. 29, 1867 to Oct. 31, 1867," entry 2307, RG 105, FB, NARA.

13. "Minutes of the Board of Police, beginning Oct. 10, 1859 through 1863," Apr. 3, 1865, WPA typescript, vol. 3, p. 243, RG 60, vol. 583, MDAH. Oxford Falcon, June 1, 1867. Rations for freedmen were for each adult one bushel of corn and eight pounds of meat per month. Each child under fourteen received one half that amount.

14. E. A. Smith, "Confederate Column," *Oxford Eagle*, Feb. 24, 1910.

15. Garner, *Reconstruction*, 86–87, 112. In March 1995 the legislature of Mississippi voted to ratify the Thirteenth Amendment.

16. On Black Codes, see William C. Harris, *The Day of the Carpetbagger: Republican Reconstruction in Mississippi* (Baton Rouge: Louisiana State University Press, 1979); Eric

Foner, *Reconstruction: America's Unfinished Revolution, 1863–1877* (New York: Harper and Row, 1988), 193–94, 199–200; Garner, *Reconstruction,* 86; Vernon Lane Wharton, *The Negro in Mississippi, 1865–1890* (1947; rpt. Westport, Conn.: Greenwood Press, 1984), 132, 83.

17. William C. Harris, *Presidential Reconstruction in Mississippi* (Baton Rouge: Louisiana State University Press, 1967), 139–40. County courts were to try all criminal cases below felonies and all civil cases involving no more than $250 in property. The act creating the county court system specifically listed the following criminal offenses over which the county court had jurisdiction: "petit larceny, assaults, assaults and batteries, riots, affrays, routes, unlawful assemblies, words of insult made indictable by our statute, violations of the Sabbath of every kind against law, disturbances of religious worship or persons assembled for that purpose, whether engaged in worship at the time or not, defaulting road overseers and all offenses concerning public roads made indictable by law, unlawful exhibition of deadly weapons, gaming, racing or shooting upon any public road, street or square, obtaining goods, money or other property by false pretences." *Laws of the State of Mississippi, 1865,* Chapter II, Section 3.

18. The three judges were A. Peterson, local government official, states' rights Democrat, owned one slave in 1860; W. H. Smither, a dry goods merchant with nearly $100,000 in property and eleven slaves in 1860, active Democrat, and local government officer; Isaac Dooley, not listed in 1860 or 1870 censuses, though others with that surname were active in local Democratic politics. Debbielee Landi, "Best Evidence: A Social History of the County Court of Lafayette County, 1865–1870" (M.A. thesis, UM, 1992),18; Julia Kendel, "Reconstruction in Lafayette County," *PMHS* 13 (1913): 230.

19. *Oxford Falcon,* Feb. 8, 1866; Landi, "Best Evidence," 27–29, 41; Harris, *Presidential Reconstruction in Mississippi,* 100–101, 148–50. Michael Wayne, *The Reshaping of Plantation Society: The Natchez District, 1860–1880* (Baton Rouge: Louisiana State University Press, 1983), details the process by which planters and freedmen in the Natchez District learned the lessons of the labor market in another part of Mississippi.

20. Case of Dave, in Feb. 1866 term of County Court, "Final Record, Lafayette County Circuit Court, 1868–1870," bound volume, UMSC. Landi, "Best Evidence," 27. These criminal laws and penalties were ostensibly colorblind, and whites were prosecuted under them, but cases involving whites led to conviction less often and only rarely involved another party providing security.

21. Markett owned 15 slaves in 1860 and 1,450 acres of land, valued at $8,000; in 1870 he claimed only $1,800 in property; LCDI.

22. "Final Record: Lafayette County Circuit Court, 1868–1870," p. 31, ledger, UMSC; Landi, "Best Evidence," 22.

23. Landi, "Best Evidence," 22, 26; "Final Record," July 1866.

24. "Final Record," January 1867; *Oxford Falcon,* Jan. 12, 1867; Landi, "Best Evidence," 49.

25. *Oxford Falcon,* July 5, 1866. On the significance of Vicksburg and the Fourth of July in Mississippi, see Malcolm Franklin, *Bitterweeds: Life with William Faulkner at Rowan Oak* (Irving, Tex.: Society for the Study of Traditional Culture, 1977), 84–85.

26. Austin was only one of several agents to serve the Oxford Bureau post. The local records indicate the following agents and times served: William Gillhousen, from sometime after the war until August 1865; Charles Austin, only briefly in Au-

gust 1865; J. W. Pancoast, September to December 1865; James M. Cook, the native Democrat, from December 1865 to April 1867; Edward Rossiter, May 1867 to June 1867; and Thadeus K. Preuss, June to December 1867, Letters Sent, entry 2307, RG 105, FB, NARA.

27. Charles Austin, Sub-Agent, to Lt. Col. R. S. Donelson, Oxford, Miss., Aug. 24, 1865, Registered Letters Received, July 1865–Mar. 1866, Jackson, Mississippi, Acting Assistant Commissioner of the Northern District of Mississippi, entry 2188, RG 105, FB, NARA.

28. LCDI.

29. Foner explains that the withdrawal of black female labor from the fields was temporary and that the hard times of the 1870s forced many back to work in the fields; Foner, *Reconstruction*, 85–87.

30. Austin to Donelson, Oxford, Miss., Aug. 31, 1865, Registered Letters Received, July 1865–Mar. 1866, Jackson, Mississippi, Acting Assistant Commissioner of the Northern District of Mississippi," entry 2188, RG 105, FB, NARA.

31. J. W. Pancoast, Sub-agent, to Bonner [?], Oxford, Miss., Dec. 13, 1865, ibid.

32. Austin to Donelson, Oxford, Miss., Aug. 31, 1865, ibid.

33. Pancoast to Bonner [?],Oxford, Miss., Dec. 13, 1865, ibid; James M. Cook to Donaldson [Donelson?], Jan. 12, 1866, Oxford, Miss., ibid.; Foner, *Reconstruction*, 201–2.

34. Thadeus Pruess, Sub-agent, to Brevet Lt. Col. H. W. Smith, Oxford, Miss., Aug 24, 1867, Registered Letters Received, July 1865–Mar. 1866, Jackson, Mississippi, Acting Assistant Commissioner of the Northern District of Mississippi," entry 2188, RG 105, FB, NARA.

35. *Oxford Falcon*, May 24, 31, 1866.

36. Wayne, *Reshaping of Plantation Society*, offers a detailed study of this learning process among freedmen and landlords.

37. A. B. W. to Dear Brother, Home Place [near Coffeeville (?), Mississippi] Aug. 15, 1866, Bryant (Clyde) Papers, MDAH.

38. Pruess to Preston, Oxford, Miss., July 18, 1867; Letters Sent, Apr. 29, 1867 to Oct. 31, 1867, entry 2307, RG 105, FB, NARA.

39. *Oxford Falcon*, Jan. 19 1867.

40. Ibid., Jan. 4, 1868, Dec. 21, 1867.

41. Ibid., Sept. 28, 1867.

42. Ibid., Jan. 8, Feb. 19, 1870.

43. Ibid., Feb. 26, Mar. 19, 1870.

44. Ibid., June 18, 1870.

45. Julia Kendel, "Reconstruction in Lafayette County," PMHS 13 (1913): 255.

46. Ibid., 254; *Oxford Falcon*, Apr. 11, 1868.

47. Statement by Thomas N. Buford, Oxford, Miss., Oct. 28, 1873, Governor's Records, R. G. Powers, vol. 81, RG 27, MDAH.

48. *Oxford Falcon*, Feb. 26, Mar. 5, 1870.

49. John K. Bettersworth, *Mississippi: A History* (Austin, Tex.: Steck Company, 1959), 348.

50. Austin to Donelson, Oxford, Miss., Sept. 1, 1865, Letters Received, entry 2188, RG 105, FB, NARA. For more on the hostility of whites to the plans for a "colored school," see FB letters from Rev. A. J. Yeater, Oxford, Miss., Nov. 28, 1865, Jan. 4, 1866; Pancoast, Oxford, Miss., Sept. 28, 1865; Register of Letters Received,

June 1865–Feb. 1866, Records of the Assistant Commissioner for the State of Mississippi, FB, mf M826, roll 6, RG 105, FB, NARA.

51. Pruess to Captain J. W. Sunderland, Oxford, Miss., Sept. 30, 1867, Letters Sent, Apr. 29, 1867, to Oct. 31, 1867, entry 2307, RG 105, FB, NARA.

52. Charles Arthur Williamson, "Reconstruction in Lafayette County," p. 3, typescript in Franklin Riley, ed., Reconstruction Essays, (UM, n.d.), UMSC. Williamson's research, like Kendel's, relies heavily on interviews with former Klansmen. Not all of his facts are accurate, and the exploits of the Klan may have been dramatized in the telling.

53. Pruess to Preston, Oxford, Miss., July 18, 1867, Letters Sent, entry 2307, RG 105, FB, NARA. See also letters from Alexander Phillips, FB teacher, Oxford, Miss., July 27, 1868, Oct. 8, 22, 28, 1868, Register of Letters Received, 1865–67, vol. 2, June 1867–Nov. 1869, Superintendent of Education, Mississippi, entry 2087, RG 105, FB, NARA. One condescending clerk in bureau headquarters noted on Phillips's correspondence: "Requests a supply of blanks, speaks in regard to school matters in Oxford (and makes nearly 30 errors)." Phillips's response was recorded by the clerk: "Acknowledges that he is incompetent to teach the common branches of the English language and states that he is willing to give up the school to a good teacher who will improve his race." Ibid., Oct. 8, 1868.

54. *Oxford Falcon*, Aug. 10, 1867.

55. Yeater to [Bureau Headquarters], Oxford, Miss., Nov. 28, 1865, Jan. 4, 1866; Register of Letters Received, June 1865–Feb. 1866, Records of the Assistant Commissioner for the State of Mississippi, Freedmen's Bureau, mf M826, roll 6, RG 105, FB, NARA, (summaries of these letters were found in the register, but the full, original letters could not be located). See also the letter from Yeater to Col. Samuel Thomas, Concordia, Miss., Jan. 18, 1866, ibid., roll 17, RG 105, FB, NARA, which reports that his enemies in Oxford stole his watch and justified this by saying to him: " 'The Yankees took their watches, and they must retaliate.' This was said by an elder in the Presbyterian Church in the presence of the P[ost] M[aster] and family."

56. *Oxford Falcon*, Aug. 17, 1867; see also ibid., Aug. 3, 1867, with a remark implying Borum (or Borrum, spelling varied) would be subverting blacks: "That's right, 'Perkins,' learn the little colored ideas about how to shoot!"

57. Williamson, "Reconstruction," 14–15.

58. Pruess to Sunderland, Oxford, Miss., Sept. 30, 1867; Letters Sent, Apr. 29, 1867 to Oct. 31, 1867, entry 2307, RG 105, FB, NARA; Rossiter to Preston, Oxford, Miss., May 12, 31, 1867, ibid; Alexander Phillips to FB Headquarters, Oxford, Miss., July 27, 1868, ibid. On Phillips, see Kendel, "Reconstruction," 234; *Oxford Falcon*, Mar. 16, 1867.

59. Pruess to Sunderland, Oxford, Miss., Oct. 15, 1867, Letters Sent, Apr. 29, 1867 to Oct. 31, 1867, entry 2307, RG 105, FB, NARA.

60. Pruess to Maj. Powers, Oxford, Miss., Sept. 12, 1867, ibid.; *Oxford Falcon*, Aug. 3, 17, 1867; Kendel, "Reconstruction," 235.

61. *Oxford Falcon*, Mar. 20, 1869, letter to editor from "Aliquis."

62. J. E. Robuck, *My Own Personal Experience and Observation as a Soldier in the Confederate Army during the Civil War, 1861–1865, also during the Period of Reconstruction* (Birmingham: Leslie Printing and Publishing Company, 1911), 71–72. Robuck may have dramatized his stories to improve book sales; in any case, his dates and other facts are not always reliable.

63. Faulkner, *Light in August* (1932; rpt. New York: Vintage International, 1990), 249, 255.

64. "The Education of the Freedmen," article written by J. N. Waddell, S. G. Burney, A. J. Quinche, T. E. B. Pegues, William Delay, and J. W. McPherson, in *Oxford Falcon*, June 14, 1866.

65. Ibid., May 31, 1866.

66. *History of Second Baptist Church, Oxford, Mississippi, Sept. 23, 1984* ([Oxford, 1984]), 1. My thanks to the Reverend Leroy Waddlington of Second Baptist for making this valuable booklet available.

67. Ibid.

68. *Oxford Falcon*, May 9, 1868. The northern Methodist church that Alexander Phillips led was forerunner to Bishop Burns Methodist Church in Oxford today.

69. Walker Jackson Coffey, *Journal of a Journey* [Oxford: N.p. 1980], 58.

70. Dewitt Talmadge Oaks, "A Survey of the Churches of Lafayette County, Mississippi" (M.A. thesis, UM, 1931), 105, 123, 142. Oakes identified forty-seven "colored" churches in 1931. Of the thirty-one with dates of organization given, two were organized before 1870, nine more before 1880, nine more before 1990, six more before 1900, two before 1910, and three before 1920.

71. *Oxford Falcon*, Aug. 31, 1867.

72. Ibid., Jan. 12, 1867. See also, Ibid., July 12, 1866, which reports that "the negroes of Brandon gave a Concert and Tableaux a few nights since, to raise money to build a church, and realized, a handsome sum."

73. Ibid., July 6, 1867. White speakers included Charles B. Howry, Dr. Waddell and Dr. Burney, Mayor James Cook, William Delay, Mr. McMahon, and Captain Rossiter, the Freedmen's Bureau agent.

74. Ibid., Apr. 5, 19, 1866.

75. Ibid., Sept. 14, 1867; official results detailed in "Final Report and List of Registered Voters of Mississippi, 1867," U.S. Army Continental Commands, Pt 1, Department of . . . 4th Military District, 18[67–70], entry 402, RG 393, NARA.

76. *Oxford Falcon*, Nov. 10, 1866.

77. Ibid., Aug. 31 1867.

78. W. G. Vaughn in 1860 was a cotton dealer, age thirty-seven, who owned six slaves and a farm that produced fifty-six bales of cotton. P. H. McCutchen in 1860 was fifty, a wealthy farmer, with property worth $37,000 including twenty-eight slaves; LCDI. They ran against two other wealthy former slave owners, T. E. B. Pegues and George Goodwin. All data on wealth and slaves from LCDI. The turnout was 1,269 voters, with 54 percent approving the convention.

79. *Oxford Falcon*, Apr. 5, 1868; Bettersworth, *Mississippi*, 320. In the *Oxford Eagle*, Mar. 10, 1910, E. A. Smith mentions Vaughn as a "good citizen, an honest merchant," and brave Confederate soldier who inexplicably "joined the army of scalawags and carpet-baggers that literally sucked for ten or twelve years the life blood of the land he fought so hard to free."

80. See SCC for individual case files on claims granted. On the white Republican vote in Lafayette, see Warren A. Ellem, "Who Were the Mississippi Scalawags," *Journal of Southern History* 38 (May 1972): 225, 229; James B. Murphy, *L. Q. C. Lamar: Pragmatic Patriot* (Baton Rouge: Louisiana State University Press, 1973), 109–11.

81. Jesse Sisk, case 4696, SCC. See *Oxford Eagle*, July 19, 1883, for an account of a shooting between Sisk and G. W. Mitchell.

82. *Oxford Falcon*, Aug. 31 1867.

83. Ibid., Aug. 31, 1867, Apr. 25, July 11, 1868, Sept. 25, 1869. See also Vernon Lane Wharton, *The Negro in Mississippi, 1865–1890* (1947; rpt. Westport Conn.: Greenwood Press, 1984), 165–66.

84. *Oxford Falcon*, Sept. 25, 1869. Kendel, "Reconstruction," 233–35. On Flournoy, see Garner, *Reconstruction*, 349, 363, 369; Wharton, *Negro in Mississippi*, 157–58.

85. Kendel, "Reconstruction," 228–35, 265–66. Jerry Fox, a black farmer from Beat Two, served three annual terms on the County Board of Supervisors (and its predecessor in 1869, the Board of Police). Mack Avent, another black officeholder, managed to be elected every year representing rural Beat Five from 1873 until well after Reconstruction in 1879. *Oxford Falcon*, July 24, Aug. 14, Sept. 4, 1869.

86. Wharton, *Negro in Mississippi*, 166, describing a similar event in nearby Holly Springs; Kendel, "Reconstruction," 238; *Oxford Falcon*, Sept. 25, 1869. Few Republican newspapers survive to give their own view of the party's events and organization.

87. Robert Flournoy to Butler, [Pontotoc, Miss.], May 23, 1867, quoted in Michael W. Fitzgerald, *The Union League Movement in the Deep South: Politics and Agricultural Change During Reconstruction* (Baton Rouge: Louisiana State University Press, 1989), 52.

88. Williamson, "Reconstruction," 11. This story is not verified in other sources, but that could be because newspaper files are non-existent or spotty for this period.

89. *Oxford Falcon*, Feb. 1, 1868.

90. Ibid., Nov. 2, 1867, June 13, 1868.

91. Wharton, *Negro in Mississippi*, 153.

92. *Oxford Falcon*, July 13, 1867. This account claims that William S. Neilson owned one hundred slaves, but the slave census of 1860 reports only nine; LCDI. See also *Oxford Eagle*, Dec. 10, 1936. A similar event was staged in July 1868; see Ibid., July 18, 1868. A picnic organized by freedmen near Oxford was attended by leading Democrats ("for all of whom a separate table was spread and offered") and reported approvingly by the *Oxford Falcon* editor, *Oxford Falcon*, July 28, 1867.

93. Ibid., Jan. 30, 1869.

94. Kendel, "Reconstruction," 253; *Oxford Falcon*, Apr. 11, June 20, July 11, 1868.

95. Ibid., July 11, 1868.

96. Gregory Scott Hospodor, "The Mississippi Ku Klux Klan during Reconstruction" (M.A. thesis, UM, 1991), examines these competing strategies in a statewide study of Mississippi counties.

97. *Oxford Falcon*, May 8, 1869. Alexander Phillips was challenged and threatened for reporting these incidents of election irregularities. Alexander Pegues in particular refuted the charge that he had open graves on his plantation. Phillips partially recanted, but his correspondence with authorities suggests that he did so out of fear for his safety.

98. 40th Cong., 3d sess., House Miscellaneous Document 53: *Condition of Affairs in Mississippi. Evidence Taken by the Committee on Reconstruction* (Washington, D.C.: U.S. Government Printing Office, [1868]), 203–12.

99. Ibid., 212–13, undated statement signed by Jack Barr, Newton Chilton, Jim Nelson [or Neilson, spelling varied], and fourteen other freedmen, all but one signed with an "X".

100. Ibid., 203–15.

101. *Oxford Falcon*, July 18, 1868. Next to the article on the barbecue was a preliminary list of the "colored Radical voters" from the recent election.

102. Robuck, *My Own Personal Experience*, 72–73; Kendel, "Reconstruction," 241–42. Kendel was confused about the time and motivation for the assault on the Raglands, which she thought was in response to Ku Klux Klan violence against blacks; that would place it too late. Later, Sam Ragland would become a leader in the Ku Klux Klan, but the local Klan did not organize until 1867. Both accounts say blacks were after money. It is Kendel's account that reports Elizabeth Ragland's escape and death by knife; Robuck thought she died immediately. See also *Oxford Eagle*, Mar. 20, 1941, an account by Ragland's grandson, which says his father and a friend were upstairs when the attack took place and intervened, saved Sam, and recognized some of the attackers. He reports nineteen "hangings" in revenge, and he also has the date in 1869 or 1870. Elizabeth Ragland's gravestone reports her death in 1866. I am grateful to W. C. Hill, Sam Ragland's great-grandson, for assisting me in this research. John B. Cullen, *Old Times in the Faulkner Country* (Chapel Hill: University of North Carolina Press, 1961), 100, identifies the Price place (renamed "Prince" for anonymity) as the model for the Old Frenchman's place. Williamson, "Reconstruction," 6, 9, mentions the "wholesale killing" of blacks following the Ragland murder and that federal troops were called in to pacify the county but the telegraph operator deliberately delayed the plea for help. There is remarkably little reliable evidence on this event.

103. William Faulkner, *The Hamlet* (1940; rpt. New York: Vintage International, 1991), 3, 5.

104. *Oxford Falcon*, Mar. 21, 28, 1868.

105. Hospodor, "Ku Klux Klan," includes analysis of the Klan, based on Kendel's information.

106. Alexander Phillips to [General Gillem], Oxford, Miss., May 2, 21, 1868, Letters Received, Jan. 1868–May 1869, Records of the Assistant Commissioner for the State of Mississippi, FB, mf M826, roll 25, RG 105, FB, NARA.

107. Phillips to Headquarters, Oxford, Miss., May 2, 1868; Phillips to General Gillem, Oxford, Miss., May 21, 1868, ibid.

108. Quote from *Oxford Falcon*, June 13, 1868; *Oxford Falcon* June 20, 26, 1868; "Riots," WPA; Kendel, "Reconstruction," 236.

109. Kendel, "Reconstruction," 240–41. The date of this episode is not made clear in Kendel, and no specific reference is found in the newspaper or other records. Between 1868 and 1875 there were constant reports of black militia in the county.

110. *Oxford Falcon*, Apr. 2, 1869.

111. Ibid., July 30, 1870.

112. Ibid., Aug. 28, 1869, on return of the U.S. Army garrison. Some details of army operations in Oxford may be found in HQ General and Special Orders Jan. 1872–Mar. 1873, Records of the U.S. Army, Continental Commands, 1821–1920, Post of Oxford, Miss., RG 393, NARA; Adjutant General's Office, Regular Army Muster Rolls, 6th Cavalry, Troop I, Aug. 31, 1867–Dec. 31, 1897, RG 94, NARA.

113. *Condition of Affairs in Mississippi*, 203–14, on election fraud and intimidation in Lafayette County; Harris, *Day of the Carpetbagger*, 194–96. Whites had an advantage of 549 registered voters, 1,964 to 1,445, going into the November 1869 election. *Oxford Falcon*, Nov. 27, 1869. James Alcorn, the Republican candidate for governor, received 1,188, Louis Dent, the Democratic nominee, 1,098. The turnout, 67 percent overall, was probably much lower among white Democratic voters, since

Dent, President Grant's brother-in-law, was of candidate with questionable loyalties. See also Harris, *Day of the Carpetbagger*, 256–59; Kendel, "Reconstruction," 236, 238; Williamson, "Reconstruction," 3–5; *Oxford Falcon*, Aug. 28, 1869. Ibid., June 26, 1869, lists new appointees to county office: DeWitte Stearns, judge, probate court; C. N. Wilson, clerk of circuit court; E. M. Main, sheriff; S. V. W. Whiting, assessor; W. H. Foard (or Ford, spelling varied), clerk of probate court. The *Oxford Falcon* noted none of the appointees had ever been a citizen of Lafayette County. Later Ames appointed to the Board of Police Jerry Fox, a freedman; A. J. Wyatte; A. G. Browning; and Moses Powell. As county aldermen, Ames named Samuel Shoup, D. J. Kennedy, J. A. Buckley, L. D. Viser, William Jenkins, and C. N. Wilson, circuit clerk of county. James M. Cook was removed as mayor, the *Oxford Falcon* claimed, for failing to join the radical wing of the Republican Party. Ibid., July 24, 1869.

114. Walter Dean Burnham, *Presidential Ballots, 1836–1892* (Baltimore: Johns Hopkins Press, 1955), 561. The vote in 1872 was 1,321 for Grant, 1,236 for Greeley. Since Mississippi had not been readmitted to the Union in 1868, there were no presidential election returns for that year.

115. Kendel, "Reconstruction," 265–66.

116. *Report of the Joint Select Committee to Inquire into the Condition of Affairs in the Late Insurrectionary States*, Mississippi, vols. 11, 12 (Washington, D.C.: U.S. Government Printing Office, 1872), 348, testimony by Edward Holman; ibid., 850–51, Samuel Gholson testimony. Roger Donald Brown, "Federal Intervention to Control Violence in Reconstructed Mississippi" (M.A. thesis, UM, 1972), 66, explains that Whissler, the man Lamar accused of threatening him, was under trial for killing a Klansmen who had been held prisoner in Corinth; Whissler was murdered by the Klan in November 1871. See also the recollections of Judge Robert Hill, *Oxford Eagle*, Apr. 27, 1937.

117. Allen P. Huggins to Ackerman, Oxford, Miss., June 28, 1871; Letters Received by the Department of Justice from Mississippi, 1871–84, Source-Chronological File, Northern Mississippi, Jan. 1871–Dec. 1875, M970, roll 1, NARA. Huggins reported that District Attorney Wells, on the previous Sunday in Oxford, "received such a dose of poison that we despaired of his life."

118. "Sometimes the Ku Klux in the people will break out and the court is so completely over awed that I do not see much chance for Justice to be meted out to these fiends in human shape." Ibid.

119. Brown, "Federal Intervention," 73; Williamson, "Reconstruction," 6.

120. Williamson, "Reconstruction," 10–11.

121. *Report of the Joint Select Committee*, 1161; Harris, *Day of the Carpetbagger*, 399–402; James B. Murphy, *L. Q. C. Lamar: Pragmatic Patriot* (Baton Rouge: Louisiana State University Press, 1973), 101, 109–11.

122. Both quotes from Foner, *Reconstruction*, 560, 562.

123. On improvements on the square, see *Oxford Falcon*, June 19, 1869, Aug. 10, 1867. See also ibid., Aug. 2, Oct. 18, 1866, Oct. 12, 1867, Jan. 23, Mar. 20, Apr. 17, 1869, Apr. 30, 1870, for further accounts of improvements on the square. On the courthouse and federal funding, see ibid., May 24, June 14, Dec. 15, 1866; Jan. 15, 1867. On jail, ibid., Apr. 10, 1869.

124. *Oxford Falcon*, Aug. 18, 1871.

125. Faulkner, *Requiem*, 42, 204.

Chapter Nine

1. *Oxford Eagle*, Mar. 17, 1910, June 1, 1911. William F. Holmes, *The White Chief: James Kimble Vardaman* (Baton Rouge: Louisiana State University Press, 1970), provides an excellent political biography.

2. William Faulkner, "Barn Burning," in *Collected Stories of William Faulkner* (New York: Vintage Books, 1977), 3. The quote refers to Flem's younger brother, Colonel Sartoris "Sarty" Snopes.

3. Eugene W. Hilgard, *Address on Progressive Agriculture, and Industrial Education* (Jackson: Clarion Book and Job Office, 1873), 3–5, 6, 9.

4. "Formation," WPA.

5. Hilgard, *Address on Progressive Agriculture*, 6, 7, 9. See also Hilgard's comments in Department of the Interior, Census Office, *Report on Cotton Production in the United States . . .* Part I (Washington, D.C.: U.S. Government Printing Office, 1884), 110–11. For a later survey of soil conditions, see A. L. Goodman and E. M. Jones, *Soil Survey of Lafayette County, Mississippi* (Washington, D.C.: U.S. Government Printing Office, 1914).

6. Robert Frank Futrell, "Economic Readjustment in Mississippi during Reconstruction, 1865–1875" (M.A. thesis, UM, 1939), 97, quoting J. B. Harrison, "Studies in the South," *Atlantic Monthly*, a series in several installments between January 1882 and January 1883.

7. Willie D. Halsell, "L. Q. C. Lamar's Taylor Farm: An Experiment in Diversified Farming," *Journal of Mississippi History* 5 (Oct. 1943): 185–96.

8. William Faulkner, *The Hamlet* (1940; rpt. New York: Vintage International, 1991), 243, 20–22.

9. Department of Commerce and Labor, Bureau of the Census, *Thirteenth Census of the United States Taken in the Year 1910*, vol. 6, *Agriculture 1909 and 1910, Reports by States, with Statistics for Counties, Alabama-Montana* (Washington, D.C.: U.S. Government Printing Office, 1913), 867. The average number of improved acres in 1910 was 33, down from 111 in 1860.

10. Skipwith Historical and Genealogical Society, *The Heritage of Lafayette County, Mississippi* (Dallas: Curtis Media Corporation, 1986), 22. Walker Jackson Coffey, *Journal of a Journey* [Oxford, Miss.: Privately printed, 1980], 23, gives colorful details on the Yugoslavian barrel stave makers whose camp was in the southern part of the county.

11. Skipwith, *Heritage*, 22.

12. Faulkner, *The Hamlet*, 190.

13. *Oxford Eagle*, Apr. 4, 1883.

14. *Oxford Falcon*, Nov. 19, 1870.

15. See, for examples, *Oxford Eagle*, Jan. 18, 1883; Feb. 1, 1883; Apr. 12, 1883.

16. Neil R. McMillen, *Dark Journey: Black Mississippians in the Age of Jim Crow* (Urbana: University of Illinois Press, 1989); Susie Marshall, interview with Don H. Doyle, Oxford, August 1994; Jack Burrage, "The *Oxford Eagle* as Seen from Its Files, 1883–1950" (M.A. thesis, UM, 1955), 14.

17. William Faulkner, *Go Down, Moses* (1942; rpt. New York: Vintage International, 1990), 324.

18. *Oxford Eagle*, Feb. 9, 1888; Vernon Lane Wharton, *The Negro in Mississippi, 1865–1890* (1947; rpt. Westport, Conn., Greenwood Press, 1984), 110, 112, 114. For a fine

study of the Delta, see James C. Cobb, *The Most Southern Place on Earth: The Mississippi Delta and the Roots of Regional Identity* (New York: Oxford University Press, 1992), chaps. 4, 5

19. McMillen, *Dark Journey*, chap. 8; James R. Grossman, *Land of Hope: Chicago, Black Southerners, and the Great Migration* (Chicago: University of Chicago Press, 1989).

20. *Oxford Eagle*, Feb. 9, 1888.

21. I am grateful to my daughter, Dr. Kelly Lynn Doyle, who shared her medical expertise on the effects of yellow fever with gruesome detail.

22. William Baskerville Hamilton, *Holly Springs, Mississippi, to the Year 1878* (Holly Springs: Marshall County Historical Society, 1984), 49; Marshall Logan, "Mississippi and the Yellow Fever Epidemics of 1878–1879," *Journal of Mississippi History* 33 (1971): 199–217; Khaled J. Bloom, *The Mississippi Valley's Great Yellow Fever Epidemic of 1878* (Baton Rouge: Louisiana State University Press, 1993), 144–53. For an account of the epidemic in Holly Springs, see Sherwood Bonner, "The Yellow Plague of '78," *Youth's Companion* 52 (Apr. 3, 1879), excerpted in John K. Bettersworth, *Mississippi: A History* (Austin, Tex.: Steck, 1959), 366–69.

23. *Oxford Globe*, Nov. 3, 1898, reprinted in *Lafayette County Heritage News* 18 (Fall 1995): 8; "Anonymous Letter, on Yellow Fever," Oxford, June 2, 1879, box 5, miscellaneous manuscripts, UMSC; Skipwith, *Heritage*, 33.

24. J. E. Bundren, excerpt from WPA Statewide Historical Research, reprinted in *Lafayette County Heritage News*, 17(Fall, 1994): 7.

25. The reference to the detention camp is found in Minnie S. Holt, "Lafayette County—General History and Points of Interest," WPA. See also Skipwith, *Heritage*, 36; Burrage, "*Oxford Eagle*," 19, quoting *Oxford Eagle*, Nov. 3, 1898; *Oxford Eagle*, Mar. 27, 1867.

26. Bettersworth, *Mississippi*, 400; Will Lewis, "The Story of Banks and Banking in Oxford through the Years" [1986] typescript in author's possession, 14, on boll weevil in Lafayette County.

27. Much of the following draws on Stephen Hahn, *The Roots of Southern Populism: Yeoman Farmers and the Transformation of the Georgia Upcountry, 1850–1890* (New York: Oxford University Press, 1983).

28. William Faulkner, *As I Lay Dying* (1930; rpt. New York: Vintage International, 1990), 42.

29. On cotton prices and production costs, see Gavin Wright, *Old South, New South: Revolutions in the Southern Economy since the Civil War* (New York: Basic Books, 1986), 118; Harold D. Woodman, *King Cotton and His Retainers: Financing and Marketing the Cotton Crop of the South, 1800–1925* (1968; rpt. Columbia: University of South Carolina Press, 1990), 339–43. Cotton production for Lafayette County had been about 19,000 bales in 1860, 9,000 in 1870, up to 15,000 in 1880, and down to 11,000 by 1890. After 1890 it shot up to nearly 18,000, 14,000 in 1910, and then down to 8,000 by 1920. On tax policy, see Stephen Cresswell, *Multiparty Politics in Mississippi, 1877–1902* (Jackson: University Press of Mississippi, 1995), 23, citing Michael R. Hyman, "Taxation, Public Policy, and Political Dissent: Yeoman Dissatisfaction in the Post-Reconstruction Lower South," *Journal of Southern History* 40 (1989): 49–76. Cresswell explains that the Redeemer government shifted much of the state taxes to the counties, which increased the local tax bills as much as six- to eightfold for many farmers.

30. Between 1860 and 1900 the total number of farms in Lafayette County grew from 913 to 3,817; more than half in 1910 were operated by tenants, and those in

turn were about evenly divided between those who pain rent with cash and those who paid with a share of the crop; LCDA. For more on tenant farming, see Hahn, *Roots of Populism*, chap. 5; Roger L. Ransom and Richard Sutch, *One Kind of Freedom: The Economic Consequences of Emancipation* (Cambridge, Eng.: Cambridge University Press, 1977); Wright, *Old South, New South*, 84–90.

31. LCDA; Bureau of the Census, *Thirteenth Census . . .* 1910, 867.

32. William Faulkner, *Intruder in the Dust* (1948; rpt. New York: Vintage International, 1991), 19.

33. Faulkner, "Barn Burning," 10. Faulkner spelled De Spain inconsistently; I have adopted the capital "D" throughout.

34. Ibid., 12.

35. Julia Kendel, "Reconstruction in Lafayette County," PMHS 13 (1913), 245 n. 60, explains the "third and fourth" method of share renting. Farming on halves meant the landlord provided the land, house, stock, and tools and received half the crop in return.

36. For a fuller treatment of sharecropping in the South, see Ransom and Sutch, *One Kind of Freedom*.

37. Faulkner, *Hamlet*, 17.

38. P. B. Parks, "Business Ledger, 1893," 39–41, bound ledger, UMSC.

39. R. G. Dun and Company, *The Mercantile Agency Reference Book, . . . Principal Cities of the United States and Canada* (New York, 1867, 1871, 1897); *Bradstreets Book of Commercial Ratings*, vol. 229, Apr. 1925 (New York: Bradstreet Company, [1925]). These and other commercial reference books were located in the Baker Library, Harvard University.

40. Faulkner, *Hamlet*, 6.

41. Skipwith, *Heritage*, 21.

42. Typical country store account books are found in "McEachin and Graham, 1877 Day Book of a General Merchandise Store in Abbeville," reprinted in *Lafayette County Heritage News* 9 (Fall 1986):4–5, ibid. 12 (Summer 1990): 11; P. B. Parks, "Business Ledger, 1893," bound ledger, UMSC.

43. Hahn, *Roots of Populism*, 60–63, 239–68.

44. Faulkner, *Hamlet*.

45. Woodman, *King Cotton*, chap. 24, offers a fuller picture of the furnishing merchant's operations. See also Thomas D. Clark, *Pills, Petticoats and Plows: The Southern Country Store* (Indianapolis: Bobbs-Merrill, 1944).

46. LCDA; Bureau of the Census, *Thirteenth Census . . .* 1910, 867.

47. Albert D. Kirwan, *Revolt of the Rednecks: Mississippi Politics, 1876–1925* (New York: Harper, 1951), 43–45; Hahn, *Roots of Populism*. On Populism, see also Robert C. McMath, *American Populism: A Social History, 1877–1898* (New York: Hill and Wang, 1993).

48. Quote from essay in "Formation," WPA; see also "Communities," WPA. Skipwith, *Heritage*, 165. Among the more notorious cases of violence in the Dallas neighborhood was the murder of Detective Wise by Dock Bishop in 1883. See *Oxford Falcon*, Sept. 24, 1885, *Oxford Eagle*, July 8, 1886. Lafayette Springs, a resort in the eastern hills, also earned a reputation for fighting and lawlessness.

49. Kirwan, *Revolt*, 44–45; Albert C. Smith, " 'Southern Violence' Reconsidered: Arson as Protest in Black-Belt Georgia, 1865–1910," *Journal of Southern History* 51 (November 1985): 527–64.

50. R. G. Dun and Company Credit Ledgers, Lafayette County, Mississippi, Baker Library, Harvard University School of Business.

51. William F. Holmes, "Whitecapping: Anti-Semitism in the Populist Era," *American Jewish Historical Quarterly* 63 (March 1974): 244–61.

52. Kirwan, *Revolt*, 45–46; Holmes, *White Chief*, 134–45; William F. Holmes, "Whitecapping: Agrarian Violence in Mississippi, 1902–1906," *Journal of Southern History* 35 (May 1969): 165–85; Holmes, "Whitecapping: Anti-Semitism in the Populist Era," 244–61.

53. Bettersworth, *Mississippi*, 336–37; Willie D. Halsell, "The Bourbon Period in Mississippi Politics, 1875–1890," *Journal of Southern History* 11 (1945): 519–37.

54. Cresswell, *Multiparty Politics*, 206–7. Stephen Cresswell, an expert on Mississippi politics in this period, shares my puzzlement as to why Lafayette County remained an island of Democratic solidarity amid a sea of agrarian discontent that centered in north-central Mississippi. Perhaps, as Cresswell proposes, the strong influence of such Democratic Party leaders as L. Q. C. Lamar explain it. The local strength of the party, for whatever reason, allowed it to implement heavy-handed measures described here, which ensured the intimidation of the opposition. Correspondence, Cresswell to author, June 20, 1996. I am very grateful for the help Stephen Cresswell gave me.

55. Lafayette County Grange, Minutes bylaws of the Lafayette County Grange, June 1, 1874–Apr. 13, 1881, ledger, UMSC. Among its achievements the Grange promoted the founding of a new land-grant college, Mississippi Agricultural and Mechanical College, in Starkville, which is now Mississippi State University. Bettersworth, *Mississippi*, 358–59.

56. Cresswell, *Multiparty Politics*, 205. Elected in 1879 were W. L. Lowrance, state senator, and Charles B. Howry and W. L. Buford, representatives. Robert Lowry and William H. McCardle, *A History of Mississippi* (Jackson: R. H. Henry and Co., 1891), 512.

57. J. H. Pierce to Alphonso Taft, Attorney General, Oxford, Miss., Aug. 21, 1876, Letters Received by the Department of Justice from Mississippi, 1871–84, Source-Chronological File, Northern Mississippi, Jan. 1876–July 1884, mf M970, roll 2, NARA.

58. Cresswell, *Multiparty Politics*, 214.

59. A. H. Kennedy to Senator H. W. Blair, Oxford, Miss., Sept. 8, 1881, Henry W. Blair Papers, New Hampshire Historical Society. All spelling as in the original. I am grateful to Professor Gaines M. Foster, Louisiana State University, who discovered this revealing letter and kindly sent it to me. One ploy of the Democratic Party was to keep the names of some eighty university students on the voter registration rolls long after they had graduated and left Oxford, allowing fraudulent voters to vote in their places. Cresswell, *Multiparty Politics*, 80. Cresswell, "Enforcing the Enforcement Acts: The Department of Justice in Northern Mississippi, 1870–1890," *Journal of Southern History* 53 (1987): 421–40. An earlier report on election practices confirms the pattern even before the rise of agrarian factionalism.

60. Cresswell, *Multiparty Politics*, 78.

61. Ibid., 101. For a variety of reasons, including concern over prohibition of liquor, many white farmers also wanted to eliminate blacks from voting.

62. Ibid., 105, 221, 220, 224; Kirwan, *Revolt*, 58–84, esp. 73. Lafayette County statistics from *Oxford Eagle*, July 14, 1892, quoted in Burrage, "*Oxford Eagle*," 23;

C. Vann Woodward, *The Origins of the New South, 1877–1913* (Baton Rouge: Louisiana State University Press, 1951), 341. The 1890 "Mississippi Plan" for disfranchisement became the model for other southern states.

63. Cresswell, *Multiparty Politics*, 187–88; *Oxford Globe*, Nov. 8, 1894. Together with the Republicans and Prohibitionists, the non-Democratic forces managed to win less than a quarter of the 701 total votes in 1894.

64. For years there had been popular agitation for primary elections that would give the people, not the party executive committees, the power to nominate candidates. In Lafayette County the local Democratic executive committee staged a local primary on its own in 1883. *Oxford Eagle*, June 21, 1883.

65. Holmes, *White Chief*, 108.

66. Ibid., 121–22.

67. Ibid., 105, 109; McMillen, *Dark Journey*, 72; James W. Silver, *Mississippi: The Closed Society*, rev. ed. (New York: Harcourt, Brace and World, 1966), 19; Walter Lord, *The Past That Would Not Die* (New York: Harper and Row, 1965), 25.

68. Chester M. Morgan, *Redneck Liberal: Theodore G. Bilbo and the New Deal* (Baton Rouge: Louisiana State University Press, 1985); Adwin Wigfall Green, *The Man Bilbo* (Baton Rouge, Louisiana State University Press, 1963). See also the essay on "Bilbonic plague" in Mississippi in Allan A. Michie and Frank Ryhlick, eds., *Dixie Demagogues* (New York: Vanguard Press, 1939); and Bilbo's own views on race in Theodore G. Bilbo, *Take Your Choice: Separation or Mongrelization* (Poplarville, Miss.: Dream House, 1947).

69. McMillen, *Dark Journey*, 228–33; McMillen estimates that approximately six hundred lynchings occurred in Mississippi between 1880 and 1945, including four in Lafayette County. A more meticulous study revealed no less than ten illegal lynchings in Lafayette County between 1865 and 1935, which may suggest McMillen's figure for the state is a drastic underestimate. I am grateful to Jan Hillegas of New Mississippi, Inc., Jackson, Mississippi, for sharing her unpublished research with me. On southern lynchings, see Stewart E. Tolnay and E. M. Beck, *A Festival of Violence: An Analysis of Southern Lynchings, 1882–1930* (Urbana: University of Illinois Press, 1995).

70. Holmes, *White Chief*, 37; Joel Williamson, *The Crucible of Race: Black/White Relations in the American South since Emancipation* (New York: Oxford University Press, 1984).

71. McMillen, *Dark Journey*, 228, citing the *Raymond Gazette*, July 18, 1885, quoted in Wharton, *Negro in Mississippi*, 224.

72. Unpublished research by Jan Hillegas, of New Mississippi, Inc., Jackson, Mississippi. On the Paris lynchings, see Skipwith, *Heritage*, 179.

73. "Bar Criminal Docket, Circuit Court, Lafayette County, [1894–]," 1907, Sept. term, p. 187, ledger, SHGSC, basement, Oxford City Hall.

74. *Lafayette County Press*, Sept. 9, 1908, "Negro Brute Cuts Woman's Throat." See also *Memphis Commercial Appeal*, Sept. 9, 1908, and *Jackson Clarion-Ledger*, Sept. 9, 1908. Each account varies in a good number of details, including not only names and spellings but also speculation on motivation and important details of the slaying of Mrs. McMillan (also spelled McMullin). I have relied on whatever details seemed most plausible.

75. John B. Cullen and Floyd C. Watkins, *Old Times in the Faulkner Country* (Chapel Hill: University of North Carolina Press, 1961), 89–90.

76. *Memphis Commercial Appeal*, Sept. 9, 1908.

77. *Jackson Clarion-Ledger*, Sept. 10, 1908.

78. *Lafayette County Press*, Sept. 9, 1908; Cullen and Watkins, *Old Times*, 91–92.

Chapter Ten

1. Rush Allen, letter to editor, *Oxford Eagle*, Dec. 12, 1935.

2. William Faulkner, *As I Lay Dying* (1930; rpt. New York: Vintage International, 1990), 66.

3. On southern town life, see Ted Ownby, *Subduing Satan: Religion, Recreation, and Manhood in the Rural South, 1865–1920* (Chapel Hill: University of North Carolina Press, 1990), chap. 2, which emphasizes the masculine domain of the town and its temptations of vice. Faulkner explores this aspect of town life in *Light in August*, when Joe Christmas finds sin in Jefferson.

4. William Faulkner, *The Hamlet* (1940; rpt. New York: Vintage International, 1991), 285.

5. *Lafayette County Press*, Sept. 25, 1907; see illustration.

6. Ibid., Nov. 7, 1906, reprints resolutions of the United Confederate Veterans to build the monument.

7. William Faulkner, *Requiem for a Nun* (1950; rpt. New York: Vintage Books, 1975), 206–7.

8. Murry C. Falkner, *The Falkners of Mississippi: A Memoir* (Baton Rouge: Louisiana State University Press, 1967), 4. These impressions refer to sometime after the boys arrived in Oxford in 1902, when Bill, the oldest, was only five and Murry was two years younger.

9. Edward Ayers, *The Promise of the New South: Life after Reconstruction* (New York: Oxford University Press, 1992), chap. 3, and passim, offers an excellent overview of the changes coursing through the South in this period.

10. William Faulkner, *The Town* (1957; Vintage Books, 1961), 29.

11. *Explanatory Rules and Rates . . . Oxford Electric Light and Water Plant* (Oxford, 1910), pamphlet, UMSC, explains the history and capacity of Oxford's new utilities. On telephones, see Telephone Directory, Oxford, Mississippi, 1917 UMSC.

12. *Oxford Eagle*, July 14, 1898.

13. Falkner, *Falkners*, 49–52, 38–43.

14. Ibid., 43–44.

15. Faulkner, *The Town*, 13; *Oxford Eagle*, Apr. 27, 1916; *Lafayette County Press*, May 13, 1908.

16. Faulkner, *The Town*, 12; Faulkner, *Requiem*, 207.

17. *Lafayette County Press*, Oct. 21, 1908; Skipwith Historical and Genealogical Society, *The Heritage of Lafayette County, Mississippi* (Dallas: Curtis Media Col;, 1986), 154.

18. Faulkner, *Requiem*, 4. It was, he added critically, "a furious beating of hollow drums toward nowhere, but merely to sound louder than the next little human clotting to its north or south or east or west, dubbing itself city as Napoleon dubbed himself emperor and defending the expedient by padding its census roll—a fever, a delirium in which it would confound forever seething with motion and motion with progress."

19. *Oxford Eagle*, Aug. 21, 1919.

20. Ibid., Aug. 21, 1919, Sept. 28, 1922, Nov. 6, 1924.

21. *Lafayette County Press*, Oct. 7, 1908.

22. Ibid., Aug. [n.d.], 1909, May 13, 1908.

23. *Oxford Eagle*, Nov. 10, 1898.

24. *Lafayette County Press*, Nov. 25, 1908.

25. Ibid., Oct. 7, 1908.

26. *Oxford Eagle*, Aug. 27, 1903; *Lafayette County Press*, Nov. 24, Dec. 1, 1909; May 18, 1910; for a list of Civic League officers and members, see the latter issue.

27. *Oxford Eagle*, Sept. 1, 1898.

28. Ibid., June 19, Aug. 7, 1919.

29. Ibid., Aug. 7, 1919.

30. E. O. Davidson, J. C. Hartsfield, Ramey and Company, H. Friedman, H. T. Smith, W. M. Woodward, J. E. Neilson, W. W. Phillips, H. L. Tate, C. E. Sisk, Joe Parks, E. E. Temple, C. A. Mcharen, and J. E. Avent were among those behind the company; *Oxford Eagle*, Jan. 8, 1920.

31. *Oxford Eagle*, Dec. 8, 1921.

32. Ibid., Dec. 8, 9, 1921, Feb. 2, April 13, 20, 27, 1922.

33. Ibid., July 13, 1922.

34. Frances R. Huff, "The Relationship of Oxford and the University of Mississippi, 1848–1947" (M.A. thesis, UM, 1947), 129 n. 364.

35. James B. Lloyd, *The University of Mississippi: The Formative Years, 1848–1906* (University, Miss.: UM, 1979), 64, 72.

36. Huff, "Oxford and the University," 130–31; *Oxford Eagle*, Feb. 5, 1920, Dec. 8, 1927, Feb. 2, 1928, Sept. 22, 1932. Though Bilbo failed to sever Oxford's hold on the university, he continued his attacks and later managed to get Chancellor Hume and several faculty members dismissed.

37. *Lafayette County Press*, Oct. 21, 1908.

38. Ibid., Feb. 27, Mar. 6, 20, 1907; *Oxford Eagle*, Oct. 10, 1907.

39. *Lafayette County Press*, June 26, 1912.

40. *Oxford Eagle*, Oct. 27, 1921.

41. Ibid., Feb. 7, Mar. 6, 1924.

42. *Lafayette County Press*, Oct. 24, 1906.

43. Ibid., Dec. 7, 1910.

44. Thomas D. Clark, "Changes in Transportation," in Richard Aubrey McLemore, ed., *A History of Mississippi*, 2 vols. (Hattiesburg: University and College Press of Mississippi, 1973), 2:274, 277, quoted in Corey T. Lesseig, " 'Out of the Mud': The Good Roads Crusade and Social Change in Twentieth-Century Mississippi," *Journal of Mississippi History* 60 (Spring 1998): 54.

45. *Lafayette County Press*, Nov. 21, Oct. 24, 1906; Falkner, *Falkners*, 70–72.

46. *Lafayette County Press*, Apr. 5, 1911.

47. Ibid., Apr. 17, 1912; this article on "Good Roads" explained that the road tax amounted to almost $16,000, while the property tax diverted to road maintenance amounted to a little over $3,500.

48. Jeanette Keith, *Country People in the New South: Tennessee's Upper Cumberland* (Chapel Hill: University of North Carolina Press, 1995), 103–17, is an excellent account of the good roads movement and its opposition in a neighboring state.

49. Lesseig, " 'Out of the Mud,' " 56–57.

50. *Lafayette County Press*, Jan. 22, 1908; see letter from A. F. Greer on race and schooling.

51. Walker Jackson Coffey, *Journal of a Journey* (Oxford, Miss.: Privately printed, 1980), 21.

52. *Biennial Report of the State Superintendent of Public Education to the Legislature of Mississippi for the Scholastic Years 1901–2 and 1902–3*, 8–9, quoted in Reuben W. Griffith, "The Public School, 1890–1970," in McLemore, *History of Mississippi*, 394n.

53. Keith, *Country People*.

54. *Lafayette County Press*, Jan. 29, February, 12, 1908.

55. *Oxford Eagle*, Jan. 12, 1922; Skipwith, *Heritage*, 190.

56. *Mississippi: The WPA Guide to the Magnolia State*, rev. ed. (Jackson: University Press of Mississippi, 1988), 487.

57. Faulkner, *The Town*, 10–11, 12–13.

58. William Faulkner, *The Unvanquished* (1938; rpt. New York: Vintage International, 1991), 231. See the summary of town government activities and election details in Skipwith, *Heritage*, 33–40.

59. Bem Price, case 20490, SCC. Price claimed losses worth $9,706 and was allowed $6,306.

60. Information on Bem Price from Dun and Company Credit Ledgers, Lafayette County, Mississippi, Baker Library, Harvard University School of Business. Paul Barringer occupied the large house on University Avenue, known as Memory House and later occupied by William Faulkner's brother John.

61. Joel Williamson, *William Faulkner and Southern History* (New York: Oxford University Press, 1993), 73; Joseph L. Blotner, *Faulkner: A Biography*, 1 vol. ed., rev., condensed (New York: Random House, 1984), 14–15; obituary *Oxford Eagle*, Mar. 9, 1922.

62. Williamson, *Faulkner*, chap. 4.

63. Susan Snell, *Phil Stone of Oxford: A Vicarious Life* (Athens: University of Georgia Press, 1991), 13–14, 16, 18, 19, 21.

64. Ibid., 23–26, 218–21, 236, 246–47, 250–51; Thomas S. Hines, *William Faulkner and the Tangible Past: The Architecture of Yoknapatawpha* (Berkeley: University of California Press, 1996), 59; Charles B. Cramer, "A History of Selected Examples of Antebellum Architecture in Lafayette County Mississippi," 14–15, typescript paper for University of Mississippi Art Department, 1965, UMSC.

65. Details of Russell's life are difficult to come by. See his obituary in *Jackson Clarion Ledger*, May 17, 1943, and Cecil L. Summers, *The Governors of Mississippi* (Gretna [La.]: Pelican Publishing, 1980), 102–4. See also Blotner, *Faulkner*, 1:81–82; Albert D. Kirwan, *Revolt of the Rednecks: Mississippi Politics, 1876–1925* (New York: Harper, 1951), 292–97. John Falkner, *My Brother Bill: An Affectionate Reminiscence* (1963; rpt. Oxford, Miss.: Yoknapatawpha Press, 1975), 143; John Corlew, "The Influence of Mississippi Politics on William Faulkner's Art: Lee Russell as Spiritual Forebear of Flem Snopes," *Journal of Mississippi History* 56 (1994): 91–106. Coffey, *Journal*, 45.

66. Allen Cabaniss, *The University of Mississippi: Its First Hundred Years*, 2d ed. (Hattiesburg: University and College Press of Mississippi, 1971), 119.

67. Blotner, *Faulkner*, 14; *Oxford Eagle*, Jan. 9, 1907, endorsement of Russell; ibid., Aug. 10, 1907, election results.

68. Blotner, *Faulkner*, 174, attributes the story of Lee Russell being shunned by Colonel Falkner at the front door to Phil Stone, William Faulkner's embittered friend who framed the story as an example of the Falkner family's snobbish pretensions. Snell, *Phil Stone*, 43. Phil Stone may have been projecting his own disdain for Russell and the Vardaman faction, which J. W. T. Falkner led and which Stone and his father

opposed vehemently. The best evidence for Russell's acceptance by the Falkners may be found Mary Metcalfe's letter to the editor, *Journal of Mississippi History* 57 (Summer 1995). Mary Metcalfe is Lee Russell's niece, and she recalls numerous friendships between the Russell and Falkner clans in Oxford. Her letter responds to John Corlew's article, "Mississippi Politics" (cited above), which interprets Russell as a prototype for Faulkner's Flem Snopes and emphasizes the alleged social distance between the "aristocratic" Falkners and the upstart "rednecks." On Russell's automotive acquisitions, see Williamson, *William Faulkner,* 170, citing *Oxford Eagle,* Oct. 14, 1909; July 21, 1910.

69. *Lafayette County Press,* Aug. 2, 1911.

70. Corlew, "Mississippi Politics," 94; Cabaniss, *University,* 119, 127, 190, 132.

71. Blotner, *Faulkner,* 149; Snell, *Phil Stone,* 58; Cabaniss, *University,* 127.

72. Blotner, *Faulkner,* 158.

73. *Oxford Eagle,* July 15, Aug. 5, 1915.

74. Russell had sold his own newspaper, the *Lafayette County Press,* in 1914 to George Price, who consolidated it with the *Eagle;* Price bought out the *Independent* as well in 1916. C. John Sobotka Jr., *A History of Lafayette County, Mississippi* (Oxford: Rebel Press, [1976?], 99; Jack Burrage, "The *Oxford Eagle* as Seen from Its Files, 1883–1950" (M.A. thesis, UM, 1955), 54–55, 35.

75. *Oxford Eagle,* Aug. 7, 26, 1919. Kirwan, *Revolt,* 295.

76. *Oxford Eagle,* Sept. 4, 1919; Blotner, *Faulkner,* 244.

77. *Jackson Daily News,* Aug. 25, 28, 1919, quoted in Kirwan, *Revolt,* 296.

78. Blotner, *Faulkner,* 285–88; Huff, "Oxford and the University," 34–35; Huff explains that the main grievance among students was a new Board of Trustees rule limiting dances to one per organization each year.

79. Kirwan, *Revolt,* 297–99. Lee Russell's death in 1943 was not even noted in the Oxford papers.

80. Kirwan, *Revolt,* 298; Skipwith, *Heritage,* 39; John K. Bettersworth, *Mississippi: A History* (Austin: Steck, 1959), 413, 419–22, 433. Corlew, "Mississippi Politics," 104, citing Wigfall Green on the Bilbo platform of 1924.

81. Avent family genealogy in Skipwith, *Heritage.* The obituary of Thomas and Sidney's son Thomas Edison Avent, *Oxford Eagle,* June 29, 1967, says the Avents moved into Oxford in 1898 to provide a good education for their five sons. It also said they had only two hundred, not two thousand acres in the Liberty Hill area. Their daughter, Etta, died in September 1900, according to cemetery records. Skipwith Historical and Genealogical Society, *Lafayette County Cemetery Records* ([Oxford, Miss.]: The Society, 1978), 1:96.

82. William Faulkner, *The Mansion* (1955; New York: Vintage Books, 1965), 332; *The Town,* 352.

83. Obituary, *Oxford Eagle,* June 29, 1967; Avent family history in Skipwith, *Heritage,* 215–18; Blotner, *Faulkner,* 1:143, 173, 234.

84. *Oxford Eagle,* Jan. 15, 1920; Joe Parks obituary, ibid., July 5, 1951; Blotner, *Faulkner,* 1:258–60.

85. Coffey, *Journal,* 24, 42–43, 51–52, 67.

86. Ibid., 57–58, 63, 69, 78.

87. Several Faulkner scholars have pointed out that Snopesism is not new to Frenchman's Bend, nor to Jefferson. Joseph R. Urgo, *Faulkner's Apocrypha: A Fable,*

Snopes, and the Spirit of Human Rebellion (Jackson: University Press of Mississippi, 1989), 149f., offers an intelligent reading of the Snopes phenomenon. See also Joseph Gold, "The 'Normality' of Snopesism: Universal Themes in Faulkner's The Hamlet," in William Faulkner: Four Decades of Criticism ([East Lansing]: Michigan State University Press, 1973), 318–27. A more recent and very penetrating treatment is found in Daniel Singal, Faulkner: The Making of a Modernist (Chapel Hill: University of North Carolina Press, 1997), 244–55, who sees Flem Snopes as an agent of modernization and change. He points out that some of the physical features of Flem Snopes, the dark eyes, thin lips, and beaklike nose, also describe William Faulkner.

88. Faulkner, My Brother Bill, 269–70.

89. Ibid., 270–71.

90. Snell, Phil Stone, 197–200, 227, 248, 287.

91. Singal, Faulkner, 244–55.

92. Katherine Davis, "Oxford, Mississippi—A Social Study," 25, typescript, Jan. 31, 1936, UMSC.

Epilogue

1. William Faulkner to Malcolm Cowley, Oxford, [Nov. 1944], in Joseph Blotner, ed., Selected Letters of William Faulkner (New York: Random House, 1977), 185; William Faulkner to Joan Williams, Oxford, Apr. 29, 1953, ibid., 348.

2. For a fine exploration of the rise of consumerism, see Ted Ownby, American Dreams in Mississippi: Consumers, Poverty, and Culture, 1830–1998 (Chapel Hill: University of North Carolina Press, 1999).

3. Nicholas Lemann, The Promised Land: The Great Black Migration and How It Changed America (New York: Knopf, 1991), provides an excellent overview of the subject.

4. Oxford Eagle, Sept. 19, 1935; Neil R. McMillen, Dark Journey: Black Mississippians in the Age of Jim Crow (Urbana: University of Illinois Press, 1989), 208, 229, 230, 387 n. 36. McMillen reports that among the six hundred victims of lynchings were twenty-four whites.

5. William Faulkner, Intruder in the Dust (1948; New York: Vintage International, 1991), 199.

6. James W. Silver, Running Scared: Silver in Mississippi (Jackson: University Press of Mississippi, 1984), 48–50. Cohran was kept in the Holly Springs jail because the filming took place in the Oxford jail, but the trial took place at the Lafayette County Courthouse. The judge recognized that Cohran was probably innocent but urged him to plead guilty, be sentenced to three years in Parchman, and as soon as the public furor died down, the governor would pardon him. He served his full sentence without pardon and left Mississippi forever.

7. Lawrence H. Schwartz, Creating Faulkner's Reputation: The Politics of Modern Literary Criticism (Knoxville: University of Tennessee Press, 1988).

8. James W. Silver, Mississippi: The Closed Society (1963; rpt. New York: Harcourt, Brace and World, 1966), xii.

9. Telephone interviews of Nathan Hodges Jr. by Don H. Doyle, Aug. 4, 1994, June 3, 1999. Some useful information on black life in Lafayette County can be found in the collection for the exhibit on African American life in Lafayette County by the Mary Buie Museum, Oxford, Miss. Information on the NAACP and the individuals

mentioned here can be found on the notes and text prepared for the exhibit. The Lafayette County Improvement Association, not Club, Nathan Hodges informs me, was the correct name.

10. Walter Lord, *The Hate That Would Not Die* (New York: Harper and Row, 1965); Silver, *Mississippi*; Silver, *Running Scared*; John Dittmer, *Local People: The Struggle for Civil Rights in Mississippi* (Urbana: University of Illinois Press, 1994); Nadine Cohodas, *The Band Played Dixie: Race and the Liberal Conscience at Ole Miss* (New York: Free Press, 1997).

11. William Faulkner, *Absalom, Absalom!* (1936; rpt. New York: Vintage International, 1990), 210.

The hundreds of historical documents and scholarly works that went into the making of this book are cited in the notes. Here I want only to highlight some of the published works that readers interested in Faulkner's Mississippi should find of special interest.

Few authors have inspired such an abundance of biographical and critical scholarship as William Faulkner. The best place to begin exploring Faulkner's world is "William Faulkner on the Web" (http://www.mcsr.olemiss.edu/~egjbp/faulkner/), sponsored by the University of Mississippi and created by John B. Padgett. It provides an up-to-date guide to scholarship on Faulkner and provides highly useful glossaries, time lines, and sketches of characters and plots. Among the most useful biographical works relating Faulkner to the history of his locale is Joseph Blotner, *Faulkner: A Biography*, 2 vols. (New York: Random House, 1974), and his revised, one-volume edition (1984). David Minter, *William Faulkner: His Life and Work* (Baltimore: Johns Hopkins University Press, 1980), is an especially good short biography with good critical summaries of the author's works. Lawrence H. Schwartz, *Creating Faulkner's Reputation: The Politics of Modern Literary Criticism* (Knoxville: University of Tennessee Press, 1988), treats the politics of literary fame in a way that helps us understand the early readings of Faulkner and Yoknapatawpha.

To better understand how Faulkner understood the relationship between his work and its historical sources, see Frederick L. Gwynn and Joseph L. Blotner, *Faulkner in the University* (1959; rpt. Charlottesville: University Press of Virginia, 1995), which are transcripts of classroom sessions at the University of Virginia where Faulkner seemed to feel unusually at ease when talking about his work. Faulkner's letters and interviews are another way of getting at some of his thinking; see Joseph Blotner, ed., *Selected Letters of William Faulkner* (New York: Random House, 1977), and Malcolm Cowley, *The Faulkner-Cowley File: Letters and Memories, 1944–1962* (New York: Viking Press, 1966). James B. Meriwether and Michael Millgate, eds., *Lion in the Garden; Interviews with William Faulkner, 1926–1962* (New York: Random House, 1968).

On Faulkner's family background, Joel Williamson, *William Faulkner and Southern History* (New York: Oxford University Press, 1993), offers a fascinating account of both the Falkner and Butler sides of the family. Daniel Singal, *Faulkner: The Making of a Modernist* (Chapel Hill: University of North Carolina Press, 1997), is an intellectual biography that stresses Faulkner's evolving affinity for modernism. Susan Snell, *Phil Stone of Oxford: A Vicarious Life* (Athens: University of Georgia Press, 1991), is an excellent portrait of Faulkner's early friend and mentor with a great interest in Mississippi history and politics.

To some extent, all of Faulkner's novels and stories about Yoknapatawpha are about the past, as I have argued above, but two stories can be read as overture and reprise to the entire saga of Yoknapatawpha: "The Courthouse, (A Name for the City)," and "The Jail (Nor Even Yet Quite Relinquish—)." Both were originally part of *Requiem for a Nun* (1951; rpt. New York: Vintage Books, 1975) and are reprinted in Malcolm Cowley, ed., *The Portable Faulkner* (1946; rev. ed. New York: Viking Penguin, 1967). Cowley's introductory essays romanticize the "southern legend" and distort Faulkner's reading of the southern past, but *The Portable Faulkner* still provides the best "historical" overview of the Yoknapatawpha. See also Faulkner's wonderful "nonfiction" essay on his state's past, "Mississippi," written originally for *Holiday* (April 1954) and reprinted in James B. Meriwether, ed., *Essays, Speeches and Public Letters* (London: Chatto and Windus, 1967).

No one did more to establish Faulkner in the canon of American literature than Cleanth Brooks, whose beautifully crafted essays helped make Faulkner's work accessible to generations of professors, students, and other readers. Brooks brought an authority as a knowing native of the South to the task and though he sometimes distorted Yoknapatawpha as an agrarian pastoral arcadia, his work still repays a reading. See Brooks's *William Faulkner: The Yoknapatawpha Country* (Baton Rouge: Louisiana State University Press, 1963); *William Faulkner: Toward Yoknapatawpha and Beyond* (New Haven: Yale University Press, 1978); *William Faulkner: First Encounters* (New Haven: Yale University Press, 1983); *On the Prejudices, Predilections, and Firm Beliefs of William Faulkner* (Baton Rouge: Louisiana State University Press, 1987).

Irving Howe, *William Faulkner: A Critical Study*, 3d ed. (Chicago: University of Chicago Press, 1975), is especially perceptive on some of the social history Faulkner was interpreting. Michael Millgate, *The Achievement of William Faulkner* (New York: Random House, 1966), stands as another classic work on Faulkner's world. See also his essay "Faulkner and History," in Evans Harrington and Ann J. Abadie, eds., *The South and Faulkner's Yoknapatawpha: The Actual and the Apocryphal* (Jackson: University Press of Mississippi, 1977). The latter is the first of a series of essays from the annual Faulkner and Yoknapatawpha Conference held each summer in Oxford. Edited by Ann Abadie, Evans Harrington, Doreen Fowler, and Donald Kartiganer, they contain the most current thinking among Faulkner scholars over the past twenty-five years.

Some Faulkner scholars have taken a genuine interest in the historical world Faulkner was exploring. Eric Sundquist, *Faulkner: The House Divided* (Baltimore: Johns Hopkins University Press, 1983), sets the theme of race in its historical context. Joseph R. Urgo, *Faulkner's Apocrypha: A Fable, Snopes, and the Spirit of Human Rebellion* (Jackson: University Press of Mississippi, 1989), looks at Snopesism in a new, refreshing light. For an acerbic review of the evolution of Faulkner scholarship, see Frederick Crews's essay in his book *The Critics Bear It Away: American Fiction and the Academy* (New York: Random House, 1992).

There are several guides to the world of Faulkner, among the more useful of which are Calvin S. Brown, *A Glossary of Faulkner's South* (New Haven: Yale University Press, 1976); Robert Warner Kirk, *Faulkner's People, A Complete Guide and Index to Characters in the Fiction of William Faulkner* (Berkeley: University of California Press, 1963). James Hinkle and Roberty McCoy, *Reading Faulkner: The Unvanquished, Glossary and Commentary* (Jackson: University Press of Mississippi, 1995), and others in this series, are helpful guides to specific Faulkner works.

Turning to the history of the South and Mississippi, one classic is W. J. Cash, *The Mind of the South*, (1941; rpt. New York: Vintage Books, 1991), whose iconoclastic portrait of the South resembles that of Faulkner. One important series on southern history by Louisiana State University Press includes Charles S. Sydnor, *The Development of Southern Sectionalism, 1819–1848* (Baton Rouge: Louisiana State University Press, 1948); C. Vann Woodward, *The Origins of the New South, 1877–1913* (Baton Rouge: Louisiana State University Press, 1951); George Brown Tindall, *The Emergence of the New South, 1913–1945* (Baton Rouge: Louisiana State University Press, 1967); and Numan V. Bartley, *The New South, 1945–1980* (Baton Rouge: Louisiana State University Press, 1995). Woodward, *The Burden of Southern History*, rev. ed. (Baton Rouge: Louisiana State University Press, 1968), is rich with insights by a historian who shared many of Faulkner's views of the southern past.

On Mississippi history, there is no recent comprehensive history of the state. John K. Bettersworth, *Mississippi: A History* (Austin, Tex.: Steck, 1959), is dated but generally reliable. Richard Aubrey McLemore, ed., *A History of Mississippi*, 2 vols. (Hattiesburg: University and College Press of Mississippi, 1973), includes essays on many important subjects.

The Indians of Mississippi have received some attention from the new historians of American Indian life. Especially useful are Patricia Galloway, *Choctaw Genesis, 1500–1700: Indians of the Southeast* (Lincoln: University of Nebraska Press, 1995); Daniel H. Usner Jr., *Indians, Settlers and Slaves in a Frontier Exchange Economy: The Lower Mississippi Valley before 1783* (Lincoln: University of Nebraska Press, 1983); Richard White, *The Roots of Dependency: Subsistence, Environment, and Social Change among the Choctaws, Pawnees, and Navajos* (Lincoln: University of Nebraska Press, 1983); and several essays in Peter H. Wood, Gregory A. Wasilkov, and M. Thomas Haltey, eds., *Powhatan's Mantle: Indians of the Colonial South* (Lincoln: University of Nebraska Press, 1989). Arrell M. Gibson, *The Chickasaws* (Norman: University of Oklahoma Press, 1971), and John Swanton, *Indians of the Southeastern United States*, Smithsonian Institution, Bureau of American Ethnology, Bulletin 137 (Washington D.C.: U.S. Government Printing Office, 1946), remain important sources. Anthony F. C. Wallace, *The Long, Bitter Trail: Andrew Jackson and the Indians* (New York: Hill and Wang, 1993), is an excellent summary of the removal debate.

On antebellum Mississippi, John Hebron Moore, *The Emergence of the Cotton Kingdom in the Old Southwest: Mississippi, 1770–1860* (Baton Rouge: Louisiana State University Press, 1988), offers a superb study of the economic development of the cotton frontier. James Oakes, *The Ruling Race: A History of American Slaveholders* (New York: Vintage Books, 1982), looks at slave owners with special attention to those moving west. For an excellent study of another county on the western cotton frontier, see Daniel S. Dupree, *Transforming the Cotton Frontier: Madison County, Alabama, 1800–1840* (Baton Rouge: Louisiana State University Press, 1997). Christopher Morris, *Becoming Southern: The Evolution of a Way of Life, Warren County and Vicksburg, Mississippi, 1770–1860* (New York: Oxford University Press, 1995), is an excellent local study that illuminates broader themes in the western expansion of the Old South. Charles C. Bolton, *Poor Whites of the Antebellum South: Tenants and Laborers in Central North Carolina and Northeast Mississippi* (Durham: Duke University Press, 1994), includes valuable insights on this neglected class with data from Lafayette County's neighbor, Panola County. On the central importance of honor, see Bertram Wyatt-Brown, *Southern Honor: Ethics and Behavior in the Old South* (New York: Oxford University Press, 1982). Randy J. Sparks, *On Jordan's Stormy Banks: Evangelicalism in Mississippi, 1773–1876* (Athens: University of Georgia Press, 1994), places the western religious experience in perspective. Ted Ownby, *Subduing Satan: Religion, Recreation, and Manhood in the Rural South, 1865–1920* (Chapel Hill: University of North Carolina Press, 1990), is a stimulating study of religious culture in opposition to traditional male culture.

On slavery, Charles Sackett Sydnor, *Slavery in Mississippi* (1933; rpt. Gloucester, Mass.: Peter Smith, 1965), is a classic that remains a reliable and informative place to begin. John Spencer Bassett, *The Southern Plantation Overseer, as Revealed in His Letters* (1925; rpt. New York: Negro Universities Press, 1968), includes fascinating correspondence from the overseers of President James K. Polk's plantation in neighboring Yalabusha County. Eugene D. Genovese, *Roll, Jordan, Roll: The World the Slaves Made* (New York: Vintage Books, 1974), is one of the major works in the field with important insights on the role of religion. Charles W. Joyner, *Down by the Riverside: A South Carolina Slave Community* (Urbana: University of Illinois Press, 1984), interprets the folk culture of slaves. Peter Kolchin, *American Slavery, 1619–1877* (New York: Hill and Wang, 1993), is a fine synthesis of the voluminous scholarship on American slavery. Winthrop Jordan, *Tumult and Silence at Second Creek: An Inquiry into a Civil War Slave Conspiracy*, rev. ed. (Baton Rouge: Louisiana State University Press, 1995), deals with an intriguing story of slave rebellion and repression.

Mississippi politics has been ably interpreted by Bradley G. Bond, *Political Culture in the Nineteenth-Century South: Mississippi, 1830–1900* (Baton Rouge: Louisiana State University Press, 1995), and the secession crisis is covered by Percy Lee Rainwater, *Mississippi: Storm Center of Secession, 1856–1861* (Baton Rouge: Otto Claitor, 1938), and William L. Barney, *The Secessionist Impulse: Alabama and Mississippi in 1860* (Princeton: Princeton University Press, 1974). James B. Murphy, *L. Q. C. Lamar: Pragmatic Patriot* (Baton Rouge: Louisiana State University Press, 1973), is a favorable treatment of the Lafayette County fire-eater.

On the Civil War, James M. McPherson, *Battle Cry of Freedom: The Civil War Era* (New York: Oxford University Press, 1988), is the most recent synthesis. John K. Bettersworth, *Mississippi in the Confederacy: As They Saw It* (Baton Rouge: Louisiana State University Press, 1961), and its companion volume, James W. Silver, ed., *Mississippi in the Confederacy: As Seen in Retrospect* (Baton Rouge: Louisiana State University Press, 1961). Some of the most exciting work in this field has involved studies of women and slaves at the home front. See Drew Faust, *Mothers of Invention: Women of the Slaveholding South in the American Civil War* (Chapel Hill: University of North Carolina Press, 1996); Lee Ann Whites, *The Civil War as a Crisis in Gender: Augusta, Georgia, 1860–1890* (Athens: University of Georgia Press, 1995); Catherine Clinton and Nina Silber, eds., *Divided Houses: Gender and the Civil War* (New York: Oxford University Press, 1992); George C. Rable, *Civil Wars: Women and the Crisis of Southern Nationalism* (Urbana: University of Illinois Press, 1989). Armstead Robinson, "Day of Jubilo: Civil War and the Demise of Slavery in the Mississippi Valley, 1861–1865" (Ph.D. dissertation, University of Rochester, 1976), is an important study of the role slaves played in the Civil War. Stephen V. Ash, *When the Yankees Came: Conflict and Chaos in the Occupied South, 1861–1865* (Chapel Hill: University of North Carolina Press, 1995), is an excellent account of the Union invasion and its impact on civilians.

Reconstruction remains one of the least reexamined subjects in Mississippi's past. James Wilford Garner, *Reconstruction in Mississippi* (1901; rpt. Gloucester, Mass., Peter Smith, 1964), is one of the best of the Dunning School state studies, but his bias against the Radicals is apparent. William C. Harris's dual volumes, *The Day of the Carpetbagger: Republican Reconstruction in Mississippi*, (Baton Rouge: Louisiana State University Press, 1979), and *Presidential Reconstruction in Mississippi* (Baton Rouge: Louisiana State University Press, 1967), revisit the subject with attention to state politics. Eric Foner, *Reconstruction: America's Unfinished Revolution, 1863–1877*, The New American Nation Series (New York: Harper and Row, 1988), is the major revisionist reinterpretation of the period. Michael Perman, *Emancipation and Reconstruction, 1862–1879* (Arlington Heights, Ill.: Harlan Davidson, 1987), is an excellent introduction to the subject; see also his *Reunion without Compromise; The South and Reconstruction, 1865–1868* (London: Cambridge University Press, 1973). James L. Roark, *Masters without Slaves:*

Southern Planters in the Civil War and Reconstruction (New York: Norton, 1977), deals with the social history of former slave masters. Vernon Lane Wharton, The Negro in Mississippi, 1865–1890 (1947; rpt. Westport, Conn.: Greenwood Press, 1984), remains a valuable source for the black experience during and after Reconstruction.

On the period after Reconstruction, Woodward, Origins of the New South, remains a major interpretation. Edward Ayers, The Promise of the New South: Life after Reconstruction (New York: Oxford University Press, 1992), illuminates the social and cultural history of the period. On state politics, see Stephen Cresswell, Multiparty Politics in Mississippi, 1877–1902 (Jackson: University Press of Mississippi, 1995), and on Mississippi's revolt of the rednecks, Albert D. Kirwin, Revolt of the Rednecks: Mississippi Politics, 1876–1925 (New York: Harper, 1951), and William F. Holmes, The White Chief: James Kimble Vardaman (Baton Rouge: Louisiana State University Press, 1970). For Bilbo, see Chester M. Morgan, Redneck Liberal: Theodore G. Bilbo and the New Deal (Baton Rouge: Louisiana State University Press, 1985); Adwin Wigfall Green, The Man Bilbo (Baton Rouge, Louisiana State University Press, 1963). A sample of Bilbo's thinking on race can be found in Theodore Gilmore Bilbo, Take Your Choice; Separation or Mongrelization (Poplarville, Miss.: Dream House, 1947).

Neil R. McMillen, Dark Journey: Black Mississippians in the Age of Jim Crow (Urbana: University of Illinois Press, 1989), is a thorough study of the systematic nature of Mississippi white supremacy. Stewart E. Tolnay and E. M. Beck, A Festival of Violence: An Analysis of Southern Lynchings, 1882–1930 (Urbana: University of Illinois Press, 1995), is one of the more recent studies of this subject.

On modern town life in Mississippi, see Ted Ownby, American Dreams in Mississippi: Consumers, Poverty, and Culture, 1830–1998 (Chapel Hill: University of North Carolina Press, 1999). Ayers, Promise of the New South, mentioned above, offers wonderful portraits of the new town culture emerging in the modern South. Don H. Doyle, New Men, New Cities, New South: Atlanta, Nashville, Charleston, Mobile, 1860–1910 (Chapel Hill: University of North Carolina Press, 1990), includes a general study of southern urbanization.

On race relations and the civil rights movement in modern Mississippi, two important social science studies of Mississippi during the 1930s are Allison Davis, Burleigh B. Gardner, and Mary R. Gardner, Deep South; A Social Anthropological Study of Caste and Class (1941; rpt. Chicago: University of Chicago Press, 1965), and John Dollard, Caste and Class in a Southern Town (1937; rpt. Madison, Wisc.: University of Wisconsin Press, 1988). Anne Moody, Coming of Age in Mississippi (New York: Dial Press, 1968), reveals a more personal experience of blacks. On the struggle against white supremacy, see Walter Lord, The Hate That Would Not Die (New York: Harper and Row, 1965); James Silver, Mississippi: The Closed Society (1963; rpt. New York: Harcourt, Brace and World, 1966). Silver's autobiographical account of life at the University of Mississippi is a very revealing story: James W. Silver, Running Scared: Silver in Mississippi (Jackson: University Press of Mississippi, 1984). Nadine Cohodas, The Band Played Dixie: Race and the Liberal Conscience at Ole Miss (New York: Free Press, 1997), looks at the same story from a more objective distance. John Dittmer, Local People: The Struggle for Civil Rights in Mississippi (Urbana: University of Illinois Press, 1994), describes the grassroots revolt against Jim Crow. Anthony Walton, Mississippi: An American Journey (New York: Knopf, 1996), is a contemplative and moving study of Mississippi by a northern black man whose father fled Holly Springs; Walton makes wonderful use of Faulkner.

416 (n. 1); ratio to men of, 103, 147;
and town, 333
Woods, Rebecca, 129, 140
Woodson's Ridge, 76, 78, 105
Woodward, C. Vann, 8, 18
Word, Thomas Jefferson, 408 (n. 13)
Works Progress Administration (WPA),
14, 122, 223
Wright, Frances, 143, 406 (n. 57)
Wyatt, Miss., 71–72, 75, 84, 92, 204,
395 (n. 54)

Yeater, A. J., 268, 427 (n. 55)
Yellow fever, 303–5
Yellow Leaf Creek, 75, 77
Yeomen, 80–83, 306
Yocona, Miss., 103
Yoknapatawpha County, 1, 5, 7, 60,
189; defined, 24–25, 387 (n. 2); and
history, 385–6 (n. 2)
Yoknapatawpha River, 1, 24, 69, 283
Young, William Humphries, 249